THE PRESS
and AMERICA

PRENTICE-HALL JOURNALISM SERIES

Kenneth E. Olson, Editor

PRENTICE-HALL INTERNATIONAL, INC.
London · Tokyo · Sydney · Paris
PRENTICE-HALL OF CANADA, LTD.
PRENTICE-HALL DE MEXICO, S.A.

William EDWIN EMERY

Professor of Journalism
University of Minnesota

THE PRESS
and AMERICA

An Interpretative History of Journalism

Second Edition

PRENTICE-HALL, INC.
Englewood Cliffs, N. J.

PN
4855
.E6

FOREWORD

Journalism history is the story of man's long struggle to communicate freely with his fellow men—to dig out and interpret news, and to offer intelligent opinion in the market place of ideas. Part of the story has as its theme the continuing efforts by men and women to break down the barriers that have been erected to prevent the flow of information and ideas, upon which public opinion is so largely dependent. Another aspect of the story is concerned with the means, or media, by which this essential news and opinion reached the public, from the days of the hand-written "newes letter" to the printed page, radio, and television. Just as important to this story are the heroes and villains, as well as the bit actors, who made the press (meaning all media of communication) what it is today. Finally, all this becomes more meaningful when the development of our journalistic tradition is related to the political, economic, and social progress of our people.

The title, *The Press and America*, reflects the emphasis placed upon correlation of journalism history with political, economic, and social trends. In this interaction, the press has had its influence upon the course taken by our country. Conversely, the conditions and influences present in each historical era have cumulatively determined the shape of the press. Within this framework emerges the story of the men and women of journalism, and of the institutions and traditions they created.

In the opening chapters, beginning with the European roots of American journalism and covering the long time-span ending with the Civil War, the primary concern is with an exposition of the principles upon which the American Fourth Estate was founded. The remaining chapters examine modern journalism—including newspapers, magazines, radio, television, and press associations— and its role in an increasingly complex society. For this edition, there have been extensive revisions of chapters dealing with the

v

53914

press associations, Washington correspondents and columnists, interpretative reporting, present-day magazines, the rise and present status of radio and television, economic pressures on the mass media and concentration of their ownership, government and press, criticisms of the social and political roles of the press, and present-day leading newspapers. Other changes have been made throughout the volume, including extensive reorganization of, and additions to, the annotated bibliographies which follow each chapter.

A word of explanation to those familiar with the first edition of this book: Henry Ladd Smith, who was a co-author, did not wish to take part in the work of preparing this edition or future editions. He preferred that his name remain associated only with the original edition, and an agreement was reached whereby his wishes could be respected. His contribution to this volume remains great. I also wish to thank again three journalism professors who gave counsel and criticism during the preparation of the original manuscript: Kenneth E. Olson, Northwestern University; Ralph D. Casey, University of Minnesota; and Frederick B. Marbut, Pennsylvania State University.

Other journalism professors to whom particular thanks are due are Harold L. Nelson, University of Wisconsin, and Warren C. Price, University of Oregon. Professor Nelson gave invaluable assistance during the preparation of the original index and offered many suggestions for text revisions, particularly for the colonial period. Professor Price's extensive work in journalism bibliography was especially useful.

Helpful in supplying information on special areas were Ralph O. Nafziger, University of Wisconsin; Fredrick S. Siebert, Michigan State University; Quintus C. Wilson, West Virginia University; Robert W. Desmond, University of California; J. Edward Gerald, Raymond B. Nixon, and Edwin H. Ford, University of Minnesota; and the late Jacob Scher of Northwestern University. I also wish to thank the many others whose comments have aided and encouraged me. To my wife, Mary M. Emery, I express appreciation for assistance and patient support.

Finally, I acknowledge my debt to the many scholars and writers whose contributions to journalism history are listed in the footnotes and bibliographies.

EDWIN EMERY

TABLE OF CONTENTS

vii

LIST OF ILLUSTRATIONS

THE PRESS
and AMERICA

Chapter 1

THE HERITAGE OF THE AMERICAN PRESS

> Give me but the liberty of the press and I will give
> to the minister a venal House of Peers . . . and
> servile House of Commons . . . I will give him all
> the power that place can confer upon him to pur-
> chase up submission and overawe resistance—And
> yet, armed with liberty of the press . . . I will
> attack the mighty fabric he has reared . . . and
> bury it amidst the ruins of the abuses it was meant
> to shelter.
> —Richard Brinsley Sheridan

WE MIGHT BEGIN our story with the appearance of the first
newspaper in colonial America—surely that would appear to be the
beginning of American journalism. But the colonial newspaper was
so closely patterned after the British product that to understand
the function of the press at that time, it is necessary to explain
a little about the English influence. Many able writers, including
Bleyer and Shaaber, have started their histories of the American
press with the appearance of the "corantos," or primitive newspapers printing foreign news, in the early seventeenth century.

But the English coranto was, in turn, traceable to similar publications on the continent. It is now generally conceded that the
modern press is the gift of no one nation, and that it was already
in the process of development in other parts of the world long

3

before the corantos began to be read in London. The oldest known and preserved copies of a primitive newspaper were published in Germany in 1609, but the existing copies do not indicate the city, printer, or publisher. From an analysis of paper, type, printing technique, political content, and religious coloring, experts conceded that the site of this earliest known newspaper had to be in North Germany. According to Dr. Ralph O. Nafziger, who has corresponded with German researchers, Bremen is the most likely birthplace of the first publication.[1]

Painstaking research has established other early newspaper publication in Strasbourg, also in 1609, and in Cologne in 1610. By 1620 it had spread to Frankfurt, Berlin, Hamburg, Basel, Vienna, Amsterdam, and Antwerp. Amsterdam printers were publishing papers in the English and French languages in 1620, but the first London publication appeared in 1621 and the first Paris paper in 1631. A court newspaper begun in Stockholm in 1645 still appears and is the world's oldest known continuously published newspaper.[2]

Other countries also contributed to the development of the press. In 1566 the Venetian Magistracy ordered accounts of the war in Dalmatia to be read and posted in public places. Persons interested in this news paid a small coin, called a *gazetta,* for the privilege of obtaining it. Thirty volumes of these "Gazettes" have been preserved in the Maggliabecchi Library in Florence.[3] Even before this the Italian peninsula was noted for its advances in the publication of current events; as far back as 59 B.C., news sheets known as *Acta Diurna* were posted in public places in Rome. These were filed each succeeding day in a special building housing records, where they were available to anyone wishing to make use of them.

During the European Middle Ages, the Chinese made important contributions to the art of printing. In A.D. 868, Wang Chieh published a book printed from blocks. Copies of it survive as man's oldest printed book. The first known use of movable type was by another Chinese, Pi Shêng, around 1045. Although the influence of

---

[1] Dr. Nafziger, director of the University of Wisconsin School of Journalism, is himself a scholar in German press history.

[2] Folke Dahl, ed., *The Birth of the European Press* (Stockholm: The Royal Library, 1960), summarizes much of this research. Dahl found local news emphasized in a Viennese paper of 1629—an unusual development. The oldest known Swedish paper was printed at Strängnäs in 1624.

[3] Venice and Florence were early news centers in Italy, but Genoa is credited with the first continuously titled paper, begun in 1645.

the Chinese craftsmen on Western pioneers would be difficult to establish, it is known that Marco Polo described Chinese printing methods when he returned to Venice from the East in 1295. It was in the same area that paper was first used in printing. The court gazette at Peiping set a record for continuous publication by appearing for more than 1,000 years, but disappeared in 1911.

The point to all this is that England had no special claim as the home of the modern press, even though it advanced beyond all other countries journalistically. And in England, as in other lands, news was exchanged long before there was even the most primitive form of newspaper. One of the great attractions at the country fairs of the Middle Ages was the opportunity to exchange gossip and information. Countrymen and gentry traveled annually to Bartholomew, Donnybrook, or Stourbridge as much to swap news as to buy yearly supplies of staples. Newspapers did not create news; news created newspapers.

It has been said that the true newspaper must meet these qualifications: (1) it must be published at least once a week; (2) it must be produced by mechanical means (to distinguish it from the handwritten "newes letters"); (3) it must be available to anyone willing to pay the price, regardless of class or special interests; (4) it must print anything of interest to a general public, as contrasted with some of the religious and business publications; (5) it must have an appeal to a public of ordinary literary skill; (6) it must be timely, or at least relatively so, in the light of technical development; and (7) it must have stability, as contrasted to the fly-by-night publications of more primitive times.[4]

Any publication that could meet all these qualifications was indeed an innovation. It might even be said that the newspaper was the most significant contribution of the printing press. There were extensive libraries of books long before there was a printing press. The so-called "cradle books," produced immediately after Johann Gutenberg introduced movable type to Europe around 1440 at Mainz and printed his famous Bible in the 1450's, were not essentially different from the handwritten volumes common before

[4] Eric W. Allen, "International Origins of the Newspapers: The Establishment of Periodicity in Print," *Journalism Quarterly*, VII (December 1930), 314; quoting from Otto Groth, *Ein System des Zeitungskunde (Journalistik)* (Mannheim: J. Bensheimer, 1928), V. I, pp. 21 ff.

that date. Both the longhand and printed books contained information bound between permanent covers. Illustrations, format, materials, and even letter characters were similar in appearance.

The newspaper, on the other hand, was something new. Not until movable type had been perfected was it possible to produce literature and printed reports cheap enough to reach the masses. The revolution was not so much in the medium, perhaps, as in the audience. At any rate, the newspaper was the most novel product of the printing press.

With a publication of this type, there was some incentive for gathering and processing information of interest to the general public—news. News thereupon became a commodity, like food or merchandise, produced for profit to meet a demand. It is significant that there was little use of the word "news" until after the invention of printing made possible the periodical of the masses. Up to about 1500, "Tydings" was the usual word to describe reports of current events. The word "news" was coined to differentiate between the casual dissemination of information and the deliberate attempt to gather and process the latest intelligence.[5]

Almost everything in the modern newspaper can be traced back far beyond the beginning of printing, with the possible exception of advertising. What we call "feature stuff" today can be traced back at least 300 years. Illustrations were common long before the newspaper appeared.[6] Comics, sports articles, political columns, and something like the modern editorial were already known. In the sixteenth century, as today, the unusual and exciting furnished the bulk of the text. The only innovation of the printing press was to expand the availability of this material. By fulfilling that one function—making news more available to a larger public—the press exerted a tremendous impact upon history.

How could movable type make such a change in thinking and habits accepted for centuries? We take the press so much for granted today that we are likely to be unaware of its significance.

[5] One example was the widespread collection of news by the great commercial house of Fugger, whose sixteenth-century news letters are famous.

[6] In 1643, before the publication of the first true English newspaper, *Mercurius Civicus* was luring the reader through the use of pictures, much as the tabloids were to do 300 years later. In Antwerp, Abraham Verhoeven was using woodcut illustrations in his newspaper during the 1620's.

By going back into the early days of journalism, when issues were not so confused as they are now, we can see what the press has meant to our society.

In the first place, printing lowered the cost of education. News letters, book manuscripts, and written materials were beyond the reach of the common man before printing, even if such a public had had the literacy skill to make use of them. The cost of a handwritten news letter was directly proportional to the number of copies produced by the copyists. Each additional copy in longhand cost about as much as the previous issue. The main expense of printing was setting the type. Thereafter, every copy produced by the press reduced the unit cost. Publications that formerly might have cost the worker a month's wages could now be purchased for a few pennies. That meant that knowledge was no longer the exclusive property of the privileged classes. It also meant that literary forms, such as the newspaper, could be tried out at slight financial risk. Reading was thus offered to a much broader base of the population. Illiteracy was then the main barrier between the publisher and his public.

Cheap publication offered the illiterate an incentive to learn to read. The more readers, the lower the cost of such material. The lower the cost, the more readers. This was a chain reaction that was certain to cause an explosion; and it did. Learning to read is likely to make a man or woman curious, simply because matters are brought into focus that have never been imagined before. Not that reading automatically produces thinking—the stacks of pulp magazines in any drugstore rack today refute any such argument—but it does make people interested in the world around them. As the Middle Ages ended, various tendencies broke the crust of fixed custom and ushered in the "age of discussion," which is progressive, inasmuch as it gives a premium to intelligence.[7]

Immediately after the perfection of printing, ideas and information reached reader publics which lacked the requisite literary background and experience for reasoning; therefore, the first appeal had to be through the emotions, rather than through reason. When people react to emotion, rather than to rational thinking, they some-

[7] Paraphrased from Walter Bagehot, as quoted by Allan Nevins, *Gateway to History* (Boston: D. C. Heath and Co., 1938), p. 245.

times forget the safety of docility. This was so in the period under discussion here. It was the reason the governing classes feared the press. The traditional elite groups possessing power stood for the orderliness of the *status quo*. They had good cause to wonder what would happen if the masses were aroused by appeal to emotions through the press.

The printing press also made a record for all to see. It offered a more responsible report of transactions, as compared with word-of-mouth information. After the invention of the printing press, people could begin to check the failures and accomplishments of their rulers more effectively. They could pin down responsibility for public policy. It is true that pamphlets were more important than newspapers in this respect, but in time the newspaper took over this function, too.

It is significant that the newspaper first flourished in areas where authority was weak, as in Germany, at that time divided into a patchwork of small principalities; or where rulers were more tolerant, as in the low countries. This explains why the development of the press lagged in England. True, William Caxton set up the first press in England in 1476, but nearly two centuries elapsed before the country had a genuine newspaper.

Caxton learned about printing on the continent, where it had been a craft since the middle of the fifteenth century. He had been governor of a chartered association of "adventurers," or merchants interested in foreign enterprise. Caxton was a learned man, the author and translator of several volumes, and a collector of fine books. He believed that it was his mission to bring the culture of the continent to his countrymen. His king, Edward IV, encouraged these ideas. Edward had just come to power, following a long civil war that had split the country. Not until 1471 was he safely in control of his government.[8] At once he began to repair the ravages of the internal conflict. Edward was responsible for progress in law, industry, and culture. It was under such circumstances that Caxton

---

[8] Relatively speaking, that is. The wars continued after his death in 1483, when his heir was pushed aside by Richard of Gloucester. Gloucester was ultimately defeated by young Henry Tudor at Bosworth Field. There was a period under Edward IV when England was peaceful, however, and it is to this time that the above passage refers.

set up his tiny press "at the Sign of the Red Pale" in the almonry of the abbey at Westminster in 1476.[9]

The Battle of Bosworth Field in 1485 brought a new dynasty into being. Henry Tudor, the victor, ended the long feud between the royal houses of York and Lancaster, thereby bringing the country back to the stability it so desperately needed. A Lancastrian by blood and a Yorkist by marriage, he emerged from the Wars of the Roses, as the civil strife was called, with powers that were eventually to make the Tudors as nearly absolute in power as English monarchs could be. The nobility, which had previously restrained the powers of the English kings, was decimated by the long years of fighting. The Tudor monarchs took full advantage of the situation. Most of them were brilliant and able administrators. Under Tudor leadership England experienced a golden age. It was not conducive to the progress of the press, however.

Caxton enjoyed relative freedom from royal interference, mostly because he never tried to test his status. Printing was not a social force for about 50 years after its establishment in England. Under the Tudors, however, the press became a matter of kingly concern, for that strong dynasty was noted for its attempts to grasp all possible power. Henry VIII started the control of the press with a list of prohibited books. This was in 1529, and the purpose was to set up a bulwark against the rising tide of Protestantism. The first licensing system under government control was established a year later, and by a proclamation on Christmas day, 1534, Henry VIII required printers to have royal permission before setting up shop. Partly as a defense against outside heresies, and partly to protect local printers, he ordered that no more foreign books were to be sold in England. The proclamation also declared that prices for books were to be reasonable.

During this period the powers of the Privy Council were also

---

[9] It is not absolutely established where Caxton set up his press, but the consensus is that it was in the Abbey. In 1660, one Richard Atkyns, a Stuart supporter, tried to prove that the first press was established by royal grant in 1468. Atkyns was trying to show precedent for royal control of printing. Caxton apparently began printing on his own initiative and without sanction. Most authorities on the subject now agree there is no validity to the Atkyns claims. See Fredrick Seaton Siebert, *Freedom of the Press in England, 1476-1776* (Urbana: University of Illinois Press, 1952), pp. 22-24.

increased, at the expense of Parliament and the older courts, but to the advantage of the crown. The Council was ostensibly to advise the king, but soon the monarchy was using it to perform much of the executive work. The Council supervised the administration of laws, regulated trade, kept an eye on the courts, and controlled the press. Beginning in 1542 the records of the Council show a continuous report of proceedings against individuals for "unfitting worddes," seditious utterances, and the like. As early as 1540 the Council made arrests for the printing of street ballads about political matters.

The proclamation (ordinance) was the tool employed by the king or his Council to give legality and force to the regulation of the press. The Tudors, who controlled Parliament, used the proclamation because it worked fast. It gave them wide powers over fields untouched by statute or common law. In 1539 Henry VIII had Parliament pass an act giving his proclamations the status of law. It was repealed in 1547, but proclamations were used effectively by kings long after that. By later standards there was no legality to such royal ordinances, but they were enforced as law by the strong Tudors.[10]

Despite these repressive measures, a kind of literary black market supplied the forbidden information and entertainment. We know, for example, that Henry VIII was angered in the thirty-sixth year of his reign by accounts of a battle in Scotland. The news was peddled by London "broadsheet" vendors, a broadsheet being a paper printed specifically to describe a certain event. The king's complaint was not so much that the reports were false, but that the news had been printed without his permission. Apparently, even the absolute powers of the king could not throttle the press, but the climate was not healthy for the steady growth of journalism.

One way to control an industry is to make it a monopoly and then to hold the directors of it responsible for abuses. The Tudors did that with the printing industry in 1557 when Queen Mary established the Stationers Company. This organization had existed since 1357 as a society of court and text writers, to which the "limners," or illustrators were admitted after 1404. By 1500 the printers had also been admitted, but by Mary's time the word "stationer" was applied to the publishers and dealers in books, as distinct from

[10] Siebert, *Freedom of the Press in England,* Chap. 1, describes the situation admirably.

the printers.[11] It was a kind of printing trust, and it made it easier for authorities to run down rebel printers not members of the elite group, or sanctioned by it. Queen Elizabeth supplemented this control by her "Injunctions," which gave the religious hierarchy a measure of control over printing. Until the upheavals of the mid-seventeenth century the Stationers Company exerted one of the most powerful controls over the press. In 1576, for example, the Stationers adopted an order for weekly search of London printing houses (where almost all printing was concentrated). Pairs of searchers reported on work in progress, the number of orders on hand, identity of customers, number of employees, and wages paid. That was an effective check on extensive bootleg printing.

The infamous Star Chamber court, originally set up to protect the public, but later the symbol of repression, was another barrier to free expression during the long period preceding the appearance of the English newspaper. By edict of the Privy Council in 1566 and of the Star Chamber in 1586 the pattern of restrictions for the next hundred years was outlined. Severe penalties were prescribed for printers foolish enough to defy the authorities. Strange as it may seem, there were printers willing to run that risk. There was William Carter, who was hanged for printing pamphlets favorable to the Catholic cause. Arrested and tortured in 1580, he was executed in 1584.[12] Puritan rebels against the Established Church included Hugh Singleton, Robert Waldegrave, John Stroud, and John Hodgkins. The attack on the monopoly control was led by John Wolfe, Roger Ward, William Holmes, and John Charlewood. Waldegrave was the printer of the first "Martin Marprelate" tracts, the Puritan arguments published surreptitiously against the Established Church. Hodgkins carried on when Waldegrave was hounded from the country. But on the whole, the repressive measures of the authorities held back the development of free discussion, in which journalism is such an important factor.

The time was coming when such pressure had to be released. During the early part of the seventeenth century news became of great importance to the English people. The religious disputes, the rise of England as a maritime power, the struggles between King and Parliament, and the changing social conditions made the pub-

[11] See *ibid.*, Chap. 3, for a detailed discussion of the Stationers Company. Siebert has found that some of these dates have been incorrectly reported.
[12] It was the only execution of this type under the Tudors, however.

lic more interested in events beyond its local sphere. The balladeers and broadsheet vendors could not meet the demand. Prose pamphlets were much more effective, as evidenced by the success of the Marprelate tracts, but such publications were not regular enough. The news letter writers, or "intelligencers," as the publishers of handwritten sheets were called, were capable journalists, but the average man could not afford their products.[13] The time was ripe for a new type of publication.

In the summer of 1621, nearly a century and a half after Caxton introduced printing to England, the very rudimentary prototypes of the modern newspaper appeared on the streets of London. These primitive news sheets were called "corantos." They lacked the regularity that is a necessary of the true newspaper, and they were too specialized in content (foreign intelligence) to meet the qualifications mentioned on page 5. But they did fulfill a need.

In 1620 the English were interested in continental developments. The popular Princess Elizabeth had married Frederick, Elector of the Palatinate, in 1613. He was a Protestant, highly favored by nonconformists, both on the Continent and in England. When he decided to accept the crown of Bohemia against the wishes of the Holy Roman Emperor, he precipitated the Thirty Years' War.

Printers in the Netherlands were quick to capitalize on this interest. At least 25 English-language corantos reporting war news were produced, nearly all at Amsterdam, by George Veseler and Broer Jonson. These single sheets, now in the British Museum, were dated December 2, 1620, to September 18, 1621. Nathaniel Butter, a bookseller, was the English distributor. Sales were so brisk that in the summer of 1621 Butter decided to do the publishing himself, pirating his news from Dutch news sheets. Thomas Archer, a printer, was probably his partner. Copies of their sheets printed in the summer of 1621 do not survive. Six similar corantos,[14] dated

---

[13] As Siebert points out, the first real English reporters were the "intelligencers" John Chamberlain, John Pory, William Locke, and the Reverends Larkin and Mead.

[14] These six corantos, bearing only the initials "N.B." as publisher, have perplexed English historians. They probably were issued by Nicholas Bourne (see page 13) but they could have been a continuation of Nathaniel Butter's summer series. The account here of the first London corantos is based upon Siebert, who found evidence in records and correspondence going beyond that offered by the surviving corantos. See also Matthias A. Shaaber, *Some Forerunners of the Newspaper in England, 1476-1622* (Philadelphia: University of Pennsylvania Press, 1929), pp. 314-18.

September 24 to October 22, do. But by that time printer Archer had run afoul of the law.

When Frederick, the newly elected king of Bohemia, led his forces to defeat in revolt against the Hapsburgs at a battle near Prague, English sentiment favored intercession by James I for his son-in-law. James could not make up his mind, however. The corantos were critical of his foreign policy, and in retaliation the king cracked down on the editors, using the old rules of the Tudors. It is significant that these restrictions riled the public in the 1620's, whereas the Tudors had probably had public opinion behind them most of the time. In December of 1620 and again in July of 1621 the king issued proclamations against "the great liberty of discourse concerning matters of state." He followed this up with an order suppressing corantos, but apparently some of the printers flouted his orders, for there is a record of the Stationers Company calling up Archer for a hearing in August. He was imprisoned.

Nicholas Bourne now enters the picture. He was a respected member of his craft and it is possible that Butter teamed up with him because of his prestige. At any rate, the two appeared before the Council to ask permission to publish a news book. They admitted the licensing power of the authorities and agreed to have the text of their proposed paper approved by the clerk of the Council. Their first coranto was authorized in September of 1621 and undoubtedly bore the legend "Published With Authority" at the top of the page, as did later issues. The earliest surviving coranto of this press is dated May 23, 1622. Archer, now out of prison, was the printer. Butter was probably the editor and Bourne was the publisher, or responsible promoter. The paper was printed on one side only, and the sheet was somewhat smaller than a page of modern typewriter paper.

Despite Bourne's prestige, he and his partners could not escape restrictions. In 1632 he and Butter were forbidden by the Council from printing more news books. They started up again in 1638, having paid large fees for the right to publish. During the interim, the unlicensed ballads and news letters had to fill the void. Butter was the first one to employ hawkers for this purpose, but the forerunner of the newsboy was actually a girl. The London "mercurie girls" were selected for their buxomness and lung power. Apparently this experiment in sales promotion was successful, but eventually it ran into moral head winds, and boys took over the job.

It was not until 1624 that the corantos began to be identified by name, thus supplying something of the continuity required of a true newspaper. The earliest known coranto published by title was *The Continuation of Our Weekly Newes*, from the office of Bourne and Butter. Because this title appeared on at least 23 consecutive issues, the offering marks another step in the development of the newspaper.

The earliest corantos printed nothing but foreign news. The first domestic reports can be traced back to the publication by the Westminster clerks of Parliamentary proceedings dated about 1628. Out of these accounts developed the "diurnals," or daily reports of local events. The diurnals flourished during the struggle between King and Parliament, when it was safe to comment on local news because neither side was strong enough to take punitive measures, and when both factions were seeking public support. Many of the restrictions on the press were modified by the Long Parliament, and after 1640 diurnals appeared by the score. Oldest known paper of this type is John Thomas' *Diurnall Occurrences*, which first appeared November 29, 1641.

The interim of the first decade of the revolution beginning in 1640 was a period of great development for the press. The Long Parliament abolished the dreaded Star Chamber in 1641. Voices began to be raised in favor of a greater freedom of expression. On November 24, 1644, the poet John Milton published his famous *Areopagitica*, probably the best known of the great pleas for a free press.[15] Milton spoke eloquently for the right of discussion and declared that

. . . though all the winds of doctrine were let loose to play upon the earth, so truth be in the field, we do injuriously by licensing and prohibiting to misdoubt her strength. Let her [truth] and falsehood grapple; who ever knew truth put to the worse, in a free and open encounter? [16]

[15] His ideas and even some of his phrases had already been expressed by Peter Wentworth, who made a speech in Parliament in 1571 on freedom of discussion. Milton's Parliament speech, later published as *Areopagitica*, arose out of his difficulties with the Stationers Company after Milton published a series of licensed and unlicensed pamphlets on divorce.
[16] Quoted from Rufus Wilmot Griswold, ed., *The Prose Works of John Milton*, Vol. I (Philadelphia: J. W. Moore, 1856), p. 189. Milton's glory is dimmed somewhat by the fact that he himself was serving as licenser and censor only seven years later.

Milton gave the most perfect expression to the idea of a free press, but just as courageous and articulate were such journalistic heroes as William Walwyn, who argued for liberty of the press following his studies on religious toleration; Henry Robinson, who based his theory of a free press on economic principles and free enterprise; Richard Overton, the Tom Paine of his day, who expanded his Separatist views on religion into principles of democracy; and John Lilburne, who did more than any of his compatriots in making his countrymen conscious of their right of discussion.[17] As a matter of fact, Milton had very little effect in bringing about any improvement. His words were not widely disseminated at the time. The ideas expressed in *Areopagitica* were picked up nearly a hundred years later by people all over the world, notably in America, struggling to obtain even greater freedom than they already enjoyed. Milton is mentioned here because he fits into the chronological pattern, but he really belongs to the rebels of a century later.

With the execution of Charles I in 1649 and the rise of the Commonwealth under Oliver Cromwell, the press again fell upon evil days. Cromwell's "Roundheads" had taken over the royal prerogatives, which had at times so restricted Puritan writers and publishers, but the new regime was no more tolerant of the press than the Crown had been. Cromwell permitted only administration organs to be published, such as *Mercurius Politicus*, censored by the great Milton, *A Perfect Diurnall*, also controlled for a time through Milton, and later the *Publick Intelligencer* (1655). All unauthorized publications were treated roughly.

The restoration of Charles II in 1660 resulted in the establishment of an exclusive patent, or monopoly, system under Henry Muddiman and Roger L'Estrange. For a time the ancient, handwritten news letters were the only means of disseminating information with any degree of freedom. Printed newspapers could be liquidated by confiscating presses, whereas news letters could be produced as long as scribes could find a hideaway, or were willing to defy authorities. During this period ultimate control was divided between Crown and Parliament. Regulations and restrictions were

---

[17] The Separatists, one of many dissenting sects, were strong believers in the separation of church and state. The Lilburne thesis was that Englishmen had a birthright in speaking out fearlessly on all measures, and that restrictions were usurpation of power.

fewer, but they were clearly stated and enforcement was effective under the Surveyor of the Press. The old alliance between the King and the Stationers Company was abandoned late in the reign of Charles, but two secretaries of state supplanted the old authority just as effectively.

It was under Charles that a new era of journalism was ushered in with the publication of the *Oxford Gazette* in 1665. Edited by Muddiman while the royal court was fleeing from the London plague, it was, strictly speaking, the first periodical to meet all the qualifications of a true newspaper. It was printed twice a week, by royal authority. After 24 issues, the publication became the *London Gazette* when the court moved back to the capital. It continued to be published right on up through the twentieth century as the official court organ.

The old licensing powers appeared to be crumbling as the Restoration period drew to a close. This was through no choice of the authorities, but more likely because of the growing tendency for class and political alignments. In 1679 Parliament allowed the Licensing Act of 1662 to lapse. It was revived from time to time, but with the increasing tension between Crown and Parliament, each side sought to protect its own spokesmen. The so-called Regulation of Printing, or Licensing, Act expired in 1694, not because authorities were convinced as to the injustice of licensing, but because it was politically unsound. From 1694 to the passage of the first Stamp Act of 1712, the only controls were the laws of treason and seditious libel, and regulations against reporting proceedings of Parliament. In vain did Charles try to restore his old prerogatives during his reign. Journalists more and more tended to ignore his authority. A few were punished, however.

One such victim was Benjamin Harris, a brash and somewhat reckless journalist. Harris was convicted of violating the King's laws. He was fined and pilloried. Unable to pay the fine, he spent two years in prison. When his office was again raided in 1686, Harris fled to Bristol with his family and took passage for America. He appears again soon in these pages as the publisher of one of the first newspapers in America.

After the Revolution of 1688, which brought a change in the monarchical institution, journalists were accorded considerable freedom. William and Mary were rulers by right of public opinion and they had the common sense not to antagonize printers and publishers, who were factors in the development of public opinion. There are no serious persecutions in their reign. By 1694 the old Licensing Act died of senility and neglect. With the rise of the two-party system during the reign of William and Mary, it was difficult to maintain licensing. Without the decisive action of the old monarchs, it was impossible to continue such an archaic system. The attack on the Act in Commons centered around the commercial unfairness of the monopoly system, the restrictions on the printing industry, the tendency of suspected violators to use bribery, and the inadequacy of censorship. But as Macaulay declared in his *History of England,* "on the great question of principle, on the question whether the liberty of unlicensed printing be, on the whole, a blessing or a curse to society, not a word is said." [18]

Today it is easy to criticise those who insisted upon strong government control of the press. But the motives of the seventeenth century authorities may not necessarily have been "bad." Sincere and honest men believed in such controls at the time. We must assume that men and women were about as reasonable then as they are today. If this is true, then there must have been some validity to the restrictive policies we are likely to hold up to scorn in a more enlightened age.

Even today there are areas of journalism where the same arguments for licensing, censorship, and restrictions apply. The principal of a modern American high school is just as likely to favor a free press as the editor of the paper in his town. But the school head will not allow just any student to start a newspaper in the school community. Before he gives permission (license), the principal will probably wish to know the purposes and aims of the editors, and the qualifications of the promoters. Perhaps this is an unfair analogy, but some of these considerations were involved in seventeenth-century restrictions. Like the modern student, the average man of the Tudor-Stuart period lacked the educational experience and background information to provide the basis for sound judgment we call "maturity." Furthermore, the average seventeenth-century editor, like the modern scholastic journalist, could scarcely compensate, either financially or otherwise, for damage to reputation or threat to community peace.

Seventeenth-century authorities who advocated certain restric-

---

[18] Siebert, *Freedom of the Press in England,* p. 262, from T. B. Macaulay, *History of England* (London: J. M. Dent and Sons, Ltd., 1906), III, 328.

tions on the press might also have pointed out that there was considerable freedom of expression at the time. Within the houses of Parliament, freedom of speech was virtually unlimited, except by the bounds of tradition or good taste. Peter Wentworth in 1571 clearly stated the thesis, but others before and after him fought the good fight on this issue. By the time the English newspaper was firmly established, even the king did not dare to infringe upon the speech rights of Parliament.

But note that the very members of Parliament who were most jealous of their own prerogatives often were the severest critics of a free press. Again, we must assume that many of these were men of good will, and that they were willing to see the press restricted not out of malice, but out of due consideration of the issues. Thus, they stood for free expression in Parliament, where a false statement or a dangerous sentiment could be corrected or refuted at once. But they might object to free expression in the press because a false or dangerous statement could not be answered before damage was done. The law of seditious libel therefore was invoked against printers and writers who affronted those in office, both in England and America, until the close of the eighteenth century. But still, there was progress made in winning more freedom of expression on issues and ideas.

This progress was speeded up by the development of the party system of government. It is significant that parties emerged at the very time that the newspaper began to be a force in the political and social affairs of a people interested more and more in government. The corantos were printed during the death throes of an outworn social system. England was moving steadily from feudalism, whose economic manifestation was production for use, to capitalism, translated economically into production for profit. The change brought social strains as power was grasped by one class at the expense of another.

A new type of citizen began to assert himself. He was the commercial man—the trader, merchant, and (later) the manufacturer. A great middle class was arising. Standing between the producer and the consumer, it profited from the processing and distribution of goods. In doing so, it helped to raise living standards to the highest level. And the wealth accumulated during this process was inevitably translated into power. Many factors accounted for this revolution. Better communications, increased population, exchange of specialized products in the European community, the development of the wool trade and the dislocation of the farm worker, and the development of financial services (credit, loans, exchange) are some of the factors involved.

Feudalism had no provision for the middle class. The ancient system provided a stability and an effective adjustment to living during a stage of human development. But it gave the Church, the landowner, the aristocrat, and the military special spheres of privilege and power. The emerging middle class could win recognition and influence only by acquiring some of the ancient privileges and powers of the traditional classes. It accomplished this through the wealth it soon acquired under the free enterprise system. But free enterprise and profit were held in disrepute by many of the old leaders. The middle class began to insist on political, social, and economic changes that would benefit the commercial man. The trader and merchant needed modification of laws restricting credit and financial transactions. He needed protection for his foreign and domestic commerce. A powerful navy was one of those needs, for example, and navies cost money. How would that money be raised? By taxation? How would such taxation be levied? On this issue alone there was certain to be an alignment of special interests.

The language of this period must be understood as ambiguous— the words were often religious, although the meaning might be social or political. Religion had been the great unifying force of the Middle Ages. The emerging middle class tended to be disruptive of old authorities, and it posed new problems in the field of religion. It is significant that the rise of Protestantism and the rise of capitalism were integrated. Both were disruptive of the established order, and the religio-politico jargon employed during this process is confusing to the contemporary reader.

Many of the issues that concerned the people of the seventeenth century appear to have been met with what sounds today like religious bickering. Implicit in the religious arguments, however, were problems still facing us today. In 1603 when James I ascended the throne, three groups struggled for power. They could have been designated almost equally as well under religious, political, and even social titles. One group was largely Anglican in religion, Tory in politics, and aristocratic as a class. The second group was likely to be Presbyterian, Whig, and middle class. The third was made up of religious dissenters, radicals, and people of more lowly station.

The Tudor control of the press was maintained in the interest of public safety. From Henry VIII to Elizabeth, the Crown acted on the principle that peace demanded the suppression of unwarranted dissent. The Tudors were able, and even brilliant, administrators on the whole. Sensitive to public opinion, they understood their people so well that they knew just how far to push their arbitrary rule. Ruthless and erratic as they were at times, their subjects admired them, with some exceptions. Under the Tudors the country had developed great national pride. The Tudors "had the feel" of the country and more often than not were interested in the general welfare. Resistance to them was negligible, therefore, at least from the journalistic standpoint.

The upheaval came when a new dynasty came to power. James I (he was James VI of Scotland) was sincere and well-meaning, but he was never in tune with the times, or with his subjects. He was the son of the unfortunate Mary Queen of Scots, whose life had been marked by scandal and violence. As the son of Mary, he was early suspected of "Papist" sympathies, in a day when that was religious jargon for treason. It was also his misfortune to succeed one of England's great rulers, Elizabeth—"Good Queen Bess." He suffered badly in comparison with this astute and able monarch. Under the Stuarts, beginning with James, the opposing factions formed battle lines. And since the press thrives in such a climate, if restraints break down, perhaps this partially explains the rapid development of journalism during the seventeenth century.

The eighteenth century of British journalism overlaps the infant years of the American press, as described in the next chapter, but because colonial editors were influenced by their British contemporaries, it is pertinent to mention some of the later press developments abroad. The first half of the eighteenth century produced some great journalists in England. Defoe, Swift, Addison, Steele, Fielding, and Samuel Johnson edited newspapers, or wrote essays and other pieces for the popular prints at one time or another. The standard set by them was widely imitated in the American colonies. While this material cannot be classed as news, it served to entertain and elevate the reader. And it did meet the craving for more popular literary fare. The newspapers were the medium for such expression, just as in modern times the popular press offers non-news material in great quantities to meet a demand. The ordinary citizen was also beginning to participate in journalism. Much of the newspaper content was contributed by readers during the eighteenth century.

The popularity of the newspaper was so great that publishers were encouraged to print daily issues. On March 11, 1702, the *Daily Courant* appeared on the streets of London. It was the first daily newspaper printed in the English language. It apparently was established by Elizabeth Mallet, and the feminists might make something of this information, except that her venture lasted only a few days.

The real hero of the *Daily Courant* was Samuel Buckley, who revived the daily and made it into a remarkable newspaper. Buckley insisted on a standard of journalism quite unheard of at the time.[19] It was a *news* paper, not a rumor-mill. He insisted upon reporting factual news, rather than opinion. He was impartial in his publication of these facts. He was careful to dateline the articles, ". . . that the Publick, seeing from what Country a piece of News comes with the Allowance of that Government, may be better able to Judge of the Credibility and Fairness of the Relation. . . ."[20] He practiced what he preached. Although Buckley was a Whig, he did not manipulate news of that party to its favor, even when the Whigs were engaged in desperate struggle for power. Printing on a single sheet of paper, with the reverse largely devoted to profitable advertising, except on exceptional news days, he had little opportunity for experimentation in makeup. Occasionally, however, Buckley used maps and tabulated figures to clarify his reports. Much of the advertising was spurious by modern standards, but Buckley made money from it. Undoubtedly this revenue made possible his excellent coverage of foreign news.

Buckley did not vouch for his news, but he did warn his readers to be on guard against bias and misrepresentation. He was so fearful of "coloring" his own writing that he often failed to

---

[19] An excellent description of the paper is given by Marvin Rosenberg, "The Rise of England's First Daily Newspaper," *Journalism Quarterly*, XXX (Winter 1953), 3-14.

[20] Rosenberg, *op. cit.*, p. 4.

The Daily Courant.

Wednefday, March 11. 1702.

From the Haflem Courant, Dated March 18. N. S.

Naples, Feb. 22.

ON Wednefday laft, our New Viceroy, the Duke of Efcalona, arriv'd here with a Squadron of the Galleys of Sicily. He made his Entrance dreft in a French habit ; and to give us the greater Hopes of the King's coming hither, went to Lodge in one of the little Palaces, leaving the Royal one for his Majefty. The Marquis of Grigni is alfo arriv'd here with a Regiment of French.

Rome, Feb.25. In a Military Congregation of State that was held here, it was Refolv'd to draw a Line from Afcoli to the Borders of the Ecclefiaftical State, thereby to hinder the Incurfions of the Tranfalpine Troops. Orders are fent to Civita Vecchia to fit our the Galleys, and to ftrengthen the Garrifon of that Place. Signior Cafali is made Governor of Perugia. The Marquis del-Vafto, and the Prince de Caferta continue ftill in the Imperial Embaffador's Palace ; where his Excellency has a Guard of 50 Men every Night in Arms. The King of Portugal has defir'd the Arch-Bifhoprick of Lisbon, vacant by the Death of Cardinal Soufa, for the Infante his fecond Son, who is about 11 Years old.

Vienna, Mar. 4. Orders are fent to the 4 Regiments of Foot, the 2 of Cuiraffiers, and to that of Dragoons, which are broke up from Hungary, and are on their way to Italy, and which confift of about 14 or 15000 Men, to haften their March thither with all Expedition. The 6 new Regiments of Huffars that are now raifing, are in fo great a forwardnefs, that they will be compleat, and in a Condition to march by the middle of May. Prince Lewis of Baden has written to Court, to excufe himfelf from coming thither, his Prefence being fo very neceffary, and fo much defir'd on the Upper-Rhine.

Francfort, Mar. 12. The Marquifs d' Uxelles is come to Strasburg, and is to draw together a Body of fome Regiments of Horfe and Foot from the Garifons of Alface ; but will not leffen thofe of Strasburg and Landau, which are already very weak. On the other hand, the Troops of His Imperial Majefty, and his Allies, are going to form a Body near Germefhein in the Palatinate, of which Place, as well as of the Lines at Spires, Prince Lewis of Baden is expected to take a View, in three or four days. The Englifh and Dutch Minifters, the Count of Frife, and the Baron Vander Meer ; and likewife the Imperial Envoy Count Lowenftein, are gone to Nordlingen, and it is hop'd that in a fhort time we fhall hear from thence of fome favourable Refolutions for the Security of the Empire.

Liege, Mar. 14. The French have taken the Cannon de Longie, who was Secretary to the Dean de Mean, out of our Caftle, where he has been for fome time a Prifoner, and have deliver'd him to the Provoft of Maubeuge, who has carry'd him from hence, but we do not know whither.

Paris, Mar. 13. Our Letters from Italy fay, That moft of our Reinforcements were Landed there ; that the Imperial and Ecclefiaftical Troops feem to live very peaceably with one another in the Country of Parma, and that the Duke of Vendome, as he was vifiting feveral Pofts, was within 100 Paces of falling into the Hands of the Germans. The Duke of Chartres, the Prince of Conti, and feveral other Princes of the Blood, are to make the Campaign in Flanders under the Duke of Burgundy ; and the Duke of Maine is to Command upon the Rhine.

From the Amfterdam Courant, Dated Mar. 18.

Rome, Feb. 25. We are taking here all poffible Precautions for the Security of the Ecclefiaftical State in this prefent Conjuncture, and have defir'd to raife 3000 Men in the Cantons of Switzerland. The Pope has appointed the Duke of Berwick to be his Lieutenant-General, and he is to Command 6000 Men on the Frontiers of Naples : He has alfo fettled upon him a Penfion of 6000 Crowns a year during Life.

From the Paris Gazette, Dated Mar. 18. 1702.

Naples, Febr. 17. 600 French Soldiers are arrived here, and are expected to be follow'd by 3400 more. A Courier that came hither on the 14th. has brought Letters by which we are affur'd that the King of Spain defigns to be here towards the end of March ; and accordingly Orders are given to make the neceffary Preparations againft his Arrival. The two Troops of Horfe that were Commanded to the Abruzzo are pofted at Pefcara with a Body of Spanifh Foot, and others in the Fort of Montorio.

Paris, Mareh. 18. We have Advice from Toulon of the 5th inftant, that the Wind having long ftood favourable, 22000 Men were already fail'd for Italy, that 2560 more were Embarking, and that by the 15th it was hoped they might all get thither. The Count d' Eftrees arriv'd there on the Third inftant, and fet all hands at work to fit out the Squadron of 9 Men of War and fome Fregats, that are appointed to carry the King of Spain to Naples. His Catholick Majefty will go on Board the *Thunderer*, of 110 Guns.

We have Advice by an Exprefs from Rome of the 18th of February, That notwithftanding the preffing Inftances of the Imperial Embaffadour, the Pope had Condemn'd the Marquis del Vafto to lofe his Head and his Eftate to be confifcated, for not appearing to Anfwer the Charge againft him of Publickly Scandalizing Cardinal Janfon.

ADVERTISEMENT.

IT will be found from the Foreign Prints, which from time to time, as Occafion offers, will be mention'd in this Paper, that the Author has taken Care to be duly furnifh'd with all that comes from Abroad in any Language. And for an Affurance that He will not, under Pretence of having Private Intelligence, impofe any Additions of feign'd Circumftances to an Action, but give his Extracts fairly and Impartially ; at the beginning of each Article he will quote the Foreign Paper from whence 'tis taken, that the Publick, feeing from what Country a piece of News comes with the Allowance of that Government, may be better able to Judge of the Credibility and Fairnefs of the Relation : Nor will he take upon him to give any Comments or Conjectures of his own, but will relate only Matter of Fact, fuppofing other People to have Senfe enough to make Reflections for themfelves.

This Courant (as the Title fhews) will be Publifh'd Daily : being defign'd to give all the Material News as foon as every Poft arrives and is confin'd to half the Compafs, to fave the Publick at leaft half the Impertinences, of ordinary News-Papers.

LONDON. Sold by E. Mallet, next Door to the King's-Arms Tavern at Fleet-Bridge.

Facsimile of the first daily newspaper in the English language.

give the interpretation we have come to expect from editorials. He used his advertising revenue to free him from political control. Thus, he made a successful enterprise of the first English newspaper to bring *news* to its readers six days a week.

The high literary quality of the eighteenth-century journalism is indicated by the "essay papers," read by students on both sides of the Atlantic even today. The *Tatler* (1709-11) and the *Spectator* (1711-12, 1714) were the products of, first, Richard Steele, and then of Steele and Joseph Addison. Printed on one side of a sheet, and selling for a penny, this type of paper was enormously popular. The *Spectator* was issued daily and at one time reached 60,000 readers, its promoters boasted. Moreover, its literary form was widely imitated, even in America.

Greatest English journalist of the period was Daniel Defoe, who edited *Mist's Journal* from 1717 through 1720. Steele probably got the idea of his *Tatler* series from reading Defoe's brilliant offerings in earlier papers. Some authorities go so far as to hold that Defoe was the father of the modern editorial. He discussed all manner of topics in a most charming and persuasive style. He, too, was widely copied by American journalists.

In the great controversy between Tories and Whigs, Dean Swift wrote some of his greatest satire. That was while he was editing the *Examiner* (1710). The conflict brought out other great writers, whose ideas were conveyed to the masses mostly through the newspapers. Influential both in England and America were the so-called "Cato Letters," written by John Trenchard and Thomas Gordon over the pen name, "Cato." The series appeared between 1720 and 1723 in the *London Journal,* later called the *British Journal.*[21] In convincing, readable form, they discussed theories of liberty, representative government, and freedom of expression. In 1724 this series was collected and published in four volumes. Copies were in great demand in the colonies, where the first stirrings of revolution were beginning to be felt. Through

---

[21] The letters were written by John Trenchard and Thomas Gordon. The first series appeared in the *Independent Whig* between January 20, 1720 and January 4, 1721. Much of the text in the 53 essays was concerned with religious liberty. After the financial crash known as the "South Sea Bubble," the authors wrote 144 more letters on the responsibilities of government in protecting citizens. These appeared in the *London Journal* and the succeeding *British Journal* between November 12, 1720 and December 7, 1723.

American newspapers and pamphlets the influence of "Cato" can be seen right up to the signing of the Declaration of Independence.

Such progress came at great cost, however. Although party conflict raised the voices of free expression, a reactionary government in control was able to force new restrictions. In 1712 the Tories succeeded in imposing a tax on newspapers and advertisements. These "taxes on knowledge" tended to curb the press by economic sanction. Even worse, they kept the price of papers high, so that the masses did not have as ready access to such publications— which was certainly one of the intentions of the authorities. The stamp tax on news sheets and advertisement taxes were not fully removed for another 140 years. The British newspaper, as a result, was low in circulation and small in size until the 1850's. Thanks to the satire of Dr. Samuel Johnson and the courage of newspaper publisher John Wilkes, whose jailing for sedition in the 1760's, aroused widespread public reaction, the ban on reporting proceedings of the Commons was dropped in 1771. But threat of trial for seditious libel still hung over those who defied authority.

It is clear from a study of this period that modern journalists can learn much from the experiences of the past. The progress of press freedom shows that the press belongs to those who rule. If power is concentrated in the hands of a monarch, or an elite group, there is no need for the public to receive information and ideas pertaining to political or social matters. Indeed, providing the public with intelligence (news) may actually constitute a threat to national security and stability, and hence the press must be confined strictly to entertainment or innocuous comment under such a system. On the other hand, if the public participates in government, it must have access to information in direct ratio to its place in the political scheme, and at this point, restrictions on the press are eased. As Siebert points out, all types of governments consider themselves responsible for the welfare of their people. The more direct the accountability of the governors to the masses, the greater the freedom of the press. As England moved from the absolute rule of the Tudors to the more limited administration of the Stuarts and on to the still more representative government after the Glorious Revolution of 1688, the restrictions on the press were withdrawn accordingly. There were setbacks along the way. Men had to suffer and die to bring greater liberty to the press. But the progress is nevertheless apparent. As absolute rule waned and other groups began to challenge authority, the press began to function as the critic, the loyal opposition, and the watchdog of public affairs.[22]

Another lesson to be learned from this period is that the more secure a government is, the less it fears undermining, and the more freedom it accords its press. This is true right up to the present century. During and after wars, when political leaders and their followers are apprehensive about national safety, liberty of speech and press is in danger of restrictions. Henry VIII's insecurity after his establishment of the English church resulted in strict enforcement of press regulations. Elizabeth cracked down on the press when her claim to the throne was in some doubt. On the other hand, the stability of the government from the end of the seventeenth century was accompanied by press freedom such as the world had never seen before. As Siebert says, "It is axiomatic that government does not exert itself in its own protection unless it is attacked, or believes itself to be seriously threatened." [23]

In the next chapter we shall see the process carried over to America, where the concept of a free press was eventually to prevail as it had in no other country. The philosophy providing the stimulus for this progress developed from the English spokesmen, however, and the American debt to English press traditions is incalculable.

ANNOTATED BIBLIOGRAPHY

Bibliographies:

An indispensable reference for students of American journalism is Warren C. Price, *The Literature of Journalism: An Annotated Bibliography* (Minneapolis: University of Minnesota Press, 1959). The more than 3,000 entries are particularly full in the areas of general journalism histories, specialized and individual histories, biographies, and narratives of journalists at work. Other sections cover press appraisals, press law, techniques of journalism, journalism education, press management, magazines, radio and television, public opinion and propaganda, international communication, periodicals of the press, and bibliographies and directories. Several hundred titles relate to British and Canadian journalism.

[22] Siebert, *Freedom of the Press in England,* p. 10.
[23] *Ibid.,* p. 10.

For listings of American newspapers see Clarence S. Brigham, *History and Bibliography of American Newspapers, 1690-1820* (Worcester, Massachusetts: American Antiquarian Society, 1947), and Winifred Gregory, *American Newspapers, 1821-1936: A Union List of Files Available in the United States and Canada* (New York: H. W. Wilson Company, 1936).

Two major bibliographies for the study of American history are *A Guide to the Study of the United States of America* (Washington: Library of Congress, 1960) and the *Harvard Guide to American History* (Cambridge: Harvard University Press, 1954). The first named, while less voluminous, carries extensive annotations lacking in the second and has a far better selection of journalistic titles.

Books:

Blagden, Cyprian, *The Stationers Company*. London: Allen & Unwin, Ltd., 1960. A scholarly account of licensing and control of printing.

Bleyer, Willard Grosvenor, *Main Currents in the History of American Journalism*. Boston: Houghton Mifflin Company, 1927. Chapter One is a good description of early English journalism, to about 1750.

Clyde, William M., *The Struggle for the Freedom of the Press from Caxton to Cromwell*. New York: Oxford University Press, 1934. This excellent study is now largely superseded by Siebert (see below).

Dahl, Folke, ed., *The Birth of the European Press*. Stockholm: The Royal Library, 1960. A 36-page brochure cataloguing an exhibition of early papers from the library's famous collection, and containing authoritative notes on first known publications in Germany, Austria, the Low Countries, France, England, and Sweden.

Ford, Edwin H., and Edwin Emery, eds., *Highlights in the History of the American Press: A Book of Readings*. Minneapolis: University of Minnesota Press, 1954. Selected articles from magazines; the first four discuss sixteenth-century ballads, journalism of the Civil War (1640) period, the eighteenth-century British press, and Daniel Defoe.

Herd, Harold, *The March of Journalism: The Story of the British Press from 1622 to the Present Day*. London: Allen & Unwin, Ltd., 1952. A condensed, readable history of British newspapers and magazines.

McMurtrie, Douglas C., *The Book: The Story of Printing and Bookmaking*. New York: Oxford University Press, 1943. Tells the Gutenberg story, and traces the spread of printing in Europe and the New World.

Morison, Stanley, *The English Newspaper: Some Account of the Physical Development of Journals Printed in London between 1622 and the Present Day*. Cambridge, England: Cambridge University Press, 1932. One of the recognized histories in its field, well illustrated.

Shaaber, Matthias A., *Some Forerunners of the Newspaper in England, 1476-1622*. Philadelphia: University of Pennsylvania Press, 1929. An authoritative, detailed study of the pre-coranto period of journalism.

Siebert, Fredrick Seaton, *Freedom of the Press in England, 1476-1776*. Urbana: University of Illinois Press, 1952. The outstanding study of the subject. Corrects many inaccuracies of older histories.

Steinberg, S. H., *Five Hundred Years of Printing*. London: Faber and Faber, 1959. A brief account of the history of printing, emphasizing the relationships of technical developments and ideas.

The Tatler and The Spectator. London: G. A. Aitken, ed., 1898-99. The complete file of the famous Addison and Steele literary papers.

Trevelyan, G. M., *England Under the Stuarts*. New York: G. P. Putnam's Sons, 1904. One of the most readable and informative histories of the period, by a great writer. See also his *England Under Queen Anne*.

von Klarwill, Victor, ed., *The Fugger News Letters*, first series. New York: G. P. Putnam's Sons, 1924. Second series, 1926. An interesting study of the content of news before the days of newspapers.

Ward, A. W., *The Counter Reformation*. New York: Longmans, Green & Company, 1893. Good background material.

Periodicals and Monographs:

Allen, Eric W., "International Origins of the Newspapers: The Establishment of Periodicity in Print," *Journalism Quarterly*, VII (December 1930), 307. Discusses qualifications of the true newspaper.

Baker, Harry T., "Early English Journalism," *Sewanee Review*, XXV (October 1917), 396. Nathaniel Butter and Sir Roger L'Estrange are highlighted in this detailed account.

Bleyer, Willard G., "The Beginnings of English Journalism," *Journalism Quarterly*, VIII (September 1931), 317. A study of foreign news in early English corantos, showing ties with the continent.

Lowenthal, Leo, and Marjorie Fiske, "Reaction to Mass Media Growth in 18th-Century England," *Journalism Quarterly*, XXXIII (Fall 1956), 442. How literary tastes were lowered by mass consumption.

Rosenberg, Marvin, "The Rise of England's First Daily Newspaper," *Journalism Quarterly*, XXX (Winter 1953), 3. An excellent description of Samuel Buckley's *Daily Courant*.

Siebert, Fredrick S., "Regulation of Newsbooks, 1620-1640," *Journalism Quarterly*, XVI (June 1939), 151.

———, "Regulation of the Press in the Seventeenth Century—Excerpts from the Records of the Court of the Stationers Company," *Journalism Quarterly*, XIII (December 1936), 281.

———, "Taxes on Publications in England in the Eighteenth Century," *Journalism Quarterly*, XXI (March 1944), 12. These monographs by Siebert are now brought up to date in his 1952 book, cited above.

Chapter **2**

THE BIRTH OF THE AMERICAN NEWSPAPER

> The way to get at the nature of an institution, as of anything else that is alive, is to see how it has grown.
>
> —A. G. Keller[1]

NEW ENGLAND was the birthplace of the American newspaper, but it was not until 1704, or 84 years after the establishment of the first successful colony in that area, that a publication meeting all the qualifications of a true newspaper appeared. Printers were available from the very beginning. William Brewster and Edward Winslow, two of the "elders," or leaders, of the Pilgrims who came to Plymouth in December of 1620, were printers. They had published religious tracts for the Separatists, the more radical offshoot of English Protestantism, and they had lived for a time near George Veseler, who was printing the first English coranto in the Netherlands while the Pilgrims were on the way to the New World in the "Mayflower." Despite this background, the Plymouth colony existed nearly a century before it enjoyed a newspaper or popular periodical.

Ten years after the arrival of the Pilgrims, another group of religious exiles settled around Boston, a day's sail to the north of Plymouth. This Massachusetts Bay Colony, as it was then known,

[1] Famous in his time as a great teacher and lecturer on sociology at Yale University.

28

was to be the cradle of American journalism. Many of its members were prosperous. The educational level was high, and some of the settlers were respected scholars. A few had held high office in the British government up to the time of the religious upheaval, with its socio-political-economic manifestations, which had forced them out. They represented the emerging middle class, some of whom stayed to fight it out for recognition in the mother country, thus precipitating conflict on the same issues on both sides of the Atlantic. Unlike the Plymouth settlement, which grew slowly, the Massachusetts Bay Colony increased rapidly in population and area of influence. From the beginning it had a high degree of self-government. All males over sixteen had the right to buy stock in the company that sponsored the colony. Stock entitled the holder to many rights and privileges. More important, the charter of the organization had been brought to America, where it served as a kind of constitution beyond the tampering of jealous officials in the home government. In effect, the colony had a form of autonomy, or at least of participating home rule, that was to be of great significance in the political development of New England.

These colonists were concerned about the education of their children. Having enjoyed educational advantages themselves, they wished to pass on the heritage to succeeding generations. Six years after the founding of the settlement, they established Harvard College (1636). The original purpose of the institution was to provide qualified religious leaders, but its educational influence extended beyond this sphere. There was progress at the primary and secondary level of education, too. Even the smaller communities around Boston, the center of the colony, required children to be taught at least the rudiments of learning. In the larger towns there were "grammar schools," which prepared boys for Harvard.

As part of this educational process, the authorities established the first press in the English colonies at Cambridge (Harvard College) in 1638. Its function was to produce the religious texts needed in school and college. Other presses were set up not long after. Later, these presses printed cultural material, including the first history of the colony and some poetry. It was this interest in education and cultural dissemination that made Boston famous as the intellectual capital of the New World. Here were all the ingredients for the development of a newspaper—high literacy, interest in community matters, self-government, prosperity, and cultural leadership—yet no successful newspaper appeared until the fourth generation.

There was good reason for the lag. At first, the wilderness absorbed the energies of the colonists. Any demand for news was satisfied well enough by the English papers, which arrived on every ship from home. For the colonists had few ties with other communities in the New World. Years after he arrived, the settler was still oriented toward the homeland, not toward his neighbors. Just as soldiers on foreign duty ignore local happenings while keeping up on home-town news, so did the colonists react in regard to community intelligence.

There was little commerce at first, and almost no intercourse with other colonies, so there was no demand for the type of news that had fostered early newspapers in Europe. Nor was there any visible means of supporting a popular press. There was little to sell and little to advertise. Yet during this period the area was producing a breed of citizen that was to expand the frontiers of social and political freedom in America, aided by an aggressive and powerful press. It took time, that is all.

The New Englander was a product of glaciation, rugged climate, and Calvinism. Glaciers had scored the country into a land of narrow valleys, swiftly flowing streams, and thin soil. The endless field stone fences of New England are evidences of the toil involved in scratching a living from such a land. It was difficult for one family to care for many backbreaking acres, and so the individual farms tended to be small. The narrow valleys and the small farms brought people closer together. This suited the New Englander, who preferred to live in towns, where he could attend church and the meetinghouse. In the South, where broad rivers drained the wide savannahs, people lived more spaciously. It is significant that here the gatherings were more in the nature of social events. A southerner met to enjoy himself. A New Englander met to improve himself—and others. His meetings were argumentative to the point of tediousness, but the endless discussions on the fine points of religious dogma sharpened his wits. Few were his equal in argument.

It was fortunate for the future of America that there could be no turning back for most of the colonists. They had come to stay. The Spaniards far to the south, in contrast, risked the dangers of conquest primarily for quick return on investment. They wished only to bring home the riches that would allow them to live in splendor. But the English colonist was often an exile from his native land. Because of social, political, but usually religious differences with authorities at home, he had committed himself to a strange new world. Other colonists were indentured servants, who found the hardships of the wilderness preferable to the hard lot of the disfranchised and exploited British pauper.

It was also fortunate for later generations of Americans that the New England settlers had great appreciation for property, especially in the form of land. Land had been the symbol of prestige and standing in England. The decline of feudalism and the emergence of the capitalist class brought many dispossessed British farmers to America. Driven from the land by the manor lord who had turned from subsistence farming to wool raising, which required much less help; sick of the stinking slums which were the only refuge of the dispossessed; unwanted—large numbers of these ex-plowmen fled to America. The country needed them, and that alone is enough to start strong loyalties. In America they could not only work the land they loved, but they could even acquire property, the mark of a superior person.[2]

The New England woman was another significant factor in the development of the region. Women came over with the original settlers. They reared large families, and the group kept its identity. In South America, and to some extent in French Canada, colonists tended to be absorbed by the native populations, because Europeans in those regions did not generally bring women along with them. The New England pioneer preserved the traditions of an old race and the characteristics of a great culture. This solidarity was even more secure in New England than in other American colonies because of the rejection of Negro slavery there. In the South, slavery was to be disruptive of homogeneity in years to come. The New Englander was saved from the curse of slavery not just because he was opposed to the system, but because it was uneconomical. The

[2] True, the farm colonist might have settled in other areas, but New England had its share, along with its middle-class emigres.

long, unproductive winters, and the small farms, were not conducive to the institution that was to exert such a baneful influence in
other sections of America.

The commercial stimulation that encourages the development of
a popular press was brought to New England in a curious way.
Because farming paid such a small return on the energy invested
in it, the New England Yankee early turned to fishing as an easier
way of earning a living. Surrounding waters teemed with fish. Soon
Yankee fishermen were the main suppliers of fish to the Mediterranean basin, where a combination of religions and diet provided
a ready market. The South might just as well have developed a
fishing industry, but plantation life was more satisfactory to the
southerner than spending cold weeks in pitching vessels on the
Grand Banks fishing grounds.

Fishing made New Englanders into great seafarers. Soon they
were building their own vessels, designed for special purposes, and
superior to anything under sail up to then. The forests provided
the raw material for a thriving industry. The region abounded in
excellent harbors. Ship-building and ocean commerce stimulated
the growth of lumbering, wood manufacture, and other small industries, for which there was abundant water power. As a result, a
class of shrewd, tough, independent business men began to win
renown for New England. Many of them became wealthy and ready
to help support a publication that could advertise wares and spread
pertinent information.

For a time the coffeehouses had sufficed as a news medium, even
as the market places and fairs had served Europe in previous centuries. Here men of congenial interests met to exchange gossip and
useful information. Notices of cargoes awaiting shipment, new imports, and customs regulations could be posted in a prominent
place. But as trade and the volume of business increased, the coffee-
house was inadequate as a means of reaching a much bigger public.

Buyers, as well as retailers, were interested in the arrival and
departure of ships. Business men were curious about conditions in
areas largely ignored by the British papers. Commerce along the
American coast was slowly increasing, for example, and there was
a thriving trade with the West Indies. The business man also
needed to know the latest proclamations of the governor, especially
if these orders applied to commerce. What was being done to dis-

perse local pirates? Was it true that a new postal system was about to be established by His Majesty's Government? Better communications would certainly benefit commerce, and the business man was eager for more information on such subjects. Finally, as rivalry spurred trade in the growing communities, the merchant discovered he could move his goods to the local customer faster if he printed notices, or advertisements, in a publication read by his customers. The emphasis on this aspect of journalism is indicated by the number of early newspapers with the word "Advertiser" in the name plate. The development of commerce, then, had an important bearing on the establishment of the first newspaper, and all the early publications appeared in commercial centers.

Commerce and Calvinism, the religion of the Yankee, fitted well together. The New Englander was usually a believer in the doctrine of John Calvin, the sixteenth-century reformer who had set up a theocratic government in Geneva. It is significant that Calvinism followed the trade routes and was most popular in commercial areas. It was strong in the Netherlands, one of the great commercial nations. The Dutch traded with the British for wool, and right behind the trader came the Calvinist minister to spread his religious beliefs. Most of this British Calvinism centered in the commercial communities. It was a disrupting influence, but the middle-class merchant, struggling for recognition, was also a disruptive force. The two attracted each other. Many of these business men fled to America, especially to the Massachusetts Bay area. They brought their philosophies with them.

The essence of Calvinism is "predestination." The Calvinist believed that the world and its people followed a plan of God. Man's salvation or damnation was thus already predetermined according to this pattern. Prosperity was a sign that God had looked upon a man with favor. A successful business man could think of himself as having passed through the eye of the needle into the circle of the elect. So, of course, every good Calvinist tried to look prosperous to show the world that he had been marked by God for salvation.

A wealthy man, who is also pious, is almost unconquerable. In New England, Bible and ledger were supplementary authorities. Calvinism was tailor-made for the Yankee. It made him not necessarily a better man, but a more sanctimonious citizen than most of his colonial neighbors. God was always very close, and since the Calvinist was in such intimate communication with the Almighty, he felt justified in giving out the "direct word" on religious matters. All who challenged him were obviously wrong. The Yankee had a dry humor, but he could not, in good conscience, be jovial, like his southern neighbors. Everything he did was for a serious purpose, and levity thus became a kind of irreverence. Indeed, fun and sin were often synonymous, because both were enemies of material productiveness in a community where the value on productiveness was high. Even when he tried to relax, the Yankee felt guilty. Actually, Calvinism as a doctrine received its biggest stimulus somewhat later, under the direction of such leaders as Jonathan Edwards, but the climate of Calvinism was identified with New England from the beginning.

The New England "Puritan" made many important contributions to the culture and society that were to prepare the way for the American experiment in self-rule and eventual independence. Other areas fortunately infused some of the more human qualities into the product, however. The South, for example, was in strong contrast to New England. Life was easier and more relaxed on the wide plantations. The general viewpoint remained agrarian, rather than commercial. Communications develop slowly in such a society. Although Virginia, the "Old Dominion," was settled 13 years before the Pilgrims landed at Plymouth, it lagged far behind in press progress. But the South contributed great ideas and spokesmen, essential to the development of democracy, with which the press was to be so closely integrated. Men and women tended to be broadminded in the spacious South. They were less constrained by religious dogma. True, religious toleration was achieved in the South only after conflict, but the general attitude on such matters was less dogmatic than in the North. The graciousness of the South was a fortunate leavening for the tough-mindedness of the Yankee, when the time came for the colonies to cooperate.

The South could even teach a few lessons on democracy in the earliest days of colonization. The New England Puritan was not noted for his tolerance. Intellectual misfits, such as Anne Hutchinson, the first great American feminist, and Roger Williams were driven into exile by the intransigent theocrats of Massachusetts because of ideas unacceptable to the leaders. It took a little while for Americans to learn the lesson that it takes ideas to keep democracy dynamic—that is, adjustable to changing conditions. The institutions of the South were not necessarily more democratic, but the areas of intolerance were different. At least the southerner appeared to have a more human outlook on life.

The Middle Atlantic, or "bread," colonies helped to fuse the regional characteristics of the colonies. Philadelphia and New York were the great commercial centers. In this respect the middle colonies resembled the New England of Boston, Salem, and Providence in this first century of colonial history. But the inhabitants tended to live more spaciously, like the southerner. Young Ben Franklin, hiding out in Philadelphia, found it to be as bustling as Boston, but more congenial to a man of his inquisitive nature. And it is significant that Philadelphia was the second American city to support a successful newspaper.

The middle colonies attracted settlers of various national and religious backgrounds. Along the Delaware river the Swedes had established communities dating from the early seventeenth century. The Dutch West India Company in 1621 established New Netherland colony, later to be renamed by the English successors New York. Later many other groups moved into the area. Areas in Pennsylvania became almost as Germanic as the cities in the Palatinate from whence the "Pennsylvania Dutch" (Deutsch) had come. The region also absorbed religious expatriates, such as Catholics, Lutherans, Quakers, and Dutch Reformers. They did not always get along well together. Sometimes, for religious or nationalistic reasons, whole communities moved to more congenial sections of the colonies. But the process of learning to adjust to different cultures and ideas went on, and this was an important contribution of the Middle Atlantic region.

By the end of the seventeenth century there were about 250,000 inhabitants of European extraction in the American colonies. Massachusetts had grown from about 100 in 1620 to 45,000 by 1700. Virginia had a white population of about 50,000. Maryland was next, with 20,000. The others were much smaller, but were growing fast. A few families had accumulated respectable fortunes by this time, but the general income level was relatively low.

The colonies reflected the religious and political troubles of the mother country. Many Americans had emigrated because of differences in beliefs, and they brought their problems with them. The restoration of Charles II after the revolution of 1640 was a period of political reaction. Once again the king exerted his old powers—or tried to. James II, who succeeded Charles, should have learned that it was dangerous to flout the good will of his subjects, but James was even more unpopular than his predecessors. Under James, revolt seethed. The unrest was reflected in the colonies.

In 1664 the British conquered the Dutch and took as one of the spoils of war the New Netherland colony. In the next few years the king tried to strengthen his power in England. It is not surprising that the same process was apparent in the colonies. The General Court of Massachusetts, for example, passed the first formal act restricting the press in 1662. The only printing plant in the colony at the time was the one at Harvard, consisting of two presses, but the authorities were taking no chances with possible subversive literature, and the law provided for rigorous censorship.[3]

The authorities made use of monopoly, as in England, to make supervision easier. In 1681 Samuel "Seawall" (the same Judge Sewall whose famous diary is still read by historians) was given the privileges and responsibilities of exclusive publication. The decision of the authorities indicates that they valued the services of the press, even though they feared its abuse, for the Sewall monopoly was clearly a compromise between restriction and utilization of the press.

One of the governors sent out to the colonies about this time was Sir Edmund Andros. He first took over the seat of government in New York in 1674. It was his understanding that his commission gave him jurisdiction over the area between the Delaware and Connecticut rivers. This was interpreted by colonial leaders as proof that the Crown wished to establish a more effective control of this area by means of centralization of authority. The charters of the New England colonies were declared invalid, and Andros believed he had a mandate to take over this region, too. By 1686 he was in control of most of the populated and prosperous sections of the American seaboard. It was during this period that Sir Edmund met what amounted to outright rebellion. Connecticut, for example, re-

[3] One of the best discussions of this period will be found in Clyde A. Duniway, *The Development of Freedom of the Press in Massachusetts* (New York: Longmans, Green & Company, 1906).

fused to give up its charter to the crown official. According to legend, the document was hidden in a hollow tree (the Charter Oak at Hartford) when the governor's agents came to demand it. Other colonies joined in opposition to Andros, just as in England an important class of the citizenry opposed the king.

Two years later (1688) Parliament deposed James II in the "Glorious Revolution." The crown was then offered jointly to his eldest daughter, Mary, and her husband, William of Orange. William and Mary were wise rulers. Aware of the circumstances under which they had been offered the crowns, they tended to be conciliatory. The counterpart of these events in America was the revolt against royal authority in the guise of Andros. He was sent back to England in 1689 for trial.[4]

It was at this very time that an ex-London bookseller and publisher decided to offer a periodical that the ordinary person could afford and could understand. Boston then had a population of nearly 7,000 and was the largest city in America. It offered sufficient sales potential for the type of publication the promoter had in mind. Cultural and literacy levels were sufficient to warrant the financial risk. There was a demand by the commercial interests for such an organ, and they could offer the essential support. The situation was made to order for a newspaper, and the man of the hour was at hand, although he never did quite achieve the honor of producing the first American newspaper.

The hero of this episode was the exiled printer, Benjamin Harris, who was last seen fleeing from the law (page 16). Harris arrived in Boston in 1686. Already he had had considerable experience in the London publishing business. Unfortunately, Harris had also been engaged in less legitimate enterprises. For a time he operated a kind of underground press engaged in attacking the Catholics. The group publicized a fictitious Catholic conspiracy to murder Charles II and to make the Duke of York (later James II) king. Harris was an accomplice of the perjurer, Titus Oates, whose false testimony resulted in the execution of innocent citizens. He was also a party to the Rye House plots, another alleged conspiracy against the king. The purpose of all this, of course, was to discredit the hated Catholics.

[4] He was never tried. Indeed, he was soon returned to favor, and came back to America as governor of Virginia.

Harris was a trouble-maker, and shortly after he had started his London newspaper in 1679, he was arrested for having seditious literature in his possession. He was sentenced to the pillory, which was erected in front of his own office. Friends kept passersby from throwing refuse at the prisoner, but they could not help him pay the stiff fine imposed, and Harris had to go to jail. From his cell he continued to edit his paper. In 1686 his shop was again raided. Officers seized a quantity of pamphlets connecting Harris with subversive organizations, and a warrant was issued for his arrest. Warned of the danger, Harris fled with his family to America. In the fall of 1686 he opened a combined coffee and book shop in Boston at the corner of State and Washington streets.

The shop was a favorite meeting place for some of Boston's most interesting citizens. Judge Sewall, chronicler of his times and a former publisher, was a regular customer. Most of the local wits and writers made the shop their headquarters. The progressive views of the proprietor are indicated by the fact that his was the only coffee shop in the city where respectable women were welcome.

Harris was a shrewd business man. He succeeded against formidable opposition. There were seven booksellers in the neighborhood when Harris set up shop. He sat down and wrote a spelling book that was a best seller in the country for many years. He published books for a distinguished clientele, and thus acquired a respect and prestige that some of his rivals lacked. He was not a printer at this time, but rather the promoter of literary works. The downfall of Andros gave Harris the opportunity to go back to his first love, the publication of a newspaper.

On September 25, 1690, the printing shop of R. Pierce issued a four-page newspaper. It was printed on only three sides. The fourth page was blank so the reader could add his own news items before passing it on. The pages measured only 6 x 10¼ inches. There was very little attempt at makeup. This was Harris' *Publick Occurrences, Both Forreign and Domestick,* called by some authorities the first American newspaper. It might very well have been, except that it was banned after the first issue, and one of the qualifications of a newspaper is periodicity, or continuity. If continuity is ignored, a publication printed the year before might just as logically be called the first American newspaper. This was *The Present State of the New-English Affairs.* It was printed in 1689 as a report from the Rev. Increase Mather to Governor Broadstreet of Massachusetts. The Reverend Mather was representing the colony in London, and the publication was designed to let the public know what progress had been made in colonial problems. This was certainly news, and was printed as such. There are even earlier examples of broadsheets and reprints of big news events. The characteristic that set *Publick Occurrences* apart was that it looked like a newspaper, it read like a newspaper, and it was intended as a permanent news organ, unlike the others.[5] Harris was a good reporter for his time. His style was concise—"punchy," the modern editor would call it. The paper included both foreign and local news—another distinction from earlier news publications. Indeed, his "occurrences" covered a multitude of interests. Thus, we find at the bottom of the outside column on page one:

The *Small-pox* which has been raging in *Boston,* after a manner very Extraordinary is now very much abated. It is thought that far more have been sick of it than were visited with it, when it raged so much twelve years ago, nevertheless it has not been so Mortal. The number of them that have dyed in *Boston* by this last Visitation is about three hundred and twenty, which is not perhaps half so many as fell by the former. . . .[6]

Harris knew what would interest his readers. He included intelligent comment, but he knew that most of his readers would be attracted more by appeals to basic emotions and by reference to familiar persons and places. Conflict and fear were two such emotions emphasized in this early paper. The pattern has been used successfully right up to modern times, which is not to say that this is the *only* means for winning subscribers.

Harris got into trouble with the local authorities, not because he printed libels, but because he printed the truth as he saw it. He had also violated licensing restrictions first imposed in 1662. One of Harris' items reported that Indian allies of the "English Colonies & Provinces of the West" had forced an army under Gen-

---

[5] Even on this count it would fail to qualify technically as a newspaper, according to the criteria listed on page 5, because Harris intended to issue the paper only once a month, unless an "unusual glut of occurrences" made greater frequency of publication practicable.

[6] From a facsimile filed in the London Public Office (1845), as reprinted in Willard G. Bleyer, *Main Currents in the History of American Journalism* (Boston: Houghton Mifflin Company, 1927), p. 45.

eral Winthrop to postpone an attack on the French. The Indians, Harris wrote, had failed to provide "canoo's" for the transportation of the forces into enemy territory. War chiefs had explained that the redmen were too weakened from smallpox to fulfill their commitments, and that was probably true. They were not too weak to make individual raids, however. From one of these raids, Harris reported, they "brought home several *Prisoners,* whom they used in a manner too barbarous for any English to approve." [7] The journalist referred to these Indian allies as "miserable savages, in whom we have too much confided."

All these remarks could be taken as criticism of colonial policy, which at that moment was concerned with winning, not alienating, Indian neighbors. Harris was also accused of bad taste. He had spiced up his paper by reporting that the French king had been taking immoral liberties with the prince's wife, for which reason the prince had revolted. Judge Sewall wrote in his diary that the Puritan clergy was scandalized by this account in a publication reaching the Boston public.

It was the Massachusetts licensing act that ended Harris' career as an American newspaper publisher, however. How he expected to get around that restriction is not at all clear. There is every evidence that the content of the paper was not enough to alienate the authorities indefinitely. Harris' connections in Boston were good. Soon after the banning of *Publick Occurrences,* Harris was appointed government printer, apparently as compensation for the arbitrary action of the authorities.

Harris eventually returned to England. One wonders why he did not succeed better in later life; he deserved fame and prosperity, after all his bold attempts to pioneer new frontiers. The relaxing of press controls in England after the Glorious Revolution should have made it possible for a clever journalist like Harris to publish a popular newspaper. History shows us that he thrived only on persecution, however. Once the obstacles were out of the way, he had no more success in journalism. He fades out of the scene as the penurious vendor of quack medicines.

Not for another 14 years was there a newspaper in the American colonies, and when one did appear, it operated alone for 15 years. The example of *Publick Occurrences* may have warned away any

[7] *Loc. cit.*

journalistic promoters during this interim. When the next newspapers did appear, they were inclined to be stodgy and dull, partly because the publishers lacked Harris' color and boldness, and partly because all news had to be "safe" to pass the licensers. Each of the successful Boston publishers in the next 30 years was careful to notify his public that he printed "by authority." Editors also took the precaution to water down their words so as to anger no one deliberately. More important; they had the protection of an important office—for the journalists who followed immediately after Harris were all postmasters.

In Europe there had been a long tradition of affiliation between the postal service and journalism. Many of the early continental newspapers had been published by postmasters. They were not necessarily printers; in fact few of them were. But for generations the postmasters in central Europe had taken a hand in promoting popular periodicals. There was good reason for this. Postmasters were especially interested in disseminating information. That was their principal business. They had access to most of the intelligence available to the community. They broke the seals of official pouches and delivered important dispatches. Postmasters then, as today, heard much of the local gossip. They were "in the know." The post office has always been a logical place to spread news. Proclamations and notices were posted there. And in colonial times, as in modern times, the postmaster was likely to be an important political figure. That was how he usually earned his office.

As the appointee of the administration in power, he had some kind of political bond with the higher authorities. It was unlikely that he would antagonize his sponsors, so he got into less trouble than independent publishers. If he did make a mistake, powerful political friends might help him in returning to grace. But his biggest asset as a newspaper promoter was his right to send out printed material free, under his "frank." That gave him a great advantage over independent rivals.

But such advantages do not necessarily produce good newspapers. Softness and safety never beget great journalism—then or now. Newspapers have progressed farthest in times of strife. Yet the early postmaster-publishers contributed much to American journalism. At least they understood that the main problem was survival, which is more than could be said of Harris. It was the ability to adjust to conditions that enabled a postmaster to produce the first genuine newspaper in America. And if he lagged 14 years behind Harris, the fault was not all his. Until 1692 there had been no official postal service in the colonies. In that year the British government authorized an intercolonial mail system; an indication that the respective colonies were beginning to take note of each other.

One of the postmasters appointed by the Crown for the new intercolonial service was John Campbell. He took over the Boston post office in 1700. From the very beginning he made use of the postal service to supply information to special correspondents in other colonies. He issued this intelligence in the form of a news letter—the primitive, handwritten report that had been the common medium of communication in Europe before the invention of printing. Most of the information sent out by Campbell was concerned with commercial and governmental matters. Boston was the most important city in the colonies then, and the postmaster's information was therefore highly pertinent all along the Atlantic seaboard. Meetings, proclamations, complaints, legal notices, actions in court, available cargo space, and the arrivals of Very Important Persons provided the grist for Campbell's news mill. There was such a demand for his news letter that Campbell began to look around for some way of relieving the pressure upon his time and energy. He got his brother, Duncan, to help, but even together they could not supply the demand for news. They just couldn't write longhand fast enough. A shrewd Scotsman, Campbell decided there must be an easier way to earn a living. He set out one afternoon to make a call on Bartholomew Green. Green was one of the few printers in the area. That day the two struck a bargain.

In Green's shop on Newbury street there was printed on the morning of April 24, 1704, the first genuine American newspaper. It was called the *Boston News-Letter*, an appropriate title, since it was merely a continuation of the publication the Campbells had been producing since 1700. The *News-Letter* was printed on both sides of a sheet just a little larger than the dimensions of Harris' paper—that is, slightly larger than a sheet of typewriter paper.

The news in the first issue was not very startling. The publisher-editor-postmaster had simply clipped the incoming London newspapers, already weeks old, and had inserted the items as foreign exchanges. Since he did not have space for all the European dispatches, he put aside excess information for future use. As a result, some of his news was months old before it reached the reader. On the other hand, local news was fairly timely. It was terse, but surprisingly informative. For example:

Boston, April 18. Arrived Capt. Sill from Jamaica, about four Weeks Passage, says, they continue there very sickly.

Mr. Nathaniel Oliver, a principal Merchant of this place dyed April 15 & was decently inter'd. April 18, Aetatis 53. . . .

The 20 the R'd Mr. Pemberton Preached an Excellent Sermon on 1 Thes. 4:11. "And do your own business"; Exhorting all Ranks & Degrees of Persons to do their own work, in order to a REFORMATION; which His Excellency has ordered to be printed.

The 21 His Excellency Dissolved the Gen. Assembly. . . .[8]

But it was savorless journalism, after Harris' reports on bloodthirsty savages and lustful kings. Campbell cleared all the copy with the Governor, or with his secretary. That made his paper libel-proof, censor-proof, and well-nigh reader-proof. Though we have noted that it was the only newspaper in the colonies for 15 years, Campbell never had enough subscribers to make his venture profitable. The first advertisement in an American newspaper was concerned with this problem of circulation. It was what the trade would call a "blind ad," or piece of promotion. Campbell discovered, as many another editor-publisher was to find out later, that the public is never willing to pay the full price for the information it must have to exert its rights. The postmaster was frantic on several occasions because so many subscribers were in arrears. His circulation seldom exceeded 300. Twice Campbell was saved from bankruptcy by a government subsidy. The paper was valuable for the publication of official notices, which could be reproduced cheaper in the *News-Letter* than by private printing. Despite this support, the publisher had to suspend publication for eight months at one critical period for lack of funds.

Even Campbell's embryonic journal contributed to the traditions of an honorable craft. He had a strong sense of responsibility to his public. That is proved by his determination to print the news in spite of public apathy and financial distress. It was also evidenced by his sincere policy of printing "for a Publick Good, to

[8] From a facsimile in the Wisconsin Historical Library.

The Boston News-Letter.

Publifhed by Authority.

From **Monday** May 1. to **Monday** May 8. 1704.

London Gazette, from *Novemb.* 8 to 11. 1703.

Weftminfter, *Novemb.* 9.

THE Parliament *met here this day , and Her Majefty being come to the Houfe of Peers, and feated on the Throne in Her Royal Robes, with the ufual Solemnity, the Gentleman Ufher of the Black Rod, was fent with a Meffage to the Houfe of Commons, requiring their Attendance in the Houfe of Peers, whither they came accordingly, and Her Majefty was pleafed to make a moft Gracious Speech to both Houfes, which follows.*

My Lords and Gentlemen,

I Have Called you together affoon as I thought you could conveniently Come out of your Countries, that no Time may be loft in making Our Preparations for Carrying on the Prefent War, in which I do not Doubt of your Cheerful Concurrence, fince you can't but be fenfible, that on the Succefs of it depends Our Own Safety and Happinefs and that of all *Europe.*

I Hope I have Improved the Confidence you Repofed in Me laft Year, to your Satisfaction and the Advantage of Us and Our Allies, by the Treaty with the King of *Portugal,* and the Declaration of the Duke of *Savoy,* which in great Meafure may be Imputed to the Cheerfulnefs with which you Supported Me in this War, and the Affurance with which you Trufted Me in the Conduct of it : And We cannot fufficiently Acknowledge the Goodnefs of Almighty God, who is pleafed to Afford Us fo far a Profpect as We now have, of bringing it to a Glorious and Speedy Conclufion.

I muft therefore Defire you, *Gentlemen of the Houfe of Commons,* to Grant Me fuch Supplies as fhall be requifite to Defray the Neceffary Charge of the War in the next Year, with regard, not only to all Our formerEngagements, but particularly toOur Alliance lately made with the King of *Portugal* for recovering the Monarchy of *Spain* from the Houfe of *Bourbon,* and Reftoring it to the Houfe of *Auftria,* which Treaty being in it felf of the higheft Importance imaginable; and requiring all poffible Difpatch in the Execution of it, has Neceffarily Occafion'd a great Expence even in this prefent Year, tho' not fo much as it will Require, and for which, I hope, We fhall be amply Recompenfed in the next.

The Subfidies which will now be immediately Required for the Affiftance of the Duke of *Savoy,* will likewife Occafion a further Neceffary Charge.

I muft takeNotice to you, That tho' no particular Provifion was made in the laft Seffion, either for the Charge of Our prefent Expedition to *Portugal,* or for that of the Augmentation Troops defired by the *States General,* yet the Funds given by Parliament have held out fo well, and the Produce of the Prizes has Prov'd fo Confiderable, that you will find the Publick will not be in Debt by Reafon of either of thefe Additional Services.

I may further obferve to you, That tho' the Fonds

for the Civil Government are diminifht by the War I have, in Conjunction with the *States General,* Contributed out of My Own Revenue towards fome Publick Services, and particularly the Support of the Circle of *Suabia,* whofe firm Adherence to the Intereft of the Allies under the greateft Preffures, did very well Deferve our Seafonable Affiftance : And I fhall ftill be Careful not to engage My Self in any Unneceffary Expence of My Own, that I may have the more to Spare towards the Eafe of My Subjects.

My Lords and Gentlemen,

I Heartily Wifh fome eafe and lefs chargeable Method could be found for the Speedy and Effectual Manning of the Fleet.

I muft alfo Recommend to you to make fome Regulation for Preventing the Exceffive Price of Coals, I have Examined this Matter, and taken particular Care to appoint Convoys for that Service ; but the Price has not been in the leaft Abated notwithftanding a very confiderable quantity has been Imported fince that time ; This gives great ground of Sufpicion there may be a Combination of fome Perfons to Enrich themfelves by a general Oppreffion of others, and particularly the Poor : Twill deferve your Confideration how to Remedy this great Inconvenience.

And in all your Affairs, I muft Recommend to you as much Difpatch as the Nature of them will admit ; This is Neceffary to make Our Preparations early, on which in great Meafure Depends the good Succefs of all Our Enterprizes.

I want Words to Exprefs to you My earneft Defires of Seeing all My Subjects in perfect Peace and Union among themfelves : I have nothing fo much at Heart as their general Welfare and Happinefs ; Let Me therefore Defire you all That you would Carefully Avoid any Heats or Divifions that may Difappoint Me of that Satisfaction, and Give Encouragement to the Common Enemies of Our Church and State.

London, December 9.

ON Monday the Marquefs *de Hencourt,* a French Proteftant Refugee, departed this Life, in the 72 year of his Age, leaving behind him a very good Name, for his great Piety and other Vertues, truly becoming a Noble-man. As he had cheerfully made a Sacrifice of a great Eftate to his Religion, he lived in his Exile after fo Exemplary a manner, that juftly gained him the efteem of all that knew him.

By His Excellency J O S E P H D U D L E Y Efq. Captain General and Governour in Chief, in and over Her Majefties Province of the *Maffachufetts-Bay* in *New-England.*

A PROCLAMATION for a General FAST.

UPon Confideration of the troublefome Sate of Europe, by reafon of the Calamitous Wars wherein thofe Nations are Engaged amongft themfelves, and of Her Majefties Great and Juft Intereft therein : As alfo the prefent Cir-

give a true Account of all Foreign & Domestick Occurrences, and to prevent a great many false reports of the same"—a policy still respected by honest publishers.

Despite his clumsiness at news gathering and news writing, Campbell tried his best to be fair and accurate. In one issue he apologized for misplacing a comma in a preceding number, although this was only a drop in the sea of other errors. An uninspired minor bureaucrat in an unpopular administration, he still had the good editor's sense of decency and kindness for his fellow men. Of a suicide involving a poor woman, he wrote that "he hoped the Inserting of such an awful Providence here may not be offensive, but rather a Warning to all others to watch against the Wiles of our Grand Adversary." He obviously regretted having to print the account of a prisoner's whipping, but the culprit had cheated the public by selling tar mixed with dirt. The news, Campbell explained sadly, "is here only Inserted to be a caveat to others, of doing the like, least a worse thing befal them." Clearly, Campbell deserves better of history.

Unimpressive as it was, the *Boston News-Letter* was like the Biblical mustard seed. From it stemmed the mighty American Fourth Estate, a force no single person could ignore.

ANNOTATED BIBLIOGRAPHY

Books:

The most useful books for the general reader from among histories of American journalism earlier than this volume are those by Mott, Bleyer, A. M. Lee, and Payne, listed below. The earliest attempt at a general account was that by Isaiah Thomas in 1810 (see bibliography for Chapter 3). Next were those by Frederic Hudson in 1873 and by S. N. D. North in 1884 (see bibliographies for Chapters 12 and 16, respectively). These three books remain of special use to journalism historians. Other general histories of lesser quality have been those by James Melvin Lee, *History of American Journalism* (Boston: Houghton Mifflin Company, 1917); Robert W. Jones, *Journalism in the United States* (New York: E. P. Dutton and Company, 1947); Edith M. Bartow, *News and These United States* (New York: Funk & Wagnalls Company, 1952); and Sidney Kobre, *Foundations of American Journalism* and *Modern American Journalism*, produced by offset printing from typewriting in 1958 and 1959 at Florida State University, Tallahassee. For analyses of the subject see the annotations in Price, *The Literature of Journalism*, pp. 3-7, and Allan Nevins, "American Journalism and Its

Historical Treatment," *Journalism Quarterly*, XXXVI (Fall 1959), 411.
Especially recommended for background reading in American history
are the interpretive history by the Beards and the studies of American
thought by Parrington and Curti, listed below. Other excellent general
histories include John D. Hicks and George E. Mowry, *A Short History
of American Democracy* (Boston: Houghton Mifflin Company, 1956);
Richard Hofstadter, William Miller, and Daniel Aaron, *The United
States: The History of a Republic* (Englewood Cliffs, New Jersey: Prentice-Hall, Inc., 1957); Samuel Eliot Morison and Henry Steele Commager, *The Growth of the American Republic* (New York: Oxford
University Press, 1950); and Henry Bamford Parkes, *The United States
of America, a History* (New York: Alfred A. Knopf, Inc., 1959).
Two good ready references for historical facts are the *Encyclopaedia
of American History* and the *Dictionary of American History*. Biographies
of many journalists are found in the *Dictionary of American Biography*.
The *Encyclopaedia Britannica* and the *Encyclopaedia of the Social
Sciences* contain articles on newspapers, magazines, press laws, printing,
advertising, radio and television, and other journalistic subjects.

Beard, Charles A., and Mary R. Beard, *The Rise of American Civilization*. New York: The Macmillan Company, 1930. A stimulating and
provocative history of the United States, with much economic, social,
and intellectual detail incorporated into a brilliant general narrative.

Becker, Carl Lotus, *Beginnings of the American People*. Boston: Houghton Mifflin Company, 1915. An authoritative account of the founding
of the American colonies by one of the outstanding historians of the
period.

Bleyer, Willard Grosvenor, *Main Currents in the History of American
Journalism*. Boston: Houghton Mifflin Company, 1927. One of the
standard histories of journalism—reliable and detailed. Places emphasis on leading editors after the 1830's.

Channing, Edward, *History of the United States*, Vol. II. New York: The
Macmillan Company, 1927. A learned and readable summary of events
and forces significant in colonial social and political development.

Curti, Merle, *The Growth of American Thought*. New York: Harper &
Brothers, 1951. One of the most scholarly studies of the American
social and literary heritage by a Pulitzer Prize historian.

Duniway, Clyde A., *The Development of Freedom of the Press in Massachusetts*. New York: Longmans, Green & Company, 1906. A detailed
and invaluable contribution to the history of early American journalism.

Lee, Alfred McClung, *The Daily Newspaper in America*. New York: The
Macmillan Company, 1937. A topical history with a sociological approach, especially useful for its discussions of economic factors.

Miller, Perry, *The New England Mind: The Seventeenth Century*. New
York: The Macmillan Company, 1939.

————, *The New England Mind: From Colony to Province*. Cambridge:

Harvard University Press, 1953. The first volume, covering to 1660, is a readable interpretation of the Puritan character. The second volume discusses society and thought to 1730.

Mott, Frank Luther, *American Journalism.* New York: The Macmillan Company, 1941, rev. eds. 1950, 1962. The most detailed general reference book by an outstanding scholar of American journalism. The revisions add sections for the 1940's and 1950's.

Nettels, Curtis P., *The Roots of American Civilization.* New York: F. S. Crofts & Company, 1938. The best study of economic factors leading to colonial self-development and conflict with Britain.

Parrington, Vernon Louis, *Main Currents in American Thought,* Vol. I, "The Colonial Mind." New York: Harcourt, Brace and Company, 1927. A Pulitzer Prize winning study of the social, economic, and political backgrounds of American literature, in three volumes, which ranks as a classic work for history students.

Payne, George H., *History of Journalism in the United States.* New York: D. Appleton and Company, 1920. An old history, but accurate and detailed, particularly useful for the period up to 1800.

Wertenbaker, Thomas Jefferson, *The Founding of American Civilization: The Middle Colonies.* New York: Charles Scribner's Sons, 1938. Describes contributions of region to cultural development of the country.

Wish, Harvey, *Society and Thought in Early America.* New York: Longmans, Green & Company, 1950. An excellent background study of the period under discussion. First of a two-volume work.

Wright, Louis B., *The Cultural Life of the American Colonies, 1607-1763.* New York: Harper & Brothers, 1957. A study focusing on the aristocracies of the plantations and the trade centers.

Periodicals and Monographs:

"The First American Newspaper and the 'New England Primer,'" *Bookman,* LXXVI (January 1933), 103. A brief account of the life of Benjamin Harris.

Kobre, Sidney, "The First American Newspaper: A Product of Environment," *Journalism Quarterly,* XVII (December 1940), 335. Social and economic factors leading to the founding of the press.

Parkes, H. B., "New England in the Seventeen-Thirties," *New England Quarterly,* III (July 1930), 397. A valuable appraisal of the Puritan traditions, which also discusses effect of British essay papers.

Shaaber, Matthias A., "Forerunners of the Newspaper in America," *Journalism Quarterly,* XI (December 1934), 339. Describes predecessors of *Publick Occurrences.* Reprinted in Ford and Emery, *Highlights in the History of the American Press.*

Chapter 3

THE PRESS WINS A BEACHHEAD

> They that can give up essential liberty to obtain a
> little temporary safety deserve neither liberty nor
> safety.
>
> —Benjamin Franklin

COLONIAL READERS had a choice of newspapers for the
first time after December 21, 1719, when Campbell fell from political favor. William Brooker won the appointment as postmaster. He
was encouraged by his sponsors to continue publication of a semi-
official newspaper. Campbell refused to relinquish the *News-Letter*,
however, so Brooker had to start a new publication. And so, after
15 years of monopoly, the pioneer American newspaper faced "opposition." The new rival was the *Boston Gazette*.

Competition did not noticeably improve either the semi-official
Gazette or the free-enterprise *News-Letter*. The *Gazette* started
out as an imitator, and a stodgy one, at that. Except for a market
page, it offered nothing that Campbell had not given his readers.
Brooker had one great advantage, however. As postmaster, he could
distribute his publication at lower cost.

Five successive postmasters continued the *Gazette* until 1741,
when it was merged with another rival that had appeared in the
meantime—the *New England Weekly Journal,* described at the
close of this chapter. The merger was the first such transaction in
the history of American journalism. These early newspapers were
all rather dull. Campbell, Brooker, and their successors, as minor

bureaucrats, were careful not to offend officials upon whom they were dependent for privileges and subsidies. Every issue of the papers was approved by a government representative before publication, even though formal licensing laws had lapsed.

This safe policy was brought to an abrupt end with the establishment in 1721 of the *New England Courant*. This vigorous little sheet was published by James Franklin, elder brother of the more famous Benjamin, but a notable American in his own right. James had been printer of the *Gazette* when Brooker was postmaster. When the publisher lost his appointment, and the *Gazette* passed on to the succeeding postmaster, the paper was printed in another shop. Franklin was irked by this turn of events, and when a group of leading citizens opposed to the governing group encouraged him to start another paper, he agreed to the proposal.

The spirit of rebellion was manifest in the *Courant* from the start. Although it lasted only five years, it exerted a great influence upon the American press. It was a fresh breeze in the stale journalistic atmosphere of Boston. The *Courant* was the first American newspaper to supply readers with what they liked and needed, rather than with information controlled by self-interested officials. Its style was bold and its literary quality high. James Franklin had one of the best libraries in the city. He was also familiar with the best of the London literary publications. Here was a publisher who knew how to interest readers. He lightened his pages by poking fun at rivals. His personality sketches appealed to local interests. Franklin printed feature stories, including "human interest" articles, of the type that Charles A. Dana was to popularize on the *New York Sun* a century and a half later.

James Franklin was also the first to use a device that was almost an essential of the newspaper at a much later date. This was the "crusade" type of journalism, involving an editorial campaign planned to produce results by presenting news in dramatic form. A crusading editor is not content with the mere reporting of events, but knows how to generate stories of interest to the public. Franklin was an expert in the use of this device.

James Franklin was much more than just a tough and independent newspaper man. The *Courant* also filled a great literary vacuum. Literature of a high standard for popular consumption was rare in Colonial America in the first quarter of the eighteenth century. Now and then a peddler sold a copy of some such classic as Hakluyt's *Voyages,* but most of the available reading of that day was heavily larded with moral lessons and religious doctrine. James Franklin was a cultured man, for his day and society, and while learning the printing trade in England he had enjoyed the essay papers that were then so popular.

Franklin, and many editors who followed him, offered a starved reading public something new in literary fare. Most of the *Spectator* and *Guardian* essays were reprinted in colonial newspapers. Addison and Steele were introduced to hundreds of Americans through such papers as the *Courant.* Such writers were imitated in the colonies, and some of this local material was very good. The young Benjamin Franklin, apprenticed to his brother James at an early age, secretly authored such essays for publication in his brother's newspaper. Indeed, Ben Franklin's "Silence Dogood" essays rank as about the best of the American imitations.

The literature in the *Courant* was witty, pertinent, and even brilliant at times. But the colonial press after the appearance of the *Courant* also offered more solid cultural contributions. Daniel Defoe's great book, *Robinson Crusoe,* was printed serially in many colonial papers as fast as installments could be pirated from abroad. Not every reader could discern the significance of Defoe's work, which expressed in the novel form his criticism of the existing social structure. Those who missed the social message could still enjoy the excellent narrative, and indeed it is still read for this purpose alone, as any youth can testify. In thus broadcasting the new literature, the American newspaper made another contribution to the culture of a new society.[1]

But the most important contribution of James Franklin was his unshackling of the American press from the licenser. All the other publishers had bowed to official pressures to print "by authority" despite the end of actual licensing. Franklin printed his paper not "by authority," but in spite of it. He thus helped establish the tradition of editorial independence, without which no press can be called free. Nor was Franklin cautious in the use of this new

---

[1] An excellent account of this literary phase is given in Elizabeth C. Cook, *Literary Influences in Colonial Newspapers, 1704-1750* (New York: Columbia University Press, 1912).

THE
New-England Courant.

From MONDAY April 9. to MONDAY April 16. 1722.

To ————— of the New-England Courant.

SIR, B. F. [No 3

STORIES of Lives are seldom entertaining, unless they contain something either admirable or exemplar: And since there is little or nothing of this Nature in my own Adventures, I will not tire your Readers with tedious Particulars of no Consequence, but will briefly, and in as few Words as possible, relate the most material Occurrences of my Life, and according to my Promise, confine all to this Letter.

MY Reverend Master who had hitherto remained a Batchelor, (after much Meditation on the Eighteenth verse of the Second Chapter of Genesis,) took up a Resolution to marry; and having made several unsuccessful fruitless Attempts on the more topping Sort of our Sex, and being tir'd with making troublesome Journeys and Visits to no Purpose, he began unexpectedly to cast a loving Eye upon Me, whom he had brought up cleverly to his Hand.

THERE is certainly scarce any Part of a Man's Life in which he appears more silly and ridiculous, than when he makes his first Onset in Courtship. The awkward Manner in which my Master first discover'd his Intentions, made me, in spite of my Reverence to his Person, burst out into an unmannerly Laughter: However, having ask'd his Pardon, and with much ado compos'd my Countenance, I promis'd him I would take his Proposal into serious Consideration, and speedily give him an Answer.

AS he had been a great Benefactor (and in a Manner a Father to me) I could not well deny his Request, when I once perceived he was in earnest. Whether it was Love, or Gratitude, or Pride, or all Three that made me consent, I know not; but it is certain, he found it no hard Matter, by the Help of his Rhetorick, to conquer my Heart, and perswade me to marry him.

THIS unexpected Match was very astonishing to all the Country round about, and serv'd to furnish them with Discourse for a long Time after; some approving it, others disliking it, as they were led by their various Fancies and Inclinations.

WE lived happily together in the Heighth of conjugal Love and mutual Endearments, for near Seven Years, in which Time we added Two likely Girls and a Boy to the Family of the Dogoods: But alas! When my Sun was in its meridian Altitude, inexorable unrelenting Death, as if he had envy'd my Happiness and Tranquility, and resolv'd to make me extreamly miserable by the Loss of so good a Husband, hastened his Flight to the Heavenly World, by a sudden unexpected Departure from this.

I HAVE now remained in a State of Widowhood for several Years, but it is a State I never much admir'd, and I am apt to fancy that I could be easily perswaded to marry again, provided I was sure of a good humour'd, sober, agreeable Companion: But one, even with these few good Qualities, being hard to find, I have lately relinquish'd all Thoughts of that Nature.

AT present I pass away my leisure Hours in Conversation, either with my honest Neighbour Rusticus and his Family, or with the ingenious Minister of our Town, who now lodges at my House, and by whose Assistance I intend now and then to beautify my Writings with a Sentence or two in the learned Languages, which will not only be fashionable, and pleasing to those who do not understand it, but will likewise be very ornamental.

I SHALL conclude this with my own Character, which (one would think) I should be best able to give. Know then, That I am an Enemy to Vice, and a Friend to Vertue. I am one of an extensive Charity, and a great Forgiver of private Injuries: A hearty Lover of the Clergy and all good Men, and a mortal Enemy to arbitrary Government & unlimited Power. I am naturally very jealous for the Rights and Liberties of my Country; & the least appearance of an Incroachment on those invaluable Priviledges, is apt to make my Blood boil exceedingly. I have likewise a natural Inclination to observe and reprove the Faults of others, at which I have an excellent Faculty. I speak this by Way of Warning to all such whose Offences shall come under my Cognizance, for I never intend to wrap my Talent in a Napkin. To be brief; I am courteous and affable, good-humour'd (unless I am first provok'd,) and handsome, and sometimes witty, but always,

SIR,

Your Friend, and

Humble Servant,

SILENCE DOGOOD.

Caleb Taylor.

To the Author of the New-England Courant.

SIR,

BEing lately at the Quarter-Sessions, when a certain Lawyer came upon his Tryal for cohabiting with a French Tayloress as his Wife without being married according to the Laws of this Province, it was with no small Indignation that I heard him deliver himself to this Purpose; Please your Honours, I have been render'd odious by a Company of scandalous Writers, which I need not wonder at, when even his Excellency himself, and all that is dear and sacred to your Honours, has not escap'd the Lash of those sorry Scribblers: And since the Town are so much byas'd by their Writings, I chuse not to be try'd by the Jury, but freely confess that I am not marry'd according to the Laws of this Province, and throw my self entirely upon your Honours: And if your Honours will give me your Word, that you will not prosecute the Gentleman that marry'd me, I'll tell you his Name. —I have thrown my self upon your Honours, and I value Fifty Pound no more than I value Fifty Farthings. This impudent Speech of the famous Gentleman of the Law, reflects not only on the Town in general, but in a particular Manner on the Judges and Jury. And here I am under a Necessity to observe, that besides his Crime above-mention'd a Woman who was presented by the Grand-Jury (at the same Sessions) for having a Bastard Child declared in open Court that he was the Father of it. But these and such like Offences, hinted at in the Courant, are so dear and sacred to him, that (judging others by himself) he insinuates, that they are likewise dear and sacred to their Honours. 'Tis plain, he did not think the Judges had any Regard to the Laws of the Province, otherwise he would not have had the Impudence to desire their Honours to give

James Franklin's paper, published in defiance of authorities. A sample of brother Ben's famous "Silence Dogood" series is shown here.

An **English Common Press**, used by many eighteenth century printers. Crude by modern stand ards, such equipment could produce superb work at the hands of expert craftsmen.

power. The pompous and restrictive religious and political leaders of the community were the particular targets of his editorial shafts. One wonders what motivated this brash fellow. He risked financial and physical punishment for his pains. He was fully aware that independent publishers before him had suffered for their outspokenness. There was no special immunity for him. Apparently Franklin engaged in his hazardous calling because he loved a fight. Many a career in journalism has been similarly motivated since that time, but Franklin was a pioneer along this frontier of the Fourth Estate.

The restrictive authorities were both spiritual and temporal. Censorship was supervised by government officials, of course, but the influence of the church leaders was nearly as great, if less direct. Puritan thought dominated the region, and the hierarchy was directed by two brilliant and strong-willed clergymen, Increase Mather and his son, Cotton. Many citizens of the region secretly detested the stern discipline imposed by the Mathers and their followers, but few dared challenge the dominant theocrats. This situation changed when Franklin began to publish the *Courant*.

A man of James Franklin's intellectual independence was certain to be irked by the type of restraint imposed by the Mathers. He began his attack at once, with the *Courant* as both his weapon and his defense. It was his defense because the governing officials also resented the Mathers, and as long as Franklin directed his rebellion against them, the government did not take action against the unlicensed paper, as it might otherwise have done. It was a weapon because it undermined obedience to the hierarchy dominated by the Mathers. One wishes that Franklin might have selected some other issue to contest with the Mathers, however, because in this case he actually obstructed medical progress.

The issue was smallpox inoculation. The disease took an enormous toll of life in those days, and sometimes reached the proportions of a plague. All the early newspapers described the smallpox situation from time to time. It was of considerable concern to everyone. Turkish doctors had long known that immunity to the disease could be obtained by a primitive form of inoculation. Around 1720 Dr. Zabdiel Boylston of Boston injected blood from recovered smallpox patients into the bodies of other persons. There was no doubt that an immunity could be achieved this way, but the risks were great and most physicians of the period frowned on the practice. It was almost 80 years before the great scientist, Edward Jenner, introduced the safer vaccination method.

Cotton Mather encouraged Dr. Boylston in his researches. There was considerable controversy over the subject, and because of the positions of the protagonists, the issue became political and social, as well as medical. James Franklin used the inoculation quarrel as a means of attacking the Mathers. What he did, although he did not know it at the time, was to launch the first newspaper crusade in America. He developed an issue by dramatic treatment until everyone in the area was aware of the fight. Around Franklin gathered the rebels against Increase and Cotton Mather. They contributed articles to the *Courant,* some of them so vindictive as to be libelous. The insufferable Mathers[2] discovered that the tide of public opinion was strong against them. They defended themselves in vain in the rival *Gazette* and *News-Letter;* it was the *Courant* that won the sympathy of the public.

The *Courant* was admired because Franklin said what many a reader had dreamed of saying to the stern Puritan leaders. For a time the Mathers had virtually dictated policies. When Increase returned from England at the end of the seventeenth century he had even won the right to nominate the governor. His judgment was not particularly good, however, and his political power was waning as Franklin began the inoculation crusade. The governing authorities undoubtedly welcomed the *Courant* as an ally, even if it did end the tradition of a licensed press in America.

But when the spunky journalist turned around and fired a fusillade at the administration, the authorities believed it was time to swat this gadfly. Franklin accused the government of ineffective defense against pirates in the vicinity. Called before the Council in 1722 on a charge of contempt, Franklin was as outspoken as he

[2] The Mathers were insufferable in the sense that their righteousness made them too sure of themselves, but that does not detract from their important place in colonial history. Increase was licenser of the press after 1674, in addition to his duties as the leading minister of the dominant Puritans. He was president of Harvard and was a respected agent of Massachusetts in London. Cotton opposed the arrogant Sir Edmund Andros, ousted from New England after the Revolution of 1688. The Mathers were prolific writers of considerable merit. They were also outstanding historians. In later life they became more tolerant. In all, they contributed much to the development of their community.

had been in the columns of his paper. For such impertinence the editor-publisher was thrown into jail.

During the month that James was behind bars, brother Ben produced the *Courant*. It must have been a satisfying experience. Young Ben was beginning to resent his overbearing brother. He knew he could write—the successful "Silence Dogood" series was evidence of that. But Ben knew that his brother would have turned down the offerings had he known their source, so the essays had to be written anonymously and slipped under the publisher's door at night. Ben had also demonstrated his business ability, for the paper was never operated more efficiently than it was during James' absence.

James showed not the slightest remorse for his rude appraisal of the administration, and jail had no effect upon him in this way. Once free, he stepped up his criticism of authorities—both religious and political. By the end of the year both factions agreed on one thing, at least: James Franklin was too troublesome to be allowed in the community without restriction. At this point the General Court declared that "James Franklin be strictly forbidden . . . to print or publish the *New-England Courant* or any Pamphlet or paper of the like Nature, Except it be first Supervised, by the Secretary of this Province."[3] This, of course, was a reaffirmation of the old licensing power.

James evaded the order by making his brother, Ben, the official publisher of the paper. No such restriction had been imposed upon the younger Franklin. But in carrying out this evasion, James eventually lost the services of his essential brother. James ostensibly cancelled Ben's apprenticeship in order to name the boy as publisher. At the same time, he made Ben sign secret articles of reapprenticeship, to be put into effect as soon as the restrictive pressure was relaxed.

This was the chance Ben had been awaiting. Apprentices were bound to their masters by law. James had a right to hold his brother to strict compliance with the terms of contract. But Ben was restless under his brother's somewhat overbearing mastership. The

[3] As quoted in Frank Luther Mott, *American Journalism* (New York: The Macmillan Company, 1950), p. 20. Colonial writing style called for use of many hyphens, such as in New-England, which are not used here for reasons of simplicity in identifying newspapers.

younger Franklin knew he was qualified to meet any master printer on equal terms. How to shake himself of the onerous apprenticeship? James' devious plan offered escape. True, the secret articles were binding, and under the law James could return his brother if Ben tried to run away. But if James did so, after assuring the General Court that he had relinquished his paper to his brother, he would thereby acknowledge that he had flouted the Court's order. Young Ben was clever enough to size up the situation. The next time we meet him in these pages is as a printer in his own right in Philadelphia, where he was destined to be one of the great journalists of his age.

The *Courant* declined in popularity and influence after that. Five and a half years after he had established the paper, James abandoned it. Later he accepted the position of government printer for Rhode Island. At Newport, in 1732, he founded the *Rhode Island Gazette*, first newspaper in that colony. It survived only a short time, and James never did achieve his former eminence in journalism.[4] If he did nothing else but establish the principle in America of printing "without authority," he would deserve a high place in America's journalistic hall of fame. He had accomplished much more, however. He had shown that when a newspaper is aggressive and readable in serving the public cause, it will elicit support sufficient to protect it from powerful foes.

The second largest city in the colonies at this time was Philadelphia. Two years after the founding of that city in 1683, William Bradford set up the first printing press in the colony. At first he printed only pamphlets and religious tracts for Quaker patrons, but because he had the only press in the region, he was also useful to the administration. Soon he was devoting much of his time to the printing of government documents. Unfortunately, he quarreled with his Quaker superiors, and in 1693 he moved his printing shop to New York, where he established the first newspaper in that city many years later, in 1725. We shall meet him again in the next chapter.

William Bradford's son, Andrew, published the first newspaper

[4] His widow, two daughters, and a son carried on the printing business in Newport. In 1758, James, Jr., with the help of his rich uncle Benjamin, established the *Newport Mercury*, which survived until 1934. Its name was then retained in a small weekly edition of the *Newport News*.

in Philadelphia. It was also the first newspaper outside Boston. His *American Weekly Mercury* first appeared on December 22, 1719, the day after Brooker published the first issue of the *Gazette*, Boston's first rival to the *News-Letter*. The *Mercury* was another postmaster paper, but it was a little more outspoken than the usual safe, semi-official publications of that type that were to appear in the next two decades. On occasion the *Mercury* criticised the administration. It defended James Franklin when the Boston journalist was jailed by angry authorities. It printed the controversial "Cato Letters," which had first appeared in London as popular manifestations of the movement for civil and religious liberties. As a pioneer newspaper publisher, Andrew Bradford deserves an honorable niche in a history of the press. He, too, will appear again in the following chapter, which describes the development of press freedom in colonial America. But in the period with which this chapter is concerned, Bradford was overshadowed in Philadelphia by the greatest printer-journalist of the period.

He was Benjamin Franklin, who arrived almost penniless in the City of Brotherly Love after running away from his apprenticeship to brother James. Within five years he was a successful and prosperous citizen of the town. Ben Franklin's whole career was one of success, color, and usefulness. There has never been another American quite like him. He was "the complete man," like DaVinci, Michelangelo, or Roger Bacon. Everything he did, he did well, and he did many things. He was an unusual person, but he so perfectly summed up the characteristics for which Americans were becoming known that it is pertinent to discuss him at this point.

Franklin's greatness resulted as much from his open mind as from his genius. Brought up in a Calvinist environment, he lost all trace of that narrow ideology by the time he had become important in Philadelphia. A product of the emerging middle class, he refused to be bound by the petty prejudices of the commercial group. He was equally at ease before his local Board of Trade, or before the most lavish court in Europe. A good husband, he held his wife ("dear Debby") in great affection, and some of his most charming letters were penned to keep her informed of the French fashions he knew would interest her; but he was also human clay, after all, if his numerous love affairs right up into his 70's are admissible evidence. Indeed, these very weaknesses in an acknowledged great man only endeared him the more to those who knew him well. They recognized that he was human in addition to being a great man.

Franklin was respected because he excelled in activities the American esteemed highly. He was an idealist, but he made more money than most of his "hard-headed" rivals and associates. He was rich, but he understood, respected, and represented the poor. He could talk familiarly with the dilettante on almost any subject, but he was strictly "old shoe" with simple people. Children adored him. He was as direct as his own literary child, "Poor Richard," whose sayings are quoted to this day, but he could carry to successful conclusions the most devious diplomatic negotiations. The gentry admired him for his scientific accomplishments in a day when science was a fad of the privileged class, but he was equally respected by the stodgy burghers, who knew that he worked constantly for civic improvements. He was noted for his drawing-room conversation, but he was also the careful scholar. He was a pioneer American sociologist and economist. The insurance company he founded is still thriving.

He was all this and much more—but first of all, Ben Franklin was a printer and journalist. That is how he began his rise to fame. That is the base upon which he built his fortune. He had concluded at the very beginning of his career that the quickest way to acquire influence was to gain wealth. There was nothing new in that idea, except that Franklin chose to make the press his medium for reaching that estate. That *was* a new idea. And when he achieved his goal, he showed others that journalism merited the attention of the prudent and ambitious. Franklin's later honors overshadowed his journalistic success, but it should be remembered that he did not leave the printing business until he was 42—only a few years short of the average life expectancy of that day.

Franklin took over the management of the *Pennsylvania Gazette* in October, 1729. He did not establish the paper. Instead, he obtained it from its founder by shrewd negotiations that spread his fame as a business man and printer. The publishing picture in Philadelphia must have appeared bleak to most young printers of the time. The city was far below the cultural standard it was later to achieve. Few books were sold, and almost none were printed, except for an occasional theological tract. The only oasis in this literary desert was the disordered printing shop of Samuel Keimer.[5]

Keimer has not fared well in history. He never lived down the fact that he had been the target of a famous man's jibes. But it was Keimer who started Franklin on his career in Philadelphia. And Keimer certainly had some pretensions to culture. His history of the Quakers, published in 1728, was the most important book to be printed in Pennsylvania up to that time. In 1729 he published *Epictetus*, the first translation of a classic writer offered by an American printer. On the other hand, he was erratic, a shoddy craftsman, and a miserable business man.

Keimer could not compete successfully with Bradford, who could distribute newspapers cheaply as postmaster of the area, and who also had a backlog of ballots, notices, orders, minutes, and laws as official printer for the colony. Franklin was not at all impressed by this formidable rival, however. The proof of Franklin's great ability is that he successfully met Bradford's competition and five years after arriving in Philadelphia as a penniless boy was operating one of the most profitable presses in the colonies. The secret of his success was that he was more than a printer, or editor, or publisher. For one thing, he was the best writer in America. He had also cultivated useful "connections" with influential citizens. And he had an uncanny business sense. This is indeed a rare combination. Franklin brought to the printing industry something it had lacked before. He had Keimer's interest in scholarship without Keimer's eccentricity. He could speak out fearlessly when the time was ripe, but he did not needlessly antagonize readers, as had brother James. He could wait for developments, but out of patience, not out of the overcautiousness that hampered Bradford. He also had the great gift of confidence in himself—not arrogance, but faith in his own judgment.

And so we find Franklin and his friend, Hugh Meredith, opening their printing shop in the spring of 1728. Already they were planning a newspaper. They were delayed by a jealous rival. A friend of the young partners disclosed the plans to Keimer, who was irked

[5] Andrew Bradford published a few books, but they were mostly theological, rather than literary, in content. At the time, Bradford operated a general store, an apothecary shop, and a post office, in addition to the *American Weekly Mercury*.

because Franklin had left his shop to set up one of his own. Keimer saw a way to get even. He at once announced his own plans for a newspaper, intending thereby to thwart Franklin. In December of 1728 Keimer published the first number of *The Universal Instructor in All Arts and Sciences: and Pennsylvania Gazette.* The paper was as clumsy as the title. Much of it was devoted to an item-by-item reprinting of Chambers' *Cyclopaedia.* Later, Keimer issued Defoe's *Religious Courtship* in serial form. There was some news, however.

Franklin was patient. He was certain the ponderous newspaper would fall of its own weight. At that, Keimer's product was no worse than many another such publication of the era. And it did supply a demand for information and literature. Indeed, it was about as readable as the rival *Mercury*—until a new feature began to appear in that publication. A series of clever essays in the Addison and Steele style soon brought delighted patrons to Bradford's shop for copies of the *Mercury.* The series came to be known as the "Busy-Body Papers." The anonymous author was actually Benjamin Franklin, and his most frequent target of satire was none other than Samuel Keimer. In vain did Keimer try to reply. He only made himself the more ridiculous. Keimer could not write as well as Franklin, nor could any other American of that time.

In the end, Keimer gave up the struggle. Pressed by creditors, unable to meet his publication deadlines, ridiculed for his dullness, Keimer decided to sell his shop to his former apprentice. One might feel sorrier for the man had he not started his enterprise with such vindictive motives. On October 2, 1729, Ben Franklin took over the good will and liabilities of Keimer's paper and began his career as a newspaper publisher.

He shortened the title to the *Pennsylvania Gazette,* dropped the encyclopaedia, and substituted news and literary material of a more popular type. Franklin had little difficulty winning public acceptance, and with it came a volume of profitable advertising. In addition to being a readable paper, it was a bold one. Franklin's experience in Boston, plus his innate common sense, kept him from getting into serious trouble with the authorities. But he took a stand on issues, just the same. Men have many opinions, he explained to his readers, and printers publish these opinions as part of their business.

"They are educated in the belief," he added, "that when men differ in opinion, both sides ought equally to have the advantage of being heard by the public; and that when truth and error have fair play, the former is always an overmatch for the latter [shades of Milton and his *Areopagitica*]. . . . If all printers were determined not to print anything till they were sure it would offend nobody," said he, "there would be very little printed." [6]

With Keimer out of the way, Andrew Bradford remained as Franklin's only serious rival. As postmaster, Bradford had the advantage of cheap distribution. He went beyond his rights, however, when he ordered his carriers not to pick up Franklin's paper. Franklin, who knew when to forsake common decency in favor of rough tactics when opponents refused to play fair, retaliated by bribing Bradford's carriers to distribute the *Gazette* to subscribers along postal routes, a device reminiscent of the Chicago circulation wars two centuries later.

Bradford had another early advantage. He had what amounted to a government subsidy through his contract for official printing. Franklin met that challenge by writing up an important legislative address, which he then sent to every member of the Assembly at his own expense. The same report appeared in the *Mercury,* but the *Gazette* story was so much better that Franklin made a great impression on the lawmakers. He continued this reporting. Within a year Franklin had won away the government printing contract.[7]

He now bought out his partner, Meredith, with money loaned to him by influential business men he had cultivated in his short career in Philadelphia. Thus, at the age of 24, we see him as the sole proprietor of the best newspaper in the American colonies. It soon had the largest circulation, most pages, highest advertising revenue, most literate columns, and liveliest comment of any paper in the area. Retiring from publishing 18 years later, he had made a fortune in a business that usually offered a bare subsistence to its promoters.

During this time Franklin established what amounted to the first chain of newspapers. True, each unit was independent in policy and

---

[6] As quoted in Carl Van Doren, *Benjamin Franklin* (New York: The Viking Press, 1938), p. 100.

[7] Some time before, Franklin had visited London, where great progress was being made in the printing industry. Partly as a result of this trip, he became an expert typographer and engraver.

direction, since Franklin exercised only a fatherly control over them. It was his custom to watch worthy apprentices, and then to help them set up shop when the articles of service had been fulfilled. Franklin let these young journalists pay him back out of earnings. In the meantime, he enjoyed a safe, profitable, and satisfying investment, for he picked only the best "risks" among his protégés for these opportunities. In this way he added indirectly to the power and prestige of the press by raising the standards of the craft.

It was Franklin, too, who helped establish the first foreign-language paper at Germantown, near Philadelphia. It did not survive long, but it was a forerunner of an important contribution to American journalism that would be made during the great waves of immigration that were to come in the next century.

It was also Franklin who first planned to publish a magazine on this side of the Atlantic. Again, as in his newspaper venture, he was outmaneuvered by a jealous rival who learned of the plans. Andrew Bradford's *American Magazine* appeared in 1741 three days before the first issue of Franklin's *General Magazine*. Neither was successful, although Franklin's survived the longer. He was not proud of this enterprise, apparently, for he does not mention it in his autobiography, but the incident shows how eager he was to test new ideas.

But Franklin's greatest contribution to American journalism was that he made it respectable. Campbell, Brooker, the Bradfords, and Keimer were dull fellows, on the whole. Some, like Campbell, lived and died in their communities without achieving more than casual recognition. James Franklin was too tactless to win the respect of "solid" citizens. Most of the printer-journalists had trouble meeting expenses, as their frequent pleas to delinquent subscribers indicate. Franklin showed that a good journalist and business man could make money in the publishing field. That was, and is, an effective way of making any business respectable. When intelligent and industrious youths saw the possibilities of journalism, as developed by the grand old man of the press, they began to turn more often to this calling. Getting this improved type of personnel into the craft was the best possible tonic for American journalism.

After 1725, newspapers sprouted all over the colonies. In Boston, Samuel Kneeland established the *New England Weekly Journal* on

March 20, 1727. It is worth a mention because it was the first newspaper to have correspondents in nearby communities whose duty it was to send in pertinent information about the neighborhood, a practice still followed by newspaper publishers. Kneeland discovered, as editors kept discovering on up through the years, that local news attracts readers, no matter how trivial the items. Perhaps that was why the *Journal* was so large in bulk and circulation. Kneeland also perfected the "vital statistics" column—a list of births, deaths, and marriages.

By 1741 there were five newspapers in Boston. In that year Kneeland bought the old *Gazette* and merged it with his paper, as mentioned on page 48. This was the paper that later was famous under its old *Gazette* title, after those super-patriots, Benjamin Edes and John Gill, Kneeland's son-in-law, took over the paper in the period preceding the Revolution.

Another important Boston paper was the *Weekly Rehearsal,* founded in 1731 by Jeremy Gridley, a lawyer. A year later he turned over the publication to Thomas Fleet, James Franklin's old printer. Fleet changed the name to the *Evening Post* a few years later. Under him, it became the best and most popular paper in Boston. It lasted until Revolutionary War times. Gridley, the founder, eventually returned to journalism in 1743 as the editor of the first magazine to win public support, and the third monthly magazine to appear in the colonies. This was the *American Magazine and Historical Chronicle,* which survived until 1746.

Maryland was the fourth colony to have a newspaper.[8] William Parks, a former English editor, set up the *Maryland Gazette* at Annapolis in 1727. His paper reflected good taste, literary skill, and pride in the craft he had learned so well under the best English masters. Later, in 1736, he founded the *Virginia Gazette,* first newspaper in Virginia, at Williamsburg. That little shop has been restored, and is now one of the interesting exhibits at the old colonial capital.[9] Because it tells us what the printing business must have

[8] The other colonies: Massachusetts, Pennsylvania, and New York.

[9] Other firsts in their respective colonies: *Rhode Island Gazette* and *South Carolina Gazette,* 1732; *North Carolina Gazette,* 1751; *Connecticut Gazette,* 1755; *New Hampshire Gazette,* 1756; *Georgia Gazette,* 1763; *New Jersey Gazette,* 1777; *Vermont Gazette,* 1780; and *Delaware Gazette,* 1785. James Parker, one of Ben Franklin's protégés, founded the Connecticut paper. Another of Franklin's "boys" established the South Carolina paper, although there is some doubt as to which one of two has the more valid claim.

been like in colonial days, it might be worth a moment to look into this quaint building.

The office is on the ground floor of a small brick building. In the center stands the English Common Press, shipped over in pieces from the mother country, for no presses were to be had in America until Isaac Doolittle of Connecticut began turning them out in 1769. Close at hand are the accessories: the imposing stones, upon which the type is gathered; the "horse" and "bank" tables, from which the paper is fed to the press; the wetting trough, for the preparation of the paper; an ink grinding stand; and the matrix punches, made in England by William Caslon himself, for cutting the beautiful type that bears his name. The press stands seven feet high and weighs about 1,500 pounds. It is firmly braced to floor and ceiling by heavy oak beams to insure rigidity when heavy pressure is applied to the type forms.

From this clumsy apparatus colonial printers such as the Bradfords, Greens, Sowers, Parks, and Franklins produced letter-press work of the highest quality.[10] There was much bad printing during this period, too, but that was often the fault of poor craftsmanship

---

[10] There were two great Bradford printing families. William Bradford was founder of the Pennsylvania line and was a pioneer printer in Philadelphia and New York. His son, Andrew, established the first newspaper in Philadelphia. William Bradford III was the famous soldier-editor of the Revolution and publisher of the *Pennsylvania Journal* in Philadelphia. His son, Thomas, succeeded the father as editor. John Bradford, no relative of the Pennsylvania clan, was a surveyor who founded the first paper in Kentucky, at Lexington. His brother, Fielding, was also active in journalism. James, another member of this branch, founded the first newspaper in Louisiana, and may have been the first American war correspondent, according to Mott (p. 196). The Greens were prominent in New England. Bartholomew and Samuel were pioneers in the Boston-Cambridge area; the former as printer of the first successful newspaper in America. From Samuel Green of Cambridge descended a long line of printer-journalists. Timothy Jr. founded the New London, Conn., *Summary* in 1758. His son, Timothy III, changed the name to the *Gazette*, after the death of the father. Samuel and Thomas founded the first paper in New Haven in 1767. Thomas, the brother of Timothy III, founded the *Connecticut* (now *Hartford*) *Courant* in 1764. Timothy IV was co-founder of the first Vermont paper. The Sowers were Germans who settled near Philadelphia. First in the printing dynasty was Christopher, who, with the encouragement of Benjamin Franklin, established one of the earliest foreign language newspapers, the Germantown *Zeitung*. A mechanical genius, he constructed his own press and made his own ink and paper. His sons carried on the business, but Christopher III was a Tory during the Revolution and his journalistic career was ruined by the American victory. The Franklin influence in Massachusetts, Rhode Island, and Pennsylvania has been described.

and worn equipment. There is abundant proof that the colonial printing press was capable of turning out superb work, under the supervision of a skilled printer. He had to know his business, however. A single impression, or "token" required 13 distinct operations. Two expert craftsmen and an apprentice working under the best of conditions might turn out about 200 tokens an hour. The usual four-page paper had to be "pulled" twice—the pull being the application of pressure when a stout man put his weight on the lever to print a token.

Let us watch the colonial printer as he works. The bed of the press is rolled out by means of a wheel and pulley arrangement. The type, all set by hand, is locked tight in the form and placed on the bed. A young apprentice, or "devil" applies the home-made ink to the type, using a doeskin dauber on a stick for this purpose. The paper is then moistened in a trough so that it will take a better impression. It is placed carefully over the type. The bed is rolled back under the press. The "platen," or upper pressure plate, is then pressed against the type by means of a screw or lever device. The platen is then released; the bed is wheeled out; the sheet is hung on a wire to dry before it is ready for its second "run" for the reverse side; and the printers get ready to prepare another token.

The usual colonial paper consisted of four pages, often about ten by fifteen inches in dimension. The paper was rough foolscap. There were no headlines, as we know them, until after 1750, and even then they were uncommon. The only illustrations were the colophons, or printers' trade marks, on the title page, and an occasional woodcut to embellish an advertisement. The Greens and Sowers made their own paper, but most of it was imported from England. It was made of rags and was of surprising durability, despite its mottled appearance.

With this primitive equipment the printer-journalist not only produced fine graphic art, but he had at hand an implement that was soon to make the press truly a Fourth Estate. At times it was more powerful than the government itself. In half a century times had changed the role of the journalist. No longer did he wait in the governor's outer office, cap in hand, while a representative of the administration checked his copy for statements disapproved by the authorities. Even the most obstinate bureaucrat had been forced to concede that this new engine of public opinion was not to be abused with impunity. Eighteenth-century journalists had learned a lesson that apparently has to be re-learned at regular intervals— that when the public supports them, no power is strong enough to throttle press freedom. They learned that when editors are identified with the public cause, putting responsibility to the people above whims and personal convenience, they not only win the essential backing, but help to generate other forces for freedom within the community.

ANNOTATED BIBLIOGRAPHY

Books:

Andrews, Charles M., *Colonial Folkways*. New Haven: Yale University Press, 1921. A small volume in the Chronicle of America series, giving eighteenth-century background, by the noted author of the four-volume *The Colonial Period of American History*.

Brigham, Clarence S., *History and Bibliography of American Newspapers, 1690-1820*, 2 vols. Worcester, Massachusetts: American Antiquarian Society, 1947. Gives brief descriptions of all newspapers up to 1820. An indispensable tool of the colonial press historian.

————, *Journals and Journeymen*. Philadelphia: University of Pennsylvania Press, 1950. Fifteen essays on the colonial press; one particularly interesting one on advertising.

Cambridge History of American Literature, I. New York: G. P. Putnam's Sons, 1917-21. Volume I of this four-volume work discusses Franklin (pp. 90-110) and colonial newspapers and magazines (pp. 111-23).

Cook, Elizabeth C., *Literary Influences in Colonial Newspapers, 1704-1750*. New York: Columbia University Press, 1912. Describes the role of the press in supplying the craving for popular literature.

De Armond, Anna Janney, *Andrew Bradford: Colonial Journalist*. Newark, Delaware: University of Delaware Press, 1949. Well-documented.

Kobre, Sidney, *The Development of the Colonial Newspaper*. Pittsburgh: The Colonial Press, Inc., 1944. A short, but adequate, study of the integration of political, social, and economic forces in the development of the American press.

McMurtrie, Douglas C., *The Beginnings of the American Newspaper*. Chicago: Black Cat Press, 1935. A 36-page description of colonial newspapers, including a few facsimiles.

————, *A History of Printing in the United States*. New York: R. R. Bowker Company, 1936. McMurtrie planned a four-volume history of the press during the pioneer period of each state in the union. Only the second volume, on the Middle and South Atlantic states, was completed. Well-documented and illustrated, it treats in detail Franklin, the Philadelphia press, and the early German press in Pennsylvania.

Mott, Frank L., and Ralph D. Casey, eds., *Interpretations of Journalism.* New York: F. S. Crofts & Company, 1936. Contains an excellent word portrait of Franklin, the printer, reprinting some of Franklin's own comments; see pages 101-12.

The Papers of Benjamin Franklin, Vol. I. New Haven: Yale University Press, 1959. Covers period to 1734, including Silence Dogood and Busy-Body letters. Extensive introduction by editor Leonard W. Labaree.

Parrington, Vernon L., *Main Currents in American Thought,* Vol. 1. Excellent background material and interesting comment on Franklin.

Thomas, Isaiah, *History of Printing in America,* 2 vols. Worcester, Massachusetts: Isaiah Thomas, Jr. (first printing), 1810; Albany, New York: Joel Munsell, 1874. The standard authority on colonial journalism; contains biographies of printers and accounts of newspapers in all colonies and in some states after independence.

Van Doren, Carl, *Benjamin Franklin.* New York: The Viking Press, 1938. The most readable account of a great printer-journalist by a prize-winning biographer.

Wroth, Lawrence C., *The Colonial Printer.* Portland, Maine: South-worth-Anthoensen Press, 1938. An excellent study of the printing craft.

Periodicals and Monographs:

Fogel, Howard H., "Colonial Theocracy and a Secular Press," *Journalism Quarterly,* XXXVII (Autumn 1960), 525. A study of how the colonial press won its freedom from interference by religious authorities.

Ford, Edwin H., "Colonial Pamphleteers," *Journalism Quarterly,* XIII (March 1936), 24. A scholarly discussion of the journalistic contributions of such colonial leaders as Increase and Cotton Mather, and Samuel Sewall. Reprinted in Ford and Emery, *Highlights in the History of the American Press.*

King, Marion Reynolds, "One Link in the First Newspaper Chain, the South Carolina Gazette," *Journalism Quarterly,* IX (September 1932), 257. Describes the arrangement by which Franklin financed his apprentices in setting up printing shops.

White, William, "The Maryland Gazette: America's Oldest Newspaper?," *Journalism Quarterly,* XXXV (Fall 1958), 439. The answer is "no" to this claim to the title of America's oldest continuously published newspaper, more properly claimed by the *Hartford Courant,* founded as the weekly *Connecticut Courant* in 1764 and a daily since 1837. See Frank Luther Mott, "What is the Oldest U. S. Newspaper?," *Journalism Quarterly,* XL (Winter 1963), 95.

Wisconsin Historical Society newspaper files, a leading collection. Photostats and answers to queries may be obtained by writing to Newspaper Section, State Historical Library, Madison 6, Wisconsin.

Chapter 4

RISE OF THE FOURTH ESTATE

> The question before the court . . . is not [just]
> the cause of the poor printer. . . . No! It may in
> its consequence affect every freeman . . . on the
> main of America. It is the best cause; it is the cause
> of Liberty . . . the liberty both of exposing and
> opposing arbitrary power . . . by speaking and
> writing Truth.
>
> —Andrew Hamilton's defense in
> the Zenger trial

IN THE SECOND QUARTER of the eighteenth century the newspaper became a force to be feared by arrogant administrators. True, the infant newspaper mortality rate was high, usually as a result of financial malnutrition. For example, more than half of the 2,120 newspapers established between 1690 and 1820 expired before they were two years old.[1] Only 34 lasted a generation. Nevertheless, by 1750 most literate Americans had access to some journal of information. In that year there were 14 weekly newspapers in the six most populous colonies, and soon the increase in such publications was to be rapid, as we shall see in the next chapter.

The product was better, too. Semiweekly, and even triweekly newspapers were available after the mid-century, and had first appeared even earlier. Circulation was rising. A few publishers had

[1] Clarence S. Brigham, *History and Bibliography of American Newspapers, 1690-1820* (Worcester, Massachusetts: American Antiquarian Society, 1947), p. x (Intro.).

won fame and fortune in the business. Rapid increase in population, better transportation and communication facilities, and rising political tensions partly explain the growth of the press. Many colonials had become prosperous and were looking around for ways of investing capital. Ports, such as New York, began to achieve world importance. About a third of the ships in the British merchant fleet were launched by New England shipwrights. There were 360 whalers operating from American ports. There were skillful artisans in the towns. The famous "Pennsylvania Rifle," one of the great weapons of the time, was a product of such craftsmen, for example. Despite the restrictions of the mother country, manufacture of finished articles continued to furnish employment for many hands. In one year alone during this period New Englanders shipped out 13,000 pairs of shoes.[2]

The press was useful to the ambitious trader and business man. Advertising was the cheapest way to move goods offered for sale by the rising commercial class. Business intercourse between the colonies increased, and accordingly there was need for information only American journalists could provide quickly and cheaply.

Better roads led to better communications. Early editor-postmasters had a double reason for improving roads. Franklin, who reversed the process by being appointed postmaster *after* taking up journalism, was named as deputy postmaster of all the colonies, along with William Hunter of Virginia, another printer-journalist. When Franklin took office, it required six weeks to bring the posts regularly from Boston to Philadelphia by land, and there was a mail pickup only fortnightly. Franklin, who took over most of the postal responsibility because of Hunter's ill-health, cut the travel time in half and established weekly service.

There was also improvement in education, always a factor in developing publics favorable to the newspaper. Many parents could now afford to send their children to school, and seminaries and academies were available in the urban centers. Colleges in many colonies produced not only teachers and ministers, effective foes of illiteracy, but writers and political spokesmen of the people. Samuel Adams, who emerges in the next chapter, was just such a product of the colleges.

[2] These aspects of development are admirably presented in Sidney Kobre, "The Revolutionary Colonial Press—A Social Interpretation," *Journalism Quarterly*, XX (September 1943), 193-7.

Not only were Americans more literate, but they had more opportunity to enjoy the privilege of reading. Homes were more comfortable and were better lighted. It was possible to read in the leisure of nightfall with the help of the whale-oil lamp, whereas previous generations had had to operate mostly on daylight schedules.

The great technical advances in printing were far in the future, but better type was available during this period. About 1720 William Caslon began modifying Nicolas Jenson's fifteenth-century type into a more readable form. Caslon type was adopted by American printers soon after, and it is still popular. The best standard press was the invention of Willem Janszon Blaeu, a Dutch craftsman of the seventeenth century. Not until around 1800, when Adam Ramage and the Earl of Stanhope came out with the iron press was there any great improvement in this essential equipment.

The development of commerce led to progress in the advertising field. Advertising and printing had been closely associated almost from the beginning. William Caxton, who set up the first press in England, issued a broadside advertising his service (religious) book, *The Pyes of Salisbury Use,* in 1480. Number 62 of the *London Gazette,* first complete newspaper in the English language, included an announcement of a special advertising supplement in June, 1666. An interesting use of advertising is shown in Number 94 of the same paper. After the great fire of London in the fall of 1666 the paper opened its columns to those seeking word of missing loved ones. There were also advertisements concerning salvaged furniture, addresses of scattered families, and houses offering shelter to the homeless.

Presbrey calls John Houghton the father of modern advertising.[3] Houghton was an apothecary; merchant of coffee, tea, and chocolate; book critic; Fellow of the Royal Society; and publisher. He established a newspaper for commercial readers in 1692. This prototype of the *Wall Street Journal* was the first newspaper to emphasize the role of advertising. Houghton had an appreciation of advertising ethics, in an age when the margin between quackery and professional knowledge was narrower than it is today. He was willing to advertise almost any product, but he would not give his

---

[3] Frank Presbrey, *The History and Development of Advertising* (Garden City: Doubleday, Doran & Company, 1929), p. 56.

seventeenth-century "seal of approval" to statements he believed to be dangerously dishonest. That advertising was a topic for debate and criticism two hundred years ago, as it is today, is implied by a comment of that famous pundit, Dr. Samuel Johnson, in the *Idler* of January 20, 1758:

. . . Advertisements are now so numerous that they are very negligently perused, and it is therefore become necessary to gain attention by magnificence of promises and by eloquence sometimes sublime and sometimes pathetick. Promise—large promise—is the soul of advertising. . . . The trade of advertising is now so near perfection that it is not easy to propose any improvement.[4]

Advertising in the eighteenth century emphasized the fundamental drives of human beings to make them buy goods or services. Thus, a merchant of 1750 offered tooth cleansers not only for the purpose of polishing teeth, which was the utilitarian value, but to beautify, and thus to act as an ally of love, social prestige, or business appeal. Then, as today, rival merchants knew the effectiveness of turning universal desires into sales stimulations. The advertiser of 1750 was as aware as his modern counterpart that emotional appeals bring a more positive response than logic from the general public. The more immediate the response, the more effective the sales campaign. Advertising copy writers of the eighteenth century used every device to arouse such a response, carrying novelty and imagination to fantastic limits.

The advertiser could teach the journalist some important lessons on the subject of reader response. For example, the advertiser quickly discovered that his message must be simply stated to reach the most people. It took the news writer a long time to learn this lesson. Advertisers also understood the value of attractive presentation. They led the way in experimentation with type, illustrations, makeup, and legibility. The press owes much to these practical psychologists and literary showmen.

The greatest stimulus to the development of the American press of this period was the rising political tension that was to culminate in the war for independence. The press had an essential role in the drama about to unfold. The newspaper thrives on controversy, providing it is able to take part in the discussions with any degree of freedom. The great development of the press during the first half

[4] From *ibid.*, p. 70.

of the eighteenth century was its victory over the forces that would have restricted that liberty. This victory made the press the most powerful weapon of the American revolutionaries. The press won its fight because it had the support of the public. People saw that the emergence of a free press was related to the recognition of the disfranchised, and that, in fact, all the freedoms were tied together. In effect, the struggle to free the press in America was a phase in the demand for Home Rule, government by public assent, and eventual independence.

Even Milton, perhaps the most eloquent of the pioneers for liberty of expression, admitted there was a need for some limitation on press freedom. The publication of his speech to Parliament in 1644 (*Areopagitica*) enunciated a concept that was largely ignored at the time, but which became a battle-cry a hundred years later in America. Milton had no patience with "superstitions," but he insisted that the publication of truth should be protected as a right, since "who ever knew truth put to the worse, in a free and open encounter [with falsehood]?" Milton was arguing for the right to express himself in print without having to have that expression approved in advance. Almost forgotten today are the battles and sacrifices by which this concept won general acceptance.

In 1692, before the first successful newspaper had yet been born in America, a Philadelphia printer boldly stated one of the cardinal principles of a free press. He was William Bradford, founder of a remarkable printing dynasty. Bradford had to placate both a jealous government and a sensitive Quaker hierarchy when he set up his little shop. Every now and then he was threatened by one or the other because of ideas expressed in pamphlets he turned out at regular intervals. Arrested in 1692 for a minor infraction, Bradford declared he was tired of such interference, and notified the authorities he was taking his press to a more congenial community. Officials were alarmed by this threat, for they depended upon Bradford for the dissemination of governmental, religious, and commercial information. The General Assembly therefore quashed the charge and induced Bradford to remain by granting him a yearly retainer of 40 pounds and all the printing he could handle by himself.

Because of the disposition of this case, Bradford's defense was not widely known, but it is worth a mention here because it brought up an issue that was hotly debated a generation later. For the printer had insisted that the jury in such cases was responsible for judging both the *law* and the *fact*. Now courts had held that when seditious libel (criticism of government) was charged, it was the duty of the jury only to establish the authorship of the statement. This was a point of *fact*. It was up to the judges to determine whether the statement was punishable. This was a point of *law*.

Bradford objected to this. He complained that when he was brought to trial, some of the jurymen appeared to be already convinced that he was a "seditious character." The objection was not valid, the judge ruled, because the jurors had no power to determine the seditiousness of the accused. That was a point of law, and a matter for the court to decide. But Bradford's insistence prevailed, and the judge instructed the jury to decide whether the pamphlet had a tendency toward "weakening the hands of the magistrate" and disturbing the peace. The jury could not agree, and Bradford was released, although authorities temporarily deprived him of his press and type. Some 40 years later, the issue that Bradford had successfully pressed in 1692 was to become a principal point in the trial of John Peter Zenger.

Bradford's son, Andrew, jousted regularly with the authorities on the right to express himself freely. He criticised the financial policy of the government and was brought before the magistrate for reprimand. He was ordered to print nothing about the Pennsylvania administration—or any other colonial government—unless he had express permission to do so. This was the old principle of "previous restraint" before publication, and Andrew objected. A year later we see him ignoring the injunction by referring to the officials of Massachusetts as "bigots, hypocrites, and tyrants" because they had arrested James Franklin on charges of breach of privilege (contempt) of the legislative body, when all he had done was to print the truth.

Sometime later the younger Bradford printed an essay in his newspaper. The subject was liberty versus tyranny. Andrew was not the author, but again he was hailed into court as publisher of the *Mercury*. This time the printer carried his arguments to the people. Authorities were so uncertain of popular backing that they dropped the trial. From then on, the *Mercury* appeared regularly with statements critical of the administration.

The Franklins also fought for the cause of free expression, long before that cause was generally recognized and protected by the courts. James Franklin was the first American publisher to flout the licenser. In his bouts with the authorities he argued that he had the duty to tell his readers everything he believed to be news, and that he should be protected in this duty, as long as he printed the truth. Unfortunately for Franklin, truth was not recognized as a defense in a libel action. Indeed, it was another hundred years before the courts recognized this concept of law.

Benjamin Franklin also spoke, if prudently, for a free press. He quoted *Areopagitica* on occasion and believed there was much more danger in what printers left unsaid out of fear, than in what they said. Ben Franklin seldom tangled with the authorities, but he discovered he could print almost anything with impunity, so long as public opinion sustained him. He won that support by making people respect him.

But the most celebrated case involving freedom of the press was the Zenger trial of 1734-5. It has been much overrated for its effect on legal reform, and it settled nothing because of the dubious circumstances under which it was conducted. Its inspirational impact was tremendous, however, and the space given to it in these pages is justified.

At this point we meet again our old friend, William Bradford, late of Philadelphia. The senior Bradford had moved to New York when he was offered the position of government printer there. As a subsidized business man, Bradford printed nothing that would antagonize his patrons. On November 8, 1725, he printed the first newspaper in the colony—the *New York Gazette*. Of course it favored the administration on all issues. Like many an editor who followed, Bradford rebelled when persecuted, as in Philadelphia, but conformed when offered special privileges and inducements by the same group he might have fought under different circumstances.

By 1734, New York was experiencing a mild revolution. A group of wealthy merchants and landowners insisted upon a greater share of control in the colony's affairs. This was an American manifestation of the situation in seventeenth-century England described in Chapter 1. A new commercial class was rising in the new world, as it had in the old. It demanded repeal of laws that restricted commerce. It insisted upon a devaluation of royal power and a greater emphasis upon the role of the king's (and governor's) advisers, representing the new class. In England this activity culminated in the "Glorious Revolution" and the eventual triumph of the Whig, or commercial party. This development was a little slower in America, but the issue came up shortly after Bradford began issuing his paper from his little office on Hanover Square in the fall of 1725.

What we are about to see is the beginning of the party system in America, although it does not fully flower until near the end of the century. Various groups had started to coalesce as early as 1720. The Tories, or administration group, had the power at that time. The Tories represented the aristocrats, as shown by the names of their leaders—the Van Cortlandts, Van Rensselaers, Beekmans, Delanceys, Bleeckers, Barclays, and Verplancks—names still heavy with prestige in New York, and commemorated by street signs in the older sections of the city. The opposition was made up of the leaders of the rising middle class. Wealth was bringing them power, but their prestige was largely dependent upon commercial, rather than upon social or family status. Included in this group were men with such names as Livingston, Morris, and Alexander. These were names that were to reappear in the American chronicle, but they had no aristocratic connotation in 1734.

The rising capitalist class in New York had no way of communicating its ideas. Bradford had the only newspaper, and he was firmly committed to the administration faction. However, Bradford's former partner was fit, willing, and able to take over this function. He was John Peter Zenger, an immigrant from the German Palatinate, whose family had found relief from religious persecution when they were offered asylum in the new world. Zenger had been apprenticed to Bradford as a youth of 13. The master appears to have been a bit strict with his protégé, for Zenger left his shop after a few years and went to Maryland.

Eventually returning to New York, Zenger still had some trouble with the language, and his writing shows it, but he was a good enough craftsman to be in demand. Bradford forgave his former apprentice and even offered Zenger a partnership in the *Gazette* shop. The partners soon disagreed, however, and Zenger ended up with his own shop just around the corner from the *Gazette*. Here a small delegation waited upon him late in the summer of 1733.

They were leaders of the commercial faction, and they asked Zenger if he would be willing to edit a paper that would be a medium for expressing their aspirations and policies.

The situation which prompted this meeting had a long and complex history. Governor Montgomerie of New York had died in 1731. Appointed as his successor was William Cosby. He was unable to sail from England immediately, and it was August of 1732 before he arrived at his new post. During this time the executive functions had been performed by Rip Van Dam, a 72-year-old Dutch colonial merchant of considerable means and prestige, although not identified with the "aristocracy." He had been on the governor's council for 30 years, and as senior member he was acting governor for the 13 months preceding Cosby's arrival. Van Dam was tough and powerful. He was a leader of the rising class that was becoming restless under an arrogant Tory ruling group.

Governor Cosby demanded a division of fees collected by Van Dam during the interval that the Dutchman was acting governor. Van Dam was willing to make some concessions, but Cosby stood upon his rights and refused to compromise. There was much more involved, however. In the litigation that followed, the governor demanded that the case be heard in the court of chancery—a court of special law—which he controlled. All money matters were to be tried in a regular court, however, and here Van Dam would most certainly have won. The struggle to take the case out of the hands of the governor's court involved Lewis Morris, chief justice of the highest colonial court. For his siding with Van Dam, Morris was removed by the governor. Van Dam thereupon filed a complaint against Governor Cosby and Justice Morris sailed for England to press the charges against the governor. Morris had more to complain of than the fee case. Governor Cosby was accused of demanding one-third the sale of all public lands sold under his jurisdiction. There were also suspected transactions involving illegal acquisition of land around what is now Utica, N. Y. Finally, there was evidence that the governor had rigged the elections so as to stack his council with his own puppets.[5] In the meantime, Governor Cosby

---

[5] Warren C. Price, "Reflections on the Trial of John Peter Zenger," *Journalism Quarterly*, XXXII (Spring 1955), 161, provides much new data on the Zenger case and points to the land-grabbing episode as one reason why public opinion swung to the Zenger-Morris side so heavily. "Cosby Manor" at Utica, 20 miles by 10 miles in extent, was an example of the governor's greed.

had replaced Justice Morris with one of his own henchmen, young James Delancey.[6] The new chief justice had not been approved by the council, as required under the charter, and Van Dam added this to the list of complaints against the governor. There is evidence that Governor Cosby realized he had a powerful faction seeking his removal for abusing prerogatives, and perhaps this is why he acted so ruthlessly in the Zenger case.

The leaders of the anti-administration forces were articulate and able citizens. They included men like Van Dam; Justice Morris; James Alexander, a member of the council and also surveyor general for the colonies of New York and New Jersey; and William Smith, noted for his *History of the Colony of New York From Its Founding to 1762*, and a well known public figure at the time of the trial. These, and other important citizens, were interested in having Zenger start a newspaper which would express the views of the opposition party.

The first issue of Zenger's *New York Weekly Journal* appeared on November 5, 1733. From the very first day, the *Journal* clashed with the administration. Bradford at the *Gazette* was no match for Zenger and the brains behind his venture. At once other rebellious elements gathered around the standard raised by the *Journal*. Smith and, more particularly, Alexander apparently were the hidden gunners of this journalistic ambuscade, and they laid down a continual barrage until the harassed governor and his party were driven into a desperate route.

On December 3, 1733, a story appeared in Zenger's paper attacking Governor Cosby for permitting French warships to spy out defenses in the lower bay. In the same issue were several derogatory statements about the administration. The governor was accused of letting only his favorites attend council meetings, for example. An irate New Jersey correspondent who wrote very much like Alexander denounced the colonial bureaucracy for incompetence. Indeed, the entire tone of the paper that day was critical.

The public enjoyed this show, and Zenger had to run off extra editions to satisfy customers. The governor was not so enthusiastic about such journalistic enterprise. Charging Zenger with "Scandal-

[6] "Henchman" is perhaps too strong a word to apply to Delancey. Delancey was young, and he was eager to get himself established in the colony. He was actually ill-equipped to take on such an important case. Later, he became lieutenant governor of New York and served with distinction and honor.

ous, Virulent and Seditious Reflections upon the Government," Cosby ordered his hand-picked chief justice, Delancey, to obtain an indictment against the brash editor. But the grand jury called to consider the matter refused to return a true bill. The Assembly likewise balked at filing any charges. Finally, a selected group of the governor's council agreed to start an action against Zenger, but only after much prodding by the governor, and after the original accusa-

Courtesy, Bettmann Archive

The trial of John Peter Zenger. A somewhat inaccurate artist's version of the famous fight for press freedom in America.

tion had been considerably watered down. On a Sunday afternoon, November 17, 1734, Zenger was arrested on a charge of "raising sedition."

He was bound over to the grand jury, but the case was not called at the end of the term, and the defense therefore demanded and obtained his release. It was up to Richard Bradley, the attorney general, and a Cosby man, to file an "information" against the prisoner, since the grand jury would not act. This he did, and Zenger was returned to jail to await the next term of court. During this time, the *Journal* continued to appear. The editorial attacks on the administration were intensified, if anything. One account has it that

Zenger's wife deserves credit for this chapter of the story. Others believe that Alexander and Smith were responsible for the content of the paper, with Mrs. Zenger and an old retainer doing the actual printing. In any case, the *Journal* appeared regularly while the publisher was in jail, and his paper was known far and wide.

In July, 1735, Zenger at last faced his judges. They were Cosby's man, Delancey, and Frederick Philipse. Bradley, the Cosby appointee who had filed the information against Zenger, was prosecutor. Alexander and Smith, who were to have defended the printer, had been disbarred when they had disputed the information, or prosecutor's warrant, filed against Zenger. They had denied Justice Delancey's right to sit on the bench without approval of the Council. They were trying desperately to get the help of equally able counsel, but on the day of the trial Zenger faced nothing but unfriendly faces within the court. Even the jury had been selected with an eye to their reactions favorable to the governor. One John Chambers was appointed by the court to defend the accused. Chambers demanded postponement until August, so he could prepare the case. Fortunately for Zenger, this plea was granted as was customary in all English courts.

The future looked black to Zenger, he himself reported afterward. But in the following month his friends were very active. A group called "The Sons of Liberty" spread the word to branch organizations up and down the coast. Alexander and Smith were using their considerable powers to find a worthy defense counsel. Ben Franklin, who kept abreast of all important developments, knew all about the issue at stake. No doubt he talked over the significance of the case with his good friend, Andrew Hamilton, of Philadelphia. Hamilton, one of the great lawyers of the period, was an outstanding liberal of his day, if we mean by liberal a person willing to consider new ideas for the improvement of society. He was co-builder of the state house, later to be enshrined as "Independence Hall." Although New York was outside his sphere, he was interested in promoting the cause of liberty everywhere, for he knew that defeat for his cause in one colony would affect the lives of all Americans. And so Hamilton thought over Zenger's case in his comfortable Philadelphia law office.

The trial began August 4, 1735. The process of impaneling the jury, and the preliminaries to the presentation of testimony indicated that there was little hope for the accused. Zenger was 38 years old then, but long months in prison had made him look older. He was pale and tired. On the bench the justices, Delancey and Philipse, glowered at the spectators crowding the room. In their black robes and elaborate wigs the judges looked stern and implacable. It is not difficult to reconstruct the scene:

The court listens attentively as Attorney General Bradley recites the offenses alleged in his own "information" (the equivalent of a grand jury indictment). Chambers, the defense counsel, arises at the end to enter a plea of "not guilty," but he does not appear to be very sure of himself. The spectators sit quietly. Most of them are members of the rebel group, and they are aware that their champion is in danger of defeat.

But while Chambers enters his plea, an old man stands watching from the rear of the room. His long, white hair falls to his shoulders, but his body is muscular and erect. The keen old eyes take in the scene. He bows with old-school elegance, as all eyes turn in his direction. It is Andrew Hamilton of Philadelphia, now in his 80's, who has risked the vicissitudes of travel to offer his services in behalf of the accused.

Striding majestically to the bar, he asks permission to present his credentials and to make his request. The bench must recognize such an eminent authority. He is granted the right to act in defense of Zenger. Turning half around so that both the judges and the jury can hear him clearly, he opens his remarks in a resonant, clear voice—a voice famous throughout the colonies. This is the "Philadelphia lawyer" in the original, favorable meaning of the term.

"I cannot think it proper to deny the Publication of a Complaint which I think is the right of every free born Subject to make," he declares, "and therefore I'll save Mr. Attorney the trouble of examining his Witnesses to that point; and I do confess (for my Client) that he both printed and published the two Papers set forth in the Information. I do hope in so doing he has committed no Crime." [7]

The courtroom is hushed in amazement. Is Hamilton deliberately throwing his case away? The only thing for the jury to decide is whether or not the accused is responsible for the publications, and Hamilton has now admitted that. Bradley, his eyes beaming with

[7] The descriptive parts of the trial are taken from "Freedom of the Press Vindicated," *Harper's New Monthly Magazine* (July 1878), 296.

delight at this apparent easy victory, arises to address the judges:
"Then, if Your Honors please, since Mr. Hamilton has confessed
the Fact, I think our Witnesses may be discharged; we have no
further Occasion for them."

The court functionaries must make the next step. Bradley remarks
that since publication of the offending articles has been admitted
by the defense, there is nothing more for the jury to do but to bring
in a verdict of guilty. To this Hamilton replies calmly, but firmly:
"Not so, neither, Mr. Attorney. There are two Sides to that Bargain. I hope it is not our bare printing or publishing a Paper that
will make it a Libel. You will have something more to do before
you make my client a libeller. For the Words themselves must be
libelous—that is, FALSE, MALICIOUS, AND SEDITIOUS—or
else we are not guilty."

Bradley approaches the bench and renews his arguments. One
by one Hamilton demolishes them. He goes back to the Magna
Carta and the abolishing of the Star Chamber to prove that the
concept he upholds—freedom to express justifiable truth—has long
been accepted in the older courts, and that colonial New York is
behind the times. His arguments are worded in decisive language,
but his manner is so courtly, and his voice so mild, that the fascinated judges listen as though hypnotized. When the spectators begin to cheer during a lull, however, the prosecution objects to Hamilton's statements, and when Hamilton insists that "the *Falsehood*
makes the *Scandal,* and both the *Libel,*" and then offers to "prove
these very Papers that are called Libel to be *True,*" Justice Delancey
remonstrates.

"You cannot be admitted, Mr. Hamilton," says the judge sternly,
"to give the Truth of a Libel in evidence . . . The Court is of the
Opinion you ought not to be permitted to prove the Facts in the
Papers," and he cites a long list of supporting authorities.

"These are Star Chamber Cases," answers Hamilton patiently, "and
I was in hopes that Practice had been dead with that Court."

Angered by this veiled criticism of his legal knowledge, the
youthful Delancey cries out angrily:

"The Court have delivered their Opinion, and we expect you
will use us with good Manners. You are not permitted to argue
against this Court."

Hamilton pauses a moment. He looks at the jury; then at the

audience; and then at Zenger, like a great actor sensing the mood of his public. Now he turns to the judges and bows courteously.

"I thank you," he replies without a trace of rancor. Then, turning his back upon the judges as though they no longer were to be considered, he acknowledges the jury with a courtly flourish. He speaks to the jurymen directly, in a voice loud enough to carry to all parts of the room.

"Then it is to you, Gentlemen, we must now appeal for Witnesses to the Truth of the Facts we have offered, and are denied the Liberty to prove. . . .

"I beg Leave to lay it down as a standing Rule in such Cases that the SUPPRESSING OF EVIDENCE OUGHT ALWAYS TO BE TAKEN FOR THE STRONGEST EVIDENCE, and I hope it will have that Weight with you."

Here Justice Delancey interposes to say that the jury may find that Zenger printed and published the offending papers, but only the judges may determine whether or not the statements are libelous.

"The Jury *may* do so," Hamilton answers, again ignoring the bench, and speaking directly to the panel, "but I do likewise know that they may do otherwise. I know they have the Right, beyond all Dispute, to determine both the *Law* and the *Facts;* and where they do not doubt of the Law, they ought to do so."

Now Hamilton is talking as though the judges were not even in the room. He exhorts the jury to act like freemen, and to follow their own consciences, without fear of official reprisals, as guaranteed under the English system of law. He ends:

". . . old and weak as I am, I should think it my Duty if required, to go to the utmost Part of the Land, where my Service could be of any Use in assisting to quench the Flame of Prosecutions upon Informations, set on Foot by the Government, to deprive a People of the Right of Remonstrating (and complaining too), of the arbitrary Attempts of Men in Power. *Men who injure and oppress the People under their Administration provoke them to cry out and complain; and then make that very Complaint the Foundation for new Oppressions and Prosecutions.*

". . . But to conclude; the Question before the Court and you Gentlemen of the Jury, is not of small nor private Concern. It is not the Cause of the poor Printer, nor of *New York* alone, which you are now trying; No! It may in it's Consequence, affect every

Freeman that lives under a British Government on the main of *America*. It is the best Cause. It is the Cause of Liberty; and I make no Doubt but your upright Conduct, this Day, will not only entitle you to the Love and Esteem of your Fellow-Citizens; but every Man who prefers Freedom to a Life of slavery will bless and honour You, as Men who have baffled the Attempt of Tyranny; and by an impartial and uncorrupt Verdict, have laid a Noble Foundation for securing to ourselves, our Posterity and our Neighbors, That, to which Nature and the Laws of our Country have given us a Right, —the Liberty—both of exposing and opposing arbitrary Power (in these Parts of the World, at least) by speaking and writing— Truth."

On that note, Hamilton won his case. The jury returned a verdict of "not guilty" and Zenger was freed. He has now become a hero of American journalism, and on the two-hundredth anniversary of the trial considerable attention was again given to the case by newspapers, radio, and movies. Less known, but equally as heroic, was Andrew Hamilton, who argued the cause of Liberty so ably.

But there are some negative aspects of the case. The verdict had no effect on libel law for more than half a century. Pennsylvania was the first state to recognize the principles of truth as a defense and the right of the jury to decide both the law and the fact, by including them in its 1790 constitution. New York accepted them in 1805. It was 1792 in England before Fox's Libel Act gave the jury power of decision, and it was 1843 before Lord Campbell's Act recognized truth as a defense.

It is very possible that expediency, rather than principle, guided the authorities after the trial. They admitted no new legal precedent in the Zenger case. It is quite probable that Zenger would have been rearrested for his very next offense, except for circumstances. Governor Cosby was cautious for a time after the trial ended, because Justice Morris was in England arguing for Cosby's dismissal, and the governor had no wish to achieve any further notoriety for himself. Then he fell desperately ill during the winter of 1735-6 and died the following March. Had he lived, he might not have accepted defeat so easily.

Again, all the reports of the trial are one-sided. The only complete account of the trial is in Zenger's own newspaper. The Crown never did issue a report, giving its side of the verdict. Since the accused had good reason to paint the picture in black and white, the Crown arguments and principles have been largely ignored. O'Callaghan's *Documents Relative to the Colonial History of New York* (Albany, 1849, V) include statements of Governor Cosby to the Lords of Trade, and they are the nearest thing to a presentation of the other side of the argument. But the "internal evidence" (facts that appear from close reading) indicate that the British view has never been fairly presented.

For example, Justice Delancey, who has always been portrayed as an arrogant judge, showed great restraint in refusing to set aside the verdict and in not overruling Hamilton. He might even have had the old lawyer arrested for his contempt of the bench. The British government in this case, as in many others, including the Stamp Act of 1765, did not use its powers to curb opinion, but backed down in the face of overwhelming public dissatisfaction.

This is an important point. The courts as much as the press guard the freedom so jealously maintained by a democratic people. To flout the law for the sake of expedience in a press case is dangerous precedent. Hamilton said the jury had the right to determine both the law and the fact, and that is what readers of the Zenger episode assume to be true. But the courts did not recognize that principle, either before the trial, or for more than 50 years thereafter. The jury in the Zenger case had only to determine the fact—that is, whether or not Zenger had printed the articles on exhibit. They knew, as everyone knew, that the editor was responsible for the offending stories. To turn in a verdict of "not guilty," therefore, was a direct contradiction of the evidence. It may have been a good verdict for the accused and for American press freedom, but when defendants are acquitted because of political feelings, rather than a calm appraisal of the known facts, that is a threat to a system every bit as important to our freedom as the liberty of the press. Admittedly, court procedure changes with the times, and the Zenger trial coincided with one of these transition periods. But at least two reputable colonial lawyers of the day agreed that the Zenger verdict was a perilous one for the over-all cause of justice.[8]

Justice Delancey appears to be somewhat ridiculous today in his opinion that truth could not be offered as a defense in this type

---

[8] Warren C. Price (see p. 74fn.) cites these reports from Howell's *State Trials*, published in 1783. The right of the jury to determine both the law and the fact had been exercised in England at least as early as 1649 in the trial of John Lilburne, one of Cromwell's soldiers. See *Notes and Queries*, Vol. 1, second series (London: Bell and Baldy, 1856), p. 355.

of libel action. The fact is, he had considerable precedent to back him up. For the principle recognized by the courts of that day was "the greater the truth, the greater the libel." The logic behind this doctrine was this: Public accusations, or criticisms of those in authority, might upset the entire community and cause a serious breach of the public peace. In Zenger's case, popular opinion was behind him, but this did not sway colonial writers on the subject of seditious libel. Almost all of them remained agreed that government could be libeled and that to do so was properly to be considered a crime. And many responsible citizens agreed with them. The threat of punishment—under the common law of seditious libel or under the power of a legislature to punish for contempt—for those who criticised officials remained strong until the close of the eighteenth century when the struggle over the Sedition Act of 1798 brought the issue to a climax.[9]

These negative aspects of the case are counteracted by the inspirational contributions of Zenger and Hamilton and the psychological effects of the trial. For the trial did enunciate a principle—even if it did not establish legal precedent—and this principle is vital to our libertarian philosophy of today in matters of free speech and press. The right to criticise officials is one of the main pillars of press freedom.[10] Psychologically, the Zenger trial advanced this goal, for no other colonial court trial of a printer for seditious libel after 1735 has come to light. Some were found to be in contempt by their own colonial legislatures or governor's councils, but none was tried by the Crown.[11] Popular opinion had proved its power. The Zenger case thus merits its place in history, as a forerunner of what was to follow.

[9] Leonard W. Levy, *Legacy of Suppression* (Cambridge: Harvard University Press, 1960), develops this thesis of colonial adherence to the concept of seditious libel except as it could be turned against one's own faction. Levy traces this attitude as prevailing as late as the 1790's.

[10] The others: (1) The right to publish without official license, established in America by James Franklin; (2) The right to report matters of public interest, a right not widely recognized until well into the nineteenth century, and still contested by reluctant public officials.

[11] Harold L. Nelson, "Seditious Libel in Colonial America," *American Journal of Legal History*, III (April 1959), 160-172. Professor Nelson finds the colonial assembly more effective than the courts in disciplining printers, and cites available evidence that Zenger's trial was the last.

ANNOTATED BIBLIOGRAPHY

Books:

Adams, James Truslow, *Provincial Society, 1690-1763,* A History of American Life, Vol. III. New York: The Macmillan Company, 1927. This series was the first large-scale attempt at social history and remains highly usable. Other volumes will be cited later. The series was edited by Arthur M. Schlesinger and Dixon Ryan Fox.

Bridenbaugh, Carl, *Cities in the Wilderness: the First Century of Urban Life in America, 1625-1742* and *Cities in Revolt: Urban Life in America, 1743-1776.* New York: Alfred A. Knopf, Inc., 1955. Cities studied are Boston, Newport, New York, Philadelphia, and Charleston.

Buranelli, Vincent, ed., *The Trial of Peter Zenger.* New York: New York University Press, 1957. Reprint of the text of the trial, with biographical information about participants and an analysis of its meaning.

Duniway, Clyde A., *The Development of Freedom of the Press in Massachusetts.* New York: Longmans, Green & Company, 1906. An early and scholarly study of colonial press freedom.

Levy, Leonard W., *Legacy of Suppression.* Cambridge: Harvard University Press, 1960. A prize-winning study of the English and colonial roots of freedom of expression, which documents a thesis that only a narrow concept of such freedom was held before 1800.

Mott, Frank L., ed., *The Case and Tryal of John Peter Zenger.* Columbia, Missouri: Press of the Crippled Turtle, 1954. An exact reprint of Zenger's original pamphlet on his trial.

Osgood, Herbert L., *The American Colonies in the Eighteenth Century,* Vol. II. New York: Columbia University Press, 1924. Pages 443-482 give the political background for the Zenger trial, examining the Cosby administration.

Ould, Harmon, ed., *Freedom of Expression.* London: Hutchinson International Authors, Ltd., 1945. A memoriam on the tercentenary of Milton's *Areopagitica.* Contributors are important British and foreign thinkers, writers, journalists, and lawyers. A very interesting discussion of press freedom from early days to the present.

Presbrey, Frank, *The History and Development of Advertising.* Garden City: Doubleday, Doran & Company, 1929. The best known and most complete history of advertising. Especially useful because of its numerous illustrations.

Rutherfurd, Livingston, *John Peter Zenger.* New York: Peter Smith, 1941. Reprints the text of the trial, with a biographical study of Zenger and an analysis of the political setting. The above edition is a reprint from a 1904 edition published by Dodd, Mead and Company.

Schuyler, Livingston R., *The Liberty of the Press in the American Colonies Before the Revolutionary War.* New York: Thomas Whittaker, 1905. A short history of an important period in press development.

Wood, James Playsted, *The Story of Advertising.* New York: Ronald Press, 1958. Less extensive but more readable than Presbrey. Relatively brief in its coverage of the period before 1850.

Periodicals and Monographs:

"Freedom of the Press Vindicated," *Harper's New Monthly Magazine,* LVII (July 1878), 296. A colorful and fascinating description of the Zenger trial, set forth with a realism lacking in most of the reports of that event.

Kobre, Sidney, "The Revolutionary Colonial Press—A Social Interpretation," *Journalism Quarterly,* XX (September 1943), 193. A digest of a more detailed study by the same author. Especially useful for its background information.

Nelson, Harold L., "Seditious Libel in Colonial America," *American Journal of Legal History,* III (April 1959), 160. Establishes thesis that after the Zenger trial, printers were disciplined by legislatures or governor's councils, rather than by trial courts. The colonial assembly became the major force in limiting press freedom.

Price, Warren C., "Reflections on the Trial of John Peter Zenger," *Journalism Quarterly,* XXXII (Spring 1955), 161. Deals with the negative aspects of Hamilton's appeal insofar as legal status was concerned, and examines Cosby's land-grabbing operations.

Steiner, Bernard C., "Andrew Hamilton and John Peter Zenger," *Pennsylvania Magazine,* XX (Summer 1896), 405. Since Hamilton is as much a hero of this period as is Zenger, this description of the lawyer's place in history is very useful.

Chapter 5

THE SEEDS OF REVOLUTION

> The United Voice of all His Majesty's *free* and
> *loyal* Subjects in America—Liberty and Property,
> and no Stamps.
> —Motto of various colonial newspapers

MANY BELIEVE TODAY that the American Revolution was strictly a struggle by freedom-loving people for independence from a tyrannical British king. Actually, the reasons for the revolution were much more complex. The clash of debtor and creditor was a factor. The weakness of British policy, inept leadership, and overemphasis of the mercantile system (by which Europeans exploited colonies) were all involved in the dispute. Colonists resented restraints on American development of commerce and industry. They complained that their frontier was being denied to them after the hard-won victory over the French, which they had expected to open up vast new areas to expansion. Refusal of the British to grant home rule was another point of dispute.

But these are not sufficient *reasons* for the war. All the above disputes might have been settled peaceably, some historians say. Other British colonies had similar grievances at the time, yet they did not have to resort to war. Nor can it be held that the issue was confined to Britain and her colonies. In other parts of the world the same issues were being raised. France and South America were soon to be embroiled in revolution, indicating that the War for Independence was a regional manifestation of world unrest.

Many students of the period maintain that the war was unnecessary. The American shipper might quarrel over British denial of certain markets, but he knew that the British navy made it possible for him to sail the high seas with reasonable safety from seizure. Certainly the little Atlantic seaboard communities in America could not have provided such essential protection—not by themselves, at least. Merchants resented the trade restrictions, but they knew full well that they also enjoyed great benefits through monopolies and bounties that only a great trading nation, such as Great Britain, could make possible. Frontiersmen might curse such measures as the Quebec Act, which limited westward expansion, but the same complainants were aware that the motherland provided the roads by which the frontier was developed and tamed. They knew, also, that British troops garrisoning forts up and down the colonies were the main bulwarks against ferocious and relentless savages.

How, then, did the American colonies find themselves at war with the homeland in 1775? Perhaps it can be explained that the war was as much a class struggle—a domestic rebellion, even—as it was a struggle for political separation. The fight for freedom was both internal and external, if we see it as a class conflict. This class struggle was directed by an able and articulate group of "agitators"— one of the best proofs, indeed, of the nature of the conflict. It is even possible that there might have been no shooting war, had it not been for these class leaders. Sam Adams was a typical leader of this movement. He was a spokesman for a class insisting upon a greater share of control. Having aroused his public, he proceeded to win his goals. For that reason, it is pertinent to study this period in terms of public opinion, and through the eyes of those who manipulated public support leading to war.

It is significant that the Stamp Act of 1765 alienated two very influential groups—the lawyers and the journalists. The new law placed a heavy duty on paper used in publishing newspapers. There was also a heavy tax on all legal documents. Thus, the lawyer, who swayed people by the spoken word, and the journalist, who had an even wider influence through the written word, were both turned against those who favored the unpopular act.

Yet one can scarcely blame the British for proposing some such law. After the Seven Years' War, which saw the British triumphant over the French in North America and India, Great Britain emerged as a great empire—one of the greatest of all time. On the other hand, victory found the British nearly bankrupt. Some way had to be found to pay the cost of defending the wide frontiers. Since the Americans had gained so much from the victory over the French, they should be willing to pay a small share of the defense costs, the statesmen in London insisted. No longer need the American colonists look apprehensively to sea, fearful that the morning sun would silhouette the rigging of an invading fleet. Never again would brave sons have to fall in the storming of French strongholds, such as Louisburg. No longer need they spend large sums of money as insurance against the French menace. The British victory had ended all that.

The motherland had not only provided the security of victory, but it offered the services of the greatest fleet in the world, without cost to the colonies. It should be pointed out that during this entire period the government at London paid about two-thirds the cost of frontier defense. The colonists could not possibly have paid their full share of the item. And if the colonies enjoyed peace, security, and prosperity, surely they could not begrudge the motherland aid in time of stress.

The colonists were indeed willing to offer help—in their own fashions. Colonial legislatures were ready to raise levies, but they did not raise enough, and they did not exert themselves enough to turn over such funds when needed. Since the legislatures controlled the colonial purse strings, not much could be done when levies were in arrears. Empire leaders believed the solution was the imposition of special taxes that could be collected more effectively for this purpose. The Stamp Act was one such attempt. The British themselves paid such a tax. George Grenville, sponsor of the hated measure, pointed out that even Massachusetts had imposed a similar tax in 1755. A little later New York did the same.

The colonists replied that the local stamp acts were imposed by the people paying the tax. As Sam Adams brought out in his resolutions of 1765, the colonies had no direct representation in Parliament. He recognized that this would be impracticable, considering the distance apart of the two areas. That was why he insisted that the colonies be given home rule under a common king.[1] But that

---

[1] "Resolutions of the House of Representatives of Massachusetts, October 29, 1765," in Harry R. Warfel, Ralph H. Gabriel, and Stanley Williams, eds., *The American Mind* (New York: American Book Company, 1937), p. 138.

JOHN DICKINSON

ISAIAH THOMAS

John Dickinson spoke for the American Whig, or business-minded colonial. He stirred up sentiment for greater liberties but he had little sympathy with the Independence movement. One of the greatest of American journalists, Isaiah Thomas, was a courageous spokesman for the Patriot cause. A self-taught scholar, he was the publisher of innumerable books. James Rivington, the Tory editor, had advanced ideas about objective and honest reporting until the pressure of his "Patriot" rivals made him retaliate in kind.

JAMES RIVINGTON

Thursday, October 31, 1765.

THE

PENNSYLVANIA JOURNAL;
AND
WEEKLY ADVERTISER.

NUMB. 1195.

EXPIRING: In Hopes of a Resurrection to LIFE again.

I AM sorry to be obliged to acquaint my Readers, that as The STAMP-ACT, is fear'd to be obligatory upon us after the First of November ensuing, (the fatal To-morrow) the Publisher of this Paper unable to bear the Burthen, has thought it expedient to STOP a while, in order to deliberate, whether any Methods can be found to elude the Chains forged for us, and escape the insupportable Slavery; which it is hoped, from the just Representations now made against that Act, may be effected. Mean while, I must earnestly Request every Individual of my Subscribers, many of whom have been long behind Hand, that they would immediately Discharge their respective Arrears, that I may be able, not only to support myself during the Interval, but be better prepared to proceed again with this Paper, whenever an opening for that Purpose appears, which I hope will be soon.

WILLIAM BRADFORD.

Remember, O my friends! the Laws, the Rights,
The generous plan of power deliver'd down,
From age to age, by your renown'd fore-fathers,
O let it never perish in your hands,
But piously transmit it to your children.

ADDISON's Cato.

LIBERTY is one of the greatest Blessings, which human beings can possibly enjoy...

Adieu, Adieu to the LIBERTY of the PRESS.

Courtesy, State Historical Society of Wisconsin

Facsimile of the final issue of a typical colonial newspaper on the eve of the execution of the hated Stamp Act in 1765.

was no solution to the immediate problem. Franklin, who was serving as agent for Pennsylvania and Massachusetts in London, could think of no alternative, but he knew something was wrong with the Stamp Act. It might have logic behind it, but when it alienated such vociferous groups in America, it was a stupid proposal, he believed.

The opposition of the editors took many forms. Some suspended publication. Since both the general public and the merchants had come to depend upon the newspapers for the essential information offered in such stirring times, these suspensions tended to arouse influential elements of the community to the support of the patriots. Many publishers tried to evade the law. Some publications appeared without title or masthead, which technically took them out of the newspaper classification. A few appeared without the required stamp, but with the notice that none could be procured, which may have been true, since mobs prevented the sale of stamps in every colony. Several publications satirized the event. On the day before the tax was to be enforced, the *Pennsylvania Journal and Weekly Advertiser* appeared with heavy black column margins, or "turned rules," the traditional symbol of journalistic mourning, but this time in the shape of a tombstone. The *Boston Gazette* and the *Maryland Gazette* were printed that day with skulls and crossed bones, as emblems of a dead free press.

The Stamp Act agitation was actually only an episode in a long conflict between Great Britain and her colonies. The British were leading exponents of the "mercantile system." Under this program, colonies were to be developed for raw materials, and again as markets for finished products. Essential to the system was a favorable balance of trade for Great Britain, meaning that the value of exports must exceed that of imports. This policy was fostered by whatever party gained control. That was why the British Government had imposed restrictions on trade, industry, and finances in the colonies beginning in 1651. Scarcity of money in the colonies became a serious matter, for example, but the refusal of British creditors to ease the debt burden embittered many a colonial.[2] An Act of 1751, specifically, denied the printing of paper money secured by land, which would have made money less dear. Sam Adams, often called

[2] Curtis P. Nettels, "The Money Supply of the American Colonies Before 1720." *University of Wisconsin Studies* No. 20 (1934), p. 279-283.

"The Father of the Revolution," never forgot that his father had been ruined by these restrictive laws, and that he had been cheated of his patrimony thereby.

The colonists did not make violent objection, however, until after the victory over the French. Smuggling went on openly, engaged in by respected citizens as a legitimate way around measures believed to be unsound by local consensus. But after 1763, the British began to enforce old laws and to impose new ones. A royal proclamation closed all the frontier west of the mountains to settlement and expansion, thereby raising land values in the older areas. Smuggling was reduced by an effective amendment to an old law of 1733. Currency restrictions were tightened. Commodities never before taxed were now enumerated. And just to rub it in, the home government asserted the right of Parliament to make all laws for the colonies.

These are samples of the type of laws passed for the benefit of the ruling faction in London. American colonists probably could have accepted regulations which kept them out of the wool, hat, or iron industries, but what rankled most was to be treated as inferiors by a group concerned primarily with exploitation. Americans might have agreed to many exactions, given a little more home rule, but they had the feeling they were being used, and they did not like it. The British Board of Trade philosophy simply did not take into consideration such unbusinesslike factors as the feelings of colonials. It should also be pointed out that a business recession in the colonies followed on the heels of the French war. The new laws, and the enforcement of old laws, aggravated this depression. *All* classes were affected—which is most significant, for people tend to unite under duress.

The reaction to the trend is seen in the colonial attempts to present their grievances peaceably at first, and then by more direct action when this policy failed. The Stamp Act Congress, which succeeded in bringing about the repeal of the hated law, showed the colonies what could be accomplished by united, decisive action. Granted all this—one must still conclude that economics were only a factor in the coming revolution. For ideas were stirring men, too. Indeed, it can be said that the revolution was completed by 1775, if ideas are the criteria, in which case the war was only the means of defending them against those who could not subscribe to the new thought.

Here is where the press of the time played such an important part. In newspaper and pamphlet (often reprints of weekly journals) appeared the literature of this revolution. Here it was that the passions and arguments of the revolutionaries found expression. As Beard has said:

. . . Unlike France of the Old Regime, provincial America did not produce, long before the struggle commenced, great treatises such as the *Encyclopedia* or the ringing calls for revolt such as Rousseau's *Social Contract*.

The reasons were not difficult to find: the colonists already had textbooks of revolution in the writings of Englishmen who defended and justified the proceedings of the seventeenth century—above all, John Locke's writings, wherein was set forth the right of citizens to overthrow governments that took their money or their property without their consent. . . . All that editors and publicists had to do was to paraphrase, decorate, and repeat. . . .[3]

The conflicting ideas as the revolution progressed can be followed conveniently by studying the products of three journalists who represented their respective classes or groups. They were James Rivington, the Tory spokesman, John Dickinson, "the penman of the revolution," representing the Whig philosophy, and Samuel Adams, evangelist of democracy and leader of the "agitators" or Radicals.

We are likely to think of the American Tory as something of a traitor because of his refusal to bear arms against his king in the War for Independence. Actually, it was the Tory who remained loyal to his country when others rebelled. Only defeat in war made the Tory a traitor. Readers of Kenneth Roberts' historical novel, *Oliver Wiswell*, can understand that there were many sincere and honest Americans who believed in the Tory cause in the middle of the eighteenth century.

The goal of the Tory, apparently, was to retain the basic structure of colonial society. He wished to continue governing by right of property, heredity, position, and tradition—which would appear to be the attributes of a nobility. This seems a strange and distasteful

[3] Charles A. and Mary R. Beard, *The Rise of American Civilization*, Vol. I (New York: The Macmillan Company, 1930), p. 187.

desideratum, by modern standards, but it had its persuasive proponents. Such a one was Rivington.

"Jemmy" Rivington came to the colonies in 1762, after he had lost his fortune at the race track—not the last newspaperman to suffer in this way, it might be added. Despite this preoccupation with the king of sports, Rivington was a credit to journalism and to his class. One can hardly blame him for his Tory views. For generations his family had been official publishers of religious books for the Church of England—the Established Church, and therefore the one that had the most general appeal to most good Tories. King and Bishop represented authority, by which order could be maintained most effectively, the Tory argued. Thus, an attack on the authority of the state was also a threat to the authority of the church, men like Rivington insisted, and history of revolution has shown that this is indeed the usual consequence. It was the duty of all citizens, therefore, to help the forces of law and order against anarchistic elements.

Rivington was influential in America, and could do much for the Tory cause. He was proprietor of the first chain of book stores in America, with branches in Boston, New York, and Philadelphia. He had been so successful in this venture that he decided to publish a newspaper. In 1773, on the eve of the revolt in the colonies, he founded *Rivington's New York Gazetteer or the Connecticut, New Jersey, Hudson's River and Quebec Weekly Advertis*er, a local paper, despite its impressive, regional title. The paper was well edited and was skillfully printed. It was also very profitable, as shown by the fact that it averaged about 55 per cent advertising.

Rivington merited respect for his venture because he was willing to discuss both sides of political questions—an objectivity that was not the standard in his era. Such objectivity was just what the "patriot" rivals resented, however. They were not interested in fair and accurate reports. That was no way to fight for a cause, they believed, and so we find Rivington complaining in his issue of April 20, 1775:

The Printer is bold to affirm that his press has been open to publication from ALL PARTIES. . . . He has considered his press in the light of a public office, to which every man has a right to have recourse. But the moment he ventured to publish sentiments which were opposed to the dangerous views and designs of certain demagogues, he found himself held up as an enemy of his country.

Rivington's complaint was a common one for Tories in the decade preceding outbreak of war. Power was slipping away from the English authorities, into the hands of the colonial assemblies. In their eyes, criticism of the Crown was no longer seditious libel. But criticism of the assemblies, or of the "patriot" cause, might well be seditious or contemptuous. Freedom of expression meant largely freedom for your side—and the Tory was on the losing side.

The troubles of the Tory printers came largely from public pressures generated by such Radical "agitators" as Sam Adams rather than from official actions. An organized campaign of threats and economic coercion was reinforced at times by mob action against printers who were not all-out for the Radical cause. The Tories, or Loyalists, were nearly all hounded out of business; those who tried to be neutral were either forced into the Radical camp or into suspension.[4]

In Boston, for example, the well-organized Radical group used threats to persuade some reluctant printers to use their propaganda, and to mute Tory voices. When John Mein's stoutly Tory *Chronicle* refused to cower, but instead attacked the Radical leaders, Mein was hanged in effigy, attacked on the street, and finally mobbed. He had to flee to England and his paper was suspended in 1770. Thomas Fleet's *Evening Post*, which tried to print both sides of the argument, closed down in 1775, as did the Tory *Post-Boy*. The last Tory voice, the *News-Letter*, died early in 1776. In Philadelphia, William Goddard was roughed up for publishing pro-Crown material in his *Pennsylvania Chronicle*. Rivington thus could complain about the experiences of others, as well as his own, in opposing the Radical-generated tide of public opinion.

After Lexington and Concord Rivington ceased to be objective. During the war he was as partisan as his "patriot" rivals. His wartime paper, renamed the *Royal Gazette,* reeked with unfounded charges against American leaders. He appeared to relish vicious rumors that might harm the rebels—but this was in time of war, whose first casualty is objectivity. And he had little reason to feel charitable toward his political and social enemies. He had been burned in effigy by mobs for expressing his views. Twice his shop had been raided—the type destroyed on one occasion. He had been

[4] See Arthur M. Schlesinger, *Prelude to Independence: The Newspaper War on Britain, 1764-1776* (New York: Alfred A. Knopf, Inc., 1958), for the story of the use of the press by the Radical propagandists.

forced to sign a humiliating public apology for merely voicing his opinions. He had even been driven back to England for a while. Even so, it should be pointed out that Rivington's most malicious writings were produced while the British general, Lord Howe, was breathing down the editor's neck. For the general had hoped that a bloody war might be averted if the colonists could be turned from the error of their ways. Rivington suited his purposes as an instrument for persuasion.

Tories such as Rivington stood for government "by the better sort." There are always those who, perhaps unconsciously, believe in this philosophy. They see their communities largely populated by illiterate, superstitious, and inexperienced citizens. The alternatives are either to place government in abler hands, or to let such citizens choose their own leaders. In many times and places the choice has been made in favor of the former. To allow the ignorant a voice in government is to bring charlatans in as officials. Rivington understood this. Such a system was the worst type of tyranny, he believed. It was much more dangerous than Tory control at its very worst. At least the Tory could argue that he had education, leisure for the study of government, long experience as an administrator, a sense of responsibility as a governor which would tend to keep the mob from wishing to revolt, and the *noblesse oblige* that comes from generations of duty to one's position.

A man like Rivington understood the Tory emphasis upon protection of property. Protection of property was the best insurance against the flouting of human rights, the Tory believed. A man with property has most to gain by peace. There can be peace only when general welfare is the concern of the rulers. Since revolt, the greatest threat to property, must come from the general public, it is incumbent upon the intelligent man of property to promote the best interests of the masses.

Civilization, after all, was the protection afforded to those who might have been swallowed up by the mighty, under the laws of the jungle. To prevent the strong from exploiting the weak, government had to have coercive power sufficient to control the strongest elements of society. That coercive power had to be defined by wise laws. Hence, any flouting of these laws was a threat to civilization and must, therefore, be the worst possible crime. That was why treason and rebellion were punished so severely.

But wise laws could only be drafted and administered by wise men. Where were such men most likely to be found, Rivington asked? Certainly not among the illiterate, emotionally-motivated mechanics and laborers, he insisted. The wise men were those who had the leisure, training, and tradition to study government. Obviously, then, the Tory class was the group from which such administrators should be drafted. It was all very clear to men like Rivington, and on such a basis, he was justified in writing as he did. That his opinions were respected is indicated by the large circulation and prosperity of his publication.

Spokesmen for other groups disputed these views—some mildly, and some violently. The American Tory was opposed by a rising capitalist faction—it could not as yet be called a party—often referred to as the Colonial Whigs. An articulate Whig was John Dickinson of Pennsylvania, sometimes called "The Penman of the Revolution."

Although not a publisher or printer, Dickinson deserves to be ranked with the great journalists of the period. By newspaper and pamphlet he spread the gospel of his political faith. The gist of his philosophy appeared in a series of articles entitled "Letters From a Farmer in Pennsylvania." The first such letter was printed in the *Pennsylvania Chronicle* in 1767. Eleven others followed on into 1768. They were widely reprinted up and down the seaboard. The letters not only discussed American foreign policy; they actually *were* the policy of the colonials at the time. Dickinson had no wish to bring on a war of independence, but he, more than any other writer except Sam Adams, prepared public opinion for the Revolution.

The subject matter of his writings makes him appear to be dangerously radical in his views. We recall that he was the author of the *Declaration of Rights of the Stamp Act Congress;* that he wrote the two *Petitions to the King;* and that he was coauthor of the Articles of Confederation. Actually, Dickinson was not at all the firebrand intimated above. He was as conservative as the class he represented, this mild Quaker, who had married a wealthy girl, and who recognized property as the basis of sound government.

Dickinson was as contemptuous of rabble-rousers as were Rivington and the rest of the Tories. For the Whig had rather narrow ideas of liberty. The great battle cry of the Whig, for example, was "no taxation without representation," which is strictly an economic aspect of the struggle. The Whig had no great interest in the rise of the common man. He had only the vaguest of ideas regarding the "natural rights" philosophy of social reform, for he thought more in terms of property, rather than in terms of human rights. Yet he, too, was fighting for a principle, and in the conflict he brought liberties to others less able to fight on fair terms. The curious twist to all this was that the worst enemy of the American Whig was his counterpart in England. The British Whig imposed commercial restrictions that were considered harmful to American business interests. The American argued that if British business men in control of the government both at home and abroad could impose taxes arbitrarily without colonial representation, then American business rivals could be driven into oblivion.

But note that the American Whig is always the conciliationist. Says "Farmer" Dickinson in one of his letters:

. . . The cause of liberty is a "cause of too much dignity, to be sullied by turbulence and tumults." It ought to be maintained in a manner suitable to her nature. Those who engage in it, should breathe a sedate yet fervent spirit, animating them to actions of prudence, justice, modesty, bravery, humanity and magnanimity. . . .[5]

And again:

. . . I hope, my dear countrymen, that you will in every colony be upon your guard against those who may at any time endeavor to stir you up, under pretenses of patriotism, to any measures disrespectful to our sovereign and our mother country. . . .
. . . If once *we* are separated from our mother country, what new form of government shall we accept, or shall we find another *Britain* to supply our loss? Torn from the body to which we are united by religion, liberty, laws, affections, relations, language and commerce, we must bleed at every vein. . . .
The *constitutional* modes of obtaining relief, are those which I would wish to see pursued. . . .

When the Revolution had to be defended by arms, the American Whig had to choose between loyalty to the crown, which provided the law and order he so prized; or loyalty to his local government,

[5] All the quotations on this page are from Letter Number Three, "Letters From a Farmer In Pennsylvania," in Harry R. Warfel, Ralph H. Gabriel, and Stanley Williams, eds., *The American Mind* (New York: American Book Company, 1937), pp. 142-4.

which held the promise of the unrestricted enterprise he coveted. The dilemma forced the Whig into becoming either a Loyalist or a Patriot during the shooting war, for there was by that time no place for the compromiser. Dickinson himself had to make this choice. He could not bring himself to stand for outright independence from his beloved motherland, and he refused to sign the Declaration of Independence. But neither could he accept the role of the Loyalist. When the Radicals persuaded the colonies to break away from Great Britain, Dickinson would have no part in the public demonstrations. He was roundly abused by his colleagues and had to give up honored positions. True, he carried a musket during the war in defense of his home, but his heart was not in the fighting. We hear very little of him during this unhappy interlude. Afterward, he emerges again, when the Federalist party offers an outlet for his conservative views.

One may wonder why his role in pre-Revolutionary days is emphasized here. We must look to his writings to understand his influence. As the Whig spokesman, Dickinson was largely responsible for indoctrinating the more conservative members of his group with the need for home rule. Like most other revolutions, the American had to be sanctioned first by the more stable elements. Once a revolution is under way, the extremists are likely to take over. Moderates are less adept at keeping the masses at essential war pitch. This was the pattern followed in England in the 1640's, when Parliament, made up largely of solid citizens, took control from the king, until eventually the extremists, in turn, seized power. The same thing happened in the French Revolution following the American rebellion. It is a leader such as Dickinson who persuades men of property and prestige that change is necessary. That the Dickinsons cannot maintain control of the forces they have generated is no fault of such spokesmen. They have fulfilled their functions; it is for others to carry on the fight.

Dickinson was influential because he was respected by the propertied class—a group generally regarded as hard headed, practical, and unemotional. Once convinced, the business man could do more than anyone else in swinging his neighbors in favor of a cause. For his neighbors reasoned that if a "sound" business man believed in proposed changes, there must be good reason for his attitude. Dickinson reached this group by articles geared to their interests.

His letters were brilliant, convincing, and readable. They were widely printed. All but three of the newspapers of the period carried the complete series by the "Pennsylvania Farmer." Ideas expressed in these contributions were reflected in the press for weeks, and even for years.

Dickinson lured the property group into taking a stand against the mother country by convincing them that all the repressive trade acts passed since Cromwell's day were deliberate attempts to keep the colonies in economic thralldom. It is clear, however, that he never was interested in social reform; he asked only for Home Rule that would bring greater protection to his particular class. On the other hand, by demanding even that much liberty for his group, he contributed to the emancipation of others. It is impossible to fight for the rights of one group without spreading them to others.

The weakest group at the beginning of the struggle, and the most important at the end of the conflict, was the so-called "Radical" or "Patriot"—words not at all synonymous at a later date. The Tory had great interest in hereditary rights; the Whig was preoccupied with economic issues; but the Radical carried on into a very different field. The Radicals were the only ones seriously interested in social change. They might have been overcome, as they had been in England, however, had it not been for the very effective leadership in America. Probably the best example of the Radical leader was Samuel Adams, one of the most prolific journalists of his time.

As a propagandist, Adams was without peer. He understood that to win the inevitable conflict, he and his cohorts must achieve five main objectives. They must justify the course they advocated. They must advertise the advantages of victory. They must arouse the masses—the real shock troops—by instilling hatred of enemies. They must neutralize any logical and reasonable arguments proposed by the opposition. And finally, they must phrase all the issues in black and white, so that the purposes might be clear even to the common laborer. Adams was able to do all this, and his principal tool was the colonial newspaper.

Adams believed that the American colonies were justified in repudiating the mother country because Parliament continued to ignore basic rights. It was the British who broke the contract, he argued, and hence the obligations of the colonials no longer applied. (The theory of the law of contracts was, and still is, that violation by one party releases all other contractors from obligations.) Adams made it appear as though his class and party fought for the traditional rights, now ignored by the British Parliament. Technically, then, it was the British who were in revolt—the colonists were the people maintaining the traditional ways.

Only by victory, said Adams, could America develop its resources and fulfill its destiny. He continually listed the many restrictive laws passed since Cromwell's day to prove his point. But colonial antagonism had to be channeled, he realized, and he eventually focused his propaganda upon the British King, George III, who was actually less responsible for the situation than his advisers.[6] Adams' group neutralized all Tory arguments by the simple expedient of refusing to allow expression of such sentiments. Lastly, the Radicals used the technique of putting the issues in black and white for quick understanding by the general public. Thus, the ill feeling between Boston citizens and quartered British troops culminating in an unfortunate fusillade of shots by the soldiers is at once labeled a "massacre" by the Adams group. The black-and-white technique is evident in such choices as "freedom or slavery," the branding of Loyalists as traitors, and later, asking the colonists to choose between independence and vassalage. It was a highly successful program, and some students of the period go so far as to say such propaganda was largely responsible for bringing the colonists to the pitch of rebellion.

Sam Adams was not the only propagandist of the revolution, but he was the greatest of them all. He was truly the "master of the puppets," as his enemies dubbed him. He was perfectly fitted for the role. Adams had turned away from the ministry, from law, and from teaching, although he was familiar with all these professions. He tried his hand at business—and failed. "Sammy the Maltster," he was called on occasion. Having lost his meager patrimony in the unsuccessful management of a brewery, he gave up trying to make money. For years he had no steady income, except the pittance of a minor official. He boasted both of his poverty and of his incorruptible honesty. He would have ambled along the wharves threadbare, had not his anxious friends supported him by secret charity. He was, in short, an utter failure.

[6] Adams himself excused the King for the colonial troubles as late as 1765. See his "Resolutions," cited on page 88.

Or was he? In one field he was a genius. He knew how to interpret the aspirations of the common man to the general public. The word "agitator" has been abused in the twentieth century, but the original meaning of the word aptly describes Sam Adams. He knew how to stir up the spiritless. His great success was in coaxing the underprivileged into making the big push for political liberty. He was a good journalist because he understood the "mass mind," if that term still has any meaning. His previous failures fitted him the better for his task. He understood the feelings and aspirations of ministers, lawyers, teachers, scholars, business men, and laborers. He could speak for all the aggrieved. Though not the first to expound the philosophy of the American brand of democracy, it was he who perfected the machinery that could make it work. For this reason he is top candidate for the title "Father of the American Revolution."

As a young Radical, Adams met regularly with the Caucus Club, founded by his father and other aggressive Boston spirits. The club sponsored a newspaper, the *Independent Advertiser*, and in 1748, at the age of 26, Sam Adams became editor of that publication. Later, he was a regular contributor to the *Boston Gazette and Country Journal*, descendant of the second newspaper published in the colonies.

Adams made a strike for liberty in May, 1764, when he was appointed one of a committee of five to instruct his town's representative to the legislature. Included was a denial of Parliament's right to impose Grenville's hated Stamp Act. A final paragraph of the document also suggested a union of all the colonies for the more effective expression of grievances.[7] These instructions were printed by the *Gazette*, and since this paper was closely followed as the mouthpiece of the "patriot" element, the stirring message was broadcast up and down the seaboard.

At once Adams was recognized as leader of a small but vociferous group. Two of this band were Benjamin Edes and John Gill, boyhood friends and now proprietors of the *Gazette*. By the end of 1764 the newspaper was the nerve center of the Boston Radicals. Many famous Americans wrote for the paper, especially after the passage of the obnoxious Townshend Acts of 1767, levying new

[7] William V. Wells, *The Life and Public Services of Samuel Adams*, Vol. I (Boston: Little, Brown and Company, 1865), p. 48.

duties on colonial imports, but none was more effective than Sam Adams.

He knew just how to reach his public through the printed word. The secret of his success was his close identity of himself with the times and with the masses. He knew how to interpret both the conscience and the consciousness of the general public. Sometimes he accomplished his purposes by using the techniques of the demagogue. It is significant, however, that he made his fame as a writer, not as an orator. He could speak very effectively when the need arose, but the stump was not his medium of expression. He left oratory for others. This is significant. The demagogue prefers an audience to readers. He can reach a wider base by the spoken word than by the written word. Since ignorance and illiteracy are tools of the demagogue, readers are usually just a little more difficult to sway than crowds dependent upon the spoken word. If Adams had been sheer demagogue, he would have made greater use of the spoken word. It is to his credit that he tried to organize public opinion not so much by emotional oratory as by thoughtful articles.

He was more than a writer; he was an expert news gatherer. His Committees of Correspondence, organized in 1772, kept him alert to every movement and sentiment throughout the colonies. His agents "covered" every important meeting as ably as modern reporters gather information for the press services today. In a remarkably short time all such news reached Adams' local committee, which then processed it for effective dissemination where such information was needed. This primitive Associated Press was highly efficient, yet no one in the colonies had thought of such a device until Adams came along.

He was just as successful at instilling his enthusiasm for the cause into the hearts of useful helpers. Since a man's greatness can be measured by the caliber of his associates, we must assume that Adams was a great man indeed. Cousin John, who later became second president of the United States, sometimes disappointed Sam, as in John's defense of the British soldiers involved in the "Boston Massacre," but on the whole, the two respected each other, as indicated by the fact that Sam used his influence in John's behalf even while the two argued. They were both honest men. John was useful in enlisting the more dignified members of the community, especially the legal fraternity, disdainful of Sam's noisier methods.

Another associate was Josiah Quincy, who understood what some organizers now refer to as "solidarity." Quincy argued that to think justly was not enough; citizens must also think *alike* before there could be a united force of public opinion strong enough to make warriors of the cause invincible. Quincy was one of the first of the leaders to declare openly for war with the mother country. He was always just about one step ahead of his followers, but he and Adams understood each other. Quincy, on the other hand, proved that he acted not out of malice, but out of good sense, when he agreed to serve with John Adams as defense counsel in the massacre case. That showed great courage, for he risked losing his constituents—the very followers he had whipped into a frenzy of patriotism—in the public resentment against the hated troops.

Still another great co-worker was Joseph Warren, the charming and kindly physician, who spoke with great logic for the patriot cause. Warren insisted upon taking direct action when the shooting began. He lost his life as a high-ranking officer in the first pitched battle of the war at Breed's (Bunker) Hill.

James Otis was the spellbinder of the group—one of the great orators of his day. The British feared Otis most of all, because of his persuasive powers.

But none of these leaders ever equaled the old master in the art of mass manipulation.

Sam Adams believed that sovereignty rested in the people—all the people, not just the lowly, and certainly not just the privileged. He insisted that whenever a powerful minority usurped this sovereignty, the entire political machine began to clank. Adams' purpose was to organize the rank and file so that the common man might regain his due share of power. Adams set himself as the instrument by which power would be drained from the autocratic minority into the reservoir of the democratic majority.

In carrying out this mission, Adams used every communication device known at the time, including letters, speeches, and the press. The newspaper was his favorite tool. If his language was strong, it was because it had to be in order to budge the apathetic into action. If he sometimes appeared to be in bad taste, he knew that he had to speak in the vernacular to reach some segments of the population. He could also write in language that comes close to the sublime. All his words were rebellious, however. That did not bother him. He never recoiled at the word "rebel." Rebellion was his business, and he loved his work. His mission was the "dissemination of unrest." Why deny that he was a rebel, then, he asked? There was no virtue in loyalty to a corrupt government, he insisted.

"What has commonly been called rebellion has more often been nothing but a manly and glorious struggle in opposition to the LAWLESS POWER OF REBELLIOUS kings and princes," he wrote.

If he was fanatical, he was no more so than Tories such as Governor Hutchinson, and at least he was honest. The governor's letters, discovered by Franklin in London proved beyond all doubt that many of the Tory promises to the colonists were empty—given only to win more privileges for the party in power. No such charge could be made against Adams. For a dozen years he gave all his energy to advance a cause that could offer him only meager material rewards.

Day after day Adams pressed his foes through newspaper and through pamphlet. He emphasized the need for a realignment of class power. Tory doctrine, which was made to sound so noble by such men as Rivington and Hutchinson, was only window dressing, said Adams. It could fool only the gullible. He appealed to the self interest of every type of American, shifting his style with his quill. At least 25 pen names have been recognized as in his hand. Late at night passersby looked up at the lighted window of the Adams home, and they knew the veteran revolutionary was still at work, writing a piece for the *Gazette*, perhaps, making it hot for the Tories. His neighbors could not help but be impressed. Many of his loyal followers may not have known just what all the furore was about, but they knew that Adams spoke for them, and they were certain that "whatever the old man wanted" must be all right.

Granted all this, is a public writer justified in smearing men's characters, even for a cause? The question is pertinent right on up to modern times. Adams believed that his technique was essential to victory. For years the laborer and clerk had shown inordinate deference to aristocratic "superiors." This attitude was less marked in America than in England, but the attitude had to be completely changed, if the masses were to make the big push for liberty and popular sovereignty. For if one class were to be treated with special deference, then the words and ideas of these "superior" persons would have weight all out of proportion to merit and numbers. Somehow, Adams had to whittle the aristocrat down to size. Until the common man was raised, and the aristocrat was brought down, to a common level, the majority of workers was clearly at a disadvantage. Adams knew how to find the soft spots in the Tory shell. The weakness of the Tory was his arrogance. Adams' weapon was his quill, dipped into the venom of vituperation. His skill in conducting a smear campaign has never been surpassed.

The ways of the idol wrecker may not be pretty. Governor Hutchinson was correct when he called Adams an assassin of reputations. The governor knew whereof he spoke, for the last British administrator was a favorite target for the caustic rebel journalist. In the end, Hutchinson, who traced his ancestry back to the illustrious and independent Anne (first outstanding woman in American public life), was forced to leave his native land for England. No wonder Hutchinson was so bitter. But Adams was playing a desperate game. His smear attacks were one way of helping to bring down the odds.

The "Master of the Puppets" did his work well. No one had more to do with the outcome than Adams. On the morning of April 19, 1775, the "shot heard 'round the world" was fired at the battle of Lexington and Concord. From then on, the country was in arms, fighting for the ultimate victory that Adams had helped to engineer.

ANNOTATED BIBLIOGRAPHY

Books:

Becker, Carl L., *The Eve of the Revolution*. New Haven: Yale University Press, 1918. An excellent one-volume summary of this period by an eminent authority.

Beer, George L., *British Colonial Policy*. New York: The Macmillan Company, 1907. Presents the British point of view in a way that may not be familiar to the average college student.

Bowen, Catherine D., *John Adams and the American Revolution*. New York: Little, Brown and Company, 1950. Following the school of historical writing which allows the author to describe the feelings of his subjects, this book nevertheless gives a very real picture of the times.

Davidson, Philip, *Propaganda and the American Revolution*. Chapel Hill: University of North Carolina Press, 1941. This book should be read by students of public opinion. It reveals the tremendous impact of pamphlets, broadsides, newspapers, and books in conditioning the public to rebellion.

Gipson, Lawrence H., *The Coming of the Revolution, 1763-1775*. New York: Harper & Brothers, 1954. Stresses colonial resistance to more efficient English administration. Part of the New American Nation series.

Greene, Evarts B., *The Revolutionary Generation, 1763-1790*. A History of American Life, Vol. IV. New York: The Macmillan Company, 1943. Source for social history.

Harlow, R. V., *Samuel Adams*. New York: Henry Holt and Company, 1923. Written at the time when the "new" psychology was the rage, this book is a kind of psychoanalysis of the great American agitator. Adams is shown as motivated by an inferiority complex.

Miller, John C., *Sam Adams: Pioneer in Propaganda*. Boston: Little, Brown and Company, 1936. A "debunking" treatment of Adams; sometimes vague, but useful. See also Miller's *Origins of the American Revolution* (Boston: Little, Brown and Company, 1943).

Morgan, Edmund S., and Helen M. Morgan, *The Stamp Act Crisis*. Chapel Hill: University of North Carolina Press, 1953. A scholarly study of the 1765 crisis as a "prologue to revolution."

Parrington, Vernon L., *Main Currents in American Thought*, Vol. I. John Dickinson and Samuel Adams are commented upon.

Schlesinger, Arthur M., *Prelude to Independence: The Newspaper War on Britain, 1764-1776*. New York: Alfred A. Knopf, Inc., 1958. An excellent detailed study of the role of the newspaper in promoting revolution, and a history of the press for the period.

Van Tyne, Claude H., *The Causes of the War of Independence*. Boston: Houghton Mifflin Company, 1922. This is Volume I of a great history describing the reasons behind many of the events of the pre-revolutionary period.

Wells, William V., *The Life and Public Services of Samuel Adams*, 3 vols. Boston: Little, Brown and Company, 1865. Useful for the documents published verbatim.

Periodicals and Monographs:

Adams, Samuel, "The Rights of the Colonists," *Old South Leaflets*, VII (1906), general series. This is the report of the Committee of Correspondence to the Boston Town Meeting, November 20, 1772. It is a good example of the type of activity in which Adams was engaged.

Cullen, Maurice R., Jr., "The Boston Gazette: a Community Newspaper," *Journalism Quarterly*, XXXVI (Spring 1959), 204. Tells how the *Gazette* reflected Boston life in the 1760's and 1770's.

"The Father of the Revolution," *Harper's New Monthly Magazine*, LIII (July 1876), 185. A good summary of the influence of Adams.

Hosmer, James K., "Samuel Adams: The Man of the Town Meeting," *Johns Hopkins University Studies in Historical and Political Science*, II (April 1884), 5.

Lawson, John L., "The 'Remarkable Mystery' of James Rivington, 'Spy,' " *Journalism Quarterly*, XXXV (Summer 1958), 317. Disposes of myth that Rivington was a secret spy for George Washington.

Nettels, Curtis P., "The Money Supply of the American Colonies Before 1720," *University of Wisconsin Studies* (1934). An analysis of the credit difficulties that were a factor in the developing resentment of colonials.

Schlesinger, Arthur M., "The Colonial Newspaper and the Stamp Act," *New England Quarterly*, VIII (March 1935), 63. An outstanding Harvard historian describes the influence of the newspaper medium.

Chapter 6

THE PRESS AND REVOLUTION

> Should the liberty of the press be once destroyed,
> farewell the remainder of our invaluable rights
> and privileges! We may next expect padlocks on
> our lips, fetters on our legs, and only our hands at
> liberty to slave for our worse than EGYPTIAN
> TASKMASTERS, OR—FIGHT OUR WAY TO
> CONSTITUTIONAL FREEDOM
> —Isaiah Thomas

PRINTERS, PUBLISHERS, AND EDITORS were important influences in preparing the public for revolution, and in maintaining the fighting spirit during the War for Independence. Edes and Gill, mentioned in the previous chapter as proprietors of the Radical *Boston Gazette*, were examples of the patriot-journalist. William Bradford III, grandson of the founder of a famous printing dynasty, wielded both the pen and the sword during the war. It was he who first printed Thomas Paine's original *Crisis* essay. His *Pennsylvania Journal* was dedicated to the patriot ideology. But the greatest journalist of the period was Isaiah Thomas, one of the important pioneers of the American Fourth Estate.

Thomas began his career when he was only six, as an apprentice printer. He had to help support his widowed mother and therefore missed the advantages of formal education. Later, he became a great scholar; owner of one of the finest private libraries in the country; first president of the learned Antiquarian Society; and historian of the colonial press.

Thomas once wrote that he owed his education to the type case over which he worked so long as a lad. He learned to spell from setting type. He broadened his knowledge from studying galley proof. Zechariah Fowle, Thomas' master, was an inconsiderate employer, who turned over much of the actual operation of the shop to his apprentice without appropriate recognition of the young man's worth. The resentful Thomas ran away to Halifax. In 1766, at the age of 17, Thomas was aroused by the agitation over the Stamp Act. He was so outspoken in his views that his new master had to discharge him. After a time as an itinerant printer's-helper, Thomas returned to Boston in 1770. Fowle welcomed his runaway apprentice and offered to take him into partnership. Together they founded the *Massachusetts Spy*, a newspaper that lived until 1904.

Thomas soon bought out his shiftless partner. Under his proprietorship the *Spy* became one of the most successful newspapers in the colonies. It was nominally non-partisan, but it followed the Whig philosophy for the most part in its early days. Thomas tried to be fair, however. A line under the name plate advertised that the *Spy* was: "A Weekly Political and Commercial Paper—Open to All Parties, but *influenced* by None." Until hostilities began, this was a successful formula, for at 21, the handsome publisher owned a paper exceeded only by Rivington's in circulation and bulk.

Thomas found it increasingly difficult to remain non-partisan as war loomed. He began to shift his Whig doctrine as it became apparent that conciliationists like Dickinson were ineffective. Eventually he had to make the choice all Whigs had to make—to remain loyal, or to side with the Radicals. Thomas chose the latter course. Soon he was the acknowledged spokesman for the Independence group in his area. When British troops arrived in Boston to enforce laws formerly flouted by the colonials, Thomas became a leader of the underground movement. He was one of the men who flashed the signal light from the steeple of Old North Church warning the Minutemen couriers of the impending British raid on Lexington and Concord.[1]

Next day Thomas was an eyewitness of the first battle in the War for Independence. If he did not hear "the shot heard 'round the world," he at least understood its significance. His report of the encounter remains today as the most notable war reporting of that

---

[1] Rider Paul Revere was an influential member of the patriot group and made engravings for their publications.

conflict. He would have been the first to deny that his "story" of the fight was objective. By that time he was committed to the use of his press as an instrument of war, and his report is therefore highly colored with propaganda favorable to his compatriots. Even so, his word picture of the event was probably accurate in its main theme, and there is so much color and vigor in his writing that the account deserves mention here. According to Thomas' report:

About ten o'clock on the night of the eighteenth of April, the troops in Boston were disclosed to be on the move in a very secret manner, and it was found they were embarking on boats (which they privately brought to the place in the evening) at the bottom of the Common; expresses set off immediately to alarm the country, that they might be on their guard. When the expresses got about a mile beyond Lexington, they were stopped by about fourteen officers on horseback, who came out of Boston in the afternoon of that day, and were seen lurking in by-places in the country till after dark. One of the expresses immediately fled, [this was probably Dr. Samuel Prescott] and was pursued two miles by an officer, who, when he had got up with him presented a pistol, and told him he was a dead man if he did not stop, but he rode on till he came up to a house, when stopping of a sudden his horse threw him off, having the presence of mind to holloo [the rider, of course, not the horse] to the people in the house,

"Turn out. Turn out. I have got one of them."

The officer immediately retreated and fled as fast as he had pursued. The other express, [Paul Revere] after passing through a strict examination, by some means got clear.

The body of troops in the meantime, under the command of Lieutenant Colonel Smith, had crossed the river and landed at Phipp's Farm. They immediately, to the number of 1000, proceeded to Lexington, about six miles below Concord, with great silence. A company of militia, of about eighty men, mustered near the meeting house; the troops came in sight of them just before sunrise. The militia, upon seeing the troops, began to disperse. The troops then set out upon the run, hallooing and hussaing, and coming within a few rods of them, the commanding officer accosted the militia, in words to this effect,

"Disperse, you damn'd rebels—Damn you, disperse."

Upon which the troops again hussaed and immediately one or two officers discharged their pistols, which were instantaneously followed by the firing of four or five of the soldiers; and then there seemed to be a general discharge from the whole body. Eight of our men were killed and nine wounded. . . .[2]

[2] *Massachusetts Spy*, May 3, 1775. This appeared on the inside (page 3) of the paper under a Worcester dateline. After moving to Worcester, Thomas described his paper in a page-one skyline as "THE MASSACHUSETTS SPY, or American ORACLE of Liberty."

WORCESTER, May 3.

AMERICANS! forever bear in mind the BATTLE of LEXINGTON!—where British Troops, unmolested and unprovoked, wantonly, and in a most inhuman manner fired upon and killed a number of our countrymen, then robbed them of their provisions, ransacked, plundered and burnt their houses! nor could the tears of defenceless women, some of whom were in the pains of childbirth, the cries of helpless babes, nor the prayers of old age, confined to beds of sickness, appease their thirst for blood!—or divert them from their DESIGN of MURDER and ROBBERY!

The particulars of this alarming event will, we are credibly informed be soon published by authority, as a Committee of the Provincial Congress have been appointed to make special enquiry, and to take the depositions, on oath, of such as are knowing to the matter. In the mean time, to satisfy the expectation of our readers, we have collected from those whose veracity is unquestioned the following account, viz.

A few days before the battle, the Grenadier and Light-Infantry companies were all drafted from the several regiments in Boston; and put under the command of an officer, and it was observed that most of the transports and other boats were put together, and fitted for immediate service. This manœuvre gave rise to a suspicion that some formidable expedition was intended by the soldiery, but what or where the inhabitants could not determine—however, the town watches in Boston, Charlestown, Cambridge, &c. were ordered to look well to the landing-places. About 10 o'clock on the night of the 18th of April, the troops in Boston were discovered to be on the move in a very secret manner, and it was found they were embarking in boats (which they privately brought to the place in the evening) at the bottom of the Common; expresses set off immediately to alarm the country, that they might be on their guard. When the expresses got about a mile beyond Lexington, they were stopped by about fourteen officers on horseback, who came out of Boston in the afternoon of that day, and were seen lurking in bye-places in the country till after dark. One of the expresses immediately fled, and was pursued two miles by an officer, who when he had got up with him presented a pistol, and told him he was a dead man if he did not stop, but he rode on until he came up to a house, which stopping of a sudden his horse threw him off; having the presence of mind to hollow to the people in the house, "Turn out! Turn out! I have got one of them!" the officer immediately retreated as fast as he had pursued: The other express after passing through a strict examination, by some means got clear. The body of the troops in the mean time, under the command of Lieut. Colonel Smith had crossed the river, and landed at Phipp's Farm: They immediately to the number of 1000 proceeded to Lexington, 6 miles below Concord, with great silence: A company of militia, of about 80 men, mustered near the meeting-house; the troops came in sight of them just before sun-rise; the militia upon seeing the troops began to disperse; the troops then set out upon the run, hallooing and huzzaing, and coming within a few rods of them, the commanding officer accosted the militia in words to this effect, "Disperse you damn'd rebels!—damn you disperse!" Upon which the troops again huzzaed, and immediately one or two officers discharged their pistols, which were instantaneously followed by the firing of four or five of the soldiers, and then there seemed to be a general discharge from the whole body; it is to be noticed they fired upon our people as they were dispersing, agreeable to their command, and that we did not even return the fire: Eight of our men were killed and nine wounded;—The troops then laughed, and damned the Yankees, and said they could not bear the smell of gun-powder. A little after this the troops renewed their march to Concord, where, when they arrived, they divided into parties, and went directly to several places where the province stores were deposited. Each party was supposed to have a tory pilot. One party went into the goal yard, and spiked up and otherways damaged two cannon belonging to the province, and broke and set fire to the carriages—They then entered a store and rolled out about an 100 barrels of flour, which they unheaded, and emp-

they disregarded the cries of the wounded, killing mercy, and mangling their bodies in the most sho

We have the pleasure to say, that notwithstanding provocations given by the enemy, not one instance we have heard of, was committed by our Militia the merciful dictates of the Christian religion, the er sentiments of humanity."

The following is a list of the Provincials who wounded.

KILLED. Messrs. *Robert Munroe, *Jonas Hadley, *Jonathan Harrington, *Caleb Harrington *John Brown, John Raymond, Nathaniel Wy Munroe, of Lexington. Messrs. Jason Russell and Jason Winship, of Menotomy. Deacon ——— Read, of Sudbury. Capt. James Capt. Jonathan Willson, of Bedford. Capt. D Hosmer. and Mr. James Howard of Acton. Mr. Daniel Thompson of Woburn. Mr. J Capt. William Barber's son, aged 14, of Charlotte ne, Esq; of Brookline. Mr. John Hicks of Henry Putnam of Medford. Messrs. Abednego Townsend, William Flint, and Thomas Hadley, Henry Jacobs, Samuel Cook, Ebenezer Goldthwait, Benjamin Daland, jun. Jotham Webb, and Danvers. Mr. Benjamin Pierce, of Salem.

WOUNDED. Messrs. John Robbins, John T Thomas Winship, Nathaniel Farmer, Joseph Comee, Francis Brown, and Prince Easterbrook (a n rington. Mr. ——— Hemmingway, of Framingham Lane, of Bedford. Mr. George Reed, and Mr. Woburn. Mr. William Polly, of Medford. Mr Mr. Timothy Munroe, of Lynn. Mr. Nathan Dennis Wallis, of Danvers. Mr. Nathaniel Cl

MISSING. Mr. Samuel Frost, and Mr. notomy.

Those Distinguished by this [*] Mark were killed by the enemy.

We have seen an account of the loss of the en come from an Officer of one of the men of war, that 63 of the regulars, and 49 marines were both wounded. In all 215. Lieut. Gould of who is wounded, and Lieut. Potter of the Marine soldiers, are prisoners.

Mr. James Howard and one of the Regulars pieces at the same instant, and each killed the oth

The public most sincerely sympathize with the ons of our deceased brethren; who gloriously sacrificed fighting for the liberties of their country. By th conduct, in helping to defeat the forces of an they have endeared their memories to the prese will transmit their names to posterity with the hig

It is now thirteen days since Boston was eati Sunday after the battle there were but two or th blies that met in Boston. In the Forenoon there ing, at which a Committee, consisting of the Select to wait upon General Gage, in order to get perm bitants to remove out of town with their effects. tation, we are told, the General covenanted with if the inhabitants of Boston would give up thei nition, and not assist against the King's on immediately be permitted to depart with all their dize included; finally the inhabitants gave up munition, to the care of the select-men; the C guard over the arms, &c and on Friday last some were permitted to go out with their effects, dize: On Saturday they were stopped for half a d prohibited from carrying out any merchandize wh they were stopped again, owing, it is said, to a di miral Greaves and General Gage; as some fami ferry, with their effects; the Admiral insisted

Courtesy, State Historical Society of Wisconsin

Report of "the shot heard 'round the world," in the *Massachusetts Spy*.

The war was hard on patriot editors and publishers. They had committed themselves to the cause so whole-heartedly that it was impossible to stay in business under British occupation. Both the *Gazette* and the *Spy* printing plants had to be smuggled out of Boston, if these two patriot organs were to continue beating the drums for the American cause. The *Gazette* was moved at night across the Charles river to Watertown, where it was published until the British were forced out of Boston by General Washington in 1776. Thomas had his press sent by trusted employees to Worcester on the eve of the Lexington battle, and he made that city his permanent home thereafter.

Once firmly established in Worcester, Thomas again began to thrive as a journalist and publisher. By the time his fellow patriots emerged from war triumphant, he was the leading publisher of his day. Seven presses and 150 employees kept his shop at Worcester humming. He established his own paper mill and bindery. In eight other cities his former apprentices operated branch publishing houses, with Thomas providing advice and some financial backing. And in the midst of the war Thomas found time to launch one of the earliest magazines.

He was one of the most skillful and prolific printers of his day. Under his imprint appeared more than 400 books on law, medicine, agriculture, and science. He was the first American to publish Blackstone's *Commentaries,* Bunyan's *Pilgrim's Progress,* and Defoe's *Robinson Crusoe* (in book form—it had already appeared serially in several colonial newspapers). He printed the first Greek grammar in America; the first printed music; and the first novel by a native author—William Hill Brown's *Power of Sympathy.* It was Thomas who brought out the first American dictionary, by William Perry, and more than 50,000 copies were sold. This was something of a publishing record until the same author wrote a speller, published by Thomas, whose various editions aggregated 300,000 copies. In addition to these feats of publication enterprise, Thomas produced more than a hundred children's books, including the first American versions of *Mother Goose* and *Little Goody Two-Shoes.*

It is getting ahead of the story, but the accomplishments of Thomas in his later life might just as well be mentioned here. When he retired from business in 1802 to devote his declining years to scholarly research, he was a wealthy man and the owner of a priceless store of books. This material was useful in gathering information for his two-volume *History of Printing in America* (1810), still the outstanding authority on the early days of the industry. He had enough energy left over to serve as postmaster of Worcester for 25 years and to found the Antiquarian Society.

With all these achievements, Thomas is best remembered for his contributions as a patriot journalist. He was an outstanding example of the men who aroused public opinion against the British by means of the press. At first Royalists tried to intimidate Thomas into repudiating the patriot cause. Many of them were important advertisers. When Thomas refused to change his views, these powerful interests applied pressure against the publisher. They saw to it that he was denied ship lists, available at the Custom House, which of course was under the control of the Crown officials. Such news was essential to an editor in a commercial center. Thomas replied that he was willing to give the administration space to tell its side, but he refused to delete patriot material. The alternative, said he, was to go over completely to the patriot cause. That was why the *Spy* eventually became known to the American Tories as a "sedition foundry."

When Joseph Greenleaf, one of the most outspoken patriots, wrote an anti-Royalist article for the *Spy*, Thomas was ordered before the Governor's Council to answer for this impudence. He refused to obey the order, and public opinion was so solidly behind him that officials did not dare arrest him. By 1774 Thomas was advocating union of the colonies in every issue of his paper. It was Thomas who used a cartoon as a kind of trade mark. This was a cut of a snake separated into segments representing the American colonies and facing a dragon, which, of course, was Great Britain. The snake stretched all the way across the front page of the *Spy*, and the caption was "Join or Die." This was not the first graphic appeal for colonial unity, for Benjamin Franklin had used a similar snake cartoon in his *Pennsylvania Gazette* of May 9, 1754, in an attempt to organize the colonies against the French and Indians at an Albany meeting, but the Thomas cartoon is noteworthy because it showed how far the idea of nationalism had progressed on the eve of the war. It is also significant that Thomas was one of the twelve colonials on the proscribed list of rebels to be excluded from amnesty offered by the British as an attempt to close the breach between the two antagonists. Incidentally, four of those twelve had become famous as journalists—Thomas, Edes, Gill, and Adams. The others were frequent contributors to the newspapers.

Thomas did much to *prepare* the public for the conflict. Another effective journalist of the war was a penniless and somewhat disreputable stranger to these shores.[3] He was Tom Paine, the Thetford Quaker, who arrived on the eve of the war. He was then 37 years old and his life up to that point had been anything but inspiring. He is sometimes represented as lacking in education. It is true that his meager schooling stopped when he went to work as a youth of 13, but it could be pointed out that he was once offered a position in an English school, and that his original purpose in coming to America was to establish, of all things, a girl's seminary.

His early career is not impressive. His father was a Norfolk farmer and corset maker, who subscribed to the Quaker faith. His mother, whom the boy disliked, belonged to the Established Church. Apparently there was philosophical friction between parents and son from the beginning. After an unsuccessful attempt to work in the corset-making business, young Tom Paine was appointed an exciseman. He was soon accused of incompetency and neglect of duty. Reinstated, he was discharged again for what we would now call "unionization." He had been chosen by the excisemen of his district to represent them in their agitation for higher pay, and it was partly because of his failure as an agitator that he left his homeland.

By a fortunate coincidence, he met Benjamin Franklin, then at the height of his career as our spokesman in Europe. Franklin, a shrewd judge of men, saw enough in Paine to write a letter of recommendation. Paine was advised to go to America, where Franklin's son-in-law, Richard Bache, would offer helpful advice. Paine arrived in Philadelphia sick in mind and body. He later said that the very air of America was his tonic. With every breath of freedom he grew stronger. He spoke wonderingly of being able to sit in the

---

[3] Paine is usually identified as a writer, or political philosopher. In this book the journalist is defined as one who acts as the transmission belt carrying ideas, information, and inspiration to the general public, dependent upon such resources for rational opinion. This was Paine's prime function during the American Revolution. His work for Aitken on the *Pennsylvania Magazine*, often ignored in sketches about him, also qualifies him for consideration as a journalist, in the broad sense.

same coffeehouses with the "gentry." He was accorded a dignity he had never known before. And now he had found the inspiration that was to change him from an abject failure into a propaganda genius. So imbued with the American spirit was he that within 13 months of his arrival in this country he was writing as though he had been a patriot all his life.

The background of this political philosopher and journalist is significant. Up to then, most of the thinkers of the American movement were relatively well-educated. Sam and John Adams, Josiah Warren, and James Otis were graduated from Harvard. John Dickinson was a product of the Middle Temple, London. Jefferson attended William and Mary College. Most of the other idea-men of the American movement were financially and educationally in an elite group. Men like Thomas had come up the hard way, of course, but they were the interpreters, rather than the philosophers of the cause.

Paine's first contributions were to Robert Aitken's *Pennsylvania Magazine,* one of several such periodical ventures that flowered and withered during this period. Aitken's magazine was one of the better ones. It did not survive, but Paine wrote for it long enough to establish a reputation as a stimulating commentator. Already he was arguing against the institution of Negro slavery, British arrogance, and in favor of universal suffrage and education.

His fame as a writer was achieved by means of a pamphlet copied by many of the colonial newspapers of 1776. This was *Common Sense,* which helped to bring the lukewarm patriots into the revolutionary movement. *Common Sense* appeared in January, 1776, just a little more than a year after the arrival of the uncouth English immigrant. Its popularity was instantaneous and amazing. More than 120,000 copies were sold in the first three months. "I challenge the warmest advocate for reconciliation to show a single advantage that this continent can reap by being connected with Great Britain," he wrote. This challenge was hurled at the Dickinsonian Whigs, who shuddered at the word "independence," and they replied in the local newspapers with condemnation of this upstart. In a matter of weeks, however, Paine's views in *Common Sense* were known to virtually every literate American, and it is significant that only six months later, the Declaration of Independence committed the former colonies to this doctrine. Although *Common Sense* was a "best seller," Paine would accept no remuneration for his writing. His work was strictly for the cause.

After the fighting broke out Paine offered to serve in what amounted to a foreign legion. When the unit was cut to pieces by the British at Amboy, Paine made his way to Washington's headquarters at Fort Lee, where the defeated Americans were licking their wounds preparatory to withdrawal to the Delaware River line. His curious status as a foreigner, which was neither that of an officer, nor of an enlisted man, gave him access to both groups. He talked with all types of Americans as he marched along the wintry roads. Actually, the season was unusually mild, but for the ill-clad troops the nightly bivouac brought only misery. The tattered companies were breaking up fast. In 1776 the ideology of the conflict was still vague. Many of the soldiers had only a hazy notion of what the shooting was all about.

At this crucial moment, Paine wrote his first *Crisis* paper. Whether or not he wrote it at Washington's direction, by candlelight on a drum head, is inconsequential. There is no doubt, however, that it was written from the heart, and under pressure. There was nothing new in what he said, but like a poet, he expressed what others could only feel. His work was rough, but that made it all the more appealing to the common man for whom it was written. The foot-slogging militiamen understood that one of their own was speaking.

And who can overestimate the power of words in arousing the will to fight? Down through history hopeless wars and battles have been won when words have doubled the force of arms. So it was with Paine's *Crisis*. His style had a kind of Biblical resonance and rhythm. Like Winston Churchill's "We shall fight them on the beaches" speech of World War II, the words rallied weary men by that most potent of spiritual tonics—dedication to a cause. They are words that have lived through the generations. Time and again in the bleak days of World War II, when there were no victories to report, the conquered peoples, despairing of freedom, listened with kindling hope as these words, written December 19, 1776, came through the ether to their secret radio receivers:

These are the times that try men's souls. The summer soldier and the sunshine patriot will, in this crisis, shrink from the service of their country; but he that stands it NOW, deserves the love and thanks of man and woman. Tyranny, like hell, is not easily conquered; yet we have this consolation with us, that the harder the conflict the more glorious the triumph. What we obtain too cheap, we esteem too lightly: it is dearness only that gives every thing its value. Heaven knows how to put a proper price upon its goods; and it would be strange indeed if so celestial an article as FREEDOM should not be highly rated.[4]

The first *Crisis* paper exceeded *Common Sense* in popularity. Printed on one side of a sheet and folded in half to make a pamphlet, the clarion call was echoed from patriot newspapers throughout the colonies. Washington had the *Crisis* papers read to his numb troops as the words emerged hot from the press. It is significant that the week after Paine made his first plea to the dejected, they turned on the foe and won a needed victory at Trenton. Morale rose to the point where Washington, given the troops the niggardly Continental Congress refused to supply, might have won the war before the year was out.[5]

Other *Crisis* papers appeared as the need demanded. Most of them were reprinted in the newspapers of the period. More than any other writer of the war, Paine caught the significance of the American Revolution. While others confined the issues to political and economic arguments, Paine advocated social revolt as well. In many ways, he was not an American at all, but an internationalist temporarily caught up in the American movement because it fitted his pattern. "The world is my country, all mankind are my brethren, to do good is my religion . . ." he said later in his *Rights of Man*, and this self-appraisal sums up his creed. His place was wherever the plain people needed a tribune. It is significant, for example, that he went to France after the victory in America. There he used the same weapons to arouse the laggards. For a time he served as a member of the French National Assembly. He not only carried the spirit of the American Revolution to France, but as we shall see in a later chapter, he brought that spirit back home after it nearly died out in the postwar reaction here.

Such a man of course drew attack from all sides. The Tories hunted him in packs. Stalwart Whigs, such as John Dickinson and William Smith, provost of the college that later became the Uni-

---

[4] Daniel Edwin Wheeler, ed.. *Life and Writings of Thomas Paine*, Vol. III (New York: Vincent Parke and Company, 1908), p. 1.

[5] Charles and Mary Beard, *The Rise of American Civilization*, Vol. I (New York: The Macmillan Company, 1930), p. 241.

versity of Pennsylvania, challenged his ideas on property. The latter group insisted that Paine was merely an opportunist. They said he argued as he did because he had nothing to risk for his cause. Usually the revolutionary is pictured by his critics as a madman or as a visionary, with his head in the clouds and his hands in the pockets of his betters. Paine was no exception to this stereotype. His enemies eventually conquered him, not by frontal assault, but by infiltration.

At any rate, he cannot be ignored. He was a great propagandist. He told people what they wanted to hear in terms so expressive that even the lukewarm became fiery patriots. Paine thought of government as a kind of public utility; to be operated at the least expense for the interests of the general population, not just for the current elite. In arguing his thesis, he cut through to the heart of the issue. In *Common Sense,* for example, he succeeded in making many of his readers face the alternatives. He tossed out all the philosophical quibbling. Instead, he asked one question—was independence to our advantage or not? He answered with a resounding "Yes!" England's wavering foreign policy and domestic corruption did not entitle the mother country to further consideration, he insisted. The British had never thought of the colonies as any more than areas of exploitation, he argued. He charged that the government in London had hampered development whenever Americans had threatened to become rivals. There was no hope of generosity or compromise with such rulers, he declared.

Having suffered in England for attempting to right some of the wrongs of the plain man, Paine had nothing but contempt for the Tory theory that the British system included the "total wisdom of the realm." He remembered the treatment he had received for his labor agitation in England. That had been an attempt to meet needs which Parliament failed to provide as representative of the common man. What did the so-called House of Commons do for the disfranchised worker, Paine asked? As he saw it, the British system was merely a device for dividing up the spoils squeezed out of the lowly. He attacked the aristocracy especially as a force opposing any encouragement for an increase in the dignity of the citizenry.

In the end, he was disgraced not by the formidable foes he had attacked on both sides of the Atlantic, but by a group whose influence he had sadly underestimated. Following the publication of his

Age of Reason, Paine was attacked by clergymen of most denominations as an atheist. Actually, the book was an attempt to explain God in rational, rather than in supernatural, terms. The author was technically a Deist, a far cry from an atheist. What he did attack was religious organization, including churches of every faith, sect, and denomination. The Protestant clergy, particularly, turned upon him. By the turn of the century, Paine had been driven to cover by forces he had heretofore ignored. But his great work had by then been accomplished. He died almost forgotten in 1809 in a land he had helped to free.

The skill and energy of Revolutionary journalists, propagandists, and popular political writers amaze historians. Editors used every known trick to win public support for the revolutionary movement. The first shot of the war was still echoing around the world when the battle of words began. Each side tried to race its version of Lexington and Concord back to the people of Great Britain, where the colonial stand was respected by a sizable public. General Gage's report placed all the blame for the shooting upon the treasonous minutemen. He sent this report to London by the fastest sloop at his command. Four days later the patriots had prepared their statement, which reversed the blame for the bloodshed. Captain John Darby of Salem, Massachusetts, agreed to carry the message to the mother country. Of course the British sloop had no chance of outrunning a Salem skipper who knew how to crowd sail. Captain Darby arrived 11 days ahead of his rival. His report, handed to Benjamin Franklin, the American agent in Europe, was disseminated in papers throughout the land, thanks to Franklin's skill as a publicist. General Gage's belated account was an anticlimax. The contemptible rebels had scored one of the most impressive scoops of the period.[6] On the whole, the "ragged Continentals" were alert to the importance of news and propaganda. They used communications effectively.

Only 20 of the 35 newspapers being published at the beginning of the war survived. Considering the vicissitudes of the times, that was not a bad record. Many would have disappeared had there been no war. And 35 new papers were established during the six years of fighting. Enough of these survived to bring the total num-

---

[6] An inspiring account of such activities is given in Lynn Montross, *Rag, Tag and Bobtail* (New York: Harper & Brothers, 1952).

ber of papers at the end of the war up to the pre-war figure. All were weeklies, and most of them were patriot in sentiment. Where the British held strategic bases, Tory papers continued to be printed, but by the end of the war they had succumbed to public pressure.

Revolutionary newspapers went into about 40,000 homes, but each issue had a larger number of readers per copy than would be true in modern times. Every word was read, even to the small "liners" and advertisements. Many an American first learned of the Declaration of Independence through his newspaper. It first appeared publicly in the *Pennsylvania Evening Post* of July 6, 1776, but others soon published the document.

Such enterprise is impressive. On the other hand, any student of the times becomes aware very soon of the primitive communications facilities of the period. It took six weeks for the account of Lexington and Concord to reach Savannah. Often the reporting of war events was of the most haphazard type. "The Hartford Post tells us," Hugh Gaine, the turncoat patriot editor wrote in the February 2, 1778, issue of his *New York Gazette and Mercury,* "That he saw a Gentleman in Springfield, who informed him that he (the Gentleman) saw a letter from an Officer in Gen. Howe's Army to another in Gen. Burgoyne's, giving him to understand, war was declared on the sides of France and Spain against the MIGHTY Kingdom of Britain." The news had actually come from a Boston paper already a month old, and the story was not true, in any case.[7] Some of the news was high in reporting quality, however. Often it was printed verbatim, which added to its charm and authenticity. That was how the details of the battle of Yorktown reached the office of the *Freeman's Journal* in Philadelphia:

BE IT REMEMBERED

That on the 17th day of October, 1781, Lieut. Gen. Charles Earl Cornwallis, with about 5,000 British troops, surrendered themselves prisoners of war to His Excellency, Gen. George Washington, Commander-in-Chief of the allied forces of France and America. LAUS DEO.[8]

[7] Frank Luther Mott, *American Journalism,* rev. ed. (New York: The Macmillan Company, 1950), p. 100.

[8] From *America Goes to Press*, by Laurence Greene, copyright 1936, used by special permission of the publishers, The Bobbs-Merrill Company, Inc.

That was all the paper had to tell of the greatest, and final, victory of the war. The account should have been authentic, because the reporter was none other than General Washington. The editor had printed verbatim the dispatch sent out by the general.

Some of the most popular items in the war newspapers were columns of names the Sons and Daughters of the American Revolution might find it embarrassing to read today. These items were lists of deserters and "bounty jumpers"—men who had enlisted just long enough to collect their volunteer bonuses before disappearing from the ranks. The papers were full of such information. Sometimes notices were printed in the press asking authorities to pick up entire squads and companies of men who had deserted. The temptation for men to leave the battlefields was great. Soldiers often could not collect their pay. When they did get it, it might be in the form of scrip, which declined rapidly in value. Many of the troops were under-fed, under-clothed, and under-armed. No wonder the war was too much for some of the "sunshine patriots," as Paine called them. Much more impressive was the fact that despite such discouragement, Washington's army held together and never shirked a fight. Out of 60 major battles, the Americans won 33, against the best troops in the world.

Much of the news received by war editors came from travelers, or from occasional "exchanges" with other journalists. An attempt had been made just before the war to provide patriot editors with a news service. It was a news column sent out from Boston in 1768 headed "Journal of Occurrences," or sometimes, "Journal of the Times." As a propaganda device it was useful, but the feature had to be dropped a year later. The nearest approach to a modern press service was the irregular military "handout." These releases did not always reach the editors who were most in need of such news. Post roads often were blockaded by the enemy. In other areas the postal service had deteriorated. European news, once supplied by importation of London papers, was virtually dried up because of the conflict. As a result, editors had to depend more than ever upon their own resources. Out of necessity they began to concentrate upon the report of local happenings. To their amazement, they found they had been neglecting a rich mine of news in their own back yards.

A serious problem was the shortage of printing supplies. Paper, ink, and type had come from Europe before the war, for the most part. Not until 1769 was an American press sold commercially. American paper mills could not begin to supply the demand for stock. Paper at that time was made of linen, and cloth of any kind was scarce, especially in wartime. That was why Washington did not put it beneath his dignity to issue a plea, asking patriot women to save all available material that might be converted into printing paper. That shows how important the Commander-in-Chief considered the press to be. In this connection, it is interesting to note that he contributed his prestige to encourage the founding of the *New Jersey Gazette*, which, for a time, served as a kind of army newspaper.

The fact is, the newspaper had won great respect during this testing period. "I saw it in the newspaper" began to be taken seriously in answer to the question, "How do you know that?" Some of the papers began to prosper, as the war dragged to an end. Indeed, many other industries thrived while the Continentals slogged from battle to battle. Factories forbidden under British rule appeared during the war and found profitable markets for goods. There was much greater demand than supply, as is usually the case in wartime, and for the new business man, this was a golden opportunity. British money flowed everywhere. Enemy troops had to procure the bulk of their supplies in America, and they paid for it in their own exchange. Competition for this money stimulated trade on all sides, as indicated by the heavy advertising in many wartime newspapers. Advertising rates went up accordingly. Presbrey, the well known authority on this phase of journalism, says that ten shillings for a first insertion was a standard rate by the end of the war. That was a little more than twice the average price in 1770.

An example of journalistic prosperity in wartime was the *Connecticut Courant*. By 1781 it had the then amazing circulation of 8,000 subscribers each issue. It was full of advertising. Few London papers could boast of such success. The *Courant* printed on paper from its own mill. It was one of the best-printed papers in America.

Visitors to this country, including the many who came to help us win our war, were impressed by the popularity of the American press. Although editors did not hesitate to print rumor, opinion, and even deliberate lies, most of the journalists were closely identified with their readers. Their very partisanship provided a comradeship with their publics that modern objectivity tends to discourage. If the news was not accurate, at least readers understood the editor's attitude. Each paper was spokesman for a particular public. That public willingly excused journalistic abuses on the ground that the editor, in prosecuting his case, had to use exaggeration to strengthen and to emphasize his arguments, as did lawyers in court. At least the reader of a particular paper, be it Tory or Patriot, believed that the editor was on his side. In this period, the press, the public, and the government were all working together for a common cause, once the Tories were driven to cover.

ANNOTATED BIBLIOGRAPHY

Books:

Aldridge, Alfred O., *Man of Reason: The Life of Thomas Paine.* Philadelphia: J. B. Lippincott Company, 1959. The best study of Paine since Moncure D. Conway's two-volume *Life of Thomas Paine* (London: G. P. Putnam's Sons, 1892). See also Mary A. Best, *Thomas Paine* (New York: Harcourt, Brace and Company, 1927).

Channing, Edward, *History of the United States,* Vol. III. New York: The Macmillan Company, 1927. The high literary quality and thoughtful comments make this volume of Channing particularly useful as background reading of the period.

Commager, Henry Steele, ed., *Documents of American History.* New York: F. S. Crofts & Company, 1934. Contains writings of Dickinson, the Adamses, Madison, Jefferson, etc. Very useful in checking the original sources of information. The comment preceding each document is helpful in explaining the circumstances involved.

Curti, Merle, and Willard Thorp, *American Issues,* Vol. I, "The Social Record." Philadelphia: J. B. Lippincott Company, 1941. Excellent appraisals of Dickinson, Paine, and leaders of Federalist party.

East, Robert, *Business Enterprise in the American Revolutionary Era.* New York: Columbia University Press, 1938. A scholarly review of the capitalistic development during this period.

Fast, Howard M., *Citizen Tom Paine.* New York: Duell, Sloan and Pearce, 1943. Not strictly a biography, but a more romantic interpretation of Paine.

————, ed., *Selected Works of Tom Paine.* New York: Modern Library, 1946. A handy and inexpensive reference.

Greene, Laurence, *America Goes to Press.* Indianapolis; Bobbs-Merrill Company, 1936. Goes to source materials to describe how the news of important events reached the people through the press.

Jameson, J. Franklin, *The American Revolution Considered as a Social Movement*. Princeton: Princeton University Press, 1926. Lectures on the status of the people, commerce, and industry as a result of the War for Independence.

Marble, Annie R., *From 'Prentice to Patron—The Life Story of Isaiah Thomas*. New York: D. Appleton-Century Company, 1935.

Montross, Lynn, *Rag, Tag and Bobtail*. New York: Harper & Brothers, 1952. Demonstrates that the people's army and government operated remarkably effectively, despite many mistakes. Public opinion and its manipulators are seen to have been highly important.

Parrington, Vernon L., *Main Currents in American Thought*, Vol. I. Highly recommended as background for the period.

Snyder, Louis L. and Richard B. Morris, eds., *A Treasury of Great Reporting*, New York: Simon and Schuster, 1949. This book contains excerpts from outstanding journalistic writings between colonial times and post-World War II.

Trevelyan, Sir George Otto, *The American Revolution*, Part III. New York: Longmans, Green & Company, 1907. The epoch viewed from the standpoint of a great British historian.

Van Tyne, Claude H., *The War of Independence; American Phase*. Boston: Houghton Mifflin Company, 1929. Volume two of a study by one of the leading authorities on the period.

Periodicals and Monographs:

Batchelder, Frank R., "Isaiah Thomas, the Patriot Printer," *New England Magazine*, N.S., XXV (November 1901), 284. An excellent short sketch of the great publisher.

Benjamin, S. G. W., "Notable Editors Between 1776 and 1800—Influence of the Early American Press," *Magazine of American History*, XVII (February 1887), 97. Colorful description of early personal journalism, including Royalist publications.

Boston Chronicle, 1768-69. Included here for special mention to show how even the Tory press spread ideas of Revolution. Mein & Fleeming published the "Letters of Junius," commented frequently on the free press discussions raging in Parliament, and published Dickinson's "Letters" serially.

Boston Weekly News-Letter, 1775-6. Specifically cited as the only paper in Boston during the British siege.

Massachusetts Spy, 1772-1776. Mentioned specifically because it was the leading spokesman for the Patriot cause and includes the philosophy of the Revolutionaries. Published by the highly articulate Isaiah Thomas.

Mott, Frank Luther, "The Newspaper Coverage of Lexington and Concord," *New England Quarterly*, XVII (December 1944), 489. A day-by-day analysis of how the news was spread. Reprinted in Ford and Emery, *Highlights in the History of the American Press.*

Pennsylvania Journal; and the Weekly Advertiser, 1776. Cited as a fighting publication of the middle colonies.

Siebert, Fred S., "The Confiscated Revolutionary Press," *Journalism Quarterly,* XIII (June 1936), 179. Describes how British used captured equipment to produce counterrevolutionary propaganda.

Thomas, Charles M., "The Publication of Newspapers During the American Revolution," *Journalism Quarterly,* IX (December 1932), 358. Describes the three political classifications of editors and appraises their wartime contributions.

"Tom Paine's First Appearance in America," *Atlantic Monthly,* IV (November 1859), 565. Describes Paine's propaganda activities and journalistic contributions. Reprinted in Ford and Emery, *Highlights in the History of the American Press.*

Chapter 7

THE PRESS AND THE SECOND REVOLUTION

> Men who distrust the people and the future may
> overwhelm us with their learning, but they do not
> impress us with their wisdom—thank God.
> —Gerald Johnson

DURING THE WAR the Tory had disappeared as a political
factor in America, but two other groups now struggled for control
of the Government. One of the elements was conservative in tone.
It consisted, for the most part, of citizens engaged in commerce,
banking, manufacturing, and property management. Generally, this
group was more interested in preserving and extending its economic advantages than in risking social experiments. The other
element was largely made up of the agrarian, small-farmer class;
increasingly strengthened by the city wage-earner, or "mechanic,"
as he was called then; but with a significant leavening of intellectuals and political philosophers interested in social reform.

The upheaval after 1775 was *their* war of independence. It was
the opportunity they had awaited to modify a situation they believed to have been unfair to them. At first the partisans of this
internal revolution lacked effective leadership, as compared with
their rivals. Most, although certainly not all, of the war heroes belonged to the more conservative element. So did a large number of
influential religious leaders, educational administrators, and the more
articulate writers.

125

On the other hand, an administration supported by the agrarian-labor group was in control as the war with Britain ended and the internal struggle came into sharper focus. Still fearful of the tyranny from which they had so lately freed the country, these "Radicals," as their conservative rivals called them, were determined to prevent the new central government from assuming strong powers. Under the Articles of Confederation proposed by this group in 1777 and made the charter of the central government by ratification in 1781, federal control was limited by spreading sovereignty among the several states. Here was the opportunity for the Radicals to prove the merits of popular rule and decentralized political controls. Instead, the leaders of this group failed at the very moment they should have been reaping the rewards of a successful revolution.

They might have made the confederation type of government work successfully, if given a fair chance. With some tinkering here and there, the Articles might have served as the plan of a more stable government. After all, Americans had waged a successful war under this charter, and the excellent legislation enacted as the Northwest Ordinances was a product of the Confederation. The main trouble with the system was the inability of the administrators to raise money from reluctant state governments, but reform in this area should have been no more of a problem than the complete replacement of the document that was finally carried out.[1]

The fact is, the conservatives saw to it that the bad qualities of the system devised by the rival party were widely advertised. For the confederation principle did not suit them at all. They were well-equipped to spread this story, because they had access to many of the newspapers of the period, and they had plenty of ammunition to use against their rivals. The Government under the Confederation had made many blunders during and after the war. Many of these mistakes were inevitable; most emergencies reveal ineptitude and corruption in bureaucracy, and a postwar period of adjustment is bound to be difficult, no matter which party is in power. British gold, exchanged for war supplies, no longer bolstered the economy.

[1] See, for example, Merrill Jensen, *The New Nation* (New York: Alfred A. Knopf, Inc., 1950). Curiously, the group that advocated a looser control in the form of a federation soon became known as the "Anti-Federalists," when the rival party took the name "Federalist." "Nationalist," rather than "Federalist," would have been a much more appropriate title.

Old markets once guaranteed by the mother country were now closed to American commerce. But the dreary postwar picture painted by the chroniclers of the time does not appear to be an accurate portrait.

There is no doubt that there was dissatisfaction with the situation, and the conservatives took advantage of the general attitude. In their effort to regain control of the government, the conservatives enjoyed brilliant leadership and very effective organization. The opposition was threatened with complete defeat until it, too, developed solidarity. Out of this controversy emerged the two-party system that was to have its profound effect upon American history. The press was essential to each group in this struggle for domination.

It is difficult to give meaningful names to these parties at this time. "Popular," or even "Populist" might serve to designate the group made up of the Radicals, but it is more of a problem to identify their rivals by name. They have sometimes been called the "property men" in these pages because, as a rule, that is what they were. It is an unfair label, however, because of its connotation. Indeed, almost any term used to describe this group appears to be a printed sneer. For generations leading historians have pictured the business man and his philosophy of government unattractively. Literary men have compounded this scorn for the type of person who was so influential in the development of the nation. Parkman, the Adamses, Beard, Parrington, and many other political and social historians interpreted the past in terms favorable to the more liberal philosophy of the rival group. Emerson, Hawthorne, Whitman, and Longfellow did the same in literature and poetry. When writers do take up the cause of the business man in history, they may very well arouse disapproval from their colleagues.[2]

There is no doubt that the United States owed much to the business man. If he was ruthless in reaching his goals, so was the common man, who is so much more attractive in historical perspective. The American Indian could vouch for that statement. The business man helped to make the country wealthy, powerful, and secure by his very aggressiveness and self-interest. The material progress of America was based upon the abundance of resources

[2] See, for example, Edward N. Saveth, "What Historians Teach About Business," *Fortune*, XLV (April 1952), p. 118.

and the proportion of people to the land, but the business man speeded up the development. That material well-being has had much to do with our social and political philosophies. Hopeless misery is not conducive to social progress, as even a casual look at the world's poverty areas will show. The fact is, America has found the business man essential to our peculiar development. He has sometimes acted as a brake to the exuberance of social planners, and he has provided the capital needed to tame the wilderness.

Unfortunately, history shows that if the property men are unchecked, they may destroy themselves. The check has come from the equalitarians—those who put the rights of people above the rights of property. In this group are the liberals, who are willing to risk experiment for the sake of more rapid social progress. "But the object of liberalism has never been to destroy capitalism, as conservatism invariably claims, but to keep the capitalists from destroying it," as the younger Schlesinger puts it.[3]

At the end of the American Revolution, the people of the United States had a choice to make. They might continue to experiment with social change, endorsing the ideals which had been their battle cries. Or they might consolidate strength by making right of property the fundamental consideration. Or they might work out some arrangement completely satisfactory to neither, but warranting mutual support. The record of the Confederation gave the conservatives hope that public opinion might be swung to their side. The opportunity was the proposal to draft a new national charter.

State legislatures sent the delegates to the Constitutional Convention at Philadelphia. The state assemblies were dominated by the property group. This was because the big commercial centers were strongholds of the conservatives, where land and voting qualifications disfranchised many "mechanics," or laborers. It was therefore the men of means and community standing who brought about the fundamental change in government under the Constitution. They succeeded in placing financial power in the hands of a strong, central government, and otherwise protected the position of property against attacks within individual states. But they could not have their way entirely. They could not have obtained acceptance of the new charter by the people, unless the authors had made

[3] Arthur M. Schlesinger, Jr., *The Age of Jackson* (New York: Little, Brown and Company, 1945), p. 522.

concessions. The document they produced is a marvel of balanced forces.

Many of the conservatives were brilliant, articulate, and famous men, whose every comment carried prestige, and for a time the opposition lacked such leadership. As a result, the Constitution of 1787 has been considered by many students as a victory for the counterrevolutionaries. Yet with all their prestige, they had a hard time winning the necessary popular support. Opposition was disorganized at first, but it was strong. Only by compromising on their original demands could the authors hope to "sell" the Constitution to the people. This constant pressure had important results. It is perhaps fortunate for the charter that has served us so well that the issue did not come up five years later. It might then have been submerged by the rising tide of sentiment for a greater share of control by the common man.[4]

One of the concessions offered by the conservatives was the Bill of Rights. Offered as the first ten amendments, these articles have since been considered part of the Constitution, in the sense that they were the price paid by the authors for the public consent that made the document practicable. The first article of the Bill of Rights is of special interest to journalists. It provides that: "Congress shall make no law . . . abridging the freedom of speech or of the press . . ." This is the cornerstone of our press liberty, but there is evidence that the authors of the Constitution spent little time discussing this issue. Madison's careful minutes of the convention show only casual and infrequent mention of the press.

But there was long precedent for the protection that finally was provided the press. British Common Law, as used in the various states, provided great freedom of expression for the times, even though it still recognized seditious libel laws. The same basic principles were stated in the Declaration of Rights written by John Dickinson when the First Continental Congress convened in 1774. Nine of the 13 states had already provided such constitutional protection by 1787. The Virginia Bill of Rights, of 1776, stated: "That freedom of the press is one of the great bulwarks of liberty, and can never be restrained but by despotick governments. . . ."

---

[4] For its day, the Constitution was little short of radical, nevertheless, since it provided a republican form of government at a time when monarchies were the prevailing mode of political administration.

Article XVI of the Massachusetts Bill of Rights, of 1780, expressed similar sentiments, and other states used variations of this theme to establish the principle.[5]

This probably explains why the authors of the new national charter ignored the press issue. They assumed that full protection was already granted under the states. Charles Pinckney of South Carolina did present a draft of a constitution with a clause similar to the one eventually adopted, but apparently little attention was paid to his suggestion at that time.

It soon was clear, however, that the Constitution could not possibly succeed without concessions to public sentiment. Delegates from Massachusetts reported it would be impossible to win ratification of the Constitution in that state without a clause concerning freedom of expression. Virginia could not muster enough votes for ratification until Governor Edmund Randolph called upon the framers to add the Bill of Rights. A constitutional committee was appointed to draft such a bill. The resolution was a modification of the Virginia document. Delegates were then told to return to their respective states, and to use all influence available in mustering support for ratification of the main document on the promise that the Rights clauses would be included in the charter. It was on this understanding that New York finally approved the Constitution, but even so, it was not an easy victory for the Federalists.

Because of promises given, the Bill of Rights was an important issue in the first session of Congress. Madison headed the committee charged with drafting the amendments. When his first draft was read out of committee, it stated: ". . . no state shall violate the equal rights of conscience or of freedom of speech. . . ." The select committee to which the report was referred added ". . . or of the press." Modified by House and Senate, the clause became the first amendment, as ratified in 1791.

It would appear that freedom of the press was a matter of serious concern to the authors of our charter, therefore. Some of the hesitancy in including the press protection clause in the federal charter may have been based on the fact that the revised Constitution actually afforded less freedom than many of the states provided in their charters, and it was believed by some that protection might

---

[5] Henry Steele Commager, ed., *Documents of American History* (New York: F. S. Crofts & Company, 1934), p. 104, Article XII; and p. 109, Article XVI.

thereby actually be weakened by the national document. It is more logical to argue that the press clause was forced upon the framers by expedience. At any rate, the same group was responsible for the ill-famed Alien and Sedition Acts, to be discussed in the next chapter, which would indicate little deep feeling about the press issue.

It should be noted that freedom of the press is part of our fundamental law, regardless of how it came to be included. In Great Britain, Parliament provides the protection granted by our Constitution, and presumably, Parliament could also take away that right. In the United States, such freedom could not be restricted legally without submitting the question to Constitutional amendment. Neither the President nor Congress could abridge freedom of the press without running into resistance from the courts. In Great Britain, the courts have no such check. Furthermore, the specific mention of press freedom in our Constitution *in addition* to our recognition of the common law on the subject, which the British have depended upon as a safeguard, showed that liberty of the press was more advanced on this side of the Atlantic in 1791 than it was in the freest state in Europe.

Curiously, the press, which had to be protected as a concession to the public sentiment, was the most effective weapon of the conservatives in winning support for the charter they grudgingly admitted was the best document they could obtain in favor of their interests. The best exposition of the conservative doctrine was a series of articles which first appeared in the semiweekly *New York Independent Journal* from October, 1787 to April, 1788. Reprinted throughout the country, and later published in pamphlet and (with six new essays) book form, these articles are known collectively as *The Federalist.*

They were written for mass consumption, and they were so effective that they gave their name to the party that was actually nationalist in doctrine, rather than federalist. The Federalists, as they came to be known during the publication of the 85 offerings, won their fight with this journalistic effort. Written hastily, much as daily editorials were written later on, these essays are still read, not only as revealing political studies, but as good literature. Alexander Hamilton wrote the largest number of *Federalist* articles over the pen name, "Publius." James Madison is believed to have written 29, some of which are the best in the series. John Jay, a noted New York state political leader, probably wrote a half-dozen. In clear, concise style, *The Federalist* explained the philosophy of the Constitutional party. The gist of this doctrine is described in the tenth, supposedly written by Madison. Madison stood somewhere between the two opposing leaders. He disapproved of Hamilton's financial and autocratic ideas, but he veered from his mentor, Jefferson, in sponsoring a stronger national government. Madison had attended all the meetings of the constitutional committee and had engineered many of the modifications in the document. Said he, in describing the form of government prescribed by the framers of the national charter: ". . . justice must prevail [even] over a majority," to prevent the whims of an unstable public from wrecking the ship of state. This control would be accomplished through a republican form of government, offering protection to the masses, without direct control by them, as under the true "democratic" system.

The Federalist firmly established Alexander Hamilton as leader of the party that took the title of the series as its label. He saw himself as the St. George of the anarchist dragon, for the radicalism and disorganization of the liberals could lead only to this, he reasoned. "We should be rescued from democracy," Hamilton insisted, and he looked forward to a restoration of an aristocracy, according to at least one of his biographers.[6] It has been suggested that Hamilton's respect for the aristocracy, and his continual seeking of recognition by those who valued heredity most highly, may have depended upon the uncertainty of his paternity. Why was he a patriot in the Revolution, instead of a Tory, then? Born and reared to young manhood in the British West Indies, Hamilton became an American not so much out of hatred of the British social and political structure, as out of contempt for British corruption and mismanagement.

That is why he fought for home rule, and there can be no doubt that he had strong feelings on the subject before the cause of revolution was generally endorsed. His war record was excellent. General Washington, who recognized Hamilton's virtues and who understood the youngster's faults (he was 18 at the time of Lexington and Concord) had a hard time keeping the fiery patriot out

[6] Claude G. Bowers, *Jefferson and Hamilton* (Boston: Houghton Mifflin Company, 1925), p. 31.

of battle and behind the ledgers, where he was much more useful. In spite of this restraint, Hamilton did succeed in getting into battle. He made two heroic, foolish, and soul-satisfying charges, and forever afterwards fancied himself as a military man who had reached the high point in his life on the battlefield. Actually, his value was not as a warrior, but as Washington's close adviser and subsequent "prime minister."

This was the man who led the Federalists. One cannot speak of him without indicating bias, one way or the other. In his day he was one of the most respected and reviled men in government. He had little knowledge of social forces. Never having lived the life of toil, he tended to dismiss the problems of the working people. He was quick to see that a government of fine phrases and glittering shibboleths was certain to be ineffective. He believed that the way to make government work was to let those with special interests in it control it, since they had most to lose by inept rule. Let those qualified take command, insisted Hamilton, who always imagined himself as the ideal soldier, ruling by command, rather than by consultation.

Hamilton believed it his duty to establish the credit of the country by drastic financial measures, regardless of the luckless victims of an inadequate monetary system. He had no compassion for popular leaders such as Daniel Shays, the Massachusetts war veteran who led a hopeless revolt in 1786 against a taxation and hard money policy that threatened the very livelihood, to say nothing of the freedoms, of the small farmer. Hamilton saw the danger in such uprisings of the common man, and that was one reason he wished to rush through the Constitution, which he correctly predicted would solve many problems. But he would have taken care of the Shayses by force, rather than by placating the aggrieved. He admired military efficiency. Yet his life was to prove his genius not as a soldier, but as a writer and political thinker. As Bowers says:

He was a natural journalist and pamphleteer—one of the fathers of the American editorial. His perspicacity, penetration, powers of condensation, and clarity of expression were those of a premier editorial writer. These same qualities made him a pamphleteer without peer. That he would have shown with equal luster in the reportorial room of a modern paper is shown in his description of the hurricane and in his letter to Laurens picturing vividly the closing hours of Major Andre. From the moment he created a sensation with "A Farmer Refuted" in his eighteenth year, until in the closing months of his life he was meeting Coleman surreptitiously in the night to dictate vigorous editorials for the New York *Evening Post* he had established, he recognized his power. No man ever complained more bitterly of the attacks of the press; none ever used the press more liberally and relentlessly to attack . . . Nowhere in the literature of invective is there anything more vitriolic than the attack on a war speculator and profiteer, under the signature of "Publius." . . . But usually he appealed to reason, and then he was at his best. . . . It will be impossible to comprehend the genius of Hamilton, his domination of his party, and his power, despite his unpopularity with the masses, without a foreknowledge of his force with the pen. It was his scepter and his sword.[7]

That was how the biographer, Bowers, answers those who underestimate Hamilton's journalistic role. This was the man who led the forces working for the ratification of the Constitution. Curiously, Hamilton did not like the document. It was a "shilly-shally thing of milk and water which could not last and was good only as a step to something better," he once said.[8] Although the Constitution was supposedly the product of the conservatives, it was all too liberal for an admirer of aristocracy, such as Hamilton. He sponsored it, however, by facing what he believed to be the facts. The document offered a means of drawing together the type of person Hamilton believed should control government. And although he disapproved of its populist concessions, he was shrewd enough to see that such compromise was essential, if any protection of property were to be imposed. When, on a summer day, he drifted slowly down the Hudson River on the New York packet and thereupon decided to subordinate his personal preferences in writing the first of *The Federalist* papers, he reached the height of his greatness. Had he accomplished nothing else in his lifetime, his services as a journalist that day would have justified his niche in the memory of his countrymen.

Hamilton led his forces so brilliantly that he won all his early battles against the vastly larger army of "unimportant men" opposing his policies. Under his generalship, the Federalists succeeded with the ratification of the Constitution. As first Secretary of the Treasury, he began grouping his cohorts even before the first Con-

[7] Bowers, *Jefferson and Hamilton*, p. 26. Bowers, it should be pointed out, is a respecter, but no admirer, of Hamilton.

[8] Wilfred E. Binkley, *American Political Parties: Their Natural History* (New York: Alfred A. Knopf, Inc., 1943), p. 32.

gress convened. Two months before the head of the Treasury was scheduled to make his report to Congress, the recommendations of Hamilton's "Report on the Public Credit" leaked out in some way. Public securities went up 52 per cent after the word got out that the Government would "fund" the public debt.

Hamilton's plan was to consolidate war debts and then to pay them off at face value. Few honest men could object to this program. It would help to establish national credit among nations. The domestic debt was something else. The face value of securities was about 42 million dollars. They had depreciated to about 20 cents on the dollar. Hamilton now proposed to pay at face value. His recommendations, discovered by speculators long before the Treasury report was made public, allowed the unscrupulous to reap a golden harvest. By fast ship and by speedy horse the speculators raced to the hinterlands, where news of Hamilton's plans had not yet penetrated. Thousands of original creditors sold their securities at the depreciated price. Many of the swindled were war veterans who had earned these securities in exchange for hazardous service. When they discovered they had been cheated by speculators and that these vultures were now to be paid in full by taxes collected from their victims, the resentment against Hamilton produced a violent reaction. The hatred was fanned when the same exploitation was repeated in Hamilton's program for the assumption of state debts.

Hamilton had no patience with dishonest speculators, but he was aware that his hated measures placed "Property on the side of the Government," by giving business leaders a financial interest in their rulers. Hamilton saw that the best way to build up credit was to have the financial and business interests firmly committed to it, through government. He admitted that funding and assumption of state debts had provided quick profits to the money group at the expense of the plain man. But the securities bought by the speculator at depreciated value were to be redeemed in full over a period of many years, and all this time the owners of the securities would *have* to support a government committed to their interests. And because the bankers, financiers, and businessmen thereby gravitated to the Federalist cause, many a newspaper editor and publisher, dependent for revenue upon such persons, also espoused Hamilton's group. It looked as though the "unimportant people" were hopelessly outclassed, outflanked, and overwhelmed.

The outstanding Federalist newspaper in the lush days of the party was the *Gazette of the United States*. Sponsored and supported by Hamilton, it was edited by John Fenno, who issued the first edition at the national capital, then in New York, April 15, 1789. Fenno had been a school teacher, and it is noteworthy that we are already beginning to see the development of the specialized journalist. Most of the previous editors and publishers had come up through the print shop. Fenno established his reputation as a journalist without benefit of mechanical apprenticeship. Soon his paper was the acknowledged mouthpiece of the Federalist party.

Another powerful Federalist voice was that of Noah Webster, remembered for his dictionary, but a man of many parts. Lawyer, pioneer weather man, translator, historian, economist, and scientific farmer, Webster was recognized in his day as a great editor. He started out as a lawyer and teacher. He was fascinated by words. His avocation resulted in a three-part *Grammatical Institute of the English Language*. The first part, the speller, appeared in 1784, and enjoyed a phenomenal sale—eventually 60 million copies were sold (not all within the author's lifetime, of course). The reader, which appeared a year later, did not sell as well, but was nonetheless popular. The third part, the grammar, was a relative failure. While his speller was setting sales records, Webster worked for a reform in copyright laws to protect authors like himself. He had to lobby before various State legislatures to win support for his cause, and this forced him to take an interest in politics. In 1785 he wrote a pamphlet, *Sketches of American Policy*, that brought him to the attention of leaders of the group that later became the Federalist party. He was encouraged to express his views as an editor. The *American Magazine*, which he edited in 1787 failed within a year, but after an interim period as a lawyer in Hartford, Webster came back to New York in 1793 to edit the daily *Minerva* and the semi-weekly *Herald* (after 1797 the *Commercial Advertiser* and *Spectator*, respectively).

Webster was an articulate and intelligent interpreter of the Federalist program. He defended President Washington against the smear tactics of such editors as Freneau and Bache, and stood firm for the party against opposition attacks. Webster was no mere party hack, however. He resented what he called the "betrayal" of President Adams by Hamilton, the circumstances of which will be described later. At any rate, the *Minerva* was an important organ in the Federalist attempt to regain control. Eventually Webster tired of politics, however, and returned to his old love—linguistics. He is remembered now for his dictionary, which appeared in preliminary form in 1803 and as a great contribution to lexicography in 1828.

Another great Federalist editor was William Cobbett, who never was an American at all, but who offered severe criticism of the (Jeffersonian) Republicans and who defended the Federalists between 1794 and 1800. Cobbett was a refugee in this country after exposing graft and corruption in the British army. He first showed his writing abilities in an attack on Joseph Priestley, whose scientific views were curiously related to his political views, which were leftist. Encouraged by the success of his writing, and sponsored by friends of the Federalist party, Cobbett gave up his modest tutoring position in 1797 to edit *Porcupine's Gazette and Daily Advertiser* in Philadelphia.

In the short span of three years, Cobbett made a name for himself throughout the new country. He made no pretense of objectivity. His purpose was to expose his enemies, and his weapon was his vitriolic pen. Few editors in history have surpassed the British exile in sustained vituperation. His general theme was alliance with Britain, war against France, and perdition for Republicans. Tom Paine was his special target, and his biography of the Revolution's penman was all the more readable because Cobbett never let himself be restrained by the facts. In short, he had a marvelous time lampooning his enemies and their ideas. His pseudonym, "Peter Porcupine," appeared regularly after he "told off" a magazine editor in a pamphlet entitled *A Kick for a Bite*. A reviewer of the piece likened Cobbett to a porcupine, a creature with bristles erect against those who sought to manhandle it. That was just the creature Cobbett fancied himself as being, and he gloried in the name.

The oldest Federalist paper was Major Benjamin Russell's *Massachusetts* (later *Columbian*) *Centinel*, published at Boston. Russell fought at Lexington as a lad of 13. He learned the printing trade under Isaiah Thomas and after serving his time as a journeyman, founded his paper in 1784. His first big crusade was his attempt to push his state toward ratification of the Constitution. That put him in the forefront of the forces that eventually rallied under the

Federalist banner. Russell was pro-British, anti-French, an advocate of an American nobility, and later a hater of Jefferson. His paper followed the Federalist line 100 per cent, but in addition, it had excellent news coverage, and it enjoyed great prosperity. With such journalistic big guns trained upon their hapless opponents, the Federalists rapidly consolidated their power. Had it not been for the French Revolution, they might have annihilated the ideas for which many an American had fought. As Colonel Thomas W. Higginson wrote in his voluminous notes of the period, the French Revolution "drew a red hot plow share through the history of America." [9] Whereas America had triggered the French upheaval after its own fight for freedom, the French were now repaying in kind—and just in time. The French influence stopped the American monarchists in their tracks. It destroyed the last hope of the aristocrats and it changed the trend toward realliance with the British. It also provided the literature and philosophy needed as ammunition against the skillful journalistic batteries defending the Federalist citadel. All that was needed was a great leader. As usual in such emergencies, a great one emerged.

He was Thomas Jefferson, then Secretary of State in Washington's cabinet. Jefferson was the antithesis of his colleague, Hamilton, both in temperament and in ideology. The American yeoman, rather than the commercial man, was Jefferson's ideal of the sovereign citizen. He was convinced that no other people of the world were so well off as the independent, rural landowners of the United States. Having seen the wretchedness of European cities, he was all the more certain that the benefits of the American yeoman must be maintained. It should be pointed out, however, that Jefferson did not stand as tribune for all the groups made up of the common man. He distrusted the proletariat—the workers in the cities. The slum was his measurement of a sick society.

It is commonly believed that Jefferson was an idealist, as opposed to Hamilton, the hard-fisted realist. Actually, an argument could be presented to show that just the reverse was true. If we assume that a realist is one who would make the best of the situation facing him, and the idealist is the proponent of things as they should be,

[9] Quoted from Vernon L. Parrington, *Main Currents in American Thought*, I (New York: Harcourt, Brace and Company, 1927), p. 321.

then Jefferson emerges more and more as the realist. Jefferson and Hamilton lived before the age of great industrial development in this country. Jefferson based his political philosophy on an existing agrarian economy. He faced conditions as they were, and sought to make the best of them. Under the above definition, that would make him a realist. Hamilton did everything he could to gear America for a capitalist, industrial future. He was so far ahead of his time that we can only conclude that he was an idealist.

The two clashed on every point. For Jefferson's purposes, a decentralized, States' rights government was sufficient. Since credit, commerce, and manufacturing were subordinate matters, Jefferson would have been content with no more government than was necessary to preserve internal order. Hamilton stood for exactly the opposite. Thus, the Federalist leader insisted upon a *responsible* government—one that could protect property and aid commerce—whereas Jefferson was much more interested in a *responsive* government, and was more concerned with the current needs of the people than in security.

The two champions inevitably clashed openly, as they had privately since their appointments as cabinet officers. The issue came to a head in 1791. Jefferson returned from a tour through New England with Madison to find himself the center of controversy. The two had already been mentioned in the *Maryland Journal* as potential anti-Federalist leaders. At this point, Edmund Burke in England had launched an attack upon those who defended the French Revolution. Paine had replied in his brilliant defense of democracy, *Rights of Man*. The Federalists saw to it that Burke's charges were widely reprinted in America. Paine's reply was slow in coming. Jefferson had obtained a copy from Madison, however, and it elated him; here was the answer to the Federalist gospel, he believed. Jefferson was stimulated into making some move against the Hamiltonians.

He encouraged the American publication of Paine's book. Unfortunately, Jefferson had to return the only copy of the *Rights of Man* before he had finished it, so that it could be set up in type. To save time, he sent it directly to the printer, and he inclosed a note explaining the reason for the delay: "I am extremely pleased to find it will be reprinted here," he wrote, "and that something is at length to be publicly said against the political heresies which have sprung up among us. I have no doubt our citizens will rally a second time round the standard of *Common Sense.*"

Jefferson maintained that he was surprised when he discovered the printer had used this note as a preface to the book. The general reader could only assume that the Secretary of State meant that the "political heresies" applied to such leaders as Vice President John Adams, whose tedious "Discourses of Davilla" were being accepted as holy writ by Federalists as the essays appeared serially in John Fenno's *Gazette of the United States.* This was of course a serious breach of official family etiquette. Cabinet members were not supposed to bicker publicly. As a result, a storm of abuse broke over Jefferson. His friends rose to defend him. Another result was that thousands rushed to buy copies of the Paine book. Thus, the political battle was joined, and Jefferson found himself thrust into the van as leader. He accepted the responsibility.

Jefferson's greatest weapon of attack on the Federalists was public opinion. The press was the forge upon which it was pounded out. He helped found newspapers in various parts of the country. Some of his most quotable remarks at this time refer to the press. If one of his party organs languished, he personally circulated subscription lists among friends to provide financial nourishment. His energy at this time was boundless. He never rested on his arms or went into winter quarters.

And so, by the end of Washington's administration, two definite parties had emerged. The party of the right was led by Hamilton. Included in his following were some of the ablest journalists of the day. The party of the left was directed by Jefferson. Its press was less notable at first, and its spokesmen tended to be inarticulate. The Jeffersonians soon found effective tribunes, however. For each party the press was the conduit between its leaders and philosophers, and the masses.

Newspapers and pamphlets served the Federalists well, but there were other effective ways of spreading the Hamiltonian ideology. The pulpit was largely a sounding board for Federalist philosophy, and colleges frowned on the unorthodoxy of the Jeffersonians. Finally, skillful writers of the time often loaned their talents to the Federalist cause.

One of the more famous Federalist propaganda agencies was a

PHILIP FRENEAU   BENJAMIN RUSSELL

WILLIAM COBBETT

Philip Freneau, as an Anti-Federalist editor, helped stimulate the "Second Revolution" that put Thomas Jefferson into the White House. Benjamin Russell, editor of the *Columbian Centinel,* was a pillar of the Federalist party and a noted journalist of his time. William Cobbett, better known as "Peter Porcupine," came from Britain to become a rabid Federalist editor who perhaps has never been exceeded in the art of invective. (*Magazine of American History*)

141

group known as the "Hartford Wits." Connecticut at that time was solidly behind the government of ~~the "right people."~~ ~~One of the~~ Hartford Wits was Timothy Dwight, high in the councils of his church, and president of Yale College. Dwight was known to his political opponents as "The Pope of Federalism." His dreary poem, "The Triumph of Infidelity," was an attack on Republican leaders as enemies of religion. Pompous, contemptuous of the public, but noted for his ponderous literary style, he was a potent voice in the Federalist movement. Other famous Wits were Governor John Trumbull, Lemuel Hopkins, and Richard Alsop.

An example of the journalistic product of the Hartford Wits was the *Anarchiad*, first published as a serial in the *New Haven Gazette* beginning in 1786. This was a heavily humorous epic mocking the rise of democracy. Dwight and his colleagues actually conceived of themselves as wits, and the contemporary reader of the *Anarchiad* might well concede that they were half right. In fact, they were not entirely devoid of cleverness, but they were utterly lacking in ideas. As Parrington puts it: "they sealed the windows of their minds against the disturbing winds of doctrine that were blowing freshly. They inspected the family tree of every new idea to determine its respectability." [10] They were, in short, rather precious fellows.

It is a relief to turn to the journalistic white knight of the Anti-Federalists. He was Philip Freneau, poet of the Revolution. Freneau might be remembered today as a great American literary figure, had it not been for his decision to become a journalist. Many historians have treated Freneau shabbily. They point to his vicious attacks on such heroes as Washington, Hamilton, and Adams. They accuse him of fostering what later was called "yellow journalism" —sensationalism for the sake of arousing emotions. On the other hand, other students of the period say that Freneau, more than anyone else, was responsible for turning the tide of public opinion against the Federalists. In so doing, he may have saved the country from capitulation to the monarchy men.

Those who accuse him of smearing heroes must also admit that he was not the one who started the row. When the Federalists began the campaign to sell the Constitution to the public, they did not hesitate to blacken the reputations of their opponents. The Anti-

[10] Parrington, *Main Currents in American Thought*, I, p. 367.

Federalist leaders were much more obscure than the heroes in the Federalist camp, with a few notable exceptions, and so, in the light of history, the blame of scurrility falls more heavily upon the Anti-Federalist journalists. Because leading Federalists were socially prominent, attacks on them were more devastating, and historians were ready to record the defenses of such men. But Jefferson and his lieutenants fared just as badly at the hands of such writers as Webster, Cobbett, Russell, and Fenno—and Federalists who dominated the literary field at the time showed little indignation.

Philip Freneau, who helped to start the second internal revolution, was a lifelong rebel. It is significant that he was of Huguenot extraction. The Huguenots had suffered for generations in the cause of religious freedom. Freneau was graduated from Princeton in 1771. At that time the college was a hotbed of sedition. Among the students who gathered in the room Freneau shared with James Madison were such "Radicals" as Harry Lee, Aaron Burr, and William Bradford, later a member of Washington's cabinet. Freneau was the most zealous patriot of the lot. Long before the Revolution he was writing newspaper contributions and fierce poems on liberty. After Lexington and Concord, he took an active part in the conflict—a rather pathetic little man, pitting his feeble efforts uselessly, as it turned out, against the enemy. For Freneau was far ahead of his time. While he was fighting for independence, most of his colleagues were still thinking in terms of home rule and reform. In disgust, he took to the sea in one of his father's ships.

He was in Bermuda when news arrived of the Declaration of Independence. Here was Revolution he could understand. Freneau hurried home to take an active part in the movement. With Letters of Marque (license for a civilian to wage war) from the Continental Congress, he put his available resources into a privateer, a vessel he called the "Aurora." The ship had to strike its colors in the first battle, and Freneau spent weary weeks in the notorious British prison hulks anchored in New York harbor—an experience that left him physically shattered, and which made him even a more implacable hater of the British. At length he was exchanged. Returning to New York sick and penniless, he turned to his last resource —his pen. Freneau's poem "The Prison Ship," whipped apathetic patriots into renewed efforts against the enemy. His account of the exploits of John Paul Jones instilled pride into a dejected nation.

He is not a heroic figure—this seedy wisp of a man, his pockets stuffed with poetry written on any scrap of paper he could find. Yet he did as much to fire up the morale of the patriots by poetry as Paine had through prose. His title, "Poet of the Revolution," is indeed valid. Had this been his only contribution, he would more appropriately be discussed in a history of literature, rather than in a story of journalism. His greatest work still lay ahead, however.

By the end of the war he had given his health, his fortune, and all his soul to the cause of liberty. As he saw it, the sacrifice had been in vain. He charged his old leaders—Washington included —with failure to carry out the promises of 1776. He saw Jeffersonian Republicanism as a movement to carry on the original drives of the Revolution over the opposition of the Federalists.

It was Madison, Freneau's classmate, who brought the little rebel to Jefferson's attention. Madison had told the Anti-Federalist leader that Freneau was just the man to engage in journalistic jousting with such champions as Fenno or Russell. Jefferson was always considerate of the ideas of Madison, who was like a son to the master of Monticello. He offered Freneau a small subsidy as State Department translator if he would found an Anti-Federalist paper. It was not money that lured Freneau to the capital, however. He saw himself as a journalistic crusader striving to fix the attention of the public on the prize of Revolutionary victory, which he believed had been denied by the Federalist counterrevolution.

And so it was that Freneau became editor of the *National Gazette* (often called the "Federal Gazette") in 1791. The early editions were mild enough, but there were hints of what was to come. Fenno, his rival, would never have tolerated a phrase like "public opinion sets the bounds to every government, and is the real sovereign of every free one." [11] The four short columns of comment on page one of the *National Gazette* looked innocuous in those first few months, but while Fenno was ridiculing the right of plain citizens to complain against government officials, Freneau was telling his readers that "perpetual jealousy of the government" was necessary against "the machinations of ambition," and he warned that "where that jealousy does not exist in a reasonable degree, the saddle is soon prepared for the back of the people." [12] But these were

[11] *National Gazette*, December 19, 1791.
[12] *National Gazette*, February 9, 1792.

mere ripples in the placid pool heretofore dominated by the Federalist frogs. Freneau, the poet, had yet to adopt fully the vitriolic language of the political partisan.

Then one day Freneau discharged both barrels at Hamilton over the injustices of the funding system. He used the pen name "Brutus" that day, and at once the Federalist leader discovered he had a journalistic foe worthy of his steel. Day by day Freneau sent succeeding volleys after the first one, and his brashness encouraged other articulate voices to sound the call to battle stations. Even the less gifted Anti-Federalist editors could arouse readers now, by picking up *National Gazette* "exchanges." The alarm of the Federalists was indicated by the torrent of abuse flowing from their editorial pens, but this, too, Freneau could return in double measure.

Freneau was so dangerous to Hamilton's plans that the Secretary of the Treasury made the mistake of taking up the cudgels personally. Convinced that the "Federal Gazette" had been established by his arch-rival, Jefferson, for the sole purpose of wrecking all that he had built so carefully, Hamilton tossed aside the dignity of his office to engage in public bickering. His contribution to Fenno's paper was over the signature "T.L.," but the word soon got around that Hamilton was the author. He charged that Freneau had no right to criticise the government that paid him his subsidy as a translator. Freneau answered:

The above is beneath reply. It might be queried, however, whether a man who receives a small stipend for services rendered as a French translator to the Department of State, and as editor of a free newspaper admits into his publication impartial strictures on the proceedings of government, is not more likely to act an honest and disinterested part toward the public, than a vile sycophant, who obtaining emoluments from government, far more lucrative than the salary alluded to [a reference to Fenno's printing contract with the Senate and Treasury, and his alleged business connections with the Bank of the United States], finds his interest in attempting to poison the minds of the people by propaganda and by disseminating principles and sentiments utterly subversive of the true republican interests of the country, and by flattering and recommending every and any measures of government however pernicious and destructive its tendency might be to the great body of the people. The world is left to decide the motive of each. . . .[13]

[13] *National Gazette*, July 28, 1792.

Such exchanges explain why the relations of Hamilton and Jefferson became more and more strained. They made cabinet meetings difficult for President Washington. The President performed one of his greatest services to his country when he tolerated such dissension within his official family. Washington knew how to draw out the best in each of his brilliant protégés. In the light of history it is apparent that the country profited by the fight. Jefferson took some of the conceit and arrogance out of Hamilton, and Hamilton made Jefferson test his concepts on the solid ground of public opinion. But in the summer of 1792 even the Father of His Country could not control the cabinet foes. Hamilton publicly charged that Jefferson was the real author of the *National Gazette's* vilifications, which, of course, was also an insult to Freneau. The editor replied with an affidavit denying that the Secretary of State had ever written a line for the paper, which is more than Fenno could say about the Secretary of the Treasury.

Although Jefferson, so far as is known, never did write directly for the Anti-Federalist organ, Washington called him on the carpet, along with Hamilton. Before his chief Hamilton admitted authorship of the embarrassing newspaper pieces, but he said he had been driven to desperation by his rival's political deceit. Jefferson, on the other hand, admitted that he had no faith in the party of Hamilton (and Washington), and he added that he resented Hamilton's interference in State Department matters. As to the articles written by Freneau, he said he could see no reason to censor an editor for attempting to uncover "aristocratic and monarchial principles."

Both Freneau and Fenno were rivals for public favor, Jefferson later wrote the President. Fenno courted by flattery, and the other by censure, he added, and ". . . the one has been as servile as the other has been severe." Referring to Hamilton, the Secretary of State continued: "But is not the dignity and even decency of government committed when one of its principal ministers enlists himself as an anonymous writer . . . for either one or the other of them?" As for the objections that had been made to Freneau's criticism of governmental measures, Jefferson answered with feeling that ". . . no government ought to be without censors; and where the press is free, no one ever will. If [the government is] virtuous, it need not fear the free operation of attack and defense. Nature has given to man no other means of sifting out the truth, either in religion, law, or politics. . . ." [14]

There could be no resolving of differences between leaders of two such opposite views. Freneau and his increasing corps of imitators swung into the fray all the more furiously after this attempt at mediation. Freneau even had the audacity to swing at Washington and Vice President Adams. This helps to explain the reputation he established in history. The Federalists, who controlled the leading colleges, saw to it that Freneau lost all claim to his former recognition as the "Father of American Poetry."

It must be said that he gained nothing personally for his pains. His paper was widely read and exerted great influence, but it produced little revenue. Nor did his position bring him power or prestige. And certainly the arousing of hate was not pleasant to him. He did enjoy a fight, it is true, but only for a purpose. "How oft has rugged nature charged my pen with gall," he once lamented, remembering all the enemies he had made. But if his personal war was grim and onerous, it was warfare for a cause. He was fighting with every weapon at his command for an ideal, and against a foe that offered no quarter. The victory he sought was the survival of the democratic spirit.

That was why he dared attack such demi-gods as Washington and Adams. He knew very well that the first President was great-souled. Anyone who had served with the Commander-in-Chief during the War of Independence, as had Freneau, understood that. But Washington appeared to Freneau to be a "front" for the Federalists. The editor believed that the old war hero was being used unfairly by the opposition. The only solution Freneau could suggest was to turn the hero back to human clay again. It was the same motivation mentioned in the discussion of Samuel Adams in an earlier chapter. Freneau smeared his old chief so that the words of a hero would not have undue weight with those who opposed his party. This, of course, is no *excuse* for such motives, but it is a *reason* for Freneau's policy.

We cannot blame Washington for cursing "that rascal Freneau,"

[14] This exchange can be followed in more detail in Bowers, *Jefferson and Hamilton*, pp. 168-74. The quotation is from Saul K. Padover, *Thomas Jefferson on Democracy* (New York: Penguin Books, Inc., 1939), p. 93. Copyright 1939, D. Appleton-Century Company, Inc., by permission of the publishers, Appleton-Century-Crofts, Inc., New York.

when the editor wrote such impudent items as: "The first magistrate of a country . . . seldom knows the real state of the nation, particularly if he be buoyed up by official importance to think it beneath his dignity to mix occasionally with the people." That was a low blow, indeed, to the man who had led his ragged army from Valley Forge to victory.

In the end, it was neither the opposition nor the government that defeated Freneau. The *National Gazette* simply died of financial malnutrition. There were no "angels" to come to the rescue, as there had been for Fenno under Hamilton's sponsorship. Jefferson could offer some help, but when he left the cabinet in 1793, Freneau had virtually no financial support. By that time, the editor was nearly bankrupt. When yellow fever drove his workmen out of the city, Freneau closed the office. He never reopened it. The paper had lasted only two years, but it is doubtful if any other publication had ever accomplished so much in that time. The end of the paper was just about the end of Freneau as a journalist, too. He tried his hand for a time in New Jersey and New York, but eventually he returned to the sea. Later, he was rediscovered as a poet.

There are two reasons why Freneau has been given space here at the expense of opposition editors equally well-known at the time: (1) His career emphasizes the issues of the day; (2) His party soon emerged triumphant over its opponents, and it is significant to bring out the part played by the leading journalistic spokesman of that party. As editor of the newspaper trumpeting the call for the people to rally to the standard of majority rule again, Freneau deserves serious consideration by students of journalistic history.

ANNOTATED BIBLIOGRAPHY

Books:

Bowers, Claude G., *Jefferson and Hamilton.* Boston: Houghton Mifflin Company, 1925. This book is particularly interesting to the student of journalism because the author draws heavily upon newspaper sources for much of his documentation. Strongly Anti-Federalist.

Binkley, Wilfred E., *American Political Parties: Their Natural History.* New York: Alfred A. Knopf, Inc., 1958. A clear and thoughtful study of the topic. The chapters on the early party era are good background reading.

Cobbett, William, *Selections*. Oxford: Clarendon Press, 1923. These excerpts from the journalist's detailed *Works* demonstrate the style and content of Cobbett's best contributions.

Cole, G. D. H., *The Life of William Cobbett*. New York: Harcourt, Brace and Company, 1924. This is the standard "life" of the journalist, but it is rather meager in description of the American interlude, and none of the flavor of the satirist is preserved, either in text or in example.

Faÿ, Bernard, *Notes on the American Press at the End of the Eighteenth Century*. New York: Grolier Club, 1927. A brief study, with facsimiles of leading papers.

Jensen, Merrill, *The New Nation*. New York: Alfred A. Knopf, Inc., 1950. A brilliant refutation of the dreary picture of the confederation period, as painted by such classic historians as John Fiske.

Krout, John Allen, and Dixon Ryan Fox, *The Completion of Independence, 1790-1830*, A History of American Life, Vol. V. New York: The Macmillan Company, 1944. Social history.

Leary, Lewis, *That Rascal Freneau*. New Brunswick: Rutgers University Press, 1941. The standard "life" of the Anti-Federalist editor. The preface includes a summary and brief explanation of the journalist's career.

Lodge, Henry Cabot, *Alexander Hamilton*. Boston: Houghton Mifflin Company, 1882. A sympathetic treatment of the great Federalist.

McMaster, John Bach, *A History of the People of the United States from the Revolution to the Civil War*. 8 vols. New York: D. Appleton and Company, 1883-1913. McMaster is chosen from among some of the best historians who wrote of this period, because he depended upon newspaper sources to bring out the flavor and the temper of the times.

Nevins, Allan, *American Press Opinion, Washington to Coolidge*. Boston: D. C. Heath and Company, 1928. This book is a fairly complete journalistic history, using short comment, followed by verbatim documentation. An excellent reference.

Parrington, Vernon L., *Main Currents in American Thought*, Vol. I. Philip Freneau is discussed in this rich study.

Pollard, James E., *The Presidents and the Press*. New York: The Macmillan Company, 1947. The attitude of the Chief Executive regarding the press is an indicator of journalistic prestige and power, decade by decade. This book is useful as a supplementary text.

Rutland, Robert Allen, *The Birth of the Bill of Rights, 1776-1791*. Chapel Hill: University of North Carolina Press, 1955. A documented study of the origins and passage of the 10 amendments.

Schachner, Nathan, *Alexander Hamilton*. New York: Appleton-Century, 1946. A middle-of-the-road interpretation.

Scudder, H. E., *Noah Webster*. Boston: Houghton Mifflin Company, 1882.

An adequate, concise biography of a versatile and interesting personality, who, among his other accomplishments, was a noted journalist.

Van Doren, Carl, ed., *The Federalist*. New York: Heritage Press, 1945. An annotated edition of the famous series of political editorials.

Periodicals and Monographs:

"Cobbett," *Fraser's Magazine*, XII (August 1835), 207. A personality sketch, which brings out the journalist's wit and pugnacity.

Reitzel, William, "William Cobbett and Philadelphia Journalism," *Pennsylvania Magazine*, LIX (July 1935), 223. An excellent interpretation of the journalist. Reprinted in Ford and Emery, *Highlights in the History of the American Press*.

"William Cobbett," *Littell's Living Age*, XLI (Spring 1854), 61. A short but surprisingly complete biographical sketch, with an interesting section on Cobbett's career in America.

Chapter 8

THE TOCSIN OF A NATION

The press [is] the only tocsin of a nation.
—Jefferson to Thomas Cooper

ONE OF THE LEADING JOURNALISTS who carried the torch of Anti-Federalism dropped by Freneau was Benjamin Franklin Bache, the grandson of Benjamin Franklin. Bache was just 21 when he founded the *Philadelphia General Advertiser,* better known as the *Aurora* (the name appeared in small print around the name plate). Bache was a mercurial young man—impetuous, brilliant, and often intemperate in expression. He was influenced by the style of Freneau, and his paper was even more violently partisan than the *National Gazette* had been. Too often he was downright vicious.

Not that the Federalists did not give him cause for his editorial mud-slinging. He had seen the statue of his grandfather—one of the great men of the country—desecrated by hoodlums inspired to acts of vandalism by those opposed to the principles so ably enunciated by "Poor Richard" in Franklin's famous *Almanac.* Brought up in France and Switzerland by his doting grandfather, young Bache was sympathetic to the French cause from the beginning of his journalistic career. That put him in opposition to President Washington when the old war hero backed up the anti-French party headed by Hamilton and others. Like Freneau, Bache resorted to personal attack in his campaign to wreck the Federalist party. He even tried to besmirch the character of "The Father of His Country."

151

"If ever a nation was debauched by a man, the American nation has been debauched by Washington," he wrote in the December 23, 1796, issue of the *Aurora*.

Some historians have called this period the "Dark Ages of Journalism," because of the scurrility of the press. This was a transition period, however, and perhaps violent partisanship, as reflected in the press, was a means of expending some of the venom stored up against the British after the war.[1] Adding to the tension was the war between Great Britain and Napoleonic France. It was not easy for Americans to take the advice of Washington, who warned against entangling foreign alliances in the last hours of his administration.[2] The new nation had little to gain by taking sides, but unfortunately, the war was forced upon the attentions of Americans by the belligerents.

The French and the British were about equally callous regarding American foreign policy. The "paper" blockades imposed by Napoleon violated international precedent, and American shipping interests were infuriated by unlawful seizure of their vessels by the French. But the British were annoying, too. They had fallen back upon the "Rule of 1756," which forbade neutrals from trading in wartime with nations not ordinarily regular customers. This made sense to the British, for it was clear to them that the enemy otherwise could supply himself through adjoining neutral countries, despite the blockade, but the enforcement of this rule threatened the development of American commerce.

But the Federalists saw evil only in France. They were repelled by the excesses of the French Revolution, and by the success of Napoleon. Since the Federalists were in firm control of the government, they could manipulate foreign policy to favor the British. The Anti-Federalists argued that America had the duty of siding with France in the name of Rochambeau, Lafayette, and DeGrasse, who had come from France to help us win our war with Britain. Federalists answered that our promises of assistance to France in time of trouble had been made to a government since overthrown by

[1] See, for example, B. E. Martin, "Transition Period of the American Press," *Magazine of American History*, XVII (April 1887), pp. 273-94.
[2] It is remarkable all during these critical years how all roads to safety eventually led right back to Washington. He was not a political genius, but he appeared to know instinctively the policies that would offer the greatest security to the nation he had saved in wartime.

a regime to which we had no binding ties.[3] The fact is, Federalists and Anti-Federalists were in conflict over the issue not because of persuasive logic, but because of partisan bitterness. Both sides found ammunition for their cause in the European issue. There was, for example, the case of "Citizen" Edmond Charles Genêt, minister to the United States from the French Republic. Genêt arrived in Charleston in the spring of 1793. Had he arrived in Boston he might have been sent home packing, but the South was Anti-Federalist territory, and on the Frenchman's month-long trip north, it was roses, roses all the way. By that time he was so certain he had public opinion behind him that when President Washington brushed off suggestions that the French be allowed to use American ports for refitting damaged war vessels, Genêt went right ahead with his plans. Washington was correct in slapping down such a presumptuous guest of the country, and the people, as a whole, approved. The Federalists used the incident to discredit their pro-French opponents.

Even more embarrassing to the Anti-Federalists was the so-called "XYZ Affair," in which it appeared that the unscrupulous French foreign minister, Talleyrand, had informed our diplomats that he would receive them as accredited ministers only after they had paid him a bribe. It was very difficult to defend pro-French sentiment in the face of such raw insults to national pride.

On the other hand, the Anti-Federalists were collecting a few rocks to throw at their enemies, too. Genêt's mistake hurt the Anti-Federalist cause in one way, but it did show how many countrymen were opposed to Federalist policy. Many a timid Republican was thus encouraged to enlist in Jefferson's party. The treaty signed by John Jay in 1794 was also used against the Federalists. "Jay's Treaty" was an attempt to get the British to meet agreements negotiated during the Treaty of Paris, which ended the War for Independence. It did get the British out of the frontier forts that they had promised to evacuate, but nothing was settled about impressment of American seamen, which irritated many Americans, especially those doomed to the harsh life of the British Navy. The Federalist leaders had no intention of forcing the British at this time, and the scorn of the people for Jay, one of the authors of

[b] Just as commitments to Chiang Kai-shek in World War II did not bind the United States to the succeeding Chinese Communist government.

The Federalist papers, was violent. At that, Jay did about as well as he could, what with Hamilton notifying the British authorities secretly that the administration had no wish to press its claims at that point—a policy that reduced Jay's bargaining power to zero.

Partisan feeling was running high when John Adams took the oath of office as the second president of the United States, after the election of 1796. With the Federalists in firm control, the administration began to prepare for war with France. Congress dutifully authorized an army of 35,000, which was a larger force than Washington had ever had at his disposal during the Revolution. Two new superfrigates, the "United States" and the "Constitution," were laid down as part of the war program. To pay for these items Congress levied a tax that fell particularly heavily upon the small landowner, who was least interested in foreign wars.

The result was a political and journalistic battle that passed all the bounds of decency. Even during the Revolution, when Tory and patriot clawed at each other, there had never been such a caterwaul. Bache and Fenno carried their personal feud beyond the pages of their papers by engaging in a street brawl. "Peter Porcupine" (William Cobbett) brought invective to finest flower by attacking well-known Anti-Federalists, living and dead.

This was the situation when the administration tried to throttle such violent opposition in the summer of 1798. In June and July of that year, Congress passed the Alien and Sedition Acts. One was a law aimed at troublesome foreigners living in the country; the other concerned the muzzling of irritating editors.[4]

There were then about 25,000 aliens in the United States. Many of them were refugees from stern authorities in their home lands, and they therefore tended to be on the side of the Jeffersonians, who believed in as little government as possible. Others were poor, or at least propertyless, and again such persons were more likely to gravitate into the ranks of the Anti-Federalists. Groups such as the Irish immigrants were by tradition opposed to the British, and so could not possibly see any good in the Hamiltonian policy of British appeasement. There were also many intellectuals in this category. Dr. Joseph Priestley, the discoverer of oxygen and seven other gases, was a British expatriate noted for his leftist views. The Du

---

[4] The Act was originally in four parts, but the alien and sedition items were the main issues. *U. S. Statutes at Large,* I, 577.

Ponts, at that time aggressive backers of liberalism, brought French ideas into the platform of the Anti-Federalists. And there was Albert Gallatin, destined to be a great Secretary of the Treasury under Jefferson, who was already making a name for himself in Pennsylvania, despite the difficulty of adjusting to a country so different from his native Switzerland. Men like these were almost certain to be opposed to the administration. The Alien Act, it was hoped, would reduce the ranks of these threatening foreigners.

One provision of the law was an extension of the naturalization period from five to fourteen years. Another clause empowered the President to deport aliens judged by him to be subversive. Two shiploads of foreigners were sent packing under the terms of the alien and naturalization acts. Some foreign-born Americans, such as John Burk, publisher of the Anti-Federalist *Time Piece* in New York, simply went underground until the trouble blew over. Anyone could see that the alien section applied only to enemies of the administration. Peter Porcupine (William Cobbett) was not only a foreigner who held Americans in contempt, but he was becoming obnoxious, even to some of the Federalist leaders, as the editor of a paper that attacked Vice President Jefferson in almost every issue. As a foe of Jefferson, however, he was immune to deportation by the Federalists.

The Sedition Act was even more alarming. It was an obvious attempt to control the journalistic spokesmen of the Anti-Federalists. It declared: "That if any person shall write, print, utter, or publish . . . any false, scandalous and malicious writing . . . against the government of the United States, or either house of the Congress . . . or the said President . . . or to excite against them the hatred of the good people of the United States . . . or to resist or oppose, or defeat any such law . . . shall be punished by a fine not exceeding two thousand dollars, and by imprisonment not exceeding two years." [5] The laws were to stand for two years.

One of the cornerstones of press freedom is the right to express criticism of government and its administrators freely. The Alien and Sedition laws reversed a process that had made America the envy of the oppressed. And yet there were important contributions in the laws. Nor have the repressive features been properly appraised in many accounts of the period. The original bill called for a decla-

[5] U. S. *Statutes at Large*, "The Sedition Act," I, Sec. 2, p. 596.

ration of war with France. The clauses that followed imposed penalties on all who gave any aid or comfort to this enemy. At the last minute, the war declaration was defeated by a narrow margin, but the following clauses concerning aliens and the press were allowed to stand. That was why all pro-French sentiment was so ruthlessly attacked by the administration.

And in some ways the Sedition Act can be called a *milestone* on the road to freedom of the press. The law did not forbid criticism of the government. It only attempted to curb malicious and false statements published to defame officials. And it provided a pair of safeguards: truth could be offered as a defense, and the jury could determine both the law and the fact. This was the twin argument made by Andrew Hamilton in the John Peter Zenger trial. Now it was enacted into the law of 1798. At first glance the Sedition Act may appear to merit full support. After all, why *should* an editor be allowed to defame public figures, thereby discouraging decent men and women from assuming civic responsibilities in their communities?

The weakness in the law lay in its administration. Fairly administered, it might have won respect. But experience has shown us time and again that the party in power will inevitably abuse such controls in the interests of expediency. It was so in 1798. Even Alexander Hamilton, the father of the Federalist party, was apprehensive of the measure. The ailing and retired General Washington rose from his bed to warn against the abuses he foresaw. President Adams, an honest man despite his political ineptitude, did what he could to modify the bill. Unfortunately, the leaders who had made the Federalist party dominant in all branches of government no longer had the power to impede the machine they had set in motion. Extremists had taken over control, and they were intent upon revenge for all the indignities heaped upon them by opposition editors.

The Alien and Sedition Acts gave the Anti-Federalists the unifying force their party needed. Jefferson himself began the counterattack, using the repressive laws as the battle line. He was aided in his fight by James Madison, father of the Constitution, but now concerned about the turn of events that had given the Federalists so much control. In the fall of 1798 Jefferson called his party leaders to his home at Monticello. They agreed that little could be accomplished for the time being in persuading Congress to repeal the acts. The Federalists were too strong in both houses of Congress. The hope lay in the State governments, especially in the South, and it was on this basis that the Monticello junta proceeded.

The result was the Virginia and Kentucky Resolutions. Madison wrote the Virginia document, and Jefferson was asked to write the one for Kentucky, but because the document challenged a doctrine he had sworn to uphold as vice president, Jefferson could not openly admit authorship. For the Resolutions brought up a disturbing issue that was to haunt our statesmen for many years—the principle of nullification. And so John Breckenridge, who introduced the bill to the Kentucky legislature, was believed to have been the author, until Jefferson's hand in it was disclosed 25 years later.

The two resolutions emphasized the essential role of a free press in a democracy. But in suggesting the means for restoring rights abused by the Alien and Sedition Acts, the resolutions questioned the very nature of the federal union. The documents affirmed that the federal government was created by the states, and that the states must logically be superior, therefore. On that basis, a state might repudiate, or nullify, a federal law when such a measure was clearly opposed by public opinion in a state. In giving up some of their sovereignty to the federal government, it was argued, the states had thereby entered into a contract. If the federal government violated that contract, then the states involved were no longer bound by it.

Here was a concept that later was to lead to a bloody contest between states' rights and federal authority, but it should be pointed out that in 1798 nullification was used as a weapon to return to the people a freedom threatened by an arrogant party. It is only fair to say that in this period such a principle was certain to be proposed sooner or later. In 1798 there was no such safety valve as "judicial review," or the right of the United States Supreme Court to declare a legislative act unconstitutional. Not until 1803 did John Marshall establish that function of the court in the case of *Marbury v. Madison*.

The Virginia and Kentucky Resolutions were widely reprinted in newspapers up and down the seaboard. Press reaction was generally unfavorable. Some of the editors no doubt saw that the seeds of national disintegration were implanted in the documents. But since the press was predominantly Federalist in policy, much of the opposition was strictly partisan. But in any case, the public had a chance to discuss this important issue, and there is no doubt that the cause of the Anti-Federalists was helped thereby. Jefferson sat back to await the next step.

The Adams administration played right into his hands. The Federalists abused the new laws so openly that for a time freedom of the press was seriously threatened in America. It was far from being the "reign of terror" charged by the opposition, but the record is not one of which Americans can be proud. Timothy Pickering, the Secretary of State, spent half his time reading Anti-Federalist papers so that he could ferret out violators of the law. Adams, who was just beginning to find out that some of his trusted cabinet members, including Pickering, were working for Hamilton against the policies of the President, tried to curb this hysteria. It was too late. The Federalists were enjoying an orgy of witch-hunting, and the sickness had to run its course.

One of the victims of the Sedition Act was Matthew Lyon of Vermont. Born in Ireland, Lyon had landed in America as an indentured servant. He had worked his way up to a position of respect and prestige in his community, and was Representative to Congress from his state. Lyon was one of the famous "Green Mountain Boys" in the War for Independence. Cashiered from the army for an act that should have earned him a medal, he was later reinstated and promoted to the rank of colonel. He had won the enmity of the Federalists in Congress by his outspoken criticism of their policies. The majority leaders had singled him out for reprisal, and the Sedition Act was to be the club to strike him down.

One afternoon in the House of Representatives, Roger Griswold, a leading Federalist from that citadel of Federalism, Connecticut, made insulting remarks about Lyon's war record. The Vermonter ignored Griswold at first, but when his colleague grasped his coat and repeated the insult, Lyon replied in the uncouth, but effective manner of the frontier. He spat in Griswold's eye. Next day Griswold walked up to Lyon's desk in the House and began beating him with a cane. Lyon grabbed a handy pair of fire tongs and beat back his adversary. The Federalists tried to expel Lyon from the House, but failed to muster the needed two-thirds vote.

The Sedition Act was used to settle scores with such persons. The crime charged against Lyon under the Act was the publication of a letter to an editor accusing President Adams of "ridiculous pomp, foolish adulation, and selfish avarice." For such remarks, Lyon was hailed before a Federalist judge, who sentenced the defendant to

Courtesy, Bettmann Archive

One of the earliest political cartoons was this panel of the Lyon-Griswold duel in the hall of Congress while partisanship was reaching new heights of violence in 1798.

four months in jail and a fine of a thousand dollars. The vindictiveness of the judge was indicated by the fact that although the trial was held in Rutland, Vermont, where there was a passable jail, Lyon was condemned to a filthy cell at Vergennes, some 40 miles distant. Thousands of local citizens signed a petition requesting parole for the prisoner. It was ignored. When Editor Anthony Haswell printed an advertisement in his *Vermont Gazette* announcing a lottery to raise money for paying the fine, he, too, was hustled off to jail for abetting a "criminal."

The Federalists should have heeded the warning. For the public reaction to such injustice was positive and immediate. Lyon was jailed in October, 1798, convicted by what he called a packed jury of political opponents. In December he was reelected to the House by a two-to-one vote over his closest opponent. Freed in February, 1799, after money had flowed in to pay his fine, the Vermonter returned in triumph to the capital at Philadelphia. At one time the procession behind his carriage was 12 miles long. In 1801 he was to play a crucial role in making Jefferson president.[6]

Other editors also had felt the lash of the Federalist masters. James Callender was one. He edited the *Richmond Examiner*. For criticising the President, Callender was brought to trial. He probably deserved what he got, for the man was an unprincipled political opportunist. The Federalists were not attacking him on principle, however, but on technicalities, and his case is just as significant as though he were a man of high character. Callender was defended by William Wirt, the South's leading lawyer and man of letters. The judge was Samuel Chase, who had said before he had even arrived in Virginia that he was going to give the Anti-Federalists a lesson. Just as predicted, Callender was found guilty. He was sentenced to nine months in jail.

A Connecticut editor was imprisoned because he criticised the Army and the military policies of Congress. A New York editor wrote an uncomplimentary article about the President, and was promptly jailed. Then the general public began to see through the hypocrisy of the repressive laws. It was noticed that whereas the slightest criticism of President Adams resulted in penalties, violent abuse of Anti-Federalist officials passed unpunished. Bache, for example, was indicted for criticism of Adams and others, while Fenno, who was just as violent, went unscathed. The wealthy and important persons in the Federalist camp regularly attacked Jefferson, the second highest officeholder, and nothing happened to them. Let some poor, obscure Anti-Federalist so much as object to high

---

[6] The 1800 election brought out a flaw in the poltical machinery. Jefferson was clearly the popular choice for President, but he and his running mate, Aaron Burr, both received 73 electoral votes under the indirect system of election. This threw the election into the House of Representatives, with 16 states having one vote each. The Federalists, despite Hamilton's opposition, voted for Burr. For 35 ballots Jefferson had eight states, one short of a majority. Burr had six and two state delegations were split. One was Vermont. On the final ballot the Federalist from Vermont abstained, thus allowing Lyon to cast the decisive vote. Lyon had not run again in 1800, but he was to serve in the House from 1803-1811 as congressman from Kentucky.

taxes, however, and Pickering's underlings swooped down on him. Consider the case of David Brown, for example. Brown was a middle-aged New England worker. He had fought throughout the Revolution, and apparently had taken the ideals of that conflict to heart. Semi-literate, inarticulate, and poor, Brown nevertheless had the courage of his convictions. He and a fellow worker, Benjamin Fairbanks, set up what was then called a "liberty pole" in Dedham, Massachusetts. A liberty pole was the equivalent of a modern political poster. On this particular pole the two workmen had painted: "No Stamp Tax—No Sedition—No Alien Bills—No Land Tax— Downfall to Tyrants of America—Peace and Retirement to the President—Long Live the Vice President and the Minority—May Moral Virtues be the Basis of Civil Government." For these dreadful statements Brown and Fairbanks were arrested as subversives. Fairbanks pleaded guilty and was let off with a five-dollar fine to prove Federalist "mercy." But Brown refused to recant. Accordingly, Justice Chase fined him $400 and sentenced him to 18 months. Brown was refused a pardon by President Adams, and at the end of his sentence was kept behind bars for failure to pay his fine. He and all others still in prison were pardoned by Jefferson as soon as the latter became President.

The persecutions under the Alien and Sedition Acts have sometimes been described as insignificant. In all, there were 25 arrests under the Sedition Act, 15 of which resulted in indictments. Eleven trials resulted, with 10 convictions. During the same time span there were at least five other convictions for seditious libel under the provisions of British Common Law in state or federal courts. Eight of the convictions involved newspapers. Whatever the numbers, the uproar over the prosecutions was enough to make it clear that the states had erred in enacting laws during the Revolution perpetuating the concept of seditious libel. What caught a Tory then caught a Republican now. There were a few more seditious libel cases after 1800 but the example of the Sedition Act proved conclusive. People saw that the test of tyranny is not necessarily the number of prosecutions, but the number of men and women restrained from speaking freely because of fear.

But the tide was turning. President Adams would have been undone in any case by the perfidy of his cabinet members, such as Pickering, Wolcott (Treasury), and McHenry (War), but the Alien and Sedition laws completed the undermining of the topheavy Federalist party. By 1800 the ponderous edifice, built so carefully by the high priests of property, collapsed of its own weight through insufficient support at the base. The biggest blunder of the Federalists was the passage of the repressive laws.

It should be noted, however, that the laws were never repealed. They simply lapsed at the end of the two-year limitation period. By 1800 the battle was over. Fenno and Bache both died in the terrible yellow fever epidemic that scourged Philadelphia in the summer of 1798 while Bache was still under indictment. Freneau, driven out by the fever, never re-established his *Gazette*. Cobbett had left the country, following a libel suit that forced him into bankruptcy.

On the whole, the press improved after the outstanding character assassins were silenced in one way or the other. The widow Bache married her husband's assistant, William Duane, whose wife had died of the fever. Duane made a decent woman of the *Aurora*. The *Aurora* continued to back Jefferson and his party, but it was much more reasonable in tone under Duane. He was as courageous as Freneau, without Freneau's shrillness and bad taste. He was as colorful in his writing as Cobbett, but without the Englishman's recklessness. Duane suffered for the cause, along with other Anti-Federalists. He was beaten up by hoodlums set upon him by his foes. He also was arrested under the Sedition Act, but was exonerated by the new administration just in time.

The removal of the national capital from Philadelphia to Washington ended an epoch, and began a new one. There had been a complete change in party and administration control, too. For by 1800 Jefferson's scorned "unimportant men" had risen in wrath to throw out the Federalists who had held them in such contempt. In the election year of 1800, Federalists were dominant in the House, the Senate, the Presidency, the cabinet, the courts, the churches, business, and education. Up to four-fifths of the newspapers opposed Jefferson and his party.

Against this seemingly invincible army stood the obscure men of farm, workbench, and counter. True, more and more of them were winning the right to vote, and that was to be important in the outcome. On the other hand, they were so disorganized and so individually helpless that their cause appeared to be hopeless.

They had only one weapon, but it was enough. That weapon was a free press. For although most newspapers were Federalist organs, enough editorial comment and information was offered under the free press concept to rally public opinion for the ultimate overthrow of the Federalists.

Jefferson understood the function of the press, and he used newspapers effectively. He knew that one feeble publication carrying a message of hope and encouragement could rally the aggrieved and discontented, no matter how much brilliant journalism the opposition had at its command. The little men and the little papers trounced a tightly organized coalition of powerful interests, teaching them that arrogance, force, and misrepresentation are no defenses against an aroused public opinion. The Federalists had intended and used the Alien and Sedition laws to bolster their selfish designs, but these same laws were largely instrumental in damaging the Federalist party so badly that it was more than a generation before members of its persuasion regained political control.

As the historian, Arthur M. Schlesinger, Jr., has written: "When a party starts out by deceiving the people, it is likely to finish by deceiving itself." [7] Since there is good evidence that this statement is true, the press, as demonstrated in this chapter, is more than ever essential in its role of disclosing party deceptions, for without such disclosures the vast majority of the public would not long remain free. Unfortunately, men had to suffer before this was generally understood—men like Lyon, Brown, Duane, and Thomas Adams of the *Boston Independent Chronicle*. Adams and his brother, Abijah, refused to be intimidated by their Federalist persecutors, although prison and worse confronted them. Sick and near death, they answered their detractors in double-space, double-measure Caslon bold type: "The Chronicle is destined to persecution. . . . It will stand or fall with the liberties of America, and nothing shall silence its clarion but the extinction of every principle which leads to the achievement of our independence." [8]

---

[7] *The Age of Jackson* (Boston: Little, Brown and Company, 1945), p. 282.

[8] Thomas Adams was the first important editor to be indicted under the Sedition Act. Before he could be tried, he was indicted under the common law for criticising the Massachusetts legislature. He was too sick to stand trial, but his brother, Abijah, was convicted and jailed for a month, although he too was ailing. The defiant Thomas, faced with both federal and state sedition trials, sold the *Chronicle* in May, 1799, two weeks before he died.

ANNOTATED BIBLIOGRAPHY

Books:

Commager, Henry Steele, *Documents of American History*. New York: F. S. Crofts & Company, 1934. An interesting history course could be given with this book as a text. Most of the important documents of American history are described briefly and then are printed in original form, including the Alien and Sedition Acts and the Virginia and Kentucky Resolutions, and the replies to them.

Faÿ, Bernard, *The Two Franklins*. Boston: Little, Brown and Company, 1933. A contrast between Benjamin Franklin and his grandson, Benjamin Franklin Bache.

Miller, John C., *Crisis in Freedom: The Alien and Sedition Acts*. Boston: Little, Brown and Company, 1951. A relatively brief account of passage of the laws and details of the trials.

Nevins, Allan, *American Press Opinion, Washington to Coolidge*. Boston: D. C. Heath and Company, 1928. An excellent selection of the partisan editorials of the period is included.

Smith, James M., *Freedom's Fetters: The Alien and Sedition Laws and American Civil Liberties*. Ithaca, New York: Cornell University Press, 1956. First of a projected two-volume work (the second to deal with the Virginia and Kentucky Resolutions). Detailed and documented analysis of the laws and court cases.

Periodicals and Monographs:

Conway, Moncure D., "An Unpublished Letter of Thomas Paine," *Nation*, LXII (February 6, 1896), 118. Describes French feeling during Washington's administration, and charges the American President with being a hypocrite. Conway is the best known biographer of Paine.

Padover, Saul K., "Wave of the Past," *New Republic*, CXVI (April 21, 1947), 14. A concise description of the effect of the Alien and Sedition laws on the Federalist defeat of 1800.

"Thomas Paine in England and in France," *Atlantic Monthly*, IV (December 1859), 690. Describes the post-Revolutionary influence of Paine, here and abroad.

Chapter 9

THE PRESS AND THE
EXPANDING NATION

> I have lent myself willingly as the subject of a
> great experiment . . . to demonstrate the false-
> hood of the pretext that freedom of the press is
> incompatible with orderly government.
> —Jefferson to Seymour

JEFFERSON'S VICTORY IN 1800 made his party subject to
the same type of attack that had so recently been launched against
the Federalists while they were in power. The Jeffersonian "Republicans" had gained control of the administration, but the President
estimated that up to three-fifths of the editors continued to support
Federalist policies. In some areas Federalist newspapers outnumbered their political rivals by as much as five to one. The rank and
file voter was not impressed by this "one-party" press, apparently,
for he continued to return to office a long succession of candidates
representing the Republican party (as the Anti-Federalists became
known before eventually adopting the name, Democratic party).

The disparity between public and editorial opinion in the periods of Jefferson, Jackson, and even in the administration of Franklin D. Roosevelt, has concerned students of our press. They point
to the occasions when overwhelming popular mandates coincided
with preponderant press opposition to the popular cause, and critics sometimes wonder if the American press is the power the jour-

165

nalists say it is. This history will indicate that the power of the press is not in its persuasion by opinion, but in its dissemination of information and its arousal of interest in important issues hitherto submerged in public apathy.

One of the important Federalist organs was founded by Alexander Hamilton a year after the defeat of his party in 1800. The Federalist leader believed that a reputable party paper was needed more than ever to stem the tide of Republican popularity. This was the *New York Evening Post,* destined to become the city's oldest newspaper. Hamilton chose William Coleman as the first editor. Coleman was a lawyer and former court reporter, again indicating the trend of journalism since the days when the printer-editor was the rule. He was an able editor, but while "The General," as Hamilton liked to be called, was around, it was plain to all that Coleman was subordinate in the office.

Coleman was a writer of some literary pretensions. He could express his convictions in a slashing style that often cut down wavering opposition within and without the party. He also had great personal charm and courage. Eventually, he broke with Hamilton because of Coleman's loyalty to Aaron Burr,[1] but in the founding days of the *Post,* Coleman did not make an editorial move without consulting his sponsor. It is significant that Coleman was a shorthand expert, and that was one reason he had been selected by Hamilton. Late at night Coleman could have been seen in the empty streets hurrying to the home of the Federalists' great leader to take dictation for the next day's editorial. These editorials needed no reworking. They were the work of Hamilton at his journalistic best. Picked up by Federalist editors around the country, they exerted an important party influence.

The victorious party in 1800 needed opposition, as does any party in power. Jefferson had committed himself frequently as a believer in press freedom. His party had fought against the Alien and Sedition Acts in accordance with this doctrine. He had sponsored and encouraged the Virginia and Kentucky Resolutions as an attack on press restrictions by the Federalists. He had helped Freneau and Thomas Ritchie establish newspapers to help stem the tide of Fed-

---

[1] Coleman was a great admirer of Burr and remained loyal even after Hamilton was killed by Burr in a duel in 1804. By that time the editor of the *Post* was expressing himself independently.

eralist dominance.[2] Now he found himself after the party victory accused of press restrictions by the Federalists. This is a pattern commonly found in the history of American journalism—the reversal of free expression policies, once a group wins power.

Jefferson appears to have been sincere in his defense of a free press. Even when the press humiliated him, he defended its freedom. Wrote Jefferson to his friend, Carrington, in 1787:

> I am persuaded that the good sense of the people will always be found to be the best army. They may be led astray for a moment, but will soon correct themselves. The people are the only censors of their governors; and even their errors will tend to keep these to the true principles of their institution. To punish these errors too severely would be to suppress the only safeguard of the public liberty. The way to prevent these irregular interpositions of the people, is to give them full information of their affairs through the channel of the public papers, and to contrive that those papers should penetrate to the whole mass of the people. The basis of our government being the opinion of the people, the very first object should be to keep that right; and were it left to me to decide whether we should have a government without newspapers, or newspapers without a government, I should not hesitate a moment to prefer the latter.

This part of Jefferson's letter to Carrington is widely quoted. It is bandied about particularly when press moguls fear various degrees of restriction or inconvenience from any quarter. But the second part of Jefferson's letter is not so well known, though it is a qualification essential to the above statement. For the great statesman went on to say:

> But I should mean that every man should receive those papers, and be capable of reading them.

Later, when the Federalist editors had made life miserable for him, he wrote in exasperation to a friend:

> The newspapers of our country by their abandoned spirit of falsehood, have more effectually destroyed the utility of the press than all the shackles devised by Bonaparte.[3]

[2] In 1804 the President helped Thomas Ritchie found the *Richmond Enquirer,* soon the most influential paper in Virginia. Ritchie was political boss of his state, and his views were therefore of significance throughout the South, and were widely reprinted there.

[3] From the *Letters.* The above is quoted from Saul K. Padover, *Thomas Jefferson on Democracy* (New York: Penguin Books, Inc., 1939), pp. 92-3. Copyright 1939, D. Appleton-Century Company, Inc. By permission of the publishers, Appleton-Century-Crofts, Inc., New York.

But that was in 1813, when he was very tired. His more considered views of the vicious opposition press are better summed up in the following letter:

They [Federalists] fill their newspapers with falsehoods, calumnies, and audacities. . . . We are going fairly through the experiment of whether freedom of discussion, unaided by coercion, is not sufficient for the propagation and protection of truth, and for the maintenance of an administration pure and upright in its actions and views. No one ought to feel under this experiment, more than myself. Nero wished all the necks of Rome united in one, that he might sever them at a blow. So our ex-federalists, wishing to have a single representative of all the objects of their hatred, honor me with that post and exhibit against me such atrocities as no nation has ever before heard or endured. I shall protect them in the right of lying and calumniating, and still go on to merit the continuance of it, by pursuing steadily my object of proving that a people, easy in their circumstances as ours are, are capable of conducting themselves under a government founded not in the fears and follies of man, but on his reason, on the predominance of his social over his dissocial passions, so free as to restrain him in no moral right, and so firm as to protect him from every moral wrong, which shall leave him, in short, in possession of all his natural rights.[4]

But although Jefferson's views on the press were well known to his followers, and although he wielded strong control over his party, he could not keep his subordinates from trying to impose restriction on opposition editors, now that the Jeffersonians were in power. Much has been made of this inconsistency. Actually, the victorious Republicans were rather restrained, considering their former persecution. Moreover, the preponderant Federalist press continued to spread vindictive libels against the administration. With Republican victory there came the understandable temptation to even up old scores. Granted all this, however, the prosecutions brought by the Republicans against Federalist editors did not square with the earlier statements regarding freedom of expression in the preceding period.

An example of this vindictiveness was the prosecution of Joseph Dennie for remarks deemed by Republican party leaders to be seditious. Dennie, a grandson of Bartholomew Green, Jr., onetime printer of the *Boston News-Letter*, was one of the ablest editors of his day. His *Farmer's Weekly Museum*, published at Walpole, New

---

[4] To Volney, 1802. New York Public Library, Manuscript II, 199, as reprinted in Padover, *op. cit.*, p. 95.

Hampshire, was so popular that it achieved national recognition. Later, Dennie took over the editorial direction of the *Port Folio*, an outspoken Federalist magazine published in Philadelphia. Shortly after Jefferson moved into the unfinished White House, Dennie wrote a series of editorials pointing out the weaknesses of popular rule. Although he did not attack the American Government specifically, he made it clear that he believed democracy to be futile. These remarks were declared by government officials to be seditious, and the editor was indicted on that charge. After all that Jefferson had written about the press as a rightful censor of its government, the administration action appeared to be highly hypocritical. The jury must have thought so, too, for after a brilliant defense by Joseph Hopkinson, composer of the patriotic song, "Hail, Columbia," Dennie was acquitted.

On the other hand, some measures had to be taken to make vindictive editors more responsible for injuries to public reputations. Jefferson himself declared that for all his love of press freedom, a few convictions for libel might have a salutary effect. He held that this could be done safely by bringing action under the various State laws. In other words, he advocated a "selected" prosecution of notorious and malicious offenders, rather than a wholesale throttling of an opposition press, as the Federalists had imposed under the infamous Sedition Act.

Thus the most celebrated case involving the press during this period was prosecuted under a state law, as recommended by the President. The defendant was Harry Croswell, editor of a Federalist paper at Hudson, New York. Croswell called his little weekly *The Wasp*, and it was an appropriate name. It was so vicious and annoying that respectable Federalists disdained it. *The Wasp* stung political opponents in every column. One day Croswell printed an "exchange" from the *New York Evening Post*, Hamilton's personal mouthpiece. The article reported that Jefferson had paid James Callender, the Richmond editor, to spread the word that George Washington had been a robber, traitor, and perjurer; and that other Federalist leaders were equally reprehensible. This was a serious charge against Jefferson and the dignity of his office. *The Wasp*, rather than the *Post*, was prosecuted because Croswell's paper was the type of scandal sheet Jefferson had in mind when he suggested smoking out the worst of the Federalist editors under State law.

Croswell was indicted in 1804. He was found guilty, but appealed the case. When the trial was called, a titan arose to argue for the defense. He was Alexander Hamilton, Jefferson's arch rival, and more bitter than ever, after the defeat of his party. Hamilton was the most important political figure in the state, whether or not he held office. His words were therefore followed closely. It was acknowledged that he might well "make law" in the celebrated case. The transcript of the proceedings has been lost, but Hamilton's notes indicate that this was one of the greatest speeches of his entire career.

The four judges listened with obvious respect as the brilliant pleader stated a principle as applicable today as it was in 1804. The press, Hamilton argued, had "the right to publish with impunity truth, with good motives, for justifiable ends, though reflecting on Government, Magistracy, or individuals." Since the "good motives" and "justifiable ends" would have to be disproved by the complainant, Hamilton was essentially saying that truth, and truth alone, was a defense in a libel action. In his arguments against the need for a Bill of Rights covering press freedom, Hamilton had not appeared as very sympathetic to the cause of liberty of written expression. But when he stood up at the Croswell trial and insisted upon the "right" of submitting truth as a full defense, Hamilton won his place alongside the great fighters for press freedom.

True, Hamilton had much to win in advocating this right. Presentation of the truth in the Croswell case might have disgraced the President and might have helped return the Federalists to power. The Federalist leader had every reason to believe that Callender's charges against Jefferson were true. The situation was as follows:

Callender was one of the Republican editors who suffered at the hands of the Federalists during the so-called "reign of terror" under the Sedition Act of 1798. His insolence and viciousness cannot be defended, but even so, he was treated badly by the Federalist judge who found him guilty under the law. Callender was sentenced to jail. He was released and given a full pardon when Jefferson was elected in the political revolution of 1800. Callender was not satisfied with mere vindication, however. He insisted on a reward, or balm, for his sacrifices, proving, as Jefferson had suspected all along, that he was not a man of principle, but a seeker of special favors. The editor demanded an appointment as postmaster of Richmond.

When it was refused, he turned vindictively against Jefferson and thereby offered his services to the Federalists, who were eager to "get the goods" on the President. Unfortunately for Jefferson, Callender had it within his power to make trouble, and a skillful politician like Hamilton could make much of the evidence offered by the editor.

When the shoddy Callender was poor and unknown, he had written a series of essays entitled, "The Political Progress of Britain." Jefferson had seen the series, as reprinted in a Philadelphia newspaper. He inquired about the author and discovered that Callender was actually living in the city, then the capital of the new nation. He had been driven from Richmond by his Federalist enemies and was literally starving. Always a friend of scholars in distress, Jefferson gave Callender a little money. On other occasions the great statesman made other contributions to Callender's precarious income, usually upon the pleas of the editor's friends. Once, for example, Jefferson advanced $50 to Callender for an inferior history of the country that Callender was writing. It was understood that the money would pay for as many copies of the book as the author could print for that amount. These payments to the impecunious Callender had become so common that a jury might well be convinced that there was some kind of contract between the two. A man like Hamilton could easily make it appear as though Callender had smeared Federalist leaders at the instigation of his generous patron.

There is no proof, however, that Jefferson was guilty of the charge made by Callender—that he was paid by the President to defame such heroes as Washington, John Adams, and others. He denied that he had ever stooped to writing strongly partisan public letters while serving as a key executive in the Washington and Adams administrations. That was more than could be said of Hamilton. Nevertheless, the Croswell case provided opportunities for the Federalist leader to embarrass his old rival, and Hamilton made the most of them. It is significant that an election was in the offing. That was another reason for using the Callender charges for all they were worth. But regardless of motives, Hamilton's defense of Croswell, and his establishment of truth as a defense in a seditious libel action was a milestone in the progress of a free press in this country.

It so happened that Hamilton lost the case, when the four judges were evenly divided in their opinions. The New York state laws still adhered to the old policy, "the greater the truth, the greater the libel." Truth had been recognized as a defense in the Sedition Act, but the law had lapsed four years before, and the precedent had not been accepted in the courts. Hamilton also insisted on the right of a jury to determine both the law and the fact. Both issues had been raised in the Zenger case, but only in Pennsylvania had they been recognized in law (in 1790).

The significance of the Croswell trial can be seen in legislation immediately following Hamilton's plea. Even before the judges had handed down the verdict, a bill was engrossed in the New York Legislature providing that truth thereafter was to be admitted in defense. The same bill gave the jury the right to determine both the law and the fact. By 1805, these principles had become law in New York—70 years after Zenger's trial. Soon other states followed suit and the shadow of the British common law of seditious libel was lifted. In 1812 the Supreme Court held that the federal government could not prosecute under the old common law.

The great pioneer in press freedom did not live to see his eventual triumph; ironically, it was another libel episode that brought about Hamilton's violent death. A remark attributed to Hamilton which appeared in an Albany newspaper while the Croswell case was being tried angered New York's second most imposing political figure—Aaron Burr. Burr's prestige was by this time slipping, which probably made him especially sensitive to insults, real or imagined. He challenged Hamilton to a duel. Hamilton might have declined with no great blackening of his honor, but he accepted the gage. On July 11, 1804, his seconds rowed him across the Hudson river to the grassy bank near Weehawken where his son had been killed in a duel several months before. Burr was an expert marksman, and in the exchange of shots he wounded Hamilton so critically that the great leader died the next day. If Hamilton had contributed nothing else in his life except his successful battle for a freer press, he would still be remembered.

By the end of Jefferson's second administration, the American press was growing so fast that it sometimes appeared to be too big for its breeches. There was some technical progress. Both Adam

Ramage and the Earl of Stanhope produced improved presses that were available in the United States after 1800. The latter was the first to use iron for construction. A little later George Clymer abandoned the screw platen for the compound lever that speeded the "pull" or impression. The Washington hand press, which was in general use before 1830, exceeded all others in efficiency and speed, thanks to an ingenious toggle, or knuckle, that transferred pressure from the lever quickly, and with less effort. Steam power had been applied to presses in Europe as early as 1811, but power presses were not generally available in America for another generation.

The greatest strides were made in the non-technical areas. In the first two decades of the nineteenth century the number of both daily and weekly publications increased rapidly. By the time Andrew Jackson was elected in 1828, the United States had more newspapers and more readers of newspapers than any other country in the world. The development of the daily paper was significant of this growth.

The first daily newspaper in America was established by Benjamin Towne at Philadelphia in 1783. His *Pennsylvania Evening Post* was as characterless as its publisher. Towne was a patriot in 1776, and was one of the first to print the Declaration of Independence for the public. Later, he became a Tory. After the surrender he confessed his sins and resumed a partial state of grace in his community. However his shoddy little daily lasted only 17 months.

It was succeeded by a very good daily, the *Pennsylvania Packet and Daily Advertiser*, published by the partnership of John Dunlap and David C. Claypoole. Like the *Evening Post* owned by Towne, the *Packet* was originally a weekly publication that had been founded by Dunlap in 1771. Switching from triweekly to daily status in 1784, the Dunlap and Claypoole venture was successful from the beginning.

By 1800, most big ports and commercial centers were supporting daily papers. Philadelphia had six; New York, five; Baltimore, three; and Charleston, two. But for some curious reason Boston, the home of the American newspaper, had no daily paper at this time. Many of these publications had been forced into the daily field to meet the competition of the coffeehouses, where the London papers were available, and where news was freely exchanged. The American journalists met the challenge by issuing first semiweekly, then triweekly, and finally daily editions containing commercial information not elsewhere readily obtained.

Philadelphia even had an all-day newspaper for a time. It was the *New World*, published by Samuel Harrison Smith in morning and evening editions. It was not successful, but it indicated the growing interest in fresh news presentation. Of 512 papers being printed in 1820, 24 were dailies, 66 were semiweeklies or triweeklies, and 422 were weeklies. They were still gene*r*ally slanted toward the more prosperous citizen, for the price was more than the average man could afford. Circulations were not impressive, either, by present standards. A circulation of 1,500 was considered adequate in all but the largest centers. But because the bulk of circulation was among the prosperous class who tended to gravitate to the conservative political party, most editors patterned their products accordingly. With the rising pressure of the masses for greater political recognition, the pages of these papers began to be filled more and more with political information and opinion.

In the hinterlands the press was also booming. The number of newspapers beyond the urban fringe increased six-fold during this period.[5] Advertising helped to support this newspaper boom. For although most families tended to buy their supplies in wholesale lots for seasonal storage, there was already some development of the retail trade that was to sustain the press in later years.

The development of the postal system also accounted for some of this press expansion. By postal acts of 1782 and 1792, educational and informational matter could be mailed at very low rates. For many years newspapers sent from one office to another could be mailed free of postage. In a day when distant newspapers served as the only means of obtaining outside information, legislators believed this subsidy of the press by the government was a sound educational and civic investment. It has been estimated that about half the population read nothing else but newspapers. If circulations of local papers were small, partly because of cost to the reader, and partly because of mechanical limitations, it could also be added that such figures did not represent the true reader-inter-

[5] Most of the newspaper figures and comments in this section are based on Clarence S. Brigham, *History and Bibliography of American Newspapers, 1690-1820,* 2 vols. (Worcester, Massachusetts: American Antiquarian Society, 1947).

est. For at a time when the newspaper provided much of the entertainment later provided by national magazines, movies, radio, and television, each edition in most cases was read "cover to cover," not only by the entire family, but by neighbors and friends as well. This period sees the beginning of the editorial, as we know it today. Up to that time, the standard non-news material was usually in the form of an essay. Often these were contributions from interested readers, who usually signed a pen-name, such as "Publius," "Coriolanus," "Vindictus," or just "Old Soldier." The style tended to be florid and wordy. The papers in the big cities often printed pamphlets concerned with political and social issues, and these were offered to readers through the paper. By 1800, editors had begun to see the value of short but complete summaries of controversial issues. By 1815, the day of the pamphlet had very nearly passed, and the editorial had supplanted it. This was a noticeable development. Visitors to this country were impressed with the virility of newspaper opinion. Men of ability began to specialize in this type of journalism. Expression of opinion was the freest in the world. Nowhere else was there such violent criticism of government, and such pitiless discussion of officials usually treated with the utmost respect in other countries.

The expansion of the press reflected the spirit of the country. It had taken 150 years to settle the seaboard colonies, and on the basis of the past record, it should have taken another 200 years to push the frontier to the Mississippi river. But once the Appalachian mountains were conquered, the lands to the west were rapidly taken up. Jefferson, who had always opposed national imperialism, had a chance in 1803 to purchase the vast Louisiana territory, and the bargain was too good to turn down out of principle. When this domain was added to the United States as a vast territory for exploitation, settlers poured in from the East. In time, these fertile prairies were to call millions of oppressed people from overcrowded European countries, who were to make America the great melting pot, and who would some day become an important factor in our social development, but when the lands were first opened up, most of the settlements were offshoots of seaboard communities. The lust for western lands is indicated by the numerous petitions for statehood during this period. Between 1790 and 1820, nine new States were admitted to the Union.

The waterways were the highways into these frontier regions. Along the Ohio, the Kanawha, and the Cumberland, tiny communities began to appear that would some day become teeming cities. By present standards they were mere hamlets, but each served a wide trading area. They were thus far more important as markets and social centers than their populations would indicate. If they were county seats, with courts, law enforcing agencies, and land offices, they were even more important. And usually one of the first to set up shop in such communities was the frontier printer-editor. He was the enthusiastic promoter of the village that he was certain would one day rival London. He was a leading business man. But most of all he was the man, who more than anyone else, knit the community into an organization that could begin to bring civilization to the remote areas. On flat boats and on ox carts he brought his few cases of type and his printing furniture. The local carpenter and blacksmith might help to install the primitive hand press, but sometimes he did that work, too. And not long after the main street began to take form, according to the plats in the surveyor's office, the first edition of the *Argus, Gazette, Gem of the Prairie*—or whatever its name—was ready to serve the various interests so interdependent in the midst of a savage country.

The first newspaper west of the mountains was John Scull's venture of 1786, the *Pittsburgh Gazette,* still thriving as the *Post-Gazette.* A year later, John Bradford, who bore a name well known in the printing industry, although he was only indirectly related to the famous Philadelphia publishing family, set up his shop in Lexington, Kentucky. His *Kentucky Gazette* might have been the first paper in the West, had his equipment not been wrecked in transit the year before the establishment of the Pittsburgh enterprise. The Ohio river was the most important artery of commerce in this early period, but there were also important settlements along the Wabash, and where lesser streams, such as the Muskingum, Scioto, Maumee, and Cuyahoga, opened up avenues to the hinterland. By 1800, 21 newspapers had been started west of the mountains.

There was little local news in these early frontier newspapers, for like the first of the colonial publications, content was lifted from the papers back home. Advertising was rarely adequate to support the new business, but fortunately there needed to be some means of publishing legal information in this new area, and that was often sufficient inducement to start up a paper. Elihu Stout, for example, himself poled up the Wabash with his press to found the *Indiana Gazette* at Vincennes in 1804. He had been induced to give up his business in Frankfort, Kentucky, on the promise that he would be awarded the territorial legal printing contract, which was enough of a stake for him to establish a paper.

The northern route to the frontier was along the Mohawk valley, straight across New York state from the Hudson river. This was the route of the Erie Canal, which was soon to make New York City the largest metropolis in the land, but even before that, it was an important highway. At the end of the valley, the Great Lakes served as transportation and communication routes between the vast wilderness and the East. Detroit, one of the outer bastions of the frontier then, had a newspaper, the *Gazette*, by 1817. Soon other communities in the area could boast the same. A Congressional Act of 1814 provided that all federal laws must be printed in two (later, three) newspapers in each state and territory. This was a logical way of letting electors know what their representatives were doing, but it also encouraged the founding of pioneer papers in communities not quite ready to support such ventures.[6]

By the end of the first decade of the nineteenth century, the western press was lusty and influential. Editors began to depend less on "exchanges" and to speak out for themselves on matters pertinent to readers. Editors and politicians who understood their constituencies saw that the region had its special problems. They tended to side with the Jeffersonians on the rights of the common man, but their dependence upon the federal government for defense of their sparse settlements against the Indian threat made them favor strong, centralized administration. After General "Mad Anthony" Wayne defeated a great Indian army at Fallen Timbers, just south of the site of Toledo, Ohio, the federal forces kept the savages at bay. The treaty forced upon the Indians by the hero of Stony Point in 1795 saved the eastern and southern sections of the territory from the blood bath of the earlier Kentucky and Tennessee pioneers.

[6] Regulations such as this and the law requiring publication at state cost of letters uncalled for at the post office were also a means of rewarding pro-administration editors. As administrations changed, political rivals found ready-made organs of expression.

The new states also turned to the federal government for the development of transportation, so essential to their growth and prosperity. Again, the great land companies, organized to promote colonization at a profit, were dependent upon the national administrations, rather than upon the territorial or parent-state politicians. There was a tendency, then, for the westerner to demand local and statewide autonomy to work out the destiny he believed to be peculiar to his region, but he was less touchy about state sovereignty because of his need of strong, centralized government. He insisted upon solid representation in the administration of that government, as indicated by the impatience of territories for statehood. But he visualized that government as a kind of public service corporation, not a dispenser of privileges for the wealthy and powerful. Timothy Dwight, president of Yale, and a spiritual leader of the extreme Federalists, charged that the settlers who left their Connecticut employers to develop the lands of the "Western Reserve" of that state were nothing but anarchists. He believed them to be too uncouth for serious consideration.

Men like Timothy Dwight could never understand that a people who had to depend upon the knife and rifle for livelihood were uncouth not so much by choice as by circumstance. There were drunkards and cut-throats and outlaws in the wilderness, of course, for the frontier is always both a haven and an opportunity for such persons. But the average pioneer was not of that stripe. Nor was he necessarily the hero he has been made out to be by the historians who make tin gods of all American character-types. Quite possibly he came to the frontier because he was restless, poorly adjusted in his community, dissatisfied with his lot, or downright incompetent. But he could not have stuck out the rigors of frontier life without courage, and his desire to be a man of property and a freeholder was commendable. The men and women who settled the new West raised large families, and they were eager to bring education to the areas. Under the Northwest Ordinances, land was set aside to be sold for educational revenue, and the pattern was generally followed in other areas. Despite graft and corruption in the sale of such land, education was encouraged. There were six universities in the new West by the end of the first decade, and many a small community supported an "academy" or seminary, conducted sometimes under denominational direction. Even in the backwoods, there was this passion for learning, as evidenced by the careers of future statesmen, such as Lincoln.

Slavery was forbidden by law in some areas, but in any case was uneconomical in a frontier society. That, too, was to have an influence. Industry was virtually non-existent, and the agrarian debtor soon developed an antipathy to his industrial, creditor neighbors of the Northeast. At this point the eastern Federalist and the western farmer, both of whom believed in a strong, centralized government, parted political company but more of that later. Suffrage was likely to be broader than in the more settled regions; property might be a voting requisite, but it was easy to acquire.

The West was to have a profound influence upon the development of the new nation. The importance of that influence has been disputed since Professor Frederick Jackson Turner suggested that the frontier was a political and social laboratory which had produced a distinctive American character.[7] His studies had convinced him that climate alone had as much to do with political traditions as established philosophies. He argued that regions, rather than boundaries, identified peoples. Weather might be responsible for great social change. A severe drought in a wheat area might cause a migration to more prosperous communities. Turner pointed out that the poor and underprivileged were more interested in popular rule than were the wealthy, because it gave them a chance to even

[7] For other evidence for the Turner thesis see Walter Prescott Webb, *The Great Plains* (Boston: Ginn and Company, 1931). Webb later went so far as to apply the Turner theory to world history. See his "Ended: The Four Hundred Year Boom," *Harper's*, CCIII (October 1951), 25. Other authorities have argued against the Turner thesis. Professor Fred Shannon of the University of Illinois took apart Webb's *Great Plains* line by line to show what he believed to be the fallacies of the thesis. Louis Hacker also argued persuasively against the Turner school of history. Other able historians, while denying the details of Turner's evidence, subscribe at least to the philosophy of Turner, which was to make history more scientific in approach by testing various hypotheses. Finally, there is another group of authorities which has remained loyal to Turner's teachings. In substantiation of the Turner thesis see his own *The Significance of Sections in American History* (New York: Henry Holt and Company, 1933); Joseph Schafer, "Turner's America," *Wisconsin Magazine of History*, XVII (June 1934), 448; and Webb's answer to Professor Shannon in "Critiques of Research in the Social Sciences," *Social Science Research Council Bulletin*, No. 46 (New York: The Council, 1940). Some of the objections to the Turner thesis are expressed by Fred A. Shannon in the same issue of the *Bulletin*, pp. 1-106; and by Louis M. Hacker, "Sections or Classes," *Nation*, CXXXVII (July 26, 1933), 108.

up the opportunities. Carried to its conclusion, the Turner theory would hold that "radicalism" is only the political expression of economic maladjustment. Those who are satisfied do not desire change or experimentation. But the men and women who moved across the mountains usually accepted the perils and discomforts of pioneer life because they were dissatisfied with the older community life.[8] On the frontier these pioneers lived roughly and dangerously. When people suffer and face dangers together, they tend to act together, regardless of past background, customs, privileges, or attitudes. Such people begin to make demands. They blame those in control for failing to consider their problems. When they become strong enough politically and economically, they tend to force the older society to adopt measures that have proved to be effective under the exacting tests of the wilderness. Thus, the frontier has been responsible for much of the social and political experimentation that helped to distinguish the American character and organization, the Turner school maintains.

The War of 1812 will serve as an example of how the frontier had come to influence American thought and politics. This disgraceful conflict reflects little credit on either of the belligerents. We do not like to be reminded of General William Hull's abject surrender to an inferior British and Indian force at Detroit, or the burning of our national capitol. There were heroic episodes, too, such as Commodore Oliver Hazard Perry's useless naval victory on Lake Erie; [9] the courageous, but futile, sea battles of American naval vessels and privateersmen against the world's greatest sea power; and General Andrew Jackson's victory at New Orleans, two weeks after the peace had been signed at Ghent.[10] But for better or for

---

[8] Studies have shown that by no means all of the pioneers were of this type. It took some capital to head west, otherwise the slums would have been the reservoirs of the frontier society, which they were not. But dissatisfaction can take many forms, and the statement would appear to be true, in general.

[9] A useless victory, because the armies to be supplied by the Great Lakes route, such as Hull's command, were ineffective by the time Commodore Perry cleared the enemy from the lake.

[10] The treaty was signed December 24, 1814. Jackson won his remarkable victory January 8, 1815, before news of the peace negotiations reached this country. The treaty specified that the official end of hostilities would await ratification by the respective governments. The war did not actually end until the middle of February, and as a result, many Americans believed that Jackson's victory had much to do with the successful negotiations.

worse, the force of public opinion in the West was largely responsible for that war.

Generations of Americans believed that the War of 1812 resulted from American resentment over British abuses of free transit on the high seas, and the "impressment," or forcible return, of former British naval ratings by methods insulting to our national pride. If these were major causes for war, then New England should have been preponderantly in favor of the conflict. The big shipping interests were centered in that area, and the commercial interests there suffered most from British naval arrogance. The fact is, New Englanders emphatically voiced disapproval of the war. It was the West that forced military action. Western newspapers offer the evidence on this point.

In 1810 the Indians went on the warpath under a great leader and statesman, Tecumseh, and his brother, Teuskwatawa, "The Prophet." Frontiersmen discovered that the savages were killing Americans with weapons supplied by the British through Canada. The glazed powder found on prisoners was the proof of this charge, for only from the British was this obtainable. Because the Indians were a serious problem in the West, frontiersmen insisted on direct action. They argued that "you can't get rid of the rattlesnakes until you find the den," and the den they sought was in Canada.

The leaders of the West were in favor of war to settle the dispute. These were the men who became known as the "War Hawks." They were not interested in the plight of the seamen, or the Napoleonic blockades, or the shipping embargoes imposed by the United States to boycott the arrogant Europeans at such great sacrifice to the commercial interests. It is significant that Henry Clay, perhaps the most vehement of the War Hawks, was elected Speaker of the House by the western bloc.

And poor Madison, best known for his constructive contributions to the American experiment, found himself in the role of a war President, thanks to the pressure of western public opinion. Clay controlled enough votes by 1812 to swing the election against Madison, if that great American did not go along with the War Hawks. Madison's opponent, Governor DeWitt Clinton of New York, was opposed to war, so the issue was clear in 1812. It was Madison and war, or Clinton and peace. Thus, it is easy to read the influence of the West by examining the records. The electoral vote of the Northeast, where the shipping and commercial men were important, was unanimous for Clinton and peace. Madison, who was presented to the voters as protector of the shipping interests, received not a single vote from the electors of New England. But the electoral vote of the West was unanimous for Madison and war. The middle and southern states were more evenly divided, but there was enough war sentiment in those areas to endorse the western stand, and from then on, it was "Mr. Madison's War."

It was clear that politicians thenceforth would have to regard the West with new respect. Soon this power was to be used in a much more significant manner, leading to the rise of the common man. The flimsy little weeklies of the isolated villages and booming river towns had much to do in the crystallization of public opinion that made the West a new factor in American politics. Typical of such publications was the *Argus of Western America,* at Frankfort, Kentucky. This was a scrappy, articulate, and at times profane little sheet that was soon one of the most quoted and influential organs of the region. Its editors were destined not only to help develop public opinion in the West at a critical time, but to have considerable direct influence at the top levels of government following the pending Jacksonian revolution. These two lieutenants of General Jackson, himself the very embodiment of "the western character," were Amos Kendall and Francis P. Blair.

What were they like, these newspapers that exerted such influence in the West? They were small, hand-set, scrubby publications, on the whole. It is apparent that there was no place on them for large staffs, regular correspondents, or columnists furnishing opinions for readers too busy to form their own. There was plenty of opinion, of course, but most of it was contributed by readers. Usually there was a column or two of local news, printed sometimes as scattered items, without benefit of headlines. There might be half a column of exchanges, or news gleaned from other newspapers arrived by the last post. The remaining material, exclusive of the notices, or advertisements, was very likely submitted by readers. Every subscriber who could wield a pen sooner or later appeared in the columns. All the aggrieved wrote out their pet complaints for the pages of the local mercury. Even government officials participated in this exchange, not always openly, true, but with sufficient identity to warrant spirited replies. Often this material was strident and in

ARGUS OF WESTERN AMERICA.

umber 39.]   FRANKFORT, KENTUCKY, WEDNESDAY, NOVEMBER 17, 1824   [Volume XVII.]

An example of the frontier newspaper that was influential in politics of the early nineteenth century. The *Argus*, published in Frankfort, Kentucky, had as onetime editors Amos Kendall, later President Jackson's postmaster general and "Kitchen Cabinet" leader, and Francis P. Blair, journalistic spokesman for "Old Hickory."

bad taste. "Straight news" tended toward distortion, flamboyance, and vindictiveness. But whatever its faults, it was a robust, colorful press. The great French observer, de Tocqueville, described the institution at a somewhat later period, but his remarks then were pertinent to this decade. He was impressed by the virility of the American press even while repelled by its provincialism. Western crudeness shocked him, but he was amazed at the success of the democratic experiment, and he conceded that the press had been an important implement in this development. De Tocqueville found a close relationship between the press and its public, fostered, no doubt, by the active participation of readers in the local journalistic effort. The public appeared to respect the Fourth Estate, he reported, and this was manifest in the great freedom accorded the institution.

As in most wars, the press suffered to some extent in the 1812 period. The most notorious attempt to muzzle an editor was in Baltimore, a shipping center with a strong faction opposed to administration war policies. Especially critical of the President was the *Federal Republican*, published by Jacob Wagner and Alexander Hanson. Some of their statements, made while an enemy was threatening our shores, no doubt merited censorship, but the party of Madison, which had fought so valiantly for press freedom since the days of the Sedition Act, could not take action against such publications without repudiating cherished principles.

Factions in the public were not so restrained, however. One night a mob wrecked the *Federal Republican* building and press. Hanson and Wagner were not present and probably owed their lives to this circumstance. They had been warned away by John Howard Payne, composer of "Home, Sweet Home," who urged the journalists to fight on. They set up another press, and knowing they would be mobbed again, they stocked the building with food and barricaded themselves against assault.

Following the next issue of the paper, which accused the President of perfidy and worse, editors and contributors of the paper were charged by the opposition as traitors, although two of the besieged staff members were Generals James Lingan and "Light Horse Harry" Lee, heroes of the War of Independence. When the mob descended on the office, the journalists held out until the irate citizens set up a cannon to blow the building down. At this point cooler heads negotiated a truce, including safe conduct of the besieged to the jail for protection. After the mob destroyed the press and building, its leaders ordered an assault on the jail. Some of the prisoners escaped, but nine were beaten and thrown to the mob. General Lingan was killed. General Lee was maimed for life.

Foes tried to blame the administration for this attack on press freedom. The critics apparently did not try to distinguish between the patterns of press persecution under the Federalists and Anti-Federalists, which formed the background of the dispute. Persecution of men like Matthew Lyon under the Sedition Act was deliberate. It was endorsed by party officials, prescribed by law, and upheld by courts. The attack on the *Federal Republican* was conducted in the heat of passion, not under a federal act. It was promoted neither by law nor by officials of the party. If foolish editors in wartime goaded a hysterical public into violent action, that was up to them, but it could not be said that there was any repudiation of Jeffersonian principles.

The wonder is that more Federalist editors were not held up to scorn. It was one thing to criticise administration policy in peacetime, but another to condemn the government while the enemy was threatening our shores. Even such a reputable Federalist as Major Benjamin Russell of the *Columbian Centinel* in Boston appeared to be more interested in administration discomfiture than in British defeat. Major Russell was a spearhead of New England hostility to a government desperately waging a war. There was actually a revolt in the area against continuing the war, and Russell went so far as to endorse a movement for the secession of his region from the rest of the Union.[11] During the dark days of 1814 a group of disgruntled New Englanders met at Hartford to discuss withdrawal from the Federal Union and perhaps return to British sovereignty. If this was not treason, while the British were pillaging our shores, at least one can scarcely blame members of Madison's party for feeling so bitter toward journalistic spokesmen of the Federalists. In the end, the Hartford Convention fizzled out as a mere rebuke of the administration, but that was only because the war was about over. It should be pointed out, however, that the South was not the first to advocate secession from the Union. Major Russell must have known the ultimate purpose of the Hartford Convention, but

---

[11] *Columbian Centinel*, January 13, 1813.

possible secession did not worry him. In a series of cartoons, reminiscent of his campaign during the ratification of the Constitution, he indicated his sympathy with the Hartford scheme. The cartoons showed a number of fallen pillars labeled with the names of the New England states. As each agreed to send delegates to the Hartford Convention, these pillars were raised into position.

By the election of 1816, which put James Monroe into office with no opposition from the Federalists, much of the wartime rancor appeared to be dying out. On the surface, the country seemed to enjoy peace and prosperity. There was a kind of political truce while the forces re-aligned themselves. "The era of good feeling," Major Russell called it.[12] Actually, partisan rivalry had been substituted by other controversies. Sectional and economic disputes were soon to resound, but between 1816 and 1820 some of the former bitter factionalism disappeared. As a result, it was a dull period, journalistically speaking.

The most important press development at this time was in government reporting. The right to report meetings of interest to the general public is one of the tests of a free press, by the English-American concept. Reporters had access to the national House of Representatives from April 8, 1789, two days after it was established. For a time the Senate was more secretive, since it excluded not only reporters, but also members of the House, from its debates. By December 9, 1795, the Senate had completed a gallery for reporters, however. When the capital was transferred from New York to Philadelphia, the gallery was too far from the rostrum for the reporters to hear clearly, but on January 2, 1802, the Senate (now in Washington) voted the reporters access to the floor. There was some squabbling between reporters and the House over arrangements. In Philadelphia, reporters were assigned "four seats on the window sill," and in Washington, after some agitation, they won the right to report the debates.[13]

[12] One of Russell's many colorful phrases, which were widely quoted. Another had its birth in 1812, when a man named Gerry was governor. The Republican legislature of Massachusetts had divided a political district into a weird shape in order to gain voting power. According to one account, Gilbert Stuart called Russell's attention to the new district's resemblance to a salamander. "Better say a Gerrymander!" replied the Federalist editor, although in truth the governor had had no part in the original "gerrymandering."

[13] See Elizabeth Gregory McPherson, "Reporting the Debates of Congress," *Quarterly Journal of Speech*, XXVIII (April 1942), pp. 141-8.

One of the most effective reports of government was provided by the *National Intelligencer,* an outstanding newspaper of the period. Its founder was Samuel Harrison Smith, only 28 when Jefferson induced him to give up a promising publishing venture in Philadelphia to start a newspaper in the new capital at Washington. The President was head of the learned American Philosophical Society of Philadelphia (founded by Franklin), and Smith had been secretary of the organization. Jefferson was much impressed with the young man. The *National Intelligencer* soon became the semiofficial organ of the administration, but it served papers of all factions outside Washington with its remarkably objective reporting of Congressional debates.

Smith retired from the paper in 1810, but his work was carried on ably by the partners who succeeded him, Joseph Gales, Jr., and William W. Seaton. One reported proceedings in the House, while the other covered the Senate. Both were experts in a recently-perfected shorthand technique, and they were able to offer complete, accurate reports of the debates. Actually, they served as the semiofficial recorders of Congress, until the *Congressional Globe,* predecessor of the *Congressional Record,* was established in 1834. Gales and Seaton made the *National Intelligencer* a daily when they assumed control (it had been a triweekly up to then). It is gratifying to learn that the paper was a success, financially and editorially, proving that a newspaper did not have to be partisan, noisy, or scandalous to meet competition.

But the *National Intelligencer* was not typical of the press of the "era of good feeling." Few other newspapers won historical recognition at this time. On the other hand, there was an interesting development in the magazine field during the period. Efforts to publish magazines had been made occasionally since 1741, when Benjamin Franklin was thwarted in his plans by Andrew Bradford, who published the first periodical three days before Franklin's magazine appeared.

Five magazines were established in the Revolutionary period. By that time there was some indication that the magazine might one day be self-supporting. It was the *Pennsylvania Magazine,* published in Philadelphia by Robert Aitken, that offered the American public its first taste of Tom Paine. This periodical was well edited. It was full of interesting political information, literary contributions of good quality, and discussions of important issues. Eventually it failed, but it showed that the magazine had possibilities. Isaiah Thomas, Joseph Greenleaf, and H. H. Brackenridge, able editors and publishers of the Revolutionary period, also produced monthly and quarterly publications, which might very well have succeeded under less unstable circumstances. Unfortunately, the country was still too unsettled for such undertakings. This picture was changed by improvements in education, transportation, communication, by territorial printing contracts, and by higher per capita wealth.

An interesting publication started in the period of the party press was the *Farmer's Weekly Museum,* printed at Walpole, on the New Hampshire side of the Connecticut river. Founded by Isaiah Thomas, who retained his interest in it, it gained its greatest fame under the same Joseph Dennie who later got into trouble for his attacks on democracy printed in the *Port Folio,* during Jefferson's first administration. Dennie was so witty, critical, and readable that his paper was in demand all over the nation. It was actually a forerunner of the news magazine.

Other magazines at the end of the eighteenth century are now valuable sources of information for the historian. The *Columbian Magazine,* founded in 1786, was elaborately illustrated (with copperplate engravings), thus pointing the way to the picture magazine. Mathew Carey's *American Museum,* founded a year later, was the best-edited periodical of its day, according to Frank Luther Mott, the leading authority on magazine history in this country. It has been a mine of information on political, social and economic history for students of the period. Some issues ran to more than a hundred pages.

The war with Britain ended in 1815, but magazines of that period continued to present views both favorable and unfavorable to the British. One of the anti-British publications was the *North American Review,* founded in 1815 under the auspices of the Anthology Club of Boston. It became a quarterly after three years as a bimonthly magazine, and was published until 1940. It was closely associated with Harvard, after its first few years. Jared Sparks and Edward Everett, foremost scholars of the day, were regular contributors. Although circulation was small, the magazine was read by thoughtful men and women who wielded influence in their communities.

Mott estimates that several hundred quarterly, monthly, and

weekly magazines were printed at one time or another in the first third of the nineteenth century. Most of them have long since been forgotten. One that deserves special mention, however, was *Niles' Weekly Register*. Edited by Hezekiah Niles, a printer with common sense, integrity, and a flare for concise reporting on current trends, the *Register* is known to every historian of the period. It was published in Baltimore, but was read in every state in the Union. The *Register* was the early-nineteenth-century equivalent of the modern news magazine. Niles started his publication in 1811. There was a minimum of opinion in it at first. Most of the material was a weekly roundup of speeches, important documents, and statements of leaders everywhere concerning current problems. Niles was an objective journalist. He was conservative in his views but he was also honest in his evaluation of events. Thus, both sides of a controversy found space in the *Register,* and the material was indexed for ready reference, much to the delight of the later researchers.

It is interesting to note that Niles also published a newspaper in Baltimore. As E. L. Godkin was to do later in the century, he went into the magazine field because he saw the need of a supplementary journalism. In his newspaper, Niles kept his hand on the public pulse and kept his community informed of day-to-day happenings and the significance of local events. In his magazine he analyzed trends and reported events of a more general nature. The *Register* appealed to serious, thoughtful readers. Curiously, it was the strong influence of the *Register* which led to its demise in 1849. Apparently so many newspaper publishers had seen the value of Niles' contribution, that there was no longer a need for the *Register*. But in a way, the *Register* never did die. Its files were so important to historians that the entire publication has been reprinted, issue by issue, for libraries all over the world needing an authoritative chronicle of the first half of the nineteenth century. Probably no day passes without some researcher digging into the information supplied with so much care and responsibility by Hezekiah Niles, a journalist who deserves the honorable recognition of his craft.

ANNOTATED BIBLIOGRAPHY

Books:

Adams, Henry, *History of the United States of America During the Administration of Thomas Jefferson.* New York: A. & C. Boni, 1930. The first two volumes of Adams' brilliant history; the next two cover the Madison administration. Adams' first six chapters portray magnificently the United States of 1800. The nine-volume work first appeared in 1889-91.

Bowers, Claude G., *Jefferson in Power.* Boston: Houghton Mifflin Company, 1936. A continuation of the author's *Jefferson and Hamilton.* Bowers uses newspaper sources heavily.

Ford, Worthington C., *Jefferson and the Newspaper, 1785-1830.* New York: Columbia University Press, 1936. Gives examples of how the great statesman regarded the journalists and their media.

Luxon, Norval Neil, *Niles' Weekly Register.* Baton Rouge: Louisiana State University Press, 1947. This doctoral dissertation is the best available information on this influential publication.

Mott, Frank Luther, *History of American Magazines, 1741-1850.* New York: The Macmillan Company, 1930. Volume one of a series by the outstanding authority on the subject. The author won a Pulitzer award for his study.

————, *Jefferson and the Press.* Baton Rouge: Louisiana State University Press, 1943. An excellent monograph.

Padover, Saul K., *Thomas Jefferson on Democracy.* New York: Penguin Books, Inc., 1939. Excerpts from his letters and speeches. One section is concerned with the press.

Pollard, James E., *The Presidents and the Press.* New York: The Macmillan Company, 1947. Describes relationships of Jefferson, Madison, and Monroe with the press during this period.

William Winston Seaton. Boston: James R. Osgood and Company, 1871. The biography of the great Washington editor of the *National Intelligencer,* with notes of family and friends.

Wood, James Playsted, *Magazines in the United States.* New York: Ronald Press, 1956. A study of the influence of magazines on American society. Fairly comprehensive in its coverage of general magazines, but far less detailed than Mott (above).

Periodicals and Monographs:

Bent, Arthur S., "Damon and Pythias Among Our Early Journalists," *New England Magazine,* XIV (August 1896), 666. Interesting information on Joseph Dennie, grandson of Bartholomew Green, famous Boston publisher, and his associates at Craft's Tavern, where the Walpole Literary Club met.

Callahan, North, "Jefferson's Contributions to America's Free Press," *Quill*, XLVIII (March 1960), 8. A summary written at the time Jefferson was honored by Sigma Delta Chi, professional journalism society.

Clark, Carlisle, "The Old Corner Printing House," *Granite Monthly*, XXX (August 1901), 91. Describes the *Farmer's Weekly Museum*, started by Isaiah Thomas, and later a pioneer national magazine.

Craven, Avery, "The Turner Theories and the South." *Journal of Southern History*, V (August 1939), 231. An explanation of the frontier thesis by an outstanding authority of the region.

Curti, Merle E., "The Section and the Frontier in American History: The Methodological Concepts of Frederick Jackson Turner," in Stuart A. Rice, ed., *Methods in Social Science*. Chicago: University of Chicago Press, 1931, 353. One of the ablest of modern American historians discusses the process by which the West has exerted continuing influence upon the more settled areas.

Glicksberg, Charles, "Bryant and the United States Review," *New England Quarterly*, VII (December 1934), 687. Describes early nineteenth-century periodicals and the movement to establish a national literature through such magazines as the *North American Review*.

Hacker, Louis, "Sections or Classes," *Nation*, CXXXVII (July 26, 1933), 108. A short, but persuasive argument by one of the able historians who dispute the Turner thesis.

Lee, Alfred McClung, "Dunlap and Claypoole: Printers and News-Merchants of the Revolution," *Journalism Quarterly*, XI (June 1934), 160. The story of the men who founded the first successful American daily.

Martin, Benjamin Ellis, "Transition Period of the American Press—Leading Editors in This Century," *Magazine of American History*, XVII (April 1887), 273. Describes battles between Federalist and Republican journalists. Includes interesting facsimile examples of papers.

Murphy, Lawrence W., "John Dunlap's 'Packet' and Its Competitors," *Journalism Quarterly*, XXVIII (Winter 1951), 58. The story of the struggle for survival among the first dailies.

Schafer, Joseph, "Turner's America," *Wisconsin Magazine of History*, XVII (June 1934), 448. One of Wisconsin's great scholars discusses a contemporary's views on frontier influence.

Shannon, Fred A., "Critiques of Research in the Social Sciences," *Social Science Research Council Bulletin*, No. 46. New York: The Council, 1940. Another critic of Turner argues against the frontier theory.

Chapter **10**

COONSKIN DEMOCRACY
AND THE PRESS

> A country, like an individual, has dignity and
> power only in proportion as it is self-informed.
> —William Ellery Channing

AMERICA IN THE 1820's was still largely rural, but industry
was beginning to exert the influence that was to be so profoundly
felt by society in the near future. All the new States followed the
Vermont pattern in providing suffrage for all white males. After
1810, state after state in the East dropped restrictive voting qualifications, not always peaceably. The enfranchisement of the common
man was to bring about what amounted to a bloodless revolution,
but in the 1820's the significance of the first farm-labor movement
was not generally recognized. The so-called "common man" was not
yet fully aware of the new power he had won. Until 1828, federal
administration of government was still largely by "gentlemen," like
Madison, Monroe, and John Quincy Adams. Yet it was in this period
that the pressures for popular sovereignty began to be exerted, and
the press was to play an important role in this drama.

Indeed, the press was more and more counted upon to supply
the information, inspiration, agitation, and education of a society
often unable to keep up with its need for schools. Newspapers,
books, and magazines increased so fast in this period that presses
could not meet the craving for such material. There were 375

192

printing offices in 1810. By 1825 there were three times as many. Between 1820 and 1830, publication of books alone increased 10 per cent, and still did not supply the need, for Americans continued to buy 70 per cent of their books from European publishers. Despite this literary dependence upon the Old World, Americans were offering every encouragement to journalistic promoters. It is significant that by 1820 more than 50,000 titles, including books, magazines, and newspapers, were listed as American. Sale of such products increased by more than a million dollars in the decade beginning in 1820, when publications grossed about two and a half million dollars.[1]

True, much of this American material was extremely shallow and provincial. The *Port Folio,* one of the most literate of the magazines, rarely exceeded 2,000 subscribers. The authoritative *North American Review* had a normal circulation of about 3,000 copies. The biggest New York newspapers printed up to 4,000 copies an issue, but 1,500 to 2,500 was much more common. Only in the religious field was circulation impressive. The Methodist *Christian Journal and Advocate,* for example, had about 25,000 subscribers by its own estimate in 1826. But although circulations were small, popular publications were reaching more and more citizens, and their numbers increased yearly.

Unfortunately, most ordinary citizens could not afford to pay five or ten dollars a year in advance for such publications. The prevailing wage scale gave many workers only about eight dollars a week, which put virtually all magazines, and most newspapers out of their reach. Even so, enough circulation reached the common man to give the United States the highest per capita newspaper readership in the world. In 1826, newspaper circulation in America exceeded that of Great Britain by more than three million annually. In 1810 there were 376 newspapers in the United States. By 1828, at the time of Jackson's election, there were nearly 900 (mainly weeklies). Nevertheless, what the nation needed was a newspaper press that could reach deeper into the masses.

In many communities, newspapers were the only literature available for the bulk of the citizenry. They served as the main educational device until other cultural institutions could take up the

[1] Merle Curti, *The Growth of American Thought* (New York: Harper & Brothers, 1943), p. 215.

slack caused by rapid migrations. European visitors often did not realize the obstacles to cultural progress in such a new land. They sometimes failed to see that the United States was at a stage where rudimentary education fulfilled the needs of much of the population. What had Americans, other than Franklin, contributed to science, literature, the arts, or philosophy, the Rev. Sydney Smith asked rhetorically in an article from the *Edinburgh Review* reprinted in an American newspaper. Actually, the United States was beginning to fill this vacuum. In the field of letters the country could offer Washington Irving, James Fenimore Cooper, William Cullen Bryant, Margaret Fuller, Nathaniel Hawthorne, and Ralph Waldo Emerson, all of whom would soon be recognized even in Europe.

The trend toward a more enlightened age was noticeable by the end of the 1820's. By that time there were 49 colleges in the United States. The increase in endowed institutions of learning was appreciable after the decision of the Supreme Court in the Dartmouth College case of 1819. Until then, the trend had been toward state control of such educational establishments. The apathy of the philanthropist in supporting universities is therefore understandable. The Court held in the Dartmouth College case that a state had no right to change contracts; specifically, to make a private institution into a State university. Potential patrons of endowed education had hesitated to make donations to educational institutions threatened by State control.

The Dartmouth College decision was one of a series by which Chief Justice John Marshall guided the Supreme Court in establishing a philosophy of government. Two famous decisions, *McCulloch v. Maryland* (1819) and *Gibbon v. Ogden* (1824) asserted the supremacy of the national government over the States. Other decisions limited the States in their restriction of the rights of propertyholders. They were indicative of the general attitude regarding the superiority of private controls. This was the heyday of unrestricted enterprise. The attitude on this subject is also reflected in the philosophies of Justice Joseph Story of Massachusetts, author of *Commentaries on the Constitution,* and of James (Chancellor) Kent of New York, who wrote *Commentaries on American Law.* The two eminent and influential jurists interpreted laws so as to make them fit the needs of an increasingly commercial nation. They had no sympathy for any extension of government regulation that might curb the individual business man, but they were willing to let the government come to the help of the commercial interests when such aid was convenient.

This was what Senator Thomas Hart Benton of Missouri had in mind when he argued at the end of the decade that the "East," the symbol of business and banking, saw to it that western demands for the homestead laws were obstructed in order to maintain a cheap labor supply for the eastern business man. Another instance of this philosophy in action was the passage of the tariff of 1828—the "tariff of abominations"—which protected the business promoter at the expense of other interests.

But this turn to the right had brought social and political strains. As the business man assumed a more dominant place in federal control, and as he began to exert his influence to his own advantage, there was an equal and opposite reaction. It is significant that labor unions and a labor press emerge about this time. The cries of anguish over the "tariff of abominations," especially in the agrarian areas, were a prelude to the battle cries of the War Between the States. And yet, curiously, American writers had little to say about the forces shaping the destiny of our country at this time. We can learn more by reading the reports of foreign observers who visited our shores during the first 30 years of the century.

Many, such as Basil Hall and Mrs. Frances Trollope, were devastating in their contempt for American culture and materialism. Others, such as Harriet Martineau, a trained journalist with an understanding heart, saw through the American veneer. In between were reporters such as Charles Dickens, who were generally severe, but reasonably accurate.[2] They were appalled, for the most part, by American provincialism, unmindful that the American was preoccupied with hacking a nation from a wilderness. This complete absorption in the development of our own resources had resulted in a strong nationalism obnoxious to the foreign observer. Earlier visitors had confined their observations to the more sophisticated East, but the European reporters of the 1820-30's were more interested in the western regions. They were disgusted by the boast-

[2] See Godfrey T. Vique, "Six Months in America"; Thomas Hamilton, "Men and Manners in America"; Harriet Martineau, "Society in America"; reprinted in Allan Nevins, ed., *American Social History* (New York: Henry Holt and Company, 1923).

fulness, the smugness, superior attitudes, and ill-mannered ignorance of the type of American about to step into control of the government. Most of these observers carried home a great disdain for the American concept of popular rule. From 1820 to 1830, Europe, and particularly Great Britain, was engulfed in a wave of conservatism. The Reform Bill of 1832 was threatening, but in the 1820's most of the British observers believed they were duty bound to criticise our popular philosophies.

The westerner they saw was the American "with the bark still on." The shrewdness of the horse trader, and the way he bragged of his "cute" dealings convinced the observers of the low standards of commercial morality in the country. In short, America exhibited to most foreign observers all the faults of adolescence, and only a few saw the virtues of the young society. One who did was the French observer, Alexis de Tocqueville (see page 184), whose *Democracy in America* reflects his observations of 1831-32.

The United States of course lagged far behind Europe in outward marks of civilization. Travel was still by stage and sailing vessel, although steamers plied the larger streams. The first railroad was built at the end of the decade, but the big expansion in steam travel was yet to come. Cities were mostly unpaved, and the clip-clop of horses was the most familiar street sound. Municipal light and water were rare luxuries. The oil lamp lit homes.

The church was still the main source of outside interest. Organized sport was unknown. One might wager on a horse race during the season, and bare-knuckle prizefights, properly hidden from the police, offered a possible outlet for the man of sporting taste, but even the colleges offered little opportunity for the sports-minded.

The most noteworthy development of the period was the emergence of the mass-production system. There were many factors responsible for what today we call the industrial revolution. One factor was the application of power to machinery, so that the factory came to supersede the crafts formerly carried on in the home or small workshop. In 1815 the historians were greatly concerned about the influence on society of the Congress of Vienna, following the Napoleonic wars. The results of that great meeting were not nearly so impressive as the changes brought about by obscure men in dingy workshops who showed how steam could perform the labors of man. The 1820's saw America move from the experimental period into the Age of Steam. The British blazed the way in the industrial revolution, but already some of the challenges of that upheaval were being offered in America. Steam made the factory possible. It lowered the price of goods and modified economies. It also brought with it the slum, human exploitation, and social unrest. It revolutionized transportation and the whole distribution system. It brought a shift from rural to urban society which was to have a profound effect upon the development of America.

The full consequence of the industrial revolution in America was not apparent until a later date, but the trend was already started in the 1820's. The opening of the Erie Canal in 1825 was to make New York truly the "Empire State" and its metropolis one of the world's great commercial centers. In 1830, only about 7 per cent of the people lived in cities, but the influence of industry was manifested by the obsession of political leaders in such problems as tariffs and the recognition of the working man's vote.

On the whole, the new class emerging out of the industrial revolution was at first inarticulate. The so-called "common man" appeared to be unaware of his new power. But as early as 1820 there was the beginning of populist revolt in Massachusetts, where workers were insisting upon a greater voice in government. New York experienced the same thing in 1821. In Rhode Island, where the worker was less successful at first, pressure built up into actual violence (Dorr's Rebellion), although the denouement dragged out into a later period. The issue was the rights of property versus the rights of the individual. The issue was pointed up by the provision of manhood suffrage. Slowly control began to slip from the landowner and capitalist to the farmer and mechanic. The trend brought new groups into opposition to each other. The western farmer, in debt to the eastern capitalist, tended to blame his troubles upon the men of the metropolis. The city mechanic, as the urban worker was called at that time, resented exploitation by what he believed to be a privileged class. He resented being paid in wildcat banknotes that sometimes depreciated to less than half of his contracted wage. It is significant that in 1829 about 75,000 men were jailed for debt. More than half of these victims owed less than $20. Conditions of labor, especially for women and children, brought out a long line of social reformers who insisted upon protective legislation.

Slowly the common man began to realize his power at the polls.

In 1824, only six states still chose presidential electors through the legislators, heretofore the frequent tools of the property group. By 1832, only South Carolina maintained this system, and it was in that year that the party convention took at least some of the power away from "King Caucus"—the selection of candidates by secret conclave or political leaders.

By 1824 the emergence of the common man as a power was well under way, although few probably knew it at the time. The popular vote went to Andrew Jackson, darling of the masses. There were four candidates, however, and none had sufficient popular support to carry the election. Henry Clay, with the fewest votes, swung his support to John Quincy Adams, who was declared winner by the House of Representatives. Jackson was convinced that he had been sold out, particularly after Adams selected Clay as his secretary of state. The old hero of New Orleans was therefore all the more determined to lead his followers to victory. In the melee, the old parties were shaken to pieces. The Whigs succeeded the Federalists, after some readjustments, as the party of the right, but the realignment brought greater emphasis to the business element of society. Federalism had strong roots in the aristocratic tradition. It was especially strong in the seaboard North and East. The Whig was a party member more from economic than from social pressure. The opposition group called itself the Democratic party, and its development from the older Jeffersonian components will appear in the following pages.

Jackson became the seventh president of the United States in 1828, following a period of depression and social discontent that did much to build up his popular support. His election was such a victory for new and vigorous elements that his administration has sometimes been called the "Jacksonian Revolution." By 1828, each section of the country had problems only a federal government could hope to solve. Westerners believed they were hampered in their expansion by selfish eastern interests, and it is significant that they helped elect a man who was the very personification of the "western type."

Just as significant was the support of Jackson by the industrial areas, however. He carried both New York and Pennsylvania in 1824, and was overwhelmingly favored by the laborer in eastern commercial centers in 1828. Working men saw that any relief they hoped to gain must come from the federal government. But the South also demanded attention to its troubles. Southern planters accused northern industrialists of trying to wreck the agrarian control, long acknowledged by the political economists. The "tariff of abominations," which threatened to split the regions wide open, heralded this growing rebellion against the growing power of the northern commercial interests.

Henry Clay believed he had found a way to satisfy all the dissident elements. Why Clay, the old western War Hawk of 1812, should now be a Whig leader would take too long to explain here, but his scheme may make his political affiliations appear less inconsistent. A century before anyone ever heard of "economic planning," Clay had worked out a way to make all regions and all groups happy, or so he believed. He called his plan the American System. It was based primarily upon a high protective tariff, which would assure safety to the capitalist, profit to the industrialist, and prosperity to the laborer through high wages. This economy would mean that industry would buy more from the farmer at higher prices. Unfortunately, the farmer had never been able to tap this rich urban market because of the exorbitant price he had to pay to get his goods transported to the big centers. Clay had provided for that. All the proceeds of the tariff would be devoted to improving highways, canals, and railroads. Thus, both the western and southern agrarian, and the eastern commercial interests would profit from each other and would forget their growing differences.

The plan sounded fine, but by 1828 a large part of the population began to suspect that the American System was like a deck of marked cards. They saw very clearly who would win all the big pots. And so voters turned to more direct relief. They listened to such men as Thomas Hart Benton, Senator from Missouri, who cried the loudest against eastern perfidy. Then Old Hickory threw his hat in the presidential ring, and at last common men had a leader around whom they could rally. In 1828 the populist movement swept all before it. For the first time the farm-labor coalition put its own man in the White House. The common man expected results, and Jackson did not let him down.

The press had been an essential tool in fashioning this new brand of democracy. Journalists not only helped crystallize public opinion responsible for the revolution, but for the first time they became part of the process. In other words, they took an active part in the politics they wrote about. An example was the so-called "Relief War" in Kentucky. This was a violent interlude that was the result of the depression of 1819. The war flared into rebellion when an attempt to aid the desperate farmer debtors was thwarted by the conservative interests, fearful of being repaid on their investments with "soft money." In 1823 the Kentucky Court of Appeals declared the state relief system unconstitutional, and the dominant populists now saw their measures sabotaged by a minority backed by a subservient court. The party leaders determined to remedy matters by changing the laws. Two of the most effective of these leaders were Amos Kendall and Francis P. Blair, Frankfort editors (see p. 182) soon to become identified with the highest echelons of the Jacksonian revolution. There were many other editors behind Jackson—men like Duff Green, Issac Hill, and John C. Rives—who were both journalists and political advisers. Although the populist press was actually much smaller than the opposition press, it was determined, articulate, and very persuasive. As much as any other factor, it brought about the emergence of the common man through the revolution of 1828.

The victory was actually only the culmination of the long struggle started by Jefferson to wrest control of government from the property interests. Jefferson's victory in 1800 was not complete. Jackson's victory carried majority rule to its logical conclusion, even if the price had to be administration by the uncouth and unlettered. Jefferson believed in the democratic-republican form of government, but he always assumed that people of his own class would retain the responsibility of political office. Jefferson would have had little use for the groups that needed recognition in 1828. The yeoman, not the laborer, was Jefferson's ideal citizen. Jackson's followers adopted a more hard-boiled attitude toward politics. They accepted the challenge of the new industrialism, and adjusted political philosophy accordingly. They retained a respect for the independent farmer, but they faced other problems ignored by the Jeffersonians. Jacksonians made practical the Jeffersonian ideals. They saw that economic equality was closely related to political equality, and they made more equitable distribution of wealth as much an issue as equitable enfranchisement had been in Jefferson's bravest days.

Amos Kendall, the mouthpiece of the Jacksonian administration, saw the conflict clearly. He described it as a fight between the "producing" classes—farmers, laborers, and craftsmen—and the "non-producing" capitalist, middleman, and landlord. Although outnumbered, this non-producing class remained dominant through control of banks, education, most of the churches, and the bulk of the press. Thus, Kendall pointed out, "those who produce all the wealth are themselves left poor." [3] Even an old Whig like Horace Greeley had to admit the validity of the charge, although that journalistic genius insisted he had better remedies than Kendall had to offer.

At any rate, this was "radical" thinking. The Whig party, digging in for the long battle against the invincible Democrats, was just as far to the right in its thinking. The sanctity of property was explained very comfortably by the ultra-Whig *American Quarterly Review,* published in Philadelphia, which reported just after the end of the decade: "The lowest orders of society ordinarily mean the poorest—and the highest the richest. Sensual excess, want of intelligence, and moral debasement distinguish the former—knowledge, intellectual superiority, and refined, social and domestic affections the latter." As the Pulitzer Prize historian of this period remarks: "Property, in [Whig] reflexes, became almost identified with character." Nicholas Biddle, who as head of the powerful Second Bank of the United States, believed he was the leader of a class too strong for any attempted restraint by the Jacksonians, smugly summed up the opposition Democrats as a party made up of "men with no property to assess and no character to lose." [4]

Fortunately for the Democrats, they were not so easily squelched. The complacency of the Whigs, indeed, accounted for their continued defeat. They could not believe that anything more than their own criticism of the administration was necessary to bring about a victory for them. The pompous Biddle was utterly astounded when, in the summer of 1832, Jackson vetoed a bill for rechartering the Bank of the United States. "Biddled, diddled, and undone," Charles Gordon Greene of the *Boston Post* wrote of Jackson's veto. Unconcerned about their lack of character, the Democrats tracked their muddy boots across the White House floors, just as though

---

[3] Arthur M. Schlesinger, Jr., *The Age of Jackson* (Boston: Little, Brown and Company, 1945), p. 306.
[4] All quoted from *ibid.*, p. 14.

they were as good as anyone else. And despite their crudeness and governmental inexperience, they began to accomplish some of their objectives. They won these goals through the combined efforts of the obscure lawmakers, in most cases. The fame of Webster and Clay has come down to us through history as they rolled their armies of purple rhetoric against the thin, gray replies of the little men. But Webster and Clay invariably were on the losing side. Too often they won the argument but lost the cause. On the other hand, unremembered, grubby politicians, buttonholing colleagues in cloakroom and lobby, time and again won the day. Democracy was not very heroic, perhaps, and provided little material during this period for future high school declaimers, but it was far more effective than the Whigs cared to admit.

A direct result of the industrial revolution and the growing need for recognition of the new type of citizen was the development of the labor press. Some means had to be found to answer the Biddles and the Websters. The depression during the terrible winter of 1828-9, and the rising cost of living, fostered the beginning of a labor revolt long overdue. The appearance of the first labor paper in 1827—the *Journeyman Mechanic's Advocate* of Philadelphia— was a clear signal that the laboring man intended to fight for his advantage, as the property man had long fought for his. The first labor paper lasted only a year. The times were too difficult for workers to provide sufficient support. It was a significant "first," however, for in conjunction with the success of the populists at the polls in 1828, the attempt of labor to express itself was prophetic. Two months before Jackson's election, the first working man's party was organized. It was sponsored by the Mechanic's Union of Trade Associations. In the same year the *Mechanic's Free Press* was established as the first successful labor newspaper. Until the depression of 1837 killed it, the *Free Press* had an average weekly circulation of around 1,500—very good for a period when even the biggest New York papers rarely exceeded 4,000.

In many ways, the early labor papers were superior to modern labor organs. Their functions were primarily to counteract prejudices against the working man, to supply labor information that the commercial press ignored, and to offer inspiration to the dispirited. The *Free Press* actually had much less propaganda and biased reporting than would be found in the typical modern labor paper. It offered thoughtful articles on pertinent legislation. The reports were concise, reasonably factual for the standards of that day, and well written. Such papers helped to develop labor unity, and it should be noted that labor was solidly behind Jackson.

This agitation led to the organization of the first national labor association—the National Trades Union—founded in 1834. A strong supporter of the labor organization movement was the *Working Man's Advocate*, founded in New York in 1829 by George H. Evans, an English printer. Another important publication supporting labor's cause (along with other social issues) was the *Free Enquirer*, edited in New York by the charming and talented Frances "Fanny" Wright. Fanny Wright, who came to the United States from Scotland in 1818, became a power in the New Harmony utopian experiment conducted by Robert Dale Owen. She had helped put out the *New Harmony Gazette*, published in New York from 1829 as the *Free Enquirer*. Among Miss Wright's many admirers was a young carpenter who was a great believer in democracy, and whose poems began to sing of the people. The poet was Walt Whitman, himself a journalist a little later.

Most of the standard newspapers had scant regard for this labor movement, but one or two helped the cause. William Cullen Bryant, the poet and editor of the *New York Evening Post*, pleaded the case of the working man. The stand of the *Post* indicated how far it had veered since its establishment by the father of Federalism, Alexander Hamilton. Bryant had been employed in 1825 by Coleman, the militant Federalist editor of the paper. Four years later Bryant was in full charge of the *Post*, and remained with the paper, except for a few lapses, for half a century. Under Bryant, the *Post* cast off much of its Federalist tradition. On many issues the paper sided with the Jacksonian Democrats. Thus, denouncing what it believed to be an unjust verdict against a "criminal conspiracy" (strike) by the Society of Journeyman Tailors, the *Post* said:

They were condemned because they determined not to work for the wages offered them . . . If this is not SLAVERY, we have forgotten its definition. Strike the right of associating for the sale of labour from the privileges of a freeman, and you may as well at once bind him to a master.[5]

[5] *New York Evening Post*, June 13, 1836.

William Leggett, part owner of the *Post*, and interim editor after Bryant went abroad in 1834, was even more pro-labor than was Bryant. He was so outspoken, indeed, that the more temperate Bryant had to cool him down on occasion. Later, as we shall see, the cause of the working man was taken up by another famous editor, Horace Greeley. There were magazines, too, fighting for labor during this period. One was the *Democratic Review*, edited by the fiery John L. O'Sullivan. Despite these editorial champions of the underprivileged, the press in general took a dim view of such Jacksonian policies.

The standard press was likely to be contemptuous of the fruits of democracy. Many editors harped on the "spoils system," whereby President Jackson replaced government employees of dubious loyalty with faithful Democrats selected more for their political conformity than for their tested abilities. Whatever the faults of the spoils system, however, it at least destroyed peaceably the monopoly of offices long enjoyed by a class and a party that had failed to face up to the issues. The system brought into power a fresh, alert group, which had the energy to meet the needs of the majority instead of the privileged. Very much to the surprise of the scornful Whigs, a spoils system bureaucrat almost immediately uncovered graft within the Treasury Department bequeathed to the Democrats by that unassailable man of integrity, John Quincy Adams. The spoils system was used by Jackson's enemies as positive proof of government corruption. Here was evidence that the system could destroy corruption. No doubt the political rewards offered by the victorious Democrats tended to cheapen government, but it was only by calumny in the press that Jacksonian bureaucracy suffered in comparison with that of the previous administration.

Equally obnoxious to the haters of the new order was the so-called "Kitchen Cabinet" of the President. The driving energy of any reform or revolution usually comes from a small group of like-minded leaders. That was true after 1828. Jackson depended upon a little band of men bound together by common zeal for the cause. Normally, they should have made up his official cabinet, but they were not known to the general public, and even an independent like the President had to bow to tradition in the selection of his official family. He chose important men for the ranking positions, but he paid them little heed. The President needed men around him who were closer to him ideologically and temperamentally. There-fore, he turned for advice not to the men chosen by protocol, but to an inner circle of "cronies," as the opposition called them deri-sively. This was the Kitchen Cabinet.

Some of the most influential members of this inner circle were journalists. Duff Green, the editor of the party paper in Washing-ton, was one of the cronies until his endorsement of Calhoun lost him Jackson's support. Isaac Hill, the crippled, rebellious, and vi-tuperative New Hampshire editor, was another intimate of the Pres-ident. The two most important powers behind the party, however, were Amos Kendall and Francis Preston Blair. Today, their coun-terparts would appear high up in the administrative hierarchy. Ken-dall did hold a minor office in the Treasury Department, but in Jackson's day, journalists were still considered unlikely candidates for exalted positions. Administrators had been willing to accept newspaper editors and publishers as tools, critics, and even as friends; but never as equals.[6] The old general respected the press, but he did not quite dare flout tradition by making his newspaper supporters members of his cabinet. And yet Green, Hill, Blair, and Kendall were as close to him at one time or another as any of his advisers.

Amos Kendall was the most important member of the group. Reared on a New England farm, he was too frail for such rugged work. He had a passion for scholarship, and his family recognized this bent. After he was graduated from Dartmouth College, Ken-dall headed for the frontier, where opportunities were better for inexperienced lawyers. He hung up his shingle in Lexington, Ken-tucky.

As a lawyer, Kendall easily turned his energies to politics. He was a protégé of a regional political chieftain, Colonel Richard M. Johnson, who insisted that the erudite New Englander take over the editorship of the Democratic party organ. The newspaper was the *Argus of Western America*, published at Frankfort. Kendall made it the party voice of the entire region. His position was

[6] As described in earlier pages, journalists were important in the develop-ment of the postal service. Benjamin Franklin and Richard Bache were appointed postmasters after the colonies declared their independence. The postmaster general was not given cabinet rank until 1829, however. In 1836 Kendall was appointed to this position. He had earned such recognition by that time.

achieved not without great risk, politically as well as physically. For a time he carried a pistol and a bowie knife for protection against those he had scorched in his *Argus* articles. An able, honest, and articulate journalist, his fame as a party spokesman eventually came to the attention of the party's supreme commander, General Jackson. Kendall fought courageously for the debtor's relief system which spilt Kentucky wide open during Adams' administration. After the voters of Kentucky were cheated of their victory in the "Relief War," he put all his energies into the election of Jackson.

Kendall was a social illiterate, or at least a man with a serious personality handicap, and he might have remained a frontier journalist had it not been for Martin Van Buren, Jackson's heir apparent. Van Buren, called by his foes "The American Talleyrand," was the perfect specimen of the spoils system politician brought to full flower by the Jacksonian Revolution. He was the living evidence of how mediocrity could be made to pay off politically. But this big-scale ward heeler was a shrewd judge of men, as are most successful party bosses, and he was impressed by Kendall. It was he who asked Jackson to bring the Kentucky editor to Washington. Kendall started out in the auditing division of the Treasury Department, where he at once discovered corruption left over from the previous administration. This was just what the Democrats needed to justify their clean sweep. The feat brought Kendall to the President's personal attention, and from that moment, they were fast friends.

Perhaps their physical ills gave them a common bond. The President was old and full of the miseries. Kendall was something of a hypochondriac, but he had always been frail, so perhaps his attitude was justified. At any rate, there was a strong bond between the two men. Jackson was not a polished writer, and he was happy to have Kendall edit his important statements. Time and again Kendall took down the dictation of the wan warrior. Jackson would lie on a faded sofa beneath the portrait of his beloved Rachel, while Kendall skillfully interpreted his chief's rough ideas and put them into presentable form. Jackson spoke forcefully, but there was too much of the western uncouthness in his diction. Kendall would smooth away the crudeness and read back the paragraph to the President. Perhaps they would have to try again, but eventually the old general would nod approval. Kendall was often surprised at the effectiveness of the speech as it appeared in print.

When Jackson first moved into the White House, the administration organ at Washington was the *United States Telegraph*, founded in 1826.[7] Duff Green was editor of the paper. He had worked hard to elect Jackson, but his other hero was John C. Calhoun, Jackson's party rival. The split in loyalty cost Green the support of the President. The Jacksonian faction decided to make Francis P. Blair Green's successor. Blair had taken over the editorship of the *Argus* after Kendall went to Washington. He had proved to be a very able journalist, but he had to be cleared of $40,000 in debts before he could accept the Washington proposal. There was a long delay, therefore, until Blair arrived to assume his capital duties. By this time, the party leaders were impatient to see this journalistic paragon. The man who descended from the stagecoach at the capital in the early summer of 1830 was disappointing in appearance. He was a pale, sandy-haired, somewhat seedy little man, and he looked even less impressive with the black eye he had received during a coach accident on the journey up from Alexandria. The inner guard began to have doubts about the white knight they had picked to wear their journalistic colors in place of redoubtable Green. Blair soon proved to them that he was more than equal to the task.

His paper, the *Washington Globe*, appeared at the end of 1830. By that time Jackson and Blair were on the best of terms. "Give it to Bla-ar," the President used to say when he had a particularly trenchant statement requiring journalistic finesse. From Blair's pencil, on scraps of paper held on his knee, came the fighting editorials that helped to knit the party even closer. In 1832, John C. Rives became Blair's assistant. Rives, a shaggy giant, quite in contrast to his colorless associates, also came to enjoy the confidences of the inner guard.

But Kendall was the most important of them all. As one of Jackson's rivals put it, Kendall was ". . . the President's *thinking* machine, and his *writing* machine—ay, and his *lying* machine. . . . He was chief overseer, chief reporter, amanuensis, scribe, accountant

---

[7] The *electric* telegraph had not been invented at that time. The name probably derived from the semaphore signal.

general, man of all work—nothing was well done without the aid of his diabolical genius." [8] And ex-President Adams, not given to exaggeration, once stated of Van Buren and Jackson, "Both . . . have been for twelve years the tool of Amos Kendall, the ruling mind of their dominion." [9]

The magazines of the period were important, too, in the spreading of Democratic doctrine. In the early days of the Jacksonian revolution, most of the monthly publications were conservative in political philosophy. The North American Review, virtually a house organ of that conservative redoubt, Harvard, and the New England Magazine, one of the stuffiest of Whig outlets, were typical periodicals of the time. Later, some of the liberal writers found expression in the Democratic Review, but that was not until after Van Buren's election in 1836. Inasmuch as the magazine of the post-Van Buren period reflected Democratic views held by party leaders earlier, it may not be inappropriate to include it here. It was the liveliest of the intellectual periodicals. Contributors were men like Bryant, Hawthorne, Thoreau, Whittier, Whitman, Poe, Longfellow, Lowell, and Bancroft—a galaxy of literary lights twinkling with Democratic enthusiasm.

Less brilliant, but more penetrating, was the Boston Quarterly, edited by Orestes Brownson. It was an important outlet for the intellectual ideas propounded by leading democratic philosophers of the day. One thing was clear: The Democratic party might be based upon the support of the underprivileged, but it also had the sympathy of many intellectuals. The party was proud of this, and it made practical use of more than one genius by enlisting him not only as its tribune, but as a practical adviser—what in a later century would have been called a "brain truster." Many of these intellectuals were actually appointed to government service, including Bancroft, Hawthorne, Irving, Brownson, and Leggett.

Which was all very well, but where were the publications for the masses? Surely all this democratic ferment must have had its consequences in developing a newspaper the man in the street could afford and could enjoy. As a matter of fact, the same forces that brought about the emergence of the common man also accounted for the establishment of a people's press. The industrial revolution,

[8] Schlesinger, The Age of Jackson, p. 73
[9] Loc. cit.

which resulted in cheaper goods, also made it possible to produce a cheaper paper. All the social pressures mentioned in the preceding pages shared in making possible the newspaper for the masses. There was a vast, untapped public tempting the promoter, if only the product could be made attractive. And by 1833, the technical progress had reached the point where this was possible.

Courtesy, R. Hoe & Co., Inc.

In 1814 the *Times* of London installed a press perfected by Friedrich Koenig, of Saxony. This early power press turned out only 800 impressions an hour, but at the time, this was considered marvelous. The press shown above was an adaptation of the Koenig press by the American manufacturer, R. Hoe & Co., Inc., of New York.

In 1822, Peter Smith, connected with R. Hoe and Company, printing-press makers, invented a hand press with a much faster lever action. Five years later Samuel Rust of New York put out the Washington hand press, still seen in some offices. It had many automatic devices—a platen raised and lowered by springs; an ingenious toggle device for quick impressions; a faster-moving bed; and later, automatic ink rollers.

The next step was to harness power to the press. This was the Age of Steam, and at once inventors set themselves to the problem. Daniel Treadwell of Boston had partial success in 1822. A steam book press was developed by Isaac Adams of Boston in 1830 and was popular for many years, but it was a European who perfected the process for speedy power printing. He was Friedrich Koenig, of Saxony, who, after many delays, produced the first of his presses in London in 1811. It had a movable bed which carried the type back and forth to be inked after each impression. Paper was fed into the top of a cylinder. Three years later Koenig invented a two-cylinder press that printed both sides of the paper—the so-called "perfecting press." The *Times* of London was the first to use this press for newspaper work late in 1814. The paper proudly stated that it could outstrip all rivals by printing papers at the unbelievable rate of 1,100 an hour.

In 1830 David Napier of England perfected the Koenig steam press so as to triple the speed of printing. America's R. Hoe and Company, which has now become a byword in newspaper plants, chose the Napier press as the prototype of a new product for American printers. The new Hoe was actually a great improvement over the Napier, and it could produce four thousand double impressions an hour. Such technical progress was essential to the production of a cheap paper that the masses could afford to buy.

By 1833 all the ingredients were available for the establishment of such a venture. It was possible to print a paper that would sell for one cent, in contrast to the six cents charged by the average commercial dailies. To a workman, six cents was the equivalent of a quarter-pound of bacon, or a pint of local whisky. In England, Henry Hetherington had published two periodicals for the masses. He failed, not because of the price he charged, but because he was caught evading the so-called "taxes on knowledge," which kept the price of British newspapers out of the hands of the common man, as intended. John Wight, the Bow Street police reporter, had also demonstrated by 1820 the type of news that would make the presses of the masses successful.

In 1829, Seba Smith founded a daily paper at Portland, Maine, that was smaller than a standard newspaper, but cheaper by half than the usual daily. It cost four dollars a year, payable in advance. A year later, Lynde M. Walter, a Boston brahmin, bought an exist·

ing paper and made it into the daily *Transcript*, offered at four dollars a year. More popular because it offered spicier items, perhaps, was the *Boston Morning Post*, founded as a four-dollar daily by Charles G. Greene in 1831. Two years later Captain John S. Sleeper founded the *Boston Mercantile Journal*, offered at the same price. All were successful, but they were sold by subscription, which took them out of the reach of the usual laboring man, who could not pay a lump sum in advance.

In Philadelphia, Dr. Christopher Columbus Conwell established a penny paper, *The Cent*, in 1830. Although interesting as a forerunner of the press for the masses, it survived such a short time that it is of little significance to the present summary. A serious, and nearly-successful attempt to put out a genuine penny paper for the masses, to be sold by the issue, and not entirely by subscription, was made by Horace Greeley. in partnership with Dr. H. D. Shepard, a dentist, in January, 1833. This was the *New York Morning Post*. A violent snow storm kept so many citizens indoors the first few days of its appearance that the promoters had to give up the venture.

The time was ripe for a successful penny paper, however. Indeed, the next attempt to produce a penny paper was to bring such a significant change to American journalism as to warrant the description "revolutionary."

ANNOTATED BIBLIOGRAPHY

Books:

The volumes by the Beards, Parrington, and Curti, previously cited, are basic references for this period. Others are:

Brooks, Van Wyck, *The World of Washington Irving*. New York: E. P. Dutton & Company, 1944. An interpretation of the period through the literary contributions of American writers.

Cambridge History of American Literature, II. New York: G. P. Putnam's Sons, 1917-21. Pages 160-75 describe magazines during 1783-1850; pages 176-95 describe the general newspaper picture from 1775 to 1860. Book publishing is surveyed in Volume 4 (pp. 533-53).

Commons, John R., ed., *Documentary History of American Industrial Society*, IV. Cleveland: A. H. Clark Company, 1910. Basic source.

Fish, Carl Russell, *The Rise of the Common Man, 1830-1850*, A History of American Life, Vol. VI. New York: The Macmillan Company, 1927. Social history, and a standard appraisal of the period.

Gabriel, Ralph H., *The Course of American Democratic Thought*. New York: Ronald Press, 1956. Intellectual history since 1815.

Nevins, Allan, *American Social History*. New York: Henry Holt and Company, 1923. Includes a description of American manners and culture as seen by various British observers of the period.

Olson, Kenneth E., *Typography and Mechanics of the Newspaper*. New York: D. Appleton and Company, 1930. Includes a description of technical progress in the publishing industry.

Schlesinger, Arthur M., Jr., *The Age of Jackson*. Boston: Little, Brown and Company, 1945. A penetrating study of the political background by a Pulitzer Prize winner. Includes a chapter on the press.

Tocqueville, Alexis de, *Democracy in America*. New York: Alfred A. Knopf, Inc., 1945. Most recent of editions which have been appearing since 1835 of this famous French observer's study of American democracy and its effect upon the social system.

Tyler, Alice Felt, *Freedom's Ferment: Phases of American Social History to 1860*. Minneapolis: University of Minnesota Press, 1944. Emphasizes effects of religious and reform movements.

Periodicals and Monographs:

Hage, George S., "Anti-Intellectualism in Press Comment: 1828 and 1952," *Journalism Quarterly*, XXXVI (Fall 1959), 439. Comparison of newspaper content in two presidential elections. A full study is in his doctoral dissertation, "Anti-Intellectualism in Newspaper Comment in the Elections of 1828 and 1952," University of Minnesota, 1957 (Ann Arbor: University Microfilms, 1958).

Myers, Donald James, "The Birth and Establishment of the Labor Press in the United States." Master's thesis, University of Wisconsin, 1950. An authoritative study of the labor press up to 1880.

Smith, Elbert B., "Francis P. Blair and the Globe," *Register of the Kentucky Historical Society*, LVII (October 1959), 340. Blair's role as editor of the Jackson party paper in Washington.

Smith, William E., "Francis P. Blair, Pen-Executive of Andrew Jackson," *Mississippi Valley Historical Review*, XVII (March 1931), 459. A vivid portrait of the *Washington Globe* and its editor. Reprinted in Ford and Emery, *Highlights in the History of the American Press*.

Chapter 11

A PRESS FOR THE MASSES

> But the world *does* move, and its motive power
> under God is the fearless thought and speech of
> those who dare to be in advance of their time—
> who are sneered at and shunned through their
> days of struggle as lunatics, dreamers, impractica-
> bles and visionaries; men of crotchets, vagaries,
> and isms. They are the masts and sails of the ship
> to which conservatism answers as ballast. The
> ballast is important—at times indispensable—but
> it would be of no account if the ship were not
> bound to go ahead.
>
> —Horace Greeley

WHENEVER A MASS OF PEOPLE has been neglected too
long by the established organs of communication, agencies eventually have been devised to supply that want. Invariably this press
of the masses is greeted with scorn by the sophisticated reader
because the content of such a press is likely to be elemental and
emotional. Such scorn is not always deserved. Just as the child
ordinarily starts his reading with Mother Goose and fairy stories
before graduating to more serious study, so the public first reached
by a new agency is likely to prefer what the critics like to call
"sensationalism," which is the emphasis on emotion for its own
sake. This pattern can be seen in the periods when the most noteworthy developments in popular journalism were apparent. In 1620,

1833, the 1890's, or 1920, this tapping of a new, much-neglected public started with a wave of sensationalism.

The phenomenon is clearly exhibited in the period of the 1830's and 1840's covered by this chapter. For it was in 1833 that the first successful penny newspaper tapped a reservoir of readers collectively designated "the common man." The first offerings of this poor man's newspaper tended to be highly sensational. This was only a developmental phase, however. Before long some of the penny newspapers began to attract readers from other social and economic brackets. And the common man, as his literacy skill improved, also demanded a better product. Within a decade after the appearance of the first penny paper, the press of the common man included respectable publications that offered significant information and leadership.

Before the appearance of the penny papers, publishers charged from six to ten dollars a year in advance for a newspaper subscription. That was more than most skilled workmen earned in a week, and in any case, the man of limited means could not pay that much in a lump sum. The standard newspapers usually were edited for people of means, and that partially accounted for the preponderance of conservatism in the press. It also was a factor in keeping circulations small, although mechanical limitations certainly had a similar effect. In 1833 the largest dailies in New York were the morning *Courier and Enquirer,* published by the colorful and irascible Colonel James Watson Webb, and the *Journal of Commerce,* founded by Arthur Tappan in 1827, but soon taken over by Gerard Hallock and David Hale.[1] The largest afternoon paper was William Cullen Bryant's *Post.* These and the other eight city papers sold for six cents a copy, and most of them were distributed by subscription, rather than by the street sale which was to characterize the penny press.

Journalism began a new epoch on September 3, 1833, with the appearance of a strange little newspaper, the *New York Sun* ("It Shines for ALL"). Its founder was Benjamin H. Day, who arrived in New York as a lad of 20, after an apprenticeship on Massachusetts' excellent *Springfield Republican.* That was in 1831. For two

---

[1] The paper had strong religious undertones, but it was aggressive in its news policies and business coverage. It will receive more attention in a later discussion on the development of cooperative news gathering.

years he operated a printing shop without much success; there were financial disturbances, and in 1832 a plague further cut into the city's prosperity. In desperation, Day decided to publish a paper in an effort to take up some of the slack in his declining job-printing business. He had watched the early attempts to establish penny papers in Boston, Philadelphia, and New York, and it appeared to him that such a publication would be successful if it could be sold and financed on a per-issue basis. He discussed the proposal with two friends, Arunah S. Abell and William M. Swain. They warned him against the undertaking, a bit of advice they had to eat sometime later, when they founded their own successful penny papers in Philadelphia and Baltimore. Day decided to go ahead with his plans, anyway.

The appearance of the *Sun* that September day did not give the impression that it would soon outshine all rivals in circulation.[2] It was printed on four pages, each about two-thirds the area of a modern tabloid page. The front page was four columns wide and devoid of any display devices. Emphasis was on local happenings and news of violence. Most of the material was trivial, flippant— but highly readable. Most important, it was cheap. Within six months the *Sun* had a circulation of around 8,000, which was nearly twice that of its nearest rival.

The reporting of George Wisner accounted for some of this success. Remembering the popularity of the Bow Street police-station news in the London forerunners of the penny press, Day hired Wisner, a Bow Street veteran, to write for the *Sun*. He was an instant success. Wisner received four dollars a week for covering the courts, plus a share in the profits of the paper. Within a year he had become co-owner of the paper.

"Human interest" news was a speciality of the *Sun*. Here is a sample of the *Sun* technique taken from a typical issue after the paper was firmly established:

Some six years ago a young gentleman, the oldest son of a distinguished baronet in England, after completing his course in education, returned home to pay his respects to his parents, and to participate in the pleasures of their social circle.[3]

[2] By 1837 the *Sun* was printing 30,000 copies a day, which was more than the total of all New York daily newspapers combined when the *Sun* had first appeared.
[3] *New York Sun*, January 3, 1835.

The account goes on to describe how the handsome youth fell in love with a girl his father had adopted as a ward. Eventually the couple ran off together because such marriages were forbidden, and the scion was disinherited by the angry baron. On the death of the father, however, the son was declared heir to the title. A younger son tried to wrest the estate by charging his elder brother with incest. This part of the story fills all of the *Sun's* first page for that day. No names are used. It could have been complete fabrication, except that the word "recent" is used to give a news flavor to the piece. The fate of the heir is never determined, although the account is embellished by such passages as:

. . . And while our hero was unsuspiciously reposing on the soft bosom of his bride, a brother's hand, impelled by a brother's hate, was uplifted with fratricidal fierceness for destruction.

A half column on the following page headed "Shocking Accident" described how a 19-year-old New Hampshire youth had been buried alive in a well cave-in. This had been picked out of the exchanges, apparently because of the twist to the story. It seems the poor chap was to have been wed the following week, which was the type of tear-jerker the *Sun* editors loved. There was humor of a sort mixed up in all this rubbish. Under a standing head, "Police Office—Yesterday," there was an item about the night watch being called to foil a desperate jail break, only to find that a pet squirrel in a cage was the source of the suspicious riot sounds. A Negro woman before the police magistrate made a whimsical remark based on the confusion of the words "prosecute" and "prostitute." All good, rich fare for the sensation-hungry *Sun* reader.

The only concession to the commercial interests of the community in this typical issue was a column of shipping news on the third page. Obviously, the paper was not printed for the property class. And yet anyone could see that the paper was bringing in plenty of advertising revenue. The back page was solid advertising, and about half the third page was devoted to classified notices, including "Want Ads." Even page one contained advertising, such as the one about Robert Hoe and Son, the printing-press maker at 29 Gold Street, who had just installed a new cylinder press for the *Sun* that was the fastest in the city—1,500 complete papers an hour.

Like the rise of organized labor, the development of a labor press, the growth of the factory system, and the emergence of the common man, the *Sun* was a shining example of what the Age of Steam was doing to people and institutions. Just as the factory made possible cheap products for mass distribution, so factory methods made the newspaper available to a wider and wider base of the public. Most of the employees of these journals for mass consumption had specialized jobs, as had the factory workers. Some of the satisfactions of making a product from beginning to end must thereby have been forfeited. But in any case, the penny press was as much a manifestation of the coming industrial revolution as the slum, the agitation for relief by exploited workers, and the trend toward urbanization.

The appearance of the penny press and the rise of the common man were closely integrated. The newspaper for the masses arrived just as the labor class began to win recognition under the Jacksonian democracy. Politics for the masses had some of the flaws corresponding to the faults of the factory system. Too often majority rule encouraged the spoils system, bossism, and mediocrity in government. Too often the early penny papers provoked criticism in striving to reach the public by lowering standards. The *Sun*, for example, was ready to sacrifice truth, even, if that would bring in more customers. The fact is, it nearly trebled in circulation in 1835 when one of its reporters, a descendant of John Locke, the political philosopher, wrote a series of articles purporting to describe life on the moon. The so-called "moon hoax" of Richard Adams Locke may not have increased public confidence in the paper, but readers did not appear to resent the journalistic trick that had been played on them. At that, the moon story was no more inaccurate than many of the human interest stories Wisner and his successors offered readers.

And yet there was much that was revealed as good in the sunrise of a new journalism, despite all the vulgarity, cheapness, and spuriousness of the first penny paper. The *Sun* was a recognition of the common man on the communications level. The working man had already won the right to vote. Now the penny papers could reach out to him as no other medium could. It did not take the politician long to discover this fact. The student of journalism will look in vain for any profound expressions of political philosophy in the early editions of the penny press, but after the first wave of sensationalism, the editors of these publications began to offer information of a more significant type. At the same time, readers began to show a little more interest in the government they had the power to control.

But of course it took a little time to win them away from the outright emotionalism with which they had been lured into the journalistic fold. Even in later stages of his development the common man showed little interest in the complicated and erudite opinions comprising the main fare of the orthodox press. The newly-recognized public was more interested in *news* than in *views*. The penny papers concentrated on supplying this type of intelligence—in readable form. The *Sun* and its galaxy of imitators proved that news was a valuable commodity, if delivered in a sprightly manner. The influence of the penny papers on journalistic style was apparent within a year or two. Very soon the stuffy commercial papers were copying this style for their own columns.

Another person began to take a special interest in the newspaper for the masses. This was the advertiser, who was impressed by the amazing circulations of the new medium. He saw that readership of the cheap daily cut through political interests, so that the paper reached a broad base of people, instead of a mere political faction. Putting an ad in every publication bought by small splinter groups was expensive and ineffective sales promotion. The large circulations of the penny papers now made it feasible to publicize articles for sale that formerly would not have warranted advertising expense.

On the other hand, advertising revenue made it possible for editors and publishers to expand and to experiment with new methods of news gathering. Since advertising flowed to the circulation leaders, and since news appeared to be the most popular type of literature, publishers began to invest heavily in various devices for improving news coverage. The full scope of this development will be described in the next chapter, but the relation between advertising and the penny press deserves mention at this point. As publishers began to understand the technique of obtaining mass circulations, they had to have better presses. Moses Y. Beach, Ben Day's brother-in-law, who took over the *Sun* in 1837, used part of his profits to buy a new steam-driven Hoe cylinder press capable

of producing 4,000 papers an hour. It was the most advanced printing equipment of its day.

The penny papers also brought changes in distribution methods.
Commercial and standard newspapers had been sold on the subscription basis. Workmen not only could not pay a large sum in
advance, but many also moved around too much to subscribe regularly. There were times when the worker could not read at all,
because of his job, or because of his poverty. The penny papers
reached such readers by depending primarily upon street sales,
under the so-called "London Plan." Vendors bought the papers
from the publisher at the rate of a hundred copies for 67 cents, to
be sold for one cent each. This put a premium on individual initiative, as indicated by the shrill cries of the vendors on street corners.
The distribution system also inevitably changed the appearance of
the paper, as editors tried to lure readers from rival publications
through the use of better makeup and more readable type.

The raw product of the press was also changed by the newspaper
of the masses. When the *views*paper became a *news*paper, the style
of the writer also changed. Editors were less interested in opinion,
and were more concerned with reporting straight news. This was
less a development toward objectivity than it was a shift away from
political partisanship.

But the shift in values brought about a curious modification in
the relationship of the press to its public. European observers were
almost unanimous in remarking how close the press and the public
were in America during the violent days of the partisan press. "Organs of dissent," the rival party papers were sometimes called. It
is true that the newspapers edited by such name-calling editors as
Bache, Freneau, Fenno, and Cobbett dissented violently from each
other, but the reader, selecting his favorite periodical because it
agreed with his views, assented to the policies of the paper. That
was why he, and all his fellow readers, each assenting to the various political views of their favorite editor, were so close to the
press. All through this period the reader considered his paper to
be his ally against the government, the leaders he disliked, or the
social experiments derided by his own group.

But when the newspaper was edited to appeal to no special faction, press and public tended to drift apart. Newspapers dissented

Courtesy, State Historical Society of Wisconsin

A typical issue of James Gordon Bennett's paper in 1836. The first three columns are devoted to the notorious Robinson-Jewett murder case, involving a rake and a prostitute. Format is tabloid size.

from one another on much broader issues. But the reader, who once assented to the fine shade of view expressed in his partisan journal, now found himself dissenting from many of the statements expressed in the more objective press, simply because no one paper could please the tastes of all readers. Thus, the more objective a press becomes, the more its readers may criticise it. No longer is the paper the close ally that it was in partisan days. But the critic who yearns for the good old days when press and public were integrated perhaps does not realize that vocal dissatisfaction is one price he pays for a more objective press.

One of the most successful promoters of a newspaper cutting through the partisanship of the times was James Gordon Bennett.[4] Bennett was strictly a reporter and editor, in contrast to the printer-publishers who have figured so prominently in this history. He had gained valuable experience as a Washington correspondent, which was to stand him in good stead when he began to develop national news as a commodity. As editor for Colonel James Watson Webb, he had engineered the 1829 merger of the *Courier* and the *Enquirer,* to make it the largest newspaper in New York. Twice he had tried to found a paper of his own, but without success. The newspaper he produced on the morning of May 6, 1835, changed this picture.

Bennett was 40 years old, disillusioned, and deep in debt when he founded the *New York Morning Herald.* His capital was five hundred dollars, plus some credit from his printers. His office was a cellar in the basement of a building at 20 Wall Street. Equipment consisted of a desk made from a plank spanning two dry goods boxes, a second hand chair, and a box for files. His entire staff consisted of himself. On this basis Bennett built one of the most profitable newspaper properties of his time.

There was a month's delay after the first appearance of the *Herald,* but from June, 1835, the paper boomed. The *Herald* was an imitator of the *Sun* in using sensational material, but Bennett

---

[4] It would be ridiculous to maintain that the penny press avoided partisanship. Papers like the *Herald* took up issues every day, and often fought for them as violently as in the old partisan-press days. But that was not the purpose of these papers, as it had been when papers reflected factions and parties. The newspaper was a little more impersonal than the viewspaper, but the development of objectivity had barely started, and the goal had not been reached more than a hundred years later. All such progress must be measured relatively.

added many tricks of his own. When it came to crime reporting the *Herald* knew no equal. The issue of June 4, 1836, a year after regular publication of the paper, will show the typical *Herald* treatment of such news. The whole front page, unrelieved by headlines, was devoted to the Robinson-Jewett case. This involved the murder of a prostitute in a brothel by a notorious man-about-town, and Bennett gave the sordid murder all the resources of his paper. He stirred up so much interest in the case that the court could not continue hearing testimony when the defendant was up for trial. The tone of *Herald* reporting is indicated by this "precede" to the main story of the trial and the disturbances in the court room:

> The mayor—the sheriff, all endeavored to restore order—all in vain. A terrible rain storm raged out doors—a mob storm indoors. The Judges and the Officers left the hall. Robinson was carried out of court, and the Public Authorities were trying to clear the hall of the mob, when this extra went to press.
> Why is not the militia called?
> We give the additional testimony up to the latest hour. . . . The mystery of the bloody drama increases—increases—increases.[5]

The "extra" feature of this news coverage (an "extra" is a special edition) was typical of Bennett's aggressive style of journalism. Soon this type of news treatment gave way to an increasing interest in more significant news. Bennett himself had no qualms about using violent news, for he was certain his paper was getting better every day. He got out of the penny-paper category in the summer of 1836 and defended his policy by stating that his readers were getting more for their money—the new price was two cents—than they could get anywhere else.

Year by year the *Herald* branched out into other fields of journalism. The paper appealed to the business class by developing the best financial section of any standard journal. Bennett, a former teacher of economics, wrote what he called the "money page." He had had experience in such reporting, and he took a special interest in this phase of journalism. When administrative duties at last forced him to give up this work, he saw to it that his best staff men were assigned to the Wall Street run. In the meantime, he was offering more serious background material than his rivals on the

[5] *New York Herald*, June 4, 1836 ("Morning" was dropped from the name-plate in 1835).

Sun. His editorial comment was seldom profound, but it was decisive, reasoned, and informative. The *Herald* led the pack in hounding news from all areas, local, foreign, and national, as we shall see in the next chapter. Bennett built up an interesting "letters" column, where readers could comment on the paper, as well as upon events. He helped develop the critical review column and society news. Long before other editors recognized the appeal of the subject, Bennett was offering sports news. Thus it was all along. The great contribution of the *Herald* was as an innovator and perfecter.

This aggressive policy paid big dividends. The *Herald* was full of advertising (50 cents for one insertion of 12 lines or less in 1836). Six weeks after the regular appearance of the paper it was selling 7,000 copies a day. It was fast overtaking its rival in the penny field, which must have given Bennett great satisfaction. He had been turned down by the *Sun* as a reporter just before he founded the *Herald.* Then, in August, 1835, the *Herald* plant was destroyed by fire. This would have defeated a lesser man, for Bennett had no financial resources. But he scurried around for credit from some of his Wall Street acquaintances. The reborn *Herald* (the "Morning" was now dropped in the name-plate) was stronger than ever. It had 20,000 readers in the summer of 1836 and was printed in its new shop on the latest Napier steam press manufactured by R. Hoe and Company. The paper began to appeal more and more to the solid, prosperous reader, but there was no abatement in the flood of sex, sin, and crime news that had won the initial successes.

This preoccupation with sordidness resulted in a curious reaction. This was a movement to boycott the *Herald.* The attack by Bennett's critics was started in May, 1840, by Park Benjamin of the *New York Signal.* Colonel James Watson Webb, Bennett's onetime employer, joined in the fray (he once administered a caning to the editor of the *Herald*), and soon all the opposition papers joined the "moral war" against the upstart journalist. Bennett was accused of blasphemy (he had carried his saucy style into the coverage of religious news) and some of the leading clergymen used their influence to make the boycott effective. Advertisers who feared to offend the moral experts withdrew their accounts. There is no doubt that Bennett offended decent members of the community with his bad taste, quackery, and sensationalism, but the real cause of the moral war was resentment over Bennett's amazing success. He had made his rivals appear stuffy and out-dated. Bennett solved the problem confronting the *Herald* in characteristic manner. He sent his best reporters out to cover the church beats, including all religious meetings of any consequence. A man of little religious feeling, he had the news sense to understand that here was another neglected public worth cultivating. He also toned down some of the obvious charlatanism that had made the *Herald* the symbol of publicized wickedness. The result was victory for Bennett.

Bennett put some needed ingredients into American journalism. He added spice and enterprise and aggressive news coverage. He proved that a publisher devoted to the continual improvement of his product could expect rich rewards. It cost a large fortune to provide all the machinery and personnel that put the *Herald* ahead of its rivals, but the investment paid huge dividends. Bennett left a valuable property to his son, and he died a rich man. But the *Herald* was remembered not so much for *what* it said, as for *how* it said it. Bennett's contributions were largely technical.

Other publishers spread the gospel of penny-press journalism to other cities. Benjamin Day's printer friends, William M. Swain and Arunah S. Abell, saw the *Sun* thrive despite the pessimistic advice they had offered, but they fully admitted their errors when they founded the *Philadelphia Public Ledger* in March, 1836, with Azariah H. Simmons as partner. Philadelphia had already been introduced to penny-press journalism by Dr. Christopher Columbus Conwell, who had experimented unsuccessfully with a penny paper, *The Cent*, in 1830. In 1835 William L. Drane founded the *Daily Transcript*, and was operating successfully when the three partners founded the *Public Ledger*. But the new paper was soon to become one of the great American dailies. It was a cleaned up version of the *Herald*—full of sensational news, but without the extreme bad taste of the New York paper. It was an effective policy. Within two years after its founding, the *Public Ledger* had absorbed its rival, the *Transcript*, and was printing more than 20,000 copies a day. Like the *Herald*, the *Public Ledger* made full use of the most modern technical and news coverage developments.

Swain was the dominant figure on the *Public Ledger*, and after

an interval, Abell decided to strike out for himself. He selected
Baltimore as a likely city. It was second only to New York as a
trade center, and was then third in population. Swain and Simmons
were not enthusiastic about the undertaking at first. Eventually they
underwrote the investment, but Abell promoted the Baltimore publication pretty much by himself. The *Baltimore Sun* first rose May
17, 1837. Its appearance coincided with a depression that had already closed the banks. The first issue of the paper played up the
story of a city council meeting the day before, at which $100,000
worth of fractional currency ("shinplasters") was authorized to
meet the financial crisis. This was scarcely the appropriate time to
found a new paper, it would seem, but the *Sun* prospered, like its
New York namesake, and appeared to be safely established at the
end of the first year with a circulation of 12,000. Like its Philadelphia affiliate, the *Sun* was always noted for its enterprise and technical progress. It was a pioneer in the development of telegraph
news. Both the Baltimore and Philadelphia penny papers worked
with the *New York Herald* in exchanging the latest news. The arrangement accounted for numerous scoops, especially during the
Mexican war. But the *Baltimore Sun* made a contribution of its
own. It developed the Washington bureau of correspondence in its
first year of operation. Soon other papers came to value the Baltimore publication for complete and accurate coverage of national
news. Government officials also began to follow the paper closely
for trends in political development.

The success of the penny-paper pioneers encouraged other publishers to follow the pattern. There were 35 penny papers started
in New York in the 1830's. All but the *Sun* and *Herald* succumbed,
but in other cities the promoters fared better. By 1840, the four
largest American cities had penny papers. Most of them had similar
news policies: much local news, great attention to human interest
stories, and a fat budget for entertainment material. But more and
more significant news was creeping into the columns, and the penny
papers led in aggressive news gathering.

The maturing of the press for the masses was best indicated by
the newspaper founded at the very beginning of the fifth decade
of the century. The paper was the *New York Tribune,* and its
founder was Horace Greeley, soon to become one of the most in-

fluential editors in the history of American journalism. More books have been written about him than about any other American of the period, except Lincoln.

Horace Greeley was like a character from a Dickens novel—so real that he appeared to be a caricature. He had the angularity of the Vermonter (which he was); a stiff, homespun personality, coupled with the shyness which makes the New England breed so difficult for others to understand. His inconsistencies were legendary. A professed Whig (the party opposed to popular rule), he worked all his life to bring a greater share of material and political benefits to the common man. A leader of the group standing for a continuance of the *status quo*, he was one of the most "radical" men of his age. At a time when the democratic process was under great stress, Greeley "put his faith in the unshackled mind."

He saw the ample resources of the United States, and he was certain that every American could enjoy the abundant life, if only simple justice could be made to prevail. He believed in what he called "beneficent capitalism." The practical application of this theory was the American System, sponsored by Henry Clay. Clay was Greeley's great hero. Until death ended the career of the Great Compromiser, Greeley devoted a column of his paper to discussions of current issues under the standing headline, "Henry Clay." Greeley, like Clay, honestly believed that if the proceeds of the protective tariff could be used to develop markets for the farmers, all the workers of the country would be prosperous. Because Greeley advocated the high tariff, he was sometimes suspected by the masses of opposing their interests. Because he had scant regard for agrarian dominance in an age of expanding industrialism, he was accused by the farmer of hypocrisy. Because he believed in the organization of unions to prevent exploitation by the privileged, he was frequently attacked by the property interests. Actually, his idea was to direct the forces of capitalism so that industry, labor, and agriculture could complement each other in improving the common lot. The day Greeley had in mind was one in which opportunity, work, and education would be available to all. Women would be paid at the same rate as men, for similar services, and would have equal civil rights. Temperance would prevail in all things. Labor would be well-organized for its own protection. Capital would reap the benefits of a prosperous community, but would feel responsible for better living standards. Slavery, and imprisonment for debt, would be abolished.

The man who proposed these revolutionary ideas was hardly messianic in appearance. He looked as though he had stepped out of a modern comic strip. He walked with a shambling, uncertain gait, as though he were feeling his way in the dark. His usual garb was a light-gray "duster," or gown, which he had purchased from an immigrant for $3, and which he wore winter and summer over his ill-fitting, nondescript suits. His guileless, baby-blue eyes were set in a moonlike face fringed with wispy whiskers sprouting out of his collar like reeds around a mossy stone. A high-pitched, whiny voice added nothing to this unimpressive ensemble. Yet this was the man who was to capture the loyalties of newspaper readers as few editors have in the history of American journalism.

Greeley began his career at the age of 15 as an apprentice to a printer whose business soon failed. He traveled around New York State as a tramp printer for five years, reading voraciously all the while. When he arrived in New York in 1831 he had just ten dollars to his name. After part-time work as a compositor, he finally landed a permanent position on the *Evening Post.*

Soon he and a partner, Francis Story, set up a shop of their own. They printed a small weekly on contract, but the main revenue was from lottery advertising, a circumstance his foes and rivals never let him forget later on. The attempt of the partners to found a penny paper in the winter of 1833 has already been described. In 1834, Greeley founded the *New Yorker,* a stimulating and well-edited publication mainly devoted to literary fare. While publishing this paper he wrote editorials for the *Daily Whig* and had entire charge of a political paper published at Albany by the Whig party leaders. For six months during the presidential campaign of 1840 he edited and published a campaign paper, the *Log Cabin.* He was an experienced journalist, therefore, when he announced in the *Log Cabin* that beginning April 10, 1841, he would publish a daily penny paper, the *New York Tribune.*

His political activities had made Greeley one of the New York Whig triumvirate, which included state party boss Thurlow Weed, the Albany journalist, and Governor William H. Seward. Now was the time to found a newspaper that could carry the Whig message to the comman man. It is significant that the *Tribune* appeared just a month after President William Henry Harrison's inauguration following the Whig victory of 1840. Greeley must have been aware that the climate was right for his undertaking. His influence in state and federal political circles must certainly have been a factor in the establishment of the paper. It should be pointed out, too, that Henry Clay, Greeley's hero, expected to be a key figure in the new administration, and was confident that the American System, also promoted by Greeley, would be pushed through at once. But the President died a month after his inauguration, and many ambitions were cut short thereby. Not Greeley's, however.[6]

With a thousand dollars of borrowed money, about that much of his own, plus a mortgage on his shop—a total capitalization of not more than three thousand dollars—Greeley issued the first *Tribune* as a penny paper. It was not much to look at. Its four pages were five columns wide and about the dimensions of a modern tabloid. The printing was good, however, and so was the content, apparently. At least it attracted readers, for Greeley boasted of a circulation in excess of 11,000 after the second month. This was about one-fourth the print order of the *Sun,* then the most popular paper in America, but it was enough to establish the *Tribune* firmly. Greeley was a good editor but a poor manager. He himself never shared in the fortune that his paper was to make for others. Indeed, the paper might have failed, had not the very able Thomas McElrath purchased a half interest for $2,000. The paper was then losing money. At the end of the second year the price was raised to two cents (weekly subscribers paid 1½ cents an issue) and the *Tribune* began to make money.

The *Tribune* always trailed both the *Sun* and the *Herald* in daily circulation, but part of its great reputation was to rest upon its weekly edition, which was a phenomenal success. It first appeared September 2, 1841. Offered at two dollars a year, or one dollar a year when "clubs" of 20 members bought it (which was very common) the weekly *Tribune* largely established Greeley's reputation as the greatest editor of his day. It was said to have been read in the midwestern states areas "next to the Bible."

Many able critics have declared that Horace Greeley does not

[6] Harrison's running mate, John Tyler of Virginia, proved as President to be more southern than Whig and vetoed Clay's pet bills. In the 1844 presidential year the Whigs ditched Tyler for Clay, but Democrat James K. Polk won.

deserve the acclaim that has been given to him. Victor Lawson, the great editor of the *Chicago Daily News*, knew Greeley personally. Lawson considered the *Tribune* editor to be the most overrated journalist in American history.[7] The younger Schlesinger apparently thinks of Greeley as a humbug. Says he:

Greeley's reputation (apart from his strong, if belated, stand on slavery) rests mainly on his feverish advocacy of sideshow reforms. He (Greeley) was eminently a "safe" radical. When he devoutly fought for the American System, what did it matter if he allowed Albert Brisbane to pay him a hundred dollars a week for printing a column on Fourierism [see p. 231]? Brisbane was . . . a cheap price for a progressive reputation . . .[8]

But equally reliable students say that Greeley was of heroic proportions. John R. Commons, the great authority on the labor movement, called the *Tribune* "the first and only great vehicle this country has known for the ideas and experiments of constructive democracy."[9] E. L. Godkin, one of the great journalists of the late nineteenth century, who is often misquoted on Greeley, actually had great respect for the editor of the *Tribune*. Godkin ridiculed Greeley's whimsies, but in his *Life and Letters* wrote: "The Tribune in particular excited my warm admiration. . . . The influence of such a journal was deservedly high. Greeley . . . sacrificed everything—advertisers, subscribers, and all else—to what he considered principle."[10] This was indeed an endorsement, coming from such a severe critic as E. L. Godkin. Joseph Bishop, who succeeded Godkin as editor of the influential *New York Evening Post*, wrote in his autobiography: "The 'Tribune' was a tremendous force in the country because of the personal faith of the plain people in the honesty of its editor. Every word the 'Tribune' printed was believed im-

---

[7] This statement was made after the bitter campaign of 1872, however, when Lawson opposed Greeley as the leader of a coalition party seeking to put Greeley into the White House in place of President Grant.

[8] Arthur M. Schlesinger, Jr., *The Age of Jackson* (Boston: Little, Brown and Company, 1945), pp. 295-6.

[9] John R. Commons, "Horace Greeley and the Working Class Origins of the Republican Party," *Political Science Quarterly*, XXIV (September 1909), p. 472.

[10] Rollo Ogden, ed., *Life and Letters of Edwin Lawrence Godkin*, Vol. I (New York: The Macmillan Company, 1907), pp. 166-7. Godkin's better-known appraisal of Greeley as a "trader in politics" was made during and after the Civil War, when Godkin's brand of liberalism could not square with Greeley's philosophies.

plicitly because he was the man behind it. The power he wielded was not equaled by any editor of his time—neither has it been equaled by any editor since." [11]

On the other hand, William Cullen Bryant, one of the great *Post* editors, had nothing but contempt for Greeley and refused to nod or speak to the *Tribune* editor even when they were brought together at social functions not connected with journalism or politics.

Perhaps the best way to evaluate such a controversial figure is to ignore his critics and to consider his record. The early issues of his paper offer no clue as to his greatness. The three pages of fine print describing the details of the President's funeral contain none of the stimulation and challenge for which Greeley was to become famous. And yet the very first issue indicates the significance of the *New York Tribune*. It sold for one cent, in competition with the other penny papers, and therefore was plainly intended for mass readership. But instead of pandering to emotionalism, the entire issue was devoted to serious discussion and reportage. The *Tribune* could offer its public murder stories just as sensational as those of its rivals, but that type of journalism was not the hallmark of the paper. Greeley had the curious faith that the masses could be attracted by reason as well as by emotionalism. He did not insult the common man by trying to "write down" to him. There is nothing that can raise the dignity of the scorned more effectively than honest recognition, and this appeal undoubtedly was a factor in the *Tribune*'s success.

Admittedly, much of the *Tribune*'s later content was rational only in the broad sense. Any crackpot social philosopher could express himself in the paper, if he wrote forcefully. The common criticism of Greeley, indeed, was that he was utterly irrational. But some of his "idealism" was founded on sound reasoning. He saw that Jeffersonian ideas, based on an agrarian society, were not applicable to a nation fast becoming an industrial power. He also realized the dangers of unrestricted industrialism. The slums of Europe warned of that. Allowing selfish business interests and rugged individualism to dominate American society could only lead to anarchy, Greeley reasoned. The duty of the statesman, as he understood it, was to reduce social friction between classes and economic interests. That could be done only when the state had strong regulatory powers.

So Greeley groped for the way out. Lacking formal education, he knew little about social and political philosophers. He preferred to learn by experimentation. Like Jefferson, he was more interested in a responsive government than in administrations guaranteeing only stability. And yet this strange man was a Whig—a member of the party that stood for rigid governmental structure. The Whigs wanted such a government so as to further their own special interests. Greeley demanded the same strong government, but in order to restrain such selfishness either in Whig or Democrat.

Thus, he was loyal to his party, since it offered the best chance of obtaining the government he advocated, but he was ready to lend a helping hand to those who could contribute ideas, unpopular as they might be. That is why he allowed Albert Brisbane the use of his columns. Brisbane was the American prophet of Fourierism, a scheme for curing the ills of capitalism by a form of collective living he called "associationism." In the 1850's the *Tribune* spent many pages explaining Socialism, and Greeley himself debated the issue publicly with brilliant opponents, including Henry Raymond of the *New York Times*. For a decade one of the London correspondents for the *Tribune* was Karl Marx, co-founder of Communism. Greeley fought steadily for agrarian reforms, including the Homestead Bill, offering land in the West that immigrants could afford to develop. All this completely violated Whig doctrine, and yet Greeley was one of the leaders of the party. No wonder his critics were confused.

But it should be clear that Greeley did not endorse all the opinions expressed in the *Tribune*. He was aware that most of the suggestions were impractical. But he was also aware that America was still groping toward a goal, and that it would have to continue experimenting, if democracy were to be kept dynamic. His readers appeared to understand these motives, even if rivals did not. For the *Tribune* fared about as well on a diet of indigestible ideas as the other mass newspapers did on their rations of luscious crime. *Tribune* readers possibly could not always follow the theories offered by "Uncle Horace," but they knew he was supplying a forum for all who fought on their side. They saw that Greeley was intent upon producing a better world—and a better press. If his experiments were ineffectual, they were no more so than those of a scientist who keeps working with test tubes to find solutions. To stop experimenting, Greeley believed, was to say that society must remain a pigsty, with the strongest hogs taking all the swill.

Greeley accepted his role. It is reasonable to argue that he was a "safe radical," whose "sideshow reforms," such as his demands for women's rights, were mere window dressing for a party whose real leaders were interested in more practical matters, such as the exploitation of labor. It might be pointed out that his party opposed Van Buren's 10-hour maximum day for government workers, and Greeley once editorially argued against the proposal. That seemed a curious reversal for a man who had demanded more rights for the laborer; actually, Greeley balked at the Van Buren measure because he believed labor itself should set its limitation on hours. If he had not been sincere in his efforts for the working man, why was he made an honorary president of the typographical union he had helped to rescue after the depression of 1837, and why was he always honored at meetings of labor groups?

It is much more logical to argue that Greeley's motives were sincere, and that his aberrations resulted from faulty education and a peculiar background. No one can say that he followed his party blindly. Actually, he and other party leaders bickered continually. Whig "realists," such as that political chameleon, Daniel Webster, were all for reading him out of the party at one time or another. They saw Greeley as the sower of discontent among wage earners, and the wrecker of plans to restrain the working man from moving westward.

Greeley considered himself not a merchant of discontent, but a social doctor. He knew that the health of his country depended upon thriving workers and prosperous farmers. The tonic he proposed was regulation of special interests by the government. At this point some of the Whig politicos howled for Greeley's scalp. They called him a traitor to his class and party.

Despite all this criticism, Greeley was read by all types of persons. Whether he wrote on politics, farming, labor, education, the horror of debt, the rights of women, temperance, marriage, the frontier, or slavery, all classes of society took note of the *Tribune*. He upbraided a nation for its whisky consumption—and the liquor-

SUPPLEMENT TO FRANK LESLIE'S ILLUSTRATED NEWSPAPER

PRESENTED GRATUITOUSLY WITH NO. 896 OF FRANK LESLIE'S ILLUSTRATED NEWSPAPER.

THE LATE HORACE GREELEY

FROM A PHOTOGRAPH BY E. W. BOGARDUS, 363 BROADWAY, N. Y.

Courtesy, State Historical Society of Wisconsin

How one of the pioneer picture magazines reported the death of the noted journalist, Horace Greeley, founder and editor of the *New York Tribune. Leslie's* was one of the popular magazines of the period.

loving public kept right on reading the *Tribune*. He denounced the tobacco smokers and chewers—they, too, remained regular readers. He criticised the speculator and financier—they fumed and fussed, and read on. Even the business men, who loathed his ideas, read Greeley. They disagreed with every column, but they respected the editor who wore no man's collar.

Why should such persons, many of whom resented all this "radicalism," not only have tolerated Greeley's paper, but have supported it loyally? There was no doubt of its success. It was full of advertising—its front page was usually solid with commercial notices—universally read, and highly respectable. The weekly edition had more readers than any other publication of the period. Many of its 200,000 subscribers were farmers in the Middle West, who had no sympathy with many of Greeley's ideas on industrial society. The daily lagged behind the *Sun* and the *Herald,* but the circulation was always high. Could such a paper succeed today? It had more inflammatory material in it than even the labor papers of the time. Was it popular because the reader trusted the sincerity of its editor?

The secret of Greeley's popularity was his consciousness of responsibility to the reader. His flights into socialistic fancy were erratic and irresponsible, perhaps, but the average reader appeared to understand that the motives were sincere. That was why the farmers, who often disagreed violently with Greeley's views, read the "Try-bune," as they usually called it, "next to the Bible." How could anyone doubt the sincerity of a man who advocated a fairer distribution of wealth and who lived up to his advice by giving away to his employees all but a few shares of the gold mine he had made out of the *Tribune*? He changed the press of the masses from the vulgar level of sensationalism to a promoter of culture and stimulating ideas, and made it pay dividends. His protégés also raised the standards of the Fourth Estate. For many years Charles A. Dana, who will appear again in these pages, was Greeley's assistant, and much of the early success of the *Tribune* has been ascribed to Dana. Henry J. Raymond, soon to establish the *New York Times,* started out under Greeley. Margaret Fuller, one of the truly great literary figures of the period, wrote regularly for the *Tribune.* Carl Schurz, John Hay, Whitelaw Reid, Henry James, William Dean Howells, George Ripley, and Richard Hildreth, who made names for themselves in various fields of literature, journalism, and history, served under "Uncle Horace."

The identification of Greeley with his paper is brought out by an anecdote told by Joseph Bishop in his *Notes,* written after Bishop had left the editorship of the *Post.* The editor was in Vermont a year or so after Greeley's death in 1872, and made some remark about an article that had recently appeared in the *Tribune.* "Does the Try-bune still print?" asked a farmer in the audience. "Why, I thought Greeley was dead." [12]

A thesis was advanced at the beginning of this chapter that when a new public is first tapped by the mass media, the appeal is invariably upon an emotional plane. The result is a "sensational" vehicle of communication. The more literate members of society sometimes look with contempt upon such readers and upon the agencies reaching such publics. They see the grimy mechanic reading a sensational newspaper and they put him down as a moron. A learned scholar, on the other hand, takes some piece of machinery to this same mechanic for a repair that might have been made with the flick of a finger, and the mechanic thinks of the scholar as a moron. Both critics are wrong. Each may be a genius in his own field. Neither is a moron. But the mechanic may be backward in reading experience, and so he prefers a simple literary fare. He may change his habits as he acquires literary skill, however.

Readers of the *Sun* first bought it primarily for its police reports. Many of these readers matured with the years, however, for as time went on, cheap papers competing successfully with the *Sun* offered more nourishing fare. Greeley proved that a publisher could reach the masses without resorting to sensationalism. Even the *Sun* and the *Herald* offered more substantial material as time went on. They had to, to keep up with the increasing skills of their readers. Eventually, such papers left the semiliterate public behind, and another wave of sensational papers had to be established (as in the 1890's) to take up the slack. The completion of this cycle is exemplified by Henry J. Raymond of the *New York Times.*

From early boyhood, Raymond showed promise as a thinker, and he was graduated from the University of Vermont in 1840 with the highest honors. "Like most of his honors," one of his biographers

---

[12] H. L. Stoddard, *Horace Greeley* (New York: G. P. Putnam's Sons, 1946), p. 322.

has said, "they cost more than they were worth." [13] His studies almost ruined his health, and the habit of overwork established in college may have contributed to his early death.

As a college student, Raymond contributed to Greeley's *New Yorker,* which the youth admired greatly. After a visit to the New York editor, Raymond became Greeley's chief assistant in 1841, the year the *Tribune* was founded. George Jones was a colleague in the business office of the *Tribune.* Together they planned to put out the "ideal daily." Neither had sufficient money, however, for already it was impossible to establish a New York paper with $500 and a few packing-box desks, as Bennett had.

Raymond and Greeley were naturally incompatible. The younger man could never appreciate the erratic mental behavior of his employer, and soon Raymond left to work for Colonel James Watson Webb on the *Courier and Enquirer.* During this interim he established a reputation as an orator and budding politician. He was elected to the State Assembly in 1849 and became speaker in 1851. At this point he broke with Webb on the Free Soil Party issue. He took a position as an editor of *Harper's New Monthly Magazine* (established in June 1850), where he remained until 1856 as a part-time editor.

It was in 1851 that Raymond and Jones realized their old ambition of publishing a New York newspaper of their own. The first issue of the *New York Daily Times* appeared September 18, 1851. It sold for one cent, and thus showed its intention of being a paper for the masses, but it eschewed the sensationalism of the *Sun* and *Herald,* and the whimsy of the *Tribune,* as described in the policy expressed the first day: ". . . we do not mean to write as if we were in a passion [a slap at Greeley, who was regularly the butt of Raymond's jibes]—unless that shall really be the case; and we shall make it a point to get into a passion as rarely as possible." [14] One of the *Times'* strong points was interpreting of foreign news. Raymond sought to excel in reporting European events.

Raymond soon established a reputation as a reasonable and objective editor. Actually, compromise, rather than objectivity, was Raymond's chief characteristic. "The great temporizer," Maverick,

---

[13] *Dictionary of American Biography,* XV, p. 408.

[14] Willard G. Bleyer, *Main Currents in the History of American Journalism* (Boston: Houghton Mifflin Company, 1927), p. 240.

one of his biographers, called the *Times* editor, adding that this quality ruined him as a politician and eventually as a leader.[15] He appealed to readers who liked the *Herald's* aggressiveness but resented its bad taste; who admired the *Tribune,* but suspected Greeley's fanaticism; or who had confidence in the solidness of the *Courier and Enquirer,* but were bored by its pompousness.

From the very beginning Raymond used every opportunity to plague his old mentor, Greeley. By 1852 Raymond was up to his neck in politics, despite the promise he had made to his partner after Jones warned that politics and editorships did not mix. At that time the prohibition of liquor was a big issue. It was one of Greeley's pet subjects, and he expected to be elected governor of New York because of his editorial stand on temperance. But Thurlow Weed, the Albany editor who controlled the state convention that year, needed an upstate man to hold the party together on the dry issue. That meant that the lieutenant governor had to be a big city "wet" in order to hold the party together on other issues. Weed selected Raymond, rather than his old teammate, Greeley. Greeley, who had done all the temperance promotion, had to see the honors go to the man who had openly reviled him. As Greeley once said of the episode: ". . . no other name could have been . . . so bitterly humbling to me," [16] and he found it hard to forgive his old protégé for the disgrace. But again, Raymond had paid too big a price for honor. He won a minor office from the Whigs, but the party was soon liquidated. There was little political advantage either to the *Times,* or to Raymond. He had estranged his partner Jones by violating a promise. And he had hurt Greeley unnecessarily.

Indeed, from this time on, Raymond was as much a politician as he was an editor. As we shall see, the *Times* editor became a power in Republican circles. Greeley was to see his rival badly mauled in the postwar political arena, but in the 1850's Raymond rode the crest of the wave. Within two years after the founding of the *Times,* even Greeley admitted that it outsold the *Tribune*

---

[15] Augustus Maverick, *Henry J. Raymond and the New York Press* (Hartford: A. S. Hale and Company, 1870), p. 170.

[16] Letter to Governor Seward, dated New York, November 11, 1854, in Thurlow Weed Barnes and Harriet Weed, eds., *Life of Thurlow Weed,* Vol. II (Boston: Houghton Mifflin Company, 1884), p. 280.

within the city limits. He left a reputation as one of the great journalists of the century.

Raymond's contribution was the development of reasonable decency in public reporting. There was a minimum of personal invective in the *Times*. It seldom presented issues in the black and white patterns favored by Greeley. It was invariably fair in tone, if not in content, and no rival equaled it in developing the technique of careful reporting. It substituted accuracy for wishful thinking, even when Raymond was deep in politics. Curiously, Raymond, who was addicted to politics, stood for a strangely objective non-partisanship in his paper. It was as though the man had two completely different personalities.

And even Greeley, who had just cause to resent the attacks of his former assistant, had to respect the man who had tried to foster decent journalism. Raymond died in 1869 at the age of 49, and Greeley wrote one of the most touching obituaries. But a discussion of the *Times* as a journalistic force belongs in a later period.

Two other journalists of the period deserve passing mention. One was Thurlow Weed, better known as a political boss, and the other was Samuel Bowles III.

Thurlow Weed began a career of influence as an apprentice printer in upstate New York. For a time (1808-1817) he worked as a journeyman; became interested in politics as a follower of DeWitt Clinton; and worked on the *Rochester Telegraph*. By 1825 he had become a political power. He purchased the *Telegraph* that year and used it to promote his candidates. Weed had strong anti-Masonic principles in a day when Masonry was a burning political issue. The Anti-Masonic party raised funds to establish a paper at Albany, and Weed was made editor while he was still serving as a leader in the Assembly. The *Evening Journal* appeared in February, 1830, and under Weed it became virtually the official organ of the Whigs. Weed was given much of the credit for electing William H. Seward governor in 1838, and the two, plus Greeley, were instrumental in putting Harrison into the White House in 1840.

Weed was the typical party boss. It was said that Seward had the principles and Weed had the votes. Greeley was the sounding board for new ideas. The big boss was Weed, however. He had the knack of making all acquaintances believe he was a special friend. The secret of his popularity was that he sincerely liked

SAMUEL BOWLES.

death of SAMUEL BOWLES, who breathed last on the evening of January 16, has deprived American journalism of one of its most worthy representatives. The Springfield Republican, of which he was the editor, has for years exercised a national influence in politics. Although published in a comparatively small New England town, half-way between New York and Boston, and overshadowed by the press of both cities, it has held its own for half a century, is more prosperous and more widely quoted at this moment than ever it was before. It is also, after an exceptional journalistic outgrowth, remarkable at least in the theory of his treatment of public affairs, it has derived a distinctive peculiarity from its editor. Provincial in its province and aims, seeking to represent the province of a life by which it is surrounded, it is regarded as a power in the land by the politicians of all parties.

An anomaly of this sort could be produced only in America, for the reason, perhaps, that we have no London centre of thought and action, no London or Paris, so that the newspapers of every town are enabled to display whatever is in them with the certainty of adequate consideration. The Republican, in spite of its geographical position, has built up a reputation as solid as that of any of its contemporaries which happen to be issued from cities of ten and twenty times the population of Springfield.

SAMUEL BOWLES, to whom the greater achievement of the Republican belong, was the son of the founder of the paper. SAMUEL BOWLES the first was a Hartford printer, who went to Springfield in 1824, and began the publication of the Weekly Republican. SAMUEL BOWLES the second, then the third—for his grandfather bore the same name—was born in 1826. He grew up in his father's office. There is a tradition that he got the rudiments of a sound academic education in the schools of Springfield; but as he entered the service of the Republican before he was seventeen years of age, it is likely that he acquired the strong and simple writing which marked his editorial style out of an inner consciousness opened by contact with types, and purified by free and early use of printers' ink. Certain it is that he was born, as he was raised, a journalist, owing his success, like so many eminent members of his profession, to the practical tuition of the composing-room.

In 1844 he prevailed upon his father to issue the Daily Republican, and from the outset became the charge of it. The years 1846–48 brought with them the Mexican war and the telegraph, and, of consequence, a revolution in journalistic practice. At this time "Sam" BOWLES, to a friend's always called him, was just of age, full of ambition and ardor, with plenty of work in him; and here he laid the beginnings of the substantial fame and fortune he has enjoyed ever since. He did every thing—edited and made up paper, helped work it off on an old ADAMS press, acted as mailing clerk, cashier, and reporter, writing, working, and sleeping in the office. The Republican became a passion with him. The Republican was SAM BOWLES, and SAM BOWLES was Republican. It owed its character entirely to

the features impressed upon it by its editor. Its rugged independence of the politicians, its tolerance and entertainment of new and original ideas, its shrewd every-day sense, its extraordinary compilation of news adapted to a certain peculiar audience, whose wants it studies and serves in the minutest way, its racy good nature, varied just enough by an occasional ugly streak or angry flash to give it the needful quantum of snap—all were characteristic of Mr. BOWLES.

In 1857 Mr. BOWLES was induced to go to Boston as editor of a paper made by the fusion of some half a dozen journals, under the title of

The Boston Daily Traveller. It was an eight-page paper, modelled on the style of the New York daily journals. It did not take, however, and at the end of about six months Mr. BOWLES resumed the editorship of the Springfield Republican, of which he was still the owner. He gave a stanch and vigorous support to the Republican party until 1872, when he opposed the renomination of General GRANT, and in the Liberal Convention at Cincinnati pressed the name of CHARLES FRANCIS ADAMS as a candidate for the Presidency. Although deeply disappointed by his failure to carry the Convention, he supported Mr.

SAMUEL BOWLES.—(PHOTOGRAPHED BY SARONY.)

GREELEY with great warmth and ardor. At the same time he disclaimed all party allegiance, and proclaimed the political independence of the Republican.

Mr. BOWLES at one time incurred the enmity of the late JIM FISK by comments in the Republican on his career as a director of the Erie Railway, and Fisk brought a libel suit against the editor for $50,000. One evening in December, 1868, while Mr. BOWLES was talking with some friends in the office of the Fifth Avenue Hotel, he was arrested on papers issued by Judge McCUNN, and taken hastily to the jail, when the jailer denied him the privilege of writing a note to his wife or of receiving the friends who came to aid him. The numerous offers of bail were refused, as the sheriff declined to be annoyed with such matters after business hours. So Mr. BOWLES slept in Ludlow Street Jail. He was bailed out in the morning, and Mr. Fisk's contemptible trick afterward formed the subject of a very spicy correspondence between Mr. BOWLES and Fisk's lawyer, in which the editor had decidedly the best of the argument.

Mr. BOWLES was fond of travel in his own country and abroad. He visited California several times, and his book, *Across the Continent*, was the first really good picture of the Pacific slope which appeared. He was a singularly agreeable man, and was universally esteemed in society. In his family he was genial and hospitable, and some of the brightest men and women in the country were his warm friends and frequent guests. He was always a hard worker. When he supposed that he was about to die he said, with a smile, to an old friend, " Nothing is the matter with me but thirty-five years of hard work," and he added afterward, "I was never much of a boy; I had very little boyhood." The immediate cause of his death was paralysis of the brain. He had been ill with congestion of the lungs since the early part of October last, and that malady, combined with a disorder of the heart, caused him acute suffering. Toward the latter part of November he grew worse. On the 1st of December he thought the end had come, and bade his family and friends farewell. During the last two weeks of his life he gradually lost strength, though conscious all the time. He suffered little, was quiet in mind through the afternoon and evening of his last day on earth, and his death was like the peaceful closing of the eyes in sleep.

HEAD-QUARTERS OF MEHEMET ALI.

On this page we give a picture of the quarters recently occupied by MEHEMET ALI at Kamarli, which is not far south of Orchanié, on the road between Plevna and Sophia. The Russian advance from the captured stronghold of OSMAN PASHA compelled the abandonment of all the Turkish positions, and the soldiers of the Czar penetrated the passes almost without resistance, where they had expected to fight their way step by step. The city of Sophia was hastily evacuated by the Turks, and immediately occupied by the Russians, who thus obtained a footing south of the Balkans, and an excellent base of operations against Adrianople.

Courtesy, State Historical Society of Wisconsin

An obituary picture of Samuel Bowles III, as it appeared in a famous news magazine. Bowles made the *Springfield Republican,* founded by his father, one of the outstanding newspapers of its day. *Harper's Weekly* used pictures regularly, long before the perfection of the half-tone photographic engraving.

people—all kinds of people. During his heyday he was one of the important Americans of the period, and his paper was therefore influential.

Weed's power waned after Seward's defeat in 1842. He recouped his political fortunes somewhat when he backed General Zachary Taylor for president in 1848 and sent Seward to the Senate. The Whigs were doomed by 1850, however, and Weed went to Europe defeated and dejected. He accepted the new Republican party reluctantly, but was unsuccessful in promoting Seward within it. From then on, Weed's fortunes declined. He gave up the editorship of his paper in 1863. He tried to make a comeback as a journalist in 1867 by taking over the editorship of the *New York Commercial Advertiser,* but he had to give up the position because of poor health. He died in retirement in 1882.

Another outstanding paper at this time was Massachusetts' *Springfield Republican.* Its founder was Samuel Bowles II, although his son, Samuel Bowles III, is more important to this history. The father was reared in Connecticut, where the family had been driven by depression. He was apprenticed to a printer at the age of 15, after the first Samuel Bowles, a grocer, died and bequeathed his entire worldly possessions to the boy—a Bible and a watch. Bowles grew up as a poor boy, but from an early age he was interested in cultural development, as evidenced by the literary club he established.

His first regular job was with the *New Haven Register.* In 1819 he joined with John Francis of Wethersfield as a partner in the *Hartford Times,* a weekly that soon failed under the adverse conditions of the time. He and his wife and family loaded their household possessions and the *Times* press on a flatboat and poled up the Connecticut River to Springfield, Massachusetts. There, a group of Anti-Federalists helped him re-establish as a publisher. First copies of the *Springfield Republican* appeared September 8, 1824. It was a weekly, and its 250 subscribers paid two dollars a year for it. Bowles ran the paper by himself; it grew slowly, but outlasted five rivals, and by 1840 Bowles had established a reputation as a reliable publisher. By that time Springfield was beginning to boom as a railroad center, and circulation was up to 1,200. The original publisher died in 1851, but by that time the paper was largely the product of the son.

Samuel Bowles III made the most of the excellent opportunities presented to him by his father, and it is the son who established the national reputation of the *Republican*. It was he who argued his father into "going daily" in March, 1844 (it was an evening paper then, but became morning a year later). Bowles made the paper successful by skillful organization of regional correspondence, so that every little community in the upper Connecticut Valley had reason to take the paper. Young Bowles was educated for the role he was to take in journalism. He shared his room as a boy with his father's three apprentices. He grew up in the back shop. He delivered papers and knew personally all the local subscribers and their interests. At 18 he was ready to assume his place as a peer in the Fourth Estate. It was at this time that he persuaded his father to let him try a daily. It was hard going at first. He worked as much as 40 hours at a stretch without sleep. His health began to fail. The paper almost foundered financially. But in the end, Bowles produced one of the great newspapers of the nineteenth century.

Partly responsible for the success of the paper were William B. Calhoun, who wrote many of the editorials credited by readers to Bowles; Josiah Gilbert Holland, a fluent and articulate writer; and George Ashmun, friend of Abraham Lincoln and a noted politician. But the main emphasis of the *Republican* was news, and Bowles made that his special department.

He took over full control upon the death of his father in 1851 (Holland had an interest in the paper, but not enough to control it). Actually, it is not until the late 1850's and the 1860's that the *Republican* exerted its greatest influence, so that this discussion must be reserved for a later chapter. But the foundations of success were laid in the period covered in this section. Bowles was a sponsor of the new Republican party. By 1860 his weekly edition was a national institution, with a circulation of about 12,000, but with a reputation throughout the country exceeded only by that of the *Tribune*. The daily hovered around 6,000, but that, too, was good for a provincial paper. Bowles was the mainspring of this intricate mechanism. ". . . he knew everything, saw everything, dictated everything—and his dictation dictated every time," one of his biographers has said.[17]

[17] George S. Merriam, *Life and Times of Samuel Bowles*, Vol. I (New York: The Century Company, 1885), p. 104.

He was his own slave driver, and expected others to keep up to him. There were no 40-hour weeks, daily hours, or regular holidays on the *Republican*. As Holland once described the routine,

> The sparkle, the vivacity, the drive, and the power of the *Republican* cost life. We did not know when we tasted it and found it so charged with zest that we were tasting heart's blood, but that was the priceless element that commended it to our appetites. A pale man, weary and nervous, crept home at three o'clock in the morning, and while all nature was fresh and the birds were singing and thousands of eyes were bending eagerly over the results of his night's labors, he was tossing and trying to sleep.[18]

Yet seldom was complaint heard about working hours in the *Republican* office. Its reporters and editors were craftsmen, proud of their product, and absorbed in their work. Young men from all over the United States tried to get on the *Republican* staff. A tour with the Springfield paper was a kind of advanced degree in journalism. A "*Republican* man" was welcome on the biggest papers in the country.

Bowles was a charming and cultivated conversationalist, although he tended to be "often a gossip and never a safe confidant," according to Wendell Phillips Garrison,[19] who knew the editor well. He believed in what he called "the higher journalism"—a responsibility not to party, social group, or class—but to conscience alone. He was not always tactful. Because of a ruthless determination, he turned associates into enemies at times. This was apparent when a group of former *Republican* newsmen founded the rival *Union*. But Bowles' contributions to journalism were much more important than his few faults. He was the prophet of responsible provincial journalism, and the institution owes much to the standards he helped to establish.

ANNOTATED BIBLIOGRAPHY

Books:

Barnes, Thurlow Weed, and Harriet Weed, eds., *Life of Thurlow Weed.* 2 vols. Boston: Houghton Mifflin Company, 1883-4. The first volume is the politician's autobiography, edited by his daughter, Harriet. The

---

[18] *Dictionary of American Biography,* II, p. 516.
[19] *Ibid.,* p. 517.

second volume comprises the memoirs, documents, and letters compiled by Weed's grandson.

Bigelow, John, *Retrospections of an Active Life,* IV. New York: The Baker and Taylor Company, 1909-13. The journalistic field of the period described by a well-known *Post* executive.

Brown, Francis, *Raymond of the Times.* New York: Norton, 1951. A first-rate biography of a great editor.

Carlson, Oliver, *The Man Who Made News.* New York: Duell, Sloan & Pearce, 1942. The best biography of James Gordon Bennett, Sr.

Davis, Elmer, *History of the New York Times, 1851-1921.* New York: The New York Times Company, 1921. Valuable for the early period of the great newspaper.

Greeley, Horace, *Recollections of a Busy Life.* New York: J. B. Ford and Company, 1868. The editor's own version of his career.

Hale, William H., *Horace Greeley: Voice of the People.* New York: Harper & Brothers, 1950. A good modern biography.

Hooker, Richard, *The Story of an Independent Newspaper: One Hundred Years of the Springfield Republican, 1824-1924.* New York: The Macmillan Company, 1924.

Isely, Jeter Allen, *Horace Greeley and the Republican Party, 1853-1861.* Princeton: Princeton University Press, 1947. An examination of Greeley's writings for the eight years.

Maverick, Augustus, *Henry J. Raymond and the New York Press.* Hartford: A. S. Hale and Company, 1870. An outstanding authority, this book contains many valuable documents.

Merriam, George S., *Life and Times of Samuel Bowles.* New York: The Century Company, 1885. More complete than the Hooker study, above, and full of interesting letters and documents.

O'Brien, Frank M., *The Story of The Sun.* New York: George H. Doran Company, 1918. Revised ed., New York: D. Appleton and Company, 1928. The standard history of the first successful penny newspaper.

Parrington, Vernon L., *Main Currents in American Thought,* Vol. II. Greeley, Margaret Fuller, and Bryant are discussed.

Parton, James, *Life of Horace Greeley.* New York: Mason Brothers, 1855. The standard reference, written by a contemporary.

Seitz, Don C., *Horace Greeley, Founder of the New York Tribune.* Indianapolis: Bobbs-Merrill Company, 1926. A standard biography of the editor, largely replaced now by later studies.

Stoddard, Henry L., *Horace Greeley: Printer, Editor, Crusader.* New York: G. P. Putnam's Sons, 1946. Not as deep as some of the other biographies of the editor, but much more human, readable, and convincing than the earlier studies.

Van Deusen, Glyndon Garlock, *Horace Greeley: Nineteenth Century Crusader.* Philadelphia: University of Pennsylvania Press, 1953. This is the best, and most detailed, of the Greeley biographies of recent years, and was awarded the Albert J. Beveridge Memorial Prize of the American Historical Association. The same author is the biographer of Thurlow Weed and Henry Clay, who were so closely associated with Greeley.

Periodicals and Monographs:

Abbott, Lyman, "Reminiscences," *Outlook*, CVI (April 25, 1914), 897. Sidelights on Raymond's brush with the courts on a contempt citation.

Borden, Morton, "Some Notes on Horace Greeley, Charles Dana and Karl Marx," *Journalism Quarterly*, XXXIV (Fall 1957), 457. It was Dana who kept Marx on the *Tribune's* payroll. *See also* Summer 1959 issue for texts of five letters from Dana to Marx (p. 314).

Bradford, Gamaliel, "Samuel Bowles," *Atlantic Monthly*, CXVI (October 1915), 487. An excellent character study. Reprinted in Ford and Emery, *Highlights in the History of the American Press*.

Browne, Junius Henri, "Horace Greeley," *Harper's New Monthly Magazine*, XLVI (April 1873), 734. Describes Greeley's idiosyncrasies.

Coleman, Albert E., "New and Authentic History of the Herald of the Bennetts," *Editor & Publisher*, LVI-LVIII (March 29, 1924 to June 13, 1925).

Commons, John R., "Horace Greeley and the Working Class Origins of the Republican Party," *Political Science Quarterly*, XXIV (September 1909), 468. A significant article by a great authority and writer on American Labor.

Peebles, Paul, "James Gordon Bennett's Scintillations," *Galaxy*, XIV (August 1872), 258. A revealing and rewarding study of the editor. Reprinted in Ford and Emery, *Highlights in the History of the American Press*.

"Personal Reminiscences of Horace Greeley," *Bookman*, XIII (April 1901), 126. Sympathetic and readable anecdotes.

"Sketches of the Life and Labors of Horace Greeley," *National Quarterly Review*, XXVI (December 1872), 153. Strong posthumous defense of the editor's character.

"The *Herald*—Onward," *Democratic Review*, XXXI (November 1852), 409. A favorable appraisal of a maligned newspaper.

Turnbull, George, "Some Notes on the History of the Interview," *Journalism Quarterly*, XIII (September 1936), 272. An authority on journalism history holds that Greeley was the father of the modern interview.

Chapter 12

THE RACE FOR NEWS

Journalism is literature in a hurry. . . .
—Matthew Arnold

THE PIONEERS OF THE PENNY PRESS probably did not
realize what a profound change they were to bring about in American journalism. As the historian-journalist, Gerald W. Johnson, once
pointed out, editors like Day, Bennett, Greeley, and Abell lived in
a period of great change—changes so profound that by comparison
the modifications after the War of Independence were slight.[1] Many
institutions were to be drastically altered after 1830, but none more
than the press.

Three factors control the development of the newspaper. They
are: (1) the reading public, (2) the system of communications,
and (3) improvements in production. In the second quarter of the
nineteenth century, all three factors exerted great influence on the
press. The public was more discerning as it acquired a greater literacy skill, and as more and more publications of various types
were offered. The system of communications was developed beyond
the wildest dreams of its promoters. The steam press, the beginning
of automatic printing, and the perfection of paper-making also
helped to change the character of the press. The pioneers of the
penny press thus found themselves engaged in a game, all the rules
of which had been cancelled, while the new regulations were still

[1] Gerald W. Johnson, et al., *The Sunpapers of Baltimore* (New York:
Alfred A. Knopf, Inc., 1937), p. 50.

245

in the process of formulation. As Johnson says, "To survive, it was necessary to guess what the new rules would be, and to guess correctly most of the time. Conditions demanded alert and supple intelligence, backed by sturdy common sense; for policies whose necessity is as plain as day now were then wrapped in obscurity." [2]

Many Americans think of the period between 1830 and 1850 as a kind of historical doldrums. Few can recall the presidents of the period. Actually, this is one of the most interesting and productive periods prior to the twentieth century. There were interesting developments in literature, economics, and education. Most striking, however, was the technical progress of the age. This was the beginning of the railroad building era. The steamboat, the power loom, and the magnetic telegraph were to bring about profound changes in the American way of life. Industrialization was to modify society and create social strains that would eventually rend the country.

Successful publishers learned to adapt themselves and their papers to the new times. Most of them reacted intuitively. Arunah S. Abell, who was as articulate and shrewd as the greatest of his peers in the newspaper business, never did understand the forces around him. He believed the secret of his success was his policy of avoiding violent controversy, forgetting that some of the great papers of the day were continually so embroiled. The secret was in presenting news instead of the usual glut of opinion. The successful penny papers concentrated on presenting straight news, while rivals, once rich and powerful, died from circulation starvation on a diet of editorial comment. Bennett and Beach (successor to Day of the *Sun*) exceeded Greeley's *Tribune* in local circulation in just about the proportion that they offered news against Greeley's views. Greeley and Raymond, on the other hand, while famous for editorials, offered far more news than some of their older rivals who were rapidly going to seed.

News of this period could be classified into five categories. One budget of information tied up interesting national and world events with community experience. Another classification included reports of crime, violence, and the activities of the famous or infamous— news that played on the chord of universal passions. Local events, often presented in the form of a crusade, accounted for another

[2] *Op. cit.*, p. 51.

news budget. A category that we now call "human interest" is also discernible—stories with appeal based on writing skill, rather than upon news value. Lastly, there was news of economic and political significance that could be made popular by emphasis upon speed of transmission and "exclusiveness."

The increased value of news meant that editors now were willing to invest heavily in means for obtaining and processing it. That was why the cost of newspapers went up so amazingly. Bennett started his paper on $500. Six years later, Greeley needed $3,000 to begin publication of a daily. Ten years later Raymond and his associates had to put up $100,000 to get the *Times* under way. Gathering the news and processing it quickly with complicated machinery accounted for most of this increased cost.

The colonial editor took his news as he found it. If someone came in with the report of an event it was inserted as news, but there was no systematic news gathering except in rare instances. No newspaper in the eighteenth century hired reporters of the type common in the nineteenth and twentieth centuries. The use of correspondents for the gathering of neighborhood gossip was common enough, but little of this material required investigation. Foreign and national news was largely gleaned from "exchanges," or newspapers traded back and forth. True, Sam Adams' "Committees of Correspondence," and the abortive cooperative news gathering agency on the eve of the Revolution were examples of organized reporting, but the effort was not destined to produce lasting results. During the early 1800's, newspapers began to seek ways of speeding up the arrival of news, particularly news from Washington and from Europe. But not until the penny press era did the idea of generating a newspaper's own news reports really take hold.

After 1833, newspapers began to go out after news. Editors still depended upon exchanges for outside sources of information, but more and more they began to work out organized systems of news gathering. One of the innovations of the first successful penny paper, as pointed out in the previous chapter, was the development of police news. This required a full-time reporter, who specialized in that type of news. Bennett assigned men to various "beats," such as Wall Street, the churches, society, and even sports. Thus the day of the specialist reporter was already at hand.

One of the first news sources to be tapped methodically was Congress—and the White House, of course. At the beginning of the century most metropolitan editors depended upon papers like the *National Intelligencer* to furnish such information. This continued to be the rule, but in a few cases special Washington reporters appeared. James Gordon Bennett was a pioneer Washington correspondent before he established the *Herald,* and he promoted this type of news in his successful penny paper. Bennett covered Congress for the *New York Enquirer* while the two houses were in session, and served as roving correspondent in the interim. When Colonel Webb bought the *Enquirer* in 1829 and merged it with the *Courier,* Bennett remained as Washington reporter. He wrote in a light, colorful style, and interspersed accounts of boarding-house life in his reports of legislative proceedings.

An authority on this subject has said that no one man can be singled out as the first Washington correspondent, but there was the beginning of such news coverage as early as 1808.[3] On January 4 of that year the *United States Gazette* announced that it had made arrangements to obtain earlier and "more full and correct information" about the government "than can be had from the Washington papers."[4] The *Gazette* used its own correspondent for the remaining weeks of the session, but reverted to the Washington *Federalist* and *Intelligencer* in November. In December, 1808, the *Freeman's Journal* of Philadelphia printed dispatches which it described as "From Our Correspondent at Washington." It began sending proof sheets of this material to the *New York Evening Post* in advance of the Philadelphia publication. The *Post* also credited the copy "From Our Correspondent," but gave credit to the Philadelphia source. Although the correspondent was not identified, he was actually James Elliott, a Vermont Congressman who concealed himself when necessary under the name "Ariel." After 1811, however, the *Post* and the *Freeman's Journal,* like the *Gazette* earlier, reverted to the old system.

The beginning of a permanent press corps in Washington can be traced to the establishment by Nathaniel Carter of a capital service for his paper, the *New York Statesman and Evening Advertiser,* as announced December 11, 1822. The first report was printed

---

[3] Frederick B. Marbut, "Early Washington Correspondents: Some Neglected Pioneers," *Journalism Quarterly,* XXV (December 1948), 370.

[4] *Ibid.,* p. 370.

December 19. Carter was the first to use the phrase "Washington Correspondence" more or less regularly, but the service was discontinued in 1824 without explanation.

Eliab Kingman perfected the system. He was well known in the capital as a correspondent for out of town papers, and he actually prospered in this branch of journalism. He was one of the first accredited Washington correspondents. He came to the capital in 1822 or 1824, but none of his work has been identified before 1830. Kingman's significance is his permanent status as a stringer and correspondent, and as a pioneer in the development of the Washington press corps.

Bennett was a Washington correspondent in the full sense of the word. He knew the value of such news and promoted it to new standards of excellence after he founded the *Herald*. Soon the *Herald* had established a reputation for its Washington news coverage which made it widely read in Europe, especially in Great Britain, and it continued to lead in this branch of journalism as long as the elder Bennett was in control. Others profited by this lesson, however, and by 1850 the Washington news corps was well established. The reporters appear to have been, as at the present writing, a hand-picked group of able journalists who were intimates of the nation's important political figures, and who enjoyed special prestige among their peers.

Foreign news, taken from European papers, had always been presented in American newspapers. But not until after 1800 was there much concern shown in offering foreign news reports while they were still fresh. As such news became more popular, editors vied with one another to offer it ahead of all rivals. The organized attempt to gather such intelligence can be traced back to 1811. British naval vessels were then searching American ships at sea for British deserters. War was imminent, and every message from Europe told of new threats to American commerce. To satisfy the craving of his customers for such information, Samuel Gilbert had provided a reading room in his seven-story Exchange Coffee House, which dominated the Boston waterfront as the tallest building in America. The reading room was typical, in that it supplied available foreign newspapers, as was the custom of coffeehouses. Gilbert's special contribution was a Marine News Book, which offered much more current and local intelligence for the edification of his merchant and shipping office clientele. When the preparation of the news books began to take too much time, Gilbert hired an assistant to carry on this work. On November 20, 1811, he announced in the *Columbian Centinel* that young Samuel Topliff, Jr., would henceforth be in charge of the "Marine and General News Books."

Samuel Topliff was the son of a sea captain who had been murdered by a mutinous crew. He had planned to follow the sea, like his father, but had been forced to find a means to keep his widowed mother and her family together. That was the reason he had accepted Gilbert's offer of a position. Topliff began to meet incoming ships in his rowboat, so that he could return sooner with important news. It was the first systematic attempt in this country to gather foreign news. Later, Topliff hired correspondents in Europe to prepare the dispatches he received from incoming ship captains. The Topliff reports were so much more accurate and complete than the old haphazard accounts had been that other papers began to use them.

Other cities perfected similar services. The *Charleston Courier* was first in America with news of the peace with Great Britain in 1814, its ship-news reporter having learned of the event only seven weeks after its occurrence. By 1828 New York had taken the lead in such news gathering. The most enterprising news merchant in that fast-growing city was David Hale, manager of the *Journal of Commerce,* published by Arthur Tappan. The paper was the newest of the 10 dailies then being published in New York. Hale soon found that the older publications had combined to run him out of business. They had established a service for obtaining news from incoming ships, and they used rough tactics to keep Hale's boats from threatening the monopoly. In desperation, Hale purchased a fast sloop, which met the European packets as they were trimmed off Sandy Hook for the run up the bay to the city wharves. He was able to return with news hours before the merchantmen hove into view from Battery Place. Rivals tried to duplicate this feat, but Hale was able to maintain his leadership for some time. This was the beginning of organized competition for incoming news.

When the New York combine set up a semaphore system from Sandy Hook to the Battery, Hale countered by establishing a pony express route across Staten Island, connecting his Sandy Hook sloop base with the Battery ferry. The rival semaphore was faster, but the news was hopelessly meager, and Hale had no difficulty in out-performing his competitors.

Not long after this Hale and his partner, Gerard Hallock, purchased the *Journal of Commerce* and made it into the most aggressive of the six-penny papers. Like the penny-press editors, the partners understood the value of news as a commodity. They sometimes put out extras when there were important stories to offer the public. They made the front page the show window, as in modern newspaper practice. But above all, they promoted any system that would speed the gathering and dissemination of news. It was Hale and Hallock who inaugurated the pony express service between Washington and New York. The *Courier and Enquirer* offered stiff competition, but until Bennett came along and out-performed the partners, Hale and Hallock led the New York pack in sniffing out the news.

Bennett was of course not content with anything short of the best in news gathering. When Daniel Craig began using carrier pigeons to fly news reports from distant points, Bennett subscribed to the service, and even provided his own pigeons. When the steamship, the railroad, and the magnetic telegraph superseded sailing ships, ponies, and pigeons, Bennett was quick to use the new means of communication. But so were his competitors, and the intensified racing for news made its publishing increasingly expensive. Men like Hale began to see that while competition for the news was important, some degree of cooperation was necessary. There was a limit to what most newspapers could spend for news gathering, and gradually the competitors began to share the expenses. Eventually Hale, Bennett, and other New York publishers formed a cooperative association for the gathering of news—the forerunner of the modern press association. But before this logical development took place, the news enterprisers experimented further with the faster means of communication at their disposal.

The United States government had a hand in developing the rapid processing of news during this period. Following the lead of the newspapermen, Postmaster General Amos Kendall established regular pony express service between Philadelphia and New York, taking over a route from the *Courier and Enquirer* in 1835.[5] By

---

[5] The *Courier and Enquirer* had found the cost of maintaining a pony route too great. But the *Journal of Commerce* continued its private express,

1836 this express service had been extended across the main routes, cutting the travel time between New York and New Orleans to less than seven days. Express riders did not carry the full newspapers, but rather proof sheets of important stories. These "slips," as they were called, preceded the regular papers by as much as a week on such long routes as the New Orleans system. The arrangement enabled newspapers around the country to work out cooperative exchange systems for beating rivals to big news.

From the days of pony express to giant airliners, the government has fostered rapid travel through subsidies and air mail payments. This support has enabled private companies to provide the best equipment and the most convenient service even though traffic was insufficient to warrant private investment. Many of the railroads in the early days were aided by government grants of land, which could be sold to help finance construction.

In the 1830's and 1840's, railroads gradually began to replace the pony expresses. From 23 miles of track in 1830, construction went up to 9,000 miles by 1850. The railroad was a great boon to the newspapers. It not only provided fast distribution, but served also as a communications agency. In May, 1837, the *Baltimore Sun* rushed President Van Buren's message from Washington in less than two hours by way of the Baltimore & Ohio Railroad. Previously, Abell and his associates would have had to wait until the following morning to obtain such news from the Washington papers.

In 1841, Bennett, Swain (*Philadelphia Public Ledger*), and Abell (*Baltimore Sun*) together hired a special locomotive to carry President Harrison's inaugural address from Washington to Baltimore, Philadelphia, and New York. The *Baltimore Sun* was able to put out an early afternoon extra covering the noonday speech. Proofs of the speech were mailed to the paper's exchanges, who thereby scored a 24-hour scoop over rivals.

The steamship also contributed to the development of fast news gathering. Travel across the Atlantic was reduced from weeks to days. In 1845, when the Oregon question brought a threat of war with England, leading papers cooperated in meeting fast ships at Halifax, the first port of call for the Atlantic steamers. Horses

---

extending it to Washington so as to gain a day over rival New York papers depending on the government's Philadelphia-New York express. Other papers were showing similar news enterprise, particularly those in Boston, the *Providence Journal*, and the *Charleston Courier*.

brought the news across the Nova Scotia peninsula to the Bay of Fundy, from where a fast steamer relayed the information to Portland, Maine. A railroad train brought the news to Washington less than 50 hours after it had been received in Halifax.

But the biggest boost in speedy transmission of news was given by the telegraph. On May 25, 1844, Samuel F. B. Morse sat at a table in the old Supreme Court chamber in Washington and tapped out a message in code. His assistant in Baltimore decoded the sounds. The message: "What hath God wrought?" Later that same afternoon, Morse sent the first telegraphic message published in a newspaper, the *Baltimore Patriot:* "One o'clock—There has just been made a motion in the House to go into committee of the whole on the Oregon question. Rejected—ayes, 79; nays, 86." This was one of the significant reports of the century—not because of the intrinsic news value, but because it portended a whole new system of communication.

Swain, the Philadelphia publisher, was one of the incorporators of the Magnetic Telegraph Company, which promoted Morse's invention. Abell, in Baltimore, used the columns of his paper to demand help of Congress in subsidizing the inventor's work. He also helped finance the Washington-Baltimore test of the new device. But for some strange reason, the *Baltimore Sun* gave very little space to one of the big stories of the nineteenth century. The Monday paper relegated the first telegraphic news dispatch to the second page under local news headed "Magnetic Telegraph." Eleven lines had to tell the story of the experiment that was to do so much for communication throughout the world. The paper gave 17 lines in the same column to a tawdry police court report and two and a half columns on page one to a dreary religious conference. True, space and placing were not as important in news rooms then, but down through history the press has invariably misjudged the importance of great technical advances. The cotton gin, reaper, sewing machine, telephone, automobile, airplane, and radio were also ignored by the press when they first appeared.

Newspapers were quick to make use of the new invention, however. In May, 1846, President Polk's message to Congress calling for war with Mexico was telegraphed to Baltimore for the exclusive use of the *Sun.* Bennett became famous for his use of the invention to help him outperform his rivals.

The telegraph also stimulated the growth of small-town dailies.

It was high time. Unchecked, the metropolitan papers might soon have dominated the field, as they did in Great Britain. In Illinois, where city dailies from St. Louis, Cincinnati, and other big publishing centers had absorbed more and more of the circulation, 30 daily newspapers were founded during the decade following the adoption of the telegraph to press service. The cost of this service made all of them likely customers for a cooperative news gathering agency. For example, when the wire from New York reached Utica, via Albany, early in 1846, the *Daily Gazette* there received its first telegraphic bulletins. The news was so fresh, and the transmission so novel, that the editor devoted about a column to the dispatches. To cover the cost, the Utica publishers enlisted the cooperation of dailies to the west. They were to share the Utica tolls. In return, they were to receive copies of the wire stories, distributed from Utica by pony express.

Development of a recognized agency to serve all these far-flung publications and to meet the needs of the big New York newspapers now seemed a logical step. Many persons had their eyes on the business, including Dr. Alexander Jones, a physician turned reporter, Daniel Craig, the pigeon expert, and various promoters of telegraph services. But the enterprising New York City dailies proved able to control the situation.

Frederic Hudson, the *Herald's* managing editor who later wrote a history of journalism, credits Hale of the *Journal of Commerce* with breaking the ice by calling on Bennett, whom he despised, and suggesting that the rivals pool their news gathering resources for the reporting of the Mexican War in 1846.[6] Cooperation did result, although there was still continued rivalry in obtaining news from the Mexican front. Abell in Baltimore and Swain in Philadelphia were also invited into the alliance. The arrangements were satisfactory enough so that Hale decided to work out a more permanent organization.

Supposedly the publishers of the leading New York papers met in the *Sun* offices in May, 1848, and reached an agreement. No record was kept, but later accounts named as those present Bennett

[6] Frederic Hudson, *Journalism in the United States* (New York: Harper & Brothers, 1873), pp. 366-67. Oliver Gramling, in his *AP: The Story of News* (New York: Farrar and Rinehart, Inc., 1940), presents a dramatic account of the beginnings of the Associated Press, but the historical basis for the details he relates has never been established.

and Hudson of the *Herald;* Colonel Webb and his assistant, Henry Raymond, of the *Courier and Enquirer;* Greeley of the *Tribune;* Beach of the *Sun;* Erastus and James Brooks of the *Express;* Hale and Hallock of the *Journal of Commerce.* On May 13, 1848, Raymond was writing to the telegraph agent in Boston, telling him those six papers wished "to procure foreign news by telegraph from Boston in common"—including both news arriving by steamships which docked in Boston before proceeding to New York and news relayed from Halifax. A week later Raymond was agreeing to a contract on behalf of the "Associated Press," providing for a payment of $100 for 3,000 words of telegraphic news and stating that the news would be forwarded also to newspapers in Philadelphia and Baltimore.[7]

The name "Associated Press" did not come into general use until the 1860's, but the New York City group was the forerunner of that modern-day press association. Dr. Alexander Jones became superintendent of the service, and was succeeded in 1851 by Daniel Craig. That year the *Times* became the seventh newspaper member of the combine. In 1856 the group tightened its organization by adopting what was called the "Regulations of the General News Association of the City of New York." [8] Soon called the New York Associated Press, the group established a firm grip on cooperative telegraphic news reporting, selling its service to outsiders.

The Mexican War provided the newspapers an excellent opportunity to demonstrate their enterprise. When war was declared in 1846 the telegraph lines reached only as far south as Richmond, Virginia. There was very little railroad development south of that city. Papers closer to the war events were depended upon to furnish the news. For that reason the New Orleans dailies became nationally known during this period.[9] The South was particularly interested in the war because of its ultimate impact upon slavery and sectional balance. But the North was interested, too (a "criminal war," some editors called it). Bennett led the way, as usual, with a special pony express across the nation from New Orleans, although he soon joined forces with Abell and Swain in sharing the

---

[7] Victor Rosewater, *History of Cooperative News-Gathering in the United States* (New York: D. Appleton and Company, 1930), pp. 64-66.

[8] Reprinted in *ibid.,* pp. 381-88.

[9] There were nine of them; the best known were the *Picayune, Delta, Crescent, Tropic,* and *Bee.* All had correspondents in Mexico to cover the war.

venture. The *Charleston Courier* and *New York Sun* ran another important service, to bring the news of the war from New Orleans, whither the correspondents sent their dispatches.

Star reporter of the Mexican War was the publisher of the *New Orleans Picayune*, George W. Kendall. He covered all the big battles from Monterey to Chapultepec, and gave accurate accounts of the military strategy involved. The biggest scoop of the war can be credited to the *Baltimore Sun*. In April, 1847, one of the pony expresses serving the paper brought the news that Vera Cruz had fallen. The capture of this fortress was a decisive victory for the invading forces. Abell was aware that his rider was at least a day ahead of the War Department courier, and so the Baltimore publisher sent a telegram to President Polk. It was the first news of the victory to reach the White House. The *Sun*, curiously enough, played its news beat on page two, in the column where editorials ordinarily appeared. But the single column head, topped with cuts of running ponies, bespoke the pride of a news enterprise paper. It had 11 decks, using 14 different type faces. The first six read: [10]

By Special Overland Expresses of
Nearly One Thousand Miles
Exclusively for The Baltimore Sun
Independent of All Telegraphic Communication!

Unparalleled Effort of
Newspaper Enterprise

Highly Important
From the South

Unparalleled Achievement
of the
American Arms!

The Greatest Military Exploit
of the
Present Century

[10] As reprinted in Johnson, *The Sunpapers of Baltimore*, p. 80.

Fall, Surrender,
And Unconditional Capitulation of
The City of Vera Cruz
and
The Castle of San Juan D'Ulloa

It had taken 12 days for the news to reach Baltimore by runner, steamer, and pony express. This is typical of the energy and aggressiveness that went into news coverage during this period. Publishers and editors were providing more facts and accurate information than the public had ever had before. The result was that more and more of the flimsy, insignificant material that had characterized the early penny papers could now be relegated to inside pages, or to weekly editions. All the evidence showed that these policies brought new readers. In 1845, the *New York Herald* had a daily circulation of 12,000. By 1849, circulation had increased to 33,000, and new presses had to be installed to meet the demand for papers.

This brings us to the final factor in developing the press. Mass circulation, and all the changes it brought about, could not have been accomplished unless papers could be produced cheaply, quickly, and in greater bulk. This problem had to be solved by the technical expert, especially the builder of printing presses. Mechanical development is as important as the other progress noted in this chapter. It would have been futile to spend much on rapid and complete news gathering if slow presses delayed processing by hours or even days. There could be no newspaper for the masses unless press runs could be stepped up.

The improvement in presses and the need for fast printing is indicated by the experience of the *Philadelphia Public Ledger*. It was founded in 1836 as a penny paper dependent upon circulation for success, but its printing equipment consisted of the usual hand press, seen in a majority of newspaper shops. In six months the paper acquired a circulation of nearly 8,000, and it was no longer possible to meet the demands of the public with the cumbersome Clymer press. Swain thereupon installed the finest equipment obtainable at the time—a Napier single-cylinder press powered by steam. A year later the publisher had to order another press, this time a double-cylinder machine. Bennett's progress was even more amazing. Ten years after he founded his paper without even a press of his own, he was using four double-cylinder presses with four men to each unit, in order to get out enough papers.

The first cylinder presses merely rolled back and forth over the flat type-bed—like some of the proof presses seen in printing shops today. Speed could be doubled by using two cylinders at a time. But even these presses were not fast enough to keep up to the circulations developed by the penny papers. The problem was solved for the time by Richard Hoe's type-revolving press, first installed in the *Public Ledger* shop in 1846. Hoe substituted a horizontal cylinder for the flat bed. Countersunk in these cylinders were curved iron beds, one for each page in the paper. Type matter was locked in these beds by an ingenious system of wedge-shaped rules to keep the type from flying out as the cylinders revolved at high speed. In 1849 the *New York Herald* installed one of these "lightning" presses with six cylinders capable of printing 12,000 impressions an hour. Other New York papers had presses with up to ten such cylinders during the 1850's. By the outbreak of the Civil War it was possible for an enterprising publisher to print up to 20,000 impressions an hour.

The type-revolving press speeded up the processing of news, but it also imposed limitations on the editor and publisher. On such a press it was difficult to print anything except one-column headlines. It was not practicable to hold type matter in place on the whirling cylinder when it was set in two- or three-column measure, because the wedges did not have enough purchase on the curved sides of the cylinder. Thus, as long as the type-revolving press was standard equipment, we find very few banner or display headlines used. And because the single-column headline became a habit with editors during this period, it was a long time before they got around to different makeup, even when more advanced presses made multiple-column headlines feasible.

Another improvement in the technical process was the use of stereotype plates. James Dellagana, a London printer, produced curved, solid plates of type instead of the columns of loose type that presented such a hazard on the revolving cylinders. This was accomplished by making an impression of the type forms in a soft mold, curving this mold to fit the cylinder, and then pouring hot lead onto the mold or "matrix" to make a type plate. In 1854 Charles Craske, an American engineer, adapted this process to the presses of the *New York Herald*—another of that remarkable paper's "firsts." Stereotyping made it possible to make duplicates of pages so that several presses could run off an edition at the same time, thereby speeding the printing to a point limited only by the amount of equipment a publisher could afford. Bennett, for example, had five presses printing from duplicate stereotype cylinders at the

Courtesy, R. Hoe & Co., Inc.

The "Hoe Type-Revolving Machine" was first used in the publication of the *Philadelphia Ledger* in 1846. By an ingenious locking device, the individual pieces of type were attached to cylinders rotating at a fairly high speed. As the need for faster presses increased, publishers bought presses with more and more such cylinders. The one shown above was first used in 1855. It had 10 cylinders, each fed by an attendant, and it was capable of turning out 20,000 sheets an hour.

same time, during the Civil War demand for papers. Stereotyping made possible bigger headlines, appropriate for war news. It also enabled advertisers to develop display devices.

But costs also mounted as the engineers provided the equipment necessary for mass circulation. Plant inventories by 1860 amounted to tens of thousands of dollars. Enterprising publishers substituted superior presses long before the old equipment was worn out, and that in itself had a share in improving the nation's press, for it made it possible for publishers in smaller communities to buy better machinery second-hand, with their lower budgets.

The small city newspapers changed much less radically than did their big city rivals, but even in the hinterland the press was experiencing the impact of the communications revolution. The telegraph lines reached Portland, Maine, by 1846, Charleston in the South the next year, as well as St. Louis in the Middle West, and were extended to Chicago and Milwaukee in 1848. Pony expresses continued to operate beyond the ends of the lines—notably the overland pony express from St. Joseph, Missouri, to Sacramento, California, which opened in 1860 and continued until the telegraph reached the Pacific in October, 1861. By that time there were more than 50,000 miles of wires.

Newspaper publishers in the interior did the best they could to publish creditable papers. They scrambled to get the Washington and foreign news from proof slips, exchange papers, and meager telegrams. Cincinnati and St. Louis, particularly, were major publishing centers and both had several daily newspapers by the 1850's. The leaders in Cincinnati were the *Gazette,* founded in 1815 as a weekly and transformed into a daily in 1827, and the *Commercial,* begun in 1843. St. Louis had as its top dailies the *Missouri Republican,* founded as the *Gazette* in 1808, and the *Missouri Democrat* of 1852. Second-hand presses, printing equipment, ink, and paper moved out from these centers to smaller towns as the newspaper followed the lines of settlement.

Population was booming in the Great Lakes area, where Chicago and Milwaukee became prominent. Chicago's first paper was the *Weekly Democrat,* begun in 1833 and made into a daily in 1840. The *Chicago Tribune* appeared in 1847, and after its purchase by Joseph Medill and his partners in 1855, it became the leading daily, absorbing the *Democrat* in 1861. Milwaukee's initial weekly was the *Advertiser,* which was founded in 1836 and which lived to become the *Wisconsin News.* The *Milwaukee Sentinel,* started in 1837, became the city's first daily in 1844. The transformation from weekly to daily publication was repeated elsewhere; the *Minnesota Pioneer* of 1849, the state's first paper, became a daily in 1854 and had several competitors in St. Paul. Even the smaller towns had competing papers in this era.

Establishment of rival papers as spokesmen for political groups accounted for some of the growth. Some of the western papers were founded as means of promoting settlement and sale of lands, like the *Oregon Spectator,* begun in Oregon City in 1846 as the first Pacific Coast publication. Others were missionary papers, like the first publications in Kansas and the Oklahoma region. Army posts also contributed papers. The weeklies typically carried a good deal of literary material, in addition to local news. The dailies, too, attempted to satisfy the hunger for reading matter as well as news. The *Alta California,* which began in San Francisco in 1849 and which became that city's first daily in 1850, later achieved fame for publishing the writings of Bret Harte and Samuel Clemens, better known as Mark Twain. Nevada's *Territorial Enterprise,* founded in 1858, boasted Mark Twain as city editor in the early 1860's.

The push into the Far West and into the mining country produced other early newspapers: the *Oregonian* in Portland in 1850; the *Sacramento Union* (1851), *Los Angeles Star* (1851), and *San Francisco Bulletin* (1855) and *San Francisco Call* (1856); the Mormon Church's *Deseret News* in Salt Lake City in 1850; and the *Rocky Mountain News* in the Denver mining area in 1859. Easterners who flocked to the California gold fields and to the Nevada and Colorado mining towns wanted more news than the local papers offered, however. New York papers, particularly the *Herald* and the *Tribune,* issued California editions which were sent by steamer around the Horn, or by overland stage. Papers in other eastern cities soon followed suit. For wherever an American went in the expanding nation, he wanted the news which an aggressive press corps was providing.

ANNOTATED BIBLIOGRAPHY

Books:

Copeland, Fayette, *Kendall of the Picayune.* Norman: University of Oklahoma Press, 1943. An interesting account of the life and times of a pioneer New Orleans editor and war correspondent.

Dabney, Thomas E., *One Hundred Great Years.* Baton Rouge: Louisiana State University Press, 1944. The centennial history of the *New Orleans Times-Picayune.*

Gramling, Oliver, *AP: The Story of News.* New York: Farrar and Rinehart, Inc., 1940. A colorful account of the rise of the Associated Press. Its content cannot always be substantiated by document and evidence, however.

Harlow, Alvin F., *Old Wires and New Waves: The History of the Telegraph, Telephone, and Wireless.* New York: D. Appleton-Century Company, 1936. First half of the book covers the pre-Civil War period.

Hoe, Robert, *Short History of the Printing Press.* New York: R. Hoe and Company, 1902. Obviously a promotional venture, but valuable in describing the various presses of the period.

Hudson, Frederic, *Journalism in the United States, 1690-1872.* New York: Harper & Brothers, 1873. One of the oldest journalism histories, but especially useful in the description of the mid-nineteenth century period because the author knew many of the persons he discusses.

Johnson, Gerald, et al., *The Sunpapers of Baltimore.* New York: Alfred A. Knopf, Inc., 1937. An excellent case history that reveals the significance of the penny press outside New York.

McMurtrie, Douglas C., and Albert H. Allen, *Early Printing in Colorado.* Denver: Hirschfeld Press, 1935. McMurtrie also wrote articles about the journalism of other western states, for *Journalism Quarterly* and other periodicals.

Rosewater, Victor, *History of Cooperative News-Gathering in the United States.* New York: D. Appleton and Company, 1930. Not as colorful as the Gramling book, but more factual. Describes services other than the Associated Press.

Periodicals and Monographs:

Carter, John D., *The San Francisco Bulletin, 1855-1865.* Ph.D. thesis, University of California, 1941. A study in the beginnings of Pacific Coast journalism.

Firebaugh, Dorothy Gile, "The Sacramento Union: Voice of California, 1851-75," *Journalism Quarterly,* XXX (Summer 1953), 321. The story of a dominant early California paper.

Marbut, Frederick B., "Early Washington Correspondents: Some Neglected Pioneers," *Journalism Quarterly,* XXV (December 1948), 369.

———, "The United States Senate and the Press, 1838-41," *Journalism Quarterly,* XXVIII (Summer 1951), 342.

———, "Decline of the Official Press in Washington," *Journalism Quarterly,* XXXIII (Summer 1956), 335. Articles by an authority on Washington correspondence and the capital press corps.

Pickett, Calder M., "Technology and the New York Press in the 19th Century," *Journalism Quarterly,* XXXVII (Summer 1960), 398. Based on "Six New York Newspapers and Their Response to Technology in the 19th Century," Ph.D. thesis, University of Minnesota, 1959.

Weigle, Clifford F., "San Francisco Journalism, 1847-1851," *Journalism Quarterly,* XIV (June 1937), 151. The beginnings of a colorful journalistic tradition are recounted by a Stanford University journalism professor.

Chapter 13

THE PRESS AND THE RISE
OF SECTIONALISM

He who opposes the public liberty overthrows his
own.
—William Lloyd Garrison

THE JACKSONIAN ERA brought out clearly the increasing
absorption in sectional differences. The beginning of the "irrepressible conflict," as one historian has called the War Between the
States, can be traced back to colonial times.[1] The petitions to the
King long before 1776; the arguments over the Constitution at the
Philadelphia convention; the drafting of the Kentucky and Virginia
Resolutions after the Alien and Sedition Acts were passed; and the
debates over the tariff of 1828 are some of the evidences of the
fault-line along which the country would one day split. By 1848,
people were no longer voting by party, but by section.

Up to about 1820 there was no great southern unit with the regional cohesion that was apparent a decade later. The South actually was more torn apart by dissension than any other section up
to 1820. The upland communities had fought against the tidewater
elite in the Revolution, largely as a result of social strains. Large
areas of the South had more in common with the West. And the
Negro added another source of social friction.

[1] Arthur Charles Cole, *The Irrepressible Conflict* (New York: The Macmillan
Company, 1934). See also Avery Craven, *The Repressible Conflict* (Baton
Rouge: Louisiana State University Press, 1939).

There is a tendency to think of the South as turning away from American traditions when it seceded in 1861. It was the North, meaning the industrial Northeast, not the South, that developed a different way of life after 1820. Generally speaking, the South was about the same in 1861 as it had been in 1761. On the eve of the War Between the States, the South retained the impress of the eighteenth century. It was still, in the middle of the nineteenth century, about what the founding fathers had apparently expected of the country when they wrote the fundamental document—a land dominated by the agrarian interests. Certainly Jefferson would have approved of the country developing as the South had developed, without the slave institution, of course. Curiously, the section where slavery flourished was also the region where some of the great national heroes of democracy emerged, including Washington, Jefferson, Madison, John C. Calhoun, and many others.

All this time the South provided more than its share of political leadership. The Speaker of the House of Representatives was likely to be a southerner. The section abounded in great orators, great statesmen, great humanitarians, and great literary spokesmen. This is in contrast to the virtual bankruptcy of southern leadership in the 75 years following the Civil War.[2] There was good reason for the South to lead politically. Life centered in the plantation, and so commercial cities did not assume the importance they had in the Northeast. Lacking such centers, the South had only a small middle class, and virtually no white proletariat. Southerners looked to foreign markets, and they usually negotiated directly with British cotton and tobacco buyers, who took a large share of the southern products. The southerner usually shipped from his own, or from a local, wharf, rather than from a great seaport. This was inefficient, perhaps, but it was pleasanter.

From this environment came a governing group with a high sense of honor and morals. Family and land counted for more than money in the South, because money was not so essential to the agrarian as it was to the northern capitalist and wage earner. Money was the sign of success in the North. Land was the criterion in the South.

[2] There were of course important leaders in the South after the Civil War, but which of them approached the greatness of the pre-war southern statesmen?

But land values declined in the South some time after 1800, as the staple crops exhausted the soil. Little was known of fertilization of soil then, and so immigrants moved to fresh land, thereby reducing the demand for, and consequently the value of, the older lands. Since there was no profit to be made in land speculation, trade, or industry, the capitalist tended to leave the agrarian in full control. Disbarred by circumstance from commerce, which was attracting some of the best young brains in the North, promising careerists in the South turned to politics as one of the outlets for their abilities. Northern industrialists resented this southern political leadership. That is indicated by the growing friction over legislation. The struggle between capitalistic and agrarian ideologies was disclosed in the great Webster-Hayne debate of 1830. In this enunciation of principles the northern and southern spokesmen publicly presented the courses their respective sections would henceforth follow. And here it is evident that it was the North, not the South, that had changed.

The South had reason to fear for its future. The industrial North was growing much faster than the South. Population pressure would inevitably give the North political dominance. Already the "tariff of abominations" of 1828 had disclosed what the North would impose upon the South if given free rein. The tariff, which protected northern industry, might ruin an area dependent upon Europe for exchange of necessities. The North was willing to spend enormous amounts of tax money on the improvement of harbors and transportation systems, all very useful to an industrial economy but only a drain on southern financial resources.

Both sections turned to the West as an ally, when it became clear that the frontier region would determine the outcome of the conflict. The West was agrarian, like the South. It also suffered from high tariffs. Westerners had natural antipathies to the industrial North. They resented the northern sabotage of every legislative attempt to ease the debt of the farmer and to open up free lands. On the other hand, the westerner was not as dependent upon world markets as was the southerner. The westerner was interested in reaching local or regional markets. His problem was to get his produce to these markets cheaply and easily, and here he found an ally in the northern capitalist. Roads, canals, steamboat subsidies, and railroads were the prices paid by the North for the temporary allegiance of the West against the South.

The westerner also demanded the opening up of the frontier to homesteaders. Both the North and the South were opposed to this, in general. Some of the bitterest debates in Congress, from 1832 on, took place over this question. The West was certain it was being held back from its manifest destiny by the selfishness of the southern and northern blocs in Congress. Southerners feared the opening of new lands would lead to a preponderance of free states, which would add to the overwhelming weight against the South. Northerners, on the other hand, tended to block westward expansion because it depressed property values in their section and because free land kept wages higher than they would otherwise have been, or else reduced the reservoir of cheap labor in the industrial areas. The point here is that western victory on this issue was a kind of bribe paid by the North for the support of the West. One evidence of this is the Homestead Act, passed on the eve of the war after years of northern objection. Once the West had committed itself, the South had only two choices. It could admit defeat and modify its way of life to suit the North, or it could cast off from an alien system and go its own way—secede.

So far, nothing has been said about slavery as a main cause of the Civil War. If slavery had been such an important issue, time alone would have solved the problem. For slavery was already doomed. World opinion was against it. Already it had proved itself to be uneconomical in the upper tier of slave states. By 1860 these states were unloading surplus slave labor as fast as planters in the deep South could absorb it. The capitalist of the North had demonstrated that it was cheaper to pay a man only while he was useful than to support him as a slave throughout the unproductive years of his life.

Slavery was not a primary cause of the conflict, but it became important as the means for joining the battle, and here the journalist played his big role. There would probably have been sectional strife with or without slavery. But slavery, like the religious double-talk of two centuries earlier, was the basket in which all the differences of peoples, regions, and ideologies could be carried. The slavery shibboleth was the rallying standard for all the various belligerents. It was the simplification of complex problems and summed up the attitudes of those who had to do the dying in battle.

Horrid Tragedy!
BLOOD CRIETH!

Liberator, November 24, 1837

An inside page of the militant abolitionist newspaper published by William Lloyd Garrison at Boston. The black, inverted column rules indicate mourning for the killing of Elijah Lovejoy, the Alton, Illinois, abolitionist, who was the victim of a mob. The story is told in column five.

It is unfortunate that slavery had to be the issue upon which the concept of the American union had to be tested. When the South seceded, it did so on the principle that the minority had the right to protect itself from the tyranny of a majority. Secession meant allegiance to states' rights, a principle that many honest men could uphold. That was more than could be said for the northern leaders who had suggested secession at the Hartford Convention in 1814, not on principle, but on expediency. At least the North had no right to attach stigma to the word "secession." When the South withdrew from the Union, it did so with profound regret. "The Union—next to our liberty, most dear," Calhoun, the spokesman of the South, once said.

Slavery lifted the doctrines and philosophies of North and South on to a plane that made them more discernible to the average man. Few would be willing to die for economic principles. But slavery could supply the hate transference that could make a John Brown, for example, die for such a cause at Harper's Ferry in 1859. To Ralph Waldo Emerson, "Old Ossawatomie" Brown had "made the gallows glorious like the cross." And Walt Whitman, poet and some-time journalist, wrote of Brown's execution:

I would sing how an old man, with white hair, mounted the scaffold in Virginia,
(I was at hand, silent I stood with teeth shut close, I watch'd,
I stood very near you old man when cool and indifferent, but trembling with age and your unheal'd wounds, you mounted the scaffold . . .)[3]

This indicates what the slavery issue meant to men of lofty senti-ment. It took some time to sweep the masses into the movement, but eventually the people of the North and South made slavery a fighting issue, and the press was effective in bringing this about. Advocates of the campaigns against slavery were known as "abo-litionists." An outstanding abolitionist editor was William Lloyd Garrison. He makes an excellent case study of how the press be-came such an important factor in the struggle.

Garrison was born in Newburyport, Massachusetts, of English and Irish stock. The father was a drunkard who abused his family, and the boy must have been influenced by these circumstances when

[3] Both quotations are reprinted in Louis L. Snyder and Richard B. Morris, eds., *A Treasury of Great Reporting* (New York: Simon and Schuster, 1949), pp. 124-5.

he took up the temperance issue while still a youth. He was a jack of all trades until he became a printer. That appeared to be his proper niche. Like Benjamin Russell and Isaiah Thomas, Garrison received most of his education at the type case. It was an education that made him literate rather than learned. As an editor, Garrison took an interest in politics, but he never appeared to master the political principles and traditions, and he had little knowledge of party backgrounds. He started out as a Federalist, more out of editorial imitation than of conviction, presumably. Day by day he became more dissatisfied with the way the world was run. Many men and women are radicals in youth and conservatives as they grow older. Garrison reversed this pattern. As he grew older, he became more rebellious. He was like some wines, which sour rather than mellow with age.

He was in his thirties when he met Benjamin Lundy, the gentle Quaker, who had started out as a temperance missionary, but who had since carried this reforming zeal over into the antislavery movement. It is significant that Quakers had been important in the successful antislavery movement in Great Britain. At any rate, Garrison became one of Lundy's recruits. Soon Garrison had been satisfactorily persecuted—an essential step in the progress of any effective zealot. He had libeled one of his neighbors by calling him a "blackbirder," or importer of slaves. The complainant offered to drop the case if Garrison would print an apology. It was characteristic of the man that he preferred to suffer seven months in jail. He emerged a confirmed abolitionist, and with that supreme gift— a cause so absorbing that life itself is not too great a price for it. He moved to Boston, and on January 1, 1831, he issued there the first copy of the *Liberator*.

The paper was well edited and ordinarily consisted of four pages. It was a throwback to an earlier day, when views, rather than news, characterized the press. The *Liberator* was more like an abolitionist house organ. But there was also plenty of news pertaining to all aspects of the movement. Indeed, the paper is almost a complete textbook of the antislavery issue. All the gag rules imposed by irate politicians are recorded, for example. One can see how attitudes crystallized month by month, in reading the pages even at this late date.

It wasn't very impressive, this voice of the abolitionist. Garrison

said in 1837 that his publication had never exceeded 3,000 subscribers. Much of the time it hovered around 1,500, and about
one-fourth of the circulation was in Negro areas, where the readers
were either disfranchised, or had little political influence. The editor
was always losing entire blocks of readers because of his tactless
scorn of men, institutions, or traditions sacred to certain publics.
And yet this was part of the medium that was to rouse the North
to battle.

Garrison did not begin the antislavery movement. Indeed, the
issue was as old as the country. It had been seriously considered
by the framers of the Constitution. In the Confederation period,
slavery was prohibited under the Northwest Ordinances. Great
leaders, such as Washington, John Adams, Hamilton, Madison, and
Patrick Henry had publicly spoken out against the institution. "I
tremble for my country when I reflect that God is just," Jefferson
wrote in his *Notes* about slavery. Southern leaders had themselves
moved in this direction when they tried to end the slave traffic in
1819. That measure was defeated not by southerners, but by New
Englanders thriving on the trade. Garrison thus was fighting on a
trampled battlefield. But whereas the early leaders suggested orderly
reform, Garrison made slavery a moral issue, requiring immediate
and drastic treatment.

His cause appeared to be hopeless at first. In 1831 he had 50
subscribers to his paper, and no following at all. He was so poor
that he lived on little more than bread and water to conserve his
meager resources for the *Liberator*. He was bitterly opposed—even
more in the North than in the South, when the Whigs and others
were putting all their faith in compromise as the solution to northern and southern differences. Garrison had one weapon, his press,
but it was to make him invincible. Through this press he spread his
creed far and wide, until the abolitionist movement began to work
on the minds of the apathetic. He reached such persons with words
like these:

He who opposes the public liberty overthrows his own. . . .
There is no safety where there is no strength; no strength without
Union; no Union without justice; no justice where faith and truth
are wanting. The right to be free is a truth planted in the hearts of
men. . . .[4]

[4] Wendell Phillips Garrison and Francis Jackson Garrison, *William Lloyd
Garrison: The Story of His Life Told By His Children*, Vol. I (New York:
The Century Company, 1885), p. 200.

This describes Garrison, a man of courage and determination, imbued with righteousness, narrow and fanatical. These are the men who override all obstacles. They reach their goals when the broad-minded reformer has long since bogged down in the quicksand of his own objectivity. Men like Garrison are not easy to love or admire, but they cannot be ignored. He aroused the conscience of a people long lulled by politicians fearful of disturbing the false balance so artfully maintained. What he said was bad for business. Most of this time the country was prosperous. When people are comfortable, conscience is often half asleep. Garrison jerked consciences awake—always an unpopular move. Even the religious leaders resented the man, particularly his self-righteousness. One clergyman complained that abolitionists like Garrison did not do their work like "Christian gentlemen." To which Garrison replied:

These are your men of "caution" and "prudence" and "judiciousness." Sir, I have learned to hate those words. Whenever we attempt to imitate our Great Exemplar, and press the truth of God in all its plainness upon the conscience, why, we are imprudent; because, forsooth, a great excitement will ensue. Sir, slavery will not be overthrown without excitement— a most tremendous excitement.[5]

Garrison caused the most violent public reaction since Tom Paine drew his red hot ploughshare through American history. Even the standard newspapers gave chase to the troublesome abolitionist. James Gordon Bennett, who had argued in defense of free expression during the moral war against the *Herald,* now saw nothing inconsistent in throttling the abolitionist editors. Amos Kendall, himself a great journalist, and a leader of Jacksonian democracy, believed that Garrison should be gagged. As postmaster general he allowed abolitionist papers to be rifled from the official mail sacks by southern "committees" charged with that task.[6] The state of

[5] Vernon L. Parrington, *Main Currents in American Thought,* (New York: Harcourt, Brace and Company, 1927), II, p. 356. Parrington's fascinating analysis of the abolitionist leader quotes many such statements of Garrison.

[6] Kendall justified his action by holding that each issue of the *Liberator* reaching a southern state was a criminal libel; that is, a threat to public peace. He tried to explain the situation in his annual report for 1835, when he asked Congress for an official banning of "obnoxious" literature in southern states. This would have taken the responsibility out of the hands of the postmaster general, and indicates that Kendall knew his past actions had been arbitrary. It is interesting to see the South's great leader, John C. Calhoun, challenge the constitutionality of Kendall's request. Calhoun's alternative was a recommendation for states with appropriate laws to ban such literature at the source.

Massachusetts was ready to forbid the export of the *Liberator*, and in many states, distributors of the paper were intimidated without redress.

Such opposition only made Garrison the more rabid. It also made it impossible for him to compromise. Before long, he considered himself as not even an American. Every Fourth of July his paper printed a long editorial exposing the fallacies of American democracy. Long before the South proposed secession, Garrison called upon abolitionists to repudiate a government that could tolerate slavery. The right "ear," or upper corner, of his paper regularly attacked the very foundations of the state, a standard statement being: "The existing Constitution of the United States is a covenant with death and an agreement with hell." One of his favorite stunts on the lecture platform was to burn a copy of the Constitution to show his contempt for a national charter that sanctioned human bondage. He held that the law of conscience was superior to the law of the land.

James G. Birney, one of the more reasonable abolitionists, was mobbed when he began printing his paper, the *Philanthropist*, at Cincinnati. Note that this was a city in a northern, not a southern, state. From that day on, Birney began to devote his energy to fighting for a free press along with his fight for freeing slaves. The abolitionists saw very clearly that the slavery issue would sooner or later affect all the freedoms in both the North and the South. One of the most stirring messages on this subject, "Free Speech and Free Inquiry," appears in the April 2, 1847, issue of the *Liberator*.

At least one abolitionist died for this cause. He was Elijah Lovejoy, editor of the *St. Louis Observer*, a strident abolitionist weekly founded in 1835. A mass meeting of irate citizens resulted in a resolution informing Lovejoy that free expression as guaranteed in the Bill of Rights did not extend to editors such as Lovejoy who threatened the peace of the community. Lovejoy replied that public resolutions could not fetter an editor. As to the argument, in the choice between peace or principle, the righteous editor could only choose the latter. "The truth is, my fellow citizens," Lovejoy told his neighbors in answer to their arguments, "if you give ground a single inch, there is no stopping place."

As an act of good faith, however, Lovejoy moved his press across the river to Alton, Illinois. His office was at once wrecked by a mob. He appealed nationally for support and received enough help to set up another press. This was also demolished. Again he appealed for assistance, and again there was a quick and positive response. The climax came while he was setting up his third press in Alton. A group of citizens decided that the Lovejoy nuisance should be abated. They called a mass meeting to devise plans. Lovejoy refused to be intimidated and boldly attended the meeting to present his side. He promised to suspend publication if his readers requested him to, but he declared he would not be ruled by mob hysteria. He said he would return to his office and would defend his right to publish with his life, if need be. When the mob marched down the street after the meeting, it was motivated not by the desire just to destroy a press, but to destroy a man who refused to renounce his right to think and to express himself. Lovejoy was killed by the mob.

His murder served the abolitionist cause far better than his writings ever had. The abolitionists had a martyr. People who had never pondered the matter were horrified by the brutality. They began to wonder what the price of peace was to be. Slowly public opinion turned. Ministers began to see a moral relationship between slavery and sin. Respectable business men, once haters of abolitionists, saw that the movement could combine righteousness with an attack on southern economic obstructionism.

Sincere thinkers began to see the light. Fanatical abolitionists had glutted Congress with antislavery bills. Since Congress was still dominated by the South (thanks to the three-fifths rule that gave added representation for a part of the non-voting slave population), the legislators passed the so-called Gag Law, which prevented any consideration of such measures. This was an attack on a fundamental right of popular sovereignty. Men who had no respect for fanaticism, but who recognized a growing threat, now became allies of the abolitionists. One such group was made up of responsible newspaper editors.

Curiously, many of the abolitionist papers first appeared in southern or border states. That was before 1832. In that year occurred the most frightening of the slave revolts under an educated Negro, Nat Turner. Turner was defeated, of course, but from then on, abolitionist literature was driven from the slave states, although there is no indication that such writing had instigated the revolt.

By 1836 the southern press was completely muzzled on the slavery issue. There were laws against any "tendency to incite to insurrections" in most of the slave states; understandable, perhaps, when an entire population lived in fear. A Georgia code of 1835 made any such breach of the law punishable by death. By 1859 it was a prison offense in some states merely to subscribe to an abolitionist paper. Even southern editors winced at such control. Most southern editors had about the same views on slavery as their legislators, but it is noteworthy that a southern editor most seriously challenged the press laws. Samuel Janney, editor of the *Leesburg Washingtonian* in Virginia, had written an editorial refuting Biblical sanction of slavery in denial of the persuasive arguments for slavery presented by Thomas Dew, later president of William and Mary College. Janney was brought to trial under a Virginia law forbidding "agitation" through the printing of opinion detrimental to slavery. In a magnificent speech before a jury of slaveowners, the courageous editor called up the state's great traditions of freedom. He was acquitted.

By 1850 the South was driven to the defensive by the violent attacks of the abolitionists. Public opinion in the North began to demand overt action. Slaveholders were held up as beasts and sinners. Southerners had to devote more and more energy to defending themselves and their institutions. By 1850 world opinion was also forcing the southerner into a humiliating position. The irony was that he had to fight for a noble principle (states' rights) on terms made odious by his enemies. To maintain self-respect, the best brains of the South were devoted to a vindication of slavery. In the North, new ideas were in a ferment, and the tested ones were being used to increase standards of living. In the South, once a hotbed of radicalism, every new idea had to be filtered so as to separate any element that might corrode the institution of slavery. The slave appeared to be dominating his master.

The southern counterpart of the abolitionist was the "fire-eater." Outstanding fire-eaters were William Lowndes Yancey, Edmund Ruffin, and Robert Barnwell Rhett. Yancey was one of the great orators of his era. It was Yancey who led the South from the Democratic convention of 1860. Ruffin was an agricultural writer, who introduced marl as a fertilizer to restore exhausted tobacco land. He was a tireless and indomitable southern patriot. When more timid souls hesitated to fire upon Fort Sumter in 1861, it was Ruffin who snatched the lanyard of the nearest cannon and sent the first ball screaming its message of war. And it was Ruffin who committed suicide rather than take the oath of allegiance after Appomattox. But of all the fire-eaters, Rhett was most effective.

Rhett, sometimes called the "father of secession," had close ties with the North, as did many a leading southerner. Calhoun, for example, was educated at Yale. Rhett went to Harvard. His real name was Smith, but he changed it to Rhett in 1837 when the lineage of an honored colonial forefather was about to die out. Rhett was a distant relative of John Quincy Adams, but he more nearly resembled Sam Adams, who was no kin.

Like Sam Adams, Rhett was a born revolutionist. He and Adams both hated the government under which they grew up. Each vowed to destroy it. Both were expert in the use of every trick that could arouse the public to rebellion. They understood the technique of agitation. Both used the newspaper as the primary medium for transmitting these ideas.

Robert Barnwell Rhett was born into modest circumstances, but he knew how to win friends and influence people. As a youth he "read law" for one of South Carolina's leading barristers. As a successful lawyer, and even more successful real estate operator, he acquired valuable property in Charleston. One such acquisition was the *Mercury*, which Rhett edited. He made it one of the leading papers in the deep south. Through the *Mercury* Rhett became so powerful that he eventually succeeded to the position of his rival, Calhoun, one of the great statesmen of the era.

Rhett emerged as the leading fire-eater of the South following the debate over the 1828 "tariff of abominations." He saw clearly where the North was heading. By 1832 he was declaring openly that the only safety for the South was for it to go its own way. Long before Calhoun had faced the facts, Rhett was arguing for nullification. Obviously, nullification carried to its logical conclusion could lead to disintegration of the Union. Rhett did not dodge the consequences of his arguments. South Carolina, he insisted, could exist by itself, although he hoped to find company for a new confederation.

No one paid much attention to Rhett at first. He was treated about as coldly in the South as Garrison had been in the North. He lost his seat in Congress because of his intemperate speeches on the issue. But as the North was whipped by the abolitionists into heaping more and more abuse upon the South, southerners began to heed Rhett's warnings. After such magnificent propaganda as *Uncle Tom's Cabin,* the South began to depend upon its Rhetts, Yanceys, and Ruffins for justification. By 1848, Rhett was once again powerful politically. In 1851 he succeeded to the Senate seat of the great Calhoun.

Ironically, Rhett had no intention of involving his section in a war. He had aroused the South to fighting pitch, but he had assumed all along that the North would not dare fight. On the day Sumter was fired upon, Rhett was still reassuring readers of the *Mercury* that the South would secede peaceably. He should have known better. Lincoln's refusal to evacuate the fort peacefully was proof that this time the North meant business.

The Rhetts and the Garrisons must take much of the blame for the hates engendered during this period. Writing to John Bigelow of the *New York Evening Post* in 1860, Rhett boasted that South Carolina would treat a Yankee reporter to the secession convention as a spy. But Rhett must not be dismissed as the villain of a tragedy. He was as much a contradiction as was his beloved South. A believer in constitutionalism, he did more than anyone else to wreck the National Charter. A champion of democracy, he fought to keep a class in bondage. He was accused of being overambitious, as indicated in his attacks on Confederate President Jefferson Davis, yet he gave up his cherished Senate seat after only a short incumbency, because of his belief in a principle.

Rhett's friends said that if the South had followed his leadership a decade earlier, it would have won its victory peacefully, as proposed by the editor. His bitterest opponents respected his integrity. J. L. Petigru and Benjamin Franklin Perry, South Carolina Unionists, thought of the *Mercury* editor as a worthy foe.[7] But in the light of history, Rhett appears somewhat unstable—the forlorn

---

[7] Perry founded the *Southern Patriot* at Charleston in 1850 to express pro-Union sentiment in that most violently secessionist state. Petigru, once called "the greatest private citizen South Carolina has ever produced," opposed the state's course up to 1861. Despite their unpopular policies, both men were highly respected, and even loved, in their communities. It was typical of them to have accorded Rhett, their implacable adversary, the same respect they expected from him.

leader of a lost cause. On his deathbed in 1876, he was still predicting that the South would one day be separate and free.

The important standard papers of the day picked up the slavery issue presented to them by the abolitionists and fire-eaters. By 1852 Horace Greeley's weekly *Tribune* had a circulation of more than 200,-000, much of it in the crucial West. Greeley's critics charge that he ignored Negro slavery until he was jolted from his complacency by the abolitionists. It is more likely that the editor understood that those who put slavery on a moral plane did not interpret the fundamental issue correctly. Greeley was opposed to all forms of slavery, including industrial exploitation of the defenseless, or what the South's William Grayson referred to as "northern slavery." But an editorial of November 7, 1842, refutes the critics who challenge Greeley's attitude on the South. His weekly editions of April 8 and 22, 1843, describe in detail plans for the freeing of slaves by public indemnity. A letter from a contributor in the latter edition applauds the editor for his stand. The fact is, Greeley was openly and strongly opposed to the slavery institution from the beginning of his editorship.

He was also accused of confusion on the secession issue. At one time he was all for letting the "erring sister" states of the South depart in peace. Later, he insisted on aggressive and even bloody tactics to win the war. The explanation is not difficult to find. Greeley was ready to let the South go, if it could do so peaceably. When that turned out to be impossible, he advised all-out war to end the carnage as quickly as possible. His critics, who had once chided him for cowardice, now accused him of brutality when one of his most effective editorials appeared on January 5, 1854. It attacked slavery, and it put Greeley at the forefront of the group that was to coalesce as the Republican party, standing for union and free soil. Replied Greeley to a critic who resented his strong language in favor of drastic action: "No other language . . . would faithfully express our convictions. . . . The conflagration it [slavery] threatens is not to be extinguished by jets of rose water."

By 1850, the *Tribune* was the acknowledged leader of the standard dailies opposed to slavery. Greeley felt so strongly on the subject that he was willing to cast off the lifetime allegiances of the Whig to help organize a new party originally called to stop the extension of slavery in new territories and states. Lincoln, still an obscure

politician at the time, read the *Tribune* regularly, and was an admirer of "Uncle Horace." Greeley attended the convention of the
new Republican party at Chicago in 1860 as the special delegate
of Oregon, just admitted to the Union. There appears to be little
doubt that he was influential in winning the nomination for Lincoln. Greeley's old partner, Seward, was the favored candidate. The
Tribune editor had broken with Seward and Weed over the free
soil issue, in the dying days of the Whig party, and in Chicago
Greeley let it be known he preferred "any candidate but Seward."

On January 20, 1861, Greeley published the first of his "stand
firm" editorials—accepted by readers, at least, as Lincoln's own com-
mandments. In February he called for unity against the South by
a slogan in large type at the head of the editorial column: "NO
COMPROMISE/ NO CONCESSIONS TO TRAITORS/ THE
CONSTITUTION AS IT IS." When the first shot of the war was
fired April 12, 1861, Greeley wrote: "Sumter is temporarily lost, but
Freedom is saved! It is hard to lose Sumter, but in losing it we
have gained a united people. Long live the Republic." He asked
for patience when critics, including Raymond, offered unreasonable
suggestions, but by summer, he, too, was demanding action. On June
26 appeared the memorable editorial: "The Nation's War Cry: 'Forward to Richmond! The Rebel Congress must not be allowed to
meet there on July 20. By that date the place must be held by the
National Army.'" This was repeated in subsequent issues. After all
this pressure, Greeley had a heavy conscience, following the hor-
rible defeat of the Union Army at the first battle of Bull Run. It
did not matter that Lincoln's cabinet had independently agreed on
the advance; that General Winfield Scott was fully aware that his
army was unfit for battle; or even that Greeley had nothing to do
with the "Richmond" series of editorials.[8] Since everything in the
Tribune was believed by most of its readers to be the work of
Greeley, the editor had to bear the burden of public scorn. He suffered a serious collapse that kept him in bed for days.

All this time the "reasonableness" of Henry Raymond's *New*

[8] The actual author of the editorials was Fitz-Henry Warren, the Washington
correspondent for the paper. Greeley was not even around the *Tribune* while
the articles were being printed. He had left his managing editor, Charles
A. Dana, in full control of the paper while he made a speaking trip through
the West. It was Dana who pounded out the war cry every day for a week.
But because of his close identity with the *Tribune,* Greeley took the blame.

York Times had made the paper and its editor important journalistically and politically. When Greeley broke with Seward and Weed, Raymond largely succeeded as the mouthpiece of the old group. When the Whigs foundered on the free soil issue, Raymond threw in his lot with the new Republican party. He was always quick to discover what was politically expedient. As a Republican leader, he was again up against his old employer, Greeley, one of the founders of the party. Raymond wrote the statement of principles at the Pittsburgh convention in 1856. It is noteworthy that he was lukewarm on abolitionism, however, until after Sumter. An early critic of Lincoln (possibly because his rival, Greeley, had helped nominate the rail-splitter) Raymond quickly adjusted to circumstance, as usual. Once the fighting began, Raymond was a staunch defender of the President.

Samuel Bowles III, who took over the *Springfield Republican* in 1851 after the death of his father, was faithful to the obsolete Whig party up to the eve of the war. He attacked the abolitionists at every opportunity, on the presumption that they were more interested in causing trouble than in solving problems. His concern over the growing quarrel between the two sections was shown in his approval of the Fugitive Slave law. He did not approve of slavery certainly, but neither did he approve of the agitation over it that might wreck the nation. His conversion came after passage of the Kansas-Nebraska bill in 1854, which junked the old compromises and once more opened up the question of slavery in the West.

By the end of 1854 Bowles had repudiated the wishy-washy Whig leadership. He urged a new party, "able to win the great contest to be fought in '56 with the slave power of the country." Bowles tried to fuse various splinter groups together for this purpose, but he was confused by the apparently hopeless differences that had split the old Whigs. He exposed the so-called Know-Nothing, or Native American, party for the fraud that it was.[9] He believed that the Free Soilers, another alternative, lacked leadership. And so Bowles turned to the new party for rescue. The *Republican* was one of the first important newspapers to endorse the Republican party.

The *Republican* denounced the execution of John Brown, following the raid on the federal arsenal at Harper's Ferry. "John

[9] And violated the confidence of a friend at the party convention in doing so.

Brown still lives," the editorial of December 17, 1859, insisted. For Samuel Bowles saw that the disreputable fanatic symbolized a principle that could not be drowned by the logical reasoning of the politicians. Bowles supported Lincoln on most issues. He preferred less drastic measures for freeing the slaves than proposed by the President, mild as they appear to be today, and he offered some criticism of the wartime threats to civil liberties. But the paper supported the President's postwar program, and continued to support President Johnson's sorry efforts to carry them out.

The *New York Herald*, on the other hand, was mostly opposed to the abolitionist movement. It endorsed the Kansas-Nebraska Act, which the South looked upon as a victory for slavery. Bennett wrote on February 28, 1854: ". . . for twenty odd years, through good and evil report, the *New York Herald* has been the only Northern journal that has unfailingly vindicated the constitutional rights of the South." Naturally, the *Herald* was popular with southern leaders, who quoted it often. The *Herald* was the most popular American newspaper in Great Britain, and because the British were inclined to favor the South, through the close relationship of their textile industry and the cotton growers, it was widely reprinted. As a result, many British readers had a very false notion of the temper of the North on the eve of the war. Bennett gave grudging support to Lincoln, once the fighting began, but continued an annoyance.

The *New York Evening Post* under the guiding hand of William Cullen Bryant and his trusted assistants continued to offer the same enlightened editorial leadership to its readers as it had during the era in which the common man was emerging as a more important force. Bryant was especially eloquent in espousing freedom of the press when he believed it was being threatened during the persecution of abolitionist editors. It was Bryant who first put the more responsible elements of the standard press on the side of such men as James G. Birney, whose paper, the *Philanthropist*, was wrecked by anti-abolitionists at Cincinnati. Birney had asked if freedom of the press were possible when slavery had to be protected from its critics. If freedom of expression were to be repudiated permanently by such measures as the southern gag laws, could democracy continue to exist? he asked. Bryant picked up these arguments and made them respectable. The *Post* under Bryant became one of the most effective spokesmen for freedom in all its forms. When the Republican party was organized from the remnants of splinter groups who upheld such freedoms, Bryant gave it his support. Throughout his long and honorable career Bryant offered reasonable leadership to men of good will.

In the West, Joseph Medill's *Chicago Tribune* was a thunderer against slavery. Founded in 1847, the paper made rapid progress after Medill and five partners took it over in 1855. Medill was one of the western leaders of the Republican party and was said to have suggested the name of the new political organization. The *Tribune* was an early supporter of Lincoln. Medill was largely responsible for the Lincoln boom. He enthusiastically followed the future president, reporting the speeches that are now history. Usually Medill followed his reports with a lively editorial on the subject. Lincoln often came to the *Tribune* office for conferences with the West's leading spokesman. Medill's intimacy with Lincoln is indicated by the crude familiarity with which he conversed with the rising politician. "Dammit, Abe, git yore feet off my desk," Medill is said to have told the lanky backwoodsman on one occasion.

By 1860, the newspaper press of the United States was highly developed. The typical daily was likely to be drab, by modern standards, but the makeup and readability had improved since the advent of the first penny papers. The standard paper was six columns wide. Eight pages usually sufficed, although Raymond's *Times* often ran to ten pages. There were few pictures or graphic illustrations. Many of the penny papers actually sold for twice that by the end of the period, and the *Times* was up to three. Headlines were mostly confined by the column rules to one-column labels, and the great development in display headlines was still waiting on the war. Advertising was increasing steadily. Three of the eight pages of the conservative-looking weekly edition of the *Springfield Republican* usually were devoted to classified notices, and this was common throughout the country.

As a whole, the press was strong and prosperous. It was well that the publishing industry was so healthy, for it was about to be tested as it never had been before. The test began on the day Edmund Ruffin sent the first shot of the Civil War toward Fort Sumter, April 12, 1861.

ANNOTATED BIBLIOGRAPHY

Books:

Many of the references cited at the end of Chapter 11 will be found to be useful in a study of the period covered by this chapter, including the biographies of Greeley, Raymond, Bennett, and Weed, and the histories of the *New York Times* and *Springfield Republican*.

Cole, Arthur Charles, *The Irrepressible Conflict*, A History of American Life, Vol. VII. New York: The Macmillan Company, 1934.

Craven, Avery, *The Repressible Conflict*. Baton Rouge: Louisiana State University Press, 1939.
Both of these books present the debatable issues leading up to the war in a frame of reference still being investigated by historians.

Garrison, Wendell Phillips and Francis J., *William Lloyd Garrison*. 4 vols. New York: The Century Company, 1885-89. The life story of the famous abolitionist, told by his children.

Garrison, William Lloyd, *Selections*. Boston: R. F. Wallcut, 1852. Excerpts from speeches and writings of the famous abolitionist.

———, *The Spirit of the South Towards Northern Freemen, etc.* Boston: R. F. Wallcut, 1861. Extracts from southern newspapers and speeches bringing out the slavery issue as attacked by Garrison.

Gill, John, *Tide without Turning: Elijah P. Lovejoy and Freedom of the Press*. Boston: The Beacon Press, 1958. A well-documented biography of the martyred abolitionist.

Isely, Jeter Allen, *Horace Greeley and the Republican Party, 1853-1861*. Princeton: Princeton University Press, 1947. Analysis of Greeley's writings in the *Tribune* about slavery.

Nevins, Allan, *The Evening Post: A Century of Journalism*. New York: Boni and Liveright, 1922. See especially chapters 4, 5, 6, and 7.

———, *Ordeal of the Union*. 2 vols. New York: Charles Scribner's Sons, 1947. *Emergence of Lincoln*. 2 vols. New York: Charles Scribner's Sons, 1950. The first two volumes cover the years 1847-57 and the next two, 1857-61. They are part of Nevins' massive history of the Civil War.

Nye, Russel B., *Fettered Freedom: Civil Liberties and the Slavery Controversy, 1830-1860*. East Lansing: Michigan State College Press, 1949. How the abolitionists finally won popular support.

Parrington, Vernon L., *Main Currents in American Thought*, Vol. II. The sections on Garrison and Rhett are particularly revealing.

Snyder, Louis L., and Richard B. Morris, eds., *A Treasury of Great Reporting*. New York: Simon and Schuster, 1949. Outstanding newspaper articles of the period.

White, Laura A., *Robert Barnwell Rhett*. New York: The Century Company, 1931. Describes the southern "fire-eater" and his part in the slavery issue.

Periodicals and Monographs:

Babcock, Havilah, "The Press and the Civil War," *Journalism Quarterly*, VI (March 1929), 1.

C.A.B., "The Political Press in America," *Fraser's Magazine*, LII (December 1855), 678. An unfavorable comparison of the American with the British press, but containing background information.

Cullen, Maurice R., Jr., "William Gilmore Simms, Southern Journalist," *Journalism Quarterly*, XXXVIII (Summer 1961), 298. A South Carolina editor first opposes secession, then defies the invading Union army.

Eaton, Clement, "The Freedom of the Press in the Upper South," *Mississippi Valley Historical Review*, XVIII (March 1932), 479. A study of the muzzling of press freedom prior to the Civil War.

Kennedy, Fronde, "Russell's Magazine," *South Atlantic Quarterly*, XVIII (April 1919), 125. Analysis of the periodical published at Charleston, which argued the pro-slavery viewpoint.

Martin, Asa Earl, "Pioneer Anti-Slavery Press," *Mississippi Valley Historical Review*, II (March 1916), 509. Describes the *Philanthropist*, an early abolitionist paper, and discusses other such publications of the early period.

Nye, Russel B., "Freedom of the Press and the Antislavery Controversy," *Journalism Quarterly*, XXII (March 1945), 1. Discusses one of the main considerations of this chapter.

Chapter 14

THE IRREPRESSIBLE CONFLICT

> Come with a sword or musket in your hand, pre-
> pared to share with us our fate in sunshine and
> storm . . . and I will welcome you as a brother
> and associate; but come as you now do, expecting
> me to ally the reputation and honor of my country
> and my fellow soldiers with you, as the representa-
> tive of the press, which you yourself say makes
> so slight a difference between truth and falsehood,
> and my answer is, NEVER.
> —General Sherman to Knox, of the *Herald*

THE WAR BETWEEN THE STATES affected all aspects of
journalism. Reporting, editing, circulation, printing, advertising, and
illustration were all modified during the conflict. Relations between
press and government also changed during this period. One of the
serious problems of the war was how to keep the public properly
informed without giving aid and comfort to the enemy. This was the
world's first modern rehearsal of mass warfare—involving both armies
and civilians. It was one of the costliest wars in terms of men and
money ever fought up to that period. And because large elements
of the populations opposed the bloody strife on both sides of the
lines, there was continuous and outspoken criticism of both administrations. The most usual medium for this expression was the
newspaper.

In contrast with World Wars I and II, reporters in the War
Between the States were much more irresponsible. But it should

be pointed out that the communications lessons of 1861-1865 were of invaluable assistance in working out later policies. For experience has shown that when a country with a free press tradition mobilizes, leaders must adjust themselves to a dilemma.

War calls for strict discipline in the armed forces and drastic reorganization of civilian living. In both cases, peacetime liberties must be relinquished for the duration. But the American theory of free discussion assumes that it is good for the public to have an idea of what sacrifices to expect. The American believes he also retains the right of knowing how efficiently his leaders and representatives are working. But if the press maintains its right to criticise leaders and programs, does not that right jeopardize national security by creating confusion? On the other hand, if the press surrenders its peacetime rights, is there not danger that leaders will conceal their failures and attempts to hold power unjustifiably? The problem in wartime is to preserve this nice balance between national security and the right of the public to know.

The Civil War serves as a case history of this problem, which was aggravated by several factors never before considered in this country. One was the power that the press had won in the previous 20 years. Another was the development of new communications systems, including the railway post and the telegraph, capable of spreading dangerous information to distant areas in a relatively short time. Lastly, the military authorities in both the North and the South did not understand the true function of censorship. It took time to learn that unless some news service is provided by the government, means will always be found to get around censors.

It is also noteworthy that the war aroused hate and bigotry to a pitch that the country had never known before. That is a common phenomenon when countrymen fight each other. The attitudes during and after the war are in contrast to the tolerance and free inquiry that had amazed foreign observers before the war. Up to 1861 there was a willingness in America to experiment with new ideas promising a more abundant life for the ordinary citizen. The various utopian plans; the rise of aggressive religious and literary liberal movements as exemplified by the Unitarians and the Transcendentalists; the encouraging agitation for women's rights, temperance, public education, free soil, and universal suffrage—all these were manifestations of free inquiry reflected in the press of the second quarter of the nineteenth century. Most of these enthusiasms were early casualties of the war. By 1861, the idealistic resources of the nation were temporarily bankrupt. Journalism reflects this trend. For example, there was Charles A. Dana, once a power in the utopian movement, an avowed socialist after his newspaper experiences in the European revolutions of 1848, and one of Horace Greeeley's most trusted lieutenants. But by 1870 Dana, as reflected in his editorials in the *New York Sun,* was a disillusioned and vindictive misanthrope—a man who knew the price of everything and the value of nothing. That is what war can do to a strong man.

A few voices still answered the roll call of the once-great legion of progress. Greeley did not change but he, too, was overwhelmed by the war. He lived to see all his illusions shattered on the rock of postwar public cynicism, but at least he stuck to his principles. His regard for mankind made Greeley abhor war. At one time he favored letting the South secede peacefully. But once the shooting began, Greeley concluded that the most humane course for the Unionists was to end the war quickly.

Lincoln liked the atmosphere of newspaper offices. He had made the *Springfield Journal* in Illinois virtually the official voice of his party previous to the inauguration. The President met reporters easily and corresponded with some of them. Of all journalists, Greeley was his greatest concern. Lincoln was sometimes exasperated by the editor's temperamental outbursts, but he respected the man. By the close of 1861 the *Tribune* was engaged in a campaign to free slaves in conquered areas. The President had already discussed the issue with his cabinet, and he had definite plans for accomplishing emancipation. The climax of the *Tribune* crusade was Greeley's famous "Prayer of Twenty Millions" editorial of August 20, 1862, which was a call for action on the slavery issue. Lincoln replied by a personal letter to Greeley, which he also gave to the *National Intelligencer* for publication on August 23. The letter included the paragraph now so familiar to students of the period:

My paramount object in this struggle *is* to save the Union, and is *not* either to save or destroy Slavery. If I could save the Union without freeing *any* slave, I would do it; and if I could save it by freeing *all* the slaves, I would do it; and if I could do it by freeing some and leaving others alone, I would also do that.

Greeley wrote another open letter to the President urging more concern with the issue. When Lincoln announced his preliminary Emancipation Proclamation a month later, to be effective January 1, 1863, many readers of the *Tribune* assumed that "Uncle Horace" had done it again. "It is the beginning of the new life of the nation," Greeley exulted in his September 23 issue. The President and his cabinet had worked out the details without any help from the editor, but surely a man so sensitive to public feelings as Lincoln must have been aware of the popular pressure.

By the time of the election of 1864, Lincoln and Greeley appear to have tired of each other. The war was increasingly unpopular in many sections. Greeley's criticism of the Administration for failing to find some means of achieving a just peace had strained Lincoln's good nature. On the other hand, the editor had lost face by his unsuccessful attempts to work with southern peace factions. He tended to take out his frustration on the Chief Executive. "You complain of me—what have I done, or omitted to do, that has provoked the hostility of the *Tribune?*" asked the weary President.[1]

But eventually Greeley swung around behind his old friend again. Of the 17 New York daily newspapers, only five were solid supporters of the administration. They were the *Tribune, Times, Evening Post, Sun,* and *Commercial Advertiser.* Greeley did not hesitate to take unpopular stands, when wartime passions made such outspokenness highly dangerous. When Greeley supported the President in his call for more troops under the draft, the *Tribune* was stoned. That was in 1863. Next year another mob threatened bodily harm to the editor after his vain attempt to work out a peace agreement with unofficial representatives of the Confederacy. When Greeley went to Richmond in 1867 to serve as co-signer of Jefferson Davis' bail bond, there was some doubt as to whether the *Tribune* could survive the storm of public resentment, for by that time, the once-maligned Lincoln was "the martyred President," and Davis, the Confederate chief, was the focus of northern hate. These pressures had little effect upon Greeley. The founder of the *Tribune* had many weaknesses, but cowardice was not one of them.

War was the golden age for Henry J. Raymond, who had made the *New York Times* one of the outstanding dailies of its time. The

[1] For relations of Lincoln and the press see James E. Pollard, *The Presidents and the Press* (New York: The Macmillan Company, 1947), pp. 312-397.

paper offered reasonable, penetrating, and thorough reportage. The feeling for objectivity on the part of *Times* writers is indicated by the four open letters Raymond wrote to Yancey, the southern fire-eater. They were able and dispassionate antisecession arguments that showed an understanding of the southern viewpoint. On occasion the *Times* was highly critical of the administration. Raymond's enemies said he was jealous of the part Greeley had played in the selection of Lincoln over Seward at the Chicago convention. But on essential issues, the *Times* gave the President strong support.

Raymond had become contemptuous of his old employer, Greeley. He often criticised the *Tribune* editor for meddling in politics. Raymond, however, was up to his eyes in politics. At one time he was much more a politician than a journalist. Raymond helped write the 1856 platform of the Republican party. He took an active part in the convention of 1860, where Greeley won sweet revenge for the way Weed and Raymond had treated him during the recent New York state election.

Raymond was drafted after the war began, but he bought a substitute to take his place, which was a common procedure. This is no reflection upon his courage, for he was under fire as a correspondent for his paper at the first battle of Bull Run, and he acquitted himself well. He was an expert correspondent and writer, and his partner, George Jones, had wisely gotten him to confine his energy to journalism rather than politics. The temptation was too great, however. By the time the war was well under way, Raymond was devoting less time to his paper and more to politics. By 1863, he was chairman of the Republican National Committee, one of the key political positions in the nation. He managed the 1864 campaign, wrote the party platform, and was elected to the House of Representatives.

When Congress convened in 1865, Raymond seemed to be its most important member. It was assumed that he represented the administration and the party. That gave him great power in the councils of the House. He was so obsessed with making friends with everyone and in preserving harmony, that the more ruthless rising leaders succeeded in using him. The editor who prided himself on his reasonable approach to issues offered no objection to Thaddeus Stevens' proposal for a joint committee to handle Reconstruction problems. Raymond was a shrewd and experienced politi-

HARPER'S WEEKLY.
A JOURNAL OF CIVILIZATION

Vol. XIII.—No. 653.]   NEW YORK, SATURDAY, JULY 3, 1869.   [SINGLE COPIES, TEN CENTS. $4.00 PER YEAR IN ADVANCE.

Entered according to Act of Congress, in the Year 1869, by Harper & Brothers, in the Clerk's Office of the District Court of the United States, for the Southern District of New York.

HENRY J. RAYMOND.

On Friday, June 18, we were startled by the sad intelligence of the death of HENRY J. RAYMOND, the founder and editor of the New York *Times*. He had died suddenly that morning of apoplexy. Thus passed away in the prime of life—for he was only in his fiftieth year—one of the four most eminent journalists in this country, and also one of the most prominent politicians of this State.

HENRY JARVIS RAYMOND was born in the village of Lima, Livingston County, New York, January 24, 1820. His father, who died only a few months since, was a hard-working farmer of moderate means and of sound integrity. His mother—a woman of strong character—encouraged his early tendencies toward a life of study. After a short period of education in the district school during the winters of his boyhood years, he continued his studies at the village academy, and in 1833 commenced Latin and Algebra at the Genesee Wesleyan Seminary. He entered the University of Vermont in the summer of 1836, and there was graduated in 1840 with the highest honors of his class.

The youth of twenty then came to New York city, where he entered upon the study of law in the office of Mr. E. W. MARSH. But he had his living to earn, and the only prominent men of the city with whom he was at all acquainted were Mr. MANN, then a law-student in Wall Street, and HORACE GREELEY, then the proprietor of the *New Yorker*, a weekly newspaper, to which Mr. RAYMOND had contributed during his college course. He still wrote for that paper, and also earned $5 a week by daily news-letters to the *Cincinnati Chronicle*, then edited by E. D. MANSFIELD, since known as the "Veteran Observer." Meantime he received an offer of a school in North Carolina at $100 a year; but as Mr. GREELEY offered him the same for his services on the *New Yorker*, he declined the first offer, and remained in New York. In 1841 Mr. GREELEY established the *Tribune*, and retained Mr. RAYMOND's services as assistant editor. In this position he demonstrated his ability as a journalist. No one could make so rapid or so accurate a report of a speech; and he was also equally prepared to write a leading editorial. Whatever he did he did well. His report of WEBSTER's speech at Bunker Hill was a memorable event in those days when short-hand writing was unknown.

Mr. RAYMOND accepted an editorial position on the New York *Courier and Enquirer* in 1843. It was in this paper that part of the celebrated controversy with Mr. GREELEY on the doctrine of Fourierism was published. It was during his connection with this journal that he became a reader in the publishing-house of HARPER & BROTHERS, a position which he held for ten years.

Mr. RAYMOND's political life began in 1849, when he was elected a member of the New York State Assembly by the Whigs. He was re-elected the next year, and was chosen speaker. In 1851 he started the *Times* newspaper. In 1852 he went to the Baltimore Convention to report the proceedings for his paper, but was given a seat as a delegate, and made an eloquent speech in exposition of Northern sentiment. In 1854 he was elected Lieutenant-Governor of this State, receiving 157,166 votes, a majority of 28,333 over LUDLOW, his principal opponent. As an organizer of the Republican party Mr. RAYMOND was an active worker. The "Address to the People," which was issued from Pittsburg in 1856, was from his pen. He was a supporter of FREMONT after the meeting of the first National Convention. In 1857 he refused to be a candidate for Governor of this State. The next four years were devoted to his profession. In 1856 he sided, apparently, with the supporters of Mr. DOUGLAS, but in the end resumed his relations with the Republican party. In 1860 he was a warm supporter of Mr. SEWARD for the Republican nomination, and he was peculiarly satisfied that Mr. SEWARD was placed in the Cabinet of Mr. LINCOLN.

In 1861 Mr. RAYMOND was again elected to the Assembly and was chosen Speaker. In 1864 he was elected to the United States House of Representatives from the Sixth District of this city. His career in that body, during a critical era of our political history, will be reviewed in another column.

His speech on the 29th of January, 1866, was his first elaborate effort in Congress. It was upon the Fourteenth Constitutional Amendment. In concluding this speech Mr. RAYMOND thus expressed his views as to what the Government ought to do:

"In the first place, I think we ought to accept the present *status* of the Southern States, and regard them as having resumed, under the President's guidance and action, their functions of self-government in the Union. In the second place, I think this House should decide on the admission of Representatives by districts, admitting none but loyal men who can take the oath we may prescribe, and holding all others as disqualified; the Senate acting, at its discretion, in the same way in regard to Representatives of States. I think, in the third place, we should provide by law for giving to the freedmen of the South all the rights of citizens in courts of law and elsewhere. In the fourth place, I would exclude from Federal office the leading actors in the conspiracy which led to the rebellion in every State. In the fifth place, I would make such amendments to the Constitution as may seem wise to Congress and the States, acting freely and without coercion. And, sixth, I would take such measures and precautions, by the disposition of military forces, as will preserve order and prevent the overthrow, by usurpation or otherwise, in any State, of its republican form of government......Above all, I beg this House to bear in mind, as the sentiment that should control and guide its action, that we of the North and they of the South are at war no longer. The gigantic contest is at an end. The courage and devotion on either side which made it so terrible and so long no longer owe a divided duty, but have become the common property of the American name, the priceless possession of the American Republic through all time to come. The dead of the contending hosts sleep beneath the soil of a common country and under one common flag. Their hostilities are hushed, and they are the dead of the nation for evermore. The victor may well exult in the victory he has achieved. Let it be our task, as it will be our highest glory, to make the vanquished, and their posterity to the latest generation, rejoice in their defeat."

On the expiration of his term Mr. RAYMOND, having declined the renomination that was pressed upon him by prominent men of both parties, withdrew almost wholly from public life, and devoted all his energies to the conduct of his paper. He was offered the Mission to Austria by President JOHNSON in 1867; but his name was sent to the Senate without his consent, and after he had notified the President that no consideration could induce him to accept the position. The last article written by Mr. RAYMOND for the *Times* was an editorial on Mr. SEWARD, which appeared on the morning of June 17.

"A remarkable instance of Mr. RAYMOND's working ability," says the New York *Tribune*, in an obituary sketch, "occurred on the occasion of the death of DANIEL WEBSTER, a statesman for whom he had the greatest admiration. The news of Mr. WEBSTER's death reached here on a Saturday afternoon. Mr. RAYMOND wrote an admirable biography, which appeared in Monday's paper, covering twenty-six columns of the *Times*, and in addition he wrote three columns of editorial on the same subject. Of this extraordinary biography by Mr. RAYMOND wrote sixteen columns without stopping a moment for rest. As a feat of editorial labor we doubt its ever having been equaled."

Mr. RAYMOND passed the afternoon previous to his death in Greenwood, making arrangements for the interment of his son WALTER's remains, and called at the office of the *Times* about six o'clock in the evening. After a few minutes' conversation on matters pertaining to the business of the paper he returned home. After dinner he sat with his family and some friends who came in until between nine and ten o'clock, when he left them to attend a political consultation; and his family saw no more of him until he was discovered, about half past two next morning, lying in the hall-way unconscious and apparently dying. He had locked the outside door and shut the inner one, and was then apparently stricken with the malady that closed his life. The most eminent medical aid was at once summoned, and the utmost that science and skill could do were done,

THE LATE HON. HENRY J. RAYMOND.—[PHOTOGRAPHED BY BRADY, NEW YORK.]

Courtesy, State Historical Society of Wisconsin

Portrait of Henry J. Raymond, founder of the *New York Times*, as it appeared in the popular news and picture magazine, *Harper's Weekly*.

James Gordon Bennett, Sr., (*left*) and Horace Greeley (*right*) founded the *Herald* and *Tribune*, predecessors of the *New York Herald Tribune*.

Arunah S. Abell (*left*), founder of the *Baltimore Sun*, and Joseph Medill (*right*), who mad* the *Chicago Tribune* a leading midwestern paper.

cian, and he must have seen what the fanatical Stevens was striving to achieve. This was the beginning of the policy of punishment for the South. As an administration spokesman, Raymond should have had no part in the program. One will look in vain, however, for any objections from the *Times* or its editor as the Stevens "Directorate" prepared to submit the conquered states to the ravages of "Reconstruction," a term the South will never forget.

It was at this time that Raymond received the title, "The Trimmer," by voting for the Freedman's Bureau and then supporting President Johnson's veto of it. He opposed the Civil Rights bill, but approved its substance in the Fourteenth Amendment. Even Stevens, who had exploited Raymond so openly, was contemptuous of such wishy-washy conduct. When Raymond once suggested that he "pair" (match with an opponent) his vote on some division in the House, the acidulous chief of the Directorate suggested this should be no problem for Raymond—he could simply pair with himself.

Raymond was failing as a politician because of his indecisiveness. He knew he was beaten when he failed to sell his platform at the Philadelphia convention of 1866. The Stevens "Radicals" were now strong enough to have him rejected from the National Committee. Under the circumstances Raymond believed it less painful to decline his renomination to Congress. Greeley was gleeful. He declared Raymond had been treated as a Judas deserved to be treated. In the end, after some unsuccessful attempts to regain his former position with the help of tired old Thurlow Weed, Raymond bolted the party. That was the end of him politically. "Shocking Cruelty to a Fugitive Slave," Greeley headlined the account of the episode in the *Tribune*. Later, Raymond and the *Times* returned to solid ground with the Republicans, but the point is made clear that with all of Raymond's contempt for Greeley's "impractical" enthusiasms the *Times* editor was no more successful as a realist. He died of a cerebral hemorrhage in 1869 while waging an editorial fight against the infamous Tweed ring of political corruptionists which was looting the city treasury.

If the above is a somewhat less favorable picture of the *Times* founder than is usually presented, let it be pointed out that the darker periods of Raymond's life were concerned with politics. The indecisiveness and "trimming" that weakened him as a politician made him great as a journalist. When the country was crying for a responsible press, Raymond led the way—not always happily, perhaps, but to the best of his very great ability.

Bennett and his *Herald* caused the Lincoln administration considerable annoyance. The paper was politically independent, but it was definitely "soft" toward the South, where it had great influence. Because of its extensive news coverage, particularly of business and commerce, the *Herald* was the most popular American newspaper in Europe. The British government at this time was making friendly overtures to the South, which provided British mills with cotton in normal times. The attitude of the widely-read *Herald* was therefore of concern to Lincoln and his cabinet, for it was important that European neutrals have a fair evaluation of the American issues.

After the first battle of Bull Run, Bennett gave his full, but somewhat grudging, support to the Lincoln administration and the war. Even so, it was necessary from time to time for the President to "sweeten up"—as Lincoln put it—the aggressive editor of the *Herald*. "I write this to assure you that the Administration will not discriminate against the *Herald,* especially while it sustains us so generously. . . ." Lincoln wrote to Bennett after personally interceding for a *Herald* reporter who had been refused a pass to go down the Potomac river with a military detachment.[2] As a former pro-southern newspaper, the *Herald* continued to attack specific issues of the Republican party, but its intentions were not subversive.

In their zeal to satisfy the amazingly aggressive news policies of their employers, *Herald* reporters sometimes had to be rebuked by the higher authorities of the administration. There was the case of Henry Wikoff, known to some of his colleagues as "Chevalier." Wikoff was very attractive to the ladies, apparently. He was accused of using this charm to obtain information from Mrs. Lincoln. Parts of the President's first message to a regular session of Congress in December, 1861, appeared in the *Herald* the morning the document was presented to the legislators. Chairman John Hickman of the House Judiciary Committee turned aside from an investigation of telegraphic censorship to find out about this leak. It was traced to Wikoff, although the affair was hushed up before all the facts could be made public.[3]

[2] Pollard, *The Presidents and the Press,* p. 360.

[3] These and some other episodes of Civil War reporting are from a manuscript, as yet unpublished, by Professor Frederick B. Marbut, Pennsylvania State University, on Washington press correspondence.

There were other instances in which *Herald* reporters tangled with authorities. At times, the *Herald* retaliated, as in its editorial attacks on Hickman during the Wikoff case, but the government also held an ace card in this game—namely, the right to restrict *Herald* coverage of the war to the advantage of Bennett's rivals. Actually, the aggressiveness of the *Herald* could have caused it much more trouble, if military officials had exerted their authority. At any rate, the editorial tactics paid off, for the *Herald* climbed to a circulation of more than 100,000 soon after the beginning of the war. It was then the most popular newspaper in the United States.[4]

Few presidents suffered more from editorial abuse than Lincoln. Opposition editors and disappointed favor-seekers accused him in print of vicious deeds, which the patient President usually ignored. He was falsely accused of drawing his salary in gold bars, while his soldiers were paid in deflated greenbacks. He was charged with drunkenness while making crucial decisions, with granting pardons to secure votes, and with needless butchering of armies as a result of his lust for victories. Once he was accused of outright treason. Typical of his press detractors was the *La Crosse Democrat*, a Wisconsin weekly, which said of the draft: "Lincoln has called for 500,000 more victims."

Continuous and unlicensed criticism was voiced by political opponents. Democrats actually polled a larger vote than Republicans in 1860.[5] They were so split by sectional differences, however, that they could not agree upon a candidate. The Republicans were aware that they had won by default. That was one reason Lincoln tried to be conciliatory where decisiveness was not absolutely essential.

Most northern Democrats were loyal during the war, although they tended to welcome almost any peace overtures from the South.

---

[4] The *New York Times* climbed from 45,000 to about 75,000 in the same period. The daily *Tribune* trailed behind, but the weekly edition, largely responsible for Greeley's national reputation, reached more than 200,000. This was the largest circulation of any single American paper. The *New York Ledger* had almost twice that many subscribers, but it was not a newspaper, as its nameplate would indicate, but a weekly story periodical.

[5] Lincoln had only 40 per cent of the popular vote in 1860, and he won by only 400,000 votes in 1864, when none of the southern Democrats had any voice in the elections. This was a serious consideration for Republican leaders contemplating the postwar political problem.

But another group of northern Democrats served as a kind of fifth column for the South. Their sympathies for the Confederacy were of varying degrees, but often their overt actions smacked of treason. This faction of the Democratic party was known as Copperhead, after the dangerous reptile that gives no warning of its attack. One of the more fanatical Copperhead organizations was called "The Knights of the Golden Circle," later supplanted by the underground "Sons of Liberty." By 1863 they had been officially declared traitors, to be treated accordingly when captured.

This presented a nice problem to Lincoln. At what point did criticism of the government exceed the limits of free expression? A test case was that of Clement Laird Vallandigham, Ohio editor and politician. Vallandigham was hero or villain, depending upon the viewpoint. There is no doubt that he was courageous and sincere. He risked his life and all his property for what he believed to be his right of free expression. On the other hand, he gave great aid and comfort to the enemy in standing upon these principles.

Vallandigham was the youngest member of the Ohio legislature when he was elected to it in 1845. His skill as a politician in a region of master politicians is indicated by the fact that he maneuvered himself into the speakership at the age of 26. In 1847 he became co-owner of the *Dayton Empire,* soon the leading anti-abolitionist publication in the Middle West. The abolitionists brought about his defeat in the Congressional elections of 1852, but he gained his seat in 1858, and at once used his office as a forum from which to attack the Republican party for its stand on secession. As secretary of the Democratic National Committee in 1860, he tried to work out a compromise. His credo was "To maintain the Constitution as it is, and to restore the Union as it was." This was legitimate until the outbreak of war, but when he continued his activities after April, 1861, Vallandigham became a threat to the North. He was by this time leader of the above-ground Copperheads, or the "peace party," as he called it. In the spring of 1863, General Ambrose E. Burnside issued his General Order Number 38, warning the Copperheads that they would be arrested if they continued to make public statements harmful to the northern war effort. Vallandigham defied the order at Columbus, and again at Mount Vernon, Ohio. He was arrested, tried in a military court, and sentenced to prison. Lincoln commuted the sentence to banishment behind the Confederate lines.[6]

The leniency and patience of Lincoln, often mistaken for weakness, kept the press reasonably free through the terrible war period. He made full use of the press as a sounding board of public opinion, and he respected the institution. The President had no official newspaper after he left Springfield. For a while the *National Intelligencer* aspired to that title, but Lincoln soon devised a much more effective way of communicating with the public. He began speaking openly with reporters, trusting he would receive a "good press" thereby, and that his cause would be presented fairly to the public. The New York Associated Press was particularly effective in this regard. Since it had to reach publishers of various political and social faiths, the AP confined its dispatches to straight reporting, minus the usual biased interpretations common to most news accounts of the time. If any part of the press served as Lincoln's organ, it was the AP. This policy caused the President much trouble, but apparently he believed the price he paid was warranted.[7]

No war had ever been so fully and freely reported before. New York newspapers usually devoted at least a third of their space to war news. But sooner or later the press had to work out an understanding with military authorities in the interests of public security. There is no record in War Department files of military censorship prior to the Civil War. There was no knowledge of the technique of censorship. A system therefore had to be developed by trial and error. As a result, both the press and the government made many mistakes in working out the problems, and criticism from all sides was often bitter. Yet many valuable lessons were learned in the Civil War about controls of communication agencies. This experience was put to good use in World Wars I and II.

The problem was aggravated by the fact that the American press

[6] Later, Vallandigham returned openly to Ohio, by way of Bermuda and Canada. He even ran for office while officially a fugitive from justice. Crowds cheered him when he appeared in Chicago. Lincoln ignored him at this time so as not to make a martyr for the Copperheads. After the war Vallandigham was accepted back in his community as a practicing lawyer. He accidentally killed himself while demonstrating a pistol used in a murder case.

[7] See Robert S. Harper, *Lincoln and the Press* (New York: McGraw-Hill Book Company, 1951).

had become so prosperous, aggressive, and independent in the years preceding the war that it was sensitive to any form of restriction. The telegraph and the railway posts were other factors to be considered. They made it possible to disseminate news much faster than before. The potential danger of information useful to the enemy was therefore all the greater. On the other hand, this was the first of the all-out wars, involving civilian populations, and since public morale was now a much more important factor in prosecuting the war, the channels of information had to be kept open.[8]

Military censorship evolved from the political censorship with which the press and public were already familiar. In most instances such restrictions came to the attention of the average man when the press defended its freedom, but there were times when even the press appeared willing to submit to certain controls. Only three newspapers complained when Amos Kendall restricted abolitionist newspapers from the U. S. Post Offices 25 years earlier. The southern gag laws and the various attempts of State legislatures to deny communications tending to incite to violence are other examples of the tradition of political control of the press.

There were three stages in the development of Civil War military censorship. The first period of fumbling ended about 1862. It began with the denial by the Post Office of messages sent to enemy areas. Curiously, this was not until the war had been under way for several days. In this instance, the editors appear to have been more aware of the danger than the government, for there had been several newspaper warnings about the laxness of communication restrictions where the enemy was involved.

The high command in Washington began to realize that the enemy was obtaining valuable military intelligence through the free flow of information to the press and to persons in private life. The authorities began to do something about the situation when they were handed thousands of telegrams which had passed through the northern states in recent weeks. Federal officials in New York, Washington, and other large cities seized these telegrams on May 20, 1861. This is noteworthy as the first step toward an official censorship policy.[9] The telegrams revealed the names of traitors in the

[8] The outstanding study of this problem is Quintus Wilson, "A Study and Evaluation of the Military Censorship in the Civil War" (Master's thesis, University of Minnesota, 1945).

[9] *Ibid.*, p. 39.

North and plans of the secessionists. One of those caught in the net was James E. Harvey, former *Tribune* reporter, friend of Lincoln, and recent appointee as minister to Portugal.

On July 8, 1861, General Winfield Scott, commander of the Union armies, issued an order, backed up by Secretary of War Simon Cameron, forbidding the telegraph companies from sending any information of a military nature. This was illegal, but it served the purpose until Congress gave the President such control in January, 1862.

The first drastic use of the telegraph censorship was after the first battle of Bull Run, July 21, 1861. Raymond, who had turned in a bulletin to the *Times* announcing a Union victory and was thereby put to shame by the reports of his rivals, maintained that his follow-up story had been blocked by the censors. The same thing happened to Lawrence A. Gobright of the Associated Press. But there was no doubt as to the need of censorship, and the legitimate correspondents themselves began to see the necessity for control. It would serve to protect them in the transmission of the type of news the public needed, but it would discourage the correspondent intent upon reporting fake news as a means of arousing interest at any price. Already it was clear that if the government had to restrict certain types of information, it was just as necessary to provide the news to which reporters were entitled.

Since honest journalists and military planners both recognized the problem, it was natural that they should try to work out some agreement. On August 2, 1861, General George B. McClellan, commanding the Army of the Potomac, called a historic press conference of Washington correspondents. He presented to them an unprecedented plan that was the forerunner of modern voluntary censorship. The meeting was held while editorial skepticism and military resentment were issues after the disastrous Union rout at Bull Run. Each of the delegates to the conference signed a document binding him to transmit no information of military value to the enemy. On the other hand, the general agreed to use all his considerable influence to facilitate the gathering of news that was of interest to the public. The men who left the meeting that day congratulated them-selves on the wisdom of the plan.

Unfortunately, the program was unsuccessful, not because of any serious flaw in the agreement, but because of division of authority.

The official censor was H. E. Thayer, who understood nothing about the problem. He was not under the supervision of the War Department, but was under the direction of the Secretary of State. The jealousy of the War and State Departments resulted in a complete breakdown of the voluntary censorship plan less than three months after it was proposed. For on October 22, Secretary of State Seward instructed Thayer to prohibit telegraphic dispatches from Washington which related to military *and civil* operations of the Government. Since this violated the very spirit of the McClellan agreement, the press reverted to its old system of getting news as best it could.[10]

The failure of a promising plan led to the first Congressional investigation of censorship. On December 5, 1861, a special House panel heard the complaints of the correspondents and turned a sympathetic ear to the demands for a revision of the State Department order. The committee was curious as to why the Associated Press should have been specifically exempt from the restrictions. This was explained by L. A. Gobright, chief of the AP's Washington bureau. Gobright said his association had achieved the status of what amounted to a semi-official Gazette by confining reports to facts and by deleting political and military opinion. On March 20, 1862, the committee issued a report demanding an end to restrictions on reports of non-military actions of the government.

There was considerable improvement when the censor was taken from the State Department and was put under the direction of the Secretary of War. Lincoln had been hesitant to give Secretary of War Cameron any more powers. His appointment had been strictly a result of political expedience, and as soon as possible he was replaced by the tough, but very able Edwin M. Stanton. He quickly brought order out of chaos, and one of his first steps was the revision of censorship. By an order of February 25, 1862, Stanton clarified the triple set of restrictions under which correspondents had been bound by voluntary, State Department, and War Department censorship. By the Stanton order, correspondents were to submit copy to provost marshals for approval before transmission, but it was understood that deletions would apply only to military matters. Now the reporters knew just about how far they could go in reporting battles, and the press was able to serve much more effectively.

In the meantime, the President had authorized the Commander

[10] Wilson, "Military Censorship in the Civil War," p. 50.

of the Armies to suspend the writ of habeas corpus, an action which made it possible for the authorities to make arrests without presenting charges immediately. Such action was provided for in the Constitution under the emergency powers, but there was some doubt as to whether the President or Congress had the power of suspension. Since Congress was not in session, Lincoln resolved the doubt by taking the responsibility on himself. The President's action was challenged by Chief Justice Taney, and had to be considered by the Supreme Court, but by that time, the action of the President had accomplished what he intended.

The second period of censorship, which began after Stanton's order of February 25, 1862, showed a better understanding of the principles involved, but was marred by faulty administration. The Stanton directive was poorly enforced, and depended too much upon individual interpretation. Another serious fault was the abuse of prerogatives by ambitious military leaders. Many of these were political appointees. They were interested in favorable publicity. Through their power of censorship, they could exert pressure upon correspondents attached to them. General Grant discouraged this habit by removing from command one of the worst offenders, General John A. McClernand, during the siege of Vicksburg in July, 1863.

General Sherman contributed to the development of organized censorship. The general had been bedeviled by reporters, who were irked by his press relations. Sherman was certain much military failure could be blamed on information leaks. On several occasions he spoke his mind on this matter. The press retaliated by spreading the story that he was insane. The issue came to a showdown after Thomas E. Knox, a correspondent for the *Herald*, transmitted information that clearly violated military regulations of censorship. Sherman had the reporter arrested and held as a spy. He had no intention of shooting the man, as he had every right to do, but he was convinced that this was a good test case. In the end, the President intervened, Knox got out of his predicament, and Sherman got what he wanted—the understanding that all correspondents must be *accredited,* or recognized, journalists; and that they must be *acceptable* to commanders in the field. Thus was established a precedent followed ever since by military correspondents.

The controversial and colorful General Benjamin Butler also contributed to the lore of censorship during his occupation of New Orleans. His proclamation outlined censorship procedures that are still followed in conquered areas. It included instructions to local editors as to what they could or could not print. It prescribed the duties of censors in the interests of the best possible adjustment between the needs of the public and the necessities of the army in control.

During this second period of development some system for control of information to foreign countries also had to be worked out. Too much harmful intelligence was leaking to the Confederacy by way of British correspondents. After April 5, 1862, British reporters were excluded from the battle areas. That was an effective brake upon correspondents such as William Howard Russell of the *Times* of London, whose caustic comments on the battle of Bull Run and adverse criticism of Union political and military leaders had made him unpopular in the North. Since there was a strong bloc of British sentiment in favor of the South, such reporting could be damaging to the Federal cause. Indeed, Union failure to meet the Confederate propaganda in Europe was one of the criticisms of the administration. In the fall of 1861, John Bigelow of the *New York Evening Post* was sent to France to see what he could do about damming the stream of abuse flowing from some of the British and French papers, but the task was far too great for one man.

From 1864 to the end of the war, censorship entered its third and successful phase. General Sherman marched all the way to the sea in hostile country without once having his plans disclosed by the press. On the whole, the press was cooperating by the end of the war. Curiously, as the North tightened its censorship, the South relaxed its controls, which had been so much more effective at the beginning of the conflict. The southern press will be discussed later in this chapter, but the point appears to be that censorship will not apply where the people will not consent to it. The South had an excellent press organization until defeat and the need for drastic action resulted in a breakdown of censorship.

On the whole, the northern press enjoyed great freedom throughout the war. The great power of the President after his suspension of habeas corpus was used sparingly. Most of the punitive actions were taken by military commanders. In June, 1864, the *Chicago Times* was suspended for three days by order of General Ambrose

Burnside, commanding the Department of Ohio, which included the military districts in Illinois. This was one of the so-called "Burnside Decrees," based on the right of a commander to silence public expression of ideas and information deemed harmful to the military effort. The general appears to have had plenty of provocation for his action. Wilbur F. Storey, publisher of the *Times*, lacked both conscience and principle. He used the most violent language in attacking Lincoln after the Emancipation Proclamation was issued. He repeatedly ignored military warnings to stop fomenting Copperhead dissatisfaction in the area. Pushed beyond endurance by the anti-Federal sentiments of the *Times*, General Burnside ordered the newspaper padlocked. Lincoln's reaction was typical. He wished to back up his own general, and he knew Burnside had much to complain about, but the President also had definite ideas about freedom of expression. After three days he rescinded the military order.

Other newspapers ran afoul of the censor. One was the *New York World*, established in 1860 as a penny paper with religious overtones. At first it was a supporter of the Lincoln administration. It lost money and continued to fail even after it absorbed the assets of the famous old *Courier and Enquirer*. Eventually it was taken over by Manton Marble, an able editor, who increased circulation by espousing the cause of the "Peace Democrats." After the Emancipation Proclamation, the *World* was openly hostile to the administration. It became the focus of Copperhead infection in an area where the war was already unpopular. In May, 1864, the military authorities had a chance to strike back.

The *World* and the *Journal of Commerce* published a forged presidential proclamation purporting to order another draft of 400,000 men. The document was actually the product of Joseph Howard, Jr., city editor of the *Brooklyn Eagle*. He had hoped to make a profit in the stock market by this hoax, although this was the least of his crimes. Such a story in the tense metropolis was almost certain to cause bloodshed and probably death by rioting. Other editors refused to carry the story, after checking the facts, but the *World* and *Journal of Commerce* appeared with the article prominently displayed. General John A. Dix promptly suppressed them. After a lapse of two days, during which the editors were severely reprimanded, they were allowed to resume publication.

It was not the first time the *Journal of Commerce* had brushed with the authorities. Gerard Hallock, who had contributed so much to journalism and cooperative news gathering, was publisher of the paper. Editorial policy was definitely pro-South. It was so critical of the Union that a grand jury was summoned to investigate the paper and four other publications in the area for indulging in "the frequent practice of encouraging the rebels now in arms against the Federal Government." The postmaster general then ordered the New York postal authorities not to accept these papers in the mail. At that point Hallock retired from the paper. His successor followed a less antagonistic policy, and the *Journal of Commerce* was allowed to use the postal services again.

The *Daily News*, one of the other papers involved in the grand jury investigation, was the organ of the Tammany Democrats. In 1861 Benjamin Wood, brother of Fernando, the Mayor of New York, bought the paper for political purposes. It was a violently anti-Republican paper. Mayor Wood had once suggested that the city secede, along with the South, and the relationship of this politico with the *Daily News* editor is of some significance.

Elected to Congress, editor Wood continued his attacks on the administration from the Union forum. In August, 1861, the paper was denied mailing privileges. The management tried to distribute papers outside the city through private express companies, but its copies were confiscated. The paper then ceased publishing for 18 months. It reappeared as full of fight as ever, but nevertheless was permitted to use the mails.

One of the most celebrated suspension cases outside New York was that of Samuel Medary, editor of the *Crisis* and of the *Ohio Statesman* at Columbus. The *Crisis* was a special organ of the Copperheads, and it supported C. L. Vallandigham, the Copperhead candidate for governor. In 1864 Medary was indicted by a federal grand jury as the spokesman for a group then declared to be subversive. He was released from jail on bond furnished by the editor of the *Cincinnati Enquirer*, who wished to test the wartime freedom of the press. Medary died before the case was tried in court.

Much more effective repression was carried out by unofficial means. Many of the Copperhead papers, including the *Crisis*, mentioned above, were wrecked by mobs. So were pro-administration papers from time to time. The *New York Tribune* was seriously threatened on two occasions. Pro-southern editors sometimes had to flee from mob violence whipped up by returning veterans. In 1861 the pro-southern New York papers were warned by placards that national security was more important than their right to criticise. But three years later, the same type of mob actions forced editors to modify extreme opposition to northern peace feelers. A year later, other waves of public violence followed the assassination of Lincoln, and those who were known to have made it difficult for the President ran the risk of physical harm. But the fact remains that the press was relatively free throughout the war, and that considering the tensions, the responsible press emerged unscathed.

Indeed, when it came to the reporting of military actions, Civil War correspondents, or "specials," as they were then called, enjoyed a freedom that would not be tolerated in modern times. Many of the battles were fought in remote areas, and the struggle to get back first-hand accounts often was heroic. Some of the best reporting in American journalism was offered the public by the hundreds of correspondents during this test of a nation.

Newsmen were everywhere. They roamed the South long after their detection might have resulted in their execution as spies. Some of them were famous already, including Raymond of the *Times,* who was at Bull Run, and William Howard Russell, the world-renowned British war correspondent fresh from his triumphs in the Crimea.

Some of the best war reporters earned their spurs after the conflict began, however. One of these was B. S. Osbon, a minister's son who had embarked on a life of seafaring and adventure. He was working for the *New York World* at nine dollars a week on that April morning in 1861, when the curtain went up on one of the great American tragedies. From the deck of a naval cutter, Osbon watched the bombardment of Fort Sumter. The lead of the story he sent back was a prototype of the news style developed during the war:

CHARLESTON, APRIL 12—*The ball is opened. War is inaugurated.*
The batteries of Sullivan's Island, Morris Island, and other points were opened on Fort Sumter at four o'clock this morning. Fort Sumter has returned the fire, and a brisk cannonading has been kept up.[11]

[11] Louis L. Snyder, and Richard B. Morris, eds., *A Treasury of Great Reporting* (New York: Simon and Schuster, 1949), p. 130.

Later Osbon shipped back on the U.S.S. "Baltic," carrying the exhausted Major Robert Anderson, commander of the fort's garrison. It was Osbon who disclosed in a published interview that a junior officer had raised the flag of surrender after Anderson had ordered the last round to be fired, and further resistance appeared to be hopeless.

Not long after, Bennett hired Osbon to report for the *Herald* at $25 a week. He was on the quarterdeck with Admiral Farragut at the siege of New Orleans. He seemed to be wherever a good story was about to break.

But there were other stars, too. Albert D. Richardson of the *Tribune* sent reports from the deep South through the line by transmitting his stories in cipher by way of the New York banks. He watched the great battle of Fort Henry from a treetop observation post. He saw Island Number Ten at the Vicksburg approaches reduced to rubble as he stood with Commodore Foote on the hurricane deck of a Union ironclad. He ran the blockade of Vicksburg; was knocked from the deck by the shock of a cannon ball that nearly struck him; and then was picked from the water and imprisoned by the Confederates. His escape through the lines was one of the exciting journalistic feats of the time.

George W. Smalley, later one of the pioneer foreign correspondents, first gained fame while covering the war for the *Tribune*. At the battle of Antietam, where he served as a dispatch rider for General Hooker, he lost two horses by gunfire. It was Smalley who first got the news of the battle to Washington, where Lincoln was anxiously waiting for some encouraging report before announcing his plans for emancipation.

Many of the correspondents wrote under a pen name. There was "Agate," for example, who was actually Whitelaw Reid, the successor to Greeley on the *Tribune* in the early 1870's. He was already famous for his report on the battle of Shiloh when he sent in a dispatch one day from Gettysburg. His story, datelined "Field of Battle, Near Gettysburg, July 2," took up 14 of the 48 columns of the *Cincinnati Gazette*. It remains as a classic of Civil War reporting. Standing on Cemetery Hill, the point most exposed to rebel fire, Reid turned in an eyewitness account of the decisive battle, of which the following is an excerpt:

. . . Hancock was wounded; Gibbon succeeded to command—approved soldier, and ready for the crisis. As the tempest of fire approached its height, he walked along the line, and renewed his orders to the men to reserve their fire. The rebels—three lines deep—came steadily up. They were in pointblank range.

At last the order came! From thrice six thousand guns there came a sheet of smoky flame, a crash of leaden death. The line literally melted away; but there came a second, resistless still. It had been our supreme effort—on the instant we were not equal to another.

Up to the rifle pits, across them, over the barricades—the momentum of their charge, the mere machine strength of their combined action swept them on. Our thin line could fight, but it had not weight enough to oppose this momentum. It was pushed behind the guns. Right on came the rebels. They were upon the guns, were bayoneting the gunners, were waving their flags above our pieces.

But they had penetrated to the fatal point. . . .[12]

In the Confederate camp near Hagerstown, Maryland, the reporter for the *Richmond Enquirer,* retreating with Lee's army, sent back this eloquent version of the same battle to soften the blow to the bereaved at home:

. . . Though many a Virginia home will mourn the loss of some noble spirit, yet at the name of Pickett's division and the battle of Gettysburg, how the eye will glisten and the blood course quicker, and the heart beat warm, as among its noble dead is recalled the name of some cherished one. They bore themselves worthy of their lineage and their state. Who would recall them from their bed of glory? Each sleeps in a hero's grave. . . .[13]

The *New York Herald,* true to its tradition, exceeded its rivals in aggressive war coverage. It had more than 40 specials in the field at any given time. One of its foremost reporters was a young Bavarian immigrant, Henry Hilgard, who soon changed his name to Villard after his arrival in 1853. While learning the language, he edited the *Volksblatt,* a German paper published at Racine, Wisconsin. Later he covered the Lincoln-Douglas debates for the *Staats-Zeitung* of New York. His account of Lincoln's departure for Washington, and of the long ride under increasing national tension, established Villard as one of the best correspondents of his day. He was only 25 when he began reporting the war for the *Herald.* He is

[12] Snyder and Morris, *A Treasury of Great Reporting,* p. 146.
[13] *Ibid.,* p. 149.

best remembered for two great reporting "scoops." The first was his account of the first battle of Bull Run. His was the first accurate report to reach New York. It made Raymond's false announcement of victory appear ridiculous. The second exclusive account was his report of the battle of Fredericksburg.

A small army of artists covered the war, describing events in almost photo-like drawings. These were printed only by a laborious process of engraving by hand on a wooden block. Such woodcuts were not new, but they were used in newspapers much more regularly after 1861 to depict battle scenes and the likenesses of leading wartime figures. In another development, some of the metropolitan papers printed large maps to illustrate campaigns, thereby leading the way to new makeup no longer limited by column rules.[14] The *Herald* of September 12, 1863, is a good example of this technique. The paper was a little smaller than a modern standard daily and ran to eight pages, six columns wide. About a quarter of page one of this particular issue was devoted to a map accompanying a story on the Arkansas campaign. On page three a huge map of the Morris Island success in Charleston harbor filled all but two columns of the page from top to bottom.

Magazines also began to use illustrations more frequently. Because the publishers had more time to spend on engraving and printing, the magazines were able to offer excellent pictures. *Harper's Weekly* and *Frank Leslie's Illustrated Newspaper* were actually the forerunners of the picture magazines that were to flourish 75 years later.[15] Their artists' drawings were superb.

The most notable contribution to pictorial journalism in the 1860's was the photograph. Pioneer war photographer was a lovable Irishman, Mathew Brady. True, his photographs could not be used in newspapers of the time, since a practical method for transferring light and shade in the printing process was not perfected for an-

---

[14] It was not impossible to print spread headlines and large maps on the earlier type-revolving presses, but it was hazardous and inconvenient, because the column rules had to be locked tight to keep the metal type from flying out as the presses revolved. It was accomplished now and then, however. Big maps were printed by the newspapers in the Mexican War period and after.

[15] An excellent study of this contribution has been made by Donald Christian Peterson in "Two Pioneer American Picture Magazines" (Master's thesis, University of Wisconsin, 1953).

other decade.[16] But Brady was famous for his war pictures, and his photographic record of the conflict comes down to us as one of the finest examples of reporting.

Brady was everywhere during the war, apparently. He recorded on his clumsy plates the scene at Fort Sumter. His photographic interpretations of famous battles and war leaders could not be matched in mood and accuracy by the printed word. It is surprising how many of the great men of the period posed for Brady.[17] And because he was so successful in using this new medium of reporting, he is worthy of recognition at this point.

Brady was born about 1823, either in Cork, Ireland, or more probably, in upper New York state. As a youth he worked for A. T. Stewart, the pioneer New York department store owner. Stewart took an interest in the bright lad. When Brady took up the study of photography, the wealthy merchant brought his protégé to the attention of Samuel F. B. Morse, famed as the inventor of the telegraph, but equally interested in the science of optics. Morse made Brady his understudy. Together they worked with Professor J. W. Draper of New York University, who was to make the first instantaneous photographic exposure in America.[18] In 1839, Morse took Brady to Europe, where they met Louis Jacque Mandé Daguerre, inventor of the "daguerreotype," a photograph on metal.

Brady returned to America and set up a daguerreotype shop at the corner of Broadway and Fulton Street, opposite Barnum's museum. That was about 1842. Soon he was famed as a photographer

[16] The pioneer in the photo-engraving, which made possible the printing of various shades of black and white so as to give a photographic effect, was Frederic Eugene Ives. His "half-tone" process was first demonstrated at Cornell University in 1877 (see pp. 405-08).

[17] As must happen to all news photographers, Brady missed some great picture opportunities. He had his camera trained on President Lincoln at the time the immortal Gettysburg Address was delivered. Edward Everett, famous orator, and main speaker at the memorial, talked so long that Brady had to keep changing his plates, which had to be exposed while still wet with sensitizing solution. He was in the midst of removing a dried-out plate when the President arose to speak. The inspiring message was so short that Brady's assistant could not fetch a fresh plate from the portable dark room in time to photograph Lincoln before he bowed and retired. One of the great "news shots" of American history was thereby lost to posterity.

[18] The word "instantaneous" had a much broader meaning then than now. It could mean anything up to several minutes.

of the great and near-great.[19] Five years in a row he won the American Institute award for his contributions to photography. He was famous and prosperous.

But Brady was not satisfied with this success. The daguerreotype was too slow to be adaptable to anything but portrait work, and he sought a faster process. In 1855 he went to Scotland to learn about a new and faster "wet plate" developed by the scientist, Scott-Archer. Brady returned with Alexander Gardner, Scott-Archer's associate, and they set up offices in Washington as semi-official government photographers. When the war loomed, Brady gave up this lucrative business.

He persuaded his friends, President Lincoln and Allan Pinkerton of the Secret Service, to let him make a photographic record of the war with Gardner. They were permitted to go anywhere, protected by the Secret Service. Soon Brady's little black wagon, which was his portable dark room, was a familiar sight on the active fronts. He had an uncanny knack of knowing where the fighting would start. Soldiers dreaded the sight of Brady arriving on the scene, for they knew that soon thereafter the shooting would begin. He was often under sniper fire as he set up his camera at exposed vantage points. By the end of the war he had collected about 3,500 photographs.[20]

These pictures give us an entirely different impression than the usual reports of people and events. Although Brady's equipment was inferior to the simplest box cameras of three generations later, he produced amazing pictures. Some of them were the equal of any produced in World War II, although he could not stop fast action, of course. Despite the limitations of his equipment, somehow he was able to capture through his lens the hysteria, horror, and occasional glory of war.[21]

[19] This period is well described in Robert Taft, *Photography and the American Scene: A Social History, 1839-1889* (New York: The Macmillan Company, 1938).

[20] Some of the best of these are available in a single volume, Roy Meredith, *Mr. Lincoln's Camera Man, Mathew S. Brady* (New York: Charles Scribner's Sons, 1946).

[21] The sequel to this episode is not so happy. Neither Brady, nor Frederic Ives, who made the photo-engraving such an essential part of the printed press, ever profited much from their contributions. Brady spent a hundred thousand dollars obtaining his pictures. Subsequent administrations were slow in turning over promised remuneration. He was finally offered $25,000 for the

Not much has been said about the southern press up to this point, although it played an important part in the fortunes of the Confederacy. In many ways editorial reactions were the same in the North and South. Southern editors were highly critical of military strategy, and journalists such as Rhett, for example, attacked the Confederate administration just as violently as Lincoln was being attacked in the North. War aims were not so much an issue as they were in the North, however, nor was there anything quite corresponding to the Copperhead press.

Most of the news of the battles was supplied to southern editors by the Press Association of the Confederate States of America, better known as "PA," which, appropriately enough, was just the reversed logotype of the biggest northern news agency, the AP.[22] When the war began, the South had no system for preparing or transmitting news of public interest, such as had been developed in the North. An Augusta editor began sending out a brief daily summary by telegraph to a few papers willing to pay for the service, but this was never widely used. In 1862, the combined newspapers of Richmond tried to establish a more effective organization. Publishers realized that to meet the enormous expense of covering a war, they would have to work together. They also saw that in order to place correspondents where they were needed, they would have to pool resources. It was soon evident that the Richmond papers could not achieve these results by themselves.

Following a series of conferences, Joseph Clisby of the *Macon Telegraph* summoned the editor of every daily in the South to attend a meeting at Augusta on February 4, 1862. The Association of the Richmond Press had just been organized, and the plan was to expand the idea by organizing the PA. A board of directors hired a

originals and for the duplicates he had made of every scene. By that time Brady, who had always been prosperous before, was in desperate financial straits. The panic of 1873 bankrupted him. His lucrative business had been taken over by creditors and rivals. By 1883 Brady did not even know where his pictures were stored. In 1895 he was injured in Washington by a runaway horse. He died the following year. Later, the magazine *Review of Reviews* published one of the sets after its accidental discovery in the vaults of the photographic supplier who had taken the pictures in debt.
[22] This subject is presented in detail by Quintus C. Wilson, "The Confederate Press Association: A Pioneer News Agency," *Journalism Quarterly*, XXVI (June 1949), 160-166.

superintendent, J. S. Thrasher, "at a salary not to exceed $3,000," and the organization was ready to function.

The value of the association was at once apparent in the signing of contracts with telegraph agencies and the abolishing of onerous postal regulations. On May 15, 1863, the directors passed a resolution defending Thrasher for his stand against unwarranted military censorship.

On the whole, the PA served its clients well. When Gen. P. G. T. Beauregard began to hold up dispatches, Thrasher called on him personally and told the general that the aim of the press association was to obtain accurate reports for the good of the public, consistent with military security. The general was impressed. He told Thrasher that the PA reporters "should have every facility for early access to intelligence compatible with the public interests," and he wrote letters to high military authorities recommending similar cooperation. Thrasher won the confidence of other leaders. In return, he instructed PA correspondents to send no opinions or comments on events—the procedure that had so irritated northern commanders. They were warned to sift rumors and to offer no information that would aid the enemy. The objectivity of the PA stories has been regarded as constituting a "complete revolution" in journalistic writing.[23]

The superintendent, in return, was jealous of arrogant commanders who held up legitimate copy, and he used the power of his office to enforce cooperation from the military. Correspondents were ordered to send to the home office copies of dispatches unreasonably censored at the telegraph office. These reports were to include the name and rank of the responsible censor, and these documents were then used to pry greater concessions from those in higher authority.

The development of PA was a big step in the progress of southern journalism. There were 43 daily papers in the South, and all were members of the association. The editorial weight of this group was impressive. Dispatches were transmitted over the Military Telegraph Lines, the army system, at half rates. There was also a satisfactory arrangement with the private South-Western Telegraph Company. Newspapers that had seldom had access to regular wire news budgets were now able to keep readers up to date on the war.

[23] Wilson, "The Confederate Press Association," p. 162.

Short, but complete, reports supplanted the rambling, confused accounts of prewar days. Reporters with the armies were paid $25 a week, which was good for that time, and the writing was of good quality. On the whole PA gave a good account of itself until the crumbling Confederacy saw a collapse of restraints and organization. As in the northern armies, reporters were sometimes ejected for releasing information believed useful to the enemy. But Thrasher appears to have perfected a great news gathering agency. He offered relatively high objectivity. He kept the press as free as possible, considering the circumstances. It was on this basis that he won his argument with the Confederate Congress when the private telegraph company tried to sell PA news unfairly to special clients.

The manipulation of public opinion through the press of both belligerents was an influence in military decisions. Public opinion, reflected and reinforced by shrewd editors, often put pressure on political and military leaders. Sometimes this forced leaders to act against their better judgment. One example was the editorial pressure against the popular George B. McClellan. After the first battle of Bull Run, the general saw that this was to be no summer war. He settled down to train an army for the long fight. McClellan was correct in his judgment, and his work as a drillmaster was an important contribution. But the press was impatient for victories, and when the general continued to report "All quiet along the Potomac," the reporters began to use the term derisively. Eventually public opinion brought about McClellan's removal from command. On the other hand, public opinion consented to Grant's bloody slugging through the Wilderness campaign.

But there was a reverse to this, too. If the press sometimes picked out battle fronts and leaders for attention, politicians and generals also used the press to win support for favored plans. The press, if properly courted, could build up, as well as tear down, reputations. There were generals, such as the Union's McClernand, who appeared to be waging war primarily for the press. Even within the President's cabinet this technique was used. Secretary of the Navy Welles broke the news of Vicksburg's fall, as sent to him by Admiral Foote, apparently to beat out his colleague, Secretary of War Stanton. The press appreciated such favors and could repay handsomely in publicity.

What the press did for morale on either side cannot even be

estimated. It was through the press after Bull Run that each side was conditioned for the tasks ahead. Northern editors used the incident to whip up the laggards. Actually, the Confederate army was more disorganized by the battle than was the defeated Union force, General Joseph E. Johnston told the press after the battle. Both sides worked feverishly to regroup and retrain.

In the South the morale-crushing Federal blockade of ports was counteracted for years by expert newspaper propaganda. In the North, Grant won his reputation through the press, after very unfavorable early reports. The man with the inferiority complex who took over command largely by happenstance in August of 1861 at Cairo, Illinois, started then and there on the road to the White House. That was shown in his independent action under the incompetent General Fremont in the campaign around Paducah. By his terms to the enemy at the fall of Fort Donelson he won the nickname "Unconditional Surrender" Grant. That was the kind of name that could rally the public during the dark days, and its reiteration in the press began to make Grant emerge as the military leader who could eventually sell the administration on the feasibility of the war in the West, which was to turn the tide for the North.

War brought important technical changes to the press. Dependence upon the telegraph led to modification in news writing, as correspondents tried to save tolls by striving to be more concise. One way to compress stories was to omit opinion and coloration. By modern standards, Civil War reporting was rambling and colored, but compared with the journalism of an earlier day it was much more readable. Some of the copy, such as that transmitted out of Washington by the Associated Press, and out of Richmond by the Confederate Press Association, would not be much out of place in a modern newspaper.

The summary lead, which put the main feature of the story in the first paragraph, was developed during the war by reporters in the field who feared that their complete dispatches might not get through. Bennett once said that the cable, rather than the telegraph, was responsible for this, but the cable was not in successful operation until 1866, and the summary lead was fairly common by that time. Here is the way the *New York Times* started off one of its important front page articles of April 16, 1865, for example:

WASHINGTON, Saturday, April 15—12 A.M. Andrew Johnson was sworn into office as President of the United States by Chief Justice Chase today, at eleven o'clock. . . .

Because vital news streamed from the telegraph by the hour, metropolitan papers began to bulletin the highlights, and soon the smallest papers were imitating this procedure. These bulletins led to the modern newspaper headline, which summarizes the story in a few lines. The main story in the *New York Times* of May 10, 1864, is typical of this primitive headline system. It began:

VICTORY

———

"On To Richmond"

———

Lee's Defeat and Retreat
Confirmed

There followed *nineteen* crossline bulletins, which filled most of the column.

Most of the newspapers continued to use the eight-page, six-column makeup carried over from before the war. By modern standards they were likely to be drab, with their small type, lack of pictures, and the dreadful uniformity of one-column makeup limitations. But the use of huge maps was breaking down the confines of the column rule, and the experimentation with headlines indicates the contrast with the page dress of only a decade earlier.

Presses had to be fast to keep up with the other developments in journalism. On the Sunday following the fall of Fort Sumter, the *Herald* printed 135,000 newspapers—a record press run up to that date. In 1863, William Bullock brought out the web perfecting press, which printed both sides of a continuous roll of paper on a rotary press. Although it was not until 1871 that R. Hoe and Company produced such presses as standard equipment, the stimulus of the war is nevertheless apparent.

One other wartime development of the press should be mentioned. That was the rise of the "feature syndicate." Many a small-city publisher was on the brink of ruin as his skilled employees marched off to battle. One such victim was Ansel N. Kellogg, who published a weekly newspaper at Baraboo, Wisconsin. Left stranded by his back-shop staff, Kellogg made arrangements with David Atwood and Horace Rublee, publishers of the nearby *Wisconsin State Journal*, at Madison, the capital. They agreed to send Kellogg sheets printed on one side with a summary of the war news. The blank side could be used for local advertising or news. Use of this "ready-print" saved hours of laborious hand-setting of type. Four other Wisconsin editors soon made similar arrangements.

Such success invited imitation. Publishers of the *Evening Wisconsin* at Milwaukee copied the system and began selling advertising space in advance. This permitted the sale of ready-prints at very low prices. The type of advertising gave the product the name "patent insides," from the patent medicines commonly promoted by the copy. Kellogg, the originator of the plan, moved to Chicago in order to compete with his rivals. By 1865 he had 53 clients.

Magazines also flourished in this period. A newcomer, *Harper's Monthly*, won a record 200,000 circulation within a few years after its founding in 1850, by featuring fiction and woodcut illustrations. Another popular magazine deserves special mention. It was *Godey's Lady's Book*, founded in 1830. From a circulation of 25,000 in 1839, it jumped to 150,000 on the eve of the war. Louis A. Godey, the publisher, lavished money to make his magazine a beautiful product, and the investment paid off, for he was the first magazine publisher to leave an estate of more than a million dollars. The magazine indicated the growing recognition of women in the economic picture. It carried many hand-colored engravings, fiction and poetry and department material designed especially for women.

It was indeed an exciting era that came to a close on the evening of April 14, 1865. Lawrence A. Gobright of the Associated Press was working late in his office. He had already sent out dispatches about President Lincoln's theater party, reporting that General Grant had declined an invitation to see the play, "Our American Cousin," in order to go to New Jersey with Mrs. Grant. The door burst open and an excited friend rushed in with news of the tragedy at Ford's Theater. Gobright quickly wrote out a bulletin before going to work on an extended account of the evening's development. No modern reporter could have broken the news more succinctly. The lead said:

WASHINGTON, FRIDAY, APRIL 14, 1865—The President was shot in a theater tonight, and perhaps mortally wounded.

ANNOTATED BIBLIOGRAPHY

Books:

Andrews, J. Cutler, *The North Reports the Civil War*. Pittsburgh: University of Pittsburgh Press, 1955. Most extensive (813 pages) of histories of Civil War reporting, and thoroughly documented. Lists several hundred northern reporters and their papers.

Catton, Bruce, *Mr. Lincoln's Army*. New York: Doubleday & Company, Inc., 1951. Includes many instances of military-press relations.

Commager, Henry Steele, ed., *Documents of American History*. New York: F. S. Crofts & Company, 1934. See especially Vol. I, p. 398, on the Merryman case and Vol. II, p. 22, on the Milligan case.

Crozier, Emmet, *Yankee Reporters, 1861-65*. New York: Oxford University Press, 1956. A readable account of correspondents' work.

Fahrney, Ralph Ray, *Horace Greeley and the Tribune in the Civil War*. Chicago: University of Chicago Press, 1929. Documented.

Gobright, Lawrence A., *Recollections of Men and Things at Washington during a Third of a Century*. Philadelphia: Claxton, Remsen, and Haffelfinger, 1869. By the Associated Press correspondent.

Harper, Robert S., *Lincoln and the Press*. New York: McGraw-Hill Book Company, 1951. Readable and detailed account of Lincoln's press relations after 1858, written from newspaper sources.

Horan, James D., *Mathew Brady: Historian with a Camera*. New York: Crown Publishers, 1955. A good biography, with 453 pictures.

Klement, Frank L., *The Copperheads in the Middle West*. Chicago: University of Chicago Press, 1960. Wilbur Storey, C. L. Vallandigham, and Samuel Medary are among those covered.

Mathews, Joseph J., *Reporting the Wars*. Minneapolis: University of Minnesota Press, 1957. History of war news reporting since the mid-eighteenth century. See also F. L. Bullard, *Famous War Correspondents* (Boston: Little, Brown and Company, 1914).

Meredith, Roy, *Mr. Lincoln's Camera Man, Mathew S. Brady*. New York: Charles Scribner's Sons, 1946. A colorful account of the pioneer war photographer, with some of the best of his reproductions.

Nicolay, John George, and John M. Hay, *Abraham Lincoln, A History*. New York: The Century Company, 1890. 10 vols. Of all the histories of the Lincoln administration, this remains as one of the most comprehensive and readable. An account by the President's private secretaries.

Photographic History of the Civil War. New York: Review of Reviews Company, 1911. 10 vols. A very complete collection of Brady's pictures, with explanatory material in chronological order.

Pollard, James E., *The Presidents and the Press*. New York: The Macmillan Company, 1947. The chapter on Lincoln and the press is very useful for those wishing to read a concise discussion of the problem.

Salmon, Lucy B., *The Newspaper and Authority*. New York: Oxford University Press, 1923. The chapters on Civil War threats to a free press offer stimulating ideas on the subject.

Sandburg, Carl, *Abraham Lincoln: The War Years*. New York: Harcourt, Brace and Company, 1939. 4 vols. Contains excellent portraits of leading Civil War editors and newspapers.

Snyder, Louis L., and Richard B. Morris, eds., *A Treasury of Great Reporting*. New York: Simon and Schuster, 1949. Examples, with pertinent comment, of Civil War news stories are included.

Starr, Louis M., *Bohemian Brigade: Civil War Newsmen in Action*. New York: Alfred A. Knopf, Inc., 1954. One of the best studies; considers all aspects of the newspaper in wartime, including reporting, editing, censorship.

Weisberger, Bernard A., *Reporters for the Union*. Boston: Little, Brown and Company, 1953. Mainly a study of correspondents' political biases and criticisms of the military; least useful of such books.

Periodicals and Monographs:

Blackmon, Robert E., "Noah Brooks: Reporter in the White House," *Journalism Quarterly*, XXXII (Summer 1955), 301. Brooks was the Washington correspondent of the *Sacramento Union* in wartime.

Goldsmith, Adolph O., "Reporting the Civil War: Union Army Press Relations," *Journalism Quarterly*, XXXIII (Fall 1956), 478. A good summary of the problem.

Guback, Thomas H., "General Sherman's War on the Press," *Journalism Quarterly*, XXXVI (Spring 1959), 171. A well-done account, featuring Sherman's famous clash with the *Herald's* Knox.

Peterson, Donald Christian, "Two Pioneer American Picture Magazines." Master's thesis, University of Wisconsin, 1953. A detailed study of *Harper's Weekly* and *Frank Leslie's Illustrated Newspaper*.

Randall, James G., "The Newspaper Problem and Its Bearing Upon Military Secrecy During the Civil War," *American Historical Review*, XXIII (January 1918), 303. Long the main authority for a discussion of Civil War censorship, by a leading historian of the period. Criticises conduct of the press; admires skill of correspondents.

Wilson, Quintus C., "A Study and Evaluation of the Military Censorship in the Civil War." Master's thesis, University of Minnesota, 1945. This is the most complete and best documented study of the subject, and largely supersedes Randall's monograph.

———, "The Confederate Press Association: A Pioneer News Agency," *Journalism Quarterly*, XXVI (June 1949), 160. A digest of a chapter in Wilson's censorship study.

Chapter *15*

THE MATURING OF THE OLDER PRESS

> . . . he was the last of those editors who wrote
> with the power of ownership.
> —Arthur Krock, about Watterson

AMERICAN HISTORY in many respects starts afresh at the close of the Civil War. This is not to deny the obvious fact that two and a half centuries of the American experience had produced fundamental guiding forces which would continue to influence the maturing of the nation's economy and the development of its political and social fabric. But great new forces were at work, and between 1865 and 1900 the United States was to pass through a revolution which affected every phase of the national scene. The forces were those of intensive industrialization, mechanization, and urbanization, bringing with them sweeping social, cultural, and political changes. At some point between the Civil War and the turn of the century, the slow maturing process of virtually every aspect of American life was given powerful new impetus or redirection.

So it was with the nation's journalism. The great development of communication and of journalistic techniques which had come in the Jacksonian period of American growth was continuing through the war period. There was a popular press which had appealed to the human interests of its readers, which had utilized the new

315

communication facilities to develop news enterprise, and which had sometimes developed editorial force. But the patterns which had emerged, the techniques which had been created, were to be drastically affected by an intensive new effort born of the impact of the new environment.

No one man's actions, no single date, no crucial event may be selected as a dividing point in this story of the transformation of American life and of its journalistic expression. The account begins in this chapter and continues in three succeeding chapters with gathering intensity—the same gathering intensity which was felt by those who lived in that period of change and who finally pieced together many small impressions to form a new picture of their society.

Emphasizing this change is the passing from the scene of famous figures of the newspaper movement which had begun in the 1830's. Between 1869 and 1878, five leaders of the era of personal journalism died: Henry J. Raymond, founder of the *New York Times,* James Gordon Bennett, Sr., founder of the *New York Herald,* Horace Greeley, founder of the *New York Tribune,* Samuel Bowles III, most famous of his name to edit the *Springfield Republican,* and William Cullen Bryant, for half a century editor of the *New York Evening Post.*

The newspaper builders who followed them appeared not only in New York but from coast to coast as the nation rushed to complete its geographical expansion and began in earnest to consolidate its economy. The new leaders were maturing and refining the processes and practices of their predecessors. Soon, sensing the opportunities presented by the changing environment in which they worked, some were to create what came to be known as the "new journalism."

Among those who replaced the departing leaders of journalism were some editors who represent a middle group, bridging the gap between the old and new: Charles A. Dana of the *New York Sun,* Edwin Lawrence Godkin of the *Nation* and *New York Evening Post,* Henry Watterson of the *Louisville Courier-Journal,* and Harvey W. Scott of the *Oregonian* in Portland. But even while these men and others like them were making their contributions to journalistic advancement as the leaders of a transitional period, the representatives of the new order were appearing. For example, rising in the dozen years between 1876 and 1887 were Melville E. Stone and the *Chicago Daily News,* Edward Wyllis Scripps and the *Cleveland Press,* Joseph Pulitzer and the *St. Louis Post-Dispatch* and *New York World,* William Rockhill Nelson and the *Kansas City Star,* and William Randolph Hearst, at the *San Francisco Examiner.* These are among the most famous names of men and newspapers in American journalism, as we shall see later in detail, and their appearance with others of note in such a brief period testifies to the opportunity for journalistic advances which the revolution in American life afforded. By the time Hearst had invaded New York with his *Journal* to do battle with Pulitzer in the late 1890's—at a time when the careers of Dana and Godkin were closing—the transition from the older era to the new had been achieved. American journalism, like American history, is marked by what historian Henry Steele Commager calls "the watershed of the nineties," whose topography is as blurred as those of all watersheds, but whose grand outlines emerge clearly.[1]

There are several general characteristics of this new movement in journalism, including the ever-increasing concentration of effort on impartial gathering and reporting of the news as the basic function of the press; growing independence of editorial opinion from partisan pressures; active and planned crusading in the community interest; intensified popularization of content, through style of writing and choice of subject matter; utilization of new mechanical developments and format techniques to create a more interesting product; and a lessening of personal influence as the daily newspaper became a complex corporate institution. It is with the first two of these characteristics that we are most immediately concerned.

Recognition of the news function as the primary obligation of the press had been a gradual process, encouraged by access to rapid communication of news by telegraph and railroad in the two decades before the Civil War. Those newspapermen who took the lead in seeking out the news, and reporting it in the interest of the reader alone, found their ranks increasing during the war years and the following decade. They realized that while their subscribers wished to have editorial opinion presented, readers wanted to be

[1] Henry Steele Commager, *The American Mind* (New Haven: Yale University Press, 1950), p. 41.

certain that they could form their own opinions based upon a factual and comprehensive presentation of the news.

Similarly, the postwar political and social situation stimulated some editors to an examination of their roles in expressing opinion. Those who rebelled against giving uncritical partisan support to a single political camp, while still in the minority, found themselves at great advantage over editors who maintained traditional loyalty at the expense of editorial freedom. And by the end of the century the editor who felt himself to be a part of a political party or group, bound to give unswerving loyalty to its dictates, was a liability to his newspaper.

There was good reason for the development of new approaches to news reporting and editorial expression. The problems which the United States faced in the years after the Civil War were heavy ones. The political leadership which was at hand was not equal to the tasks, and for a generation the talent exhibited in public life was far less than that shown in industry and business. There was no really great president between 1865 and the turn of the century, although Grover Cleveland won considerable recognition, primarily for his honesty and courage. But whatever the shortcomings in presidential leadership, the remainder of the political scene was far more depressing. The effort at political reconstruction of the South degenerated into an ugly battle between a vengeful Congress and an inept president; carpetbaggers and scalawags put in power in the South through arbitrary reconstruction policies gave way in turn to southern home rule without participation by the Negro; scandals rocked the Grant administration and corruption permeated city governments; a "consistent rebellion" flared against economic maladjustments, money supply inequities, and life-squeezing transportation and interest rates assessed against the farmer. In such a setting an editor with notions of independent thinking and devotion to presentation of the news was definitely encouraged.

Before we consider what the editors did, we should examine in more detail the political and socio-economic situation in which they worked. The long debate over the status of the Federal Union, which had preoccupied Americans and split their allegiances so sharply, had come to an end with the verdict of the war. And in the years which followed, the revolution in industry and communication insured the national character of American society and subordinated the importance of the individual states. This latter development could not be known to those who were living through the transition, however. Until the late 1870's there was widespread fear that the effort to destroy the Federal Union had not ended, and that the fruits of victory would be lost if the political rights of the South were restored. For another ten years, on into the 1880's, some political leaders found it useful to continue a pretended fear of a new challenge to the union.[2]

The Republican party, which had elected Abraham Lincoln as its first president in 1860, found it necessary to run a Union ticket in 1864, pairing Lincoln with a Tennessee Democrat, Andrew Johnson. Even then, Lincoln polled only 400,000 more votes than the Democratic candidate, General George B. McClellan, with the South excluded from voting. In light of this, many Republicans viewed the immediate return of the South to full voting privileges with real alarm. They feared the result of accepting Lincoln's theory that since the Union was indissoluble, southern states would automatically return to their former status when fighting ceased. Freed from this policy by Lincoln's death, Representative Thaddeus Stevens of Pennsylvania and Senator Charles Sumner of Massachusetts gave leadership to a group which maintained the South had committed "state suicide" and should be considered as conquered territory. They and their followers, who came to dominate the postwar Congresses, were named the "radical Republicans."

In Andrew Johnson, the radical Republicans found an opponent who was made vulnerable by personality weaknesses which obscured his other qualities. When southern states readmitted to the union by Johnson ignored Negro political rights, the radical Republicans moved to handle the South on their own terms. They passed a civil rights bill; they submitted the fourteenth amendment to the Constitution for ratification; they passed over Johnson's veto the reconstruction acts which forced all southern states to again seek re-entry into the Union on radical-Republican terms; and they instituted military rule in the South. Northern carpetbaggers and southern scalawags who took advantage of the unpreparedness of Negro voters for democratic responsibilities disrupted southern life, and home rule was not fully restored until 1877. The contest

[2] Frederic L. Paxson, *Recent History of the United States* (New York: Houghton Mifflin Company, 1937), p. 2.

between the radical Republicans and the president was climaxed by the impeachment of Johnson, who was saved from removal from office by a single vote in the Senate. Thereupon the Republican party turned to General Ulysses S. Grant as its candidate in 1868, and won the election easily.

Political reconstruction thus was a controversial problem, but financial reconstruction was even more so. Commodity prices in the North had doubled during the five years of war. Running of the printing presses to create legal tender paper money, dubbed "greenbacks," had driven coinage into hiding, intensifying the usual wartime inflationary trend. Congress in 1866 therefore voted to retire the greenbacks gradually over an 11-year period. The argument was advanced that retirement of the greenbacks, which constituted a part of the large federal debt, would deflate prices and increase the value of the dollar. Such action would be to the benefit of creditors, and of wage earners whose incomes had not kept pace with prices. But farmers, who generally were debtors, would find money dearer and prices for their products lower. Opposition to retirement of the greenbacks from circulation began to develop in the Middle West agricultural areas, and of course in the South, whose economy had been prostrated by the collapse of the Confederate currency and the ravages of war. The movement to keep the greenbacks, and even to issue more paper money as a means of easing the load of debts, became known as the "Ohio Idea." By 1868, pressure had mounted until Congress repealed the greenback redemption act. The debate continued, however, and the opponents of paper money forced final retirement of the greenbacks beginning in 1879, further intensifying the problem of an inadequate money supply for the rapidly-expanding American economy.

Currency supply was not the only complaint of the agricultural West and South. Farmers found interest rates on their borrowed money excessively high, and impossible to pay in years of poor crops or low prices. They found the railroads, which were extending their tracks across the country, were basing their rates on the axiom "charge all the traffic will bear." And they found grain elevators and other storage facilities usually were under the control of those who bought the crops. The system generally worked so that the farmer had to sell immediately after harvest to pay his debts, and could not hold his grain in storage for more advantageous prices. Transportation rates were inflexibly high, regardless of market conditions and the level of the nation's economy.[3]

By the early 1870's a depression was closing in on a country which had fought a costly and devastating war, which had plunged into a postwar expansion of capital investment at a faster rate than it was producing wealth, and which was still borrowing large amounts of money from European investors for its expansion. When the financial crash came in 1873, with declining prices for agricultural products, the farmers were certain that their lot was unbearable. A "consistent rebellion" began as the agricultural West and South sought economic redress. Currency reform, banking reform, regulation of railroad and grain elevator rates, and lowering of interest charges were the major political issues. The Greenback party flourished as a result, to be followed by the rise of the Populists. The Patrons of Husbandry formed their Grange organizations which forced passage of state laws in the Middle West fixing maximum railroad rates, and the United States Supreme Court in a famous decision (*Munn v. Illinois*, 1877) upheld the doctrine that the railroads were subject to regulation in the public interest.

In this troubled political and economic setting, the press found much significant news. And as the news principle gained ascendancy, the editorial columns showed definite signs of rebelling against unswerving loyalty to political parties and their beliefs. The way was eased by rebellion within the ranks of the political parties themselves, and particularly by the emergence of a "liberal Republican" faction opposing the radical Republicans and their President, General Grant. Independence of editorial expression meant primarily the freedom to criticise the leaders and policies of the party which the editor might normally support; but for some it also meant freedom to bolt the party and support a rival. Those who bolted were called "mugwumps" by their opponents.

The mugwumps of 1872 were led by a group of editors. The liberal Republicans, meeting in convention to find a suitable candidate to oppose Grant, included many newspapermen, the most important of whom were Samuel Bowles of the *Springfield Republican*, Horace White of the *Chicago Tribune*, Murat Halstead of the

[3] This is a brief summary of the farmers' problems, which are given full analysis in such studies as John D. Hicks' *The Populist Revolt* (Minneapolis: University of Minnesota Press, 1931), and Solon J. Buck's *The Granger Movement* (Cambridge: Harvard University Press, 1913).

Cincinnati Commercial, and Carl Schurz of the St. Louis *Westliche Post.* The convention ended with the selection of a famous editor, Horace Greeley, as the candidate. Greeley also was nominated by the Democrats, and thus an important segment of the Republican-aligned press found itself allied with pro-Democratic papers. But Greeley's bid for the presidency was ill-starred. Many liberals could not find their way clear to support the aging editor, and others commented cruelly on his eccentricities. Thus such critics of the Grant administration as the *New York Evening Post* and *New York Sun,* and the influential magazines, *Harper's Weekly* and the *Nation,* shied away from the Greeley cause. And despite growing discontent with the radical Republicans' reconstruction policies, the administrative shortcomings of the Grant regime, and unsolved economic problems, Grant was re-elected handily.

Even though the Greeley campaign had failed, the effect of the mugwump rebellion by such influential editors was a substantial gain in journalistic prestige. It added new proof that editors could shift their political positions and survive, and encouraged those newspapers which felt obliged to attack strong political groups. Previously, Henry J. Raymond of the *New York Times,* William Cullen Bryant of the *New York Evening Post,* and Charles A. Dana of the *New York Sun*—all supporters of the Republican party—had opposed the radical Republicans in their attempt to remove President Johnson from office in 1868. Now each successive episode strengthened the determination of some newspapers to put reporting of the news and maintenance of editorial independence ahead of partisan political considerations.

Scandals in government offer a tempting target for any editor, and the political ineptness and moral laxity which characterized the postwar years further stimulated newspapers and magazines to action. The most notorious example of corruptness at the city level was in the operations of the Tweed Ring in New York City. Tammany boss William M. Tweed and his Democratic party cohorts, who milked the city of an estimated hundred million dollars, had grown so brazen by 1870 that they had listed a plasterer's pay at $50,000 a day for an entire month while constructing a courthouse. The Tweed Ring controlled some newspapers, and frightened others into silence, but it met its masters in the *New York Times* and *Harper's Weekly.* The *Times,* published by George Jones and edited by Louis J. Jennings after the death of Raymond in 1869, obtained documentary proof of the Tweed Ring's thefts in 1871 and broke the astounding story. *Harper's Weekly,* ably edited by George William Curtis, provided a gallery for Thomas Nast, the great political cartoonist who invented the donkey and elephant symbols for the two major parties. Nast used his pen and ink against Tweed in such devastating fashion that he was offered a bribe to halt his attacks. The answer was the driving of the Tweed Ring from power.[4]

The scandals which left the reputation of the Grant administration blackened were being hinted at before the 1872 presidential election, but it was not until the closing days of the campaign that the *New York Sun* publicized what became known as the Crédit Mobilier affair. When the evidence was developed fully after the election, it proved that promoters of the Union Pacific and Central Pacific railroads had developed a simple system for influencing legislators and others whose support was needed in the obtaining of federal land grants for railroad construction. The railroad builders, operating under the name Crédit Mobilier of America, had sold stock to many public men, lending them the money to pay for the stock and then declaring such huge profits that the loans could be repaid in a single year. Exposure of what amounted to gifts from those seeking legislative favor ruined some politicians, and cast suspicion on many more, including the prominent Republican leader, James G. Blaine of Maine.

Other disclosures of weaknesses of the Grant administration came rapidly: the whiskey tax frauds in the Treasury Department, the bribing of the Secretary of War, W. W. Belknap, and the acceptance of improper gifts by Grant's private secretary. The dazed Grant was himself untouched by the scandals, but his party lost control of the House of Representatives to the Democrats in 1874, and politics became a see-saw affair. The country was entering a period of "dead center" government. For 16 of the next 22 years, control of the two houses of Congress and the presidency was split between the two major parties, so closely was the popular vote divided. Little political progress could be made in such a situation, and eventually the protective tariff became the principal issue of

[4] Fuller details are given in Gustavus Myers, *The History of Tammany Hall* (New York: Boni and Liveright, 1917).

frustrated political aspirants who could not cope with the problems which were generating the "consistent rebellion" of the economically discontented West and South.

Of the editors who worked in this turbulent postwar period, two in particular stand out as leaders. Their contributions are sharply different. Charles A. Dana in his years as editor of the *New York Sun* taught the journalistic world new lessons in the art of news handling and writing. Edwin Lawrence Godkin in his years as editor of the *Nation* and of the *New York Evening Post* provided solid editorial page leadership. With the deaths of the older New York leaders—Bennett, Greeley, Raymond, and Bryant—Dana and Godkin became the strong men who influenced the maturing of the older press.

Dana and his *Sun* in many respects represent the bridge between the older press and the new journalism which was to develop before the end of the century. A New Englander who had been attracted to the Brook Farm socialist experiment in the 1840's along with other intellectuals seeking the answer to the problems created by the industrial revolution, Dana had met Horace Greeley there. He joined Greeley's staff and became managing editor of the *Tribune* in 1849—the first American to hold such a position. When the Dana-Greeley association was broken in the early days of the Civil War as the aftermath of the *Tribune's* mistaken military predictions, Dana entered government service, and emerged to struggle for a year as editor of a new Chicago paper, the *Daily Republican* (forerunner of the famous *Inter Ocean*). The newspaper venture was successful, but Dana wearied of Chicago. Returning to New York, he obtained sufficient backing to buy the *Sun*, the original penny newspaper. Its plant and 43,000 circulation were priced at $175,000 by Moses S. Beach, whose father had taken over Ben Day's paper. A career with Greeley on the *Tribune* already behind him, Dana in 1868 began a 29-year career as editor of the *Sun*.

Dana's audience consisted mainly of average New Yorkers, workers and small merchants. To them he addressed his first editorial in the *Sun*, which expressed his ideas on newspaper making. The *Sun*, he said, would present "a daily photograph of the whole world's doings in the most luminous and lively manner." Its staff would write simply and clearly as it tried to present that photograph of the life of the people of New York, as well as of the world's doings.

Editors of the post-Civil War transition period: Charles A. Dana (*left*), *New York Sun*, and Edwin Lawrence Godkin (*right*), *New York Post*.

Harvey W. Scott (*left*), of the *Oregonian* in Portland, and Henry Watterson (*right*) of the *Louisville Courier-Journal* raised strong voices.

Founders of "New Journalism" dailies: Melville E. Stone (*left*), *Chicago Daily News*, an
William Rockhill Nelson (*right*), *Kansas City Star*.

Two southern leaders: Henry W. Grady (*left*) of the *Atlanta Constitution* and Josephu
Daniels (*right*), builder of the *Raleigh News and Observer*.

The *Sun* would be low-priced and readable, yet it would use enterprise and money to be the best possible newspaper.

The journalist, Dana insisted, must be interested not only in politics, economics and government, but first of all in people. The average American, Dana knew, was hard at work but yet loved sentiment and fun, and enjoyed stories reflecting a skillful touch of tenderness or wit. As one of the biographers of Dana and the *Sun* put it, Dana had "the indefinable newspaper instinct that knows when a tomcat on the steps of the City Hall is more important than a crisis in the Balkans." [5]

Writers who could make their stories come alive were prized on the *Sun,* and as a consequence reporters prized the *Sun* in turn. It became what the craft calls a "newspaperman's newspaper." Those who worked there were refining the sensationalized techniques of the penny press, as they wrote with increasing ability and discernment, seeking to report all manner of events, but looking especially for those happenings which make up "the poetry of life." The rule of the *Sun* was "be interesting," and its reporters obeyed whether they were writing about the doings of the Astors and the Vanderbilts, the commercial and financial life of the city, a murder, a political debate, or merely about a crying child on a curb, a neighborhood quarrel in one of New York's many sections, or the latest style in whiskers. Other newspapers were in quest of the same goal, of course, but the *Sun* under Dana's direction was more diligent and therefore more successful. Its readership doubled in the first two years of Dana's tenure and circulation reached 130,000 by 1876.

The office cat was one of the most celebrated members of the *Sun's* staff, and the subject of a famous editorial which reflected the paper's spirit. One night in the 1880's the *Sun's* copy of a message from President Cleveland to Congress blew out an open window. There was considerable concern, for the publishing of every presidential message was a must. One staff member, however, was unconcerned and suggested, "Oh, say the office cat ate it up." This Dana did, and soon the cat was a familiar trademark of Dana's *Sun.* [6]

[5] Frank M. O'Brien, *The Story of The Sun* (New York: George H. Doran Company, 1918), p. 231. New edition (D. Appleton and Company, 1928) p. 151.
[6] *Ibid.,* pp. 287-89, carries the editorial in full.

Brilliant as the *Sun* was, however, it had serious weaknesses. Since Dana insisted on limiting its size to four pages, comprehensive coverage of significant news suffered. And the editorial page which could originate such ringing phrases as "No king, no clown, to rule this town!" to combat Tweed, and "Turn the rascals out!" to harass Grant, could also be so intellectually "smart" as to approach cynicism. Dana's fondness for wit and levity made for entertaining reading; but his cynical and sometimes perverse comments on public issues greatly weakened the character of his newspaper.

In politics, Dana steered an erratic course. The *Sun* opposed the impeachment of Johnson by the radical Republicans in 1868, but supported their candidate, Grant, in the fall presidential election. By 1872 it had turned on Grant, but could not restrain itself from laughing at the candidacy of editor Greeley. Dana supported the Democratic presidential candidate, Samuel J. Tilden, in 1876 and was so enraged when the disputed electoral votes of three southern states were finally awarded to the Republicans that the *Sun* always referred to President Rutherford B. Hayes as a "fraud" and, in a drawing of him, printed that word across his forehead. In 1880 Dana refused to support any candidate, but devastatingly remarked that the Democrat, General Winfield S. Hancock, was "a good man, weighing 240 pounds." Perversity reached a climax in 1884 when Dana violently attacked the "tainted" candidacy of Republican James G. Blaine, then ignored Democrat Grover Cleveland and put the *Sun* behind the politically discredited candidate of a third party, Benjamin Butler. Butler's campaign failed dismally and the *Sun* lost a third of its readers. Dana then supported Cleveland in 1888, only to see him lose the presidency to Benjamin Harrison. When Cleveland ran again in 1892 and rewon the White House from Harrison, Dana was against him because it was Cleveland's third campaign. And in 1896, the year before he died, Dana bowed out opposing William Jennings Bryan.

In its discussions of issues, the *Sun* became increasingly conservative, in contrast to Dana's earlier beliefs. The paper detested labor unions. It poked fun at civil service reform advocates and others interested in good government, even though the *Sun* itself crusaded against misconduct in office. And it long advocated imperialistic schemes for the annexation of Canada, Cuba, and other neighboring areas.

It remained for an English-born journalist to give the United States the vigorous and intelligent editorial leadership which it needed in the postwar period. He was Edwin Lawrence Godkin, the founder of the magazine, the *Nation,* and successor to William Cullen Bryant as the driving spirit of the *New York Evening Post.*

Of Godkin, historian Allan Nevins has written: "Godkin showed at once a distinctive style, a refreshing penetration, and a skill in ironic analysis never before equalled in American journalism." And because this was so, philosopher William James could write: "To my generation his was certainly the towering influence in all thought concerning public affairs, and indirectly his influence has assuredly been more pervasive than that of any other writer of the generation, for he influenced other writers who never quoted him, and determined the whole current of discussion." [7] President Charles W. Eliot of Harvard University, President Daniel Coit Gilman of Johns Hopkins University, James Russell Lowell, James Bryce, Charles Eliot Norton—the intellectual leaders of Godkin's generation—all publicly acknowledged the debt they owed to the pages of the *Nation.* Not, of course, that they always agreed with its editor's viewpoints.

Godkin had been a reporter and editorial writer for English newspapers, and had written editorials for Henry J. Raymond's *New York Times,* before deciding that the United States needed a high-grade weekly journal of opinion and literary criticism, similar to those in England. In 1865 he found the financial backing for the *Nation,* and announced its aims.

The *Nation,* Godkin said, would discuss the political and economic questions of the day "with greater accuracy and moderation than are now to be found in the daily press." It would advocate "whatever in legislation or in manners seems likely to promote a more equal distribution of the fruits of progress and civilization." It would seek to better the conditions of the Negro. It would fix "public attention upon the political importance of education, and the dangers which a system like ours runs from the neglect of it in any portion of our territory." And it would print sound and impartial criticisms of books and works of art.[8]

[7] As quoted in Allan Nevins, *American Press Opinion* (New York: D. C. Heath and Company, 1928), p. 299.

[8] Godkin's full statement of purpose is found in Rollo Ogden, *Life and Letters of Edwin Lawrence Godkin,* I (New York: The Macmillan Company, 1907), pp. 237-38.

Godkin was a mid-Victorian English liberal, of the John Stuart Mill school of economic thought. Therefore he believed that government should not intervene in economic matters. But unlike many of his time, he did believe that government should take action in social spheres. To a twentieth-century world which has used government as a regulatory force in both economic and social situations, Godkin thus appears at times to be reactionary and at other times liberal.

For example, Godkin fought the protective tariff which had been hiked to high levels by the Republicans during the Civil War, because tariffs represented government intervention in economic affairs. This placed him in the liberal camp. But he argued relentlessly against what he considered improper attempts by debtor groups to obtain legislation which would increase the money supply or regulate high interest rates. And he opposed any recognition of the right of labor unions to strike or to bargain collectively, although he admitted that an individual workman had little chance to bargain effectively. His use of cold, intellectual arguments against liberal groups with whom he at other times showed sympathy led his critics to call him cruel and snobbish.

But in many other areas, Godkin was in the forefront of progressive thought. He urged complete reconciliation with the South during the period of military rule; he was one of the earliest advocates of civil service reform to end the spoils system; he believed in women's suffrage when it was an unpopular idea; he was a strong supporter of public education and the new land-grant universities; and, as mentioned above, he wrote in behalf of the Negro. Above all, the *Nation* spoke out against corrupt and inefficient government, and ceaselessly badgered politicians who were interested more in personal gain than in progressive improvement of government. The magazine had other writers, and well-known contributors. But it was Godkin's opinions, written usually in a measured and convincing style but pointed up with pungent phrases, which won it the enthusiastic attention of its 10,000 or so readers. And they in turn, as ministers, teachers, editors, writers, and other leaders of society, transmitted the *Nation's* arguments to millions of other Americans.

In 1881, Godkin moved onto a bigger but actually less influential journalistic stage. That year Henry Villard, a Civil War correspondent who later won a fortune building railroads, purchased the *New*

York Evening Post, and obtained a trio of outstanding editors for
the newspaper. One was Horace White, who had edited the *Chicago Tribune* from 1866 to 1874, taking that newspaper into the
liberal Republican camp for a brief period as he advocated tariff
reduction, civil service reform, and currency policies favorable to
the farmers. A second was Carl Schurz, the former editor of the
St. Louis *Westliche Post* who had become Secretary of the Interior
in President Hayes' cabinet, and a leading American liberal. The
third was Godkin, who sold the *Nation* to Villard but continued to
edit it as the weekly edition of the *Evening Post.* Within two years,
Schurz and Godkin quarreled over Godkin's antilabor union views,
and Schurz resigned, leaving Godkin in control of the *Evening Post*
with White as his assistant.

With Godkin, the *Evening Post* and the *Nation* rose to new fame
in the presidential election year of 1884. The contest lay between
James G. Blaine, the Republican congressional leader from Maine,
and Grover Cleveland, Democratic governor of New York. Godkin,
declaring that Blaine was unacceptable because of the post-Civil War
scandals, fought his election with all his editorial skill. As the campaign progressed, charges of immoral conduct were made against
Cleveland, and emotionalism ran high. Some stalwart Republican
newspapers in leading cities found themselves opposing Blaine in
company with the usual dissenters—the *Evening Post,* the *New
York Times, Springfield Republican, Harper's Weekly,* and the *Nation.* Dana of the *Sun,* who would support neither major party candidate, fastened upon these papers the name "mugwump," indicating desertion of party regularity. It applied particularly to the *Evening Post,* which had been Republican since the founding of the
party in 1856.

The *Evening Post's* particular contribution was Godkin's famous
"deadly parallel" column, in which he matched Blaine's campaign
statements and congressional record against his personal associations
with railroad builders and financiers. The campaign became exceedingly bitter, and it was evident that the New York State vote would
decide the election. When Cleveland carried New York by 23,000
votes and became the first Democrat to win the presidency since
the Civil War, many explanations were advanced. A Blaine supporter who had described the Democrats as a party of "rum, Romanism, and rebellion" received heavy blame, as did the antilabor

New York Tribune, whose advocacy of Blaine was judged to be a handicap in the wooing of working men's votes. But Godkin asserted, with some justice, that the victory was proof of the creation of a group of independent voters who would put the public welfare ahead of party loyalty, as had the mugwump newspapers and magazines.

Another great crusade against Tammany Hall in the 1890's found Godkin and the *Evening Post* in the forefront of a newspaper attack upon the revived political machine. Godkin called Tammany "an association for plunder" and began publishing before elections a "voter's directory" in which he exposed the police records and other shortcomings of Tammany men. Eventually the directory ran to 6,500 names, and anguished politicians filed as many as three suits for libel in one day against the *Evening Post's* editor, to no avail. By 1894 the voters of New York had elected another of the city's periodic reform administrations.

Godkin stood in the early 1880's as New York's leading editor primarily because of his great ability, but also because of the shortcomings of his contemporaries. The *Times,* after the death of Raymond, was slowly going downhill and exhibited spirit and influence only sporadically. Dana's *Sun* was erratic, and the Bennetts' *Herald* had little editorial force. Greeley's *Tribune,* after the founding editor's death in 1872, switched position and became the spokesman for the dominant conservative wing of the Republican party. The *Tribune's* new editor was a famous journalistic figure, Whitelaw Reid, but his editorial stand lacked the qualities of independence shown by an increasing number of editors. While Godkin was urging reconciliation with the South, the *Tribune* was waving the bloody shirt as late as 1880 to preserve Republican supremacy. Godkin was for tariff reform; the *Tribune,* for high tariffs and protection of the industrial interests of the expanding capitalism. Godkin long favored civil service reform, which found favor with the Republican leadership only after the assassination of President James A. Garfield. And the *Tribune* more than matched Godkin's opposition to labor unions, fighting a printers' strike against itself for 15 years.[9] Still, the *Tribune's* standards of news coverage and

---

[9] As previously noted, the *Tribune's* founder, Horace Greeley, had been the first president of New York City's Typographical Union No. 6, founded in 1850.

presentation were such that it was a formidable competitor for the readership of those whom the *Post* called the "gentlemen and scholars."

Unfortunately, Godkin was not a newspaperman despite his editorial genius. He cared little for the news policies of the *Evening Post*, beyond his specialized interests. He disliked sentiment and color in the news, and he would have liked to have kept all news of crime and violence out of the paper's columns. Whatever merit there was to his viewpoints, they put the *Evening Post* at a serious disadvantage in the competition for circulation, and the paper never attained the readership its editorial leadership deserved.

Godkin retired as editor of the *Evening Post* and the *Nation* in 1899. He died in 1902. When Henry Villard died in 1900, his son, Oswald Garrison Villard, became publisher and editorial leader of the two publications. They continued to be fighting liberal organs.[10]

Other strong editorial voices were raised outside New York during the period of Godkin's dominance. The most notable were those of Henry Watterson of the *Louisville Courier-Journal* and Harvey W. Scott of the *Oregonian* in Portland. Both enjoyed long careers which began at the close of the Civil War and continued until World War I, but both belong primarily in this transitional period of journalism history. Arthur Krock, an associate of Watterson on the *Courier-Journal* staff before becoming a *New York Times* fixture, offers one reason for setting Watterson apart from later editors: ". . . he was the last of those editors who wrote with the power of ownership."[11] The same was true of Scott. Other editors, like Godkin, exercised free rein because of their relationship to owners of their papers, and they have continued to do so since, but admittedly with increasing difficulty as the newspaper became a corporate institution.

Watterson was editor of the *Courier-Journal* for 50 years, and his personality did much to make the newspaper one of the foremost in the country. He was a colorful representative of the era of personal journalism who loved to engage in editorial-page duels with other editors. One of his first foes was Dana and he lived to banter with the editors of another journalistic generation in the twentieth

---

[10] The younger Villard sold the *Evening Post* in 1918 but remained at the helm of the *Nation* until 1933.

[11] Arthur Krock, ed., *The Editorials of Henry Watterson* (Louisville: The Courier-Journal, 1923), p. 15.

century. He himself said that he belonged to the era of "the personal, one-man papers—rather blatant, but independent." [12]

Watterson had varied youthful ambitions: to be a great historian, a great dramatist, a great novelist, a great musician. He came no closer to those dreams than writing a rejected novel and serving as a music critic in New York, but his catholic interests served in time to make him a versatile and engaging writer of editorials. He was an editorial writer in Washington when the Civil War began, and he cast his lot with the South, editing a Tennessee newspaper named the *Rebel*. After stints on newspapers in Cincinnati, Atlanta, and Nashville, Watterson at the age of 28 found his lifetime work in Louisville.

There Walter N. Haldeman, editor of the *Courier*, was in the process of consolidating the *Journal* and the *Democrat* with his newspaper, and the editorship and part ownership of the new *Courier-Journal* went to Watterson. The year was 1868. Watterson, who despite his work for the southern cause had believed secession to be wrong, raised his voice in behalf of reconciliation of the North and South, and gave advice freely to both sections. He told the North that military rule should be relaxed, and he was listened to because he also was a hard-hitting spokesman for the Negro. He told the South that Lincoln was a great man, and that much of its misery had come about as a result of his assassination. And the South listened, because Watterson was a southerner of good family, not a reforming Yankee. Soon the *Courier-Journal* editorial columns, and particularly its weekly edition, won a position as a leading voice of the new South.

Watterson enhanced his position by exchanging fire with other leading editors, and by his picturesque and powerful comments, particularly in the field of politics. Although often verbose and sometimes florid, he was telling in his attacks upon those with whom he disagreed. The victims were legion; Watterson rarely was in harmony with those in authority, and he was a stalwart defender of the rights of the individual. When he used such phrases as "whack-whaddle," "pot-wholloper," and "bandy-shanked," or said of Theodore Roosevelt, "as sweet a gentleman as ever scuttled a ship or cut

[12] Tom Wallace, "There Were Giants in Those Days," *Saturday Evening Post*, August 6, 1938 (reprinted in John E. Drewry, ed., *Post Biographies of Famous Journalists*).

a throat," the reader was encouraged to continue perusing editorials which ran as long as three columns of type.

The combination of the Haldeman family and Watterson prospered. The editor looked and acted his part as a southern gentleman, equipped with shaggy eyebrows and mustache, and "Marse Henry" became a newspaper tradition. He lived in a country home graced with fine wines and fine cooking, and talked and wrote about politics, literature, music, and the arts. While the *Courier-Journal* advanced steadily and surely into the modern era of journalism, its "Marse Henry" contentedly remained in his role of personal journalist.

In the Far West, another voice was raised by an editor whose intellectual powers and forceful writing brought him attention as the leading spokesman of his area. He was Harvey W. Scott, who for 45 years edited the *Oregonian* in Portland. The *Oregonian*, founded in 1850 in a village near the junction of the Willamette and Columbia rivers, grew with the community. Scott gave up a law career to become its editor in 1865, and in 1877 he and Henry L. Pittock became the owners.[13]

Like Godkin, Scott was scholarly and forceful in his expression of opinion, but like Godkin, too, he lacked Watterson's human touch. There was one major reason why Scott's editorials were widely read and quoted; he had the ability to grapple with complex problems which many an editor shied away from, and to present new viewpoints originating in his own reasoning and analysis. His range of information seemed unlimited, and he used this resource as he thought an editor should, to guide public opinion in the public interest. The *Oregonian* was Republican by choice, but Scott wrote as an independent editor, taking his stand on the basis of his conception of the public good. An editor with Scott's abilities is rare in any period, and his fame spread from the home city in which he was a leading figure, as the *Oregonian* won statewide circulation and its editorial voice became nationally recognized.

Dana, Godkin, Watterson, and Scott—particularly the latter two— lived through the enormous changes which were occurring in American life as the industrial revolution hit full stride. They were aware

[13] The Scott and Pittock family heirs retained control of the *Oregonian* until 1950, when the 100-year-old paper was sold to Samuel I. Newhouse. See the *Oregonian*, December 11, 1950.

of change, and accepted it, but their journalistic roles were more of the older order than of the new. There were other men among their contemporaries who might well be named, but these were the leaders and the symbols of a transitional era. They and their fellow workers contributed new strengths to American journalism as it approached the "watershed of the nineties."

ANNOTATED BIBLIOGRAPHY

Books:

Baehr, Harry W., Jr., *The New York Tribune Since the Civil War.* New York: Dodd, Mead and Company, 1936. One of the better histories of newspapers.

Casual Essays of The Sun. New York: R. G. Cooke, 1905. A collection of *Sun* editorials including "Dear Virginia."

Fuess, Claude M., *Carl Schurz.* New York: Dodd, Mead and Company, 1932. A biography of the famous liberal, whose own *Reminiscences* (1907) are rewarding reading.

Hicks, John D., *The American Nation.* Boston: Houghton Mifflin Company, 1955. A standard text for American history since 1865.

Josephson, Matthew, *The Robber Barons.* New York: Harcourt, Brace and Company, 1934. A scathing description of the low state of public morality after the Civil War, focusing particularly upon corruption in railroad building. *The Politicos* (1938) is a companion volume.

Krock, Arthur, ed., *The Editorials of Henry Watterson.* New York: George H. Doran Company, 1923. Excellent preface.

Nevins, Allan, *The Emergence of Modern America, 1865-1878,* A History of American Life, Vol. VIII. New York: The Macmillan Company, 1927. A rich social history, whose extensive documentation is accompanied by highly skillful writing.

———, *The Evening Post; A Century of Journalism.* New York: Boni and Liveright, 1922. The Godkin and other eras are presented against a general social and political background.

Nye, Russel B., *Midwestern Progressive Politics; a Historical Study of Its Origins and Development, 1870-1950.* East Lansing: Michigan State College Press, 1951. A comprehensive survey. For more specialized studies, see Solon J. Buck, *The Granger Movement* (Cambridge: Harvard University Press, 1913), and John D. Hicks, *The Populist Revolt* (Minneapolis: University of Minnesota Press, 1931).

O'Brien, Frank M., *The Story of The Sun.* New York: George H. Doran Company, 1918. Revised, New York: D. Appleton and Company, 1928. One of the most readable histories of newspapers.

Oberholtzer, Ellis P., *History of the United States since the Civil War.* New York: The Macmillan Company, 1917-37. A five-volume history in the McMaster tradition but not as successful; valuable mainly for socio-economic picture after Civil War.

Ogden, Rollo, *Life and Letters of Edwin Lawrence Godkin.* New York: The Macmillan Company, 1907. The standard biography.

Paine, Albert Bigelow, *Th. Nast, His Period and His Pictures.* New York: The Macmillan Company, 1904. Well-illustrated with Nast's famous cartoons.

Rhodes, James Ford, *A History of the United States Since the Compromise of 1850.* New York: The Macmillan Company, 1892-1906. A nine-volume political history ending with the turn of the century, written with conspicuous success by a conservative businessman turned scholar.

Stone, Candace, *Dana and the Sun.* New York: Dodd, Mead and Company, 1938. The top-ranking biography of Dana, critical in tone.

Wall, Joseph F., *Henry Watterson: Reconstructed Rebel:* New York: Oxford University Press, 1956. A well-documented study.

Watterson, Henry, *"Marse Henry"; An Autobiography.* New York: George H. Doran Company, 1919. The Louisville editor's own pungent story.

Wish, Harvey, *Society and Thought in Modern America.* New York: Longmans, Green & Company, 1952. The second volume in Wish's social and intellectual history, beginning with 1865.

Woodward, C. Vann, *Origins of the New South, 1877-1913.* Baton Rouge: Louisiana State University Press, 1951. Prize-winning study of the South's emergence from the Civil War.

Periodicals and Monographs:

Mitchell, Edward P., "The Newspaperman's Newspaper," *Scribner's,* LXXVI (August 1924), 149. A vivid portrait of Dana and his *Sun* by a longtime *Sun* editor.

Nevins, Allan, "E. L. Godkin: Victorian Liberal," *Nation,* CLXXI (July 22, 1950), 76. An interpretive essay, followed by a study, written by Lewis Gannett, of Oswald Garrison Villard's editorship.

Plummer, L. Niel, "Henry Watterson's Editorial Style: An Interpretative Analysis," *Journalism Quarterly,* XXIII (March 1946), 58.

Pringle, Henry F., "Godkin of 'The Post,'" *Scribner's,* XCVI (December 1934), 327. A well-balanced article by a newspaperman turned biographer. Reprinted in Ford and Emery, *Highlights in the History of the American Press.*

———, "Kentucky Bourbon—Marse Henry Watterson," *Scribner's,* XCVII (January 1935), 10. Reprinted in Ford and Emery, *Highlights in the History of the American Press.*

Quarterly of the Oregon Historical Society, XIV, No. 2 (June 1913). An issue devoted to Harvey W. Scott, editor of the *Oregonian*.

Turnbull, George, "The Schoolmaster of the Oregon Press," *Journalism Quarterly*, XV (December 1938), 359. A study of the influence of Harvey W. Scott by the author of the *History of Oregon Newspapers* (1939).

Wallace, Tom, "There Were Giants in Those Days," *Saturday Evening Post*, August 6, 1938. The color of the Marse Henry Watterson days is recaptured by another longtime Louisville editor. Reprinted in John E. Drewry, ed., *Post Biographies of Famous Journalists* (Athens: University of Georgia Press, 1942).

Chapter *16*

A REVOLUTION IN
NATIONAL LIFE

> The newspaper has a history; but it has, likewise,
> a natural history. The press, as it exists, is not, as
> our moralists sometimes seem to assume, the wilful
> product of any little group of living men. On the
> contrary, it is the outcome of a historic proc-
> ess. . . .
>
> —Robert E. Park

THE JOURNALISM OF DANA AND GODKIN was the prod-
uct of an American society in transition; what was happening to the
national life for the first dozen years after the close of the War
Between the States could be called a transition. But then, the swell-
ing tide of economic and social change brought not transition, but
revolution.

In journalism, as in all other aspects of American life, the result
was an emergence of new concepts and practices more akin to the
twentieth century than to the immediate past. New leaders were to
revolutionize the newspaper and the magazine by responding to the
abruptly changed environment rather than by clinging to the older
patterns. The contrast, by the 1890's, between Dana's cranky,
change-resisting journalism and that of the dynamic symbol of the
new order—Joseph Pulitzer—was glaring indeed. It was no more
glaring, however, than the differences which had developed in literature, in science, in political and economic thought, in business
and industry, in the way Americans lived and worked.

What was happening? Industrialization was happening on a major scale: mechanization of production processes, the rise of the city, vast expansion of communication facilities, the coming of the age of steel, the harnessing of electricity for light and power, and a host of inventions and new businesses.

This was the true nationalization of the United States, the achievement of economic and social interdependence.[1] National growth and increased wealth meant cultural progress in literature, science, and the social sciences. But the wealth was not equally distributed, and there was sharp questioning of the theory of individualism which permitted unrestrained exploitation, enormous concentrations of wealth and economic power, and the many injustices of a materialistic-minded age. Political unrest, the rise of labor unions, and demands for economic and social reform thus were added to the scene.

America was a rich continent for the aggressive and the ingenious to master. Between 1865 and 1880 the national wealth doubled, and by 1900 it had doubled again. The population doubled in those 35 years. The nation's iron ore, its oil, its lumber, and its western agricultural lands were sources of yet untapped wealth. Its people, who by and large admired the successful enterprisers, eagerly provided investment and speculative capital. Only when it became clear that the division of the spoils had been in favor of a few to the detriment of the many, did the protests take effect. In the meantime, the patterns had been set. The dynamic capitalism of an expanding America, seizing upon unparalleled natural resources and utilizing the new machines of the industrial revolution, had transformed the national economy.

Some of the figures which show what was happening to the United States are these:

Total manufacturing production increased sevenfold between the end of the Civil War and 1900: Using a base figure of 100 for the years 1909-1913, the index figure for 1865 was 8.5; in 1880 it was 27, and by 1900 it was 61.[2]

[1] Best surveyed in Allan Nevins, *The Emergence of Modern America, 1865-1878* (New York: The Macmillan Company, 1927), and Ida M. Tarbell, *The Nationalizing of Business, 1878-1898* (New York: The Macmillan Company, 1936).

[2] This and following statistical information is from U. S. Department of Commerce, *Historical Statistics of the United States, 1789-1945* (Washington: U. S. Government Printing Office, 1949).

There were 140,000 industries of all types in 1860. By 1880 there were 250,000, and by 1900 the number was over 500,000. The number of persons employed in those industries doubled in each of the 20-year periods. The percentage of the labor force engaged in non-agricultural work was 41 per cent in 1860, 50 per cent in 1880, and 62 per cent in 1900.

Estimated national wealth in 1865 was 20 billion dollars. By 1880 it was 43 billions, and by 1900 the figure was 88 billions. Bank deposits tripled between 1865 and 1880, then quadrupled in the next 20 years.

A look at some production figures tells a similar story. In 1865 the country mined 24 million tons of coal, produced less than one million tons of pig iron, smelted 10,000 tons of copper, and produced only small amounts of steel, petroleum, and cement.

By 1880 the figures were 71 million tons of coal, over four million tons of pig iron, 30,000 tons of copper, one and one-quarter million tons of steel, 26 million barrels of petroleum, and two million barrels of cement.

And in 1900 the figures read 270 million tons of coal, 15 million tons of pig iron, 300,000 tons of copper, 10 million tons of steel, 63 million barrels of petroleum, and 17 million barrels of cement.

The rate of increase was greatest in the twenty years, 1880 to 1900. Coal and pig iron production quadrupled; copper smelters scored a tenfold increase; steel and cement production increased eight times. Petroleum output more than doubled. While the production totals continued to climb steadily after 1900, the rate of increase declined, except in the case of petroleum.

Familiar symbols of this new economic order are John D. Rockefeller and the oil monopoly, and Andrew Carnegie and the steel combine. But similar concentrations of wealth and business control developed throughout American industry and trade—Cornelius Vanderbilt, Jay Gould, and J. Pierpont Morgan in finance; Leland Stanford, Collis P. Huntington, James J. Hill, and George Pullman in railroading; C. C. Washburn and Charles A. Pillsbury in the milling industry which centered in Minneapolis as the great plains opened; Philip D. Armour and Gustavus F. Swift in the meat packing industry which grew in Chicago and Kansas City as cattle raising became big business; the makers of machine-sewed shoes, ready-made clothes, packaged foods, watches, cameras, farm machinery, and hardware; the lumbermen, the mining kings—all rose to dominate the American scene in the late nineteenth century. The captains of industry and finance obtained power through a variety of means. Some gained control of large segments of natural resources. A few held patents on basic inventions. Others, of whom Rockefeller was the most noted, won supremacy in part through manipulation of transportation rates and ruthless competitive tactics. Some were lucky in the world of financial speculation. Most important, the Rockefellers and the Carnegies usually were successful because they had, or could hire, the brains necessary to create a new manufacturing or financial empire.

But, as usual, there was a flaw in the new order. As the machine revolutionized the American economy, it brought with it the threat of overproduction and disastrous competition among the new producers. The dislocation of labor which resulted, and the bankrupting of weaker businesses, also promoted economic instability. The captains of industry cast about for ways of avoiding the industrial and financial panics which threatened the strong as well as the weak.

One effort to overcome these dangers took the form of the pool agreement. Direct competitors sought by voluntary secret agreement to limit industry-wide production, to allocate production quotas, and to stabilize prices. The trouble was that in times of distress the rule quickly became "every man for himself."

A more successful form of industry control was the trust, developed by the Standard Oil group around 1880. By this method the shareholders in the original companies assigned their capital stock to a board of trustees and received trust certificates in return. The trustees thus obtained legal control of the individual units. They could decide production quotas, set selling prices, and eliminate competition.

Hosts of other industries followed the lead of the oilmen before 1890. Sugar, salt, whiskey, rope, lead, tin plate, crackers, matches, newsprint, fence wire, and many other products fell under near monopolistic control. The number of producing companies declined sharply in such fields as woolen goods, iron and steel, leather, and farm machinery. Congress passed the Sherman Anti-Trust Act of 1890 in an attempt to restore open competition, but the end result was hardly satisfactory to opponents of industrial monopoly. The sugar trust simply became an incorporated company under the laws of New Jersey, and the Standard Oil group developed the holding-company technique. The amalgamation of many businesses now took the form of a single great corporation, whether in manufacturing, in railroading, or in mining and cattle raising.

The basic trend in this economic revolution was one which came to be intensified in twentieth-century America. It involved an increasing change from production of a small number of units at a comparatively large profit per unit to production of a large number of units at a smaller profit per unit. The familiar story of mass production by a decreasing number of producers was chronicled in many fields of business.

The American newspaper could not fail to be affected along with the rest of the national economy. Mass production methods meant that more and more businesses needed regional or national distribution of their goods. The result was the rise of new techniques in advertising and merchandising to popularize brand names. Newspapers thus received added advertising revenue, not only from this new source, but more important, from the retail stores of the expanding cities.

The blessings of the new order were mixed, however. Metropolitan papers, particularly, began to feel strong pressures for efficient operation which the increased mechanization of printing processes and pyramiding capitalizations entailed. It was costing more and more money to produce a competitive daily newspaper, and the publisher who wished his newspaper to grow—or even to survive—had to match the skills of his rivals. His increasing production costs had to be met by increased revenues from advertising and newspaper sales. This race for larger circulations, and expanded advertising volumes based upon readership, could only bring the eventual elimination of those competing newspapers which failed to match the pace, either in the quality of their product or in their business ability.

Because of the community flavor of the newspaper, however, the publishing industry scarcely could be amalgamated into one giant national corporation or be consolidated into a few major production units. Here, fortunately, the new economic pattern did not apply. Successful publishers could own a group of newspapers, as E. W. Scripps was to prove before 1900, but the newspaper by its nature remained predominantly a home-owned enterprise. The competitive battles were to be fought out in each local publishing field and later in regional publishing areas.

The industrial concentration which was maturing between 1880 and 1900 was of vital significance, but it was only a part of the enormous change in American life. Mechanization, industrialization, and urbanization brought swift and extensive social, cultural, and political developments. People were being uprooted physically and mentally by the effects of the economic revolution, and in the new environment no social institution could remain static. Even a brief examination of the character of this new environment will indicate the basic causes of the tremendous changes which developed in the daily newspapers of American cities by the 1880's.

Arthur M. Schlesinger, Sr., has chosen the phrase "the rise of the city" to characterize the period from 1878 to 1898.[3] Census figures show that the number of American towns and cities of 8,000 or more population doubled between 1880 and 1900. The total population of those urban places more than doubled, jumping from some 11 million to 25 million. In 1880 there were 50 million Americans, of whom 22.7 per cent were living in towns and cities of more than 8,000. By 1900 that figure had risen to 32.9 per cent of a total population of 76 million.

The most rapid gain in urbanization occurred during the ten years between 1880 and 1890, which were the years of greatest ferment in the daily newspaper business. The rise of the city was particularly evident in the northeastern industrial states, where urban centers now predominated over declining rural areas, and in the older states of the Middle West. New York City jumped in population from a million to a million and a half during the decade. Chicago, the rail and trade center of inland America, doubled its size, passing the million mark in 1890 to become the nation's second city. Next in line were Philadelphia, at a million; Brooklyn, at 800,000; and Boston, Baltimore, and St. Louis, in the half-million class. Altogether there were 58 cities with more than 50,000 population in 1890. Eighty per cent of them were in the East and Middle West, and half of them were in the five states of New York, Pennsylvania, Massachusetts, New Jersey, and Ohio.

[3] Schlesinger's *The Rise of the City, 1878-1898* (New York: The Macmillan Company, 1932) is the best study of the transformation of American life stemming from the economic revolution.

Into these cities was pouring an ever-rising tide of immigration, which brought new blood and new problems for American society. Again the decade of 1880-90 stands out, since in those ten years more than five million immigrants came to America, double the number for any preceding decade. All told, approximately nine million foreign-born were added to the population in the 20 years between 1880 and 1900, as many as had come during the 40 years preceding 1880. As a result the newspapers of New York City in 1890 were serving a population that was 80 per cent foreign-born or of foreign parentage, and as might be expected, the character of some of the newspapers changed. Other American cities had from 25 to 40 per cent foreign-born residents. To the older Irish, British, and German streams of migration were added great numbers of Scandinavians, Poles, French-Canadians, Italians, Russians, and Hungarians. Of these, the Germans and the Scandinavians particularly migrated to the Middle West, while the other groups tended to remain in the Atlantic states.

The rest of the country was advancing steadily, if less conspicuously than were the East and the older settled sections of the Middle West. The South, slowly recovering from the effects of the Civil War, was establishing a substantial amount of new enterprises. Southern cotton mills multiplied until they challenged the older New England supremacy; between 1860 and 1900 the number of southern spindles increased from 300,000 to 4,300,000. Tobacco manufacturing, the cottonseed industry, and southern lumber and oil production developed rapidly. Large coal and iron ore deposits were worked in southern states, and Birmingham, Alabama, became a center of iron production. In comparison with the East and the Middle West, however, the South was far behind.

In the western plains and mountain regions, pierced by the transcontinental railroads built in the 1870's and early 1880's, the major economic activities were agriculture, cattle raising, and mining. The plains area doubled its population between 1880 and 1890, as the line of the frontier disappeared from the map of the United States, and the process of creation of new continental states neared its end. Major population centers were still scarce in the South and West in 1890, but the trend toward urbanization was under way. The isolation which had been characteristic of farm life was breaking down, and the villages and towns of rural America more and more were becoming trade and social centers for the surrounding countryside.

The rise of the city meant a quickening of material progress, reflected first in the life of the city dweller and transmitted gradually to the rest of the country. The new American cities hastened the installation of water and sewage systems in the years following the Civil War. They paved their streets with asphalt and bricks, and they bridged their rivers with steel structures patterned after the Roeblings' famed Brooklyn bridge of 1883. A ten-story Chicago building, constructed around a steel and iron skeleton in 1885, heralded the coming of the skyscraper. Horsecars and cabs no longer could carry the throngs of city dwellers, nor could they serve adequately the suburbs which mushroomed about metropolitan centers. The first answers were New York's elevated trains and San Francisco's cable cars, adopted by other large cities in the 1870's. Then came the electric railway and streetcar, perfected in 1887, to meet the urban transportation problem. By 1895 some 850 electric lines were in operation.

Electricity was becoming a great new servant, both as a source of power for industry and transportation and as a source of light. American cities barely had begun to install arc lights in 1879 when Thomas A. Edison invented a practicable incandescent bulb. When the current flowed out from his Pearl Street generating station in 1882 to light the Stock Exchange and the offices of the *New York Times* and *New York Herald*, a new era in living had begun. By 1898 there were nearly 2,800 central electric power stations in the country, as businesses and homes were lighted, electric elevators were installed in the new tall buildings, and electric motors became widely used in industry.

America was being tied together by its industrial revolution, and its communications network kept pace with the sense of urgency which was characteristic of the new order. The telephone, invented by Alexander Graham Bell in the 1870's, already had one user for every thousand persons in 1880. By 1900 there was one telephone for each hundred. Intercity lines multiplied during the 1880's, until by 1900 the Bell System covered the country. Western Union quadrupled its telegraph lines between 1880 and 1900. The railroads, with 93,000 miles of track in 1880, reached a near-saturation point of 193,000 miles by 1900. The federal postal service, still the primary means of communication, greatly extended its free carrier service in cities during the two decades and instituted free rural delivery in 1897. Congress, by clearly defining second-class matter in the Postal Act of 1879, and by providing a one-cent-a-pound rate for newspapers and magazines in 1885, opened the way for cheap delivery of publications. In business offices the invention of the typewriter and adding machine speeded the work pace and simplified the handling of increased correspondence and records.

Each of these material advances and changes in the physical character of American society had its impact, large or small, upon the nation's journalism. The nationwide financial and industrial expansion which took the name of "big business" transformed the big city newspaper into a corporate enterprise rather than a personal venture. Increasing mechanization, spurred on by inventive genius, revolutionized the printing processes just as it had other industrial processes. The tremendous growth of the cities permitted larger newspaper circulations, which were in turn made necessary by larger investments and operating expenses. And a steady increase in the number of urban communities, as population expanded and the economic benefits of industrialization spread across the country, offered a host of new publishing opportunities which were seized upon quickly.

The most striking evidence of what was happening to the newspaper is to be found in a bare statistical summary. Between 1870 and 1900, the United States doubled its population and tripled the number of its urban residents. During the same 30 years the number of its daily newspapers quadrupled and the number of copies sold each day increased almost sixfold. Both in numbers and in total circulation the daily newspaper was rising even more rapidly than the city which spawned it. The number of English-language, general-circulation dailies increased from 489 in 1870 to 1,967 in 1900. Circulation totals for all daily publications rose from 2.6 million copies in 1870 to 15 million in 1900.[4] A similar advance was being made by weekly newspapers, serving mainly the small towns and rural areas, but also the suburbs and sections of the cities. Between 1870 and 1900, the number of weekly publications tripled, increas-

---

[4] The census figures for totals of all types of dailies were 574 in 1870 and 2,226 in 1900. The figures used above are more comparable to twentieth-century statistics.

ing from approximately 4,000 to more than 12,000. The weeklies, however, still represented personal journalistic ventures, and the revolution in newspaper methods was taking place at the big city daily level.

There were many less tangible reasons why the newspaper was making such tremendous strides as an American social institution. The forces of social and economic interdependence, products of industrialization and urbanization, played a leading part in the creation of the lusty "new journalism." The peoples of the cities, being molded together as economic and cultural units, increasingly turned to the daily newspapers for the story of their urban life and their common interests. At the same time the country itself was being rapidly unified by the rush toward economic interdependence. Improved communications facilities were a manifestation of this nationalizing influence which pervaded all American life. And again, the daily newspaper was the chronicler of the national scene, the interpreter of the new environment. The city reader, whether he was seated in new-found comfort on a streetcar or in his better-lighted home, was the eager customer of the publisher who met successfully the new challenge to journalism.

As American social and economic life became more complex and as the national wealth accumulated, many cultural advances were possible which in turn promoted new interest in the newspaper. The cities, with their concentrated populations and earning capacities, naturally led in expansion of social and intellectual activity. But they also set the pace for a nationalized cultural development. The bookstores, libraries, art galleries, museums, theaters, opera houses, churches, retail stores, schools, and newspapers which brought higher standards in the cities stimulated the interests and the desires of all the country. Progress in education, the result of this general thirst for knowledge and a better life, was particularly important to the expansion of the mass media—newspapers, magazines, books. The percentage of children attending public schools in the United States rose from 57 to 72 per cent between 1870 and 1900, while illiteracy declined from 20 to 10.7 per cent of the population. The number of high schools jumped from approximately 100 in 1860 to 800 by 1880, and then skyrocketed to 6,000 by 1900.

At higher educational levels, growth of state universities and of private colleges financed by America's new men of wealth resulted in notable advances in the social sciences, as well as progress in the natural and physical sciences and the humanities. Federal land subsidies provided by the Morrill Act of 1862 encouraged the founding and expansion of state universities, particularly in the Middle West and West, where such state-supported universities as Wisconsin, California, Minnesota, and Illinois began to flourish. The private colleges and universities gained in numbers and influence with the founding of Cornell University in 1865 by Ezra Cornell, whose millions came from the electric telegraph; of Johns Hopkins University in 1876 by a Baltimore merchant; of Leland Stanford University in 1885 by a California railroad and business man; of the University of Chicago in 1892 by John D. Rockefeller's benefaction. Johns Hopkins, by emphasizing the role of research in higher education, and Harvard, by giving its students an elective choice of courses, set new patterns for the universities. And university presidents such as Charles W. Eliot of Harvard, Daniel Coit Gilman of Johns Hopkins, and Andrew D. White of Cornell gave effective leadership. No longer was it necessary for Americans interested in scholarly pursuits to go abroad; and the number of graduate students in the United States increased from 400 in 1880 to some 5,600 in 1900. Nor were women ignored in the new spread of education. The state universities became coeducational institutions; Smith College was founded in 1875, soon to be followed by Bryn Mawr and Radcliffe, as fruits of the woman suffrage movement.

The scholars of the universities, and other men and women whose intellectual and cultural achievements were supported by the new wealth of the nation, made great advances in the years between 1880 and 1900. Most importantly, they challenged the socio-economic philosophies which had developed in nineteenth-century society, and suggested new concepts better fitted to the revolutionized character of American life. They organized areas of knowledge which were needed if the country was to understand its problems and cope with them, and in doing so they laid the groundwork for the vast growth of research and interpretation in the twentieth century.[5]

A socio-economic theory of individualism had been well developed by 1880 to bolster the argument that government should not inter-

[5] Well-discussed in Henry Steele Commager, *The American Mind* (New Haven: Yale University Press, 1950).

fere in economic affairs. The individual, this school of thought declared, supplies the enterprise which makes possible industrial progress, wealth, and national power. Therefore government should do nothing which would adversely affect individual economic enterprise. Government's function, ran the argument, is to provide an orderly society in which the individual is protected as he fulfills his destiny.

Powerful support for the theory of individualism was drawn from the work of the English scientist, Charles Darwin, who published his *Origin of Species* in 1859 and his *The Descent of Man* in 1871. Darwin's emphasis upon the struggle for individual existence in the process of evolution fitted nicely into the pattern. Another major influence on American thinking came from the writings of the English philosopher, Herbert Spencer. The Spencerian doctrine declared that man's ultimate achievement of a perfect society would be the result of a natural process—an inevitable development which men themselves should not attempt to hasten or to alter. In the United States, sociologist William Graham Sumner, historian John Fiske, and political scientist John W. Burgess shaped their teaching and writing to conform with Darwin's and Spencer's ideas of individualism. The influence of this socio-economic doctrine became so strong, particularly in the rendering of Supreme Court decisions nullifying reform legislation, that Justice Oliver Wendell Holmes was led to protest that Spencer's *Social Statics* was not part of the Constitution.

Those who decried the negativism of this theory of individualism were being heard by the 1880's. They contended that man did have the ability to control his destiny, and to shape his economic and political actions as the general welfare of society might require. Unrestricted exercise of individual power by some only brings misery and poverty to others, and the outcome is not national strength, but national weakness, said this school of thought. True progress, they said, depends upon cooperation and the use of government's powers in the common good.

A sociologist, Lester Ward, who published the first volume of his *Dynamic Sociology* in 1883, provided logical arguments for the belief that government should be regarded as a positive force, and that it should actively seek ways of achieving social improvement. Economist Richard T. Ely attacked the pat theories of the laissez-faire advocates, theories which he and other economics professors pointed out did not conform to the facts of industrial life. Ely's *Socialism, Its Nature, Strength and Weakness*, published in 1894, made definite proposals for reasonable reform legislation. Economist Thorstein Veblen compared the theories of economic individualists with the actual practices of industrial capitalism, and voiced his bitter protest in 1899 with his *Theory of the Leisure Class*. Henry George assailed the unearned increment of wealth through land ownership in his *Progress and Poverty* (1879), and Henry Demarest Lloyd denounced the oil monopoly in *Wealth against Commonwealth* (1894), an effective plea for socio-economic cooperation.

Newspaper editors Dana, Godkin, and Reid, as we have observed, were supporters of the theory of individualism, and opposed government interference in economic spheres. One might expect, in light of what was happening, that other editors would appear who would support the principles of social cooperation and use of governmental power to regulate economic life. And indeed, one of the characteristics of the "new journalism" came to be the expression of editorial-page support for the "common man." What publishers and editors like Joseph Pulitzer and E. W. Scripps represented in the field of journalism was only an expression of a larger movement in American thought and life.

Those who thus argued directly with the supporters of individualism were aided by those whose contributions to knowledge widened the country's understanding of its history, its government, and human thought and action. The period of the 1880's and 1890's was one of intense activity in study and publication, and in every field there were major achievements which helped Americans to meet the challenge of economic and social change.

Historians broke new ground by studying and writing about social and economic history, as well as politics. John Bach McMaster pointed the way by using newspapers as source materials for his significantly-titled *History of the People of the United States*, begun in 1883. Henry Adams produced his brilliant history of the Jefferson and Madison administrations in 1889, and James Ford Rhodes began publication of his *History of the United States* in 1892. Frederick Jackson Turner's famous essay on the "Significance of the Frontier in American History" appeared in 1893, to father a whole new school of historical interpretation. Colonial history was being rewritten by men with an understanding of economic and social conditions of the early American period.

The landmark for this period in the field of government and political science was James Bryce's *American Commonwealth,* in which the talented Englishman gave to the United States a description of its new environment. The same year, 1888, Frank W. Taussig wrote his *Tariff History of the United States.* Woodrow Wilson's *Congressional Government* appeared in 1885, and by 1903 Charles E. Merriam had completed his *History of American Political Theories.*

The list of men and books could be extended: anthropologist Lewis Henry Morgan's *Ancient Society* (1877); philosopher William James' *Principles of Psychology* (1890); philosopher Josiah Royce's *The Spirit of Modern Philosophy* (1892) and *The World and the Individual* (1900); historian Brooks Adams' *The Law of Civilization and Decay* (1895); educator John Dewey's *School and Society* (1899); jurist Oliver Wendell Holmes' *The Common Law* (1881).

Literature offered Henry James' *Portrait of a Lady* (1881); Samuel Clemens' *Life on the Mississippi* (1883) and *Huckleberry Finn* (1885); and William Dean Howells' *The Rise of Silas Lapham* (1885), an early example of the rise of realism in American literature. In the 1890's, poets Emily Dickinson and Edwin Arlington Robinson and novelists Stephen Crane and Hamlin Garland were making major contributions, while such realistic writers as Theodore Dreiser and Frank Norris were on the verge of fame.

Nor was this great cultural stirring and extension of factual information limited to an intellectual class. Millions shared in the new knowledge through the chautauquas and public study courses which became of major importance toward the close of the century as means of adult education. The world fairs and expositions which caught America's fancy in this period were another means of mass education. At the Philadelphia Centennial of 1876 and Chicago's Columbian Exposition of 1893, millions of Americans viewed the material and artistic achievements of their generation. Free public libraries, spreading across the country after 1880, found their great benefactor in Andrew Carnegie. In these libraries were available the literary triumphs and the popular writings of American and British authors.

Magazines came to have increasing influence upon American life. Earlier ventures like the *North American Review* (1815) and the *Knickerbocker*, a more popular magazine published from 1833 to 1865, had been eclipsed by *Harper's Monthly*, begun in 1850 by the New York book publishing firm. *Harper's* introduced extensive woodcut illustrations, published the writings of leading English and American authors, and ran up a world record circulation of 200,000 before the Civil War. Two women's magazines, *Godey's Lady's Book* and *Peterson's*, began their careers in 1830 and 1842, respectively, and offered hand-colored engravings of fashions and fiction stories to more than 150,000 readers each by the 1850's.

In 1881, the *Century* joined *Harper's* in the highly literary and artistic class of magazines. *Scribner's* made it a trio in 1886. Unillustrated, but of equal literary quality, was the *Atlantic Monthly*, begun in 1857 and specializing in publishing the writings of the New England authors. In the weekly field were two illustrated periodicals, *Frank Leslie's Illustrated Newspaper* (1855) and *Harper's Weekly* (1857). The latter exercised strong influence in public affairs, along with E. L. Godkin's weekly, the *Nation* (1865). In addition, the *Independent* (1848), the *North American Review*, and such newcomers as the *Forum* (1886), the *Arena* (1889), and the *Outlook* (1893) all discussed the new political and social environment. The *Literary Digest* began summarizing contemporary editorial opinion in 1890.

Coming into the field were publications which depended upon humor, cartoons, and political satire. *Puck* (1877) featured Joseph Keppler's dynamic color cartoons. The others were *Judge* (1881), and *Life* (1883), famed for its publication of the "Gibson girl" drawings of Charles Dana Gibson. In the children's magazine competition, *Youth's Companion* (1827) was joined by *St. Nicholas* (1873).

Helped by the cheap postage rates established by Congress under its 1879 act, some new leaders struck out in the 1880's for the mass readership which still awaited American magazine publishers. One was Cyrus H. K. Curtis, who founded the *Ladies' Home Journal* in 1883, and with Edward W. Bok as his editor, soon won a half million circulation. Curtis bought the *Saturday Evening Post* in 1897 and with editor George Horace Lorimer quickly made it a leader in the low-cost weekly field, which *Collier's* entered in 1888. The older high quality monthlies found stiff competition from three low priced popular magazines: *Munsey's,* begun in 1889 by Frank Munsey; *McClure's,* started in 1893 by S. S. McClure, and the *Cosmopolitan* (1886). It was these magazines, circulating more extensively than any of their predecessors, which were to open the minds of more readers to social and cultural trends.

It must be noted, however, that the general level of cultural attainment was still low. Even by 1900 the average American had received only five years of schooling in his lifetime. If the public bought encyclopedias galore from the book publishers because it wanted to know more, it also bought dime novels by the millions. If the chautauqua was a booming institution, so were horse racing, prize fighting, and baseball. Cultural and business organizations were expanding in number, but growing even faster were fraternal and social groups. In the newspaper world Adolph Ochs would be able to find enough serious readers in the metropolis of New York to support the reborn *New York Times,* but the great mass of readers was attracted by the devices of a journalism which sought a popular level as it both entertained and informed.

It should be noted briefly, too, that not everybody was successful or contented in this new economic and social environment, despite the general blessings that industrialization had bestowed upon the country. Political and economic events became of more than ordinary interest to masses of people whose new livelihoods in the cities and in the factories were immediately affected by financial panics, labor disturbances, and even by political debates over the tariff and free silver. The newspaper reader of the 1880's and 1890's might devour all the details of the doings of America's new-rich society, as it built its great mansions, its country estates, its private art museums, and its marital alliances with European nobility. The reader might find himself admiring the financial coups and the graceful living, but he also was disturbed by the excesses of economic individualism. Newspapers which attacked the traction company bosses of Chicago and Kansas City, or the manipulation of freight rates in favor of a great corporation, or the dangers of reckless market speculation found widespread popular approval.

A running political battle was being fought during the closing years of the nineteenth century between those who believed that government should not interfere with the course of economic development, except to protect business in its onward drive, and those who believed that government regulation must be invoked to maintain an equitable society and economic freedom. In general the protests, while loud and widespread, served only to alleviate the worst features of excessive individualism. The drastic proposals of Marxian Socialism found but few adherents, even among the immigrant populations of the cities. And the idealistic writings of Edward Bellamy and Henry George stirred popular thinking, but did not result in the socialistic solution of economic ills which the authors advocated. The practical victories, such as they were, were won by the advocates of moderate regulation of the capitalistic economy, who obtained progressive state statutes and federal legislation restricting the abuses of the railroads and the trusts, and forwarding the status of social reform.

Sharp divisions began to appear between those who had gained wealth in the process of national economic upheaval, and those who had gained only a crowded room in a city tenement, a poverty-stricken tenant farm in the South, or a precarious existence on the dry plains of the West. Falling farm prices in the 1880's spurred the political activities of the discontented in the South and West. There the Grangers, the Greenbackers, the Farmers' Alliance, and the Populists arose to demand economic equality for agriculture, and launched third party movements which showed real strength. Not until 1896 did one of the major political parties answer the call of the "consistent rebellion"; at that time, the merging of the forces of free silver coinage, paper money, and general political and economic reform under the Democratic banner of William Jennings Bryan provided America with the greatest political excitement of a generation. But despite the bitter experience of the depression of 1893, the advocates of William McKinley and political and economic conservatism won the decision.

In the cities the rise of the labor movement on a nationally organized scale provided a much sharper clash than that between business and agriculture. Some craft unions, such as those of the bricklayers, railroad engineers, and printers, had become established before the Civil War, and a National Labor Union of some stature was organized in 1866, only to disintegrate during the depression of 1873. The Knights of Labor, carrying on the "one big union" plan under the leadership of Terence V. Powderly, reached a peak membership of 700,000 during the two years of industrial turbulence which followed the panic of 1884. Powderly advocated moderate cooperative action by all working men to better their pay and working conditions, and the use of the strike weapon when necessary. Unfortunately for the Knights of Labor, their aggressive action was at its peak in 1886, when anarchists who advocated deeds of violence and terror touched off the Haymarket riot in Chicago. Public reaction coupled Powderly's legitimate labor movement with the troubles caused by the anarchists, and the Knights of Labor movement fell away. As a result the steadier American Federation of Labor, built in 1881 as a national organization of the various craft unions, became the principal voice of the labor movement. Its nationwide strikes in 1886 for a shortening of the ten-hour workday won a reduction to eight or nine hours for some 200,000 workers out of the 350,000 involved, and newly elected AFL president Samuel Gompers became the individual leader of labor. The reaction in many industries was the formation of employers' associations which raised defense funds to fight the carefully planned demands and strikes of the individual craft unions.

In such a swiftly changing and exciting environment, then, the daily newspaper was coming of age. From 850 English-language, general-circulation dailies in 1880 to 1,967 in 1900; from 10 per cent of adults as subscribers to 26 per cent—these were the statistical evidences of its arrival as a major business. The enormous success of Joseph Pulitzer's *New York World,* which between 1883 and 1887 broke every publishing record in America, was evidence that a "new journalism" had been created which would change the character and the appearance of the daily newspaper and enormously increase its mass influence.

But before focusing attention on the *New York World,* whose triumphs caught the attention of even the most unobservant in the newspaper business, we should briefly examine the changes which were occurring in other cities. Certainly Henry W. Grady in Atlanta, Edward W. Scripps in Cleveland and Cincinnati, Melville E. Stone and Victor Lawson in Chicago, and William Rockhill Nelson in Kansas City also were engaged in the creation of the "new journalism" in the same years that Joseph Pulitzer was exhibiting his skill, first in St. Louis and then in New York. And in many another city, older newspapers were being challenged by bright-faced newcomers which in some cases were destined to take their places among America's best. The new papers were low-priced, aggressive, and easily read. They believed in the news function as the primary obligation of the press; they exhibited independence of editorial opinion; they crusaded actively in the community interest; they appealed to the mass audience through improved writing, better makeup, use of headlines and illustrations, and a popularization of their contents. These were the general characteristics of the "new journalism"; the individual newspapers, of course, exhibited them in varying degrees. And while their application did not always result in a better kind of journalism, if popularization of the product gave rise to an overpowering and crude sensationalism, still the over-all result was a great expansion of the influence of the newspaper.

The rise of evening newspapers was a feature of this growth of the daily. The evening field claimed seven-eighths of the increase in numbers of daily newspapers between 1880 and 1900, and by 1890 two out of three papers were evening editions. The swing toward evening publication was due in part to the changed reading habits of the city populations, and it was strengthened by the discovery that the woman readers to whom retail store advertising was directed favored afternoon-delivered newspapers. Mechanical and news-gathering innovations permitted the evening papers to carry "today's news today," particularly in the Middle West and West where time differentials aided inclusion of news from the East and from Europe on the same day events occurred. Some morning papers found an answer by publishing afternoon editions under the same nameplate, while others established separate evening papers.

New York remained primarily a morning-paper city, with only the *Evening Post* achieving distinction as an afternoon paper before the Pulitzer invasion. Two additions to the field in 1867 were the *Evening Telegram,* begun by James Gordon Bennett as the afternoon edition of the *Herald,* and the *Evening Mail.* The *Mail* was merged with the older *Express* in 1882 to form the *Mail and Express.* The circulation winner of the period was the *Daily News,* a one-cent evening paper dating back to 1855 (see also p. 300). The *Daily News,* cheap in content as well as in price, circulated in the tenement districts so widely that it challenged the *Sun* and *Herald* throughout the 1870's, and its success suggested to other publishers new ways of reaching the immigrant-crowded tenement sections of the city.

In Philadelphia, two newcomers in the 1870's were the *Record* and the *Times*. The *Record*, begun in 1870, was taken over in 1877 by William M. Singerly, a millionaire railroad builder, who cut the paper's price to one cent, brightened its makeup and writing, and engaged in popular crusades against local abuses. By the early 1880's the *Record* was outselling its famous competitor in the morning field, the *Public Ledger*, which had been purchased from the Swain family in 1864 by the able George W. Childs. The *Times* (1875),[6] published by reform-conscious Alexander K. McClure, also pushed into the top circulation bracket, along with the *Evening Item* (1847), which hit its stride in the 1880's as a crusading penny paper, and the *Press* (1857). The *Evening Bulletin* (1847) and the *Inquirer* (1829), ultimately the two survivors in the Philadelphia field, trailed the *Public Ledger* in prestige and the other papers in circulation.

Boston's quiet journalism was upset by the appearance of the *Globe*. Founded in 1872, it had only 8,000 circulation when General Charles H. Taylor became publisher in 1877. Taylor established an evening edition, cut the price to two cents, ran big headlines, emphasized local news, and gave editorial support to the Democratic party. By 1890 the *Globe*, with combined morning and evening circulation of 150,000, ranked among the top ten papers in the country. The staid *Herald* (1846) and the sensationalized *Journal* (1833) kept pace by establishing evening editions. But the morning *Advertiser* (1813) and *Post* (1831), and evening *Transcript* (1830) and *Traveller* (1825), contented themselves with limited circulations. The *Advertiser* did establish an evening edition, the *Record*, in 1884.

The trend was similar in other eastern cities. Baltimore's new entry was the *Evening News* (1872), which in the 1890's under fighting editor Charles H. Grasty rose to challenge the famous *Sun*. The *Evening Penny Press* of Pittsburgh appeared in 1884 as the forerunner of the *Pittsburgh Press* and promptly undertook civic improvement campaigns. The Butler family's *Buffalo News* dates from 1880, and it immediately asserted leadership in the newspaper field as an aggressively run evening paper. Another influential

* Figures in parentheses indicate founding dates of newspapers.

leader in the 1880's was the evening *Brooklyn Eagle,* begun in 1841. In Providence, the *Journal* (1829) saw the trend early and established the *Evening Bulletin* in 1863. The Noyes and Kauffmann families gave Washington a local evening paper in 1852, and by 1890 their *Evening Star* had as its only competitor the morning *Post* (1877).[7]

In the South, Henry Watterson's well-established *Louisville Courier-Journal* started the *Times* as an evening edition in 1884 and soon saw it outsell the parent morning paper. New Orleans' morning leader, the *Picayune* (1837), found new competition from two evening papers, the *Item* (1877) and the *States* (1879). Two other New Orleans morning papers, the *Times* (1863) and the *Democrat* (1875), found the going more difficult and merged in 1881. A famous editor appeared in Raleigh, North Carolina, in 1885, when Josephus Daniels took over the *State Chronicle,* which he soon merged into the *News and Observer,* thereby establishing what became a great Daniels family newspaper.

Most brilliant of the southern newspaper-makers of the period was Henry W. Grady, who in his brief 39 years demonstrated the qualities of a great reporter and managing editor. Grady's talents were widely exhibited in the dozen years before he became managing editor of the *Atlanta Constitution* in 1880. Indeed, when Grady became editor and one-third owner of the *Atlanta Herald* in 1872, he nearly put the *Constitution,* founded four years before, out of business. But the *Herald,* for all its journalistic superiority, fell victim to the financial depression of 1873 after a four-year struggle. Grady then became a free-lance correspondent for such enterprising newspapers as the *Constitution,* the *New York Herald,* the *Louisville Courier-Journal,* the *Philadelphia Times,* and the *Detroit Free Press,* distinguishing himself for his coverage of politics and for his use of the interview technique in reporting and interpreting the news. He traveled widely and his grasp of events and his acquaintanceships increased accordingly.

When the *Constitution,* published by Evan P. Howell after 1876, obtained Grady as a part owner and managing editor, things began to hum. A network of correspondents was built up, and Grady spent

---

[7] Crosby S. Noyes and Samuel H. Kauffmann were leading men in the early years of the *Star;* Noyes' sons, Frank and Theodore, became active before 1890 and guided the *Star* down to the 1940's.

lavishly to get all the news coverage possible in every field from politics to baseball. Grady continued to report major news events and political affairs himself. His brilliant story of the Charleston earthquake of 1886 won him national attention as a newsman. The same year his address entitled "The New South," which advocated industrial advancement of the South as a means of re-establishing national solidarity, won him national fame as a spokesman for his area. As a consequence Grady devoted increased attention to the editorial page of the *Constitution* until his death in 1889, and his influence furthered the paper's position as sharing southern leadership with Henry Watterson's *Louisville Courier-Journal*.

Grady's biographer, however, points out his real function with these words:

The success of the *Atlanta Constitution* was due, furthermore, to the fact that it had in its managing editor a great reporter and a master news executive. Just as in his public policies Grady belongs to the New South rather than to the Old, so in his journalistic methods he exemplifies not the personal journalism which the Civil War rendered obsolete, but the modern era, with its emphasis upon the gathering and interpreting of news. The South, certainly, has never seen his like as one who "perceived instantly the multitudinous interesting things of life" and who could picture even the most difficult of subjects in colorful strokes that caught the public fancy.[8]

With Grady's death, Clark Howell, Sr., son of the publisher, became managing editor of the *Constitution*. The other event of the 1880's in Atlanta journalism was the founding in 1883 of the *Journal*, an evening paper which was destined to out-maneuver the Howells' *Constitution* by the 1950's.

To the West, the newspaper which is now the *Dallas News* was established in 1885, and its future publisher, George B. Dealey, appeared in Dallas that year. The *Los Angeles Times*, begun in 1881, saw Harrison Gray Otis assume its leadership in 1882. In San Francisco, the major event of the period was the sale of the *Examiner* (1865) to George Hearst in 1880, and the turning over of the paper to young William Randolph Hearst in 1887. San Francisco journalism had been lively before the Hearst entry, with the morning

[8] Raymond B. Nixon, "Henry W. Grady, Reporter: A Reinterpretation," *Journalism Quarterly*, XII (December 1935), p. 343. The full-length biography is Nixon's *Henry W. Grady, Spokesman of the New South* (New York: Alfred A. Knopf, Inc., 1943).

Chronicle (1865) leading in civic campaigns and political clean-up movements. Its publisher, Michel H. de Young, one of two brothers who founded the paper, remained in control of the *Chronicle* for 60 years.

What has been described thus far would suffice to prove the point that things were happening to the nation's journalism, everywhere. Singerly's *Philadelphia Record*, Taylor's *Boston Globe*, Grady's *Atlanta Herald* and *Constitution* exhibited the major characteristics of the "new journalism." The appearance of the Butler family in Buffalo, of the Noyes family in Washington, of Josephus Daniels in Raleigh, of the Howell family in Atlanta, of George B. Dealey in Dallas meant in each case the beginning of the building of a noted American newspaper. But it was in the Midwest of the 1870's and 1880's that the biggest revolution in newspapering was brewing— Detroit, Cleveland, Cincinnati, Chicago, Kansas City, Milwaukee, St. Louis.

The name Scripps is written boldly into the story of midwestern newspaper-making in the 1870's and early 1880's. James E. Scripps, elder half-brother of the famed Edward Wyllis Scripps, started the family on its journalistic mission when, after working on newspapers in Chicago and Detroit, he founded the *Detroit Evening News* in 1873. By the end of 1880, the Scripps family had fostered newspapers in Cleveland, Cincinnati, St. Louis, and Buffalo. The story of the rise of the Scripps newspaper chain belongs later (Chapter 20), but the story of the early successes is a part of the general pattern of the rise of the "new journalism." Scripps newspapers were low-priced evening publications; small in size, but well-written and tightly edited; hard-hitting in both news and editorial page coverage of the local scene. Above all, they were distinguished for their devotion to the interests of the working man.

When James Scripps needed help to keep his *Detroit News* afloat, he called upon his brother George and sister Ellen, and eventually upon young Edward, who was the thirteenth child of a thrice-married Englishman now settled on an Illinois farm. Edward helped to build circulation routes for the *News* and reported for it while the struggle to win advertising support was in progress. Detroit had well-established papers, such as the morning *Free Press* (1831), but by the 1880's the *News* emerged as a leading evening paper known for its business operation as well as for its qualities as a newspaper.

Scripps money went into four one-cent evening papers: the short-lived *Buffalo Evening Telegraph*, the ill-fated *St. Louis Chronicle*, and the famous *Cleveland Press* and *Cincinnati Post*. These two latter papers became the products of Edward Wyllis Scripps' own publishing genius, and the parent papers of his eventual chain.

Cleveland of 1878 had three going newspapers, the *Leader* (1854), the *Herald* (1835), and the *Plain Dealer* (1842). When the *Penny Press* appeared as a four-page, five-column evening paper, it looked no more permanent than the alley shack in which it was published. But the editor, Edward Wyllis Scripps, paid the top salary to his advertising solicitor, and put his own tremendous energy into the venture in a fashion which drove the circulation to 10,000 within a few months and foreshadowed the rise of the Scripps publishing empire.

What happened to Cleveland journalism as a result of the rapid growth of the *Press* can be briefly told. The *Plain Dealer* shifted its emphasis from the evening to the morning field in 1885 as one of the first acts of a new owner, L. E. Holden. Holden bought the plant and morning edition of the *Herald;* the evening editions of the *Leader* and the *Herald* were combined as the *News and Herald*. But the *Press* continued to harass its evening competitors, and in 1905 the other afternoon dailies were combined into a new paper, the *Cleveland News*.

The Scripps opposition in Cincinnati was more formidable. The evening *Times* (1840) and *Star* (1872) were merged in 1880 by Charles P. Taft (half-brother of the later president, William Howard Taft). The *Times-Star* was a two-cent, conservative Republican paper; the Scripps entry that year was one-cent and Democratic. But in the morning field were the *Enquirer* (1841), published by John R. McLean as a Democratic paper which was noted for its adoption of the techniques of sensationalism, and the *Commercial Gazette*, edited by the distinguished liberal Republican supporter, Murat Halstead.[9] The Scripps paper, which became the *Cincinnati Post* after Edward Wyllis Scripps took control in 1883, nevertheless soon gained circulation leadership as the *Press* was doing in Cleveland.

[9] The *Commercial Gazette* resulted from an 1883 merger of the *Gazette* (1815) and the *Commercial* (1843), which Halstead had edited since 1865. After Halstead left Cincinnati in 1890 to go to Brooklyn, the *Commercial Gazette* became the *Commercial Tribune* in 1896. It disappeared into the *Enquirer* in 1930.

Another star which was rising in the Midwest was that of the *Chicago Daily News*. Together with another newcomer, the *Herald*, the *Daily News* quickly won equal prominence with older Chicago papers. The *Tribune* (1847), with Joseph Medill as controlling owner and editor after 1874, was continuing its development as a substantially edited, alert newspaper leader. The *Inter Ocean* (successor to the *Republican* founded in 1865 with Charles A. Dana as first editor) became widely known for its enterprise in news-gathering and in adoption of new journalistic and printing techniques. But the circulation went to the newcomers, the *Daily News* and *Herald*.

Melville E. Stone, the founder of the *Daily News*, was a product both of Chicago journalism and of the new national newspaper environment. Stone became managing editor of the *Republican* in 1872, as an inexperienced young man of 24, and ended up as city editor when the paper became the *Inter Ocean* later that year. In the fall he went on tour for the paper, studying conditions in the South. He records in his autobiography an association with Henry W. Grady and his *Atlanta Herald* partners: "They spent almost every evening with me talking over the profession of journalism. In these discussions we all learned much." [10] On the same trip, Stone studied New Orleans and St. Louis papers, and in St. Louis met a talented young newsman, Eugene Field.

When Stone returned to Chicago he became managing editor of the *Post and Mail*, but almost immediately he left for Washington to serve as correspondent for his and other papers. And in his autobiography, Stone records another major influence; he was watching the successful one-cent *New York Daily News* and deciding that he would try the same price formula in Chicago. He experimented briefly in 1874, then returned to Washington for more seasoning as a correspondent, and laid his plans to leave the *Post and Mail*.

In January, 1876, the *Daily News* appeared as a four-page, five-column sheet with only a few thousand dollars in capital investment. Stone believed that his first responsibility was to print news; his second responsibility was to guide public opinion; and his third, to provide entertainment. The paper did not reject sensational techniques; Stone's personal favorite was the detection of criminals by the news-

[10] Melville E. Stone, *Fifty Years a Journalist* (Garden City: Doubleday, Page & Company, 1921), p. 44.

paper. Nor did the *Daily News* fail to entertain; Stone brought Eugene Field to Chicago in 1883 from his earlier St. Louis and Kansas City surroundings, and until his death in 1895 Field conducted the famous "Sharps and Flats" column, in which he commented upon politics and people in a witty and highly literary style. But the paper won its place by its style of news presentation, by its determination to remain free of political and outside financial pressures, and by its aggressive editorial page policies.

The going was difficult at first, however. There was a chronic shortage of pennies in circulation, so Stone had to import pennies for Chicago banks to handle and promoted "99-cent sales" in stores in order to put a sufficient number of pennies in Chicagoans' pockets to sell his papers. In the first year a young Chicago financier, Victor F. Lawson, took over the business managership of the paper and two-thirds of the stock. But by 1878 the *Daily News* had bought out the *Post and Mail,* obtaining its Associated Press news rights. A morning edition, eventually named the *Record,* was begun in 1881, and by 1885 the combined circulation had passed the 100,000 mark. When Stone sold his interest to Lawson in 1888 for $350,000, only Pulitzer's *New York World* had a larger circulation among American newspapers than the *Daily News'* 200,000.

The editorial staff which Stone had built was a famous one: Eugene Field as a columnist, Slason Thompson as an editorial writer, George Harvey, George Ade, and Finley Peter Dunne (Mr. Dooley) as young reporters; literary figures, scientists, and professors such as Chicago's James Laurence Laughlin and Wisconsin's Richard T. Ely as special contributors. Lawson continued the same type of leadership until his death in 1925; Stone comes into the story again as the general manager and builder of the modern Associated Press.

Rivaling the *Daily News* as an exponent of the new order in journalism was the *Herald,* founded by James W. Scott in 1881 as a low-priced, liberal-independent morning paper. Scott had difficulties providing sufficient capitalization for his expanding paper, but it quickly won the runner-up position to the *Daily News* in circulation. The ambitious Scott followed William M. Singerly of the *Philadelphia Record* as the second president of the newly formed American Newspaper Publishers Association, serving from 1889 to 1895. With his business associates, he founded the *Evening Post* in

1890 and in 1895 he consolidated the older *Times* (1854) with the *Herald* as the *Times-Herald*.[11] At this moment of glory, Scott died and his papers passed into less talented hands.

Taking his place with Scripps and Stone as one of the great figures in this midwestern newspaper revolution was William Rockhill Nelson, founder of the *Kansas City Star*. Nelson had been a lawyer and a building contractor before buying into a Fort Wayne, Indiana, newspaper in 1879. But by the time he appeared in Kansas City in the fall of 1880 he was ready to follow the pattern of the times. He and his editors created a small, two-cent evening newspaper, well written and filled with entertaining material as well as news, and possessed of the crusading urge. Notably, however, the *Star* shunned sensational treatment of the news in use of headlines and illustrations.

One other difference stands out strongly. Unlike the other great figures of journalism before him, Nelson was not a writer. He believed that the reporter was the heart of the newspaper, and had seven of them on his initial staff, and he sought the best news editors and editorial writers. And he was constantly a part of the news, editorial, and business activities of the *Star,* but only as the publisher who guided the actions and writing of his staff. If he had something to say, as he usually did, he told it to others who put the ideas into the printed page. One of Nelson's biographers ascribes the reasons for the development of the *Star's* sparkling qualities in this fashion:

> Next to Nelson, but always through Nelson's triumphant spirit, it was the work of Nelson's editors and their staff of inspired reporters and editorial writers. Possibly Nelson's greatest genius lay in his ability to select editorial talent, to exploit it by giving it freedom, and to cherish its flowering, both by positive encouragement to expression and avoidance of negative rules of suppression. . . . By adhering to this policy, Nelson succeeded in exploiting the ablest men and gaining their loyalty despite a salary and wage scale which was niggardly.[12]

---

[11] The *Times*, under editor Wilbur F. Storey, had become known for its shocking sensationalism. Its most famous headline, over an 1875 story of the hanging of four repentant murderers, read "Jerked to Jesus."

[12] Charles E. Rogers, "William Rockhill Nelson and His Editors of the *Star*," *Journalism Quarterly*, XXVI (March 1949), p. 15. The article is based upon *William Rockhill Nelson: Independent Editor and Crusading Liberal* (Ph.D. thesis, University of Minnesota, 1948).

Nelson had great co-workers, such as managing editor Thomas W. Johnston and associate editor James B. Runnion (a former managing editor of the *Chicago Tribune*). The staff was blessed with a succession of young men willing to be "exploited" for the glory of being a *Kansas City Star* man: William Allen White, of *Emporia Gazette* fame; Eugene C. Pulliam, later publisher of the *Indianapolis Star;* Frank L. Martin, who became dean of the University of Missouri School of Journalism; and in later years, editor Wesley Stout of the *Saturday Evening Post,* columnist Raymond Clapper, and writers Ernest Hemingway and Russel Crouse. But for all their contributions, the personality of the *Star* was that given it by Nelson. When he died in 1915, the institution which he had built continued without a quiver.

Kansas City was a rough, growing town of little beauty when Nelson came in 1880. It was the gateway to the plains, and the receiving point for western cattle. Half-built, cursed with the usual political corruption and vice of the utilitarian America of the 1880's, it offered a great chance for a strong editor. Nelson was that: a big man, with massive face and head, stubborn qualities of independence, and an air of dignity which gave him the title of colonel. William Allen White, writing about him the year he died, commented: "Not that he was ever a colonel of anything; he was just coloneliferous." [13]

Nelson gave Kansas City what he thought it needed, through his relentless crusades for big and little things. He fought for cheap and efficient public transportation, bringing cable cars to the city's hills. He battled against politicians and gamblers. He campaigned for years to establish Kansas City's famous parks and boulevards, then himself built model homes along the boulevards, and saw that those who lived in them planted trees and flowers. The *Star* helped to inaugurate the commission form of government in the city, and by its espousal of progressive reform in government, spread the doctrine throughout its circulation area in the Missouri Valley.

Kansas City and the state of Kansas were captured by 1890, and before Nelson's death the *Star*'s circulation hit 170,000. The subscription price was ten cents a week at the start, but even after a Sunday edition had been added and the morning *Times* (1868) had

[13] William Allen White, "The Man Who Made the Star," *Collier's*, LV (June 26, 1915), p. 12.

sold out to Nelson in 1901, the price for morning, evening, and Sunday editions remained at a dime. A weekly edition, selling for 25 cents a year, climbed to 150,000 circulation. The price formula, plus the *Star's* intensive coverage of its area and its human interest and literary qualities, made the paper invulnerable to the attacks of competitors who tried to win by using the sensational techniques which Nelson shunned.[14]

Characterizations of Nelson are sometimes seemingly contradictory. To William Allen White he was both "coloneliferous" and "a big, laughing, fat, goodnatured, rollicking, haw-hawing person who loved a drink, a steak, a story, and a fight." He was niggardly in paying salaries, yet he spent large sums in courts of law to defend the victories won in his crusades, and practiced many private charities. He inspired his men to work and write as they had never done before, yet one of his editors described him as a fighter, a hater, and a despot who loved power and used it arbitrarily. He did not write himself, but he would get up in the middle of the night to reread the columns of the *Star* and glory in its triumphs. In politics he supported Democrats and Republicans alternately—Grover Cleveland, Theodore Roosevelt, Woodrow Wilson. But this was no contradiction; the strong editor admired the strong men in political life, and his newspaper was following the main currents of American life.

In other midwestern cities, changes in newspaper fortunes were in the air. Milwaukee's several dailies greeted a new competitor in 1882, Lucius W. Nieman and his *Milwaukee Journal*, which at once began to show some of the zeal which drove all its competitors, except the morning *Sentinel* (1837), to cover in the next 60 years. In Minneapolis another *Journal* began its career as a leading evening newspaper in 1878, while William J. Murphy gave the morning *Tribune* (1867) new life in the 1890's. St. Paul's *Pioneer Press* (1849), run by the distinguished team of editor Joseph A. Wheelock and manager Frederick Driscoll, found competition in the evening *Dispatch* (1868). Another aggressive evening newspaper was the *Indianapolis News* (1869).

But it was in St. Louis that the climax was reached. The river city long had been a newspaper center. The *Missouri Republican*

---

[14] Two of the challengers were Scripps with his *Kansas City World* (1897) and the Denver team of Bonfils and Tammen, who operated the *Kansas City Post* from 1909 to 1922. Neither paper survived.

(1808), which became the *St. Louis Republic* in 1888; the *Missouri Democrat* (1852), and Carl Schurz' German language *Westliche Post* (1857) were leading papers. The first shock was the arrival of J. B. McCullagh from Chicago, and his consolidation of the newly founded *Morning Globe* with the *Missouri Democrat* to start the *Globe-Democrat* on its way in 1875. The great event was the appearance of Joseph Pulitzer, a penniless immigrant who within ten years built the *St. Louis Post-Dispatch* and then turned to startle the publishing world with his *New York World*. All around him in America, a new daily newspaper was developing in keeping with the changed character of the national life, but Joseph Pulitzer by his spectacular genius became the recognized leader of the "new journalism." His story becomes the story of the emergence of the modern newspaper.

ANNOTATED BIBLIOGRAPHY

Books:

Aaron, Daniel, *Men of Good Hope: A Story of American Progressives.* New York: Oxford University Press, 1951. Studies, among others, Henry George, Edward Bellamy, Henry Demarest Lloyd, Thorstein Veblen, William Dean Howells, and Theodore Roosevelt.

Adams, Henry, *The Education of Henry Adams.* Boston: Houghton Mifflin Company, 1918. A classic personal reaction to a changing society.

Beard, Charles A. and Mary R., *The Rise of American Civilization.* New York: The Macmillan Company, 1930. The chapter in Vol. II, "The Second American Revolution," is the best interpretation of the rise of industry in the Civil War and postwar periods.

Cochran, Thomas C. and William Miller, *The Age of Enterprise.* New York: The Macmillan Company, 1943. A balanced portrayal of industrial and financial expansion from 1800 to 1930.

Commager, Henry Steele, *The American Mind.* New Haven: Yale University Press, 1950. A provocative and sweeping introduction to intellectual and social trends since the 1880's. It carries the reader past the uncompleted closing of Vernon L. Parrington's *Main Currents in American Thought.*

Dorfman, Joseph, *Thorstein Veblen and His America.* New York: The Viking Press, 1934. A study of rebellion against the rugged individualists and their economic thinking.

Faulkner, Harold U., *American Economic History.* New York: Harper & Brothers, 1954. Standard one-volume college textbook.

Goldman, Eric F., *Rendezvous with Destiny: A History of Modern Amer-

ican Reform. New York: Alfred A. Knopf, Inc., 1952. An interpretive synthesis which traces the tradition of dissent from post-Civil War years to the times of the Fair Deal.

Hart, Jim Allee, *A History of the St. Louis Globe-Democrat.* Columbia: University of Missouri Press, 1961. The story of founder J. B. McCullagh and of the paper, within a social framework.

Hofstadter, Richard, *Social Darwinism in American Thought, 1860-1915.* Philadelphia: University of Pennsylvania Press, 1955. A harshly critical study.

Johnson, Icie F., *William Rockhill Nelson and the Kansas City Star.* Kansas City: Burton Publishing Company, 1935. The best published study of Nelson.

Mott, Frank Luther, *A History of American Magazines.* Vol. II, 1850-1865; Vol. III, 1865-1885; Vol. IV, 1885-1905. Cambridge: Harvard University Press, 1938-57. The continuation of Professor Mott's authoritative study. Vol. V, 1905-1930, is projected.

Nixon, Raymond B., *Henry W. Grady: Spokesman of the New South.* New York: Alfred A. Knopf, Inc., 1943. The definitive biography of a leading southern editor, with emphasis upon his contributions as a newsman in stimulating the rise of the "new journalism."

North, Simeon N. D., *History and Present Condition of the Newspaper and Periodical Press of the United States.* Washington: Government Printing Office, 1884. Published as a part of the 1880 census; valuable particularly for its picture of the press in that year.

Paxson, Frederic L., *History of the American Frontier.* Boston: Houghton Mifflin Company, 1924. Records the passing of the frontier by 1893.

Schlesinger, Arthur M., *The Rise of the City, 1878-1898,* A History of American Life, Vol. X. New York: The Macmillan Company, 1932. The best social history of a crucial period. See Ida M. Tarbell, below, for reference to companion volume.

Sharpe, Ernest, *G. B. Dealey of the Dallas News.* New York: Henry Holt and Company, 1955. A favorable biography; covers to 1946.

Stone, Melville E., *Fifty Years a Journalist.* Garden City: Doubleday, Page & Company, 1921. The first portion deals with Stone's Chicago newspaper career and the *Daily News;* the latter portion with the rise of the Associated Press. An excerpt on the founding of the *Daily News* is reprinted in Mott and Casey, eds., *Interpretations of Journalism* (New York: F. S. Crofts & Company, 1937).

Tarbell, Ida M., *The Nationalizing of Business, 1878-1898,* A History of American Life, Vol. IX. New York: The Macmillan Company, 1936.

U. S. Department of Commerce, *Historical Statistics of the United States, 1789-1945.* Washington, D. C.: U. S. Government Printing Office, 1949.

Ware, Norman J., *The Labor Movement in the United States, 1860-1895.* New York: D. Appleton and Company, 1929. More compact than the massive history of labor by John R. Commons and associates, this book emphasizes the Knights of Labor. See also Lloyd Ulman, *The Rise of the National Trade Union* (Cambridge: Harvard University Press, 1955), and autobiographies of Powderly and Gompers.

Webb, Walter P., *The Great Plains.* Boston: Ginn & Company, 1931. A classic study in the Turner frontier theory tradition.

Young, John P., *Journalism in California.* San Francisco: Chronicle Publishing Company, 1913. Principally a history of the *San Francisco Chronicle*, consistently one of the West's leading newspapers.

Periodicals and Monographs:

"Fifty Years of Harper's Magazine," *Harper's,* C (May 1900), 947.

Irwin, Will, "The Power of the Press," *Collier's,* XLVI (January 21, 1911), 15. The first article in Irwin's "The American Newspaper" series, discussing the birth of modern journalism and such publishers as William Rockhill Nelson of the *Kansas City Star* and Harrison Gray Otis of the *Los Angeles Times.*

Mott, Frank Luther, "Fifty Years of Life: The Story of a Satirical Weekly," *Journalism Quarterly,* XXV (September 1948), 224.

Nixon, Raymond B., "Henry W. Grady, Reporter: A Reinterpretation," *Journalism Quarterly,* XII (December 1935), 341. Reprinted in Ford and Emery, *Highlights in the History of the American Press.*

Rogers, Charles E., "William Rockhill Nelson and His Editors of the Star," *Journalism Quarterly,* XXVI (March 1949), 15. Based upon the author's *William Rockhill Nelson: Independent Editor and Crusading Liberal* (Ph.D. thesis, University of Minnesota, 1948).

Rosser, J. E., "Dealey of the News," *Southwest Review,* Autumn 1946, p. 327. Also see obituary story, "George Dealey Dies at 86" in *Editor & Publisher,* LXXIX (March 2, 1946), 8, for additional material on the publisher of the *Dallas News.*

White, William Allen, "The Man Who Made the Star," *Collier's,* LV (June 26, 1915), 12. A portrait of William Rockhill Nelson by the editor of the *Emporia Gazette.* Reprinted in Ford and Emery, *Highlights in the History of the American Press.*

White, Z. L., "Western Journalism," *Harper's,* LXXVII (October 1888), 678. A contemporary picture of Ohio journalism, including the Scripps enterprises, and journalism farther west.

Chapter **17**

THE NEW JOURNALISM

> . . . every issue of the paper presents an oppor-
> tunity and a duty to say something courageous and
> true; to rise above the mediocre and conventional;
> to say something that will command the respect of
> the intelligent, the educated, the independent part
> of the community; to rise above fear of partisan-
> ship and fear of popular prejudice.
>
> —Joseph Pulitzer

JOSEPH PULITZER was one of those many immigrants who
helped to build the new America of the post-Civil War period. In
so doing, he both gave and received: the two great newspapers
which he established won for him the honor of being named as the
leading American editor of modern times,[1] and they also built for
him a fortune appraised at his death at nearly 20 million dollars,
one of the largest ever accumulated in the newspaper field.

The story of Joseph Pulitzer's journalistic success climaxes the
story of the emergence of the modern newspaper born of the new
national environment. Pulitzer made his own contributions to the
creation of the "New Journalism," but more important, he achieved
his leadership by being receptive to the ideas of others. His immense
energy and his highly developed journalistic sense enabled him to
adapt and to develop in his own way the publishing concepts and

[1] In a poll of American editors conducted by *Editor & Publisher* in 1934.

techniques of his time, and to satisfy his passionate desire to win unquestioned recognition as the builder of the brilliant staff and the complex mechanism of a great modern newspaper. This was a notable achievement, but it alone was not enough to win him his reputation as the most useful and worthy American editor in the estimate of his craft. His true greatness lay in his high-minded conception of a newspaper's purpose, particularly in exercising editorial leadership, and in the way in which he made that conception live in his newspapers.

Pulitzer was born in Hungary in 1847. His father was Magyar-Jewish, his mother Austro-German. At 17, after receiving a good private school education, he ran away from home to join an army. But he had weak eyesight and an unmilitary look which brought rejections from the Austrian army and the French Foreign Legion. Less particular, however, was an American agent who was seeking Europeans who would volunteer for the Union Army in that Civil War year of 1864. The agent enlisted Pulitzer, who became a member of the Lincoln cavalry.

Pulitzer's experiences with the army were all unfortunate. One of his biographers describes the youthful Pulitzer as clearly unfitted for soldierly life.[2] He was tall and thin, with long, thick black hair, a large head, and an over-sized nose. His complexion was pink, his hands were those of an artist. Ungainly in appearance and awkward in movement, he seemed to be the ideal subject for the practical jokes of his fellow men. His only saving grace was that his eyes revealed a searching intelligence. He added to his troubles by continually asking questions, trying to find the reasons for army practices. These were admirable qualities for a newspaperman, but not for a recruit.

When the war ended, without his seeing real action, Pulitzer found himself in New York, virtually penniless, and handicapped by language difficulties in the competition for jobs. He tried to ship out on a whaler, but was turned down. He tried the newspapers on Park Row, but since he spoke only a little English along with his German and French, he was rejected. Eventually he decided that he would go to an inland city containing few immigrants, where he would

[2] Joseph W. Barrett, *Joseph Pulitzer and His World* (New York: Vanguard Press, Inc., 1941), pp. 3-4.

by necessity improve his command of English. He asked his German acquaintances, and they played a final practical joke on him by sending him to St. Louis, a center of the German-speaking population.

In St. Louis he first fired a steamboat boiler, then became a hostler for 16 army mules. Most of his engagements were short; the mule-tending lasted two days. He became successively a river stevedore, a livery stable tender, and a waiter until he plopped a beefsteak upon a customer's head. Finally he won a position as assistant bookkeeper in a lumberyard, seemingly the measure of his ability.

But his restlessness, his tremendously inquisitive nature, and his unbounded energy led him upward. At the public library he was reading, learning, and studying for admission to the bar. In 1867 he became an American citizen. About the same time he became friendly with Carl Schurz, then the liberal editor of the leading German-language daily, the *Westliche Post*. When the *Post* needed a new reporter in 1868, the city editor interviewed two candidates and chose Pulitzer because he thought the other candidate the more likely threat to the city editor's job security.

Now Pulitzer was at home in his work. Everything was his meat—beat reporting, politics, civic news, the important and the trivia, the obvious and the hidden news. He worked from 10 a.m. to 2 a.m. writing columns of copy each day. Other reporters laughed at his mannerisms, but after Pulitzer had surpassed them with his incredible reporting zeal, the laughter stopped.

One more practical joke helped to shape the Pulitzer career. He was nominated as the Republican candidate for the Missouri State Assembly in what was assumed to be a certain Democratic district. But Pulitzer made a house-to-house campaign and won the election. At the capitol, he became legislative correspondent for the *Westliche Post*.

Pulitzer's growing interest in public affairs led him to join with Schurz in the liberal Republican movement of 1872, and he stumped the German-speaking areas of Missouri for the presidential candidate, Horace Greeley. When the liberal Republican movement collapsed in defeat, Pulitzer became a Democrat. He also became a part owner of the *Westliche Post*, some of whose stockholders sold out cheaply because they thought the Greeley campaign had ruined the paper. But Pulitzer exhibited too much aggressiveness to suit Schurz and Dr. Emil Preetorius, the principal owners, and they soon paid him $30,000 to give up his stock.

The next year, 1874, Pulitzer again showed his financial ability by purchasing a mediocre St. Louis paper whose only virtue was an exclusive membership in the Associated Press of the time. Pulitzer foresaw that Joseph B. McCullagh, the highly qualified Chicago newspaperman who had entered the St. Louis morning field, would need the press association membership for his new *Globe-Democrat*. McCullagh did, and the price paid to Pulitzer was $20,000.

Again Pulitzer left St. Louis newspaper work. During the next few years he visited Europe four times, was married, and was admitted to the District of Columbia Bar. He took the stump for Samuel J. Tilden, the 1876 Democratic presidential nominee, and reported for Dana's *New York Sun* on the activities of the electoral commission which decided that disputed election in favor of Rutherford B. Hayes. His command of the English language was now excellent, and he had greatly increased his knowledge of his adopted country. Then, in 1878, he returned to St. Louis journalism.

Pulitzer's destiny now was to be fulfilled. The *Dispatch*, founded in 1864 and now bankrupt, was on the block at a sheriff's sale. Pulitzer won it with a $2,500 bid on December 9, 1878, again obtaining as his principal prize an Associated Press membership. Within three days he had used the AP franchise to effect a combination with the *Post*, started by John A. Dillon in 1875 (Dillon lasted for a year as a partner but remained as a Pulitzer associate).

Thus was born the *Post-Dispatch*, a newspaper which was to become one of the country's greatest in the next 75 years. Almost immediately Pulitzer's newspaper sense began to produce a financial reward, and by 1881 the *Post-Dispatch* was the leading evening paper in St. Louis, netting $45,000 a year and rivaling the powerful morning *Globe-Democrat*.

Behind this achievement lay the talents of the editor-publisher. Pulitzer in his early thirties was a commanding figure: six feet two inches tall, thin and erect in stature, now wearing a short red beard. He was an ambitious and self-contained man, confident of his powers, in whom were combined intellectual capacity and a consuming energy. He had the artist's love for good music and good

eph Pulitzer, founder of the *St. Louis Post-Dispatch*, and great editor of the *New York World*.
From the portrait by John S. Sargent.

Edward Wyllis Scripps, founder of "people's papers" in industrial cities, pictured aboard yacht near the close of his career.

writing; he had the scholar's interest in economic, political, and social trends. But above all, he had a driving passion for accomplishment. His maturing facial features and his flashing eyes expressed the Pulitzer will; those who met him felt the full force of his nervous energy and his determination. He was not easily approachable and held even close associates at a distance, but in his own way he showed high appreciation for the work of men who measured up to his exacting standards for newspaper achievement.

Many capable newsmen were to serve under the Pulitzer banner in the years ahead, but one of the most influential was the right-hand man of these early years, John A. Cockerill. Cockerill came to the *Post-Dispatch* as managing editor in 1880, when the burden of supervising the expanding paper forced Pulitzer to find an able associate. Cockerill had none of Pulitzer's artistic qualities; he was a hard-fighting extrovert who carried the title of "Colonel." But he was a good news executive who had been trained in the journalism of Cincinnati, Columbus, Washington, and Baltimore. He had served as a war correspondent during the Russo-Turkish War of 1877-78 and was managing editor of the *Baltimore Gazette* when Pulitzer discovered him. Upon the hard-working and pugnacious Cockerill fell much of the responsibility for carrying out Pulitzer's commands, and he responded ably. He also brought with him a keen sense of newspaper methods, which was to serve Pulitzer well for the next 10 critical years.

But it was Pulitzer who imparted to the *Post-Dispatch* its distinctive spirit. His statement of policies for the new paper contains memorable words:

> The *Post and Dispatch* will serve no party but the people; be no organ of Republicanism, but the organ of truth; will follow no causes but its conclusions; will not support the "Administration," but criticise it; will oppose all frauds and shams wherever and whatever they are; will advocate principles and ideas rather than prejudices and partisanship. . . .[3]

Even more memorable are the words written by a more mature Pulitzer in 1907, near the end of his career, which have become the *Post-Dispatch* platform, printed on the editorial page:

[3] As quoted in Don C. Seitz, *Joseph Pulitzer: His Life and Letters* (New York: Simon and Schuster, Inc., 1924), p. 101. The name of the paper was soon changed to the *Post-Dispatch*.

I know that my retirement will make no difference in its cardinal principles; that it will always fight for progress and reform, never tolerate injustice or corruption, always fight demagogues of all parties, never belong to any party, always oppose privileged classes and public plunderers, never lack sympathy with the poor, always remain devoted to the public welfare, never be satisfied with merely printing news, always be drastically independent, never be afraid to attack wrong, whether by predatory plutocracy or predatory poverty.

"Never be satisfied with merely printing news" was a cardinal Pulitzer policy. By that phrase was meant the kind of reporting Pulitzer himself had done, getting more than surface news or that which came by itself to the city room. It meant, too, the kind of crusading in the public interest which Pulitzer demanded when he wrote to an editor: "Never drop a big thing until you have gone to the bottom of it. Continuity! Continuity! Continuity until the subject is really finished." [4]

Crusading of this type, through both news and editorial columns, was a distinctive Pulitzer contribution to the "new journalism." For although crusading was a common characteristic of leading contemporary papers, the impact of the Pulitzer-inspired crusade was heightened both by the intensity of the effort and by the techniques employed in writing and in news display. In its first years the *Post-Dispatch* printed lists of wealthy tax-dodgers in the city; it fought the granting of an extortionate franchise to a public utility corporation; it warred constantly for three years to break up a police-protected gambling ring; and it poured editorial fire on crooked politicians.

At the same time the staff was taught to cover the news of the city incessantly, and to look for both the significant news and the "original, distinctive, dramatic, romantic, thrilling, unique, curious, quaint, humorous, odd, apt to be talked about" news. Pulitzer considered the day a loss if his newspaper did not have one distinctive feature—a crusade, public service, or big exclusive story.

Post-Dispatch men also came to know the famous Pulitzer dictum: "Accuracy! Accuracy!! Accuracy!!!" This meant not only avoiding simple errors, but also the half-truths and inadequate statements of sloppy reporting. Another Pulitzer command which became familiar was: "Terseness! Intelligent, not stupid, condensation." As the years

[4] As quoted in *The Story of the St. Louis Post-Dispatch* (St. Louis: Pulitzer Publishing Company, 1949), p. 3.

went by, Pulitzer news executives and newsmen received thousands of reminders from their publisher-editor on these subjects, and many proddings to do a full job of covering the news. An example of a Pulitzer memo on how to write a story is this one, sent to one of his New York editors in the last year of his life:

> Apropos of enclosed clipping from the London *Times* showing that there were 185 homicides in New York during 1910, this would make a good magazine feature article if properly worked up. Pick out the most interesting cases. What were these homicides? Who committed them? What was the motive? Give a table of motives, of social rank, of age, of nationality, etc. But print the facts more reliably, more strikingly than would the magazines. But don't print it from the standpoint of mere sensationalism, but rather from the moral point of view. It should be a thoughtful article with a great moral to it. Compare the figure with Paris, and with London, and with other great European cities. Allude also to the administration of justice and the methods of dealing with murder cases in the different countries, with statistics of indictments, convictions, executions and failure to punish or to solve murder mysteries.[5]

There is no record of how well the editor succeeded.

In every field of newspaper publishing, Pulitzer, Cockerill, and their associates on the *Post-Dispatch* were learning the lessons they were soon to apply in New York. There were many mistakes, many stories and editorials falling short of the Pulitzer goals. But there were successes, for as the *World* commented in 1890, "The foundation of the *New York World* was laid in St. Louis. . . . The battle of new ideas and new theories of journalism was fought there under the banner of the *Post-Dispatch*." [6] The *World* might have added that the editors of the *Post-Dispatch* were watching and learning from the other new midwestern papers: Nelson's *Kansas City Star*, Stone's *Chicago Daily News*, Scripps' *Cleveland Press*, McCullagh's rival *Globe-Democrat*—just as they in turn were watching Pulitzer.

By 1883 Pulitzer was a 36-year-old physical wreck. His poor eyesight was failing; his nerves were badly impaired by incessant work. Matters had not been helped when Cockerill shot and killed a prominent St. Louis attorney whom the *Post-Dispatch* had attacked in its columns. Cockerill successfully pleaded self-defense, but public indignation hurt the paper. Discouraged by this turn of events,

---

[5] As quoted in Seitz, *Joseph Pulitzer*, p. 423.
[6] As quoted in Willard G. Bleyer, *Main Currents in the History of American Journalism* (Boston: Houghton Mifflin Company, 1927), p. 325.

Pulitzer was enroute to Europe for a long vacation in May, 1883, when he heard in New York that the *World* was for sale.

Founded in 1860, the *World* had been well-edited by Manton Marble as a Democratic morning newspaper, but had suffered financial reverses. Sale of the paper in 1879 to the unscrupulous financier, Jay Gould, had further damaged its prestige, and the *World* was losing $40,000 a year. Gould offered to sell for what he claimed he had in the paper—$346,000.

The situation looked unpromising. The *World* had but 15,000 circulation for its two-cent, eight-page paper. Its more powerful morning rivals were Bennett's *Herald*, printing from 12 to 16 pages at three cents a copy; Dana's *Sun*, still publishing but four pages for two cents; Whitelaw Reid's *Tribune* and George Jones' *Times*, both selling at four cents for eight pages. There was a personal factor involved, however. Joseph Pulitzer's younger brother, Albert, also had come to the United States, and after working as a newspaperman had started the *Morning Journal* in New York in 1882 with $25,000 capital. It was catching on as a breezy, one-cent paper (he eventually sold it for a million dollars). The two brothers had little to do with each other, and Albert's successful gamble in New York journalism may have stimulated the ailing Joseph to make his own bid.

The deal with Gould was closed on May 9, 1883, and Pulitzer paid the first installment on the price of the *World* from *Post-Dispatch* profits. To Gould's surprise the remaining installments were paid from the profits of the *World*.

Pulitzer issued the first edition of the *World* under his editorship May 11. He fired some of the old editors; stole his brother's managing editor, a man who soon proved to be incompetent; wired St. Louis for two good *Post-Dispatch* men; changed the nameplate and the format; and sat down to edit the first issue.

His lead story was an account of a million dollar storm in New Jersey. Other front page features were an interview with a condemned slayer, the story of a Wall Street plunger, a Pittsburgh hanging, a riot in Haiti, and the sad story of a wronged servant girl. Then Pulitzer ordered a press run of 22,000 copies and sold out by noon. Only the *Herald* had matched him in sensational coverage.

Next day the *World* blushingly admitted that it was the talk of the town. It took two columns to report the praises of New Yorkers, from the mayor to shop girls. In the upper corners of page one, alongside the short nameplate, what became known as "ears" appeared, expounding the virtues of the *World*. Here was exhibited another important factor in the Pulitzer formula—aggressive promotion of the newspaper's qualities. Within a week the *World* had found its first popular cause to promote: that the Brooklyn Bridge, just being opened as one of the new wonders of the world, should be a free bridge.

But all was not sensation and promotion. The *World* was presenting good news coverage, and it was establishing its new editorial policies. In a signed statement in his first issue Pulitzer said:

> There is room in this great and growing city for a journal that is not only cheap but bright, not only bright but large, not only large but truly Democratic—dedicated to the cause of the people rather than that of the purse-potentates—devoted more to the news of the New than the Old World—that will expose all fraud and sham, fight all public evils and abuses—that will serve and battle for the people with earnest sincerity.[7]

A concise ten-point program soon appeared on the editorial page: tax luxuries; tax inheritances; tax large incomes; tax monopolies; tax the privileged corporations; a tariff for revenue; reform the civil service; punish corrupt office-holders; punish vote-buying; punish employers who coerce their employees in elections.

To cap his fighting entry into New York, Pulitzer published a strongly worded editorial denouncing the aristocracy of Park Avenue, the aristocracy of the moneyed classes, and those who he said were aping foreign nobility. The *World*, he declared, believed in the aristocracy of labor, the aristocracy of brains and honor, the aristocracy of virtue. The editorial ended: "Money alone makes no aristocrats." To those who worshiped the successful dollar-chaser, this was unbelievable heresy. But it was delightful reading for many New Yorkers who resented the excesses of economic individualism and who, like Pulitzer, were believers in the necessity for economic and social reform.

Pulitzer's liberal political and social stands editorially were to pay handsome circulation dividends in 1884, when the *World* supported Grover Cleveland, Democratic governor of New York, for the presidency against the conservative Republican champion, James G.

[7] *New York World*, May 11, 1883.

Blaine. Dana's *Sun,* which attacked both major party candidates and supported the discredited third party candidate, Benjamin Butler, lost a good share of its circulation to the hard-hitting *World,* which in both editorial spirit and news appeal was directing its attention to the mass of New York residents. Pulitzer himself was elected to Congress that year, but soon abandoned this political career.

Much of the success of the news policy is credited to Cockerill, the *Post-Dispatch* managing editor who had now become managing editor of the *World.* Cockerill was adept in both playing up human interest stories and in maintaining a solid presentation of significant local, national, and international news; for despite the attention given to sensational material, the *World* tried to give its readers full coverage of the day's events.

Typographically, the new *World* was using smaller and lighter type faces than its predecessor. But some of the headlines printed during the first month spoke for themselves: "Death Rides the Blast," "Love and Cold Poison," "All for a Woman's Love," "A Heroine or a Criminal?" "Screaming for Mercy," "A Bride but not a Wife," "The Wall Street Terror," "Terrible Times in Troy," "Little Lotta's Lovers," "Baptized in Blood." [8] Alliteration was frequent; so were sex, conflict, and crime.

Use of illustrations also contributed to the success of the *World.* Cockerill found that the use of woodcuts spurred circulation, and when they were omitted because Pulitzer disliked their crude appearance, circulation slumped. Back went the woodcuts along with line drawings, particularly as illustrations for feature articles in the *Sunday World.* Valerian Gribayédoff began to draw the likenesses of prominent New Yorkers in early 1884, and cartoonist Walt McDougall did a front page series of political drawings to further the presidential candidacy of Cleveland. The *Journalist,* newspaper trade publication, asserted in 1885: "It is the woodcuts that give the *World* its unparalleled circulation." [9]

And unparalleled circulation it was. The average daily circulation of the *World* doubled during the first three months of Pulitzer's editorship. Other New York papers cut their prices to meet the threat, and the *Herald* even resorted to advertising itself in the

[8] As quoted in Bleyer, *Main Currents in the History of American Journalism,* p. 328.
[9] *Journalist,* August 22, 1885.

World's pages. But the *Herald,* in cutting its price, got into a war with newsstand dealers who were given smaller commissions, and thus further benefited the newcomer.

Daily circulation of the *World* at the end of a year was more than 60,000—a fourfold increase. Four months later the *Sunday World* hit the 100,000 mark, and Pulitzer's promotion men presented each employee with a tall silk hat and fired a hundred cannon shots in City Hall Park by way of celebration. When in 1887 the 250,000 figure was reached by the *World,* a silver medal was struck off in honor of America's largest newspaper circulation.

. Most importantly, by the end of 1884 the *World* had passed the *Herald* as the leader in number of advertising columns printed, partly because of its low rate in relation to circulation figures and partly because of the city's interest in the new paper. The size of the newspaper jumped to 12 or 14 pages daily and 36-44 pages on Sunday. As expenses mounted, advertising rates were raised, but the sale price remained at two cents. Within three years the *World* had become the talk, not only of New York, but of the country's newspaper fraternity. For Joseph Pulitzer's brash new paper had broken every publishing record in America and its annual profit was at the half million dollar mark.

What had Pulitzer done? First of all, he had recognized the characteristics of his potential audience. The population of New York City was increasing by 50 per cent during the 1880's, and Pulitzer worked to attract the attention of the newcomers to his newspaper. As an immigrant himself, he was alive to the fact that four out of five of the city's residents were either foreign-born or children of foreign-born parents. And as one who was aware of the social and economic trends of his time, he understood the desire of his readers for effective leadership reflecting progressive attitudes, as well as for entertainment.

Therefore he had enlivened the *World's* significant news coverage to satisfy one set of changing conditions, and he had achieved sensationalism both in news content and in newspaper appearance to satisfy another trend. He had combined great promotional skill with a popular editorial aggressiveness and crusading spirit to make the mass of readers feel that the *World* was their friend. He had plowed money into the building of a competent staff of newsmen and he had kept pace with mechanical innovations. He had given the readers their money's worth in size, in solid news and editorials, in entertaining human interest stories and illustrations. And he had never let his readers forget that the *World* was a dynamic newspaper of a dynamic era.

His critics said Pulitzer had done something else that did not reflect to his credit. He had revived, they said, the sensationalism which had marked the first mass newspapers of the penny-press period of the 1830's. Sensationalism was as old as the newspaper press, but no one had depended upon its devices so much in recent years as had Pulitzer. His success encouraged imitation, and this was viewed as a disastrous trend in journalism which made Pulitzer's constructive contributions seem not worth the price.

Pulitzer's answer was that human interest and sensational stories were needed to win a large circulation and that having won the circulation he would create sound public opinion through enticing readers into the editorial columns and news stories about public affairs. He admired the work of the talented Edwin Lawrence Godkin in the *Evening Post,* although he disagreed with Godkin's economic theories, but when he was chided about the contrast between the news policies of the *Post* and the *World* he made his famous retort: "I want to talk to a nation, not to a select committee." [10]

Undoubtedly the critics were right in accusing Pulitzer of rationalizing when he presented this defense of the *World's* revival of coarse sensationalism. But they were not correct if they wrote Pulitzer off as a cynic. Pulitzer recognized the weakness of the sensational approach, and struggled much of the time to temper its uses. If he failed during conspicuous periods of his editorship, it was because of human frailty, whose consequences no editor has escaped.[11] The man who set an example for his profession in the creation of newspapers with a crusading spirit and an aggressive editorial leadership was basically high-minded in his conception of his responsibilities. This passage from a letter written by Pulitzer to

[10] James Creelman, "Joseph Pulitzer—Master Journalist," *Pearson's,* XXI (March 1909), p. 246.

[11] Indicative of that frailty was Pulitzer's admiration in particular of three publishers whose newspapers utilized sensational techniques, but did not measure up to the *World* in high-quality performance. They were William M. Singerly, *Philadelphia Record;* Charles H. Taylor, *Boston Globe,* and the British newspaper popularizer, Alfred Harmsworth, who later became Lord Northcliffe.

one of his editors in later life reflects the spirit which won for him recognition as a courageous, worthy, and effective editor:

. . . every issue of the paper presents an opportunity and a duty to say something courageous and true; to rise above the mediocre and conventional; to say something that will command the respect of the intelligent, the educated, the independent part of the community; to rise above fear of partisanship and fear of popular prejudice. I would rather have one article a day of this sort; and these ten or twenty lines might readily represent a whole day's hard work in the way of concentrated, intense thinking and revision, polish of style, weighing of words.[12]

Pulitzer's newspapers on many days fell short of attaining this high goal of journalism, but they approached it often enough to stimulate the efforts of other editors and to win their admiration.

The World did not rest upon the laurels it had won during the first three years of the Pulitzer regime. In every area of activity it continued to exploit its success. Sensational crusades were carried on against big corporations, bad tenement housing, white-slave traffic, city aldermen who accepted bribes. The paper inaugurated a series of public services—Christmas dinners for the poor, free ice for tenement dwellers in summer, a staff of 35 doctors to serve the needy, entertainments for thousands of children. Its most noted early success was a campaign to raise funds for the building of a pedestal in New York harbor on which was to be placed the Statue of Liberty. The World pointed out that the statue had been given to the people of the United States by the people of France, and it said that "the people's paper now appeals to the people to come forward and raise this money." Within five months news stories and editorials brought in the needed $100,000, mostly in nickels and dimes from 120,000 loyal World readers. Pulitzer later named his yacht the "Liberty" in honor of this campaign.

Stunts, as distinguished from useful crusades and promotions, were another World specialty. Most ambitious was the sending of Nellie Bly around the world in 1889 to see if she could beat the time suggested by Jules Verne in his fictional Around the World in Eighty Days. Nellie Bly was a by-line name for Elizabeth Cochran, a girl reporter who had brightened the pages of the World by inviting the attention of mashers and then exposing them, and by

[12] As quoted in Seitz, Joseph Pulitzer, p. 286.

Joseph Pulitzer announces the completion of the *World's* campaign to raise $100,000 for a pedestal for the Statue of Liberty. Columns three and four contain a sensational murder story, as contrast.

feigning insanity in order to write about conditions in the New York asylum. As Nellie traveled around the world by ships, trains, horses, and sampans, the *World* ran a guessing contest which drew nearly a million estimates of her elapsed time. Nellie didn't fail her newspaper; a special train brought her from San Francisco to New York with banners flying as the country applauded her time of 72 days.[13]

Expanded size of the *World* permitted its editors to enliven its pages with stunts and features and still maintain coverage of serious and significant news. A large staff of ambitious reporters covered the city in the same manner Pulitzer had blanketed St. Louis. News editors sought equally hard to get national coverage and cabled news from abroad. Gradually the coarser sensationalism of the first few years of *World* publication under Pulitzer began to disappear, although there was no letup in the demand for well-written human interest stories and for reader-pulling illustrations.

The editorial page continued its political support of the Democratic party, backing Cleveland in 1888 and 1892. Yet at the same time it exhibited its independence by opposing the local Tammany Hall machine. Labor found the *World* a solid champion in 1892 when several strikers were killed by Pinkerton guards during the bitter Homestead steel strike in Pittsburgh. The *World* splashed the story on its front pages and denounced Andrew Carnegie's plant manager, Henry Clay Frick, on its editorial pages. The frailty which stems from the responsibilities of ownership was illustrated by the aftermath of this editorial stand, however. The *World's* editorial-page chief, William H. Merrill, had placed the paper on the side of the workers while Pulitzer was absent in Europe. The publisher, hearing of the uproar and conscious of the isolated position of the *World* as one of the few newspapers to take such an extreme stand, attempted to tone down Merrill's writing. In general, however, the "people's paper" took its stand on the side of fair play and progressive reform.

Pulitzer's publishing empire was expanded in 1887 with the establishing of the *Evening World*, on the heels of Dana's decision to publish an evening edition of the *Sun*. The evening paper sold for

---

[13] Three New York newspapers repeated the stunt in 1936. H. R. Ekins of the *World-Telegram* won with a time of 18½ days, defeating Dorothy ("Nellie Bly") Kilgallen of the *Journal* and Leo Kiernan of the *Times*.

one cent, and soon outdid the morning edition in popular appeal. It never attained the distinctive character of the morning edition, however, and to newspapermen the name *World* still meant the original paper.

A new $2,500,000 home for the three *Worlds* was the next order of business. It was an impressive building, among the tallest of its time, topped with a gilded dome and filled with the newest machines of the printing arts. But before the building was finished, tragedy struck. Pulitzer had become completely blind. His nerves were shattered as well, and he was under the care of European specialists. In October, 1890, he announced his retirement from active editorship of his newspapers, and the *Herald*, thinking that it was bidding him goodby, said "We droop our colors to him."

But Pulitzer was not gone. He was to live until 1911, and he was to continue to build his personality into the newspapers. His affliction left him incapable of bearing even the slightest noise, and he went to incredible lengths to isolate himself from tormenting sounds. His associates found him infuriatingly difficult, but they also found him keenly aware of the progress of the newspapers. No matter where the blinded and bearded Pulitzer was—aboard his yacht; at Bar Harbor, Maine; or on the Mediterranean coast— he was constantly in touch with the *World* staff. Copies of each issue were read to him by young men secretaries and streams of instructions and suggestions came to the offices in the *World's* gilded dome by cable, mail, and messenger.

There were important editors and managers there in the *World* offices. Some of them in the late eighties and early nineties included Cockerill, who became editor-in-charge; William H. Merrill, who had come from the *Boston Herald* to be chief editorial writer; Ballard Smith, former managing editor of both the *Louisville Courier-Journal* and the *New York Herald*, who served as managing editor; S. S. Carvalho, ex-*Sun* newsman who was city editor of the *Evening World* and later a Pulitzer executive; Colonel Charles H. Jones, a colorful southerner who served as publisher for Pulitzer in both New York and St. Louis; George Harvey, later to become an important political figure.

Conflicts between strong-willed rivals for authority and for Pulitzer's favor were inevitable under this policy of assembling many men of high talent under the *World's* dome. But no editor or manager became too powerful or long ignored the wishes of the absent owner. Cockerill lost his place in 1891 during one of the upheavals by which Pulitzer enforced his will upon the staff. Jones, who was given complete editorial control of the *Post-Dispatch* in 1895, was forced out two years later when he flouted Pulitzer's wishes. By a constant process of seeking loyal and able assistants from among the country's newsmen, Pulitzer was able to keep the *World* steadily progressing in the manner which he had conceived, as the leading exponent of what newspapermen were calling the new journalism.

ANNOTATED BIBLIOGRAPHY

Books:

Barrett, James W., *Joseph Pulitzer and His World.* New York: Vanguard Press, Inc., 1941. A colorful, rambling story of Pulitzer and the *New York World* by the last city editor of the *World.*

Ireland, Alleyne, *Joseph Pulitzer: Reminiscences of a Secretary.* New York: Mitchell Kennerley, 1914. Reprinted as *An Adventure with a Genius,* New York: E. P. Dutton & Company, 1920. The eccentricities of the great publisher, and his struggles against physical handicaps, are recounted by a personal secretary.

Seitz, Don C., *Joseph Pulitzer: His Life and Letters.* New York: Simon and Schuster, Inc., 1924. The best Pulitzer study; others draw upon it. Written by Pulitzer's onetime business manager.

The Story of the St. Louis Post-Dispatch. St. Louis: Pulitzer Publishing Company, 1954. A booklet written by Charles G. Ross in 1928 and since revised, which recounts many of the paper's campaigns.

Periodicals and Monographs:

Brisbane, Arthur, "Joseph Pulitzer," *Cosmopolitan,* XXXIII (May 1902), 51. An intimate contemporary portrait by an editor who jumped from Pulitzer's *World* to Hearst's *Journal.*

Inglis, William, "An Intimate View of Joseph Pulitzer," *Harper's Weekly,* LV (November 11, 1911), 7. An article with considerable insight, published at time of Pulitzer's death.

Outlook, XCIX (November 11, 1911), 603 and 608, contains two estimates of Pulitzer and the *World.*

Seitz, Don C., "The Portrait of an Editor," *Atlantic Monthly,* CXXXIV (September 1924), 289. Reprinted in Ford and Emery, *Highlights in the History of the American Press.*

Chapter *18*

THE MODERN NEWSPAPER EMERGES

> The magnitude of financial operations of the
> newspaper is turning journalism upside down.
> —Lincoln Steffens (1897)

MUCH HAD HAPPENED to the nation's journalism during
the first decade of Joseph Pulitzer's New York publishing career.
He had bought the *World* in 1883 for $346,000. In the mid-nineties
it was housed in a $2,500,000 building and its estimated worth was
$10,000,000. Expenses for a year ran to some $2,000,000 and guesses
at the annual profit hovered around $1,000,000. The number of full-
time employees totaled 1,300.

This was big business. And what was happening to the *World*
was happening to other metropolitan papers, and to a lesser degree
to smaller dailies. Editorial staffs were growing in size and the quest
for the world's news was sharpening. Circulation and advertising
departments were becoming of major importance. Operating problems of these complex business institutions—mechanical innovations, labor contracts, newsprint supply—required constant attention. An examination of these changes in daily newspaper publishing
will demonstrate the fact that the modern era was at hand.

The editorial staff of the metropolitan daily newspaper had taken
recognizable modern form by 1890, in numbers and in departmentalized activities. Specialization of duties was necessary as the editing process became more complex, and as staffs grew in size. Look-

ing back at the growth of the editorial staff after the founding of the popular press of the 1830's, we can see its evolution from a one-man status to the organization of scores of newsmen who constituted the staff of the *World.*

Regularly employed reporters were rare even after the penny press had become well established in the 1840's. Newspaper editors ran what local news they encountered or had time to cover, used their telegraph news, clipped their exchanges, and printed the contributions of correspondents, such as the group who covered Congress after the mid-1820's. Some owner-editors added chief assistants, notably Horace Greeley, who employed first Henry J. Raymond and then Charles A. Dana to help him handle the news on the *New York Tribune* in the early 1840's. The chief assistants soon became known as managing editors, two of the earliest to hold that title being Dana of the *Tribune* and Frederic Hudson of the *New York Herald.* In the 1850's chief reporters emerged, as forerunners of the city editors. The *Tribune* of 1854 had 14 reporters and 10 editors, and had introduced editorial writers, literary editors, and other specialists. But these editorial staff advances were only found on leading newspapers.

Intensified reporting of the Civil War by hundreds of correspondents in the field did much to stimulate the rise of news staffs. Some of the Civil War reporters who thus demonstrated their journalistic skill rose to become editors or owners of newspapers— Murat Halstead, Whitelaw Reid, Henry Villard. Others went on to cover wars in Europe, the Indian wars on the western American plains, and other major news events at home and abroad.

George W. Smalley was an example of the new type of newsman. A graduate of Yale and of the Harvard Law School, he covered the Civil War for the *Tribune,* then reported the Franco-Prussian War and remained in Europe as London correspondent for the paper. Henry M. Stanley of the *New York Herald* covered the Civil War and the Indian wars, went to Asia and Africa as a *Herald* correspondent, and climaxed his career with his expedition to Africa in 1871 to find the missing missionary, David Livingstone. Jerome B. Stillson, another *Herald* reporter, obtained an exclusive interview with the Indian chief Sitting Bull in 1877 that filled 14 columns of the paper. John A. Cockerill, Pulitzer's ace newsman and editor, had covered the Russo-Turkish War. Again, these are examples of a limited activity, but they foreshadow the intensified reportorial achievements of the 1890's.

Emphasis increasingly centered upon the reporter. Dana and Pulitzer, as editor-publishers, prized their reporters because they themselves had handled the news. Raymond put news coverage first in his *Times,* and himself covered the Austro-Italian War. Henry W. Grady, who served as a free-lance correspondent before becoming managing editor of the *Atlanta Constitution,* did as much as any man of his times to advance the status of the newsman. Grady's leadership in advancing the art of interviewing, as a means both of gathering and interpreting the news, made it more necessary for newspapers to have larger staffs.

By the 1870's the leading metropolitan dailies had a chief editor, a managing editor or night editor in charge of the news, a city editor who directed the work of as many as two dozen reporters and selected the stories which were to run, a telegraph editor who handled the increasing volume of wire and cable news, a financial editor, literary editor, drama critic, and editorial writers. The city editor, it should be noted, was becoming a key man on the large newspaper staff.

Further specialization of editorial staff duties came with the upsurge of competition in the 1880's. The coming of the telephone in newspaper offices meant that reporters could call in with news on fast-breaking stories. Increased numbers of editions also demanded more rapid handling of local news. Before the close of the century the leg-man on the beat and the rewrite man in the office began to appear as distinct personalities on the editorial staff, although special assignment men continued to write their own stories. The rewrite men learned to use typewriters, and they also began to favor the summary lead as a means of condensing stories. The literary stylists and the writers of rambling chronological stories were still numerous, however.

Deskmen who specialized in selecting and condensing news, and in writing headlines in the long and involved style of the day, became necessary assistants to the chief editors of newspapers whose volume of news was becoming greater each year. Growth of Sunday papers meant addition of special Sunday staffs for the major newspapers, along with cartoonists and artists.

Sports news, which had been covered since the 1830's in fairly good fashion, was a natural feature for a mass-circulated newspaper. One of Pulitzer's first acts on the *World* was to organize a separate sports department. Horse racing, prize fighting, international yacht racing, and baseball were attracting widespread popular interest, and specialized writers began to appear in each field.[1] Although regular sports pages did not appear until after the turn of the century, several columns of sports stories were run in big newspapers by 1890, and sports departments were on their way toward gaining their modern status. In the next few years bicycle racing was added to their coverage, and football became more important. And when the Corbett-Fitzsimmons heavyweight title fight was staged in Nevada in 1897, dozens of writers turned up from all parts of the country to herald the arrival of the sports "gigantic."

A rapid influx of women staff members was another development of the 1880's. Women were entering into the business offices of America as the industrial boom brought them new opportunities; they were working in the expanding retail stores; they were graduating from women's colleges and coeducational universities; they were winning some battles for recognition of women's rights. There had been women journalists of note before the Civil War—Margaret Fuller of the *New York Tribune*, for example, and Jane Grey Swisshelm as a Washington correspondent and newspaper editor—and the *New York Sun* had employed Mrs. Emily Verdery Bettey as a general reporter as early as 1868. Now in the late 1880's several hundred women were in newspaper work and some of them became leading reporters and feature writers. Others by the 1890's became the first specialists in women's news, as newspapers began to run fashion articles, recipes, and other women's interest news in conjunction with society items.

Salaries for the editorial staff were generally low except for a few top men. The principal editors were paid from $25 to $60 a week in 1870; by 1890 managing editors of large papers received up to $125 a week, and city editors and star reporters made from $50 to $100 a week. These were very good salaries in 1890 dollars. But many of the staff stayed at the same $15 to $25 a week level which

---

[1] Henry Chadwick of the sports-conscious *New York Herald* became in 1862 the first of a long line of baseball writers.

had existed for reporters after the Civil War, because there was no pressure on publishers to pay more. The "new journalism" attracted many hopeful cub reporters; if one man quit, another was waiting to try his luck, and there was no effective labor organization in the editorial offices as there was in the mechanical departments. Many beginners were paid only on space rates, and some volunteered their services free of charge. Willis J. Abbot, who ended his career as editor of the *Christian Science Monitor*, records that he worked 14 hours a day in 1886 for the *New York Tribune* and received only $2.85 a week in space rate payments.[2] He did it willingly, he said, because that was the only way to learn the newsman's skills.

Some newspapers became training centers for reporters who migrated to other cities and other staffs. They included older distinguished newsgathering organizations, such as the *Sun, Herald, Tribune,* and *Times* in New York, and newcomers like Nelson's *Kansas City Star,* Stone's *Chicago Daily News,* and Pulitzer's *World.* Managing editors of the type of Cockerill of the *World,* John C. Reid of the *Times,* and Henry W. Grady of the *Atlanta Constitution* were able exponents of journalistic techniques. Perhaps the most famous were the leading editors of the *New York Sun:* Amos J. Cummings, managing editor and expert in the human interest story, John B. Bogart, city editor, and Chester S. Lord and Selah M. Clarke, managing editor and night city editor, respectively, after 1880. The *Sun* developed great reporters—Julian Ralph, Arthur Brisbane, S. S. Carvalho, Edward W. Townsend, Richard Harding Davis. It shared with the *Tribune* the reporting career of Jacob A. Riis, who wrote with discernment about conditions in the New York slums and the tragedies they bred.

There was competition for the services of reporters such as those developed on the *Sun.* Ralph, who once wrote an 11,000 word story in seven hours, and whose speed and writing style made him the foremost idol of the cub reporters, eventually became a prized Hearst correspondent. Brisbane, who joined the *Sun* in 1883 at the age of 19 and was sent to London two years later, became managing editor of the *Evening Sun* in 1888, joined the *World* in 1890 and then left to win a fortune with Hearst. Carvalho became the first city editor of the *Evening World,* rose to a managerial position and

[2] Willis J. Abbot, *Watching the World Go By* (Boston: Little, Brown and Company, 1933), p. 29.

later was a Hearst executive. The dashing war correspondent, Davis, left the *Sun* to join Hearst, then achieved greatest fame as a *Herald* writer.

Newspapermen who gathered in the small hours of the morning from the various city staffs—in Doctor Perry's drugstore in New York or in the Whitechapel Club and Press Club in Chicago—admired the literary style and news skill of the leading reporters. They envied the "Van Bibber" stories of Davis and the "Chimmie Fadden" stories of Townsend, and the more enthusiastic of the young newsmen reveled in what they preferred to call a bohemian atmosphere—which to others looked more like hard work at long and irregular hours for low pay.

Some of the newspapermen of this period, like Henry Grady, were intelligent, perceptive men who were sensitive to the requirements of society and who helped to create a more comprehensive and interpretive journalism. Some, like Pulitzer, possessed a crusading spirit and outstanding editorial page ability. Some, like Ralph, were excellent reporters of news events. Some, like Cockerill and Cummings, were able exponents of the reader-attracting techniques of human interest writing.

But many others were less talented, more prone to seize upon the devices of sensationalism, or to substitute slovenly and dishonest work for the kind of journalism they should have produced. Many were unqualified for their work. Although more newsmen were products of colleges and universities, no one yet came into the field equipped with a professional education in journalistic techniques and responsibilities. The professional standards which were being set were those of the best qualified practitioners of newspaper work, and only a minority of newsmen worked on staffs which had able leadership. The quality of the editorial staff was improving, but in an uneven, spotty manner.

Pressure for speedier and more comprehensive coverage of the news, which stemmed both from increasing competition among the dailies and from the needs of the new social environment, brought advances in cooperative news gathering. The communications network was keeping pace with the needs of an America which was sensing the interdependency created by its industrial revolution, and which was imbued with the spirit of speed in tackling its new problems.

Newspapers had many new facilities which they could use in improving their coverage. The railroads and telegraph lines which had made possible the speed-up of news coverage which began in the 1840's spurted ahead to cover the country. Between 1880 and 1900 the number of miles of railroad tracks doubled, while those of telegraph lines quadrupled. They were joined by the Bell System's telephone lines which in those 20 years spread from city to city. The federal postal service began free rural delivery in 1897, and improved its city carrier service. The Atlantic cable, which began operating in 1866, linked the United States to London, and to another cable stretching eastward to India and the Orient.

Still at the center of news gathering on a national and international scale for American dailies in the 1880's was the Associated Press of New York. It had been founded by the city's morning papers in 1848 so that they could share the cost of telegraphing news collected from European papers brought by ship to North Atlantic ports. Similarly, they pooled routine news coverage from Washington and other major eastern cities. The New York Associated Press group then had found it could sell its news to regional, state, and city newspaper groups which arose spontaneously as telegraph lines were extended inland. It obviously was both practical and financially necessary for papers along the lines to share the telegraphed news accounts from other points.

The New York papers which controlled this early version of the Associated Press adroitly maneuvered themselves into a monopolistic position. Their agreements with the Western Union telegraph company gave their press service preferred treatment and rates, and an exchange of favors between the New York Associated Press and Western Union served to build both into positions of dominance over their competitors. Opening of the Atlantic cable facilitated reciprocal exchange of news between the AP and the press agencies which had developed in Europe: Reuters in Britain (1851), Havas in France (1836), Wolff in Germany (1849), and Stefani in Italy (1854). World news reports of these agencies could be easily collected and transmitted exclusively by the AP.

The bait which the New York Associated Press group offered to other papers in the country was an extension of the news monopoly which the New York papers held. The regional and local groups which became clients of the Associated Press could restrict their membership, and prevent new competitors from obtaining the basic news coverage afforded by the AP. Thus the AP franchise became a valuable asset, usually obtainable only by sale in competitive newspaper cities. To discourage press service competitors, the New York AP forbid those receiving its service to buy the news of any other agency.

Papers outside New York had many complaints against the AP service, however. The seven charter member New York morning papers decided what news should be included in the report, and preferred to compete among themselves for many of the major news stories, leaving only the more prosaic news for the AP. They were mainly interested, obviously, in a news report for morning papers, and did not respond to the needs of the rapidly expanding evening dailies. Their rate charges to clients were arbitrarily assessed, and the outside papers felt they were paying too much of the cost and had too little say about the operations of the service.

As might be expected, the rapidly growing newspapers of the Middle West became the most powerful regional group among the AP clients. The Western Associated Press which they formed in 1862 soon began an agitation for reform which eventually led to the reorganization of the Associated Press into its modern cooperative form by the end of the century. The fact that the Associated Press of 1880 served only half the morning dailies and a fourth of the evening papers made it inevitable that competing news services eventually would arise. Of those who tried before 1900, however, only the United Press (no relation to the present-day service of the same name) offered real competition to the AP, and it was quickly submerged in the battle between rival AP factions for control.[3]

In the meantime, however, cooperative news gathering was making forward steps. The first leased wire, reserved for the AP's use and carrying up to 20,000 words a day, was opened between New York and Washington in 1879. Chicago got this improved service in 1884. By 1890 the AP leased wires had extended to New Orleans, Denver, and Minneapolis.

Smaller dailies were given inexpensive service by the making of thin stereotyped plates, which could be expressed rapidly and set

---

[3] The standard account of this subject is Victor Rosewater, *History of Co-operative News-Gathering in the United States* (New York: D. Appleton and Company, 1930).

directly into the news columns. The leading distributor of thin plates in the 1880's was the American Press Association, which used the news report of the Associated Press. It and other syndicates also offered feature stories, illustrations, and entertainment material in plate form.[4]

Older forms of obtaining the news still continued. Leading newspapers offered their exclusive stories to strings of clients, sending proof slips by express service or mail as they had done in the past, or sometimes using the telegraph. Editors clipped their exchange papers from other cities and subscribed to the *Congressional Record* for details on Washington news. City news services, which had taken definite form during the Civil War, continued to collect the routine news within metropolitan areas, and were formally organized in New York and Chicago in the early 1890's.

The largest papers found they needed to supplement the AP news report with stories from their own correspondents, if they were to keep pace with their rivals, and sometimes spent more money on their privately collected non-local news than on the AP service. The number of newspapers which had correspondents covering Congress rose from 45 at the outbreak of the Civil War to 130 by 1870. Improved AP service from Washington left the congressional press gallery at this level until the excitement of the Spanish-American war period. The Washington correspondents formed their famous Gridiron Club in 1885, and numbered some of the country's best newsmen.

Thus the new leaders in journalism were demonstrating that they were willing to spend more effort and more money on collecting the news. But the system was as yet unsatisfactory and inadequate, despite the advances made. The New York Associated Press depended heavily upon the news collected by member papers and by foreign press services. Regional AP groups expanded their own interexchange of news, but in many instances the AP depended upon Western Union operators for coverage of spot news events. And papers outside the AP fold had to struggle along as best they could with unsatisfactory substitutes for the modern competitive news services which were to evolve with the opening of the twentieth century.

The expansion of the editorial staff and its news gathering activi-

[4] Alfred M. Lee, *The Daily Newspaper in America* (New York: The Macmillan Company, 1937), p. 511.

ties, which thus was heralding the arrival of modern journalism, was made possible by tremendous developments in the business and mechanical departments of the metropolitan daily newspaper. But these developments in turn brought an over-shadowing of the figure of the old-time editor and a relative lessening of his influence in the new era of corporate journalism.

This did not mean that editors and news executives were shunted aside, but they no longer could dominate the scene as in the days when an editor-owner stood in command of his less complex enterprise. The achieving of gains in editorial staff efficiency and in comprehensive coverage of the news was to be at the expense of the personal factor in newspaper editing.

Those larger dailies which had become complex business institutions—headed by the *New York World* with its 10-million-dollar valuation and its annual million-dollar profit in the mid-nineties—were harassed by a host of new problems. It was they who first reflected the corporate nature of the new journalism, although the pressure of the business problems they faced soon came to be felt by an increasing number of middle-sized dailies, and to some degree by any newspaper.

The scramble for advertising and circulation supremacy, widespread mechanical innovations and pyramiding capitalization costs, larger payrolls and more difficult labor relations problems, increasing concern over newsprint supply for skyrocketing circulations—these and other problems brought the rise of a managerial corps in newspaper publishing, just as managers were rising as a group in American business generally.

Thus, while men trained as reporters were assuming the leadership of the editorial staffs, men specializing in business problems were filling influential managerial posts and, increasingly, the publishers' chairs. News-trained men who also were publisher-owners found themselves forced to deal with business affairs much of the time, and to delegate their editorial responsibilities to others, who competed with the managers for the ear of the publisher. Only the strongest personalities on the editorial side could continue in such an atmosphere to exercise the kind of leadership the ablest editor-owners of the age of personal journalism could give. Where a combination of able management and effective editorial leadership existed, however, the change was all to the good, for it meant those newspapers had a firm financial basis for the expansion of their community services.

Symbolizing the ascendancy of business problems of the daily newspapers was the establishment of the American Newspaper Publishers Association in 1887 to serve as their trade association. The leaders in the association were representatives of aggressive new papers and of older papers which were alive to the problems of the new journalism. Most of the men taking part in association affairs held managerial posts on their newspapers, or were publishers who were primarily interested in business management.

Two of the early presidents were James W. Scott of the *Chicago Herald* and Charles W. Knapp of the *St. Louis Republic,* both news-trained publishers. But men like Colonel Charles H. Jones, S. S. Carvalho, John Norris, and Don C. Seitz—all of whom contended for managerial-side supremacy on Pulitzer's *World* in the 1890's—were more typical leaders of the ANPA. Seitz, who survived as manager of the *World,* and Norris, who became business manager of the *New York Times,* were particularly important leaders of the Publishers Association after the turn of the century. There they spoke for their absent publishers, Pulitzer and Adolph Ochs.

The ANPA was organized at the call of William H. Brearley, advertising manager of the *Detroit Evening News,* James E. Scripps' successful new paper. There were many state editorial associations —17 had been founded between 1853 and 1880—but most of their members published weeklies and small dailies. The National Editorial Association had been organized in 1885 by B. B. Herbert of the *Red Wing Daily Republican* of Minnesota, but it too showed little concern for the problems of the metropolitan press and became the national organization of the weeklies and smallest dailies.

What Brearley and his associates wanted primarily was a daily newspaper trade association which would help its members with the problem of obtaining national advertising. While the ANPA soon became deeply involved in problems of labor relations, newsprint supply, government mail rates, and mechanical developments, it centered much of its attention on the field of advertising and upon the advertising agencies.

The expansion of business upon a national scale, and the consequent necessity for increasing national advertising and merchandising efforts, had opened the way for a middleman between advertiser and newspaper. The first advertising agents had appeared in New York and other eastern cities in the early 1840's. Their business was a haphazard one, in which they bought space in newspapers and magazines with scanty knowledge of the worth of such space. They found that publishers would pay them discounts of from 15 to 30 per cent, and sometimes as high as 75 per cent, on stated advertising rates. The discount represented the agent's profit, since he did not then prepare copy for the advertiser or engage in research.

Larger metropolitan papers were able to deal fairly effectively with the agents, both in obtaining advertising and in limiting the agents' commissions to reasonable figures. But those newspapers which were published at distant points from manufacturing and business centers of the East, and smaller papers, were not as fortunate. The agents found they often were able to play one publisher against another and obtain handsome commissions for extending the favors they had to offer.

Not all advertising agents operated in this manner. The founding around 1870 of the businesslike and respected agencies of George P. Rowell, N. W. Ayer & Son, and Lord & Thomas helped to stabilize the situation. But there were still many sharp-dealing agents, particularly those representing patent medicine manufacturers, and there were newspapers which would deal with them.[5]

One of the problems was identifying the newspapers and magazines which were being founded in great numbers during the last decades of the century. Rowell began publication of his *American Newspaper Directory* in 1869, and N. W. Ayer & Son started its continuing annual publication in 1880. These directories listed the newspapers and periodicals and attempted, often unsuccessfully, to determine their true circulations. There was as yet no outside check on circulation statements, and to make matters worse, advertising rate cards varied widely even in relation to claimed circulations. Only after 1914, when newspaper and magazine publishers and advertisers succeeded in organizing the Audit Bureau of Circulations, was the problem solved.

For the publishers the problem was one of identifying the potential advertisers and the trustworthy advertising agents. The ANPA headquarters office in New York published regular bulletins notifying members of prospective advertising accounts, and reporting on agents' activities. The association, after a dozen years of wrangling, agreed in 1899 to issue lists of recognized advertising agencies, and to blacklist those who engaged in unfair practices or who were bad financial risks. By common consent the discount payment to agencies became 15 per cent. In this work the publishers received the cooperation of the American Association of Advertising Agencies (the final name adopted in 1917 for a group which began to organize in the 1870's).

The amount of advertising revenue at stake was growing steadily. Advertising in newspapers and periodicals amounted to 39 million dollars in 1880; the census that year showed advertising in daily newspapers alone was worth 21 million dollars. No further breakdowns for daily newspapers are available in this period, but the spurt in advertising revenues was evident. In 1890 the advertising revenues of all newspapers and magazines totaled 71 million dollars; in 1900, 95 million dollars; in 1910, 200 million dollars. Of the 1910 figure, 148 millions is identified as advertising revenue of all newspapers, of which dailies received the greater bulk.

The percentage of the revenue of the newspapers coming from advertising, as compared to circulation income, rose from half in 1880 to 64 per cent by 1910. Space given to advertising in most dailies rose from 25 per cent of the available columns to a 50-50 ratio with editorial material by World War I.

As the amount of advertising in daily newspapers increased after 1880, the variety and quality of the content of advertising columns improved. Retail store advertising gained steadily, with the impetus given it by three successful pioneer department store merchants, John Wanamaker of Philadelphia, Marshall Field of Chicago, and A. T. Stewart of New York. National advertising of soaps and foods —Ivory soap and Royal baking powder were two leaders—marked the 1880's, and was supplemented in the next decade by campaigns for Eastman Kodak, Wrigley's chewing gum, bicycles, phonographs, and various new products.

Slogans like "It Floats," "Do You Know Uneeda Biscuit?" and "His Master's Voice" became familiar to all Americans. Some of them made quick fortunes for their sponsors, too, and stimulated other concerns to use the various advertising media more energetically. The first copy writers appeared in the leading advertising

pical inside page make-up of 1898, from the *Chicago Times-Herald*, showing advertising copy of two famous department stores.

agencies during the 1890's, followed by artists. As a result the layouts, type choices, and illustrations in the advertising columns improved.

Still, however, the leading advertising clients of newspapers and magazines were the patent medicine manufacturers. Their copy extolling the virtues of Castoria, Scott's Emulsion, Peruna, or Lydia Pinkham's Female Compound was the largest single type in the 1880's and continued to bulk large until World War I. These popular remedies, like Dr. Williams' Pink Pills for Pale People, didn't hurt anybody, but some of the cure-alls which were accepted as substitutes for medical attention in remote areas and in crowded tenements did. Some even contained poisons which brought death to incautious users. It is to the credit of a few publishers that they regulated this type of advertising themselves before patent medicines were regulated by Congress.

The major competitors for the advertising dollar were the newspapers and the magazines, with billboards and car-cards cutting in slightly. Growth of magazine circulation in the 1890's forced newspapers to view them with real concern as competitors both for reader attention and for advertising revenue, and caused publishers to join forces in better promoting the newspaper as an advertising medium.

There were successful new leaders in magazine journalism, just as there were in newspaper making. One was Frank Munsey, a New Englander with a sober and industrious character, who struggled for a decade in the New York magazine publishing field before achieving success with his *Munsey's,* begun in 1889. Another was S. S. McClure, who after establishing a feature syndicate service for newspapers, brought out his *McClure's* in 1893. A third competitor was *Cosmopolitan,* founded in 1886 and sold to William Randolph Hearst in 1905.[6]

These well-edited, popularized monthly magazines had found the same answer to the problem of obtaining mass circulation that the daily newspapers had found in the past. The secret was the cutting of the price to first 15 cents, and then a dime, for magazines which competed with older 35 cent publications. The cheap one-cent-a-pound mail rate, in effect from 1885 until zone rates were estab-

[6] Hearst established *Hearst's Magazine* in 1901 and consolidated the two in 1925.

lished during World War I, helped to make this possible. By the turn of the century *Munsey's* had achieved 650,000 circulation to lead other general magazines by a wide margin, and *McClure's* and *Cosmopolitan* were runners-up. The formula for all three was popular fiction, general articles, and illustrations.

Cyrus H. K. Curtis provided new leadership in the women's magazine field with his *Ladies' Home Journal,* founded in 1883. With Edward W. Bok as editor after 1889, the magazine quickly rose to a half million circulation at a one dollar annual subscription price. In the weekly five-cent magazine field the *Saturday Evening Post,* bought by Curtis in 1897, and *Collier's,* founded in 1888, pushed to even higher circulations than those of the monthlies.

These new popularly circulated magazines were the ones which made the biggest inroads on available advertising revenue, arising as they did to public notice at the moment when national advertising was expanding. But the general illustrated monthly magazines of high literary and artistic quality—*Harper's, Century,* and *Scribner's* —continued to have major influence, even though outstripped in circulation. Sharing in the competition for reader attention and revenue too were the illustrated weekly periodicals, *Harper's Weekly* and *Leslie's;* the weeklies depending upon humor and cartoons, *Puck, Life,* and *Judge;* and the children's magazines, *Youth's Companion* and *St. Nicholas,* as well as many specialized periodicals.

Newspapermen grumbled in the late 1890's that the magazines were getting too much of the advertising of the new products of American business. And the competition spurred them into doing better jobs of running their businesses and of selling their advertising space. Two new business associations were formed, the International Circulation Managers' Association in 1898 and the Newspaper Advertising Executives Association in 1900. Regional interests of the dailies were coming to be served by such organizations as the Inland Daily Press Association, the Southern Newspaper Publishers Association, the Northwest Daily Press Association, and the New England Daily Newspaper Association.

Testifying, too, to growing emphasis upon business problems and to the increased interest in what the other fellow was doing, was the growth of trade publications. The leaders were the *Journalist* (1884), the *Fourth Estate* (1894), and *Editor & Publisher* (1901), in the daily newspaper field; the *Publishers' Auxiliary* (1865), which became the Western Newspaper Union's newspaper for weekly publishers; and *Printers' Ink* (1888), in advertising.

Special advertising representatives, appointed to obtain national advertising for their client newspapers, began their work in the late 1870's. After 1900 they organized associations to promote the newspaper as an advertising medium. The Daily Newspaper Club, a group of larger newspapers, worked to the same ends after 1906. Its members persuaded the American Newspaper Publishers Association to sponsor the founding of the Bureau of Advertising in 1913. The Bureau, with a paid staff, did the most effective job yet in arguing the case of the newspapers with advertising agencies and national advertisers.

The result was that magazines, which were obtaining 60 per cent or more of national advertising revenue at the turn of the century, were forced to share the take with newspapers on an equal basis by the time of World War I. The number of national advertisers using newspapers or magazines rose from approximately 6,000 in 1900 to some 13,000 in 1914, and then leveled off, so that the 1914 figure remained a high until 1947.[7] The newspapers, of course, also had local advertising which gave them a wide lead over magazines in total advertising take, the newspapers receiving roughly 70 per cent of all advertising revenues in the early years of the twentieth century.

The growth of the modern newspaper thus far described—in editorial techniques, in circulation, and in advertising volume—went hand in hand with the development of new mechanical equipment. The practitioners of the new journalism demanded better printing techniques to increase the mass appeal of their product, and faster means of production to keep pace with their sense of speed. These demands helped to create a never-ending process of advancement in the printing arts and in editorial practices.

Mechanization of hand labor processes was one of the driving forces of the industrial revolution of the late nineteenth century— in factories, in manufacturing, in offices. Inventive genius, stimulated by the demands of a production-expanding society, brought new processes into being in many fields. In printing, the achievements were the typesetting machine, faster presses, stereotyping, color printing, dry mats and electrotyping, and photo-engraving.

[7] *Printers' Ink*, CXXV (October 29, 1948), 102.

The first casting of a line of type for newspaper use was made in 1886 in the *New York Tribune* plant on Ottmar Mergenthaler's Linotype machine. Mergenthaler, a German immigrant whose work making patent models interested him in the typesetting machine problem, successfully developed his machine after years of experimentation by himself and others. Some newspapers gave him financial backing; significantly the other principal backers along with the *Tribune* were two newspapers which were among the new leaders, the *Chicago Daily News* and the *Louisville Courier-Journal*.[8]

Mergenthaler's first Linotype was basically the same machine used today. It was operated by a keyboard, and cast a slug from a line of matrices, which were then redistributed automatically. It had at the start an output three times that of the traditional hand compositor, and it was quickly adopted by the larger papers, particularly by evening dailies which needed its time-saving performance in order to cover the day's news closer to press deadline time.

There were competitors, but the Linotype was improved in its performance and won dominance in the field. It was joined by other machines shortly after the turn of the century: the Monotype, used to cast type and rules in quantities; the Intertype, a slug-casting machine with easily changed magazines of matrices for setting copy requiring different kinds of type; and the Ludlow, which cast slugs from handset matrices for use in setting advertisements.

Some improvements in the type faces themselves were beginning to be made in the interests of legibility and reader appeal. The ugly Gothics which had dominated newspaper typographic style did not begin to disappear widely, however, until after 1900, when the newly designed Cheltenham family, the really graceful Bodoni, and other headline types began to come into favor. The *New York Tribune* was to win typographical fame by its early use of Bodoni upper and lower case headlines.

The pressrooms also were being affected by the new order. Larger circulations, and increased competition which pushed the deadline for closing the news pages closer and closer to the time for distribution of big dailies, brought demands for improved printing presses. Expanded size of editions, as the volume of advertising and news was upped, also meant larger presses were needed which could

[8] The *Tribune* was interested because it was engaged in a long and bitter dispute with its printers.

handle the large papers within the time limit of daily journalism. American pressmakers, under the leadership of R. Hoe and Company, had converted the presses of the leading newspapers from hand to steam power and from flatbed to rotary printing before the Civil War. Ingenious pressmen figured out ways of fitting the type solidly enough between column rules so that it would stick on the revolving cylinder. These type-revolving presses were widely used. The next step was the adaptation of the stereotyped plate to the newspaper press. This permitted the breaking of column rules for illustrations, headlines, and advertising—a practice not practical for users of type-revolving presses.

More importantly, use of the solid stereotyped plate, produced from the type form and curved to fit the cylinder of the rotary press, permitted a speeding-up of the hourly rate of newspaper printing. The presses could run faster, and extra stereotypes of the same page could be produced for the running of two or more presses simultaneously.

Equally necessary to this speed-up was the development of presses which used a web, or continuous roll of newsprint, and which printed on both sides of the sheet in one operation. Larger papers were casting stereotyped plates and were using web presses from the 1860's on, but the type-revolving press held its place in many shops until the 1890's. By that time automatic folders operating at press speed also had been perfected. In 1890 the finest Hoe press could produce 48,000 12-page papers in an hour. Within the next 10 years that output was tripled as New York newspaper circulations skyrocketed, and banks of presses were installed in the effort to keep pace with potential circulation sales.

New developments in press operations came fast by the turn of the century. George Pancoast, mechanical superintendent for William Randolph Hearst, made one major improvement when he perfected the use of electric-powered presses in 1896. The autoplate, a new device for casting stereotypes, cut the time required for that process by 80 per cent and thus moved the news deadline closer to press time. The fudge box, a corner of the front page which could be printed separately on a small cylinder in any desired color, came into use as a means of squeezing last-second news into an edition.

Color printing on rotary presses became another necessity for the larger metropolitan papers in the 1890's if they wanted to keep in the swim. Color inserts printed separately had been used earlier, but full color presses modeled after those being used in Paris were first built for the *Chicago Inter Ocean* in 1892 by Walter Scott. Within a year Scott had installed a color press in the *New York World* plant. Soon feature sections of Sunday papers were carrying color printing—and the Sunday comic section was on its way to becoming a part of the American newspaper.

Newspaper mechanical departments also were spending much time experimenting with matrix-casting processes. Development of fool-proof and easily cast "mats" meant that advertisers and feature syndicates could distribute material for reproduction throughout the country cheaply and easily. Mat services could provide illustrations for use in advertising columns. Introduction of electrotypes also was important in obtaining widespread reproduction of illustrated advertising copy.

Mechanical advances which made possible improvement of illustrations in newspapers were another major achievement of the 1880 to 1900 period. The leaders up to that time in providing pictures for readers to see had been the magazines. *Frank Leslie's Illustrated Newspaper* and *Harper's Weekly*, both founded in the 1850's, had competed during the Civil War in providing woodcut reproductions of drawings made on the battlefields by small armies of artists. They and other magazines continued to run illustrations of dramatic events, cartoons, and drawings. Monthly magazines like *Harper's*, *Century*, and *Scribner's* did highly artistic work with woodcuts, and women's magazines used engraved steel fashion plates. The magazines of comment and satire—*Puck, Life,* and *Judge*—which appeared about 1880 depended upon illustrations and cartoons for much of their appeal.

Newspapers had used some sort of illustrations upon occasion since colonial days, and had used small cuts in advertisements. But woodcut illustrations of news events were rare—the *New York Herald* stood out for its early work. Cuts which were symbolic of an event, or stock illustrations which could be used with any story of a general type, were the best most newspapers could do. The *Evening Telegram*, companion paper for the *Herald*, was the first to run a political cartoon regularly, in competition with the magazines, publishing a large drawing one day each week, beginning about 1870.

More than one newspaperman sensed that illustrations would be a big drawing card, but there were great difficulties involved in producing the cuts. One large woodcut might require several days' work by an engraver, after the artist had completed his drawing. A cheaper and faster process was found in the Civil War period, involving the use of plates covered with a chalk powder. The artist drew his picture on the chalk with ink, and the uncovered chalk was removed. Then the chalk drawing was hardened in an acid solution, a mold was made, and finally a stereotype. The printed reproduction was less satisfactory than that of the woodcuts, however, and the cost and time factors were still discouraging.

Zincographs, which were line cuts produced by etching on zinc plates with acid, were invented in Paris about 1860 and began to appear in American publications in the 1870's. Illustrators, meanwhile, had found that they could print photographs directly onto woodblocks or zinc plates, where they would form the guide for the artist or etcher who completed the cut.

Still in 1880 there was relatively little illustration work appearing in American newspapers. When Pulitzer and his managing editor, Cockerill, took over the *New York World* in 1883, their first successes with illustrations were woodcuts. They also could produce engravings of artists' drawings by what was called the "soft metal process," but 48 hours' time was required, and the uses of newspaper illustration seemed limited.

Then the *World* editors stumbled into a quite unexplored but perfectly obvious journalistic field—the running of sketches of prominent local citizens. The resulting furor pressed them into conducting new searches for better mechanical processes.

Valerian Gribayédoff, one of the leading artists of the period, described the rise of local illustrations, and of newspaper illustration generally, in a magazine article published in 1891.[9] The artist related that he prepared a series of caricatures of the "Wall Street Nobility," which appeared on the front page of the *Sunday World* in February, 1884. The response was overwhelming and on succeeding Sundays drawings of other New Yorkers were reproduced. Within a short time, the artist said, the *Albany Evening Journal, Detroit Journal, Chicago Tribune, Chicago Inter Ocean, Kansas City Times, Philadelphia Times,* and *St. Louis Post-Dispatch* were ar-

° *Cosmopolitan,* XI (August 1891).

ranging for similar portraits of local celebrities. Vanity played its part, too; Gribayédoff said that many New Yorkers did everything they could to get their pictures in the paper.

Establishment of an engraving company in 1884 which could turn out zinc etchings in four hours' time further spurred the spread of illustration. The American Press Association began to use its facilities to distribute cuts widely to smaller papers. Illustrations became regular features of many papers, although they were still few in number.

Gribayédoff estimated in 1891 that there were a thousand artists at work in the country supplying illustrations for 5,000 newspapers and magazines. The vast majority of newspapers depended upon cut manufacturers, but an increasing number were employing their own artists and had installed their own engraving facilities. The *Boston Globe*, for example, was spending $30,000 a year on its engraving plant in 1893.

Photo-engraving was to curtail quickly this boom for the artists, however. The halftone photo-engraving process had been developed in England prior to 1860, but the results were unsatisfactory until Frederic E. Ives went to work on the problem of reproducing photographs in the printing process. Ives was made head of the photographic laboratory at Cornell University in 1876, when he was 20. The next year he produced a photo-engraving of a pen drawing, which was published in the student paper at Cornell. In 1878 he made his first halftone. Ives saw that the way to break up masses of dark and light was to lay out a series of prominences on a plate which would transfer the ink to paper point by point. If the points were close together, the mass would be dark; and the more widely they were spaced, the lighter the mass would become. Ives moved to Baltimore, and then to Philadelphia, after 1879 and produced commercially used halftones. He perfected his process in 1886, but unhappily he failed to obtain a patent and never realized financially on his invention.

There still remained, however, the problem of using the halftones on rotary presses. One of the heroes of the struggle to get pictures into the American newspaper was Stephen H. Horgan. Horgan was the art editor of an illustrated paper called the *New York Daily Graphic*, which began in 1873 and battled bravely until 1889 when it succumbed in the big city competition. It was Horgan who succeeded in publishing a newspaper halftone of good quality in 1880, a picture called "Shantytown." And it was Horgan who first had the idea of how to run halftones on rotary presses. He was rebuffed by doubting pressmen, however, and it was not until 1897 that he perfected the method for the *New York Tribune*.

Within a short time other large papers were running halftone reproductions of photographs. Pressure for quick printing of local pictures brought installation of photo-engraving plants in larger shops; smaller papers got their cuts from centrally located photo-engraving companies.

The artists found the news photographers edging into their field in earnest, now that their photos could be reproduced directly. Both groups covered the Spanish-American War. Syndicates quickly added news and feature photographs to their stock in trade, and big city papers began to employ local photographers who carried their heavy, awkward equipment and their flashlight powder out on assignments. Pictorial journalism was on its way, although many a newspaperman scorned the new technique and lamented the waste of space.

The sweep of mechanical improvements in the publishing busines, bringing with it labor specialization and larger working forces, gave newspaper publishers some new labor relations problems. The printers, pressmen, and engravers were organized into unions which belonged to the American Federation of Labor, and the labor movement was pressing constantly for shorter working hours and higher pay in all industries.

Strikes and work stoppages were something most newspaper publishers wanted to avoid. In a highly competitive field, particularly in metropolitan areas, suspension of publication meant perhaps fatal loss of circulation and advertising. Suspension also could jeopardize the status of a newspaper which held a lucrative contract to publish legal advertising. Such arguments were more compelling at the turn of the century than later.

One factor favored the publishers in this situation. The International Typographical Union, which had been reorganized in 1852 and which had become one of the most powerful of the AFL craft unions, was splitting into four unions as specialization of labor increased in printing plants. The International Printing Pressmen and

Assistants' Union broke away from the typographers in 1886, followed by the International Photo-Engravers' Union in 1900 and the International Stereotypers and Electrotypers' Union in 1901. Publishers thus were enabled to deal with the union groups separately, and the danger of plantwide strikes was reduced.

At first newspaper publishers organized city associations so they could bargain as a unit with the unions. Then these local publishers' associations began to sign arbitration contracts with their printers which would minimize the danger of labor disputes. In 1899 the final step was taken, when the American Newspaper Publishers Association decided to enter into nationwide arbitration agreements between its members and the unions.

These voluntary agreements called first for local conciliation and arbitration procedures in event of contract disputes. Appeal could be made to a national arbitration board, whose decision would be binding on both the newspaper and the union involved. Strikes and lockouts were banned.

The arbitration agreements were signed with all four unions and they were successful enough that they were continued through the World War I period, before disputes with the typographers over their union rules resulted in a breakdown of the major contract. Thus the efforts of the organized publishers and the labor unions brought comparative peace to the newspaper industry during a period of severe labor disturbances in other industries.

All of these advances in newspaper publishing which have been traced thus far would have been impossible, however, without the appearance of the Fourdrinier papermaking machine. Newsprint is a prosaic subject, but the ability to make low-cost newsprint from wood pulp, by a process introduced into America from Germany in 1867, was the basic factor in the growth of the daily newspaper. The same process also permitted the making of higher grade magazine and book paper in the quantities needed by a modern society.

Print paper made by hand from rag stock was the product of an expensive, limited industry. When newspapers had to pay as much as $440 a ton for paper during the Civil War, the time was ripe for the introduction of a new manufacturing process. This process used water power to grind spruce logs into wood pulp, which when combined with a small amount of rag stock could be made into a usable print paper. By the 1890's a chemically produced wood pulp, called sulphite pulp, replaced rag stock as the toughening element in newsprint.

These manufacturing advances, coupled with the increased productive efficiency of papermaking machines, brought the price of newsprint tumbling downward. Paper manufacturers, stimulated by the prospect of increased demands for newsprint and higher grade magazine and book paper, slashed into the forests of Maine, Michigan, Wisconsin, and Minnesota. Newsprint cost $246 a ton in 1870, $138 a ton in 1880, $76 a ton in 1890, and $42 a ton in 1899, the bottom price until 1933.[10]

In view of this rapid decline in newsprint prices, it would seem that American newspaper publishers should have been quite satisfied with the situation at the turn of the century. But such was not the case. They were happy, of course, that newsprint was available at moderate prices. They were acutely conscious of the price of this raw material which bulked larger and larger in their operating costs, however, and they viewed the future with foreboding. As the tonnage of newsprint used by larger papers increased each year, slight price fluctuations meant sizable differences in expenditures for mass-circulation newspapers. The 1910 census figures show that 21 per cent of the total revenue of American newspapers was spent in buying newsprint, and a $10 change in the ton price might mean an annual difference of $50,000 to even a moderately sized daily.

American newspapers used about two-thirds of the amount of newsprint produced domestically in 1880, buying 100,000 tons. In 1900 domestic newsprint consumption equaled domestic supply, both figures standing at 570,000 tons. What was worse, the domestic newsprint manufacturers had obtained a good-sized tariff on newsprint imported from abroad, and they had effected a virtual monopolistic control over domestic output and sales prices.

The American Newspaper Publishers Association therefore plunged into battle. It crusaded against the newsprint trust, and forced dissolution of the largest sales organization. And it campaigned steadily to win removal of the tariff on imported newsprint, so that the vast forest resources of Canada could be opened to the papermaking industry. The Canadians wisely had refused to ship

[10] Lee, *The Daily Newspaper in America*, pp. 743-45.

logs or wood pulp to the United States for processing, knowing that eventually the entire industry would be theirs when American forests were gone.

Under the leadership of John Norris, business manager of the *New York Times,* and Herman Ridder, publisher of the German-language *New Yorker Staats-Zeitung* and president of the Publishers Association during much of the newsprint campaign, the battle went on. Newsprint prices rose to as high as $58 as supply tightened. But not until the Woodrow Wilson administration was elected in 1912 and a Democratic Congress carried out the party's pledge to lower tariffs, was the way cleared for full use of Canadian newsprint. By then the price was back at $42 a ton and a flood of Canadian-produced paper arrived on the American market. Even it was not enough to prevent a newsprint shortage and zooming prices after World War I.

It is evident, then, from this survey of the changing conditions in daily newspaper publishing that there was a "watershed of the nineties" for the American newspaper. The advance into the modern era had been accomplished, and for better or for worse, the older era of journalism was no more.

ANNOTATED BIBLIOGRAPHY
Books:

Most valuable of the journalism histories for this period are still Frank Luther Mott's *American Journalism,* Willard G. Bleyer's *Main Currents in the History of American Journalism,* and Alfred McClung Lee's *The Daily Newspaper in America.* Lee's topical treatment of the problems covered in this chapter is particularly noteworthy. The *Union List of Newspapers,* beginning where Brigham's bibliography leaves off in 1820, is supplemented by directories: *Geo. P. Rowell & Co.'s American Newspaper Directory* (1869) and *N. W. Ayer & Son's American Newspaper Annual* (1880), later called the *Directory of Newspapers & Periodicals.* The *Editor & Publisher International Year Book* dates from 1921.

Abbot, Willis J., *Watching the World Go By.* Boston: Little, Brown and Company, 1933. The experiences of a longtime newspaperman who eventually became editor of the *Christian Science Monitor.* Abbot gives a good picture of the 1890's.

Carnes, Cecil, *Jimmy Hare, News Photographer.* New York: The Macmillan Company, 1940. The biography of one of the early leading press photographers.

Downey, Fairfax D., *Richard Harding Davis: His Day*. New York: Charles Scribner's Sons, 1933. Biography of the glamor-boy of early modern journalism.

Ellis, L. Ethan, *Print Paper Pendulum*. New Brunswick: Rutgers University Press, 1948. A readable study of the newsprint supply problem, beginning in the late 1870's.

Emery, Edwin, *History of the American Newspaper Publishers Association*. Minneapolis: University of Minnesota Press, 1950. Covers the activities of the organized daily newspaper publishers in the fields of labor relations, newsprint, advertising, mailing privileges, mechanical research, and legislative lobbying, from 1887 on.

Gunther, John, *Taken at the Flood: The Story of Albert D. Lasker*. New York: Harper & Brothers, 1960. The career of a pioneer adman at the Lord & Thomas agency.

Hower, Ralph M., *The History of an Advertising Agency: N. W. Ayer & Son at Work, 1869-1949*. Cambridge: Harvard University Press, 1949.

Irwin, Will, *The Making of a Reporter*. New York: G. P. Putnam's Sons, 1942. Autobiography of a discerning newspaperman who ranked with the best.

Isaacs, George A., *The Story of the Newspaper Printing Press*. London: Cooperative Printing Society, 1931.

Jones, Edgar R., *Those Were the Good Old Days: A Happy Look at American Advertising, 1880-1930*. New York: Simon and Schuster, 1959. Illustrations of 50 years of advertising from magazines.

Knight, Oliver A., *Following the Indian Wars: The Story of the Newspaper Correspondents among the Indian Campaigners, 1866-1891*. Norman: University of Oklahoma Press, 1960. Well documented.

Loft, Jacob, *The Printing Trades*. New York: Farrar and Rinehart, Inc., 1944. An inclusive account. See also Elizabeth F. Baker, *Printers and Technology: A History of the International Printing Pressmen and Assistants' Union* (New York: Columbia University Press, 1957).

Presbrey, Frank, *The History and Development of Advertising*. New York: Doubleday, Doran & Company, 1929. The standard history in its field.

Ralph, Julian, *The Making of a Journalist*. New York: Harper & Brothers, 1903. The autobiography of another top-ranking reporter of the period.

Rosewater, Victor, *History of Cooperative News-Gathering in the United States*. New York: D. Appleton and Company, 1930. The recognized source for the early history of press associations.

Ross, Ishbel, *Ladies of the Press*. New York: Harper & Brothers, 1936. Valuable for stories of early women journalists.

Turner, E. S., *The Shocking History of Advertising*. New York: E. P. Dutton & Company, 1953. A constructively critical account.

Ware, Louise, *Jacob A. Riis*. New York: D. Appleton-Century Company, 1938. Biography of a socially conscious reporter.

Wood, James Playsted, *The Story of Advertising*. New York: Ronald Press, 1958. Fairly detailed from the 1860's on.

Periodicals and Monographs:
    The trade journals become available in this period. The leaders were the *Journalist* (1884-1907), the *Fourth Estate* (1894-1927), and *Editor & Publisher* (1901) in the daily newspaper field; the *Publishers' Auxiliary* (1865) in the weekly newspaper field; and *Printers' Ink* (1888) in advertising. The fiftieth anniversary numbers of *Editor & Publisher* (July 21, 1934) and of *Printers' Ink* (July 28, 1938) are particularly valuable sources.

Irwin, Will, "The American Newspaper," *Collier's*, XLVI-XLVII (January 21-July 29, 1911). A series of 15 articles which constitutes a history of journalism after the Civil War. One article, "The Fourth Current," which traces the rise of yellow journalism, is reprinted in Ford and Emery, *Highlights in the History of the American Press*. Another, "The Reporter and the News," is reprinted in Mott and Casey, *Interpretations of Journalism*.

Knight, Oliver A., "Reporting a Gold Rush," *Journalism Quarterly*, XXXVIII (Winter 1961), 43. The story of two young reporters from the *Inter Ocean* and *New York Herald* in the Black Hills of 1875.

Park, Robert E., "The Natural History of the Newspaper," a book chapter by a University of Chicago sociologist, originally published in *The City* in 1925 and reprinted in Mott and Casey, *Interpretations of Journalism*.

Chapter 19

YELLOW JOURNALISM

> The reason why such journals lie is that it pays
> to lie; or, in other words, this is the very reason
> for which they are silly and scandalous and inde-
> cent. They supply a want of a demoralized public.
> —E. L. Godkin

THE AMERICAN NEWSPAPER was making great strides by
the mid-nineties both as an instrument of society and as a business
institution. Thanks to the publishing concepts and the techniques of
the new journalism, many dailies had won larger circulations giving
them greater public influence and support. Their increased advertising and subscription revenues provided the resources necessary
for more intensive coverage of the news. And growing financial stability meant that conscientious publishers and editors could do a
better job of telling the news honestly and fully, and of demonstrating their community leadership, because they were better able to
resist outside pressures.

This, of course, was the brighter side of the growth of the modern newspaper. There could be shortcomings, as well. The financial
bigness of metropolitan dailies brought a lessening of the personal
element in editorial direction, and sometimes muffled the voice of
the newspaper and dulled its social conscience. Mass circulation
was achieved by a popularizing of the product, and sometimes the
primary news function was overshadowed by efforts to entertain.

It should be added, however, that corporate journalism did not need to speak in a timid voice. And popularization, while inevitable if mass readership was to be achieved, did not need to become mere sensationalism. The tools which were now available—linotypes and faster presses, more striking typography and layout, color printing, cartoons and photographs, skillful writing by larger staffs of reporters and editors, better communications facilities—all could be used constructively to build better newspapers. Stories which were written in a more readable style, or which in their nature appealed to the human interests of readers, could increase popular acceptance of the newspaper without detracting from its social usefulness. Bigger headlines, pictures, blobs of color might give the newspaper a new face, and might cause some readers to grimace at the result and yearn for the bygone days; but effectively used, these devices too could be useful and desirable.

By the same token, a modern daily newspaper could use the new techniques of editing and printing in another way. It could emphasize sensationalism at the expense of news; it could lavishly dress up its entertainment features; it could put success in snaring readers ahead of the primary obligations of journalism. Some newspaper editors proceeded in the mid-nineties to do these things, just as they had been done in earlier periods when newspapers reached out to attract new audiences. But now they had far better tools which made their sensationalism distinctive and seemingly new, and so their degrading kind of journalism became known as "yellow journalism."

Yellow journalism, at its worst, was the new journalism without a soul. True, the yellow journalists trumpeted their concern for "the people," and championed the rights of the common man; but at the same time they choked up the news channels upon which the common man depended, with a callous disregard for journalistic ethics and responsibility. Theirs was a shrieking, gaudy, sensation-loving, devil-may-care kind of journalism which lured the reader by any possible means. It seized upon the techniques of writing, illustrating, and printing which were the prides of the new journalism and turned them to perverted uses. It made the high drama of life a cheap melodrama, and it twisted the facts of each day into whatever form seemed best suited to produce sales for the howling newsboy. Worst of all, instead of giving its readers effective leadership, it offered a palliative of sin, sex, and violence.

Joseph Pulitzer had opened Pandora's box when he used the devices of sensationalism to help build the *World's* circulation during the early years of his editorship. Other papers, like the *Philadelphia Record* and the *Boston Globe,* were playing the same game, but it was Pulitzer's phenomenal success which had so strikingly demonstrated once again the appeal of this age-old technique of sensation. And now there were new devices, for super-sensationalizing the newspaper, available to those who eyed his progress and mistakenly attributed the *World's* circulation achievements to sensationalism alone. Those who became brazen yellow journalists did not understand that Pulitzer had sought to achieve a balance between informing the reader and entertaining him, so that in the end the innovations of the new journalism would enhance the stature of his newspaper above the imitators. They saw the clever promotion and the lighter side of the *World*, but they did not see—or disregarded—the solid characteristics of its news coverage and the high qualities of its editorial page.

So the high priests of the yellow press set out to show Pulitzer how it really could be done. And their antics, which paid off handsomely in newspaper sales to the casual readers of the big cities, forced competing dailies to take on the yellow hue in varying degrees all across the country. Eventually most newspapers recovered from the disease, but modern journalism has exhibited some of the effects of the curse of yellow journalism ever since.

The man who more than anyone else brought about the era of yellow journalism was watching with sharp interest while Pulitzer was setting New York journalism on its ear in the mid-eighties. He was William Randolph Hearst, who was to become the most controversial figure in modern journalism before his 64-year publishing career was ended. The youthful Hearst was a calculating witness to Pulitzer's climb to glory, and when eventually he invaded New York to challenge the supremacy of the *World*, he came prepared to dazzle the city with a sensationalized and self-promoted kind of journalism which would put Pulitzer to shame. The resulting struggle brought repercussions whose effects are still being felt.

Hearst was a Californian, born in 1863, the son of a successful pioneer who struck it rich in the silver mines of the Comstock Lode, and who later won more riches in Anaconda copper and western and Mexican ranch lands. The only child of George and Phoebe Hearst, he grew up in San Francisco under the guidance of a busy, ambitious father and a schoolteacher mother, who in later years became a noted philanthropist and able manager of the family fortune.

Having achieved wealth, George Hearst aspired to political power. In 1880 he acquired the *San Francisco Examiner,* a debt-ridden morning paper which lagged behind the *Chronicle,* and converted it into a Democratic party organ. Young Hearst showed an interest in the paper, but his father took a low view of the newspapermen who worked for him, and packed his heir off to Harvard in 1883.

The Hearst career at Harvard was sensational, if not successful. He was a free-spending westerner who drank too much beer, listened to too much band music, and who did his best job as business manager of the humor magazine, the *Lampoon.* He was suspended in his sophomore year for celebrating Grover Cleveland's election to the presidency with a noisy fireworks display, and was expelled a few months later for perpetrating a practical joke upon Harvard's professors. Distinguished faculty members like William James and Josiah Royce could see no humor, it seemed, in finding their likenesses decorating chamber pots.

But the eastern education had not been entirely wasted. Harvard may not have made its impression on Hearst's mind, but the *Boston Globe* and the *New York World* did. Hearst studied the somewhat sensational techniques of General Charles H. Taylor's successful *Globe* and visited its up-to-date mechanical plant. He was more interested in Pulitzer's *World,* however, and on one of his vacations he worked as a cub reporter for the newspaper he later was to battle. After bowing out at Harvard, Hearst again spent some time in New York studying the *World's* techniques and then returned to San Francisco.

His father didn't want to see young Hearst take over the editorship of the *Examiner*—but that was what the strong-willed "Willie" intended to do. Furthermore, the confident son assured his doubting father, money could be made from newspapers as well as from mines and ranches. The *Examiner,* he said, would become "the *New York World* of the West." In 1887 George Hearst was named

Senator from California, and as he left for Washington, 24-year-old William Randolph Hearst was given control of the *Examiner*.

The tall, blue-eyed, shy young editor, whose high-pitched voice contrasted with a commanding physical presence, immediately began to staff up his newspaper. For his managing editor he picked Sam S. Chamberlain, who had worked for both Bennett and Pulitzer, who had edited Bennett's Paris edition of the *Herald*, and who had founded the Paris newspaper *Le Matin* in 1884. Chamberlain's experience, and his grasp of news techniques, made him invaluable.

This was a typical Hearst move—to watch for a good man on another paper and then to buy him at his own figure. The salaries on the *Examiner* were good for men with ability, and word soon spread.

Coming onto the *Examiner* staff in the early years were many talented recruits. There was the brilliant Ambrose Bierce, who contributed his "Prattle" column to the paper, and who later became famous for his short stories. There were star reporters like Edward H. Hamilton, and up-and-coming newspapermen like Arthur McEwen, who became a key figure in developing Hearst-style journalism, and Charles Michelson, who some 40 years later achieved his greatest fame as publicity director of the Democratic party during the Hoover regime and the first eventful years of the New Deal. Homer Davenport began to draw his political cartoons, and artist James Swinnerton turned to the new field of comics. Giving the *Examiner* literary flavor of quite different degrees were Edwin Markham, whose poem "The Man With the Hoe" first appeared in the paper, and E. L. (Phinney) Thayer, whose contribution was "Casey at the Bat."

When Chamberlain one day decided to investigate the city hospital's management, he picked a young woman reporter and assigned her to the story. She fainted conveniently on the street, was carried to the hospital, and turned out a story "with a sob for the unfortunate in every line." She was Winifred Black, who became known as "Annie Laurie" to future generations of Hearst readers. Her greatest early hit was an appeal to raise funds for the establishment of a "Little Jim ward" in the local children's hospital—a ward for incurables like little Jim, whose plight Annie Laurie described with such intensity that San Francisco women particularly were attracted to the *Examiner's* kind of human interest appeal. Hearst early saw the importance of the woman reader in the stimulation of retail advertising revenue.

Hearst was experimenting with crusades and stunts, and with devices for presenting the news in the most luring manner. As a stalwart Democrat, he relished attacking the Southern Pacific railroad company, bulwark of the Republican state machine. When a schooner went aground outside the Golden Gate, Hearst sent out a tug boat filled with reporters, who rescued survivors "courtesy of the *Examiner*." If the Del Monte hotel burned, or a murder took place near San Francisco, a special train carrying *Examiner* men and women reporters and artists went chugging to the scene. Hearst writers sought to play up a sensational, picturesque fact in their lead paragraphs—love, power, hate, or sympathy were the preferred themes. News which was important, but dull, took a back seat. Arthur McEwen summed up the Hearst approach when he said: "What we're after is the 'gee-whiz' emotion. We run our paper so that when the reader opens it he says: 'Gee-Whiz!' " [1]

Hearst's experiments on the mechanical side were important—and constructive—contributions to the new journalism. He worked with the typography of the *Examiner* to give it readable and attractive type faces. He tried many new patterns of makeup, arranging the heads in symmetrical patterns, introducing illustrations and large headlines, and eventually arriving at a distinctive Hearst formula which many another newspaper imitated. Hearst himself often worked over the page forms, but he also sought as eagerly for mechanical experts as he did for writers and artists. His greatest genius was George Pancoast, who joined Hearst on the *Examiner* in 1888, became superintendent of all Hearst mechanical plants and remained at this job for most of his 50-year career. Pancoast perfected the electric drive for presses, improved color printing processes, and designed 14 printing plants as the Hearst publishing empire expanded.

And Hearst was ready to expand his empire. His *Examiner*, which he proudly called "The Monarch of the Dailies," had doubled its circulation in the first year, reaching 30,000. By 1893 the figure was 72,000 and the *Examiner's* circulation had passed that of M. H. de

[1] Will Irwin, "The Fourth Current," *Collier's*, XLVI (February 18, 1911), 14.

Young's *Chronicle*, the recognized leading daily of the city. Senator Hearst, who died in 1891, lived to see his son make a handsome profit on the once money-losing paper, and the profit grew until it averaged between $350,000 and $500,000 a year.[2]

The profits from the *Examiner* now were available for an invasion of New York. But Hearst needed more capital, and eventually he persuaded his mother to sell the family holdings in the Anaconda copper mines for $7,500,000 and make the cash available for new publishing ventures.[3] Later, when a friend told Mrs. Hearst that she had heard the *New York Journal* was losing a million dollars a year, and expressed fear that the family fortune was being thrown away recklessly, Mrs. Hearst replied that, in such an event, her son could hold out for 30 years more.

Somewhat ironically, Hearst entered the New York field by buying the newspaper which Joseph Pulitzer's brother, Albert, had established in 1882. The *Morning Journal* had been a successful one-cent paper appealing to casual newspaper scanners. In 1894 its price was raised to two cents, and circulation fell off. Albert Pulitzer then sold the *Journal* for a million dollars to John R. McLean, ambitious publisher of the *Cincinnati Enquirer*. McLean was no stranger to sensational methods of publishing newspapers, but he was unable to break into the highly competitive New York field. In the fall of 1895, Hearst picked up the paper from the defeated McLean for $180,000.

Joseph Pulitzer had been busy during the 10 years since Hearst had left New York to launch his career in San Francisco. Particularly he had expanded the mechanical facilities available to his editors, and he had applied the new techniques to the development of the *Sunday World*.

It was Pulitzer who first demonstrated the full potentialities of the Sunday newspaper as a profitable news and entertainment medium. There had been weeklies issued as Sunday papers since 1796. The daily *Boston Globe* put out a Sunday edition briefly in 1833, but James Gordon Bennett's *Herald* was the first daily to print a Sunday edition steadily, starting in 1841. The demand for news

---

[2] *Ibid.* Estimate by Will Irwin in 1911, for the period up to then.

[3] Ferdinand Lundberg, *Imperial Hearst: A Social Biography* (New York: Equinox Cooperative Press, 1936), p. 50. Lundberg presents much information about Hearst's finances, but paints the publisher in the blackest possible fashion.

during the Civil War stimulated Sunday publication, but even by the time Pulitzer invaded New York in 1883 only about 100 daily newspapers had Sunday editions. Most of them were appearing in eastern cities and a good share were printed in German and other foreign languages. Some carried a four-page supplement filled with entertaining features, fiction, and trivia.

Pulitzer's new *Sunday World* added many more pages of entertainment to the regular news section. Feature material for women, for young readers, and for sports enthusiasts appeared. Humorous drawings and other illustrations were concentrated in the Sunday pages. The offerings of the literary syndicates, such as that developed by S. S. McClure, added to the Sunday paper's appeal. Circulation of the *Sunday World* passed the 250,000 mark in 1887 and by the early 1890's the paper had reached 40 to 48 pages in size, as retail advertisers realized the extent of its readership by families and by women. Other newspapers were quick to follow suit, and in 1890 there were 250 dailies with Sunday editions, crowding the metropolitan areas and driving the independent Sunday weeklies out of the picture.

Heading the *World's* Sunday staff was Morrill Goddard, a college graduate who as a young city editor had shown his ability to spot the feature possibilities of significant news events. Goddard was not content, however, to present interpretive stories reporting the advances being made by American scientists and scholars in the fields of medicine, psychology, archaeology, and the physical sciences, or by the inventive geniuses of the industrial age. He jazzed up his page spreads, exaggerating and popularizing the factual information. Scientists particularly were the victims of the Sunday newspaper's predilection for distortion and sensationalism, and the pseudoscientific stories of yellow journalism made the men of science shy away from newspaper coverage for the next 50 years.

This didn't bother Goddard, however; he knew that many of his readers enjoyed what they thought was an easy way to keep up with the world's new learning. One of his staff explained the operation this way:

Suppose it's Halley's comet. Well, first you have a half-page of decoration showing the comet, with historical pictures of previous appearances thrown in. If you can work a pretty girl into the decoration, so much the better. If not, get some good nightmare idea like the inhabitants of

Mars watching it pass. Then you want a quarter of a page of big-type heads—snappy. Then four inches of story, written right off the bat. Then a picture of Professor Halley down here and another of Professor Lowell up there, and a two-column boxed freak containing a scientific opinion, which nobody will understand, just to give it class.[4]

The Sunday staff had a similar approach to crime stories, to drama and literature, to the doings of prominent persons, and to advice to the lovelorn.

When the *World* installed its color presses in 1893, Goddard had a new medium to exploit. His illustrations, which had steadily expanded in size, now could appear in color, as could the bold-type headlines. As many as five colors could be used in the Sunday color supplement for illustrations ranging from wash drawings of cathedrals to comic drawings. It was the comic drawings, Goddard knew, which were most effective in spurring circulation. The *World* began the first regular comic section in 1889, and it was the first newspaper to use color in these drawings (magazines had done so since the 1870's). These early comics were not the kind of continuous-action strips which are familiar to newspaper readers now, but they had the same kind of high reader appeal. Most successful of the artists was Richard F. Outcault, whose "Hogan's Alley" depicted life in the tenements. The central figure in each drawing was a toothless, grinning kid attired in a ballooning dress. When the *World's* printers daubed a blob of yellow on the dress, he became the immortal "Yellow Kid."

Thus, when William Randolph Hearst arrived on the New York scene, the *Sunday World* presented a variety of offerings to its readers: a good news section and editorial page: significant coverage of intellectual interests and society; lighter but high-class entertaining fare; and excursions into sensational presentations of pseudo-science, crime, and affairs of the heart. Hearst set out to buy the men who were doing the sensational jobs.

From an office which the *Examiner* had rented in the *World* building, Hearst conducted a series of raids on Pulitzer's staff. He offered Morrill Goddard a fabulous salary to come over to the *Journal*, and when Goddard explained that his staff of writers and artists did most of the work, Hearst bought them too. Pulitzer detailed S. S. Carvalho, publisher of the *World*, to woo Goddard back.

[4] Will Irwin, "The Fourth Current," *Collier's*, XLVI (February 18, 1911), 14.

but Hearst's typical unconcern for lavish spending made Pulitzer's counter offers hopeless. Before long Carvalho himself was working at the *Journal* building along with the managing editor of the popularized *Evening World*.

Now the contest was on. Pulitzer turned to Arthur Brisbane, Socialist Albert Brisbane's brilliant young son who had broken into newspaper work on the *Sun* before joining the *World* staff, and made him Sunday editor. Brisbane, like Goddard, knew how to popularize scientific advances and scholarly thinking, and he drove the *World's* Sunday circulation to the 600,000 mark. Goddard had taken Outcault and his "Yellow Kid" with him to the *Journal*, but Brisbane had George B. Luks, later a well-known painter, continue the "Yellow Kid" in the *World*. Circulation men for both papers featured the happy-go-lucky kid in their posters, and his grinning but curiously vacant features became familiar to all New Yorkers. To opposition newspapermen, the "Yellow Kid" seemed symbolic of the kind of sensational journalism which was again developing, and the public agreed. The phrase "yellow journalism" soon became widely used. Hearst settled the matter of which paper was to have the most prominent personalities of yellow journalism on its staff in his usual manner, however; Brisbane became editor of the *Evening Journal* in 1897 and Luks took his version of the "Yellow Kid" over to the enemy.

The *World* was not the only contributor to the *Journal's* staff. From San Francisco came the stars of the *Examiner:* managing editor Sam Chamberlain, editorial writer Arthur McEwen, cartoonist Homer Davenport, and sob-sister Winifred (Annie Laurie) Black. Dana's *Sun* lost its star reporters, Julian Ralph, Richard Harding Davis, and Edward W. Townsend, to the Hearst bankroll. Dorothy Dix joined the women's staff. Writers Stephen Crane, Alfred Henry Lewis, and Rudolph Block (Bruno Lessing) signed up, along with other leading newsmen, drama critics, and artists.

Two events helped Hearst build the *Journal* up as a formidable competitor for the *World* and other New York newspapers. In early 1896, when the *Journal* had won 150,000 circulation as a one-cent paper, Pulitzer cut the price of the *World* to a penny. Though the *World* gained circulation as a result, Pulitzer's action was interpreted as a recognition of Hearst's success, just as the *Herald's* price maneuver against Pulitzer in 1884 had been viewed. More importantly, the *World* deserted the Democratic party in the presidential election of 1896, leaving the *Journal* as the city's major supporter of William Jennings Bryan.

Bryan's candidacy in 1896 represented the flowering of the "consistent rebellion" by those who were dissatisfied with the theories of economic individualism which had dominated American political thinking since the Civil War. When Bryan cried, "You shall not press down upon the brow of labor this crown of thorns, you shall not crucify mankind upon a cross of gold." he not only won the Democratic nomination, but he expressed the desires of the labor movement, the populists and reformers of the Middle West, and the silver and paper money advocates who sought to break the hold of financial interests. Pulitzer, while sympathizing with many of the objectives of the movement Bryan led, refused to support his inflationary monetary program. Hearst as a silver mine owner had no great regard for the gold standard and ranged the *Journal* alongside "the people's choice," despite the conservative East's horror of Bryanism. He thus fared well among political partisans, just as Pulitzer had snatched circulation from the *Sun* in 1884 when Dana refused to support Grover Cleveland for the presidency.

But the most important reasons for the upward surge of the *Journal* were its frank adoption of the sins of yellow journalism, and its blatant promotion of what it called its journalistic achievements. The journalistic historian Willard G. Bleyer cited these headlines in issues of the *Journal* published during the fall of 1896, and undoubtedly was justified in linking them with a circulation jump of 125,000 in a single month:[5]

"Real American Monsters and Dragons"—over a story of the discovery of fossil remains by an archaeological expedition.

"A Marvellous New Way of Giving Medicine: Wonderful Results from Merely Holding Tubes of Drugs Near Entranced Patients" —a headline which horrified medical researchers.

"Henry James New Novel of Immorality and Crime; The Surprising Plunge of the Great Novelist in the Field of Sensational Fiction"—the *Journal*'s way of announcing publication of *The Other House.*

[5] Willard G. Bleyer, *Main Currents in the History of American Journalism* (Boston: Houghton Mifflin Company, 1927), pp. 357-64. This book documents the case against the *Journal*'s rampant yellow journalism.

Other headlines were more routinely sensational: "The Mysterious Murder of Bessie Little," "One Mad Blow Kills Child," "What Made Him a Burglar? A Story of Real Life in New York by Edgar Saltus," "Startling Confession of a Wholesale Murderer Who Begs to Be Hanged." Annie Laurie wrote about "Why Young Girls Kill Themselves" and "Strange Things Women Do for Love." When a *Journal* drama critic interviewed a famous actress the streamer headline read, "Mlle. Anna Held Receives Alan Dale, Attired in a 'Nightie'" —and a page-length sketch of the nightgown-clad actress accompanied the story.

The *Journal* was crusading, too, but it went beyond other New York newspapers in a manner which enabled it to shout, "While Others Talk the Journal Acts." The paper obtained a court injunction which balked the granting of a city franchise to a gas company, and pleased by its success, it took similar actions against alleged abuses in government. Hearst then solicited compliments from civic leaders across the country and printed them under such headings as, "Journalism that Acts; Men of Action in All Walks of Life Heartily Endorse the Journal's Fight in Behalf of the People," and "First Employed by the Journal, the Novel Conceit Seems Likely to Become an Accepted Part of the Function of the Newspapers of This Country." [6]

Before his first year in New York had ended, Hearst had installed bigger and better color presses at the *Journal* and had produced an eight-page Sunday colored comic section called the *American Humorist*. It was, the *Journal* said, "eight pages of iridescent polychromous effulgence that makes the rainbow look like a lead pipe." Most of the *Journal's* readers didn't catch the first few words, but they could understand the added explanation. Soon a 16-page color supplement was added under the name of the *Sunday American Magazine* (later, with Brisbane as editor, this was to become the famous *American Weekly*). Still another eight-page color supplement devoted itself to the interests of women. The result was that in late 1896, after a year of Hearst's editorship, the *Journal's* daily circulation was 437,000 and its Sunday circulation was 380,000. In another year's time, Sunday circulation reached the *World's* 600,000 figure.

[6] William Rockhill Nelson, editor of the *Kansas City Star*, also had used his own funds to fight court battles in behalf of the public interest, but not so sensationally.

Circulation figures moved up and down according to the street sales appeal of the moment; on the day following the McKinley-Bryan election the *World* and the *Journal* each sold approximately 1,500,000 copies, to break all records.

The *Journal* and its New York competitors fought to obtain exclusive and dramatic coverage of major news events. The *Journal* sewed up the rights to statements by heavyweight fighters James J. Corbett and Bob Fitzsimmons when they met in Nevada in 1897. It sent Samuel Clemens to London to cover the sixtieth anniversary of Queen Victoria's coronation. When the Greco-Turkish War began in early 1897, King George of Greece cabled an exclusive message to the *Journal*. James Creelman, Julian Ralph, and two women were among seven *Journal* correspondents covering the conflict. And going along on the Klondike gold rush were two expeditions from Hearst's *Journal* and *Examiner*. The *World*, the *Herald*, and the *Sun*, among New York papers, and leading papers in other cities, were just as active in scrambling for the news.

It was in this kind of atmosphere, then, that American newspapers approached the events which led to an international crisis—and the Spanish-American War. For the yellow journalists, trouble in Cuba meant another chance for sensational stories, excitement, and adventure. For their competitors, the problem became one of maintaining caution and losing circulation, or matching the efforts of the yellow journalists in printing fact and fiction and thereby holding their readers. Only smaller papers, and those big city dailies which contented themselves with building a solid core of appreciative readers, could face the problem calmly.

The insurrection in Cuba which caught the attention of the yellow journalists was the culmination of several decades of struggle between Cuban independence leaders and the Spanish government. The island, principal remnant of the once-great Spanish empire in the Western hemisphere, had been the scene of several revolts in the first half of the century, and from 1868 to 1878 there had been constant turmoil. Expansion of the Cuban sugar industry then had brought a measure of prosperity and a dwindling of the independence movement, but a change in American tariff policies in 1894 affected the Cuban sugar market and brought hard times, unemployment, and a renewal of hostilities in early 1895.

Insurrectionists, operating in small guerrilla bands, destroyed sugar mills and plantations owned by Spanish loyalists. In New York a Cuban junta, styling itself as a revolutionary government, sold bonds and used the money to ship arms to the island. It also intensified a long-established propaganda campaign to win the sympathy of Americans and to obtain United States intervention in the Spanish-Cuban struggle. The Spanish government, of course, sought to prevent contraband arms from reaching the island and instituted repressive measures to control the insurrection. Ruthless tactics on both sides led to the committing of atrocities, and disruption of normal life on the island brought widespread disease and starvation.

When American public opinion became aroused, the Spanish government sought to introduce reforms in Cuba which would satisfy the diplomatic demands of the United States. But just when the controversy seemed to be quieting, the United States battleship "Maine" was sunk in Havana harbor. Despite frantic Spanish efforts to prove that the Spanish government had no part in the sinking, and new diplomatic concessions, the United States Congress decided to force the issue by demanding that Spain quit the island altogether. War was the result.

Of all the wars the United States has fought, the Spanish-American War was the most painless. In fewer than four months the Spanish government was forced to request an armistice, at an extraordinarily small cost in American lives, and the American flag was floating over an empire stretching from Puerto Rico to the Philippines. Save perhaps for the Mexican War, it was also the most unwarranted war in American history.

Those who have sought to explain the causes of the war have often centered the blame on William Randolph Hearst in particular and the newspapers of the country in general. Carefully documented studies made by Marcus M. Wilkerson and Joseph E. Wisan in the early 1930's give ample evidence that Hearst's *Journal*, Pulitzer's *World*, the *Chicago Tribune*, the *Sun* and *Herald* in New York (and, as is usually ignored, many other American newspapers) so handled the news of events leading up to the crisis of the sinking of the "Maine" that a war psychosis was developed.[7] It must not be

[7] Marcus M. Wilkerson, *Public Opinion and the Spanish-American War* (Baton Rouge: Louisiana State University Press, 1932); Joseph E. Wisan, *The Cuban Crisis as Reflected in the New York Press* (New York: Columbia University Press, 1934).

forgotten, however, that the newspapers were cultivating public opinion in a favorable atmosphere.

Throughout the nineteenth century the United States had pursued a policy of expansion. Its people in general subscribed to the belief in "manifest destiny" which spurred the westward movement. The War of 1812 was forced upon a reluctant New England by western expansionists who viewed the British in Canada as their mortal enemies. The Mexican War and cries of "54-40 or Fight" brought the completion of the continental United States. Americans liked to buy the territory they wanted, but they were also ready to take it by force if necessary.

As a new industrial America emerged after the Civil War, the country's interest in international affairs steadily grew. The Monroe Doctrine which had proclaimed the freedom of the New World from the Old became an instrument for the development of an American foreign policy which aimed at a domination of the Western hemisphere by the United States. The purchase of Alaska brought protection of one flank. James G. Blaine, in two terms as Secretary of State, began maneuvering to force the British out of any share in control of the inter-oceanic canal which would be built in Panama. Blaine also sought to build a Pan-American union in which the United States would play a leading role, but a controversy between the United States and Chile, marked by Yankee diplomatic ineptitude, reduced the effectiveness of Blaine's efforts.

At the same time the United States was increasingly interested in the Pacific area. Friendly relations were cultivated with Japan, and trade with China was increased to the point where John Hay was to enunciate the famous Open Door Policy in 1899 as a means of keeping China's trade open to all comers. Agitation for the annexation of Hawaii increased during the 1880's, and the United States successfully won a foothold in the Samoa Islands, in competition with Germany and Britain. Beginning in 1882 the United States had built a modern navy symbolic of the age of steel, and Captain Alfred Thayer Mahan was revolutionizing the theory of naval warfare with his writings on the influence of sea power on history. The United States, along with Britain, Germany, France, and Japan, was entering into a world-wide race for power.

Viewed in the long perspective, the Spanish-American War was but one incident in a series of events which marked this arrival of the United States as a world power. It was preceded by the Venezuelan crisis of 1895, in which President Grover Cleveland brought his country to the verge of war with Great Britain over a test of the Monroe Doctrine. It was followed by the annexation of Hawaii, the Philippines, Guam, and Puerto Rico, and the building of the Panama Canal. American interest in affairs on the Asiatic mainland brought about the Open Door Policy in China and the negotiation of the peace treaty ending the Russo-Japanese War in a little New Hampshire town. Pan-Americanism became open American intervention in the affairs of Central American countries and the building of a Caribbean defense for the United States and its new Panama Canal. President Theodore Roosevelt, who was the guiding force in the establishment of this new policy, took his country into European affairs by participating in the Algeciras conference which settled the Moroccan crisis of 1905 precipitated by German expansionism. The United States, as a powerful force in the modern era of industry and world commerce, henceforth was to be an important participant in international affairs.

The desire for power was not the only driving force behind this American expansion of interest. There was pride felt by many Americans in the addition of new territories, and there was keen interest in the expansion of American trade and foreign investments as the domestic economy matured. But Americans also felt they had a role to play in promoting peace and justice in the world. There had been proposals for the annexation of Cuba throughout the nineteenth century, but there also had been widespread sympathy for the Cuban independence movement which had flared in ten revolts before the final crisis. Americans were disturbed by accounts of Turkish atrocities in Armenia, and many newspaper editors called Cuba "another Armenia." Americans also were following with keen interest the Greco-Turkish War of 1897, and were sympathizing with the Greeks in their struggle for independence. Many Americans wanted a Pan-American union in the full meaning of the phrase. American policy in Japan and China was friendly and forward-looking. Thus in the United States there were two major forces: a strong sympathy for another people whose freedom was being suppressed, and a growing sense of power in world affairs. Both forces came into play during the Spanish-American War period. If later the advocates of imperialism and "dollar diplomacy" gained the upper hand over the idealists, that was but one phase of America's coming of age in international affairs.

The newspapers which came to be blamed for precipitating the Spanish-American War played upon the American feeling of sympathy and social justice. They exaggerated the story of the Spanish-Cuban struggle and they presented it in a lurid manner, as will be shown. But if their stories and illustrations were sensationalized and sometimes untrue, they were nevertheless founded on a solid core of fact. Cubans were fighting for their independence against an inefficient and oppressive Spanish regime. There were atrocities committed during the insurrection. And disease and starvation were widespread. These established facts should not be overlooked, for other Americans than the newspapermen pointed them out in public discussion, and they formed the basis for acceptance of sensationalized reports and propaganda.

The newspapers involved also played upon American pride and sense of power. They openly discussed the nature of a war between Spain and the United States, and pointed to the new American navy which awaited its first test in battle. They urged the United States to use force if need be to oust the Spanish from Cuba, so that the Cuban people would be freed from oppression. They suggested that the decadent Spanish military power would be an "easy mark." They were not thinking of the economic gains from such a war; the commercial interests of the country and those newspapers which reflected the thinking of America's new big business shrank away from a war which might upset the prosperity of the country, barely regained after the depression of 1893. The newspapers advocating intervention in Cuba were, in many cases, simply reflecting a desire to flex the nation's new muscles.

Nor were they alone in this desire. For 30 years the people of both North and South had lived in the aftermath of the Civil War, honoring its veterans and reliving its struggles in story and song. As the horror of war faded, older Americans began to wonder if their country's military prowess was still secure. Younger Americans were eager to match the valor of the honored men of Blue and Gray. For them war, 1898 style, still seemed to be an exciting personal adventure. John D. Hicks, an American historian of first rank who is not unaware of the role of the newspaper as an organ of public opinion, sums up his discussion of the causes of the Spanish-American War by saying:

> Years later, Theodore Roosevelt recaptured the spirit of 1898 when he mourned apologetically, "It wasn't much of a war, but it was the best war we had." America in the spring of 1898 was ripe for any war, and the country's mood was not to be denied.[8]

Certainly the excesses of yellow journalism, and the reflections of the doings of the most guilty newspapers in the other press of the country, played an important part in the country's decision to go to war. Perhaps the crisis would have passed without a war had the newspapermen written their stories and editorials dispassionately, for in similar episodes involving American indignation and national honor peace has been maintained. But the fact remains that whatever the newspapers did to stir up sympathy for Cubans and to create a war fever, they were striking responsive chords in many Americans. The situation was one in which journalistic excesses and outright war propaganda could be effective, because other factors were combining to produce a "ripe for war" atmosphere. Enough of the reading public was willing to be convinced, and enough newspapers were willing to provide the alleged justifications, for war to come.

From March, 1895, when the Cuban insurrection began, until April, 1898, when Spain and the United States went to war, there were fewer than a score of days in which a story about Cuba did not appear in one of the New York newspapers.[9] This was due in part to the aggressive news policies of the big dailies. It was due in part to the manufacturing of stories by some of the papers, notably the *Journal*. It was due in part to increasing reader interest in a controversial story. And it was also the result of the activities of the Cuban junta which fed information and propaganda to American newsmen in New York and at the Florida news bases nearest the island.

A considerable number of Cubans had emigrated to the United States, settling in New York, Philadelphia, Baltimore, Boston, and

---

[8] John D. Hicks, *A Short History of American Democracy* (Boston: Houghton Mifflin Company, 1943), p. 605.
[9] Wisan, *The Cuban Crisis*, p. 460.

several Florida cities. The junta had its headquarters in New York, where a Cuban newspaper was published. Through the Cuban residents in the eastern cities, a program of mass meetings was established. Money was raised, and several hundred volunteers were obtained in each city for service in running arms and taking part in filibustering expeditions. Cuban agents funneled information on the progress of the fighting on Cuba to the American newspapers. The work was well underway in 1895, and as the crisis intensified, the activities of the junta reached greater heights. Ministers, educators, civic leaders, and politicians were reached by the junta's efforts to advance the Cuban cause and discredit the Spanish regime. And, of course, Cuban propagandists found the pro-Cuban yellow journalists particularly receptive. Conscientious newsmen complained that some of their colleagues made no effort to check on the veracity of rumors and stories given them by the Cubans, particularly at the Key West and Tampa news bases.

There was news from Spanish sources as well, and in early 1895 none of the New York papers did more than print the conflicting claims of the Cubans and the Spanish authorities. The first real flare of indignation came in March, 1895, when an American ship was fired upon near the Cuban coast by a Spanish patrol boat. The ship was not carrying contraband to the insurrectionists, and editors inveighed against a violation of the freedom of the seas. Later, when American ships and crews were caught running guns and supplies to the rebels, the stories assumed major proportions despite the illegality of gun-running. Considerable sentiment developed for passage of a congressional resolution recognizing belligerency, but President Cleveland set a course of strict official neutrality. Congressmen by this time were quoting the stories published in pro-Cuban newspapers, and were using information provided by the Cuban junta. And when these stories became a part of debates in Congress, they became news for papers in all parts of the country.

The Spanish decision in early 1896 to use strong repressive measures in Cuba brought the focus of attention upon what was happening to the native population. Captain-General Valeriano Weyler, a tough Spanish commander known as the "Butcher," was sent to the island to stamp out the insurrection, and quickly became the villain of the piece. Weyler ordered all loyal Cubans to congregate in small areas adjoining Spanish military bases. Those who did not obey were to be considered as enemies. This *reconcentrado* policy aroused quick resentment in the United States, for it meant in effect the creation of a military dictatorship. It was an unhappy decision for the Spanish in another way, too, since the Cubans who huddled in the towns and camps quickly became victims of epidemics, and many of them starved to death when food supplies became disrupted. Much of the newspaper copy centered about the effects of famine and pestilence, and estimates of Cuban deaths ran as high as 400,000. Wilkerson in his study sets the figure for all Cuban deaths during the three years of revolt at approximately 100,000,[10] and the discrepancy affords an illustration of the exaggeration by American newsmen of conditions in Cuba which were sufficiently serious in truth, but more striking when enlarged upon. The *reconcentrado* policy, and Spanish reprisals against revolutionary guerrilla bands, fitted Weyler's nickname of "Butcher" and he was compared in American newspaper stories to the "blood-thirsty Cortez and Pizarro" of the days of the conquistadors.

When Weyler's campaign began in February, 1896, there were correspondents in Cuba from the *World, Journal, Sun,* and *Herald,* of the New York newspapers. The *Washington Post,* the *New Orleans Times-Democrat,* and several Florida newspapers also were represented. The Associated Press had its own coverage, and also could use in its news report all the stories printed by its member papers.[11] In addition, the newspapers with correspondents on the scene sold their news services to other dailies across the country. In Chicago, for example, the *Tribune* bought both the *World* news service and the *Journal* syndicate, while the rival *Times-Herald* relied upon the *New York Herald* service. In San Francisco Hearst's *Examiner* had the *Journal's* coverage, while the opposition *Chronicle* tried to keep up in sensational news presentation by printing the offerings of both the *Herald* and *Sun.* Therefore, with the selling of the New York papers' stories to other dailies, the transmission by the Associated Press of the "news beats" of the competing papers, and the growing attention in Congress to Cuban affairs, the Cuban story was broadcast widely across the country.

[10] *Public Opinion and the Spanish-American War,* p. 40.
[11] There was competition between the Associated Press and the old United Press until 1897. After that time, all the major New York papers except the *Sun* were AP members.

The *World's* first correspondent in Cuba, William S. Bowen, was fairly accurate in his reporting of conditions on the island. But two of his successors, James Creelman and Sylvester Scovel, gave the *World* thoroughly sensationalized coverage. Creelman saw sickening scenes in 1896, but he made certain that his reading audience was impressed by giving them such lines as, "Blood on the roadsides, blood in the fields, blood on the doorsteps, blood, blood, blood!" Scovel described in nauseating detail the mutilation of Cuban men, women, and children who had stayed in the countryside in defiance of Weyler's orders, and would drop in dubious reports—such as one that the Spanish were collecting the ears of their victims as trophies. Some of their stories were supposedly based on their eyewitness reporting; others admittedly were recountings of the stories of Cuban refugees.

One correspondent after another was expelled from the island by the outraged Weyler, who caught some aiding the insurrectionists and accused others of distorting the facts. When Scovel was placed under arrest, papers other than the *World* expressed little sympathy for him. Still, the American press felt that it was challenged by Weyler's censorship and worked harder to get news unfavorable to the Spanish. If correspondents could not operate successfully in Cuba, they could get tips from Cuban propaganda agents at Key West and other Florida points, and at least the yellow journalists were satisfied with this alternative.

Hearst was not to be outdone in this competition. He persuaded Creelman to switch his allegiance from the *World* to the *Journal* in late 1896, and sent the famous team of Richard Harding Davis, the ex-*Sun* reporter, and Frederic Remington, the artist, to the island. They obliged with stories rivaling those of Scovel in exaggerated effect. The *Herald* correspondents kept to the same pace, while those of the *Sun* trailed in sensational coverage. Sketches were drawn in Cuba, or more frequently in the newspaper offices, to illustrate the stories, and many of them went beyond the facts. The impact of pictorial journalism was increased in 1897 when New York newspapers began to print photographs which sometimes were accurate portrayals of Cuban scenes and which sometimes were fakes. Enough of them seemed authentic, however, to give strong evidence to readers that what the reporters were writing was in essence true.

One of the episodes of this period did much to tag the *Journal's* owner with "Hearst's war." Creelman, in writing his reminiscences in 1901, said that Remington found his Cuban assignment an unhappy one. According to Creelman, the artist cabled Hearst that all was quiet in Cuba, that there would be no war, and that he was coming home. Whereupon Hearst was supposed to have replied: "Remington, Havana. Please remain. You furnish the pictures, and I'll furnish the war. W. R. Hearst." [12] There is no other evidence that Hearst sent this cable, so often quoted as conclusive evidence against him, but in a sense it reflected the situation. Of all the American newspapers, Hearst's *Journal* worked the hardest to create public sentiment for war.

Open advocacy of war with Spain appeared in the *Journal* by the fall of 1896, and Hearst applied to this situation the paper's boast: "While Others Talk the Journal Acts." When Congress assembled in December the *Journal* polled senators on the question of open American intervention in Cuba, and it asked state governors how many volunteers they could raise in event of war. The *Chicago Tribune* and the *World* conducted similar polls, and the results gave further emphasis to the campaign for intervention, since many prominent political leaders gave pro-Cuban answers.

Still there was not sufficient fodder for the *Journal's* intervention policy, and Hearst looked about for incidents which could be exploited. His first notable discovery was the case of a Cuban dentist named Ricardo Ruiz who was found dead in a Havana cell. Ruiz had at one time taken out naturalization papers in the United States and the *Journal* played this angle to the hilt. The *Chicago Tribune,* the *New Orleans Times-Democrat,* the *New York Sun,* the *San Francisco Examiner,* and other interventionist papers picked up the chant.

Hearst's greatest exploit came in the summer of 1897 when he built up the story of Evangelina Cisneros. Miss Cisneros, a niece of the Cuban revolutionary president, had been accused of luring a Spanish officer to her home where insurrectionists tried to kill him. Nine months after she had been sentenced to a 20-year prison term for rebellious activity, the *Journal* took up her cause. It described her as the most beautiful girl in all Cuba and pictured

[12] James Creelman, *On the Great Highway* (Boston: Lothrop Publishing Company, 1901), p. 178.

her as living in indescribable quarters in a Havana prison while awaiting transportation to an African penal settlement. Cried the *Journal:* "The unspeakable fate to which Weyler has doomed an innocent girl whose only crime is that she has defended her honor against a beast in uniform has sent a shudder of horror through the American people." When the *World* printed Weyler's version of the incident, and proved that the *Journal's* account of her sufferings was greatly exaggerated, the *Journal's* editors accused Pulitzer of unpatriotic motives.

After a month during which the *Journal* solicited pleas for Miss Cisneros' safety from scores of prominent American women, the paper acted. With giant headlines in a Sunday edition, it announced that a *Journal* reporter, Karl Decker, had succeeded in rescuing the girl from her prison cell and had smuggled her aboard a New York-bound ship. Secretary of State John Sherman, the Bishop of London, Clara Barton, Henry George, and other notables congratulated the *Journal* on its achievement. Even President William McKinley, who was firmly opposed to a war with Spain, found himself greeting Miss Cisneros at the White House. Some idea of the *Journal's* exploitation of the Cisneros case may be found in a compilation of newspaper space given the story. It was big news which no newspaper could ignore, but the figures for New York newspapers were as follows: The *World,* 12½ columns; the *Times,* 10 columns; the *Tribune,* 3½ columns; the *Sun,* one column; the *Herald,* one column; the *Journal,* 375 columns.[13]

Despite the energies of the *Journal* and other pro-Cuban newspapers, and of Cuban sympathizers in the country, it did not seem probable in late 1897 that any warlike action would be taken. Indeed, the trend was the other way. A change in the Spanish government had brought a new prime minister and promises from the Spanish crown that Cuba would be granted autonomy. The concentration camp policy was to be ended, and Weyler was recalled. The *World* and some other newspapers abated their campaigns, and President McKinley announced that American diplomatic representations in Madrid had been properly answered by the Spanish. Polls of congressional sentiment made by the *Journal* and *Herald* in December, 1897, showed most Republicans backing up McKinley, and most Democrats favoring at least recognition of

[13] Wisan, *The Cuban Crisis,* p. 331.

William Randolph Hearst, as he appeared at the peak of his career, about 1930,
when his group of newspapers had grown to include 26 dailies and 17 Sunday
papers, published in 18 cities.

,000 REWARD.—WHO DESTROYED THE MAINE?—$50,000 REWARD.

The Journal will give $50,000 for information, furnished to it exclusively, that will convict the person or persons who sank the Maine.

NEW YORK JOURNAL
AND ADVERTISER.

Copyright, 1898, by W. R. Hearst.—NEW YORK, THURSDAY, FEBRUARY 17, 1898.—16 PAGES.　　PRICE ONE CENT

The Journal will give $50,000 for information, furnished to it exclusively, that will convict the person or persons who sank the Maine.

DESTRUCTION OF THE WAR SHIP MAINE WAS THE WORK OF AN ENEMY.

$50,000!
$50,000 REWARD!
for the Detection of the Perpetrator of the Maine Outrage!

New York Journal hereby offers a reward of **$50,000** for information FURNISHED TO IT EXCLUSIVELY, which shall lead to the detection and conviction of the person or government criminally responsible for the explosion which resulted in the destruction, at Havana, of the United States war ship Maine and the loss of 258 lives of American sailors.

$50,000 CASH offered for the above information to our Wells, Fargo & Co., and will be paid upon the production of the convincing evidence.

No one be barred. Let be the hireable but misguided assassin, sking out a few miserable dollars by aiding as a spy, or the attache of a protracted secret service, plotting by any devilish means to encompass the devilish or cripple measuring resistance.

The devilish enemy has been cabled to Europe and will be made public in every capital of the Continent and in London this morning.

The Journal believes that any man who can be bought to commit murder can also be bought to betray his comrades. **FOR THE PERPETRATOR OF THIS OUTRAGE HAD ACCOMPLICES.**

W. R. HEARST.

Assistant Secretary Roosevelt Convinced the Explosion of the War Ship Was Not an Accident.

The Journal Offers $50,000 Reward for the Conviction of the Criminals Who Sent 258 American Sailors to Their Death. Naval Officers Unanimous That the Ship Was Destroyed on Purpose.

$50,000!
$50,000 REWARD!
For the Detection of the Perpetrator of the Maine Outrage!

The New York Journal hereby offers a reward of **$50,000** CASH for information, FURNISHED TO IT EXCLUSIVELY, which shall lead to the detection and conviction of the person, persons or government criminally responsible for the explosion which resulted in the destruction, at Havana, of the United States war ship Maine and the loss of 258 lives of American sailors.

The **$50,000 CASH** offered for the above information is on deposit with Wells, Fargo & Co., and will be paid upon the production of the convincing evidence.

No one be barred. Let be the hireable, but misguided, assassin, eking out a few miserable dollars by acting as a spy, or the attache of a permanent secret service, plotting by any devilish means to encompass devilish or cripple measuring resistance.

This offer has been cabled to Europe and will be made public in every capital of the Continent and in London this morning.

The Journal believes that any man who can be bought to commit murder can also be bought to betray his comrades. **FOR THE PERPETRATOR OF THIS OUTRAGE HAD ACCOMPLICES.**

W. R. HEARST.

THEIR MAGAZINE

NAVAL OFFICERS THINK THE MAINE WAS DESTROYED BY A SPANISH MINE.

George Eugene Bryson, the Journal's special correspondent at Havana, cables that it is the secret opinion of many Spaniards in the Cuban capital, that the Maine was destroyed and 258 of her men killed by means of a submarine mine or fixed torpedo. This is the opinion of several American naval authorities. The Spaniards, it is believed, arranged to have the Maine anchored over one of the harbor mines. Wires connected the mine with a magazine, and it is thought the explosion was caused by sending an electric current through the wire. If this can be proven, the brutal nature of the Spaniards will be shown by the fact that they waited to spring the mine after all the men had retired for the night. The Maltese cross in the picture shows where the mine may have been fired.

A Mine or a Sunken Torpedo Believed to Have Been the Weapon Used Against the American Man-of-War---Officers and Men Tell Thrilling Stories of Being Blown Into the Air Amid a Mass of Shattered Steel and Exploding Shells---Survivors Brought to Key West Scout the Idea of Accident---Spanish Officials Protest Too Much---Our Cabinet Orders a Searching Inquiry---Journal Sends Divers to Havana to Report Upon the Condition of the Wreck.

Was the Vessel Anchored Over a Mine?

Assistant Secretary of the Navy Theodore Roosevelt says he is convinced that the destruction of the Maine in Havana Harbor was not an accident. The Journal offers a reward of $50,000 for exclusive evidence that will convict the person, persons or Government criminally responsible for the destruction of the American battleship and the death of 258 of its crew.

The suspicion that the Maine was deliberately blown up grows stronger every hour. Not a single fact to the contrary has been produced.

Captain Sigsbee, of the Maine, and Consul-General Lee both urge that public opinion be suspended until they have completed their investigation is taking the course of tactful men who are convinced that there has been treachery.

Spanish Government officials are pressing forward all sorts of explanations of how it could have been an accident. The facts show that there was not before the ship exploded, and that, had her magazine exploded, she would have sunk immediately.

Every naval expert in Washington says that if the Maine's magazine had exploded the whole vessel would have been blown to atoms.

Cuban belligerency. The majority opposed any demand for Cuban independence, which would inevitably force the Spanish into a war with the United States.

At this point the *Journal* again acted, scoring its most significant "scoop." On February 9, 1898, the Hearst paper published a private letter written by Dupuy de Lome, the Spanish ambassador to the United States, to a Spanish newspaper editor visiting in Havana. The letter, stolen in Havana by a Cuban junta member, referred to President McKinley as "weak and catering to the rabble, and, besides, a low politician." At the same moment Theodore Roosevelt was commenting that his chief had the backbone of a chocolate eclair, but to have the Spanish ambassador say the same thing— even in a private letter—was a different matter. American indignation was universal, although not everyone called for immediate war as did the *Journal*. De Lome was recalled to Madrid, and American opinion of the Spanish government hit a new low. The significance of the de Lome letter episode lies in the fact that it preceded by just six days the sinking of the battleship "Maine" in Havana harbor, and the impact of the two events proved to be the turning point in the diplomatic crisis.

No one has satisfactorily established the cause of the explosion which sank the "Maine" with the loss of 266 American lives. The ship had been sent to Havana because Cuban independence leaders were inciting riots in an effort to forestall public acceptance of the Spanish government's autonomy policy. Resentment among the revolutionists was strong against American acceptance of the Spanish plan for a measure of Cuban self-government under continued Spanish sovereignty. If the "Maine" was blown up by an outside agent, rather than by an internal explosion as seems probable, a Cuban sympathizer could have been responsible. Certainly the Spanish government itself had every reason to avoid such an aggressive act, and no one seriously believed that the plot was hatched in Madrid. But some American newspapers set about to make it appear that the Spanish were indirectly responsible for the sinking.

The *Journal* offered a $50,000 reward for information leading to the arrest and conviction of the criminals—a fairly safe offer—but tipped off amateur detectives with its first-day streamer: "DESTRUCTION OF THE WAR SHIP MAINE WAS THE WORK OF AN ENEMY." Both the *Journal* and *World* rushed ships to

Havana harbor to conduct diving operations, and both were indignant when Spanish and American authorities preferred to conduct their own investigations. Both papers carried misleading reports on the outcome of the official inquiries, as did the Associated Press, primarily because all concerned were eager to have the news in advance of official release. Three days after the sinking the *Journal's* streamer read: "THE WHOLE COUNTRY THRILLS WITH WAR FEVER."

Godkin's *Post* played the Maine story in lead position, then column one, on February 16, saying: "BATTLE-SHIP MAINE BLOWN UP." This was the more conventional treatment of the story.

Other newspapers were reflecting the same attitude, however. The *St. Paul Pioneer Press*, for example, ran these successive headlines based on Associated Press reports during the first seven days after the sinking: "Cruiser Maine Lost"; "It Looks Suspicious"; "Americans Aspersed"; "Captain Warned" (of impending destruction of his vessel); "Done by Spaniards"; "More Than Suspicious"; and "A Hostile Nation: Spain May Be Declared Such at Any Hour." These front page headlines had more effect than the editorial urgings for calm judgment written by editor Joseph A. Wheelock, whose voice was important in his area. It was two months before the final break between the two countries but in many newspapers the ultimate verdict already had been made clear.

Large headlines and striking illustrations became common in big

AINE EXPLOSION CAUSED BY BOMB OR TORPEDO?

pt. Sigsbee and Consul-General Lee Are in Doubt---The World Has Sent a Special Tug, With Submarine Divers, to Havana to Find Out---Lee Asks for an Immediate Court of Inquiry---Capt. Sigsbee's Suspicions.

I. SIGSBEE, IN A SUPPRESSED DESPATCH TO THE STATE DEPARTMENT, SAYS THE ACCIDENT WAS MADE POSSIBLE BY AN ENEMY.

E. C. Pendleton, Just Arrived from Havana, Says He Overheard Talk There of a Plot to Blow Up the Ship---Capt. Zalinski, the Dynamite Expert, and Other Experts Report to The World that the Wreck Was Not Accidental---Washington Officials Ready for Vigorous Action if Spanish Responsibility Can Be Shown---Divers to Be Sent Down to Make Careful Examinations.

he *World's* February 17 front page, somewhat more cautious than that of the *Journal*.

439

city papers like the *Journal* and *World* during the "Maine" crisis. The first three pages of the *World* were devoted daily to the war story; in the *Journal* it was the first eight. Leading the field in yellow journalism techniques was Arthur Brisbane, editor of the *Evening Journal*. Brisbane loved big headline types, and he experimented with giant artist-drawn types which virtually filled the front page with two or three words. Writing in a popular magazine at the close of the war, Brisbane had this to say about his activities:

> Before the type size reached its maximum, "War Sure" could be put in one line across a page, and it was put in one line and howled through the streets by patriotic newsboys many and many a time. As war was sure, it did no harm.[14]

If Brisbane wrote so frankly in 1898, clearly he thought the temper of the people was with him. And it was. During February and March the newspapers began to be filled with news of preparations for war, of the formation of volunteer troop units such as the Rough Riders, of the passage of a 50 million dollar defense bill by Congress, of the marshaling of resources. President McKinley still stood against the war trend, but his Secretary of State, Sherman, who more than once made official statements based on news reports from the *Journal*, swung back to his original pro-Cuban beliefs. The young Republicans, led by Theodore Roosevelt, were so outspoken that it became obvious to McKinley that a split was developing in his party. When in mid-March a leading Republican senator, Proctor of Vermont, made a speech based on his personal investigation of conditions in Cuba, which bore out much of what the newspapers had said for three years, the swing toward war was definitely underway. By the time diplomatic negotiations with Spain had produced a complete victory for the United States on issues which were at stake between the two countries, pro-war and anti-war newspapers alike were in a frame of mind to brush the Spanish offers aside as "untrustworthy and too late." Congress passed a resolution on April 18 looking toward United States intervention in Cuba, which Spain considered as a declaration of war.

The *World* at first had urged caution in handling the "Maine" question, in its editorial comment. But gradually it had swung

[14] Arthur Brisbane, "The Modern Newspaper in War Time," *Cosmopolitan*, XXV (September, 1898), 541.

around, until by April 10 Pulitzer had published a signed editorial calling for a "short and sharp" war. The *New York Sun*, which under Dana's cynical editorship had been extremely jingoistic, stood with the *Journal* and *World* in demanding intervention. The *New York Herald*, while keeping up in sensational news coverage, opposed intervention in its editorial stands—an incongruity also true of the *Chicago Times-Herald, Boston Herald, San Francisco Chronicle,* and *Milwaukee Sentinel.* Strongly interventionist were such papers as the *Chicago Tribune, New Orleans Times-Democrat, Atlanta Constitution,* and *Indianapolis Journal.* Keeping calm were such papers as the *New York Tribune, New York Times, Chicago Daily News, Boston Transcript,* and papers which reflected the thinking of the business community in their editorial columns. Wilkerson, in his study of the newspapers for the period, ranks the *Journal* as the leader in excessive journalism, and the *Chicago Tribune* and the *World* next in order. Joseph Medill's *Tribune,* strongly nationalistic in its editorial columns, did not originate sensational news stories as did the *Journal* and *World,* but it ran the cream of those collected by both papers.

It should be pointed out, too, that the *World* was not a jingo newspaper. It opposed annexation of foreign territory by the United States, in contrast with the *Sun* and *Journal,* which were willing to expand the country in any direction. Pulitzer fought the annexation of Hawaii, and when the Spanish-American War was over, sought to prevent the annexation of the Philippines. Most of the other interventionist papers approved of territorial expansion. The *World* based its call for war on the issue of human liberty, and in subsequent actions proved that it was not merely jingoistic. Pulitzer realized the part his paper played in preparing public opinion for the war, and later regretted it; in 1907, when Theodore Roosevelt ordered the American fleet to the Pacific to impress Japan, Pulitzer requested his editors to "show that Spain had granted to Cuba all that we demanded. . . . Give further details of jingoism causing Cuban War after Spain had virtually granted everything." [15]

Indeed, only a little more than two years before the outbreak of the Spanish-American War, Joseph Pulitzer and the *World* had made a notable contribution to world peace by opposing President

[15] Don C. Seitz, *Joseph Pulitzer* (New York: Simon and Schuster, 1924), p. 312.

Cleveland's headstrong action in the Venezuelan crisis. The boundary line between Venezuela and British Guiana was in dispute, and Great Britain's demands upon the South American country violated the principle of the Monroe Doctrine, according to many Americans. Cleveland finally demanded that the British submit the dispute to arbitration, and warned that if necessary the United States would fight to uphold Venezuela's claims. The *World* immediately opposed the President, although most other New York papers rallied to his support.

Pulitzer's editorial column insisted that the spirit of the Monroe Doctrine was not being violated by the British (who, ironically enough, had helped Monroe make his statement stick in the 1820's). The *World* added that war between the two English-speaking countries would be a "colossal crime." Then Pulitzer sent cable messages to leading Englishmen, asking for their opinions. The Prince of Wales, the Duke of York, former prime minister Gladstone, and other men well known to Americans all replied that England did not want war. The *World* published their replies on Christmas eve, 1895, under a banner headline which read, "Messages of Peace, Common Sense and Humanity to the People of the United States." Secretary of State Olney and Senator Henry Cabot Lodge tried to prove that Pulitzer had carried on diplomatic activities as a private citizen in violation of the law, but a reaction against war brought both a settlement of the international dispute and a resounding victory for Pulitzer.

In this instance, the *World* stood against popular sentiment in opposing war; in New York only Godkin's *Evening Post* put up the same kind of fight. But Godkin did not spare Pulitzer when he lashed out against the pro-war newspapers of 1898. Referring to Pulitzer and Hearst he said, "It is a crying shame that men should work such mischief simply in order to sell more papers." The *Evening Post* fought to the end against the decision to force Spain from Cuba, and bitterly attacked the sensational newspapers with such statements as this:

A yellow journal office is probably the nearest approach, in atmosphere, to hell, existing in any Christian state. A better place in which to prepare a young man for eternal damnation than a yellow journal office does not exist.

Godkin was not guiltless on his side, however. When Senator Proctor made his crucial speech substantiating much of the evidence the correspondents had offered from Cuba, the *Evening Post* printed only a dozen lines in its news columns. Other newspapers carried extensive quotations from Proctor's speech, or printed the text in full. Godkin instead sought to minimize the impact of the speech by argument in his editorial column.[16]

All in all, while Godkin's criticism of Pulitzer was justified, the *World's* publisher did not deserve to be bracketed with Hearst, whose *Journal* gleefully asked in its front page ears, "How do you like the Journal's war?"

The newspapers fought the war as determinedly as they had fostered it. Some 500 reporters, artists, and photographers flocked to Florida, where the American army was mobilizing, and to the Cuban and Puerto Rican fronts. Small fleets of press boats accompanied the Navy into action. Correspondents sailed with Dewey to Manila and with Schley to Havana. They covered every battle and skirmish in Cuba and more than once took part in the fighting itself. A *Journal* correspondent lost a leg during one fighting charge. Richard Harding Davis, then reporting for the *New York Herald* and the *Times* of London, led another charge and won the praise of Rough Rider Roosevelt.

Among the correspondents were famous writers, including Frank Norris, Stephen Crane, Julian Hawthorne, and of course Davis. Murat Halstead, James Creelman, Sylvester Scovel, and other leading correspondents took in this war as they had others. So did many less qualified journalists, even including the drama editor of the *Sun* and the humor editor of the *World*. As one newspaperman of the time put it, you didn't have any influence if you couldn't get to be a war correspondent.

Leading the *Journal's* contingent was the publisher himself, who exuded enthusiasm as he directed the work of his staff of 20 men and women reporters, artists, and photographers, including a motion picture man. Creelman, who was wounded in one battle, records a picture of Hearst—wearing a be-ribboned straw hat on his head and a revolver at his belt—taking the story from his bleeding reporter and then galloping away on horseback to get to a

[16] Wisan, *The Cuban Crisis as Reflected in the New York Press*, p. 417.

Journal press boat. Even more dramatic was Hearst's participation in the battle off Santiago when Admiral Cervera's hapless fleet was destroyed as it sought to escape along the Cuban shore. Hearst's flagship had to be warned off with a shot across the bow, so close did the eager *Journal* men get to the fighting. As the battle ended Hearst leaped from his yacht to capture a band of Spanish sailors huddled on the beach. He then sailed to the American flagship, delivered the prisoners, and hustled off to record the story for the *Journal's* readers.

American correspondents were learning how to use the cables to speed their messages to the news offices. Stories from Cuba had to be brought by boat to Key West for transmission to New York, with leading papers sending several thousand words a day. All this was expensive, but the race for news was an exciting one. The *World* scored the biggest single beat when Edward W. Harden, one of three correspondents to witness Dewey's amazing victory in Manila Bay, got his story off first by paying the "urgent" priority rate of $9.90 a word. Harden's beat arrived in New York too far into the dawn for the *World* to capitalize on it with a full-blown extra, but the *World's* news client, the *Chicago Tribune*, had time to revamp its final edition and carry the most dramatic story of the war.

Circulations leaped upward with the war news, but profits went down for the big dailies. The cost of the correspondents, press boats, and cable tolls ran high; the *Journal* spent half a million dollars to lead the pack in its coverage of the four-month war. Competition in extras was an expensive business, as well as a wearing one. The *Journal* put out as many as 40 extras in a single day, and Arthur Brisbane complained that it taxed the staff's ingenuity to make each new one look different from the last. Advertising volume declined during the war period, to make certain that there was no profit in the venture for Pulitzer and Hearst. Hearst said he did not care, so long as the *Journal* beat every paper in the world with its war coverage. But Pulitzer viewed the situation with dismay. He didn't like the many extras and big headlines; he liked even less the extravagant costs and the wiping out of the *World's* profits. When the war was over Pulitzer breathed a sigh of relief.

Yellow journalism did not come to an end at the same time, however. The competing newspapers turned to the familiar subjects of sensationalism: crime, sex, the doings of the famous and the infamous, disasters, and new wars. The devices of yellow journalism continued to be used: scare-heads and sensationalized makeup; lurid stories, many of them faked; attention to the unimportant but exciting news; the colored supplements of the Sunday paper; and lavish illustrations, with photographs ever more in demand. The yellow journalist did not care where he got his pictures; photos of European women would do nicely to illustrate wire stories from other cities. By 1900 about one-third of metropolitan dailies were following the yellow trend which the *Journal* had set in New York. It was another 10 years before the wave of sensationalism subsided, as it had before, and newspapermen concentrated on intelligent use of the devices which had marked its rise—headlines, pictures, and color printing.

The *World* withdrew from the competition in sensationalism at the turn of the century. A leading critic of the press, Oswald Garrison Villard, said of Pulitzer, "like many another he deliberately stooped for success, and then, having achieved it, slowly put on garments of righteousness." But Pulitzer foresaw what Hearst did not: the excesses of yellow journalism would undermine public confidence in the newspaper. Both Pulitzer and Hearst were champions of the common man—as was almost any yellow journal publisher, at least ostensibly—and in the first decade of the twentieth century both took strong stands in behalf of social justice and progress. But Hearst continued to exploit the news in a manner which seriously impeded the effectiveness of his role as a people's champion. It is to a period of the rise to prominence of the crusading liberal and the muckraker that we now turn.

ANNOTATED BIBLIOGRAPHY

Books:

Bleyer, Willard G., *Main Currents in the History of American Journalism.* Boston: Houghton Mifflin Company, 1927. The chapter on Hearst admirably documents charges of sensationalism.

Carlson, Oliver, *Brisbane: A Candid Biography.* New York: Stackpole Sons, 1937. A good critical analysis of the famous Hearst editor.

Carlson, Oliver, and Ernest Sutherland Bates, *Hearst, Lord of San Simeon.* New York: The Viking Press, 1936. Better than other early biographies by John K. Winkler and Mrs. Fremont Older. Still useful for the early Hearst period, but supplanted by Tebbel and Swanberg (see below).

Davis, Richard Harding, *Notes of a War Correspondent*. New York: Charles Scribner's Sons, 1910. An American war correspondent in Cuba, Greece, South Africa, and Manchuria, covering four wars.

Lundberg, Ferdinand, *Imperial Hearst: A Social Biography*. New York: Equinox Cooperative Press, 1936. A bitter attack on the chain publisher; valuable particularly for financial data.

Millis, Walter, *The Martial Spirit; a Study of Our War with Spain*. Boston: Houghton Mifflin Company, 1931. A readable, critical account.

Swanberg, W. A., *Citizen Hearst*. New York: Charles Scribner's Sons, 1961. A highly readable study, covering available printed sources in meticulous detail; has some new material.

Tebbel, John, *The Life and Good Times of William Randolph Hearst*. New York: E. P. Dutton & Company, 1952. A well-balanced biography and the best documented study of the Hearst newspaper empire.

Wilkerson, Marcus M., *Public Opinion and the Spanish-American War*. Baton Rouge: Louisiana State University Press, 1932. A scholarly study of war propaganda and press influence.

Wisan, Joseph E., *The Cuban Crisis as Reflected in the New York Press*. New York: Columbia University Press, 1934. A good specialized study.

Periodicals and Monographs:

Brisbane, Arthur, "The Modern Newspaper in War Time," *Cosmopolitan*, XXV (September 1898), 541. The *Journal* editor confesses his sins. See also his "Yellow Journalism," *Bookman*, XIX (June 1904), 400.

Commander, Lydia K., "The Significance of Yellow Journalism," *Arena*, XXXIV (August 1905), 150. A contemporary analysis.

Donald, Robert, "Sunday Newspapers in the United States," *Universal Review*, VIII (September 1890), 79. A look at a then-new medium.

Hachten, William A., "The Metropolitan Sunday Newspaper in the United States: A Study of Trends in Content and Practices." Ph.D. thesis, University of Minnesota, 1960 (Ann Arbor: University Microfilms, 1960). The most complete study of the Sunday paper.

Irwin, Will, "The American Newspaper," *Collier's*, XLVI (February 18 and March 4, 1911). The sins of yellow journalism described.

Mott, Frank L., "The First Sunday Paper: A Footnote to History," *Journalism Quarterly*, XXXV (Fall 1958), 443. The *Boston Globe*.

Steffens, Lincoln, "Hearst, the Man of Mystery," *American Magazine*, LXIII (November 1906), 3. Penetrating study based on interviews of Hearst, rarely obtained.

Zobrist, Benedict Karl, "How Victor Lawson's Newspapers Covered the Cuban War of 1898," *Journalism Quarterly*, XXXVIII (Summer 1961), 323. The non-sensational *Chicago Record* and *Daily News*.

Chapter **20**

THE PEOPLE'S CHAMPIONS

> I have only one principle, and that is represented
> by an effort to make it harder for the rich to grow
> richer and easier for the poor to keep from grow-
> ing poorer.
>
> —Edward Wyllis Scripps

THE OPENING OF THE TWENTIETH CENTURY found
the United States moving toward a consolidation of its position as
an industrial nation. The framework had been completed by 1900:
the economic expansion which had begun after the Civil War, the
growth in population and the tying together of the country, the
rapid development of rich natural resources, the inventive and productive genius, the political and cultural advances—all ensured the
future of a new world power.

Vital contests still were in progress, however, which would affect
the character of the new America. These contests assumed critical
importance at a moment when the economic, political and social
trends of a new era were being shaped. How would the nation conduct itself in the world community? How democratic would it remain? Would there be a balance struck between the advocates of
unrestricted economic individualism and the crusaders for social
justice? Would the fruits of progress be shared by all the people,
in the form of better living conditions, educational and cultural
opportunities, higher health standards, and personal security? Would

447

government be responsive to the general welfare? What was to be the role of the press in advancing or retarding necessary adjustments?

Men had struggled to obtain affirmative answers to these questions now confronting America since the industrial revolution changed the character of American society. The "consistent rebellion" in the agricultural areas against economic inequities represented one phase of the struggle; the rise of the labor unions in the cities another. The growth of strong political movements which sought to place more power in the hands of the people generally; the efforts of the social scientists to impart knowledge on which wise social and political decisions could be based; the appeals of reformers, agitators, political leaders, and writers for an arousing of the country's social conscience—all these had helped to shape the direction in which the country would turn.

But in the first years of the new century there were major divisions of thought and action which indicated the crucial importance of the struggle to shape public opinion, and to enforce the popular will. Nationalists and internationalists contended in the field of foreign affairs. Economic individualists and social reformers clashed in the domestic arena. The mass media of the times—newspapers, magazines, books—played a most important role in these national debates.

America's movements on the world stage were contradictory, as might well be expected of the newcomer. Instinctive isolationism dominated the thinking of many Americans, while some advocated an aggressive nationalism. International "idealists," as they were called, had to contend with both oppositions, as they sought to put the weight of the United States behind actions which would lead to world peace and economic and social progress.

The supporters of nationalism and dollar diplomacy exercised considerable power in the years preceding World War I. The treaty which the United States wrote at the end of the Spanish-American War gave it an empire. The new American position in the Pacific was solidified by the crushing of a native revolution in the Philippines, and by Theodore Roosevelt's "showing of the fleet" as a warning to Japan. The Panama Canal was built in an annexed zone which Colombia complained had been torn from her by an American-backed revolution. This action, and the extension of American military and economic domination in the Central American and Caribbean areas, dissipated hopes for Pan-American understanding. Cuba and Panama virtually became American protectorates under the Platt amendment. The Dominican Republic, Haiti, and Nicaragua in turn were forced to accept United States intervention in their affairs under the Roosevelt corollary to the Monroe Doctrine, by which the United States undertook to preserve order in those countries and administer their financial affairs to prevent any possible intervention by European powers. The primary intent was to assure American military security in a vital area, but American trade and financial interests followed the flag—and many persons complained that they sometimes preceded it.

At the same time, however, there were powerful forces in operation which sought to commit America to a quite different role in world affairs. Cultural and religious ties were made with China after the Boxer Rebellion. The Philippines were promised their eventual independence after a period of tutelage. Roosevelt himself acted as a mediator in helping to end the Russo-Japanese War and in smoothing relations among Germany, France, and Britain at the Algeciras conference. The United States accepted the idea of an international court of arbitration, advanced at The Hague Peace Conference of 1899, and negotiated several arbitration treaties. Americans played a leading part in the unsuccessful attempt to create an international court of justice during the second conference at The Hague in 1907. Out of these movements came American leadership in proposing the League of Nations and the World Court at the close of World War I—proposals which most of the other nations of the world adopted only to see the United States slump back into isolationism.

Important as was this contest over foreign policy, it was not the major concern of the American people in the years around the turn of the century. Their attention was centered largely upon domestic problems created by the industrial revolution: the growth of trusts and centralization of economic power in a few hands; the inadequate incomes of the workingman and farmer; corruption and inadequacies in political and business life. To many Americans it seemed that national wealth and strength, while reflecting basic progress for all the people, actually were mainly benefiting a plundering few who were usurping the freedoms of the many.[1]

Concentration of economic power, which had begun to develop rapidly in the 1880's, was greatly accentuated after 1900. A study made in 1904 listed 318 industrial trusts, three-fourths of which had been incorporated since 1898. These 318 trusts, capitalized at 7 billion dollars, represented the merging of 5,300 individual plants. Seven big trusts—in steel, oil, copper, sugar, tobacco, and shipping —which had been organized in those six years were capitalized at 2½ billions. Census figures show that in 1914 one-eighth of American businesses employed more than three-fourths of the wage-earners and produced four-fifths of the manufactured products.

The newspaper and magazine editors and the reporters and writers who joined in protesting this economic monopoly were even more concerned with the seemingly insatiable appetite of capitalists for power. Those who won domination in one field promptly reached out into other spheres, until the country's financial power fell largely into the hands of two loosely organized groups, the Morgan and the Rockefeller interests and their satellites. The famous Pujo committee investigation in 1913 reported that four allied financial institutions in New York held 341 directorships in banks, railroads, shipping lines, insurance companies, public utilities, and other businesses with total resources of 22 billion dollars.

Distribution of the wealth being created was heavily one-sided. Two-thirds of the male adult workers failed to earn $600 a year in wages, which was the figure set by sociologists as the minimum needed to maintain decent standards, at the current cost of living. There were many material and social advances being made—electricity, gas, and plumbing in homes; better schools and parks; the conveniences of city life; telephones, railroads, and highways. But they did not mean much to the millions in the New York tenements whose plight had been reported on by Jacob Riis.

Labor union membership increased between 1900 and 1910, jumping from 3.5 per cent of all workers to 7 per cent. The gains were

---

[1] One excellent study of the period is Harold U. Faulkner, *The Quest for Social Justice, 1898-1914* (New York: The Macmillan Company, 1931). A full and fascinating account by a journalistic historian is found in the first three volumes of Mark Sullivan, *Our Times* (New York: Charles Scribner's Sons, 1926 ff.).

being made by skilled workers: the railway brotherhoods, building trades, machinists, miners, printing trades, and garment workers groups. Unskilled workers, women workers, and immigrants remained victims of the economic order. Immigrants were a major factor in creating the social problem. The flood of immigrants of the period 1880 to 1900 was equaled in the single decade 1900 to 1910. The great bulk of the new immigration was from southern and eastern Europe, and a fourth of those arriving were illiterate. By 1910 one-seventh of the United States population was foreign-born, and in the industrial East more than half the population was foreign-born or of foreign-born parentage. These were the "poor and ill-informed" who were to be championed by such newspaper publishers as Edward Wyllis Scripps.

Despite the fact that these conditions inevitably demanded reform, the "quest for social justice" was slow. Eugene V. Debs did see his Socialist party win nearly a million votes in the presidential election of 1912, and some 300 cities and towns elected Socialist officeholders. In the labor movement William D. Haywood and his Industrial Workers of the World sought a radical approach to the plight of the unskilled laborer. But political leadership remained in the hands of the two major political parties, and most labor followed the moderate program of Samuel Gompers and his American Federation of Labor.

The instruments for political action on the national level were Theodore Roosevelt's "Square Deal" and Woodrow Wilson's "New Freedom." But the decisions which these two administrations won in the fields of monetary reform, government regulation of business, welfare legislation, and tariff revision stemmed from the spirit of the times. This spirit was reflected in various forms by the agitation of the Populists, the great crusade headed by William Jennings Bryan in 1896, the governmental reforms being proposed by Robert La Follette and his individualistic Wisconsin progressives, the work of the labor union leaders, and the thinking and writing of the intellectuals.

In the Roosevelt years the winning of an antitrust suit against the Northern Securities Company, preventing a monopoly of railroad transportation west of the Mississippi, turned the tide against extreme concentration of economic power. The Hepburn Act brought effective government regulation of transportation rates.

And Roosevelt's conservation policies saved a sizable residue of America's natural resources from ruthless exploitation. In the Wilson administration the creation of the Federal Reserve banking system brought a modern currency and credit system to the country for the first time; the Clayton Act struck at the abusive use of court injunctions and contempt citations against striking labor unions; the Federal Trade Commission was given power to regulate unfair business practices; and in other areas government extended its influence to a greater degree than ever before in American history.

But the progress which was being made, while substantial, was hampered and often balked by the supporters of big business. Senators like Nelson Aldrich of Rhode Island were frank spokesmen for the conservative cause and they had great influence. Congressmen like George Norris of Nebraska could clip the wings of House Speaker Joe Cannon, a powerful ally of the big-business forces, but they nevertheless lost many battles to their conservative opposition. William Howard Taft, succeeding Roosevelt as president, was unable to cope with the big-business elements of his Republican party, and an irate Roosevelt launched his third party Progressive movement in 1912. The Bull Moose crusade failed, but it split the Republican party so thoroughly that Woodrow Wilson entered the White House with a minority of the popular vote to inaugurate a Democratic administration.

Many of the gains were made at state and local levels. Popular election of United States senators, presidential primaries, and adoption of the referendum, initiative, and recall were manifestations of the new trend. State laws protecting working women and children, regulating hours of work, providing for workmen's compensation, and advancing social security generally ran the gauntlet of unfavorable court decisions. In the cities, reform movements led by such men as Samuel M. Jones in Toledo, Tom Johnson and Newton D. Baker in Cleveland, Seth Low in New York, and the advocates of commission government in Galveston did yeoman work in restoring governmental decency. Corruption in municipal councils and in state legislatures was a common mark of the times, and newspaper editors who wished to join with the reformers had almost unbelievable instances of bribe-taking and graft to expose.

The crusading spirit is as old as journalism, but never in American history had there been more opportunity for "the people's champions" than in these years following 1900. Voices of protest were raised in colonial days by men like James Franklin and Samuel Adams, in the early years of the republic by Jeffersonian and Jacksonian editors, by the creators of the first mass press before the Civil War, by the leaders of the "new journalism" before the close of the century. The struggle between big business and workers and farmers was as old as the struggle between the Hamiltonians and Jeffersonians for control of the government. The battle for the rights of labor and for a more equitable distribution of wealth was a basic issue of similar standing. And warring upon corruption in city governments had been a job for conscientious newspapermen since the rise of urban life. In the ebb and flow of these contests, however, the years following 1900 became critical ones.

Some newspapers were conspicuous in their response to the challenge. So were some of the new popular magazines, which became important vehicles for those whom Teddy Roosevelt eventually termed the "muckrakers." And the school of realistic writers which flowered at the turn of the century added important books to the American literature which dealt with life and problems of the day. Joining hands with politicians and labor leaders, reformers and agitators, professors and ministers, social workers and philanthropists, the men of journalism and literature helped to shape the course of the great crusade.

Joseph Pulitzer and his *New York World* became increasingly effective as "people's champions" in the years which followed the Spanish-American War. In foreign affairs the *World* vigorously opposed the annexation of the Philippines and the imperialism of the Caribbean policy. It continued to support the internationalist movement and the policy of peaceful arbitration of the world's problems, which it had espoused during the Venezuelan crisis. In domestic politics, this stand of the *World* on foreign policy led it to support William Jennings Bryan for president in 1900 on an "anti-imperialism" platform, ignoring Bryan's radical monetary policies which Pulitzer disliked.

The independent qualities and the crusading spirit of the *World* reached new heights, both on local and national issues. This was not a sudden manifestation of interest in crusading, as in the case of some other newspapers of the period, but a flowering of the Pulitzer editorial-page philosophy. Pulitzer, while agreeing that the

World was Democrat in political sympathy, argued that his newspaper was independent of party and supported only those elements
in a political party whose objectives coincided with those of the
World. In looking at the major political parties of his day, Pulitzer
put little trust in a Republican party with strong elements representing the big business interests of the country, although he admired
and supported Republican insurgents who fought to break the power
of Speaker Cannon, or Republican candidates of the caliber of
Governor Charles Evans Hughes of New York. Pulitzer decided
that the Democratic party best represented the political philosophy
in which he believed, and was most likely to act as the defender of
individual liberties, grass-roots government, and progressive democracy. The *World's* role, he believed, was to fight unceasingly for
that kind of a Democratic party.

Thus the *World* fought bossism, whether that of Tammany Hall
in New York City Democratic politics or that of Senator Thomas
C. Platt in New York State Republican politics. The *World* lashed
out against the conservatism of Mark Hanna, Nelson Aldrich, and
other Republican defenders of big business interests, and editorialized unceasingly against the "money power" of J. P. Morgan.
But it also opposed what it called the "socialistic and paternalistic"
policies of Bryan and what it called the "personal government" of
Theodore Roosevelt, even though both men were in the liberal
movement of their time. The *World* feared that centralization of
governmental power would result in bureaucratic control of the
business and individual life of the country—and it particularly
feared that a centralized government of great power created by
liberals would only fall under the domination of reactionary property and money interests. The *World,* like any other organ of
opinion, was not always consistent in the application of its basic
beliefs to specific events, however. While it feared Theodore Roosevelt's attempts to strengthen the powers of the federal government
and the presidency, it favored Woodrow Wilson's extensive program
of legislation enacted under Democratic auspices, from which came
many of the results the *World* had feared in the Roosevelt period.

But the *World* did not follow blindly a political leader it admired
nor did it oppose automatically one it disliked. It had first won
national attention by supporting Grover Cleveland for the presidency in 1884, but it did not hesitate to oppose him on the Vene-

zuelan issue. And while the *World* opposed Theodore Roosevelt personally, it applauded his mediation of the Russo-Japanese War, his prosecution of the Northern Securities case, and his efforts to intervene in business and industrial affairs as the champion of the public interest. When the lengthy coal miners' strike of 1902 became a paramount public issue, the *World*, unlike many conservative papers, agreed that Roosevelt was right in cooperating with John Mitchell, the coal miners' union leader, and forcing the mine operators to arbitrate the issues involved. This was a highly significant episode, for it not only involved recognition of the labor movement, but also the recognition by business management of the joint interests of owners, workers, and the public in the economic life of the country. The White House had intervened before in labor disputes of national import, but only to maintain order and to protect life and property. Henceforth the executive branch of the government, and the president, would take part in similar major crises as an interested party representing the public—a step which the *World* approved, even though its editors were fundamentally opposed to Roosevelt's "big stick" tactics.

Part of the *World's* new strength in its editorial columns was the result of a revamping of its editorial page staff. The ailing Pulitzer, tortured by the acute nervous disorders which made the last few years of his life a nightmare, found in 1904 a brilliant young editor who was destined to become the central force of the *World's* editorial page. His name was Frank I. Cobb.

Realizing that William H. Merrill, the effective editorial-page editor for 15 years, was nearing the end of his career, Pulitzer looked about for a successor. He had lost most of a talented staff of editorial writers, including George Cary Eggleston, David Graham Phillips, and John A. Dillon. So one of Pulitzer's personal secretaries was sent across the country, looking for an editorial writer who would disprove Pulitzer's epigram: "Every reporter is a hope; every editor is a disappointment."

The secretary found his man in Detroit. Cobb was then 35, a veteran of 15 years' newspaper experience who had been for four years the chief editorial writer for the *Detroit Free Press*. His somewhat limited formal education had been greatly supplemented by his scholarly interest and wide reading in the fields of history, government, and philosophy, and by his experiences as a newspaper reporter and as a political correspondent covering several Michigan legislative sessions and three national political conventions. Cobb early had demonstrated the maturity of his judgment and his great intellectual capacity; but he also was a man who understood human nature and who attracted others to him by his friendliness, his eagerness, and his enthusiasm for living.[2]

The secretary telegraphed to Pulitzer that the man had been found who could be entrusted with control of the *World's* editorial page while the editor-owner was absent, cruising on his yacht or sojourning in Europe in quest of the relaxation and quiet his health demanded. But Pulitzer's answer illustrates the extreme concern he had for the quality of the *World's* editorial columns and the heavy demands he made upon those who wrote for it:

> What has Cobb read in American history, Rhodes, McMaster, Trevelyan, Parkman? What works on the constitution and constitutional law? Has he read Buckle's history of civilization? Where did he stand during the Bryan free silver campaigns? What about the state of his health? How tall is he? Is his voice harsh or agreeable? My ears are very sensitive. Take him to dinner and note his table manners. Is his disposition cheerful? Sound out his ambitions. . . . Describe minutely his appearance, color of eyes, shape of forehead, mannerisms, how he dresses. Search his brain for everything there is in it. JP[3]

Cobb passed the examination—particularly in his knowledge of American history—and joined the *World* staff. Pulitzer put him in competition with other editorial writers and subjected him to a rigorous, and to Cobb an infuriating, hazing on points of writing style, clarity of expression, and logical thinking. More than once Cobb was on the point of returning to Detroit. But within a year he had become the recognized chief editorial writer, who would succeed to the editorship upon Pulitzer's death.

Cobb now became an important force in conducting the *World's* editorial page. But Pulitzer remained the guiding spirit and mentor of his editorial writers. In an editorial published at the close of Pulitzer's life in 1911, Cobb himself described the continued influence of the tired and blinded editor to the moment of his death:

[2] For a sketch of Cobb and a collection of his important editorials, see John L. Heaton, *Cobb of "The World"* (New York: E. P. Dutton & Company, 1924).

[3] As quoted in James W. Barrett, *Joseph Pulitzer and His World* (New York: Vanguard Press, Inc., 1941), p. 184.

His chief concern centered in the editorial page as the expression of the paper's conscience, courage and convictions. To that he devoted infinite care and attention. Sick or well, it was never wholly absent from his thoughts. When he was well he had it read to him every day and expressed his opinion about every editorial article, the style in which it was written, the manner in which the thought was expressed, whether the editorial was strong or weak, whether it served any useful public purpose, whether it said the thing that a great newspaper ought to have said.

When ill-health made it impossible for him to have the editorial page read every day he would keep the files for weeks, and then when his condition permitted, he would go over them with painstaking care, always from the point of view of a detached critic, seeking only to determine whether the page was taking the fullest advantage of its opportunities for public service and whether it was measuring up to the high standards that he had set for it.

Nothing was ever allowed to interfere with its independence and its freedom of expression. There were certain questions about which he became convinced that in spite of all his efforts he was possibly prejudiced. In these matters he exacted a pledge that no suggestions or instructions or even commands from him would ever be followed, but that the paper would always say what an independent, untrammelled newspaper ought to say in performing its duties to the people. This pledge was never violated. . . .[4]

The most famous of all the *World*'s crusades began in 1905, just as the new editorial-page staff—composed of Cobb, John L. Heaton, Samuel E. Moffett, Ralph Pulitzer, the publisher's son, and others —was proving its strength. A battle had developed for control of the management of the Equitable Life Assurance Society, one of the life insurance companies which had built up great financial resources as Americans took up the purchase of policies and benefits to provide for their personal and family security. Evidence was presented by two *World* reporters, David Ferguson and Louis Seibold, that officials of the company were using funds paid in by policy-holders for their own private investments and thereby were building huge personal fortunes—gambling with the people's money, the *World* said. A series of editorials by William M. Speer on "Equitable Corruption" caught Pulitzer's attention and a full-fledged campaign was ordered under Cobb's direction. Other editors, like Ervin Wardman of the *New York Press,* joined in the battle and

[4] *New York World,* October 31, 1911.

the spotlight was turned on the Mutual Life and New York Life companies as well.

Demand rose for an investigation by a legislative committee. As legal counsel for the committee, the newspapers suggested Charles Evans Hughes, a young and forceful attorney who had attracted attention by assisting in a campaign against the "gas trust" in New York City a few months before. Hughes documented the case against the insurance companies, proving that their vast assets were being used by those in control for investments of profit to themselves. He also substantiated the *World's* charges that the companies maintained a large fund of money to exert political influence and affect the progress of legislation in various states. The specter of the "money interests" dominating the life insurance companies and using their power to corrupt legislatures so aroused public opinion that strict regulatory legislation was enacted in New York State; Hughes rode into the governorship in 1906.

One other of the *World's* crusades deserves mention, for it involved the always-present issue of the freedom of the press. Late in 1908, Cobb wrote a lengthy editorial demanding a congressional investigation of what he called the "entire Panama Canal scandal." Cobb's ire had been aroused by "a scandalous personal attack" by President Roosevelt upon Delavan Smith, editor of the *Indianapolis News,* who had raised questions about the canal. Cobb said Roosevelt had made "deliberate misstatements of fact" and proceeded to outline a story of intrigue and needless purchase of the rights of the French company which originally had attempted to construct a canal. Roosevelt sent an unprecedented special message to Congress attacking Pulitzer by name and said the government would prosecute him for criminal libel.

Cobb welcomed the suit, crying "Who got the money?" and "The World will not be muzzled." Two suits were brought by the United States Attorney General under Roosevelt's instructions, one against the *Indianapolis News'* editors and the other against the *World* and Pulitzer. Indictments were returned in the District of Columbia on the government's complaint that copies of the newspaper had circulated in a federal reservation in New York. Federal judges in both Indianapolis and New York ruled that the editors could not be forced into federal court in this manner, since the Sixth Amendment to the Constitution guarantees an accused person the right to

a trial in the state or district where the crime was allegedly committed. The United States Supreme Court upheld the newspapers,
declaring that Roosevelt was without power to institute the suits
except in the state courts. The practical result of the decision was to
stop cold any effort by the federal government to seek criminal libel
actions against newspapers through its own courts, and Cobb declared that the *World* had won "the most sweeping victory for
freedom of speech and of the press in this country since the American people destroyed the Federalist party more than a century ago
for enacting the infamous Sedition law." While the outcome of the
case left the original libel charges unanswered, later events proved
Cobb essentially correct in his statements concerning the canal
episode. Eventually Congress compensated Colombia for the loss of
the Panama area.

While the *World* was thus rising to greatness, its chief competitor for mass circulation in New York was just as determinedly
making a claim to leadership as "the people's champion." William
Randolph Hearst, having seen the country start toward annexation
of the Philippines and Hawaii, the development of military bases
in the Caribbean, and the adoption of other nationalistic policies
advocated by the *New York Journal,* turned his attention to domestic
affairs. In early 1899 he set forth an editorial platform calling for
public ownership of public franchises, the "destruction of criminal
trusts," a graduated income tax, election of United States senators
by popular vote rather than by state legislatures, and national, state,
and local improvement of the public school system. Soon Hearst was
urging that the coal mines, railroads, and telegraph lines—the symbols of the new industrial era—all be nationalized. And he gave
strong encouragement to the economic and political powers of labor
unions.

Not only was this a more radical program than that of the *World*
and other liberal newspapers of the day, but the impact of the
Hearst editorial technique was bitter and extreme. In the presidential campaign of 1900, Homer Davenport's cartoons depicting
President McKinley as the stooge of a Mark Hanna wearing a suit
made of dollar signs were crude but effective. Hearst was supporting Bryan's domestic policies and ignoring his anti-imperialism, just
as Pulitzer was doing the reverse, and the *Journal* was venomous
in its attacks upon McKinley and his party. But the *Journal* did

not subside when McKinley and his running mate, Theodore Roosevelt, won the election.

In April, 1901, the *Journal* declared editorially that "if bad institutions and bad men can be got rid of only by killing, then the killing must be done." Two months before, on February 4, Ambrose Bierce had written a quatrain for the *Journal* which read:

> The bullet that pierced Goebel's breast
> Can not be found in all the West;
> Good reason, it is speeding here
> To stretch McKinley on his bier.

Goebel was Governor Goebel of Kentucky, a victim of an assassin. When in September, 1901, President McKinley was fatally wounded by an anarchist, the offending lines in the *Journal* were recalled, along with the Hearst paper's continual assaults upon McKinley. Hearst found it advantageous to change the name of his morning New York paper to the *American*. But the incident was to haunt him for the rest of his life.

Hearst now sought to advance his political beliefs by seeking office himself. He served two terms in Congress from a Democratic district in New York City, from 1903 to 1907, but his eye was on the White House. His high point came in 1904 when 204 delegates cast votes for him in the Democratic national convention (Judge Alton B. Parker, the successful nominee, received 658). The next year Hearst ran as an independent candidate for mayor of New York and lost by some 3,500 votes as the result of Tammany's counting him out at the ballot boxes.

This was a notable achievement, and Hearst decided to make the race for the New York governorship in 1906, as a stepping stone to the White House. He won the Democratic nomination in convention, but found himself up against Charles Evans Hughes in the November election. Theodore Roosevelt's close associate, Elihu Root, recalled the McKinley assassination episode in a public speech; the *World* and other New York newspapers turned against Hearst; and so did Tammany, which he had challenged the year before. Hughes won by 60,000 votes—the only Republican to be elected that year in the statewide balloting—and Hearst's political star had set. In 1908 he stage-managed a third party ticket for the presidency which polled few votes, and in 1909 Hearst himself was decisively beaten in another try for the New York mayoralty.

In his political races and in his newspapers Hearst was making a heavy play for the support of the working man, the small businessman, and other ordinary people. His slashing attacks upon the "criminal trusts"—the ice trust, the coal trust, the gas trust—and crooked political bosses found favor with those who had grievances against the established order. His forthright support of the labor unions won him the backing of the American Federation of Labor. And the popularized content of his newspapers appealed to the mass of readers. Emphasis on sensational crime and vice stories, human interest features, pictures and cartoons, and readable typographical display helped draw crowds of new readers to Hearst papers.

New publishing ventures brought Hearst to the attention of three more large cities in the first few years of the twentieth century. To his *San Francisco Examiner, New York American,* and *New York Journal,* Hearst added four more papers which put him in the business of chain publishing. In Chicago, the evening *American* was begun in 1900 and the morning *Examiner* in 1902. Boston saw the birth of an evening *American* in 1904. Los Angeles was invaded in 1903 with the founding of the morning *Examiner.* The Los Angeles entry was welcomed with open arms by local labor unions, which had been engaged in a bitter fight with the anti-labor *Los Angeles Times.* The *Times,* published by General Harrison Gray Otis, had become open shop in 1890 after a typographers union strike, and the labor unions cooperated with Hearst in establishing direct competition for the powerful Otis paper. Otis and his son-in-law, Harry Chandler, continued their fight against organized labor until the feud was climaxed in 1910 by the dynamiting of the *Times* building, a crime to which two radically-minded union men, the McNamara brothers, eventually confessed. Amid all this controversy in Los Angeles the Hearst *Examiner* established itself as one of the chain's strongest papers. In Chicago, against Medill's *Tribune,* and in Boston and New York the going was tougher.

Despite the following which Hearst had attracted, there was widespread doubting of his journalistic and political motives. Admittedly Hearst journalism then was powerful; its master advocated progressive beliefs; his newspapers were widely read and were financially successful; and Hearst himself was a potent force in political life. But Hearst journalism was degrading in its use of techniques to snare the reader; its master lacked, in the final analysis, the responsible feeling a worthy publisher or political leader must have for his public mission; and above all, Hearst and his journalism lacked depth.

There were varying expressions of the criticism that Hearst journalism lacked depth: depth of intellectual appeal; depth of sincerity; depth of understanding of social issues; depth of responsible conception of public trust. In general the intellectual leaders of the time spoke out against both the degrading characteristics of Hearst's news techniques and the tone of his editorial opinions. His opponents viewed Hearst as the leader of a political movement which was tinged with fanaticism in its bitter criticism of the social and economic order. And they saw in Hearst's own political efforts a bid for personal power rather than a bid for public service.

Pulitzer, while applauding Hearst's fights against the Tammany machine in New York, viewed his rival as one who would destroy the existing Democratic party and substitute for it a party which would be semi-socialistic in its nature. The Socialist party leader, Norman Thomas, said later that as a young man in 1905 he admired Hearst's crusading but quite distrusted the sincerity of his beliefs. The Republicans condemned Hearst unequivocally as a rabble-rouser. And indeed, the platform written for the third party he created in 1908 was a bitter, radical document which appealed to all the discontented.[5]

Will Irwin, writing about Hearst in 1911, said that his editorial policies might well represent a marriage of convenience and sincerity, but added that "those who knew Hearst best in this early era declare that under his cold exterior he kept a real sympathy for the submerged man and woman, a real feeling of his own mission to plead their cause." [6] If that were so, Hearst failed to convince many persons whose support he needed of the sincerity of

[5] For further comments about the Hearst of this period see Oliver Carlson and Ernest Sutherland Bates, *Hearst, Lord of San Simeon* (New York: The Viking Press, 1936), pp. 132-38.

[6] Will Irwin, "The Fourth Current," *Collier's*, XLVI (February 18, 1911), 14.

his newspapers. They were alienated by his sensationalized treatment of the news; by his unblushing agitation for war in 1898; by Arthur Brisbane's frank explanation of how the *Journal* had capitalized on the war fever; and by the popularized editorial page.

The Hearst editorial page, following the "gee-whiz" approach, spoke in one-syllable words. It talked about human virtues, religion, science, and love more easily than it talked about significant current issues. And when it approached social and economic issues it often did it in this fashion, under an editorial page cartoon:

> Trusts and unions are both combinations, beyond question. But a pronounced difference distinguishes them, and we shall endeavor to make it clear.
> You see a horse after a hard day's work grazing in a swampy meadow. He has done his duty and is getting what he can in return.
> On the horse's flank you may see a leach sucking blood.
> The *leach* is the *trust.*
> The *horse* is the labor *union.*
> Possibly you have read "Sinbad the Sailor," with its story of the Old Man of the Sea. The Old Man of the Sea rode round on the sailor's back squeezing his neck with tightly twisted legs.
> The *old man* is the *trust.*
> The *sailor* is the labor *union.*[7]

Hearst preferred the cartoonist and the man who could thus simplify an argument—Davenport and Brisbane, among others—to the editorial thinker. He had no men of the intellectual caliber of William H. Merrill and Frank Cobb of the *World* or Charles R. Miller of the *Times* in command of his editorial pages. As evidence of this, the testimony of Willis J. Abbot about life on the *New York Journal* in the late 1890's may be quoted. Abbot, who later became editor of the *Christian Science Monitor,* records the following in his autobiography about his introduction to Hearstian methods:

> Within an hour after meeting him (Hearst), I was engaged as "Editor-in-chief" of the *New York Journal.* The resonant title was most grateful to my still youthful and ingenuous mind. . . . It took months of cruel disillusionment to reveal to me the two facts that despite a liberal conferring of titles, Mr. Hearst was the only editor-in-chief of any of his papers, and that of all his newspaper pages the editorial page of which

---

[7] As quoted in *Editorials from the Hearst Newspapers* (New York: Albertson Publishing Company, 1906), pp. 170-71.

I had charge was the one on which he looked with most tolerant contempt.[8]

Abbot continues by asserting that for three weeks he conducted the editorial page of the *Journal* without a single scrap of instructions from Hearst or any other editor. (Shades of Pulitzer and his rigorous training of Frank Cobb for his duties in heading the all-important *World* editorial page!) Abbot adds, however, that around 1910 Hearst himself took up in earnest the writing of editorials, and proved to be more effective than any of his editors. Thereafter he held the editorial page in slightly higher esteem, Abbot says.

Here, then, was an important reason for intellectual distrust of Hearst. The editorial page lacked depth of appeal, and to many this indicated lack of sincerity. In the New York morning field the combination of the sensationalism of the Hearst news policy and the popularized editorial page made the future of the *American* (the renamed *Journal*) increasingly insecure. Against the competition of the *World,* the *Times,* the *Tribune,* and the *Herald,* the Hearst entry gradually lost ground until in the newspaper world it was known as the "vanishing *American.*" This was not true of Hearst enterprises generally, however, for they remained as a continuing force in American journalism and will appear again in this story.

Another type of "people's paper" was emerging, meanwhile, under the direction of Edward Wyllis Scripps, the Ohio farm boy who had successfully started the first of his many Scripps newspapers by the time he was 24. Scripps got his start in the Middle West at the moment that Pulitzer was achieving his first success in St. Louis, and when Stone was succeeding in Chicago and Nelson in Kansas City. The *Detroit News,* on which Scripps had served his apprenticeship under his brother James, had been one of the early practitioners of the "new journalism." His own first two papers, the *Cleveland Press* and the *Cincinnati Post,* were low-priced afternoon dailies appealing to the mass of readers.[9]

But unlike Pulitzer and Hearst, who sought giant circulations in big cities, Scripps set his sights upon the working people in the smaller but growing industrial cities of the country. For them he

[8] Willis J. Abbot, *Watching the World Go By* (Boston: Little, Brown and Company, 1933), pp. 134-35.
[9] See pages 359-60 for Scripps' early career.

published brightly written, easily read newspapers, small in size but big in heart. Closely edited news, human interest features, fearless news coverage and local crusades, and hard-fighting independent editorial opinion constituted the Scripps formula.

What made Scripps a distinctive leader as a "people's champion" was his conception of his responsibility to the working man. "The first of my principles," Scripps said, "is that I have constituted myself the advocate of that large majority of people who are not so rich in worldly goods and native intelligence as to make them equal, man for man, in the struggle with the wealthier and more intellectual classes." [10] Scripps viewed his newspapers as the only "schoolroom" the working man had. He believed that nearly all other newspapers were capitalistic and opposed to the working class or else too intellectual in appeal, and he said sadly that the educational system was a failure in its service to his "large majority." So he sought to drive home through his editorial columns the necessity for labor union organization and collective bargaining as the first prerequisite to a better life for the poor and ill-informed. To him the struggle was to keep the rich from getting richer and the poor from getting poorer, and his papers invariably lined up on the side of the have-nots.

Scripps was the first to admit that his papers did not always maintain the noble objectives he set for them, and that they sometimes made mistakes in "always opposing the rich, always supporting the working man." But Scripps believed that if he kept the focus on such a basic policy he would further the long-range pattern of society which he hoped would emerge in an industrialized America. And he exerted through his newspapers published in the growing industrial cities of the country a great influence on changing social and political attitudes. The Scripps papers struck closer to the hearts and the minds of working men than did Pulitzer's *World;* and they exhibited a more consistent liberal political and economic policy than that of Hearst, and won their readers without resorting to the extremes of sensationalism which marked the Hearst press.

Above all, the Scripps newspapers reflected a "spirit of protest" which was inherent in the character of their owner-editor. Scripps

[10] As quoted in Negley D. Cochran, *E. W. Scripps* (New York: Harcourt, Brace and Company, 1933), p. 235.

declared that he protested against everything; his motto was "Whatever is, is wrong." He protested against antiquated governmental systems, against undemocratic political actions, against usurpation of power and prestige by the rich and the intellectuals, against inequality of opportunity, against all sorts of authority in religion and law and politics save those exercised for the benefit of mankind, against corruption, against the power of business interests. His spirit of protest led him to ignore advertisers unless they came seeking the circulations which he had built, and to resist any kind of pressure they might seek to use to influence him. He pictured himself as a "damned old crank" who was in rebellion against society. But actually he was seeking to build a progressive democracy by raising the level of the working classes, and he was enough of a capitalist to urge the worker to better himself by increasing his production and thereby adding to the wealth to be distributed.[11]

Scripps started his newspaper career with an investment of $600 in one share of stock in the *Detroit News.* With that collateral, and with the help of his brothers James and George, he started the *Cleveland Press* in 1878. In 1880 the Scripps family flirted with an ill-fated paper in Buffalo, the *Evening Telegraph,* and bought the *St. Louis Chronicle* (which faded out in 1905 in competition with the strong *Post-Dispatch* and *Globe-Democrat*). In 1883, with an income of $10,000 a year, Scripps turned to Cincinnati and took over management of a struggling penny paper which became the *Post.* A fourth paper, the *Kentucky Post,* was established in Covington in 1890 as an affiliate of the Cincinnati paper.

These were the formative years of the Scripps newspaper empire. In Cleveland Scripps found an editor, Robert F. Paine, who for more than 30 years was a leader in editorial policy-making. In Cincinnati Scripps found a business manager, Milton A. McRae, who was to become the managerial leader of the chain. Scripps and McRae formed a partnership in 1889, which in 1895 was expanded to include George Scripps. The organization took the name Scripps-McRae League of Newspapers. McRae was to be the speech-maker, the front man, the operations chief. Scripps was to set policy and live as he pleased on a California ranch. And in 1890, at age 36,

---

[11] Scripps' personal views are set forth in a collection of his writings edited by Charles R. McCabe, *Damned Old Crank* (New York: Harper & Brothers, 1951), particularly in Chapters 12 and 13. Scripps deliberately painted a "shocking" self-portrait in these letters to his sons, however.

Scripps did "retire" to a great ranch near San Diego, named Miramar, where he lived a burly life, wearing ranch clothes and cowhide boots, playing poker, drinking whisky, and smoking innumerable cigars.

Much has been made—particularly by Scripps himself—of his many affairs with women, of his intemperate drinking, and of his general violation of all of Horatio Alger's rules for success. Scripps claimed that he drank as much as a gallon of whisky a day for many years—undoubtedly a gross exaggeration—and he delighted in such proverbs as "Never do today what you can put off until tomorrow." But the rough-living and bearded Scripps also was a lover of poetry and music and the wife whom he took to Miramar was the daughter of a Presbyterian minister. At Miramar, too, he was still the director of the Scripps newspaper ventures, with which he kept in intimate touch through a mass of correspondence and through occasional conferences with his principal editors and managers. He also managed to live to the age of 71, and to build himself a fortune of some 50 million dollars.

The Scripps plan for expansion was simple. He and McRae looked for a growing industrial city, usually fairly small and with stodgy newspaper opposition. They put up a few thousand dollars and sent a young, ambitious editor and business manager off to start a paper. If the young journalists succeeded, they could obtain as much as 49 per cent of the stock; if they faltered, new faces replaced them. If the paper failed to make a profit within ten years, it was abandoned as a failure. Scripps papers, as a result of this policy had a good many employee-stockholders, but they also paid the usual low journalistic salaries of the times to those who were not so blessed. In this respect, Scripps was typically capitalistic in his publishing behavior.

Since the papers were cheap afternoon dailies relying principally on circulation revenue they had to be edited carefully. Scripps saved newsprint costs by insisting upon small headlines and short, concisely edited stories. Saving those extra words so that a Scripps newspaper would be packed with the most news possible became a fine art for Scripps newsmen. Word economy meant also that after the essential news had been told there would be plenty of space for editorial opinion and features—and, of course, space for the advertising which the Scripps newspapers sought for as avidly as any others, provided that their advertising space was bought on a strictly business basis.

Between 1897 and 1911 the Scripps-McRae League added 14 more papers to the original four. The first venture, the *Kansas City World* (1897) was a failure, for Nelson in Kansas City was as tough a competitor as were the St. Louis opposition papers. In Ohio, the new papers were the *Akron Press*, founded in 1899; the *Toledo News-Bee*, bought in 1903, and the *Columbus Citizen*, purchased in 1904. The League brought the *Des Moines News* into the fold in 1902. Then in 1906 eight new papers were started: the *Evansville Press* and *Terre Haute Post* in Indiana; the *Memphis Press* and *Nashville News* in Tennessee; the *Denver Express* and *Pueblo Sun* in Colorado; and the *Dallas Dispatch* and *Oklahoma City News*. The *Houston Press* followed in 1911. By the time of Scripps' death in 1926, 11 of these 18 first Scripps-McRae papers remained. Those which were abandoned or sold to competitors were the papers in St. Louis, Kansas City, Des Moines, Pueblo, Dallas, Nashville, and Terre Haute.

Scripps himself was building his own chain of West Coast newspapers, meanwhile. He started by buying the *San Diego Sun* in 1893, and in the next 15 years opened up shop in 10 other coast cities. Flying the Scripps banner were the *Los Angeles Record*, the *Seattle Star*, the *Spokane Press*, the *Tacoma Times*, the *Portland News*, the *San Francisco News*, the *Sacramento Star*, the *Fresno Tribune*, the *Berkeley Independent*, and the *Oakland Mail*.

Here in an only slightly industrialized West the Scripps record was extremely poor. The *San Francisco News* eventually emerged as a strong unit in the Scripps chain. But the Fresno, Berkeley, and Oakland papers in California all were unsuccessful; the *Sacramento Star* flickered out in 1926; and the *San Diego Sun* eventually died. The *Los Angeles Record* and the four Pacific Northwest papers seceded from the parent Scripps organization after a quarrel between Scripps and his son James in 1920, and formed the basis for the Scripps League. But all five of those papers succumbed in due time. While each paper lived, however, it breathed the Scripps fire so long as the founder and his policies remained a factor—and each city felt the "spirit of protest."

Scripps tried another experiment in 1911, when he established an adless tabloid in Chicago, named the *Day Book*. Negley D.

Cochran was the editor, and poet Carl Sandburg was chief reporter. The little paper, which represented Scripps' fondest dream, reached a circulation of 25,000 and was within $500 a month of breaking even when the rising newsprint costs of the first war year, 1917, caused its suspension. A second adless paper, the *Philadelphia News-Post,* started in 1912 but also failed.

Through the years the Scripps papers continued to fight for the right of workers to organize. They crusaded for public ownership and against utility abuses. They attacked political bossism and corruption. They supported Theodore Roosevelt's reforms and his third party candidacy. And they backed Woodrow Wilson's "New Freedom" and his re-election campaign. In appearance and in content they were closer to being "labor papers" than any other general circulation newspapers, yet they also won the support of the intellectual liberals whom Scripps sometimes tried to avoid.

There is more to the Scripps story. Later chapters will describe the founding of the United Press Associations by Scripps and its growth under Scripps' eventual successor, Roy W. Howard. Scripps and his talented editor, Robert F. Paine, began the Newspaper Enterprise Association in 1902 as a general feature syndicate, and in 1921 Scripps sparked the formation of Science Service, a specialized news agency. Also in the Scripps fold were United Features, Acme Newspictures, and the surviving newspaper organization, Scripps-Howard. But what happened to the empire which Edward Wyllis Scripps built in his years as a "people's champion" is another episode in another era.

Pulitzer, Hearst, and Scripps were far from being the only champions of the common man among newspaper publishers and editors of the years around the turn of the century. Nor can all those who opposed the business trusts, who fought against one-sided public utilities franchises, who exposed political inadequacy and corruption, be listed. Some idea of the contributions made by newspapermen can be gained by a look across the country, however.[12]

One battle against a tightly run political machine was that waged by Charles H. Grasty, editor of the *Baltimore Evening News,* and by the *Baltimore Sun.* Grasty, who came to Baltimore from the *Kansas City Star,* was a fighting editor in the Nelson tradition who

[12] One account, not confined to this period, is Silas Bent, *Newspaper Crusaders* (New York: Whittlesey House, 1939).

had exposed the policy racket in Baltimore despite a criminal libel charge brought by his political opponents. When in 1895 the *Sun* broke with its Democratic party traditions and attacked Senator Arthur P. Gorman's state Democratic machine, Grasty pitched in to help oust the Gorman group. Maryland elected its first Republican administration since the Civil War and Gorman lost his senate seat for one term. Later, Grasty sold the *Evening News,* and after two years in St. Paul as part owner of the *Dispatch* and *Pioneer Press,* returned to Baltimore in 1910 as owner of the *Sun.* He supported Woodrow Wilson in the 1912 election before retiring from the *Sun* in 1914.

Across the country the spectacular but contradictory career of Fremont Older was being unfolded in San Francisco. Older, a typical roving newspaperman in his early years, settled down as managing editor of the *Bulletin* in 1895. He built the struggling evening sheet into a fairly substantial paper by his sensational methods, and then decided to join the solid civic leader, the *San Francisco Chronicle,* in its fights against city machine politics. The target was a Union-Labor party headed by Mayor Eugene E. Schmitz and a political boss, Abram Ruef. Older stepped out of his role as a newspaperman to become a civic reform leader, and his dominating personality made him the rallying point for the public-spirited of the city. Older printed sensational stories detailing charges of bribery of city officeholders by public utilities and the street transit company, and in one instance trapped city supervisors in a bribe-taking plot. The reform group brought Schmitz and Ruef to court on indictments for accepting payoffs from houses of prostitution, and saw Ruef sent to prison. Others involved escaped conviction, despite the work of prosecutors Francis J. Heney (who was shot and critically wounded in the courtroom) and Hiram W. Johnson. Older then confounded his admirers by insisting that Ruef was a victim of his environment, and that since he was the only one of his gang to be sent to prison, he should be released. His last great crusade was in behalf of Tom Mooney, who Older eventually decided had been unjustly convicted of the Preparedness Day bombing of 1916 in San Francisco. Breaking with the *Bulletin* management on the Mooney issue, Older joined Hearst's *Call* as editor in 1918, saw it become the *Call-Bulletin* in 1929, and died in 1935 before Mooney won his freedom.

Older had been kidnaped and nearly killed during the height of the San Francisco trials. In South Carolina, two editors were assassinated—Francis W. Dawson of the *Charleston News and Courier* in 1891 and N. G. Gonzales of the *Columbia State* in 1903. Gonzales was one of three brothers who battled against political boss Ben Tillman with their newspaper, founded in 1893. The paper continued to exert leadership, however, calling for compulsory public education and opposing child labor and "lynch law."

A less spectacular, but solid, champion of decency was Josephus Daniels, North Carolina's famous editor. Daniels fell in love with newspaper work as a school boy, went to work on a weekly at 18, and was running two weeklies and serving as president of the North Carolina Press Association at 22. He then studied law at the University of North Carolina and went to Raleigh to edit the *State Chronicle* in 1885. The paper was a weekly, started by Walter Hines Page two years before.

In his first few years in Raleigh, Daniels campaigned against the Southern Railway and its attempt to extend its control over other lines. He advocated a state public school fund as a means of equalizing educational opportunity, urged financial support of the state university, supported establishment of teacher training colleges, and argued for compulsory education as a means of overcoming illiteracy. When the American Tobacco Company was organized by the Duke family in 1890 he began his long campaign against the "tobacco trust."

The established daily in Raleigh was the *News and Observer*. Daniels made the *State Chronicle* a daily in 1891, but sold out in 1892 to a buyer who in turn sold out to the *News and Observer*. Daniels meanwhile established another weekly, the *North Carolinian*, and entered government service in Washington. Then in 1895 his chance to buy the *News and Observer* came and he returned to Raleigh to build one of the South's leading newspapers. Significantly, the Daniels paper in Raleigh was the first in the state to have Linotype machines and a perfecting press.

Daniels continued his fights against the railroads and the tobacco trust. He called for the establishment of a railroad commission, for reduced rates, and for abolition of passes granted to politicians and editors. He urged prosecution of the tobacco trust, and pointed out to farmers that the price of tobacco in the field had fallen 50 per cent since the smaller companies had been combined into one giant organization. The railroad and tobacco interests put another paper in the field against him, but it failed.

When a fusion party combining the support of Republicans, Populists, and Negroes won control of the state government, Daniels backed a "white supremacy" movement. But he was a strong opponent of lynching and he continually advocated equal educational opportunities for Negroes. For all working men he urged a three-point program: shorter hours, better wages, and abolition of child labor competition.

Daniels was a fervent supporter of the Democratic party, campaigning for Bryan in his three races for the presidency and supporting Woodrow Wilson with full enthusiasm. Wilson made him his Secretary of the Navy in 1913 and the Daniels political career was under way. In his autobiography Daniels says the greatest influence upon his early career as an editor was his admiration for Samuel Bowles III and his regular reading of the *Springfield Republican*.[13] Bowles, he said, taught him the principles of journalism and a conception of his public trust. And the newspaper which he established and continued to edit until the 1940's was evidence of lessons well learned and of the strength of his own personality.

In Chicago, the *Tribune* which Joseph Medill had built enjoyed a varied record. In the last years of Medill's editorship, before his death in 1899, the *Tribune* was strongly nationalistic in foreign policy and generally conservative in its outlook. It fought the liberal Illinois governor, John P. Altgeld, and bitterly attacked the Debs-led Chicago labor unions. But the *Tribune* vigorously crusaded against utility and street-railway franchise grabs, and used John T. McCutcheon's front page cartoons with effectiveness after the artist transferred from the *Record* to the *Tribune* in 1903.

James Keeley, the *Tribune's* outstanding managing editor, helped develop one of the state's biggest exposés in 1910 when the paper published evidence that William Lorimer had won election to the U. S. Senate by bribing state legislators. Despite the evidence which Keeley had obtained, it took two years of campaigning by the *Trib-*

[13] Josephus Daniels, *Tar Heel Editor* (Chapel Hill: University of North Carolina Press, 1939), p. 92. The second volume of his autobiography, *Editor in Politics,* continues his story through this period.

une and the *Record-Herald* before Lorimer was ousted from the Senate. Keeley also sponsored the *Tribune's* lengthy crusade for a "safe and sane" Fourth of July, in which carefully collected lists of victims of dangerous fireworks eventually led to restrictive legislation.

Other newspapers kept the crusading spirit at full force. Nelson's *Kansas City Star* editorialized continually for civic improvements. In national politics Nelson became an admirer of Theodore Roosevelt and backed his Progressive party in 1912, calling for state laws establishing the initiative, referendum, and recall. Pulitzer's *St. Louis Post-Dispatch* conducted one of its outstanding campaigns from 1898 to 1902 when it charged that two-thirds of the municipal assembly had been bribed by the local traction company, and battled for four years before one of the culprits confessed and sent eight officials to the penitentiary. In New York, Ervin Wardman's *Press* accused city officials of bribery and joined in the fight against the insurance companies. And in Boston the *Traveler* centered fire upon the "bucket shops," which conducted a form of investment gambling and fleeced the unsuspecting.

Many a public service campaign was carried out by American newspapers. The *Chicago Daily News* sponsored a tuberculosis sanitarium. The *New York Herald* promoted an ice charity for sweltering tenement dwellers. Newspapers everywhere collected Thanksgiving and Christmas baskets for the poor, before the Community Chest movement came on the scene, and raised funds for the relief of disaster victims. Campaigns for better schools, for city parks, for recreation facilities, and against child labor were equally widespread. Few newspaper editors had as full an appreciation of the basic economic problems of the "poor and ill-informed" as did Scripps, but many of them caught some measure of the spirit of the times.

Highly important as "people's champions" were the magazines which in the dozen years after 1900 developed a literature of exposure which Theodore Roosevelt dubbed the work of the "muckrakers." Roosevelt used the expression in a derogatory sense, comparing the more sensational writers to the Man with the Muckrake in *Pilgrim's Progress*, who did not look up to see the celestial crown but continued to rake the filth. The reformers, however, came

McClure's Magazine

VOL. XX   *JANUARY, 1903*   NO. 3

THE SHAME OF MINNEAPOLIS

The Rescue and Redemption of a City that was Sold Out

BY LINCOLN STEFFENS

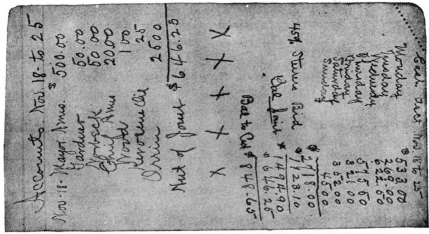

FAC-SIMILE OF THE FIRST PAGE OF "THE BIG MITT LEDGER"

An account kept by a swindler of the dealings of his "Joint" with City Officials, showing first payments made to Mayor Ames, his brother, the Chief of Police and Detectives. This book figured in trials and newspaper reports of the exposure, but was "lost"; and its whereabouts was the mystery of the proceedings. This is the first glimpse that any one, except "Cheerful Charlie' Howard, who kept it, and members of the grand jury, has had of the book

WHENEVER anything extraordinary is done in American municipal politics, whether for good or for evil, you can trace it almost invariably to one man. The people do not do it. Neither do the "gangs," "combines," or political parties. These are but instruments by which bosses (not leaders; we Americans are not led, but driven) rule the people, and commonly sell them out. But there are at least two forms of the autocracy which has supplanted the democracy here as it has everywhere it has been tried. One is that of the organized majority by which, as in Tammany Hall in New York and the Republican machine in Philadelphia, the boss has normal control of more than half the voters. The other is that of the adroitly managed minority. The "good people" are herded into parties and stupefied with convictions and a name, Republican or Democrat; while the "bad people" are so organized or interested by the boss that he can wield their votes to enforce terms with party managers and decide elections. St. Louis is a conspicuous example of this form. Minneapolis is another. Colonel Ed. Butler is the unscrupulous opportunist who handled the non-partisan minority which turned St. Louis into a "boodle town." In Minneapolis "Doc" Ames was the man.

One of the articles which made *McClure's* the leading muckraking magazine. This was the second of Steffens' celebrated series.

to accept the designation as a badge of honor, and in the history of American magazines the period is known as "the era of the muckrakers." [14]

When in 1893 three new popular magazines—*McClure's, Cosmopolitan,* and *Munsey's*—cut their prices to a dime, their circulation figures started on an upward climb. After the turn of the century these magazines and such others as the *Ladies' Home Journal, Collier's, Everybody's,* and the *Saturday Evening Post* had circulations running into the hundreds of thousands. Most of them joined with great enthusiasm in the crusade against big business, against corruption, and for social justice. Their writers, who came largely from newspaper ranks, had national audiences for articles which were sometimes original but which also sometimes were drawn from the stories published by crusading newspapers in various cities. However the articles were obtained, the magazines performed the service of coordinating and interpreting information about social, economic, and political problems for a nationwide audience, and thus had great impact.

Touching off the muckracking era was S. S. McClure, whose magazine began three significant series of articles in late 1902. McClure and his associate editor, John S. Phillips, had selected a staff of talented and responsible writers to handle the nonfiction section of *McClure's*. One was Ida M. Tarbell, whose specialties were biographies and research work. Another was Lincoln Steffens, former reporter for the *Evening Post* and city editor of the *Commercial Advertiser* in New York, who was to become one of the country's most famous crusading liberals. A third was Ray Stannard Baker, who came to *McClure's* from the *Chicago Record* in 1897 and who later was to achieve fame as Woodrow Wilson's biographer. Beginning in late 1902 Miss Tarbell exposed the business practices of John D. Rockefeller and the Standard Oil Company; Steffens opened his attack upon corruption in city and state governments; and Baker began discussing the problems of the working man. The circulation of *McClure's* mounted past the half million mark and the muckraking trend in magazine editing was in full swing.

[14] The full story is told in C. C. Regier, *The Era of the Muckrakers* (Chapel Hill: University of North Carolina Press, 1932). Regier, however, ignores the contribution of newspapers in crusading and thus distorts the picture.

What McClure was doing was not entirely new to the magazine field. The older magazines of high quality—*Harper's, Scribner's,* the *Century,* and the *Atlantic Monthly*—had paid some attention to current affairs, although they were primarily literary in tone. There were several journals of opinion which had relatively small but influential audiences: Godkin's *Nation,* Albert Shaw's *Review of Reviews,* Lyman Abbott's *Outlook,* the *North American Review,* the *Forum,* and the *Independent.* In the same class but taking an early leadership in crusading for socio-economic and political reform was Benjamin O. Flower's *Arena.* These magazines and others were giving attention to the rising business trusts, graft, and political machines, but it was *McClure's* which first made a frontal assault of real magnitude.

Miss Tarbell's "History of the Standard Oil Company" ran in *McClure's* until 1904, and her detailed, thoroughly documented account of the unfair business practices used by the company to squeeze out competitors put Rockefeller on the defensive for many years to come. Steffens began his series on "The Shame of the Cities" by recounting the situation in St. Louis which had first been exposed by the *Post-Dispatch* and followed up with reports on corrupt government in Minneapolis, Pittsburgh, Philadelphia, Chicago, New York, and other cities. George Kibbe Turner, an alumnus of the *Springfield Republican,* continued the city series later in the decade. Baker dealt with labor problems, including child labor and the economic status of the Negro. Other contributors to *McClure's* included Burton J. Hendrick, who wrote about the New York life insurance companies, Kansas editor William Allen White, and newspaperman Will Irwin.

Cosmopolitan joined the muckrakers when the magazine passed from John Brisben Walker to Hearst, by running the series "The Treason of the Senate" which appeared in 1906. The author was David Graham Phillips, one of Pulitzer's editorial writers on the *World* staff, who retired from newspaper work to write a series of books examining problems of his time. Phillips denounced a score of conservative senators—both Republican and Democrat—as spokesmen of "the interests." Among other prominent muckrakers, Alfred Henry Lewis attacked the International Harvester Company in *Cosmopolitan* and followed up with a series examining the careers of America's leading millionaires. Charles Edward Russell, who had been managing editor of the *Minneapolis Journal* at 21 and who had worked for several New York and Chicago newspapers, surveyed the weaknesses of state governments in a 1910 series. Active in the fray, too, was *Everybody's*, founded in 1899 and edited by John O'Hara Cosgrave. When in 1904 it persuaded a colorful Wall Street financier, Thomas W. Lawson, to write "Frenzied Finance," the public appetite for Lawson's inside information drove the magazine's circulation from 200,000 to 735,000 within a year. *Everybody's* also was a vehicle for Charles Edward Russell, who attacked the beef trust in its columns in 1905 and contributed a savage assault on Wall Street financiers in 1907. Less important, but influential, were *Pearson's*, *Hampton's* (which built a readership of 440,000 in the years 1907 to 1911), and *La Follette's Weekly*, the voice of the Wisconsin progressive movement.

Taking the lead from *McClure's* in muckraking after 1905 was *Collier's*. Published by Robert J. Collier and edited by Norman Hapgood, the magazine developed an effective editorial voice in national political affairs. Its articles ranged over many social and economic problems, but it caught popular attention for a series of articles by Samuel Hopkins Adams on the patent medicine trade, called "The Great American Fraud," published in 1905 and 1906. Adams exposed the false claims of many of the popular "cure-alls" and demonstrated that some of the patent medicines contained poisonous ingredients not identified on the labels. Newspaperman Mark Sullivan also contributed to the *Collier's* drug exposé, as well as covering Washington politics for the magazine.

Equally prominent in the attack on the patent medicine business was Edward W. Bok, editor of the *Ladies' Home Journal*. It was Bok who shocked his women readers by proving that Lydia E. Pinkham, to whom American women were supposed to write for advice, had been dead for 22 years. And he, too, crusaded for legislation which would force proper labeling of drugs and medicines, and prevent dishonest advertising of the products.

The attack on the patent medicines coincided with a drive against adulterated foods and unsanitary practices in packing plants. Under the leadership of Dr. Harvey H. Wiley, chief chemist of the Department of Agriculture, federal and state officials had proved widespread adulteration of food and addition of chemicals and artificial dyes by food manufacturers. But the lid was blown off when Upton Sinclair wrote *The Jungle* in 1906, a novel intended to portray the plight of immigrant workers in Chicago's packing houses, but which was so terrifying in its charges of unsanitary and callous practices in meat handling that it caused a nationwide revulsion.

Passage of the Pure Food and Drugs Act of 1906 was the outcome. This regulated the activities of manufacturers, but the problem of "truth in advertising" remained. Some newspapers, like those of the Scripps-McRae League, had banned unethical advertising from their columns, as had the *Ladies' Home Journal.* But some state newspaper editorial associations, and the American Newspaper Publishers Association, had attempted to defend the patent medicine business against regulation. Some newspapers had obtained testimonials from their readers, extolling the virtues of the medicines, and had run them in their news columns. This use of "readers," as they were called, also had been extended to cover publicity stories sent out by all manner of businesses and paid for by the column inch. As the campaign for "truth in advertising" grew, more newspapermen saw the need for reform. State laws making untruthful, deceptive or misleading advertising statements a misdemeanor were adopted after *Printers' Ink* drafted a model statute in 1911, and the federal Newspaper Publicity Law of 1912 required that all matter published for money should be marked "Advertisement."

Other magazines should be noted. One was the *American Magazine,* which was purchased in 1906 by a group of McClure's writers. A disagreement in policy led John S. Phillips, associate editor of *McClure's,* to leave its staff. He took with him Miss Tarbell, Steffens, Baker, William Allen White, and Finley Peter Dunne, America's "Mr. Dooley." These were the leaders of the muckrakers and for a few years they constituted a distinguished editorial board for the *American.* The high point of muckraking had been reached in 1906, but liberal insurgency continued, climaxed in 1912 by Theodore Roosevelt's third party candidacy and Woodrow Wilson's election as president. The *New Republic* began its career in 1914 under editor Herbert Croly, whose *The Promise of American Life* (1909) became a creed for Wilsonian liberals. Croly and staff member Walter Lippmann supported Wilson in wartime. Not so *The Masses,* edited by Max Eastman, and a brilliant voice of protest from 1911 to 1917 when its pacifist-socialist line led to wartime persecution and demise. Among its contributors were Lippmann, Carl Sandburg, Sherwood Anderson, and cartoonist Art Young.

Playing a role, too, in the quest for social justice were a group of America's writers. William Dean Howells and Henry James had pointed the way toward the realistic novel. Joining them in this movement were novelist Stephen Crane and short story writers Ambrose Bierce and Hamlin Garland. Of the same school were poets Walt Whitman and Emily Dickinson. From this literary heritage, and from the pressure of the times, came a flowering of realism in literature after 1900.

Californian Frank Norris contributed two volumes of a planned trilogy on the "Epic of Wheat" before his career was cut short by death at 32. His *The Octopus,* appearing in 1901, told the story of the struggle of California farmers against the power of the Southern Pacific Railroad. His protest against Chicago wheat speculators, *The Pit,* made an equally deep impression. Another Californian, Jack London, captured in his stories of adventure and raw, brutal experience a full expression of the rising protest against the capitalistic system. London's *The Iron Heel,* published in 1907, and Upton Sinclair's *The Jungle* were high points in relentless realism. So were Theodore Dreiser's *Sister Carrie,* which was at first suppressed by a frightened publisher, and his later books, *The Financier* and *The Titan.*

More Americans, it is true, were reading historical novels, adventure stories, and popular favorites like *David Harum* and *Mrs. Wiggs of the Cabbage Patch* than were reading the works of Norris, Sinclair, London, and Dreiser. More Americans, too, were reading fiction in *Munsey's* and the *Saturday Evening Post* than were reading the exposés by Lincoln Steffens, Ida M. Tarbell, and Samuel Hopkins Adams. And among newspaper readers, relatively few were absorbing the editorial arguments of Edward Wyllis Scripps, Joseph Pulitzer, and their contemporaries of equal stature. Still, at a critical moment in American history, when an arousing of public opinion was needed to ensure economic and political progress and a more equitable social pattern, journalism and literature played their part and produced effective leaders.

The most common criticism of the muckrakers and the crusaders of this period has been that many of them offered nothing but protests against the injustices and inadequacies of American economic and political life. They aroused discontent, they exposed corruption and greed, they pointed to the inevitable growth of corporations and trusts, but they had few constructive solutions to offer, few alternatives to suggest. So the criticism runs, with some validity, although it should be tempered by the realization that the noisy, persistent radical often prods more cautious people into making needed reforms which keep society in balance. It should be remembered, too, that this criticism applies equally, when valid, to political leaders, labor organizers, ministers, teachers, reformers, and other persons as well as to newspaper and magazine editors and writers.

But it does not apply to those individuals who saw that the problem was one of making reasonable adjustments to changing conditions, rather than fighting blindly against the transition from one socio-economic situation to another. There were leaders who so saw the problem, and they had many followers. There were La Follettes and Wilsons in politics who offered reasonable solutions; there were constructive leaders like Mitchell and Gompers in the labor movement; and there were journalists like Scripps and Pulitzer who rose to equal heights, as effective champions of progressive democracy. Together they helped to develop a new main current of American thought and action, in keeping with the requirements and the wishes of the majority.

ANNOTATED BIBLIOGRAPHY

For references to the literature about Pulitzer see the bibliography for Chapter 17; for the Hearst references see Chapter 19. Vol. IV of Mott's *History of American Magazines* covers this period (see Chapter 16).

Books:

Baker, Ray Stannard, *An American Chronicle.* New York: Charles Scribner's Sons, 1945. The autobiography of one of the *McClure's* writers.

Bent, Silas, *Newspaper Crusaders.* New York: Whittlesey House, 1939. A general study.

Bok, Edward W., *The Americanization of Edward Bok.* New York: Charles Scribner's Sons, 1920. The famous autobiography of the editor of the *Ladies' Home Journal.*

Bowers, Claude G., *Beveridge and the Progressive Era.* Boston: Houghton Mifflin Company, 1932. A distinguished study of the times of Theodore Roosevelt and the Bull Moose progressives, of whom Senator Albert J. Beveridge was one.

Cochran, Negley D., *E. W. Scripps*. New York: Harcourt, Brace and Company, 1933. A more factual biography than Gilson Gardner's *Lusty Scripps* (New York: Vanguard Press, Inc., 1932).

Daniels, Josephus, *Tar Heel Editor*. Chapel Hill: University of North Carolina Press, 1939. The first volume of the Daniels autobiography, it deals with his early newspaper career.

Editorials from the Hearst Newspapers. New York: Albertson Publishing Company, 1906. Selected reprints of the Hearst editorial page offerings at the turn of the century.

Ellis, Elmer, *Mr. Dooley's America*. New York: Alfred A. Knopf, Inc., 1941. The life and times of Finley Peter Dunne, humorist and reformer.

Faulkner, Harold U., *The Quest for Social Justice, 1898-1914*, A History of American Life, Vol. XI. New York: The Macmillan Company, 1931. This volume of the series measures up as a work of social history.

Filler, Louis, *Crusaders for American Liberalism*. New York: Harcourt, Brace and Company, 1939. A study of the liberals and the muckrakers which is based on the political problems of the era.

Forcey, Charles, *The Crossroads of Liberalism*. New York: Oxford University Press, 1961. A case study of Herbert Croly, Walter Weyl, Walter Lippmann, and their *New Republic* of 1914.

Hapgood, Norman, *The Changing Years*. New York: Farrar and Rinehart, Inc., 1930. Reflections of the editor of *Collier's*.

Heaton, John L., *Cobb of "The World."* New York: E. P. Dutton & Company, 1924. Includes a sketch of Frank I. Cobb and a collection of his *New York World* editorials.

Link, Arthur S., *Woodrow Wilson and the Progressive Era, 1910-1917*. New York: Harper & Brothers, 1954. A volume in the New American Nation series by the biographer of Wilson.

Linn, James W., *James Keeley, Newspaperman*. Indianapolis: Bobbs-Merrill Company, 1937. The biography of the *Chicago Tribune's* crusading managing editor.

McCabe, Charles R., ed., *Damned Old Crank*. New York: Harper & Brothers, 1951. A collection of autobiographical essays by E. W. Scripps, written with more design to startle than to inform, but nevertheless valuable.

McClure, S. S., *My Autobiography*. New York: Frederick A. Stokes & Company, 1914. The story of the magazine publisher.

McRae, Milton A., *Forty Years in Newspaperdom*. New York: Brentano's, 1924. Autobiography of E. W. Scripps' partner and business manager.

Marcosson, Isaac F., *David Graham Phillips and His Times*. New York: Dodd, Mead and Company, 1932. The biography of a muckraker.

Mowry, George E., *Theodore Roosevelt and the Progressive Movement*. Madison: University of Wisconsin Press, 1946. Traces the relationship of Roosevelt to radicalism.

Older, Fremont, *My Own Story*. New York: The Macmillan Company, 1926. The fighting San Francisco editor tells his piece.

Pollard, James E., *The Presidents and the Press*. New York: The Macmillan Company, 1947. Covers the newspaper relations of Theodore Roosevelt.

Pringle, Henry F., *Theodore Roosevelt*. New York: Harcourt, Brace and Company, 1931. A Pulitzer Prize biography of the key figure of the muckraking era by a former newspaperman.

Regier, C. C., *The Era of the Muckrakers*. Chapel Hill: University of North Carolina Press, 1932. An exhaustive study of the crusading magazines and their writers. Unhappily it ignores newspapers, thus implying that they lacked interest in muckraking.

Sedgwick, Ellery, *The Happy Profession*. Boston: Little, Brown and Company, 1946. Includes a description of the hurly-burly times at *Leslie's*, the *American*, and *McClure's* before Sedgwick became owner and editor of the *Atlantic* in 1909.

Steffens, Lincoln, *The Autobiography of Lincoln Steffens*. New York: Harcourt, Brace and Company, 1931. One of the great journalistic autobiographies. Steffens' advice on writing is included in Mott and Casey, *Interpretations of Journalism*.

Sullivan, Mark, *Our Times*. New York: Charles Scribner's Sons, 1926 ff. Newspaperman Sullivan's six volumes are crowded with the color and the drama of the years 1900 to 1929, and in addition are historically sound. *Our Times* is a treasure house.

Tarbell, Ida M., *All in the Day's Work*. New York: The Macmillan Company, 1939. The chief woman muckraker reviews her career.

Villard, Oswald Garrison, *Fighting Years*. New York: Harcourt, Brace and Company, 1939. The autobiography of the publisher of the *Nation* and *New York Evening Post*.

Weinberg, Arthur and Lila, eds., *The Muckrakers*. New York: Simon and Schuster, 1961. A compilation of some of the best magazine articles by the muckrakers, with comments by the editors.

Periodicals and Monographs:

Grenier, Judson A., "Muckraking and the Muckrakers: An Historical Definition," *Journalism Quarterly*, XXXVII (Autumn 1960), 552. A study of the movement and leading individuals from 1902-14.

Morrison, Joseph L., "Josephus Daniels as 'Tar Heel Editor,' 1894-1913." Ph.D. dissertation, Duke University, 1961 (Ann Arbor: University Microfilms, 1961). The first biographical study of Daniels, scheduled for 1962 publication by the University of North Carolina Press.

Pringle, Henry F., "The Newspaper Man as an Artist," *Scribner's*, XCVII (February 1935), 101. The artist was Frank I. Cobb, editor of the *New York World*.

Chapter 21

THE GREAT AND THE
COLORFUL

It will be my earnest aim . . . to give the news
impartially, without fear or favor. . . .
—Adolph S. Ochs

THE SEVERAL PRECEDING CHAPTERS have been con-
cerned with the historical development of patterns of press behavior.
A segment of the press was involved successively in important
general trends: the rise of the new journalism, the spread of yellow
journalism, and service as "people's champions." But it is difficult
to fit newspapers into such patterns, because each newspaper has
an individuality born of its publishing environment. In some cases
a newspaper's individuality is so pronounced that its story is best
told apart from discussions of trends and patterns.

One conspicuous example is the *New York Times*. The *Times* was
rescued from near-oblivion in 1896 and began a rise to greatness
as a journalistic institution which eventually approached the status
of a national newspaper. In the same years, fame also came to a
unique and colorful Kansas editor, William Allen White, whose
name was known to more persons than was that of the publisher of
the *Times*, even though the *Emporia Gazette* was always a small-
town paper. Across the country, other newspapers and newspapermen achieved distinctive notice within and without the craft, for
varying reasons. Some are more colorful than great, but they are a

483

part of journalistic lore. It is with their stories that this chapter is concerned.

The story of the *New York Times* is the story of the man who rescued it from bankruptcy in 1896 and who guided it until he died in 1935. He was Adolph S. Ochs, a onetime printer's devil from Tennessee, who salvaged the glories of the *Times* of Henry J. Raymond's day and set its course as America's leading newspaper. It was the men and women he selected to staff the *Times* who made it an institution.[1]

Ochs, like many another great publisher, struggled up from the ranks to win his place. His parents were Germans of Jewish faith, who emigrated to the United States before the Civil War. Adolph, born in 1858 in Cincinnati, was the oldest of six children. His father fought in the Civil War and at its close took his family to Tennessee in a covered wagon. For a brief two years the family enjoyed Captain Julius Ochs' business success in a Knoxville drapery shop, but the postwar depression brought quick ruin. The captain thereafter eked out a small income as a magistrate and United States commissioner.

The oldest son went to work, in the tradition of the times. Appropriately enough young Ochs became a carrier boy for the *Knoxville Chronicle* at 11, covering four square miles on foot beginning at 4 a.m. He worked in a grocery store, as a druggist's apprentice, and sandwiched in some schooling. When he was 14 he landed the job as the *Chronicle*'s printer's devil. For three years the lad tended the fires and lamps, cleaned the press, ran errands, and learned to set type.

For a few months in 1875 Ochs tried his hand at newspaper work in Louisville. He became assistant composing room foreman of the *Courier-Journal* and did some reporting for Henry Watterson. But he was a colorless and awkward writer; his genius lay in his business ability and in his capacity for developing ideas and exhibiting journalistic leadership.

Back in Knoxville in 1876 and setting type on the *Tribune*, young Ochs got his chance. The paper's business manager had $100, an

[1] Ochs' story is told in Gerald W. Johnson, *An Honorable Titan* (New York: Harper & Brothers, 1946). The *Times*' story was first told in Elmer Davis, *History of the New York Times, 1851-1921* (New York: The New York Times, 1921). The panorama of 100 years is presented in Meyer Berger, *The Story of the New York Times: 1851-1951* (New York: Simon and Schuster, 1951).

impressive sum in the money-less South of postwar days. The editor, a black-bearded Scotsman of 45 who had all the education Ochs lacked, wanted to start a newspaper in Chattanooga. The three joined forces to publish the *Chattanooga Dispatch*. Ochs was the advertising solicitor and put out a city directory on the side, but within a few months the venture had collapsed.

Chattanooga was an unlikely spot in which to seek success in journalism. It was a city of 12,000 but it was still in the frontier stage, with no sidewalks, muddy streets, and little interest in newspapers. The city had seen 16 newspapers come and go in 40 years and the only survivor was the *Times*, a paper with a decrepit printing shop and a circulation of 250. Ochs had the frontiersman's faith, however, and persuaded a businessman to endorse his note for a $300 bank loan. He got control of the *Times* for $250 and persuaded the old *Dispatch* staff to join him in his new venture. The Scottish editor, Colonel John E. MacGowan, agreed to work for $1.50 a day until times were better. A reporter was added signing on with a publisher who had exactly $12.50 working capital.

It was July, 1878, and Ochs was not yet 21. But he and his editor promised Chattanooga big things. They would carry all the local news, the latest news by telegraph, and particularly all the commercial news which was available. Chattanooga would become the capital of a commercial and agricultural area, Ochs said, and the *Times* would be its indispensable newspaper. He said flatly that he expected community support for "a paper primarily devoted to the material, educational and moral growth of our progressive city and its surrounding territory."

Ochs was a born gambler, and he gambled almost daily to save the *Times*. He borrowed money with one hand, and paid an old loan with the other. He paid his staff in orders on the town's merchants, and took whatever cash and goods he could from advertisers and subscribers. Business improved, but Ochs went deeper in debt in order to buy better presses and type. He built up a string of correspondents through the South to widen his news coverage. He started a weekly edition of the paper, as well as a trade journal for southern industrialists, an agricultural journal, and a religious newspaper. His editorials in the *Times* called for a nonpartisan city government, for improved river transportation, for sewers, parks, and schools, and for a Chattanooga University. When a fever of land speculation hit the town, the publisher was caught up in the enthusiasm. Seemingly Ochs was a smashing success. His family moved to Chattanooga and his father and a brother, George, took positions on the newspaper. The *Times* by 1892 was clearing $25,000 a year and was regarded as one of the South's best newspaper properties. That year Ochs built a $150,000 gold-domed newspaper building which was the pride of Chattanooga. But in the meantime the real estate bubble had burst, and Ochs was in great financial trouble. To pay off his debts, he required more money than he could make with the *Chattanooga Times*. What he needed, Ochs decided, was another newspaper. He looked about the country for four years, and in March, 1896, he heard that there was a gambler's chance to buy the *New York Times*.

Ochs was properly impressed by this opportunity. He knew how respected the *Times* had been since its founding by Henry J. Raymond in 1851. After Raymond's death in 1869, the paper had come under the direction of its business manager, George Jones. Jones, editor Louis J. Jennings, and chief assistant John Foord had helped to smash Boss Tweed in the seventies. John C. Reid had served well as managing editor from 1872 to 1889 and the paper had maintained its place until the death of Jones in 1891. By then the impact of the "new journalism" was having its effect.

The new guiding spirit on the *Times* became Charles R. Miller, a graduate of Dartmouth and former staff member of the *Springfield Republican*, who assumed the editorship in 1883. With associate editor Edward Cary and other staff members, Miller negotiated purchase of the *Times* from the Jones family heirs in 1893 for approximately a million dollars. But the paper did not prosper. It had the smallest circulation of the city's eight morning dailies, a paltry 9,000 paid circulation concealed in a 21,000 press run. This was not far behind the *Tribune*'s 16,000, but far below the *Sun*'s 70,000 morning circulation, the *Herald*'s 140,000, and the *World*'s 200,000 morning figure.

Ochs did not have the money to save the *Times*, but he convinced Miller that he had the know-how and the vision which would be needed to put the paper in a sound competitive position. An elaborate re-financing plan was advanced, which would give Ochs control of the paper within four years if he succeeded in revitalizing it. Ochs trudged through the Wall Street district for months persuading financiers, even including J. P. Morgan, to buy bonds in the new enterprise. Finally, in August, 1896, an agreement was completed, with Ochs putting up $75,000 of his own money and risking his Chattanooga paper on the outcome. The 38-year-old Tennessean, with 24 years of experience since his printer's devil days, now was competing with Pulitzer, Hearst, Dana, Reid, and Bennett in the New York field. Though he stood in awe of the journalistic greats, he felt confident that he would restore the *Times* to a position of leadership. After all, he told himself, he had sold J. P. Morgan on investing in a newspaper which currently was losing $2,000 a week.

The plan of attack which Ochs had devised to save the *New York Times* was simple. He would not attempt to match the sensationalism of Hearst and Pulitzer, nor would he popularize the paper's offerings in a half-way effort to keep up with the mass circulation leaders, as some other New York publishers were attempting to do. Instead he would publish a paper with solid news coverage and editorial opinion which would be designed for readers who did not like overemphasis of entertainment and features.

Ochs' declaration of principle contained these lines:

It will be my earnest aim that the *New York Times* give the news, all the news, in concise and attractive form, in language that is parliamentary in good society, and give it as early, if not earlier, than it can be learned through any other reliable medium; to give the news impartially, without fear or favor, regardless of any party, sect or interest involved; to make the columns of the *New York Times* a forum for the consideration of all questions of public importance, and to that end to invite intelligent discussion from all shades of opinion.[2]

In the years which followed Ochs and his staff made good on these promises. The effort to give all the news with the greatest possible speed became the *Times'* working principle. "To give the news impartially, without fear or favor" became the *Times'* creed. And the promise to make the newspaper "a forum for the consideration of all questions of public importance" was carried out in both news and editorial columns.

Ochs' first steps were unspectacular, but effective. He used his printer's ability to revamp the paper's typographical appearance and to improve the mechanical department. With Henry Loewen-

[2] *New York Times*, August 19, 1896.

thal, a veteran of 20 years of *Times* service whom Ochs named managing editor, he set out to develop news coverage which other papers were handling inadequately. The *Times* began to publish a guide listing the out-of-town buyers who were in the city. It reported daily real estate transactions. And it expanded its market reports, adding to the daily coverage a weekly financial review. The business and financial community began to find these *Times* features increasingly valuable. Lawyers similarly were attracted by another column listing court cases and records.

The class of readers to which Ochs was appealing also liked the emphasis placed upon reporting of news of government. It liked Ochs' Sunday magazine, which featured articles of current news significance rather than entertainment. It liked the *Times* book review section. It liked the expanded "letters to the editor" column which presented the comments and opinions of all contributors without regard to the paper's editorial policy. And it enjoyed an editorial-page feature begun in 1896 by Frederick C. Mortimer and continued by him for 30 years, consisting of paragraphs written in a lighter style and called "Topics of the Times."

On the business side Ochs found two valuable associates. One was Louis Wiley, who came from the *New York Sun* to become manager of the *Times*. Wiley soon established himself as Ochs' personal representative in civic and newspaper trade affairs, the relationship being similar to that between McRae and Scripps. As the "front man" and business manager, Wiley served ably until his death in 1935. Associated with him in the management was John Norris, from the *World* staff, an active leader in newspaper advertising and business affairs. Advertising linage passed that of the *Tribune* in the first year, and the *Times* used every device to increase its circulation, even becoming the first paper to solicit by telephone.

Still the *Times* was not prospering. Ochs determinedly set his face against the popular features of the new journalism, refusing to run "stunt" stories, banning comics from his columns, and giving pictures short shrift. He sniped at the yellow journalists, advertising the *Times* under the slogan "It Does Not Soil the Breakfast Cloth" before choosing the famous front-page ear, "All the News That's Fit to Print." But circulation in 1898 was still at the 25,000 mark. It was dwarfed by the huge circulations of the *World* and *Journal* during the Spanish-American War period, when the *Times* was hurt by its lack of resources to compete with its rivals for exclusive war stories.

Ochs decided in late 1898 to make one last gamble. The *Times* was selling for three cents, the *World* and *Journal* for two. Why not cut the price of the *Times* to a penny and thus win the circulation which was needed to ensure solid advertising support? His associates were skeptical. But Ochs insisted that the kind of readers who wanted to buy the *Times* could be found at all economic levels. Poor men and women, and those of limited incomes, would welcome the paper at a price they could afford, Ochs argued. They soon would discover that the *Times* was a different kind of penny paper than the usual venture at that price.

Once again the old formula of price adjustment was successful. The *Times* as a penny paper jumped to 75,000 circulation in 1899 and passed the 100,000 mark in 1901. Its advertising linage doubled within two years. The red ink turned to black and Ochs won majority control of the paper's stock under his purchase agreement. He promptly went into debt again to build the Times Tower on Broadway, in what became Times Square, putting $2,500,000 into what was in 1904 one of New York's most spectacular buildings. The strategic location of the *Times* plant in what became the city's nighttime heart and the later development of its moving electric news bulletins helped to establish the paper as one of the city's institutions.

Far more important to the future of the *Times* was another event of 1904, however. That year Carr V. Van Anda, America's foremost managing editor, began his 25-year career as the guiding genius of the *Times* news staff. With Miller directing the editorial page, Wiley the business office, and Van Anda the news room, Ochs had completed the quartet which would build the *Times* to greatness by the 1920's. Of them all it was Van Anda who contributed most directly to the *Times'* reputation as a great news-gathering organization.

To single out Van Anda as America's foremost managing editor perhaps seems extraordinary, for comparisons of the accomplishments of men in different eras and different publishing situations are difficult to make. But it is generally agreed that the chief architect of the superior news department of the *New York Times* was Van Anda, a man who shunned personal publicity so completely that despite his incredible achievements he became almost a legendary figure even to his own craft.[3]

Alexander Woollcott once remarked that Van Anda "loved the editing of a newspaper more than anything in the world." Apparently he was born with this love, for as a boy of six in an Ohio village in 1870, he was pasting clippings on sheets of paper and selling them for 10 cents a copy. At 10 he made a press out of a wooden frame, an ink roller from a cloth-wrapped broom handle, and printed with type salvaged from the village paper. Next he acquired a small press and did job printing, using the profits to finance his study of chemistry and physics. When he entered Ohio University at 16 he specialized in mathematics and science and had not the lure of journalism been so strong he likely would have become a scholar in the realms of astronomy and physics. As it was, he became a layman who could keep step with the keen minds in those fields.

Van Anda left college at 18 to become foreman for his village paper. Next he set type and reported for the *Cleveland Herald* and other Cleveland papers. When he was 22 he applied for work on the *Baltimore Sun* and was selected for the important post of night editor. Two years later, in 1888, he moved to the *New York Sun*, where after five years he became night editor. Dana and his managing editor, Chester S. Lord, recognized the genius of the young night editor who had no thought other than to obtain all the news for the next morning's edition. Later, Van Anda described the work of a night editor in words which reflect his own ability:

> The man most to be envied is the night editor. The night editor's work, always of world-wide scope, is never dull. He is the appraiser of events. He is the keeper of a St. Peter's Ledger of the news of the day. To him the excellence of a newspaper is due. He can make or mar it. The night editor passes finally on every item. He is the retriever of errors and must always be on the lookout for shortcomings and neglected opportunities.
>
> He should be keen, alert, and well-informed. He must be sympathetic, imaginative, human. As he sits quietly reading proof slips, it is he who

[3] See Davis, *History of the New York Times*, p. 274, and Berger, *The Story of the New York Times*, p. 160, for two estimates of Van Anda's role in building the *Times*. Many tributes to Van Anda from leaders in his profession are found in a short biography: Barnett Fine, *A Giant of the Press* (New York: Editor & Publisher Library, 1933). Berger carries the story of Van Anda's achievements through several chapters.

is framing the reflection of itself the world will see at the breakfast table. When you have achieved this post you have reached the highest place in your profession. It is true there are a few figures ahead of you, the managing editor and the editor-in-chief, but these are only offices to absorb the profit of other people's work.[4]

Van Anda set standards for the night editor which few other men could attain. He combined intellectual ability with a rare sense for news and news play. The qualities of imagination and integrity were both his to a high degree. And he had the physical stamina to edit the news thoroughly, accurately, and intelligently day in and day out, reading every story in copy or proof and yet standing ready to meet "shortcomings and neglected opportunities."

When Ochs decided in 1904 that his first managing editor, Henry Loewenthal, should devote full attention to business news, Van Anda's name was suggested to him. The association was to be an ideal one. Ochs was willing to spend money to get the news; Van Anda was more than willing to spend it for him. Both Ochs and Van Anda put every emphasis on getting all the news possible for the reader. The almost unlimited freedom which Van Anda found at the *Times* to utilize his skills was recognized by business manager Louis Wiley at a 1929 banquet celebrating the twenty-fifth anniversary of the Van Anda managing editorship, when he said, "It is well known that the *Times* prints only advertising for which Mr. Van Anda's news leaves room, in a paper of the size determined by him." [5] As the years went by there was an ever-increasing volume of both news and advertising, but the news came first.

Although he was now a managing editor, Van Anda never stopped serving as night editor. His routine at the *Times,* for 20 years, never varied. He appeared in the news room at 1 p.m., went home at 6 p.m. for dinner and a rest, and returned at 10 p.m. to stay until the last man departed at 5 a.m. Usually he was the last man. Twelve hours a day, seven days a week, Van Anda was riding the news, giving as much attention to the flow of stories as to the major news breaks. He loved to match his speed and wits against a deadline. He loved to exploit an important but undeveloped story and give it painstaking coverage and significant play. But he never lost sight of

⁴ As quoted in Fine, *A Giant of the Press* (New York: Editor & Publisher Library, 1933), p. 29.
⁵ *Ibid.*, p. 103.

the importance of conscientious and intelligent handling of the bulk of the news, and he transmitted this spirit to his staff. He was not a colorful, dynamic leader; rather he was reserved and cold in appearance and his piercing gaze was called the "Van Anda death ray." But those who worked with him found him a modest, sympathetic chief who backed his men completely and who never flew into a rage. His secret was in doing his own job so well that the impress was made both upon the newspaper and upon its staff.

Some paragraphs from advice once given by Van Anda to journalism students indicate the qualities he sought in his staff:

All who expect to become journalists must begin as reporters. The first requirement is a knowledge of the language. You must know your language as a musician knows his instrument. You must be able to detect the false word as readily as the musician does a false note. . . .

When you go to work in a newspaper office, regard your particular task as the biggest thing in the world. Learn to distinguish what you know and what you think you know and write only what you are certain of. The vice of guessing is never eradicated. Don't use slang unless you have the faculty of seizing on those slang expressions of today that will be the idioms of tomorrow. You may not invent, but you may imagine. If you possess the gift of imagination to any degree, you'll be qualified to adorn your profession. . . .

The first test of a good reporter is the collection of facts and impressions. He must be eager and curious about everything under the sun and beyond it. Next, he must have industry, and lastly, he must possess the ability to distinguish the true from the false, to differentiate the dull from the common-place. Here lies the opportunity to make journalism a profession, not a trade. . . .

Let me commend the copyreader to you. His work is no less essential to the paper than that of the reporter. A first rate copyreader can make a first rate newspaper out of third rate copy. On the other hand a poor copyreader can spoil the work of the best reporter. . . . He must possess keen literary appreciation. If he cannot write brilliantly he must write well enough to convert bad copy into good. He must be able to apply sandpaper to the bodily excrescences of an article, but not to its soul. His range of information must be wide and at instant command. He must know where to lay his hands on the facts he cannot draw from his memory. His chief joy is in the headlines. A two or three column story is told in a few words, luring the reader on if the subject interests him, warning him to pass on if it doesn't. In writing headlines . . . stick to honest nouns and verbs.[6]

[6] As quoted in Fine, *A Giant of the Press,* pp. 81-83.

There are many stories of Van Anda's almost legendary ability to practice what he preached. Soon after he became managing editor of the *Times*, word arrived that the decisive naval battle of the Russo-Japanese War might be at hand. Van Anda recognized the importance of the event and readied himself to handle the story. When the bulletin came, at 4:30 one morning, that the Japanese admiral, Togo, had smashed the Russian fleet, all of Van Anda's elaborate research and preparation went into play. Within 19 minutes the *Times* had put an extra to press with three columns of news on page one, running under banks of headlines written by Van Anda as the story was pieced together. Inside was a page of advance material which Van Anda long before had made ready for this moment. Forty thousand copies were run off and the managing editor rode about the city with a fleet of horse-drawn wagons at dawn seeing personally that his news play beat was prominently displayed on the newsstands.

It was Van Anda who took over when a big story broke at deadline time. He scanned the copy, and then sometimes ran to the composing room to set the headlines into type himself. He was "setting from the case," never stopping to write the heads—yet they always would fit. Van Anda's delight in beating an edition deadline in this manner often gave the *Times* a lead over its rivals in rushing the news to the readers.

More important than speed was Van Anda's ability to sense the news, to plan for expansion of a story, to calculate the true significance of an as-yet-undeveloped event. His classic achievement was his handling of the story of the sinking of the liner "Titanic" in 1912. Here, as in other situations, it was Van Anda's personal ability and the functioning of a well-trained staff of high caliber which combined to produce superior news coverage.

It was 1:20 a.m. Monday, April 15, 1912, when the first Associated Press bulletin reached the *Times* newsroom reporting that the luxury liner "Titanic" had struck an iceberg on its maiden voyage from Britain to America. An SOS had been picked up by the Marconi wireless station in Newfoundland. The "Titanic" supposedly was unsinkable, but Van Anda's rapid calls to *Times* correspondents in Halifax and Montreal and to the offices of the White Star Line told him that the ship's wireless had fallen silent a half hour after

"All the News That's Fit to Print."

The New York Times.

THE WEATHER.

Unsettled Tuesday; Wednesday, fair, cooler; moderate southerly winds, becoming northerly.

VOL. LXI...NO. 19,595. NEW YORK, TUESDAY, APRIL 16, 1912.—TWENTY-FOUR PAGES. ONE CENT

TITANIC SINKS FOUR HOURS AFTER HITTING ICEBERG; 866 RESCUED BY CARPATHIA, PROBABLY 1250 PERISH; ISMAY SAFE, MRS. ASTOR MAYBE, NOTED NAMES MISSING

Col. Astor and Bride, Isidor Straus and Wife, and Maj. Butt Aboard.

"RULE OF SEA" FOLLOWED

Women and Children Put Over in Lifeboats and Are Supposed to be Safe on Carpathia.

PICKED UP AFTER 8 HOURS

Vincent Astor Calls at White Star Office for News of His Father and Leaves Weeping.

FRANKLIN HOPEFUL ALL DAY

Manager of the Line Insisted Titanic Was Unsinkable Even After She Had Gone Down.

HEAD OF THE LINE ABOARD

J. Bruce Ismay Making First Trip on Gigantic Ship That Was to Surpass All Others.

The Lost Titanic Being Towed Out of Belfast Harbor.

CAPT. E. J. SMITH,
Commander of the Titanic.

PARTIAL LIST OF THE SAVED.

Includes Bruce Ismay, Mrs. Widener, Mrs. H. B. Harris, and an Incomplete name, suggesting Mrs. Astor's.

Biggest Liner Plunges to the Bottom at 2:20 A. M.

RESCUERS THERE TOO

Except to Pick Up the Hundreds Who Took to the Lifeboats.

WOMEN AND CHILDREN FIRST

Cunarder Carpathia Rushing New York with the Survivors.

SEA SEARCH FOR OTHERS

The California Stands By on Chance of Picking Up Other Boats or Rafts.

OLYMPIC SENDS THE NEWS

Only Ship to Flash Wireless Messages to Shore After the Disaster.

Continued on Page 2.

One of the great news stories of the twentieth century was that of the sinking of the "Titanic" with the loss of 1,500 lives. The handling of that story by Carr Van Anda, managing editor of the *New York Times*, won him attention of newspapermen everywhere. Van Anda had been ahead with the news the day before the edition reproduced above appeared, April 16, 1912. See page 493.

the first call for help, and convinced him that the ship must have gone down.

Before 3:30 a.m. Van Anda and his staff had organized the story. Among the more than 2,200 aboard were many famous persons. A background story was prepared on the passenger list, and a picture of the "Titanic" was prepared for page one. Two other vessels had reported close scrapes with icebergs in the North Atlantic area; this fitted the pattern of the news available about the "Titanic." The *Times* in several columns of type reported Monday morning that the ship had sunk, while other papers were handling the story in incomplete and inconclusive form.

Tuesday, Wednesday, and Thursday, the story commanded the world's attention, as the liner "Carpathia" sailed toward New York with survivors. Van Anda on Tuesday hired a floor in a hotel a block from the "Carpathia's" pier and installed four telephone lines directly connected to the *Times* city room. The entire staff was mobilized under the direction of Arthur Greaves, city editor, to cover the arrival of the rescue ship Thursday night. Van Anda persuaded Guglielmo Marconi, the wireless inventor, to board the ship to interview the wireless operator—and a *Times* reporter slipped through the police lines with the inventor. He got an exclusive story of the last messages from the "Titanic."

Within three hours after the arrival of the rescue ship the *Times'* first edition had appeared, with 15 of its 24 pages devoted to the story of the loss of 1,500 lives in the "Titanic" disaster. In coverage and in organization of a great news story that edition of the *Times* remained a masterpiece.[7]

Van Anda and Ochs both loved speed in the gathering of the news and this love had led the *Times* to leadership in the use of correspondents and communications facilities in such instances as the "Titanic" sinking. Both men had watched the work of Marconi, the Italian scientist who between the years 1895 and 1900 devised a practical system of sending telegraphic messages through space by means of electromagnetic waves. Marconi's "wireless" telegraphy was based upon the experiments of others, but it was he who obtained the basic patents and formed the first commercial wireless company in London in 1897.

[7] For the full story of the "Titanic" coverage see Berger, *The Story of the New York Times*, pp. 193-201. A contemporary account by Alexander McD. Stoddart appeared in the *Independent*, LXXII (May 2, 1912), 945.

Ship-to-shore communication and the use of the wireless by English newspapers and the *New York Herald* to cover sporting events soon followed. In December, 1901, Marconi successfully transmitted signals from England to Newfoundland. But it was not until 1907 that a headline in the *Times* reported: "Wireless Joins Two Worlds. Marconi Trans-Atlantic Service Opened With A Dispatch To The *New York Times*." [8]

The front page carried the *Times'* promotional stories and congratulatory messages from notables in Britain. Wireless was faster and less expensive than the commercial cable, and as operating difficulties were overcome, the *Times* began to present two to three pages of wireless news from Europe each Sunday. During the first World War, correspondents in Germany used the wireless to reach the United States with their stories without intervention of British censorship, until American entry into the war. By 1920 the *Times*, as well as the *Chicago Tribune*, had built its own trans-Atlantic wireless receiving station, and the activities of these and other newspapers led to the establishment of Press Wireless, Inc. The development of short-wave transmission after 1924 enabled the *Times* to complete its own radio facilities to receive press messages from any point in the world. Fred E. Meinholtz became the *Times* communications chief who kept his paper in the front rank technically so that the world's news could be received directly and exclusively.

The team of Van Anda and Ochs was spending money freely to establish a network of correspondents in the United States and abroad so that the *Times* would have its own men reporting the news and augmenting the press association services. The *Times* invested heavily in thorough coverage of world political and economic news. It found drama and excitement in stories on exploration, about the new field of aviation, and in the world of science generally.

One Van Anda beat was his signing of Commander Robert E. Peary to a contract giving the *Times* exclusive rights to his personal story of his 1909 expedition to the North Pole. Word of Peary's discovery of the Pole was flashed to the *Times* by wireless while the world was digesting the claims of Dr. Frederick A. Cook that he

[8] *New York Times,* October 18, 1907.

had reached the Pole the year before. The *New York Herald*, which had purchased rights to Cook's account, saw the Peary story eventually discredit Cook's tale.

The *Times*, like other newspapers, sponsored several cross-country flights during the early period of aviation. In the 1920's it carried exclusive stories of adventure and science, with wireless communication to provide immediate reporting of such exploits as those of William Beebe on the ocean floor and Auguste Piccard in the stratosphere. When Commander Richard E. Byrd flew over the North Pole in 1926 the *Times* carried his exclusive story of the historic flight and when the dirigible "Norge" went over the Pole three days later a *Times* reporter aboard wirelessed his story with the dateline "North Pole." Because the *Times* had its eye on every possible exclusive story, it held the world rights to the personal account of Captain Charles A. Lindbergh when the "Lone Eagle" made the first New York-to-Paris flight in 1927. The *Times* sponsored the Byrd expedition to the South Pole in 1929, with reporter Russell Owen winning a Pulitzer Prize for his widely-syndicated stories.

Van Anda, the scientist, also kept a close watch on the world of physics and mathematics. In 1919, when British astronomers decided to test the revolutionary mathematical formulae of the then obscure Albert Einstein, Van Anda assigned his London bureau to the story. The result was a copyrighted piece reporting the confirmation of the Einstein theory. Later, according to *Times* legend, Van Anda edited a story containing extremely complicated material from an Einstein lecture and spotted an error which professional mathematicians had missed.

The field of archaeology provided Van Anda with one more triumph in 1922. An Associated Press story based on a dispatch to the *Times* of London reported in 250 words the discovery of the tomb of an Egyptian Pharaoh, Tut-ankh-Amen. Van Anda quickly obtained exclusive rights in the United States to the story of the opening of the tomb. The dispatches and pictures from Egypt gave the *Times* one of its greatest syndicated offerings as all America came to know "King Tut." Van Anda, it turned out, had added a knowledge of Egyptology to his many accomplishments and astounded the staff by himself deciphering the hieroglyphics in a photograph late one night when a translator was not available. He also detected a 3,500-year-old forgery on the tomb and duly reported it.[9]

There also was space for the lighter side of the news in the *Times* of the Van Anda era. It paid handsomely in 1910 to have ex-prize fight champion John L. Sullivan cover the Jeffries-Johnson title bout in Reno. Van Anda preferred non-sportswriters for his featured stories on the big fights, and had Irvin S. Cobb cover the Dempsey-Carpentier bout. Elmer Davis, a young reporter fresh from studies as a Rhodes Scholar, reported the Dempsey-Gibbons match. The *Times* also gave extensive coverage to major crime stories of the period. When Ochs was twitted about this departure from usual *Times* policy he replied, "The yellows see such stories only as opportunities for sensationalism. When the *Times* gives a great amount of space to such stories it turns out authentic sociological documents."[10] Ochs knew that even the audience to which the *Times* appealed was interested in this brand of sociology.

Ranking above all else in bringing the *Times* to greatness, however, was its coverage of the events of the first World War. It was in this period that the paper began to publish the texts of documents and speeches, a policy which led to its becoming the leading reference newspaper for librarians, scholars, government officials, and other newspaper editors. The compilation of the *New York Times Index* further ensured the paper this position.

Six full pages in an August, 1914, issue of the *Times* presented the British White Paper to American readers. The *Times* had been the first American paper to obtain a copy of the British Foreign Office's correspondence with Germany and Austria, and printed it in full. Next day it published the text of the German version of events leading up to the war declaration, brought from Berlin by a *Times* correspondent, for another exclusive.

Van Anda meanwhile was giving his readers minute coverage of the military news, using press association accounts, the reports of his own correspondents with the various armies, and stories obtained from the *London Chronicle*. War pictures were carried in a rotogravure section, added by Ochs in 1914 after Van Anda had

[9] According to Russell Owen, writing in the *New York Times Magazine*, December 21, 1947, p. 2.

[10] As quoted in Berger, *The Story of the New York Times*, p. 258.

Investigated rotogravure printing in Germany. Political and economic reporting from European capitals was given proper emphasis with the military news. On the editorial page, editor Charles R. Miller ably documented the Allied cause and placed the blame for the war upon the German and Austrian governments.

When the United States entered the war the *Times* expanded its coverage. Costs of cabled news reached $750,000 a year but Van Anda did not hesitate to order the most elaborate coverage, sent at costly "urgent" rates if necessary, in order to give the *Times* the lead on a significant story. As a result the paper piled up a record number of exclusive interpretive stories and news beats which gave it additional prestige. Among its own war correspondents or syndicated contributors were Walter Duranty, Philip Gibbs, and Wythe Williams, three of the leading foreign correspondents of their era; Charles Grasty, the onetime Baltimore publisher; and a young *Times* staffman named Edwin L. James, who was destined to become the paper's managing editor. For its wartime coverage the *Times* was awarded one of the first Pulitzer Prizes in 1918.

The *Times* climaxed its wartime coverage with the only publication by a newspaper of the text of the Treaty of Versailles, a document which filled eight pages. Ochs and Miller wholeheartedly supported President Woodrow Wilson's fight for American entry into the League of Nations and the paper covered the lengthy peace negotiations and the postwar American political situation in detail, presenting official documents in increasing numbers even though advertising had to be curtailed to obtain the necessary space during a time of newsprint shortage. If there is a complaint to be registered against the *Times* of the Ochs and Van Anda period it centers upon its voluminous presentation of the news without sufficient interpretation for the average reader, who was lost in the columns of information presented in a "dead pan" objective fashion.

After 25 years of Ochs' ownership, the *Times* of 1921 had achieved major stature. There was one great reason for this success. The paper had taken in some $100,000,000 in those 25 years and had paid out but 4 per cent in dividends. Ochs had poured the millions into the *Times* for buildings and equipment, for staff, and for the tremendous news coverage which Van Anda had built. Circulation had reached 330,000 daily and more than 500,000 Sunday, while advertising linage had increased tenfold in the 25 years, passing the 23 million line mark. Ochs was a great builder and the *Times* was the symbol of his business success.

Politically the *Times* had been Democratic except during the Bryan campaigns. But it was essentially conservative in tone, particularly in its economic outlook. It was progressive in its social viewpoint but Ochs was not one of the crusaders of the "people's champions" variety. After going down to defeat on the League of Nations issue with the 1920 Democratic ticket of James M. Cox and Franklin D. Roosevelt, the *Times'* favorite Democrat of the early 1920's was John W. Davis, the New York lawyer who was defeated by Calvin Coolidge in the 1924 election. The *Times* supported Alfred E. Smith in 1928 and Franklin D. Roosevelt in 1932 in the final campaigns before Ochs' death.

The 1920's saw one era of *Times* history ending and another beginning. Editor Miller died in 1922 and was succeeded by Rollo Ogden, longtime *New York Post* editor. Van Anda went into semi-retirement in 1925 although he continued to hold the title of managing editor until 1932. Frederick T. Birchall, his distinguished associate in the newsroom and also a leading foreign correspondent, continued the Van Anda tradition. Appearing on the staff in the early twenties were such future *Times* luminaries as Mrs. Anne O'Hare McCormick, foreign correspondent; Lester Markel, Sunday editor; and Louis Stark, labor reporter. Following them were Waldemar Kaempffert and William L. Laurence in the field of science and Arthur Krock in the Washington bureau. David H. Joseph became city editor in 1927 for a 21-year term, and Edwin L. James became managing editor in 1932 after his European assignments.

While still active in management, Ochs groomed his son-in-law, Arthur Hays Sulzberger, and his nephew, Julius Ochs Adler, to succeed him. The deaths of Ochs and his business manager, Louis Wiley, in 1935 removed the last of the quartet which had been instrumental in building the *Times*. But the organization which they had created continued to carry the paper to new heights in the succeeding years. What the newspaper and its staff contributed to recent American journalism becomes a part of a later story.

While Ochs was guiding the destinies of the *Times* in his comparatively impersonal role as head of a journalistic institution, a small town Kansas editor was making a highly personal impact upon American society. William Allen White was born in Emporia,

Adolph S. Ochs (*above*) rescued the *New York Times* from bankruptcy in 1896 and made it one of the world's great newspapers before he died in 1935. His longtime managing editor, Carr Van Anda (*right*), achieved fame as the man most instrumental in developing the *Times*' superb news coverage. It was Ochs, however, whose leadership made the achievements of Van Anda and other staff members possible. (*New York Times* photographs)

William Allen White became the best known of America's small-town editors, not only for w
he wrote in the *Emporia Gazette* for his Kansas readers, but for the role he played in natic
political affairs. He is shown seated at his cluttered desk in the editor's cubbyhole office
1938, near the close of his career.

Kansas, in 1868, and died there in 1944. But between those years he became a citizen of America and a spokesman for its small towns —of which Emporia became the symbol. The editor of the *Emporia Gazette* was anything but a typical representative of his kind of journalism, but nevertheless his newspaper editorship was the foundation for his larger activities.

White in his *Autobiography* declared that never in his life did he want money for the necessities of life or for his few extravagances. He was in many respects a typical member of the American middle class, with an impulsive, sentimental streak that saved him from being as dull a small-town editor as he might have been expected to be, and a perceptiveness and understanding of changing American social and economic conditions which enabled him to be a thoughtful leader of his class. The historian Allan Nevins describes White admirably in this paragraph:

> White developed a burly, genial, neighborly personality which endeared him to a wide audience. Loving his profession of country editor, to him Emporia was a microcosm of the world. He liked the opportunity his editorial chair gave him of surveying human weaknesses and virtues, of being teacher and helper to the whole community, of expressing his own audacious opinion today upon some problem which affected a single family or block, and tomorrow upon some issue of world importance. His informality, the trait of a really great and transparently sincere personality, was captivating, and in combination with his spontaneous literary talent, enabled him to touch chords of humor and pathos, and to rise to occasional levels of literary beauty, which would have been quite impossible under the restraints of ordinary urban journalism. In his outlook upon national affairs, he began as a conservative, but rapidly worked around to a vigorous political and social insurgency, which in turn gave way to a philosophic tolerance of liberal stamp.[11]

White's father died before the son entered the University of Kansas and he decided he should earn his own way. So he worked as a printer and reporter for a weekly newspaper and as a college correspondent for several papers. After a year as a reporter and legislative correspondent for the *Kansas City Journal,* White went over to William Rockhill Nelson's *Star* in 1892 as an editorial writer. During his three years of exposure to the *Star's* journalistic atmosphere he wrote the first of his several books and married Sallie Lindsay, his lifelong helpmate. Then in 1895 he scraped together

[11] Allan Nevins, *American Press Opinion* (New York: D. C. Heath and Company, 1928), pp. 455-56. Nevins reprints several of White's editorials.

$3,000 and bought the *Emporia Gazette,* which had been started by the Populist party five years before. It had a poor reputation, a run-down shop, and fewer than 600 subscribers. But William Allen White, age 27, was home in Emporia.

Kansas had been captured during the 1893 depression by the Populists and the Democrats. White was an active Republican editor and politician—he loved politics all his life and remained a party worker and an intimate of politicians from the time of William McKinley and Theodore Roosevelt to that of Wendell Willkie and Franklin Roosevelt. On August 15, 1896, White exploded with anger at the Populists in an editorial which shot him into national fame. It was "What's the Matter with Kansas?" which White later referred to as representing "conservatism in its full and perfect flower." The editorial cited evidence that Kansas was declining in population and economic standing and placed the blame in fully unrestrained and effective style upon the "shabby, wild-eyed, rattle-brained fanatics" of the reform movement.[12] It was reprinted in virtually every Republican newspaper in the country, as ammunition against the Democratic candidate for president, William Jennings Bryan. William McKinley's campaign manager, Mark Hanna, adopted the young editor. But Bryan and the Democrats won the election in Kansas.

White now moved to the national stage. He became the friend of political leaders, and came to know the young New York Republican, Theodore Roosevelt, to whom he became deeply attached and who was his lifetime political hero. Publication of a volume of stories about life in Kansas had brought White to the attention, too, of literary and intellectual circles and he met William Dean Howells, Hamlin Garland, and other writers of the developing school of realism. More importantly, he met S. S. McClure and became a member of the circle which included Lincoln Steffens, Ray Stannard Baker, John Phillips, and Ida M. Tarbell. His articles and stories about Kansas and politics appeared in several magazines. White was now in tune with the times, hob-nobbing with the muckrakers and becoming with his wife a frequent visitor at the Oyster Bay home of the Theodore Roosevelts. The *Emporia Gazette* began to demand reforms: conservation of natural re-

[12] The editorial is reprinted in *The Autobiography of William Allen White* (New York: The Macmillan Company, 1946), pp. 280-83. It also appears in Nevins, *American Press Opinion,* pp. 419-422.

sources, railroad rate control, working men's compensation, direct primaries, the initiative and referendum, abolition of child labor.

When Roosevelt split with William Howard Taft in 1912, and the Progressive party was formed, White was Kansas national committeeman for the new third party. He admired the liberal principles of Senator Robert M. La Follette of Wisconsin and of Governor Woodrow Wilson of New Jersey, but he followed Roosevelt and campaigned furiously for "the Colonel." He hoped that the Progressive party would supplant the Republican party in the national political scene, but when the insurgent movement eventually collapsed, White re-entered Republican politics. He was a supporter of the League of Nations—an internationalist in isolationist territory—and when World War II came, he was a leader in the Committee to Defend America by Aiding the Allies. He admired the social gains of the New Deal, but he preferred the leadership of Theodore Roosevelt to that of Franklin Roosevelt.

In these later years White was forced to print a special weekly edition of the *Gazette* as a service to subscribers throughout the country. His most important book was *Puritan in Babylon,* a study of the America of the twenties as well as of Calvin Coolidge. But his most famous single piece of writing is the editorial, "Mary White," which appeared in 1921 when his teen-age daughter died in a horseback riding accident. In it is embodied the artistic soul of William Allen White.[13] His son, William L. White, became a newspaperman and writer in his own right and assumed the editorship of the *Gazette* when his father died in 1944. But although the *Gazette* continued to prosper, its peculiar qualities were no more.

Another of America's distinctive small town editors also lived and worked in Kansas. He was Ed Howe, who in 1877 at the age of 22 founded the daily *Atchison Globe* with $200 capital. Howe was a superlative reporter. He knew people and how to report their little doings. However, he had none of White's expansiveness and sentimentality, but rather an amazing ability to make trouble for himself. He told the people of Kansas that religion was all bosh, and he asserted in a time of agitation for women's rights that a woman's place was strictly in the home. His terse, sardonic editorial paragraphs often reflected a keen understanding of human nature,

---

[13] The editorial has appeared in many anthologies of literature and is reprinted in *The Autobiography of William Allen White,* pp. 606-609.

however, and they were widely requoted in the country's newspapers as the work of the "Sage of Potato Hill." His excellent novel, *The Story of a Country Town*, added to his national fame.

Among the great and colorful editors of the years immediately preceding and following World War I were the aging editor of the *Louisville Courier-Journal*, Henry Watterson, and the dynamic editor of the *New York World*, Frank I. Cobb. Watterson, though reaching the close of a career which had started in Civil War days, was vigorously and colorfully attacking Theodore Roosevelt in his columns, expressing his distrust of "Professor" Woodrow Wilson, and delighting in an exchange of editorial argument with men like Cobb. Two months after World War I began, Watterson adopted the simple but effective battlecry: "To Hell with the Hohenzollerns and the Hapsburgs!" His more intellectual arguments for American entry into the war won for him the 1918 Pulitzer Prize for editorial writing as a fitting tribute to a great journalistic figure.

Cobb's editorial page represented the realization of Joseph Pulitzer's hopes for the full development of the *New York World*. The editor whom Pulitzer had carefully trained before his own death in 1911 was unexcelled in his forcible expression of logically developed opinions. The *World* commanded deep respect for its intelligent and fair-minded approaches to issues of public importance, for its progressive and hard-hitting crusades which combined the reporting abilities of its news staff and the support of the editorial writers, and for its brilliant, if sometimes erratic, news play. It became one of those favorites of the press world which are called "newspapermen's newspapers."

The *World* helped to "discover" Woodrow Wilson as a presidential candidate, and Cobb and Wilson became close friends. Cobb's often-expressed fear of centralization of authority was in part overcome by his association with Wilson, and the *World* vigorously supported the far-reaching New Freedom program of economic and social reform which gave the federal government vast new powers. Cobb was one of Wilson's advisers at the Versailles peace conference, giving expression to the hopes for international cooperation which the *World* had long held. His battles in the columns of the *World* for American participation in the League of Nations and the World Court were unavailing, but they further established the paper as the leading spokesman of the Democratic party.

Tragedy struck the *World* in 1923 when Cobb died at the height of his powers. For just eight years later the *World* itself succumbed, and many a sorrowing newspaperman muttered, "If only Cobb had lived. . . ." Probably there would have been no difference in the fate of the *World* but it was true that after Cobb's death the newspaper lacked the genius of leadership which it had enjoyed since its purchase by Pulitzer in 1883.

During the middle twenties the *World* seemed to be continuing its powerful position. Cobb had left behind a distinguished editorial page staff, headed now by Walter Lippmann. Among the editorial writers were Maxwell Anderson and Laurence Stallings—more famous for their play, "What Price Glory"—and Charles Merz, later to become editor of the *New York Times*. Appearing on the *World's* "op. ed." page were Heywood Broun, the liberal-thinking columnist of "It Seems to Me" fame, Franklin P. Adams, conductor of the "Conning Tower," and Frank Sullivan, who like Anderson and Stallings moved to other creative fields. Rollin Kirby, the cartoonist, won three Pulitzer Prizes in this period for the *World*.

Despite this brilliance and the distinguished record of the paper, Joseph Pulitzer's creation was losing the battle in New York morning journalism. Pressing it on one side were Ochs' *Times* and the merger-created *Herald Tribune*. Soaking up circulation on the other side were the tabloids which appeared in the early twenties. The *World* failed to keep pace with its orthodox rivals in complete coverage of the news, even though it sometimes performed brilliantly, and it saw some of its subway-riding readers succumbing to the lure of the tabloids. Of the Pulitzer heirs, Joseph Pulitzer, Jr., had shown the most ability but he had assumed control of the *St. Louis Post-Dispatch*. His brothers, Ralph and Herbert, delegated much authority to Herbert Bayard Swope as executive editor, but Swope left the *World* staff in 1928. Already the newspaper was running a deficit, and in the depression of 1930 Pulitzer family losses on the morning, evening, and Sunday editions reached nearly two million dollars. Rumors of an impending sale began to be heard, and staff members made a desperate effort to raise enough cash to buy the *World* themselves. They argued, too, that the Pulitzer will forbade the sale of the paper, but in February, 1931, a New York court approved its purchase by Roy W. Howard for the Scripps-Howard interests. The evening *World* was merged with the *Telegram*. The morning *World*—symbol of Pulitzer's journalistic genius—was dead, and there was scarcely a newspaperman who did not feel that something peculiarly precious and irreplaceable had been lost to the craft.[14]

There were other newspapers which, like the *World,* were regarded as "newspapermen's newspapers." Very few combined a conception of public responsibility and journalistic brilliance to the degree which made the *World* great. But wherever oldtime newsmen gathered in this period there likely would be mentioned the work of men who wrote for and edited the *New York Sun* and *New York Herald.* Quite likely, too, the name of the *Chicago Inter Ocean* would be mentioned. These papers, now dead, are a part of the colorful story of American journalism, and the alumni of their excellent training grounds were legion. They lagged behind in the journalistic advance into the modern era but they and the men who worked for them had proud traditions and moments of glory.

The *New York Sun* of the days of editor Charles A. Dana and managing editor Amos J. Cummings had emphasized reporting skill, writing style, and human interest techniques to a degree worthy of the admiration of the practitioners of the "new journalism." It was a city editor of the *Sun,* John B. Bogart, who told a young reporter for the first time: "When a dog bites a man, that is not news; but when a man bites a dog, *that* is news." It was an editorial writer for the *Sun,* Francis P. Church, who in 1897 answered the "Is There a Santa Claus?" inquiry of a little girl named Virginia with an explanation which was reprinted widely for many years. It was a reporter for the *Sun,* Will Irwin, who in 1906 wrote the journalistic masterpiece, "The City That Was," in memory of a San Francisco being destroyed by earthquake and fire.[15]

Heading the *Sun* news staff from the eighties to the World War I period were managing editor Chester S. Lord and night city editor Selah M. Clarke, called "Boss" by his associates. They helped to train reporters like Irwin, Arthur Brisbane, Julian Ralph, Samuel

[14] The last city editor of the *World* told the story of its death in James W. Barrett, *The World, the Flesh, and Messrs. Pulitzer* (New York: Vanguard Press, Inc., 1931). See also Barrett's *Joseph Pulitzer and His World* (New York: Vanguard Press, Inc., 1941).

[15] Some of the color of the *Sun* is found in Frank M. O'Brien, *The Story of The Sun* (New York: George H. Doran Company, 1918). Church's "Is There a Santa Claus?" is reprinted on pp. 409-10.

Hopkins Adams, Richard Harding Davis, and Jacob Riis. From their night desk, too, Carr Van Anda went to his great career on the *Times*. Succeeding Dana as editor was the highly competent and graceful stylist, Edward P. Mitchell. The *Sun* was regarded as a "school of journalism" for young journalists and its graduates formed an alumni association. They were dismayed when control of the *Sun* passed in 1916 to Frank A. Munsey, a business-minded purchaser of newspapers who understood little of the journalistic traditions of the craft. The famous morning edition of the *Sun* disappeared in 1920 and the evening *Sun*, bearing little resemblance to the paper of old, trudged on toward eventual oblivion.

The *New York Herald*, under the guidance of founder James Gordon Bennett, had achieved leadership in news enterprise. When James Gordon Bennett, Jr., took control in 1872 the *Herald* ranked first in collecting and presenting the news. Its reporters and correspondents were the best and its insistence upon use of the fastest means of communication made it a hard-hitting rival for Pulitzer and Hearst when they invaded New York. Its traditions were still those of its adventurous correspondent of the early seventies, Henry M. Stanley, who spent two years searching in Africa on an assignment from the younger Bennett before he found the missing missionary and inquired, "Dr. Livingstone, I presume?" The *Herald* remained a news enterprise paper in the early twentieth century, contesting vigorously for complete and dramatic coverage of the world's events.

In the struggle for survival in New York, however, the *Herald* was handicapped by the personality and practices of its owner, the younger Bennett. He was intelligent and alert, and his driving force dominated the paper. He established the *Evening Telegram* in New York and the Paris edition of the *Herald*. But in his 45 years as a publisher he proved to be a dictator who put his personal whims first. He lived in Paris most of his life, rarely visiting the *Herald* office, and his royal manner of living drained an estimated $30,000,-000 from the profits of his papers.[16] No other publisher, save William Randolph Hearst, equaled Bennett in irresponsible personal control of a journalistic enterprise.

George Jean Nathan has described Bennett as he appeared in

---

[16] Don C. Seitz, *The James Gordon Bennetts* (Indianapolis: Bobbs-Merrill Company, 1928), p. 377.

1909, at the age of 67.[17] He was tall, slender, full of nervous energy, but bearing himself with a military erectness accented by steel-gray hair and moustache. Though he lived in Paris, his editors could neither hire nor fire a reporter without his consent. His editorial committee met at a table with an empty chair at the head—that was Bennett. At his place were set fresh copies of the paper each day, as though he might walk in at any moment.

Bennett's connection with the paper was far from being a psychological one, however. Cabled instructions arrived from Paris each day. Frequently department heads were called to Paris for conferences. Bennett kept close watch on the work of each employe, and practiced a policy of seeing to it that no individual achieved personal importance. Men were shifted from one position to another apparently at the publisher's whim, but usually to emphasize Bennett's desire that it was the *Herald* as an institution which came first. An entire department might be fired if it missed a good story; other men might find themselves handsomely rewarded by a suddenly indulgent ruler. Bennett had many good news instincts, but he also forced the paper to observe many rules of conduct based upon his personal idiosyncrasies and ordered promotion of his personal beliefs. It was not surprising that by the time of Bennett's death in 1918 the *Herald* had slipped badly and was destined to disappear into the *Herald Tribune* in 1924.

A newspaper in Chicago's past journalism history which for a time attracted a following of newspapermen was the *Inter Ocean*. It started its career in 1865 as the *Chicago Republican,* edited by Charles A. Dana for the first year. It became the *Inter Ocean* in 1872, a staunch Republican spokesman owned by William Penn Nixon. Through its reporting enterprise on the frontier, its religious news, and its agricultural news coverage it built up a midwestern circulation. It also led in introducing mechanical improvements, installing a color press in 1892 in advance of other American newspapers. During the nineties the paper lost money and was sold to Charles T. Yerkes, Chicago's traction line boss. Despite its record for conducting crusades in the public interest, the *Inter Ocean* suffered under Yerkes' ownership until he sold it in 1902 to George W. Hinman, who had come from the *New York Sun* to be the *Inter Ocean's* editor.

[17] In *Outing,* LIII (March 1909), 690.

Under Hinman the *Inter Ocean* won notice as a training school for newspapermen. The paper had been one of those which had catered to the "tramp reporters" of the period and by so doing had obtained the services of many young men with journalistic futures. Belonging to the *Inter Ocean* alumni association were Marquis James, William Cuppy, and Ring Lardner, writers; Walter Howey, later a famous Hearst executive; Richard J. Finnegan, later editor of the *Chicago Times* and *Sun-Times;* and a score of other prominent newspapermen. In 1914, however, the *Inter Ocean* fell victim to Chicago's newspaper competition and was added to the list of newspapers which have become reminiscences.[18]

No account of American journalism history is complete without a mention of the *Denver Post* of the days of Harry H. Tammen and Fred G. Bonfils. With its giant bannerlines printed in red ink, its startling and helter-skelter makeup, and its highly sensationalized news play the *Post* won fame as a dynamic but irresponsible paper. Its owners won fame, too, as ruthless operators of a journalistic gold mine. Tammen, a onetime bartender, and Bonfils, who had come West to make money in real estate and the lottery business, joined forces in 1895 to buy the *Post.* Their yellow journalism tactics succeeded in the rough-and-tumble newspaper warfare of Denver and at the height of their fortunes in the 1920's the paper was making more than a million dollars a year.

The *Post* was filled with features and sensational stories, but it also engaged in stunts and crusades which spread its fame in the Rocky Mountain area, where it advertised itself as "Your Big Brother." The partners operated from an office with red-painted walls, which Denver promptly called "The Bucket of Blood." Victims of the *Post*'s crusades and exposés filed libel suits against Tammen and Bonfils and accusations of blackmailing were leveled against the owners. No such charges were ever proved in court, however, and the *Post* continued in its proclaimed role as "the people's champion."

After Tammen's death in 1924, the *Post*'s luck began to change. The conduct of the paper in withholding news of illegal oil leases at Teapot Dome, until Bonfils was in a position to force the lessees

[18] The story of the *Inter Ocean* is told in Walter E. Ewert, "The History of the Chicago Inter Ocean, 1872-1914" (Master's thesis, Northwestern University, 1940).

to make a contract by which the *Post* would profit by half a million dollars, led the committee on ethics of the American Society of Newspaper Editors to recommend that Bonfils be expelled from membership. Instead, however, he was allowed to resign. His reputation was further darkened just before his death in 1933 when he sued the rival *Rocky Mountain News* for libel and then lost interest when the *News* undertook to document many of the stories about the partners.

Still the *Post* roared on, while the stories about life on Denver newspapers multiplied.[19] Entry of the Scripps-Howard chain into intensified competition with the *Post* in 1926 through purchase of the morning *Rocky Mountain News,* and of the evening *Times* for merger with the Scripps-owned *Express,* brought about one of the country's greatest competitive struggles. No holds were barred by city desks and circulation departments for the next two years, and Denver gorged itself on sensational news and free premium offers. In 1928 a truce was arranged by which the *Times* was killed, leaving the *Post* alone in the evening field, and the *News* in the morning. The journalistic habits of the days when anything went continued to haunt Denver, however, for another two decades, until a change in management at the *Post* brought new policies which pushed memories of the Tammen-Bonfils era into the background.

ANNOTATED BIBLIOGRAPHY

Books:

Barrett, James W., *The World, the Flesh, and Messrs. Pulitzer.* New York: Vanguard Press, Inc., 1931. The best story of the sale of the *World,* by the paper's last city editor.

Berger, Meyer, *The Story of the New York Times, 1851-1951.* New York: Simon and Schuster, 1951. Mainly the story of the *Times* after Ochs bought it; other books are better for the pre-Ochs period. But reporter Berger gets many reporters into his story, too rare an event in newspaper history-telling, and thus has a lively and interesting book. The *Times* also issued *One Hundred Years of Famous Pages from The New York Times* in its centennial year.

Bond, F. Fraser, *Mr. Miller of "The Times."* New York: Charles Scribner's Sons, 1931. The biography of *New York Times* editor Charles R. Miller.

[19] Many of the colorful stories are found in Gene Fowler, *Timber Line* (New York: Covici-Friede, Inc., 1933).

Davis, Elmer, *History of the New York Times, 1851-1921.* New York: The New York Times, 1921. Still good for its period.

Fine, Barnett, *A Giant of the Press.* New York: Editor & Publisher Library, 1933. A short biography of Carr Van Anda, the great managing editor of the *New York Times.*

Fowler, Gene, *Timber Line.* New York: Covici Friede, Inc., 1933. The colorful story of the Bonfils and Tammen era at the *Denver Post.* No tale was too tall for Denver newsmen.

Howe, E. W., *Plain People.* New York: Dodd, Mead & Company, 1929. The story of an unusual small-town Kansas editor in the usual small town, and of the *Atchison Globe.*

Johnson, Gerald W., *An Honorable Titan.* New York: Harper & Brothers, 1946. A good, but comparatively uncritical, biographical study of Adolph S. Ochs.

Johnson, Walter, *William Allen White's America.* New York: Henry Holt and Company, 1947. Important not only as a biography of the *Emporia Gazette* editor, but as an interpretation of the swiftly changing half-century in which White was a national figure.

Mahin, Helen O., ed., *The Editor and His People.* New York: The Macmillan Company, 1924. An excellent collection of William Allen White's editorials.

Mitchell, Edward P., *Memoirs of an Editor.* New York: Charles Scribner's Sons, 1924. By the distinguished editor of the *New York Sun.*

Nevins, Allan, *American Press Opinion.* New York: D. C. Heath and Company, 1928. Nevins' brilliant interpretive essays and selected editorials continue through this period.

Perkin, Robert L., *The First Hundred Years: An Informal History of Denver and the Rocky Mountain News.* Garden City: Doubleday & Company, 1959. By a staff member of Colorado's first paper.

Seitz, Don C., *The James Gordon Bennetts.* Indianapolis: Bobbs-Merrill Company, 1928. The younger Bennett brings the *New York Herald* to its downfall.

White, William Allen, *The Autobiography of William Allen White.* New York: The Macmillan Company, 1946. No one should miss this autobiography, and few do.

Periodicals and Monographs:

Ewert, Walter E., "The History of the Chicago Inter Ocean, 1872-1914." Master's thesis, Northwestern University, 1940. An excellent account of a famous newspaper.

Fine, Barnett, "When 'Boss' Lord Ruled 'The Sun,'" Editor & Publisher, LXVI (April 22–July 15, 1933). A series of articles about Chester S. Lord, managing editor of the *New York Sun* during 33 of its best years.

Howe, Gene, "My Father Was the Most Wretchedly Unhappy Man I Ever Knew," *Saturday Evening Post*, October 25, 1941. A dramatic story about E. W. Howe, reprinted in Drewry, *Post Biographies*.

Irwin, Will, "The New York Sun," *American Magazine*, LXVII (January 1909), 301. The story of the *Sun's* school of journalism, by one of the pupils.

Nathan, George Jean, "James Gordon Bennett, the Monte Cristo of Modern Journalism," *Outing*, LIII (March 1909), 690. The drama critic criticises an erratic publisher.

Stolberg, Benjamin, "The Man Behind 'The Times,'" *Atlantic Monthly*, CXXXVIII (December 1926), 721. A discerning study of Adolph S. Ochs. Reprinted in Ford and Emery, *Highlights in the History of the American Press*.

Chapter **22**

CONSOLIDATION BEGINS

> There was nothing new about newspaper consolidations in these years except the large number of them.
>
> —Frank Luther Mott

IN THE YEARS OF THE RISE of the "new journalism" it 'seemed that newspaper individuality was on a definite up-grade. As the daily newspapers took modern form and multiplied, a striving for innovations and for individual appeal was the goal of an unusual number of publishers, editors, and newsmen. The Pulitzers, the Scrippses, the Gradys, and the Van Andas joined the Franklins, the Bennetts, and the Greeleys of the past who by achievement of new techniques and appeals enriched the total journalistic output. Their successes in creating newspapers with distinctively individualized appeals, combined with a doubling of the number of dailies between 1880 and 1900 (from 850 to 1,967), seemed to indicate that variety of competitive appeal was a permanent feature of American journalism.

But the forces which created the modern mass newspaper—industrialization, mechanization, and urbanization—made for less individuality and more standardization of the product as the twentieth century unfolded. The great and the colorful, representing individualistic deviation from the norm, survived in some instances, but variety of competitive appeal tended to decline in the cities and towns of a standardized civilization. Competition for the mass

513

market in the urban centers, and other socio-economic pressures stemming from technological change, led to an inevitable contraction of newspaper publishing. The story of newspaper consolidation, already suggested in the preceding chapter, now becomes a dominant theme.

The years 1910 to 1914 mark the high point in numbers of newspapers published in the United States. The census of 1910 reported 2,600 daily publications of all types, of which 2,200 were English language newspapers of general circulation. General-circulation weekly newspapers numbered approximately 14,000. The totals hovered at these peaks until the economic pressures of the first World War were felt by American newspapers.

Wartime pressures, while of marked effect upon publishing, only accented trends which were developing as early as 1890. These trends were toward suspension of some competing newspapers, merger of others with their rivals, concentration of newspaper ownership in many cities and towns, and creation of newspaper chains. Before 1930, each of these trends had been clearly developed, to set the pattern for twentieth-century American journalism.

Statistics often can be confusing, and this is true of those concerned with the number of American newspapers published over the years. For example, it might be assumed that if there were 2,200 English-language daily newspapers of general circulation in 1910, and but 1,942 in 1930, then 258 newspapers died in those two decades. Actually, 1,391 daily newspapers suspended publication or shifted to weekly status in those 20 years, and another 362 were merged with rival papers. In the same two decades, 1,495 dailies were being born.[1] The turnover among established dailies was less drastic than these figures might seem to indicate, however, since one-fourth of the newcomers died within the first year of publication, and another one-half eventually joined the suspension list. But some of the newcomers were healthy ventures in the growing small towns and cities of an increasingly urbanized country.

Between 1910 and 1930 the population of the United States in-

[1] Royal H. Ray, *Concentration of Ownership and Control in the American Daily Newspaper Industry* (Columbia University Microfilms, 1951), pp. 401-08. A summary of this Ph. D. dissertation was published in *Journalism Quarterly,* XXIX (Winter 1952), 31.

creased 30 millions, from 92 to 122 million persons. Industrialization, steadily mounting in intensity after the great spurt prior to 1900, brought an increase in urban population of 25 millions. The number of towns and cities of 8,000 or more persons jumped from 768 to 1,208 between 1910 and 1930. Daily newspaper circulation increased at a faster pace, from 22½ million copies a day in 1910 to 40 million copies in 1930. Sunday newspaper circulation more than doubled in the two decades, moving from 13 million to 27 million copies. Total newspaper advertising revenue tripled in the years 1915 to 1929, increasing from an estimated 275 million dollars to 800 millions.[2]

Yet despite this great growth in advertising revenue, in numbers of readers, and in numbers of urban centers which could support daily newspaper publication, there was a net loss of 258 daily newspapers in the 20 years. Reduction of the number of competing dailies in larger cities, elimination of all but one newspaper in smaller towns, and suspension of daily newspaper publishing in some fading communities more than offset the number of new dailies started in growing towns and older publishing centers.

The figures given in Table 1 illustrate daily newspaper publishing trends from 1880 to 1930. Those for 1960 are included to indicate the full extent of the decline in number of dailies and of the rise in number of one-daily cities and one-combination cities (one owner of two papers). The pattern was clearly set by 1930.

A study of country weeklies made for the decade years from 1900 to 1930 shows similar trends, as illustrated in Table 2. The figures are only for weekly newspapers published in towns of 15,000 population or less, excluding publications in larger cities and some suburban weeklies. The percentages for one-weekly towns run higher than the percentages for one-daily cities given in Table 1. They show that by 1930 half the dailies and three-fourths of the country weeklies in the United States were published as the only newspapers in their respective communities. Seventy-one per cent of daily newspaper cities and 86 per cent of country weekly towns had but a single newspaper by 1930.

[2] Census population figures and newspaper circulation totals are conveniently tabulated in the appendices of A. M. Lee's *The Daily Newspaper in America* (New York: The Macmillan Company, 1937). Advertising revenue totals are from figures of the ANPA Bureau of Advertising.

TABLE 1

GROWTH OF ONE-DAILY CITIES

	1880	1900	1910	1920	1930	1960
Number of English-language general circulation dailies	850	1,967	2,200	2,042	1,942	1,763
Number of cities with dailies	389	915	1,207	1,295	1,402	1,461
Number of one-daily cities	149	353	509	716	1,002	1,222
Number of one-combination cities	1	3	9	27	112	178*
Number of cities with competing dailies	239	559	689	552	288	61
Percentage of daily cities with only one daily paper	38.3	38.6	42.2	55.3	71.5	83.6
Percentage of daily cities with competing dailies	61.4	61.1	57.1	42.6	20.6	4.2
Percentage of all dailies published in one-daily cities	17.5	17.9	23.1	35.1	51.6	69.3
Number of one-daily cities above 25,000 population	4	8	25	47	93	293
Number of one-daily cities above 100,000 population	0	1	1	5	6	23
Total daily circulation (millions)	3.1	15.1	22.4	27.8	39.6	58.9

* Includes 18 cities where two owners merged business and printing facilities.

Sources: For 1880: Data tabulated from S.N.D. North, History and Present Condition of the Newspaper and Periodical Press of the United States (Washington: Government Printing Office, 1884). For 1900-1920: W. Carl Masche, "Factors Involved in the Consolidation and Suspension of Daily and Sunday Newspapers in the United States Since 1900: A Statistical Study in Social Change," Master's 'hesis, University of Minnesota, 1932; and Morris Ernst, The First Freedom (New York: The Macmillan Company, 1946), p. 284. For 1930: Alfred McClung Lee, "The Basic Newspaper Pattern," The Annals of the American Academy of Political and Social Science, CCXIX (January 1942), 46, except figures for one-daily cities of specified population, from Masche. For 1960: Raymond B. Nixon and Jean Ward, "Trends in Newspaper Ownership and Inter-Media Competition," Journalism Quarterly, XXXVIII (Winter 1961), 3. Figures for one-combination cities since 1910, and total circulation, are from the Nixon-Ward article.

For numbers of English-language general circulation dailies: 1880, tabulated from North; 1900, from Masche; 1910, from Royal H. Ray (see footnote 1); 1920-1960, Editor & Publisher International Year Book figures. The census counts of daily publications, which included foreign language, religious, trade, and technical dailies, were 971 dailies in 1880, 2,226 in 1900, 2,600 in 1910, and 2,441 in 1920. But those figures do not compare with the Editor & Publisher International Year Book figures available after 1920. Masche, Ernst, and Ray tabulated their data from Ayer directories; Lee and Nixon used Editor & Publisher International Year Book data, which Nixon adjusted through additional research.

TABLE 2

GROWTH OF ONE-WEEKLY TOWNS

	1900	1910	1920	1930
Number of weeklies published in towns of 15,000 population or less	11,310	11,802	10,462	9,522
Number of towns of 15,000 population or less with weekly papers	7,827	9,260	8,798	8,295
Number with but one weekly	5,177	7,079	7,285	7,172
Percentage of country weekly towns with but one paper	66.1	76.4	82.8	86.5
Percentage of all weeklies studied published in one-weekly towns	45.8	60.0	69.7	75.3

Source: Malcolm M. Willey and William Weinfeld, "The Country Weekly and the Emergence of 'One-Newspaper Places,' " *Journalism Quarterly,* XI (September 1934), 250. The authors tabulated data from Ayer directories.

By 1960, with continued growth of both one-newspaper cities and one-combination cities, competition remained in only 4.2 per cent of daily cities and 5.2 per cent of country weekly towns.[3]

Many reasons can be listed for the decline in numbers of newspapers published, for the curtailment of competition in most communities, and for the increasing concentration of ownership. They fall under seven general headings: (1) economic pressures stemming from technological changes in the publishing pattern; (2) pressures resulting from competition for circulation and advertising revenues; (3) standardization of the product, resulting in loss of individuality and reader appeal; (4) lack of economic or social need for some newspapers; (5) managerial faults; (6) effects of wartime inflation and general business depressions; (7) planned consolidation of newspapers for various reasons.[4]

Technological change—the mechanical innovations of the 1880's and 1890's—brought increasing financial responsibility and risks for newspaper publishers, large and small. Typesetting machines, high-speed presses, engraving plants, and other expanded mechanical facilities meant not only constantly enlarged investments, but increased operating costs. The publisher who wished to keep abreast

[3] For weeklies, see Wilbur Peterson, "Loss in Country Weekly Newspapers Heavy in 1950s," *Journalism Quarterly,* XXXVIII (Winter 1961), 15.
[4] See bibliography at the close of this chapter for citations to the literature in this field.

of technological developments had to increase his revenues from circulation and advertising; the larger number of pages to handle a greater volume of advertising and the printing of more copies in turn made necessary more elaborate mechanical departments. The new entrant in the business was faced with a greater financial problem as each decade passed. Melville E. Stone established the *Chicago Daily News* in 1876 with a few thousand dollars capital; Albert Pulitzer founded the *New York Morning Journal* in 1882 with $25,000 capital. Hearst paid $180,000 for the *Journal* in 1895; Ochs was able to take over the *New York Times* in 1896 with $100,-000 working capital. But such opportunities were disappearing, as tremendous plant investments and other factors increasing the value of newspaper properties were putting metropolitan daily prices at million-dollar levels. Stone's *Chicago Daily News* sold for 13½ million dollars in 1925. The change was equally dramatic in smaller towns. In Spokane, Washington, the weekly *Review* founded in 1883 was printed on a Washington hand press by a printer-editor. After a decade of mechanical and editorial innovations William H. Cowles took control of the daily *Spokesman-Review* by assuming responsibility for an $80,000 mortgage and operating costs too heavy for numerous other competitors.[5]

Competition for circulation, upon which advertising rates are based and upon which advertising volume largely depends, thus was heightened by economic necessity stemming from the changing business character of newspaper publishing. Weaker publications were eliminated in many localities as the newspaper fell into the general economic pattern of a mechanized and industrialized country, a pattern which favored those who produced for a mass market at the most efficient unit cost.

Advertisers deemed it more efficient to buy space in one metropolitan daily newspaper with substantial general circulation, than in several papers with overlapping or specialized circulations. In smaller cities and towns, advertiser preference for the larger in

---

[5] Ralph E. Dyar, *News for an Empire* (Caldwell, Idaho: The Caxton Printers, Ltd., 1952). Dyar's early chapters trace the economic changes in Spokane newspaper publishing as daily newspapers came to a frontier town at a moment when American newspapers were being revolutionized by the impact of the "new journalism." The *Spokesman-Review* and its evening affiliate, the *Chronicle,* are the only survivors of Spokane's score or more of weekly and daily newspaper ventures.

circulation of two papers often spelled disaster for the smaller. Advertiser preference for evening dailies, based particularly upon knowledge of readership habits of American women-shoppers, helped speed the decline of morning papers. In the field of national advertising, increased competition of other media—magazines, billboards, and by 1930, radio—complicated the problem of newspaper survival, although this factor did not become a critical one for newspaper owners until after 1930.

Standardization of the product, which was encouraged by economic pressures, also accounted for a reduction in the number of newspapers. Competition for the mass market discouraged individuality; the newspaper which appealed to a specialized group of readers by the distinctive nature of its news or editorial policy often found it had lost the race to a mass appeal newspaper whose circulation attracted an increasing volume of advertising revenue. Loss of individuality in turn discouraged readership of more than one newspaper by most persons. Contributing to standardization were the press associations, which supplied increasingly better news coverage, but also a uniform news content and standardized writing style; and the syndicates, with their mass distribution of the efforts of columnists, cartoonists, comic strip artists, and feature writers. Newspapers which came to rely too heavily upon such sources of content, at the expense of their own staff enterprise and local news initiative, jeopardized reader support.

It was not always desirable that all existing newspapers in a community should survive, however. The typical American town saw more newspaper publishing ventures attempted than its economy could support. Even after the initial weeding of newspaper ventures, steadily increasing costs of publishing required further adjustments of the number of newspapers which the community's business volume justified. Nor were all newspapers deserving of community support. Some were founded solely as voices for political parties or business groups. Such newspapers, inveterately partisan in their outlook and appeal, had little to recommend them to modern readers. Other newspapers were founded by men who were in the business to make money. They were attracted by the conspicuous successes of the "new journalism" and became publishers much as they might have become store owners or shoe manufacturers. If too many such hopefuls set up shop in one community, a contraction inevitably resulted, without much loss to journalism. The newspapers of the frontier communities of the Middle West and West often were of a transient variety. Some were founded to promote the settlement of a town, or to lure easterners and immigrants to the farm lands for sale along the railroad rights-of-way. When they had served their purposes, they disappeared from the newspaper statistics which they had helped to bulk larger. Others were started as editorial spokesmen for the Republican, Democratic, and Populist parties, or even for factions of political parties. The 1880 census figures showed that 174 towns of less than 25,000 population had competing daily newspapers, as compared to 146 towns of similar size with only a single daily. By 1960 there were only 13 out of 956 daily newspaper towns of less than 25,000 population which had competing dailies. Publishing economics forced the elimination of the second, and sometimes third and fourth, dailies in these towns, as well as competing weeklies.

There were other changes in economic and social needs which affected newspaper publishing. Foreign language papers which flourished during the peak years of immigration disappeared as the process of Americanization inevitably dried up their circulation potential. Movements of population in various sections of the country either decreased possibilities for publication or encouraged new starts. Improved transportation facilities, the advent of the automobile and paved roads, and better communications meant that newspapers in urban centers could expand their coverage on regional and statewide levels. Nearby dailies in smaller towns found sharper competition as a result. Among the weeklies, the county seat paper tended to squeeze papers in adjacent villages out of business. Movements of population from rural to urban areas further restricted opportunities for multiple publication, as communities with declining business activity or stagnant population saw their newspapers reduced to one or eliminated entirely.

Managerial faults sometimes have contributed to the reduction in numbers of newspapers, and consolidation of ownership. Newspapers traditionally have lagged in setting advertising and circulation rates which realistically reflect current business conditions. Too often newspaper rates have been changed only after the business has gone into the red ink because of a sudden fluctuation in general economic conditions—or they have been set so low that in a period of inflation the publisher is unable to adjust rates to meet a new level of costs. Rigidity of newspaper rates is a complex problem, in part inherent in the business, but some managements have been more successful than others in providing adequate financial cushions for their papers in times of stress. And some managements have displayed conspicuous lack of ability as newspaper publishers. Continuity of efficient business direction and competent editorial leadership through stable ownership for long periods of time has been a key factor in the survival of many American newspapers. Loss of that leadership by death or sale has sometimes meant the sudden decline of a hitherto distinguished newspaper.[6]

Periods of general business inflation or depression affect newspapers drastically. The economic pressures attending World War I reduced the number of dailies by 112 in four years, one of the sharpest contractions in American journalism history.[7] Weekly publications of all types slumped one-eighth in the same period, with nearly 1,800 disappearing. A newsprint shortage, and a tripling of the price between 1916 and 1921, spelled ruin for many a marginal paper. Wartime price-fixing by the federal government, with the cooperation of the publishers, held the price of a ton of newsprint to a rise from $42 in 1916 to $80 in 1918. But a post-war runaway market after government controls ceased sent the figure soaring to $137 a ton at the 1921 peak. A gradual decline to $62 by 1929 brought newsprint prices into line with other price levels. Also affecting publishers was a wartime revenue measure which established zone rates for second-class mail, thereby increasing newspaper and magazine mailing costs. Other rising costs, including wages, forced increased circulation and advertising rates which weaker newspapers could not justify. Finally, when the "high cost of living" era was followed by a sharp post-war recession, sudden losses of advertising revenue by newspapers operating on a narrow margin of profit, and still paying inflated prices for materials and

---

[6] Examples of the benefits of stable ownerships are *The New York Times, Chicago Tribune, Louisville Courier-Journal,* and *St. Louis Post-Dispatch*, among a score or more of similar leading papers with longtime continuous and effective direction. Examples of newspapers set adrift are the *New York World, Chicago Inter Ocean, New York Sun,* and *Chicago Record-Herald,* among others.

[7] Ray, *Concentration of Ownership and Control in the American Daily Newspaper Industry,* p. 6.

higher wages to workers, brought additional suspensions and mergers.

Calculated planning sometimes has played a part in the consolidation of newspapers. Publication of both a morning and evening newspaper from the same mechanical plant is more efficient than operating separate newspapers in two plants, and by 1931 there were 152 cities with local combinations, including both those with and without other competition.[8] Before the news facilities of the Associated Press were opened more easily to non-AP newspapers in 1945 by a Supreme Court decision, the only practical way to obtain an AP membership was to buy the franchise of a member paper. Many a daily was bought and merged with another for this reason. In other cases, ambitious publishers, particularly those creating chains of newspapers, strengthened their positions by buying competitive papers.

Reduction of the number of American newspapers, and concentration of ownership of the remaining dailies, has caused a continuing debate over the social and political consequences of those trends. More will be said about that debate in a later chapter, but it is evident that the causes of newspaper consolidation were largely beyond the control of either the publishers or the reading public. In some cases newspapers have been sacrificed unnecessarily by inept management or by cold-blooded elimination, but these examples are in the minority. Economic pressure has been the dominant cause for newspaper consolidation. In such circumstances, the survival of one financially stable newspaper in a community is preferable to the continued existence of two or three weak and mediocre ones—always provided that the "monopoly" newspaper strives to justify its community support and is edited by newspapermen who recognize their full responsibility to all segments of the community. Nevertheless, decline in variety of competitive appeal and loss of individuality in news presentation and editorial opinion have affected public opinion concerning newspapers. The trend toward one-owner newspaper operations in smaller communities ordinarily was recognized as inevitable, but the spread of one-owner control

---

[8] Lee, *Daily Newspaper in America*, p. 222. Ray counted 31 local combinations formed between 1909 and 1919, and 142 formed between 1920 and 1929, the peak decade for such activity. The total between 1909 and 1948 was 302. Some did not survive, however.

to good-sized cities, and the reduction of the number of competing dailies in even the largest cities, neither was anticipated nor readily accepted. It is important, then, that the historical development of these trends be understood. New York City boasted 15 general-circulation, English-language daily newspapers in 1890. Eight were morning papers and seven were afternoon papers. Twelve owners were represented. By 1932, when Joseph Pulitzer's famous *World* and Bernarr Macfadden's infamous tabloid *Graphic* had followed other New York dailies into oblivion, only three morning papers, four afternoon papers, and two tabloids remained. The nine papers represented seven ownerships. Since the list still retained seven papers in the early 1960's, it is evident that the story of the consolidation of New York's dailies is an old one.

The name of Frank A. Munsey plays a large part in that story. Munsey was a successful New Englander whose career had a Horatio Alger ring. He was a young telegraph operator in Augusta, Maine, with no assets but a fierce determination to break into the New York publishing business. When he reached the city in 1882, he had a stack of manuscripts for a juvenile magazine and $40 cash.

Several years of struggle and great promotional ability made his *Golden Argosy* a success; he then turned to the general magazine field with his *Munsey's*. As a ten-cent monthly, *Munsey's* hit 650,000 circulation by 1900 to lead its competitors by a wide margin. Its publisher had a million dollar a year income by 1905 and was engaged in running a grocery chain, hotels, and banks in addition to his journalistic ventures.

Munsey apparently wanted even greater power and income, however. He dreamt of a great national chain of newspapers, directed from a central headquarters by the most brilliant of American editors and business managers. To Munsey, the successful business man, the newspaper business was a disorderly, if not chaotic, enterprise. In keeping with the trend of his times—toward concentration of control of segments of a business—he proposed to bring efficiency to the newspaper world, and thereby improve the product.

"There is no business that cries so loud for organization and combination as that of newspaper publishing," Munsey declared. "For one thing, the number of newspapers is at least 60 per cent greater than we need." And in another vein he added:

Think of the possibilities involved in a chain of 500 newspapers under a single control! Such a faculty could be so maintained as no college could support; the greatest authors, artists, engineers, essayists, and statesmen could write with authority on every question of importance, each of the 500 papers getting the benefit of these great minds, while maintaining their individuality on purely local matters. There could be a $100,000 or $200,000 a year man at the head of the editorial force and another God-made genius in charge of the business end . . . and the combined genius of the men in control would be the most uplifting force the world has ever known.[9]

Munsey's first newspaper venture was buying the *New York Star* in 1891. It was a one-time political paper, which had been reinvigorated in the 1880's but which was losing out in the Pulitzer-era competitive struggle. Munsey, from his magazine experience, reasoned that a newspaper with pictures and human interest stories would sell, and he made the paper, renamed the *Continent*, a tabloid. His perfectly logical editorial formula failed to jell, however, and after losing $40,000 in four months he retired to his magazine business. The paper became the *Morning Advertiser* and was sold to William Randolph Hearst in 1897 for its AP membership rights.

By 1901 Munsey was ready to try again. He bought the old *New York Daily News* and the *Washington Times* that year as the nucleus of his chain. The *Boston Journal* was added in 1902, and in 1908 he invaded two more eastern cities, buying the *Baltimore Evening News* and founding the *Philadelphia Evening Times*.

The *Daily News*, founded in 1855, had prospered as a penny paper edited for the tenement districts of New York, until the Pulitzer-Hearst duel affected its circulation adversely. Munsey set about to improve the paper, installing color presses, featurizing its Sunday edition, and seeking to break into higher level readership groups. Again the public failed to respond, and the paper died in 1906 after Munsey had lost an estimated $750,000.

Munsey did no better with his other ventures. The Boston paper was sold at a loss in 1913; the Philadelphia paper was killed in 1914. Disappointed at the failure of his chain, Munsey sold his two successful papers in Baltimore and Washington before 1917. He, like

Hearst, had been interested in politics, and he had been a solid champion of Theodore Roosevelt and the Bull Moose progressive movement, but his dream of attaining journalistic influence on a national scale was ended.

Not so his dream for bringing efficiency of operation to the newspaper business. There were too many small units operating in journalism, he said, and the only answer was orderly consolidation, similar to that taking place in manufacturing, railroading, oil, and retail selling.[10] He proposed to perform this service for New York City.

Munsey still owned one newspaper, the *New York Press*, which he had added to his chain in 1912. The *Press*, under the editorship of Ervin Wardman, had been effective in the newspaper crusades at the turn of the century, and it still had a comfortable circulation. But Munsey eyed the New York field for a newspaper which could be combined with it, and his choice was the *Sun*.

The *Sun*, founded in 1833 as the city's first penny paper, had slumped in circulation with the coming of Pulitzer and Hearst, but it was still a proud newspaper, edited after the death of Charles A. Dana in 1897 by Edward P. Mitchell. Munsey paid 2½ million dollars for the *Sun* and the *Evening Sun* in 1916, and merged the *Press* into the morning edition, making Wardman publisher, Mitchell editor, and the *Press's* renowned Keats Speed, managing editor. The price was cut to a penny, and Munsey poured two million dollars more into the venture. But wartime publishing difficulties cost him the profit he hoped to make, and in 1920 he looked about for another prospect for consolidation. In the next five years, Munsey, who already had failed to resuscitate the old *Star* and *Daily News*, and who had killed the *Press*, was to remove four more newspapers from the publishing scene.

New York in 1920 still had 14 established general circulation newspapers. In the morning field were the *Times, World, Tribune, Herald, Sun, American*, and a new *Daily News*, first of the postwar tabloids and just founded by Robert R. McCormick and Joseph M. Patterson of the *Chicago Tribune* dynasty. In the evening field were the *Post, Evening Sun, Evening World, Telegram, Evening Journal*,

---

[10] Munsey's philosophy and his career are detailed in George Britt, *Forty Years—Forty Millions; the Career of Frank A. Munsey* (New York: Farrar and Rinehart, Inc., 1935).

Mail, and *Globe and Commercial Advertiser.* There were 10 owner-ships, the *Telegram* being the evening edition of the *Herald,* and Hearst owning both the *American* and *Journal.*

Munsey's first move was to buy the *Herald,* the *Telegram,* and the Paris edition of the *Herald* for four million dollars. The younger Bennett had spent lavishly during his long lifetime, and when he died in 1918 his newspapers were in neither a financial nor competitive position to continue. Munsey merged the morning *Sun* into the *Herald* and gave the historical name *Sun* to the evening edition, which he continued to operate despite his ownership of the evening *Telegram.*

The next victim was the *Globe.* Started in 1904, it had been consolidated the next year with the *Commercial Advertiser,* founded in 1793 by Noah Webster as the *American Minerva.* The *Globe* was considered a healthy, liberal newspaper when Munsey bought it for two million dollars in 1923 for its evening AP membership and merged it in the *Sun.* The next year Munsey paid another two millions for the conservative *Mail,* merging it with the *Telegram.*[11] Both the *Sun* and *Telegram* gained circulation and advertising as a result of the mergers.

Munsey's morning paper, the *Herald,* was not faring as well. High operation costs in the postwar period and difficulties with advertising rates plagued the businessman-publisher. He turned his eyes toward the *Tribune,* lowest in circulation of the morning dailies and the only remaining morning newspaper supporter of the Republican party along with the *Herald.* Munsey argued that it was only logical that the two papers should merge. But the *Tribune*'s owners, Ogden Mills Reid and his able wife, Helen Rogers Reid refused to sell the family paper and its modern publishing plant. Munsey, true to his belief that further consolidation was necessary, thereupon sold the *Herald* and its Paris edition to the Reids for five million dollars. Happily, the new *Herald Tribune* successfully added the bulk of the old *Herald*'s subscribers to its list and saw its advertising volume expand under the business direction of Mrs. Reid. Of all Munsey's newspaper maneuvering, his part in the

---

[11] The *Evening Mail* dated from 1867. It had been consolidated in 1882 with the *Express* (1836), as the *Mail and Express.* Wartime charges that the paper had engaged in German propaganda efforts blighted its reputation.

creation of the *Herald Tribune* was the happiest, even though it meant the merger of the historic Bennett and Greeley papers. Death claimed Munsey in 1925. His *Telegram* passed to the Scripps-Howard chain, which combined it with Pulitzer's *World* in 1931. The *Sun* became a staff-owned newspaper under the direction of William T. Dewart, and prospered for a while under editor Frank M. O'Brien and managing editor Keats Speed as a solid, conservative newspaper, but it too was to disappear into the Scripps-Howard *World-Telegram* in 1950. Undoubtedly the New York newspapers would have gone through a consolidation process whether Frank Munsey had lived or not, but undoubtedly, too, he had hastened the deaths of several of the city's dailies. Newspapermen generally were bitterly resentful of the cold and business-like approach which Munsey had both toward them and their profession. William Allen White best expressed the rebels' sentiments in his famed terse obituary published in the *Emporia Gazette:*

Frank A. Munsey contributed to the journalism of his day the talent of a meatpacker, the morals of a money-changer and the manners of an undertaker. He and his kind have about succeeded in transforming a once-noble profession into an eight per cent security. May he rest in trust!

Another magazine publisher played a major role in the consolidation of Philadelphia's newspapers. He was Cyrus H. K. Curtis, who founded the *Ladies' Home Journal* in 1883, and drove it to leadership with Edward W. Bok as editor. His second major triumph had been the rejuvenation of the *Saturday Evening Post,* which as a nickel weekly led its field within 10 years after Curtis bought it in 1897.

Philadelphia had 13 general circulation dailies of importance in 1895, of which eight remained when Curtis entered the newspaper field in 1913. Coming to the top in circulation during this period was the *Evening Bulletin,* purchased by William L. McLean in 1895 and given a new home and a solid editorial character which solid Philadelphia admired. Within ten years the *Bulletin* rose from 6,000 to 220,000 in circulation, upsetting the city's newspaper balance. One of the losers in the circulation battle was the one-time crusading penny paper, the *Evening Item.* Another was Munsey's ill-fated *Evening Times.* Going downhill, but staying in business, was the *Record,* William M. Singerly's highly popular paper which passed to the control of Thomas B. Wanamaker in 1902.

Curtis entered the Philadelphia newspaper picture by buying the historic *Public Ledger,* founded by William M. Swain in 1836 in the first wave of penny papers. Ably edited by George W. Childs from 1864 until his death in 1894, the *Public Ledger* had gone up for sale in 1902. The purchaser was Adolph S. Ochs, who put his brother George in charge of the Philadelphia paper and himself remained interested solely in the *New York Times.* Ochs also bought the lively *Philadelphia Times* in 1902 and merged it with the *Public Ledger.* By 1913 Ochs was ready to sell to Curtis for two million dollars, $250,000 less than the purchase price.

Curtis' first move was to give Philadelphia another newspaper, the *Evening Public Ledger,* in 1914. But then, like Munsey, he moved in on the competition. The *Evening Telegraph,* dating back to 1864, was bought for its AP membership in 1918 and killed. The *Press,* founded in 1857, was purchased in 1920 for its newsprint contracts. Newspapermen mourned again in 1925 when the *North American,* on the scene since 1839 and with a reputation as a crusading force under editor E. A. Van Valkenberg, was killed.

Curtis poured money into his newspapers, building them a 15 million dollar plant and developing a famous foreign news service which was widely syndicated. When Lee Ellmaker started the tabloid *Daily News* in Philadelphia in 1925 Curtis protected that flank by publishing the tabloid *Sun,* but it failed within three years. Meanwhile Curtis had bought the *New York Evening Post* in 1923, turning it from its traditional liberal course.

The expanded Curtis newspaper enterprises were financially unsound by depression time in 1930. In a final effort, Curtis bought the *Inquirer,* plunging an estimated 18 million dollars into the deal with the Elverson family owners which gave Curtis control of both the big Philadelphia morning dailies. When he died in 1933, leaving control of the newspapers to his business associate and son-in-law, John C. Martin, the empire crumbled. The *Public Ledger* was merged into the *Inquirer* and the property reverted to the Elverson family, to be sold in turn to Moses L. Annenberg in 1936. The *Evening Public Ledger* lived until 1942, competing with the *Bulletin* and the tabloid *Daily News.* The *Inquirer's* morning rival was the *Record,* rejuvenated after 1928 as a liberal, New Deal-supporting paper by J. David Stern. Stern also rescued the *New York Evening Post* from the Curtis regime.

Curtis' record in the newspaper business is an unhappy one. Of the seven Philadelphia newspapers he owned only one remains. He did succeed, however, in giving the *Public Ledger* additional glory, principally through an expansion of its foreign correspondence during World War I years and on through the 1920's.

Herman Kohlsaat was the chief figure in Chicago's newspaper consolidations. Enriched by a chain of bakeries and lunch counters, and enamored of the newspaper business, Kohlsaat bought into the *Inter Ocean* in 1891. Dissatisfied, however, by lack of complete control and dismayed by the activities of his less idealistic associates, he sold out and bought the *Times-Herald* and *Evening Post*. The *Times* and *Herald* had been consolidated by James W. Scott just before his death in 1895, with the *Mail*—evening edition of the *Times*—disappearing.

Scott's successful morning paper had been a Democratic party supporter. Kohlsaat was a Republican, and he turned the *Times-Herald*'s editorial course to parallel that of a competitor, Joseph Medill's redoubtable *Tribune*. By 1901 Kohlsaat was in trouble, which he hoped to solve by buying the *Record*, morning edition of Victor Lawson's *Daily News*. Kohlsaat's resources were not as extensive as those of Munsey and Curtis, however, and before the end of 1901 he had to dispose of his properties. The *Record-Herald*, as the paper was now called, went to Lawson. The *Evening Post* was sold to John C. Shaffer.

Chicago in 1902 thus had four morning papers: the *Tribune*, *Inter Ocean*, *Record-Herald*, and William Randolph Hearst's newly established *Examiner*. In the evening field were the *Daily News*, *Post*, *Journal*, and Hearst's *American*. The highly successful *Tribune* and *Daily News*, and the well-financed Hearst papers, were to squeeze out their competitors in the next 30 years.

One victim was the well-edited *Record-Herald*, which, when Lawson brought Frank B. Noyes from the *Washington Star* to run it from 1902 to 1910, ranked as one of the country's best. It boasted John T. McCutcheon's cartoons before the *Tribune* enticed the artist away, and was aggressive and distinctive in its news coverage. But the *Tribune*'s competition was too much and Noyes resumed his Washington career in 1910. Kohlsaat returned as editor, and the *Record-Herald* had one more moment of glory when it joined the *Tribune* in a crusade which exposed the bribery accompanying the election of William Lorimer to the United States Senate. Lorimer lost his Senate seat, but Kohlsaat's brave campaign did not save the *Record-Herald*. In 1912 he turned again to the *Inter Ocean*, hoping to save that dying paper.

Failing this, too, Lawson and Kohlsaat had one constructive move left. If they could not defeat the *Tribune*, they could join the enemy, in effect, by selling out to one of the *Tribune's* most brilliant staff members, managing editor James Keeley. This they did in 1914, and the new paper arising from the ruins of the *Record-Herald* and the *Inter Ocean* became known simply as the *Herald*. But Keeley failed in his mission and sold out to Hearst in 1918. The new *Herald & Examiner*, sole competitor to the *Tribune* in the morning field, thus represented five journalistic ventures, the *Times*, *Herald*, *Record*, *Inter Ocean*, and *Examiner*.

In the evening field, the *Daily News* continued to excel. Lawson had started its distinguished foreign service and the paper was operating in full stride when its veteran publisher died in 1925. Control passed to a syndicate headed by Walter A. Strong, *Daily News* business manager, for 13½ million dollars, record price for a newspaper sale before Curtis' 18 million dollar investment in the *Philadelphia Inquirer*. Colonel Frank Knox obtained the controlling interest in 1931. The *Daily News* bought out two weak competitors in this reorganization period—the *Journal* in 1929 and the *Post* in 1932. Joining the *Daily News* and the American in the evening field, however, was the pro-New Deal, tabloid-style *Times*, founded in 1929 by Samuel E. Thomason, last owner of the *Journal*, and edited by Richard J. Finnegan.

The sharp reduction in the number of morning dailies in New York, Philadelphia, and Chicago was part of a nationwide trend. Reader and advertiser preference for afternoon papers, and the time advantage these had in publishing European war news, helped to cut the number of morning papers from 500 in 1910 to 388 by 1930. Early in this period such morning papers as the *Atlanta Constitution*, *Indianapolis Star*, *Minneapolis Tribune*, and *St. Paul Pioneer Press* were alone in their fields. They were joined in 1915 by the *Detroit Free Press*, with the death of the old *Tribune*. Cleveland in 1917 saw the *Leader* disappear into the *Plain Dealer*, leaving the latter the only morning paper. Elimination of the *Free Press* in Milwaukee in 1919 left the *Sentinel* without morning competition. The same year the *St. Louis Globe-Democrat* bought its morning rival, the *Republic*. Merger in Buffalo in 1926 of the *Courier* (1831) and the *Express* (1846) ended that city's long morning rivalry. Pittsburgh's morning dailies were reduced to one in 1927, and Kansas City joined the trend in 1928. The *Cincinnati Enquirer* closed out its competition in 1930 by buying the *Commercial Tribune*, successor to Murat Halstead's old *Commercial Gazette*. By 1933 the journalistic historian Willard G. Bleyer could list 40 cities of more than 100,000 population which had only one morning daily.[12]

Morning paper mergers were the most spectacular in the first decades after 1900, but over-all consolidation of metropolitan newspapers, and concentration of ownership, continued from coast to coast. Entry of the Hearst chain into Detroit through purchase of the *Times* in 1921 prompted the *News* (founded by James E. Scripps) to buy out the *Journal* in 1922. Thus Detroit, with more than a million population, was left with but three newspapers, the morning *Free Press* and the evening *News* and *Times*. In New Orleans, the *Times-Democrat* and the *Picayune* were merged in 1914, leaving the new *Times-Picayune* alone in the morning field for 10 years. The *Times-Picayune*, owned by L. K. Nicholson, bought Colonel Robert Ewing's *States* in 1933 for an evening edition. The other evening paper, the *Item*, published a morning edition, the *Tribune*, from 1924 to 1941.

St. Louis afternoon journalism was dominated by Pulitzer's *Post-Dispatch*. The *Chronicle*, Scripps-McRae entry of 1880, merged with the *Evening Star* (1878) in 1905. The *Times* (1895) joined

---

[12] Willard G. Bleyer, "Freedom of the Press and the New Deal," *Journalism Quarterly*, XI (March 1934), 29. Those cities with but one morning daily but with two or more evening papers, in addition to the dozen listed above, were Baltimore, Providence, Rochester, Syracuse, Dayton, Columbus (Ohio), Louisville, Richmond, Memphis, Houston, Dallas, Fort Worth, Oklahoma City, Portland (Oregon), and Seattle. Those cities with but one morning and one evening paper were Hartford, New Haven, Tampa, Chattanooga, Knoxville, Grand Rapids, Tulsa, and Denver. One company owned all the dailies published in six cities: New Bedford and Springfield, Massachusetts; Duluth, Des Moines, Wilmington, Delaware, and Charleston, South Carolina. Springfield, however, had two morning and two evening dailies operating under a single ownership headed by Sherman H. Bowles of the historic *Republican* family.

forces with the *Star* in 1932 as the *Star-Times*, leaving St. Louis with three ownerships. Kansas City rivals of Nelson's *Star* found the going equally difficult. Nelson bought the morning *Times* in 1901. The Scripps-McRae *World*, founded in 1897, faded from the picture. The evening *Post*, started in 1906 and bought by Bonfils and Tammen of *Denver Post* fame in 1909, was sold in 1922 to the owners of the morning *Journal* (1858), and the two papers became the *Journal-Post* in 1928. Kansas City thus dropped to two ownerships.

The team of publisher Gardner Cowles and editor Harvey Ingham captured the entire Des Moines newspaper field between 1903 and 1927, foreshadowing what was to happen in other cities after 1930. The *Leader* (1849) and the *Register* (1856) ended their long rivalry in a 1902 merger and Cowles assumed control the following year. In 1908 he bought the newly founded *Tribune*, which became the evening associate of the morning *Register*. The evening *Daily News*, founded in 1886 and bought by Scripps in 1902, was eliminated in 1924. Cowles' last purchase was the evening *Capital*, dating from 1881, which surrendered in 1927 in the face of the effective Cowles promotional policies and editorial direction.

Activities of the country's two biggest chain ownerships—Hearst and Scripps-Howard—and of lesser chain aspirants caused newspaper consolidations in still other cities. The Hearst organization, in a buying splurge concentrated in the years 1918 to 1928, put 16 newspapers to death, as consolidations were carried out to bulwark the positions of Hearst-owned dailies. The Scripps-Howard group was responsible for the closing of 15 newspapers between 1923 and 1934.

Hearst's purchase of the *Chicago Herald* in 1918, to combine with his morning *Examiner*, already has been mentioned. He thus had the *Herald & Examiner* and the *American* in that city. In Boston, where the Hearst-owned evening *American* was founded in 1904, the publisher bought the century-old *Daily Advertiser* in 1917 and the *Record* in 1920. The two papers were juggled in an effort to bring tabloid publication to Boston, with the name *Record* surviving for the morning Hearst paper.[13] Meanwhile the *Boston Herald* was buying the *Traveler* in 1912 for an evening edition and was absorbing the Munsey-owned *Journal* in 1917. Thus Boston, which

[13] The name *Advertiser* was retained for the Hearst Sunday edition in Boston.

in 1900 had eleven major newspapers operated by seven owner-ships, by 1930 had eight newspapers and five ownerships. The others were Edwin A. Grozier's highly successful morning *Post*, the Taylor family's morning and evening *Globes*, and the limping but traditional *Transcript*.

New York State extensions of the Hearst chain were made in 1922, a year in which the publisher was seeking the governorship. The *Rochester Journal* was one addition, with the *Post-Express* be-ing absorbed for its AP membership. In Syracuse the *Telegram*, bought in 1922, and the *Journal*, added in 1925, were merged as the *Journal Telegram*.

Washington was one of the few large cities to add newspapers during this period, but Hearst promptly consolidated the owner-ship of two newcomers. The morning *Post* and the Noyes family's evening *Star* were challenged by the founding of the *Times* in 1894 and the *Herald* in 1906. Munsey bought the *Times* in 1901 and killed its morning edition. When he retired from the Washington field in 1917 the *Times* passed to Arthur Brisbane, who sold it to Hearst two years later. The *Herald* was added to the Hearst chain in 1922. Scripps-Howard gave Washington a fourth ownership when it established the tabloid *Daily News* in 1921.

Baltimore was less fortunate. The *Sun*, original penny paper of 1837, took over the *Evening World* in 1910 and made it the *Evening Sun*. The *Herald*, a morning penny paper, died in 1906. The *Eve-ning News*, Grasty's crusading paper which fell into Munsey's con-trol, was consolidated with the *Star* in 1921, and the paper was sold to Hearst in 1922. The *American*, dating from 1799, also passed from Munsey to Hearst and after 1928 was published only as a Sunday paper. A 1922 Scripps-Howard entry, the *Post*, was sold to Hearst in 1934. The Hearst *News-Post* thus survived as daily op-position for the *Sunpapers*.

Pittsburgh also saw its newspapers shuffled by the Hearst and Scripps-Howard organizations. The Scripps-Howard group bought the well-established *Press* in 1923 for six million dollars, under an agreement with the city's other newspaper owners that the *Dispatch* and *Leader* would be bought out and killed. Four years later Hearst and Paul Block, a Hearst associate and newspaper publisher and broker, bought the remaining four Pittsburgh dailies. The morning *Sun* and *Chronicle Telegraph* were transformed into the

Hearst-owned *Sun-Telegraph;* the evening *Post* and *Gazette Times* into the Block-owned *Post-Gazette.*

Arthur Brisbane and Hearst teamed up in Milwaukee at the end of World War I, with the result that the *Evening Wisconsin,* the *News,* and the *Telegram* were rolled into the *Wisconsin News,* Hearst-owned after 1919. The morning *Sentinel* joined the Hearst chain in 1924 to give the chain two footholds against the steadily increasing pressure of the *Milwaukee Journal.*[14] Also in the Midwest, the *Omaha News* and *Bee* were bought by Hearst in 1928 and merged as the *News-Bee,* a morning, evening, and Sunday publication.

On the West Coast Hearst created a strong evening companion for his *San Francisco Examiner* by combining three papers. He bought the *Call* (1855) in 1913 and combined the *Evening Post* with it to obtain an Associated Press membership. In 1929 the *Bulletin* (1856) was absorbed by Hearst to form the *Call-Bulletin.* The mergers left San Francisco with Hearst morning and evening papers, the locally owned morning *Chronicle,* and the Scripps-Howard evening *News.* Across the bay in Oakland the *Post-Enquirer* was formed in a 1922 Hearst double purchase and merger as competition for the Knowland family's *Tribune.*

In Los Angeles, Hearst's morning *Examiner* was augmented in 1922 by purchase of the evening *Herald.* The *Express,* founded in 1871, was swallowed up by Hearst in 1931 to form the *Herald & Express.* The *Record,* established by Scripps in 1895, died in the 1920's but was replaced by the *Daily News,* a tabloid which Manchester Boddy developed into a pro-New Deal newspaper. Hearst's solid morning competition in Los Angeles still was Harry Chandler's conservative *Times.*

Hearst's other purchases, which did not involve consolidations, were the *Atlanta Georgian,* 1912; *Detroit Times,* 1921; *Seattle Post-Intelligencer,* 1922; *Fort Worth Record,* 1923 (soon sold to the *Star-Telegram*); *Albany Times-Union,* 1924; and *San Antonio Light,* 1924. The tabloid *Daily Mirror* was added to his New York City holdings, the *Journal* and the *American,* in 1924. At its peak in the early 1930's the Hearst chain totaled 26 dailies and 17 Sunday papers, published in 18 cities.

[14] Paul Block leased the *Sentinel* from Hearst and operated it from 1929 to 1937.

Changes after World War I in the direction of the chain of newspapers started by E. W. Scripps brought newspaper consolidations to a dozen cities in the next 15 years. Scripps and his business associate, Milton A. McRae, parted company in 1914. A paralytic stroke suffered by Scripps in 1917 impelled him to put his sons, James and Robert, in charge of the chain. James withdrew from the organization after a family quarrel in 1920, taking five Pacific Coast papers with him. Two years later Roy W. Howard, head of the United Press, was given equal control with Robert Paine Scripps over what became the Scripps-Howard newspapers.

Scripps and McRae had founded 27 papers and bought five more, between 1878 and 1917. Of the 32, only 13 remained at the time of Scripps' death in 1926. Robert Paine Scripps founded seven more papers in 1921 and 1922, but with the coming of Roy Howard the chain switched its tactics, thereafter only buying existing newspapers. In the next 14 years, 14 newspapers were acquired, 6 of them for merging with other Scripps-Howard papers. At the end of this burst of activity Scripps-Howard controlled 25 dailies, published in 24 cities, and 7 Sunday editions.

Strengthening of Scripps-Howard properties by elimination of competitors took place in several cities. Knoxville saw the *News-Sentinel* created by the merger of the *News*, started in 1921, and the *Sentinel*, bought in 1926. The *El Paso Post*, founded in 1922, became the *Herald-Post* with the acquisition of the *Herald* in 1931. The *Akron Press*, begun in 1899 by E. W. Scripps, received a badly needed transfusion in 1925 with the purchase of the *Times*, to form the *Times-Press*. The *Memphis Press*, founded in 1906, became the *Press-Scimitar* by absorbing the *News-Scimitar* in 1926; 10 years later Scripps-Howard added the morning *Memphis Commercial Appeal* to the chain. The *New York Telegram*, bought in 1927, became the *World-Telegram* in 1931 when Howard negotiated the purchase of the famous Pulitzer papers. The *Pittsburgh Press* was acquired in 1923 in a deal which saw the elimination of the *Dispatch* and *Leader*.

Denver's newspapers were reshaped by a cut-throat battle between the Scripps-Howard chain and the *Denver Post*. The *Post's* evening opponents had dwindled over the years. The *Republican*, which had absorbed the *Tribune* in 1884, in turn was merged with the *Times* in 1913. The *Times* and the morning *Rocky Mountain*

News came under the same ownership in 1902 and were sold in 1926 to Scripps-Howard. Thereupon the *Express*, in the Scripps fold since 1906, was merged into the *Times*. A truce arranged between the *Post* and the Scripps-Howard newspapers in 1928 brought the demise of the *Times* and left Denver with two newspapers.

On the loss side, Scripps-Howard sold the *Des Moines News*, *Sacramento Star*, and *Terre Haute Post* to competitors during the 1920's, and the *Baltimore Post* to Hearst in 1934. The *Washington Daily News*, *Fort Worth Press*, *Birmingham Post*, and *Norfolk Post* all were founded in 1921, but the Norfolk paper died almost immediately. Scripps-Howard purchased the *Indianapolis Times* and *Youngstown Telegram* in 1922 and the *New Mexico State Tribune* in Albuquerque in 1923, while the *Buffalo Times* was acquired in 1929. It should be noted that Scripps-Howard newspapers, generally speaking, were operated in smaller-sized cities than those invaded by the Hearst chain.

Rising to third place among chain newspaper publishers in point of number of newspapers owned was Frank E. Gannett, New York publisher who began in earnest to build his chain during the 1920's. His activities brought newspaper mergers in Ithaca, Rochester, Utica, Elmira, Newburgh, and Beacon before 1930. The Gannett group, mainly in New York State, totaled 16 by 1935, and Gannett achieved some prominence and political influence.

Newspaper chain ownership boomed during the 1920's, as already observed in the cases of Hearst, Scripps-Howard, and Gannett. There was both a sizable increase in the percentage of total daily newspaper circulation which was chain-owned, and in the number of chain operations, both daily and weekly. The "menace of the chains" became a topic for study and debate. A newspaper chain ownership was defined as ownership of two or more papers in two or more cities.

In 1900 there were 8 such chains of dailies, owning a total of 27 newspapers and controlling about 10 per cent of total daily circulation in the country.[15] A study of chain ownership for the year 1923 shows that there were by then 34 daily newspaper chains, owning 158 newspapers and controlling 31 per cent of total daily circula-

[15] Frank Luther Mott, *American Journalism* (New York: The Macmillan Company, 1950), p. 648

tion. The same researcher found that by 1935 there were 63 daily newspaper chains, owning 328 newspapers and controlling 41 per cent of the country's daily circulation.[16] Chain owners controlled 42 per cent of Sunday circulation in 1923 and 52 per cent in 1935. In 1932, chain dailies represented 18 per cent of the total number of dailies, a peak figure for the period. Chains owned 27 per cent of Sunday papers the same year. As it turned out, the years of greatest influence of the big national chains were in the mid-1930's, when the numbers of their dailies and their percentages of total daily and Sunday circulations reached a zenith.

Hearst's always was the biggest chain. In 1923 his 22 dailies had 3,400,000 circulation, which represented 10.8 per cent of total daily circulation in the country. His Sunday circulation of 4,100,000 was 19.1 per cent of the total. By 1935 the 26 Hearst dailies had a total circulation of 5,100,000 representing 13.6 per cent of the country's daily circulation. The Sunday figure was 6,800,000, comprising 24.2 per cent of total Sunday circulation. This meant that in 1935 Hearst sold 13 out of every 100 daily newspaper copies issued in the country, and one-fourth of all the Sunday papers.

The McCormick-Patterson combine of the *Chicago Tribune* and *New York Daily News* ranked second in 1935 with 6.4 per cent of total daily circulation and 12.3 per cent on Sunday. Scripps-Howard was third, with 5.1 per cent daily and 2.1 per cent Sunday. No other chain had as much as 2 per cent of daily circulation.

Among the many smaller chains which developed were some achieving numerical importance.[17] H. C. Ogden owned a group of 15 newspapers in 1935, comprising nearly half of West Virginia's dailies. The Lee Syndicate in Iowa, dating from 1903, had 12 dailies by 1935. The Scripps League on the West Coast had 11. The Booth Newspapers group in Michigan, founded by George C. Booth of the *Detroit News* in 1893, totaled 8 in 1935. Newspaper publisher and broker Paul Block had a string of 7 dailies, as did the Ridder brothers of New York and Minnesota. Two other chains of long standing with 6 dailies each in 1935 were the Brush-Moore group

---

[16] William Weinfeld, "The Growth of Daily Newspaper Chains in the United States: 1923, 1926-1935," *Journalism Quarterly*, XIII (December 1936), 357.

[17] Weinfeld, *op. cit.*, carries tabulations of chain ownership in 1923 and 1935.

in Ohio, founded in 1901, and the Ira C. Copley chain in Illinois and California, begun in 1905.

The two big national chains, Hearst and Scripps-Howard, had a steadily decreasing percentage of total newspaper circulation after the early 1930's. Fears that they and other groups would gobble up most of the country's papers proved unfounded. Instead, chain owners tended to concentrate on achieving local and regional dominance. Thus Gannett focused his attention on New York State, Ogden on West Virginia, Booth on Michigan. Another pattern which was to develop was the achieving of dominance in one city and then selection of another—as the Cowles family in Des Moines was to do by invading Minneapolis. These new patterns of chain ownership had their effects upon newspaper consolidations and concentration of ownership, even more pronounced than the effects of the Hearst and Scripps-Howard ownerships.

ANNOTATED BIBLIOGRAPHY

Books:

The general journalism histories by Mott and A. M. Lee trace the process of newspaper consolidation, as does the admirable final chapter of Bleyer. The collections of articles edited by Schramm, by Bird and Merwin, and by Willey and Casey, cited below, offer important interpretations, as do others of the books and articles listed.

Bird, George L., and Frederic E. Merwin, eds., *The Press and Society: A Book of Readings.* New York: Prentice-Hall, Inc., 1951. Chapters 19, 20 and 27 particularly consider problems of newspaper economics and ownership.

Bok, Edward W., *A Man from Maine.* New York: Charles Scribner's Sons, 1923. A life of Cyrus H. K. Curtis by his editor.

Britt, George, *Forty Years—Forty Millions; The Career of Frank A. Munsey.* New York: Farrar and Rinehart, Inc., 1935. A critical biography of the newspaper consolidator.

Dennis, Charles H., *Victor Lawson: His Time and His Work.* Chicago: University of Chicago Press, 1935. The authorized story of Lawson and the *Chicago Daily News.*

Ernst, Morris, *The First Freedom.* New York: The Macmillan Company, 1946. Freedom-loving Mr. Ernst decries the trend toward newspaper consolidation.

Schramm, Wilbur, ed., *Mass Communications.* Urbana: University of Illinois Press, 1949; rev. 1960. Of these selected readings, the recommended one on newspaper ownership is Raymond B. Nixon's "The Problem of Newspaper Monopoly."

Smith, Bruce Lannes, Harold D. Lasswell, and Ralph D. Casey, *Propaganda, Communication, and Public Opinion*. Princeton: Princeton University Press, 1946. See essay by Ralph D. Casey, "Communication Channels," pp. 4-30.

Stewart, Kenneth, and John Tebbel, *Makers of Modern Journalism*. New York: Prentice-Hall, Inc., 1952. Chapter 21 tells the story of Philadelphia's recent journalism.

Villard, Oswald Garrison, *The Disappearing Daily*. New York: Alfred A. Knopf, Inc., 1944. Criticism of the trend toward consolidation and bigness.

———, *Some Newspapers and Newspaper-Men*. New York: Alfred A. Knopf, Inc., 1923. Like *The Disappearing Daily*, this book discusses newspapers in major cities as well as major publishers: New York, Boston, Philadelphia, Washington, among others.

Willey, Malcolm M., and Ralph D. Casey, eds., *The Press in the Contemporary Scene*, Annals of the American Academy of Political and Social Science, CCXIX (January 1942). An excellent survey of press problems, including an article on ownership trends, A. M. Lee's "The Basic Newspaper Pattern."

Periodicals and Monographs:

Bleyer, Willard G., "Freedom of the Press and the New Deal," *Journalism Quarterly*, XI (March 1934), 22. Report on trend toward newspaper combinations.

Duffus, Robert L., "Mr. Munsey," *American Mercury*, II (July 1924), 297. A gently critical rejection of Munsey as a newspaper owner. Reprinted in Ford and Emery, *Highlights in the History of the American Press*.

Neurath, Paul, "One-Publisher Communities: Factors Influencing Trend," *Journalism Quarterly*, XXI (September 1944), 230.

Nixon, Raymond B., and Jean Ward, "Trends in Newspaper Ownership and Inter-Media Competition," *Journalism Quarterly*, XXXVIII (Winter 1961), 3. See also Nixon's "Trends in Daily Newspaper Ownership Since 1945," *Journalism Quarterly*, XXXI (Winter 1954), 3, and "Concentration and Absenteeism in Daily Newspaper Ownership," *Journalism Quarterly*, XXII (June 1945), 97. Major studies.

Norris, Wendell W., "The Transient Frontier Weekly as a Stimulant to Homesteading," *Journalism Quarterly*, XXX (Winter 1953), 44. Based on "The Prairie Frontier Boom of the Weekly Press, 1865-1915." Master's thesis, University of Wisconsin, 1951.

Ray, Royal H., "Economic Forces as Factors in Daily Newspaper Concentration," *Journalism Quarterly*, XXIX (Winter, 1952), 31. An excellent summary of pressures for newspaper consolidation, taken from his *Concentration of Ownership and Control in the American Daily Newspaper Industry* (Columbia University Microfilms, 1951).

Robb, Arthur, "Chain Journalism in the Sixth Decade," *Editor & Publisher* golden jubilee number, July 21, 1934. A descriptive essay summarizing chain developments.

Weinfeld, William, "The Growth of Daily Newspaper Chains in the United States: 1923, 1926-1935," *Journalism Quarterly*, XIII (December 1936), 357. The first important study of the problem.

Chapter **23**

THE COMMON DENOMINATORS

> . . . when one travels through the country on a
> Sunday on a fast train and buys . . . Sunday
> papers . . . one finds the same "comics," the
> same Sunday magazines, the same special "fea-
> tures" in almost all of them and, of course, in most
> of them precisely the same Associated Press
> news. . . . The newspaper profession has turned
> out to be a business and as a result there was
> bound to be standardization . . .
> —Oswald Garrison Villard (1930)

THE RISE OF THE AMERICAN PRESS ASSOCIATIONS—
organizations dedicated to the rapid, thorough and impartial collection and dissemination of all the news—was an epochal development in the history of journalism. "The right of the people to know"
was greatly advanced by the creation of news agencies which
utilize journalistic skills and modern communications techniques
to find the news, to report it impartially, and to speed it to every
corner of the country and of the world. The development in the
twentieth century of two strongly competitive press associations,
the Associated Press and the United Press International, guaranteed
newspaper editors and readers a better kind of national and international news coverage than the world had ever known—despite
acknowledged imperfections.

While the press associations have contributed mightily to the excellence of modern newspapers, nevertheless they have become one of the common denominators of a standardized journalism. The news they supply is a vital part of any daily, together with the paper's own local news. Only a few American dailies ever have been able to maintain staff correspondents in leading news centers of the country and world, and the press association logotypes—AP, UPI—have become the symbols of trustworthy service from an outside source. At the same time the influence of the press associations upon the character of many daily newspapers has become pronounced. Their usual style of writing—summary lead, inverted pyramid story structure, jam-packed facts—affected all newspaper writing, to the detriment of original, individualistic reporting. Their decisions on the relative importance of news events, indicated by the use of "bulletin" slugs and by transmission of news budget summaries to desk editors, became accepted by most papers. Their steadily increasing news and feature offerings lessened the necessity for local staffs to dig for their own stories. In too many newspaper offices the press associations' "flashes of life" and "today's chuckles" replaced local efforts, and entertaining stories of far-away crimes, violence, and romance became too readily available to uninspired and ineffectual news editors. Even on stories immediately affecting a newspaper's own area it became easy to "let the AP do it." The result was a standardization of content going beyond the beneficial and needed cooperative coverage of significant nonlocal news.

More strikingly emerging as common denominators of journalism were the syndicates and special services. Just as entertaining or exciting news attracts an audience anywhere, so do comic strips, cartoons, Sunday magazine sections, columns, and other features. Again, the syndicates have made available to newspapers of all sizes and localities the work of talented artists and writers whose services could not otherwise be obtained by the average paper. But in more than one city the race to corral the most successful comic strips, the best-read columnists, the most colorful features has at times overshadowed the more serious aspects of journalism. And sadly enough, ability to compete in newspaper publication has been affected by possession or lack of possession of popular syndicated material. Even more sadly, some newspapers decided that two full pages of comics, several other syndicated features, and the offerings of two or three Washington columnists were a cheap and easy substitute for their own news and editorial opinion. They ignored the fact that effectively produced local material outdraws most syndicated material in reader interest. Even when syndicated material was used wisely, it had an inevitable standardizing effect, which, combined with the similarity of news display, caused many a reader to refuse to buy more than one paper because "they're all alike." Oswald Garrison Villard, the famous editor of the *Nation* and thoughtful critic of the press whose quotation opens this chapter,[1] saw both the good and the bad in such standardization. His observations of 1930 remained true in 1960. The stories of these common denominators of journalism therefore become important, not only for their own sake, but in the total newspaper pattern.

The United States has had three major press associations operating on nationwide and worldwide scales. One is the Associated Press, which arose out of nineteenth-century efforts at cooperative newsgathering. Its twentieth-century competitors were the United Press Associations, founded in 1907 by Edward Wyllis Scripps, and the International News Service, begun in 1909 by William Randolph Hearst. When these two services were merged in 1958 to form the United Press International, the new UPI became quite comparable in strength to the AP. Abroad, the UPI and AP of the 1960's sold their news and picture services to newspapers, radio and television stations in competition with two other worldwide services. These were Reuters of Great Britain, founded in 1851, and Agence France-Presse, which arose after World War II out of the ruins of the old French Havas agency (1836).

The longest history among the American press associations is that of the Associated Press. The modern cooperative news-gathering association with that name took final form in 1900 after a bitter struggle for control of the press association facilities of the country. The agreement among New York City's leading newspapers in 1848 which brought about the establishment of the Associated Press of New York set the pattern for similar associations. Midwestern dailies formed the Western Associated Press in 1862, and before 1870 a New York state AP and the New England Associated Press were organized. Other subsidiary regional groups followed. But

[1] Oswald Garrison Villard, "The Press Today," *Nation,* CXXX (June 1930), 646.

always the power of the Associated Press of New York was felt.[2] The New York AP had been well-guided by its earliest general agents, Dr. Alexander Jones (1848-1851), news-gathering pioneer Daniel H. Craig (1851-1866), and former Washington correspondent and San Francisco newspaperman James W. Simonton (1866-1882). It had held its position as disseminator of foreign news obtained from European news agencies and it had maintained a monopolistic position through agreements with the Western Union for telegraph line use. By 1882, however, the non-New York dailies were ready to challenge the autocratic control of the founding papers.

One outcome that year was a partial recognition of the growing importance of the midwestern dailies. A joint executive committee was named to administer the AP organization, with three members from the New York group and two from the Western Associated Press. William Henry Smith, who had been general agent of the Western AP since 1869, was named general manager succeeding Simonton. New York committee members were Charles A. Dana of the *Sun*, Whitelaw Reid of the *Tribune*, and James Gordon Bennett, Jr., of the *Herald*. Representing the Western AP were Walter N. Haldeman of the *Louisville Courier-Journal* and Richard Smith of the *Cincinnati Gazette*.[3]

More important was the creation in 1882 of a strong rival for the Associated Press groups. Newspapers outside the AP fold had attempted various organizations without much success. One of the promoters of a rival agency was Henry George, who 10 years before he wrote *Progress and Poverty* attempted to break an AP news monopoly in California. George and a friend, John Hasson, began a news service in 1869 which two years later became the American Press Association. Western Union quickly raised its rates to discriminatory levels in order to protect the AP, but the independents were able to use the wires of rival telegraph companies. The association was reorganized in 1877 and again in 1882, when it took the name United Press (no relation to the present-day UPI).

Giving the United Press competent direction were its general manager, Walter Polk Phillips, a former Associated Press man;

[2] See pages 254-55 and 392-94 for earlier accounts.
[3] Victor Rosewater, *History of Cooperative News-Gathering in the United States* (New York: D. Appleton and Company, 1930), p. 179.

William M. Laffan, business manager of the *New York Sun;* and John R. Walsh, Chicago financier and partner with James W. Scott in the *Chicago Herald.* Such vigorous dailies as the *Boston Globe, Detroit News, Buffalo News, Philadelphia Ledger,* and *New York Daily News* were among the members. Phillips organized a first-rate foreign news service and within three years the United Press was challenging the AP.

The reaction of the ruling groups within the AP and UP was typical of the times. The AP executive committee entered into a secret agreement with the United Press' three strong men, providing for exchange of news between the two associations and a virtual end of competition. There were financial rewards for the insiders. When Western Associated Press members uncovered these arrangements in 1891, a new battle within the newspaper ranks was inevitable.[4]

Victor Lawson, publisher of the *Chicago Daily News,* took the lead for the westerners. Various attempts were made to consolidate the AP groups, which by then included a Southern Associated Press, with the United Press. Negotiations collapsed, however, and the *New York Sun* and *Tribune* bolted to the UP in 1892, to be followed the next year by the remaining members of the Associated Press of New York. Taking control of the AP organization was a new corporation, the Associated Press of Illinois, chartered in late 1892.

Melville E. Stone, who had sold his interest in the *Chicago Daily News* to Lawson in 1888, was drafted as general manager of the AP. One of his first steps was to obtain exclusive news exchange contracts with the leading European news agencies—Reuters in Britain, Havas in France, Wolff in Germany. Stone's contracts cut the United Press off from sources of foreign news long enjoyed by the New York dailies. Lawson and Stone then went to work on the eastern strongholds of the United Press, winning over to AP membership the *New York World* and the *Evening Post,* the *Washington Star,* most of the Philadelphia and Baltimore papers, and holding the southern papers in line. A four-year struggle, which cost the Associated Press members a million dollars in added expenses, finally ended in early 1897 when all the New York papers except Dana's *Sun* and Hearst's *Journal* were admitted to the AP. The

[4] See Rosewater, *History of Cooperative News-Gathering,* pp. 182-89.

United Press went into bankruptcy, but Laffan of the *Sun*, its stubborn leader, had organized the Laffan News Bureau and thus created a creditable news-gathering organization which operated until the sale of the *Sun* to Munsey in 1916.

Laffan indirectly was to cause the Associated Press more trouble before the association's course was finally set. The *Chicago Inter Ocean* went to court in 1898 to prevent the AP from discontinuing service to it as punishment for the *Inter Ocean*'s use of Laffan News Bureau copy. An Illinois court decision, handed down in 1900, found that the incorporation papers of the AP were written so broadly as to make the press association a public utility, bound to provide its service to all newspapers wishing it. For the moment the Illinois ruling seemed to put an end to the exclusive membership character of the AP, but its leaders found a way out. The Associated Press of Illinois was dissolved, and a new Associated Press was formed as a nonprofit membership association under New York State law. Stone continued as general manager of the new AP, and Frank B. Noyes of the *Washington Star* succeeded Lawson as president, to serve until 1938.

The most important fact about the new Associated Press was that it was a cooperative. Its members were to supply each other with news originating in individual publication areas. They were to share the cost of this exchange of news, and the cost of maintaining a press association staff which would direct the flow of news and augment it with other coverage. The staff, headed by the general manager, was to be responsible only to the membership, through its officers and directors. The Associated Press thus would be an agency existing only for the benefit of its member newspapers.

There were some faults, however, in the AP organization. One was an association bylaw prohibiting members from using other news services. This was eliminated in 1915 after an advisory opinion of the U. S. Attorney General's office ruled such action monopolistic. Another complaint centered about extra voting privileges given the original members in 1900 by the issuing of low-denomination bonds carrying voting rights. The result was that the larger, older morning papers kept control of the board of directors despite the growth of evening papers and entry of many smaller dailies into the AP. Voting rights were spread more widely in 1928, and in 1937 the smaller dailies were given three directorships on a board of 18.

Directors were limited to a maximum service of three terms beginning in 1942.

Protest rights, by which an AP member could prevent the entry of a direct competitor into the association, formed the basis for charges that the AP was monopolistic in character. These rights, at first restricted to the original membership, were extended to all members in 1928. If a member protested the election of a competing paper in the same city, a four-fifths vote of the entire membership was required to override the veto. In only a few cases was a member's protest thus overridden, and as a result, newspaper owners in larger cities usually could obtain AP service only by buying an existing membership.

This restriction of AP membership was challenged by the *Chicago Sun,* founded in 1941 by Marshall Field as a competitor in the morning field to the *Tribune.* Court action was begun in 1942, and in 1945 the U. S. Supreme Court held that the AP bylaws concerning protest rights constituted unfair restriction of competition. The AP thereupon amended its membership rules and elected several newspapers previously denied admission.

Another unhappy situation in which the Associated Press found itself stemmed from the news exchange contracts it made in 1893 with European news agencies. Spheres of influence had been assigned to the major agencies for the sale of their news services. Reuters controlled the British Empire area, the Middle East, and Asia. Havas had France, Italy, Spain, Portugal, and South America in its domain. Wolff controlled Germany, Scandinavia, and eastern Europe. The Associated Press had rights in the United States and Canada and shared control in Mexico and Central America with Reuters and Havas. National news agencies in other countries were included in the arrangement by subsidiary agreements.

This meant that news of the United States which was collected by the Associated Press was distributed abroad by foreign news services. Many charges were made that Reuters and Havas mishandled American news. Foreign news given to the Associated Press by its associates likewise was suspect, since many of the foreign news services were under the control of their governments. Melville E. Stone, as AP general manager, did his best to open news channels in European countries[5] and the AP established some

[5] For a description of Stone's activities see *"M.E.S."—His Book* (New York: Harper & Brothers, 1918).

foreign bureaus before World War I to collect its own news. But lacking the right to sell its foreign news abroad, it could not build the kind of foreign service it eventually achieved. Not until 1934 was this restrictive arrangement finally broken down by the AP management.[6] An AP World Service was begun in 1946.

There were many notable names in the AP organization during its formative years under Stone's managership. Charles S. Diehl, a veteran of the Illinois AP regime, became an assistant general manager. So did Jackson S. Elliott, news chief during World War I. Frederick Roy Martin, successful editor of the *Providence Journal*, became assistant general manager in 1912 and succeeded Stone as manager in 1921. Among the noted bureau chiefs were Salvatore Cortesi in Rome, Seymour B. Conger in Berlin, and Edwin M. Hood in Washington. World War I correspondents included Charles T. Thompson, Frederick Palmer, and DeWitt Mackenzie, later an AP news analyst. Wilmer Stuart set up the Associated Press election coverage system on a state-by-state basis between 1904 and 1916, proving the completeness and accuracy of the coverage in the see-saw race between President Woodrow Wilson and Charles Evans Hughes in 1916. The AP correctly reported several hairline decisions in various states, which gave Wilson the victory after it had once been generally conceded to Hughes.[7] Helping to organize that election coverage was the then young AP traffic chief, Kent Cooper.

The name of Kent Cooper was soon to dominate the history of the Associated Press. An Indianan, he had started reporting for his local paper at 14. His college education was interrupted by the death of his father, and he left school to join the *Indianapolis Press*. From there he went to the Scripps-McRae news service, becoming head of the Indianapolis bureau of what was to become the Associated Press' major rival. There Cooper got the idea that out-of-the-way papers could be better served by a system of telephoning the news report than by telegraphing it. In 1910 he went to General Manager Stone of the AP and so impressed Stone with his knowledge of news communications methods that he was made

---

[6] The whole story, from the AP's viewpoint, is told in Kent Cooper, *Barriers Down* (New York: Farrar and Rinehart, Inc., 1942). Reuters became a co-operative, like the AP, in 1941, and invaded the American market with some success.

[7] This episode is described in Oliver Gramling, *AP: The Story of News* (New York: Farrar and Rinehart, Inc., 1940), pp. 249-55.

AP traffic chief. He became an assistant general manager in 1920 and succeeded Martin as general manager in 1925. Through his subsequent career Cooper demonstrated his strong administrative qualities, but he was never a "newspaperman's newspaperman." Cooper had plans for improving the efficiency and quality of the Associated Press service, and many changes came with his rise to control. The number of bureaus was increased and staffs were expanded. The quality of writing was improved and some interpretation was introduced into factual AP stories which demanded explanatory background material. Human interest stories, long frowned upon by the AP, gained favor. The transition was marked by the AP's first Pulitzer Prize, won by Kirke L. Simpson in 1922 for a series on the burial of the Unknown Soldier in Arlington Cemetery. The changes in writing were not so much the result of Cooper's foresight as they were of the prodding the AP was receiving at the hands of rival press associations, as will be demonstrated later in this chapter.

Other changes indicated a modernizing of the AP. A mail feature service was begun in 1928. State services, permitting exchange of regional news on wires subsidiary to the main AP trunk wires, were expanded. A news photo service was established in 1927, and after a sharp clash between picture-minded publishers and their more conservative colleagues, the AP Wirephoto system was approved in 1935. The leased wire system of the Associated Press was tripled between 1920 and 1930 and the budget doubled, reaching 10 million dollars annually. Automatic news printers, called teletypes, were first used in 1913 and gradually replaced Morse operators.

The pressures of competition from other news services and of World War II coverage requirements brought further advances. A leased cable and radioteletype circuits across the North Atlantic, European leased land circuits, and an overseas radiophoto network were added to the service. The character of the news report was subjected to an increasingly intensive review by members of the Associated Press Managing Editors Association, a group formed in 1931. The managing editors of member papers criticised the AP news coverage and writing style orally until 1947, when the reports of a Continuing Study Committee annually were put into printed form. State memberships began similar analyses of their wires. The

AP management hired readability expert Rudolph Flesch to advise its staff, and correspondents like James Marlow of the Washington bureau did excellent work in pointing the way to better writing techniques. After a bitter battle, AP began to sell its news report to radio stations in 1940, five years later than the UP and INS. Radio stations were granted associate membership, without voting rights, in 1946. The Associated Press Radio-Television Association was formed in 1954.[8]

New faces appeared in the AP management. Two of the men most respected by their colleagues for their capabilities as journalists were Byron Price and Paul Miller. Both served as chiefs of the Washington bureau. Price became the AP's first executive news editor in 1936 before retiring from the news service to become director of the Office of Censorship during World War II and later assistant Secretary General of the United Nations. Miller, after being named an assistant general manager, quit the AP to become an executive of the Gannett newspapers.

Their departures left Frank J. Starzel and Alan J. Gould as the leading AP executives under Cooper. Gould, sports editor since 1923, replaced Price as executive editor in 1941. Starzel, who was a newspaperman in Iowa and Illinois before joining the AP in 1929, became Cooper's chief assistant and succeeded him as general manager in 1948. More the traditional newsman than Cooper, he was regarded as a capable successor. Wes Gallagher and Harry T. Montgomery joined Lloyd Stratton and Oliver Gramling as assistant general managers in 1954. Stratton, who died in 1961, had directed AP service abroad until Stanley M. Swinton was named director of the World Service in 1960. On the publishers' side, Robert McLean of the *Philadelphia Bulletin* became AP president in 1938. He was succeeded by Benjamin M. McKelway of the *Washington Star* in 1957.

The names of AP staffmen should not be ignored. Serving in Washington were such newsmen as David Lawrence, who left the AP to become a columnist and news magazine publisher, and Stephen T. Early, who became President Franklin D. Roosevelt's press secretary. Pulitzer Prize winners of the 1930's were Francis A. Jamieson, who covered the Lindbergh baby kidnaping story, Howard W. Blakeslee, AP science editor, and Louis P. Lochner, Berlin bureau chief. Other noted byliners were Brian Bell, W. F.

---

[8] The radio news struggle is detailed in Chapter 26.

Press association executives: Kent Cooper (*left*) and Frank J. Starzel (*right*), general managers of the Associated Press.

Hugh Baillie (*left*), president of the United Press Associations, and Barry Faris (*right*), editor-in-chief for International News Service.

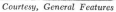

Courtesy, General Features   *Courtesy, N. Y. Herald Tribune—Warman*

Edgar Ansel Mowrer (*left*), *Chicago Daily News* foreign correspondent, and Homer Bigart (*right*), *New York Herald Tribune* war correspondent.

Joseph C. Harsch (*left*), *Christian Science Monitor*, and Mrs. Anne O'Hare McCormick (*right*), *New York Times*, foreign news analyst-reporters.

Thomas L. Stokes (*left*) and Marquis Childs (*right*), leading Washington newsmen and columnists for United Features, beginning in the 1940's.

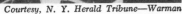

Walter Lippmann (*left*), *New York Herald Tribune* columnist, and Heywood Broun, (*right*), columnist and American Newspaper Guild founder.

Caldwell, foreign correspondent James A. Mills, and Edward J. Neil, killed during the Spanish civil war. World War II saw AP men distinguish themselves overseas. Hal Boyle, Larry Allen, and Daniel De Luce won Pulitzer Prizes as correspondents. Frank Noel, Frank Filan, and Joe Rosenthal were similarly honored as news photographers—Rosenthal for his famous picture of the Marines raising the flag on Iwo Jima's Mount Suribachi. Lloyd Lehrbas, Wes Gallagher, Don Whitehead, Edward Kennedy, Russell Brines, and C. Yates McDaniel were other leading war correspondents. In the Korean War, correspondents Relman Morin and Don Whitehead, and photographer Max Desfor won Pulitzer Prizes. Similar awards went to foreign correspondents Eddy Gilmore in 1947 and Lynn Heinzerling in 1961, and to diplomatic writer John Hightower in 1952. Whitehead and Morin repeated, with national reporting prizes, in 1953 and 1958, respectively. Morin won his covering the Little Rock school riots.

Other major figures included Paul Mickelson, general news editor, and his 1958 successor, Samuel G. Blackman; Ben Bassett, foreign news editor; William L. Beale, Jr., Washington bureau chief; J. M. Roberts, Jr., and William L. Ryan, news analysts; Jack Bell and Douglas Cornell, political writers; and Ernest B. Vaccaro and Marvin Arrowsmith, White House correspondents.

The many names of individuals mentioned illustrate the rising importance of the press associations, for all were well-known to readers or fellow newspapermen. But the men most often identified with the AP are its three general managers—Melville E. Stone, Kent Cooper, and, since 1948, Frank J. Starzel.

Rising alongside the Associated Press as aggressive competing press associations were the United Press Associations of Edward Wyllis Scripps and the International News Service of William Randolph Hearst. This new United Press and the INS were not cooperatives, as was the AP. They were regular business enterprises which sold their news services to clients on a contract basis. Both arose in answer to the Associated Press' closed-membership policy. The chain newspaper publishers who started UP and INS soon found the news they collected could be sold both at home and abroad to others who could not obtain, or did not wish to have, AP service. Serving a variety of clients, as both the UP and INS soon did, their identification with two strong-minded newspaper publishers became only incidental. Their operating staffs were as anxious to cover all the news thoroughly and impartially, for the benefit of their ultimate readers, as were AP men, or any other newsmen. As the twentieth century approached its mid-point all three American press services reached levels of mature journalistic development.

Edward Wyllis Scripps once said that he founded the United Press Associations because he was suspicious of his fellow publishers who controlled the Associated Press. He did not take his papers into the AP in 1897, when the old United Press folded up.

"I knew that at least 90 per cent of my fellows in American journalism were capitalistic and conservative," he explained, and went on:

> I knew that, at that time at least, unless I came into the field with a new service, it would be impossible for the people of the United States to get correct news through the medium of the Associated Press. . . . I have made it impossible for the men who control the Associated Press to suppress the truth, or successfully to disseminate falsehood.[9]

The rebellious Scripps undoubtedly was too critical of his fellow publishers, but his concept of competing press associations acting as checks on each other proved to be of inestimable value to American journalism.

Scripps had other reasons for establishing his own news service. The AP was most interested in the news report for its big morning paper members, and Scripps published evening papers. The closed-membership character of AP meant that Scripps would have trouble obtaining memberships for the new dailies he was establishing. If he ran his own news service, he could fashion its coverage and writing style to better serve the Scripps type of paper. And finally, he expected to make money running a press association.

After operating two regional news services for his own papers in the Middle West and West for 10 years, Scripps merged them in 1907 with the Publishers' Press Association (begun in 1898 by non-AP eastern papers) to form the United Press Associations. A young Scripps newspaperman named John Vandercook helped create the merger and became head of the United Press, but he died the following year. Succeeding him as general manager was 25-year-old

---

[9] As quoted in Rosewater, *History of Cooperative News-Gathering*, p. 354.

Roy W. Howard, destined eventually to dominate the Scripps publishing empire. Howard had served on the *St. Louis Post-Dispatch* and the Scripps papers in Indianapolis and Cincinnati before getting his big chance with the UP.

Scripps described the Roy Howard of this period as "a striking individual, very small of stature, with a large head and speaking countenance, and eyes that appeared to be windows for a rather unusual intellect. His manner was forceful, and the reverse from modest. Gall was written all over his face. It was in every tone and every word he voiced. There was ambition, self-respect and forcefulness oozing out of every pore of his body." [10]

Both Scripps and Howard exhibited a certain amount of gall when they announced the new United Press to its 250 subscribing papers and to other prospective clients. Scripps underwrote a $300,-000 preferred stock issue to start the business, but actually put no money into it. There were but a dozen staff members, a handful of bureaus, and almost no foreign news reports. Howard hustled abroad and established bureaus in the major European capitals. He made connections with leading foreign papers and with commercial news agencies not allied with the AP. Howard's biggest break came when the British cut off the cabling of German news service to belligerents and neutrals during World War I. Two leading Argentine newspapers, *La Prensa* and *La Nación*, rebelled against receiving only the one-sided reports of the French Havas agency and requested Associated Press service. The AP, under its contract agreements, could not enter the South American area, and Howard rapidly rushed in to give the Argentine papers the type of war news coverage they wanted. Soon UP was on the way to building up an extensive string of clients in South America, and established its own bureaus there.

But Howard and the United Press came a cropper in November, 1918, just when the UP was winning attention. Howard was in American naval headquarters at Brest on November 7 when a message arrived from Paris saying the Armistice had been signed at 11 o'clock that morning. Howard flashed the news to the New York UP office, and by an incredible stroke of bad luck for his news service, the message passed the censors. The UP bulletin set off wild cele-

[10] As quoted in Charles R. McCabe, ed., *Damned Old Crank* (New York: Harper & Brothers, 1951), p. 219.

brations in the United States—until several hours later the AP broke the news that the UP had cabled a false report. Although Howard argued that he did what any newsman would have done when he saw the message at naval headquarters (he decided later that the message had originated with a German secret agent in Paris), some telegraph editors never again fully trusted the United Press. Even when in the 1930's the Associated Press flashed the wrong verdict on the outcome of the trial of Bruno Richard Hauptmann for the kidnaping and murder of the Lindbergh baby, and when in 1944 the AP flashed the news of the D-Day landing in France prematurely, oldtime newsmen still recalled how "Roy Howard ended the first World War four days early." [11]

The United Press survived the false Armistice Day report, however. When Howard left it in 1920 to become a partner in the Scripps newspaper chain, the UP had 780 clients and a fairly good news service. Scripps, who held 51 per cent of the controlling common stock, estimated he received $200,000 in dividends during the first 10 years. In the Scripps custom, the remaining 49 per cent of the stock went to key United Press men. The intangible "good will" assets were then valued at $2,500,000 by Howard.[12]

There were good reasons why the United Press was making rapid progress. Its news report was dynamic, and, like the Scripps papers, conformed to the needs and interests of the mass of readers. The Associated Press in the early 1920's was still frowning upon human interest stories, and was so intent upon its strict rules of accuracy and objectivity that it served its members with only strait-laced and factual accounts. United Press staff men were backgrounding the news, personalizing it, and delving into kinds of coverage ignored by the AP. They also scuttled much of the routine commercial news which had long been the bulk of the AP report,

[11] Howard gave his explanation in Webb Miller's *I Found No Peace* (New York: Simon and Schuster, 1936), p. 96. The Associated Press blunder on the Hauptmann verdict stemmed from the setting up of a signal system to get the news out of the courtroom. An over-anxious AP man got the wrong signal and flashed news of a life sentence when the verdict was death. The 1944 premature D-Day flash by AP was sent by a girl teletype operator who was "practicing," the AP said. The UP was similarly victimized by an employee who flashed the end of the Japanese war prematurely in 1945.

[12] McCabe, *Damned Old Crank*, p. 204.

and substituted byline stories, interviews, features, sports stories, and human interest bits.[13]

A common saying among young, low-paid UP men was, "They pay you with bylines." Early in its career, the UP began giving enthusiastic young staffers some glory and a chance to develop their own writing styles and news specialties. AP men covering World War I were largely anonymous news-gatherers. The UP turned loose young correspondents like Webb Miller, Fred S. Ferguson, William Philip Simms, William G. Shepherd, and Westbrook Pegler. Their vividly written and interpretative copy attracted attention, and helped to sell the UP service as a second wire for AP member papers.

Some of the UP's young men moved up rapidly. Among the war correspondents, Miller became European news manager and stayed in command until he was killed in a London blackout early in World War II. Ferguson became general news manager, then in 1926 was put in charge of the Scripps news feature service, Newspaper Enterprise Association. Simms became foreign editor for the Scripps-Howard newspapers. Pegler became a widely syndicated columnist, as did three UP Washington staffers of the 1920's— Thomas L. Stokes, Paul Mallon, and Raymond Clapper.

The UP news operation, while dynamic, was still suffering from growing pains in the 1920's. The management expanded the client list faster than it built its news-gathering bureaus and the leased wire system. Papers which could not afford the full service purchased the "pony service," which consisted of a few hundred words of news read over the telephone from a UP bureau. Understaffed UP bureaus were at a disadvantage in competing with the AP because the UP had no member papers obligated to supply local news to the press association. But by the 1930's, partially through its success in the radio news field, the UP was greatly improving its service. Its foreign news reporting won particular favor and domestic bureaus were strengthened to make the UP a solidly organized news service, as well as one showing frequent flashes of

---

[13] Estimates of the character of the UP service are found in Will Irwin, "United Press," *Harper's Weekly,* LVIII (April 25, 1914), 6, and in Rosewater, *History of Cooperative News-Gathering,* pp. 340-55. See Gramling, *AP: The Story of News,* pp. 175 and 313-18, for characterizations of AP service. The full UP story is told in Joe Alex Morris, *Deadline Every Minute* (Garden City: Doubleday & Company, Inc., 1957).

brilliance in developing a major story through individual initiative. Howard's successors as president of the United Press all came up through the ranks. His assistant, William W. Hawkins, held the post from 1920 to 1923. Then a second strong man of the UP, Karl A. Bickel, moved into the top command. Bickel possessed abilities that made him a respected leader in journalistic circles. He had worked first for the Scripps papers and the United Press on the West Coast, then had won his spurs in the foreign service. As UP president, he became a leader in furthering freedom of international news coverage, and he did much to advance the UP's own position in worldwide service.

Hugh Baillie, who succeeded Bickel in 1935, also rose from the West Coast Scripps organization. At 19, after two years of college, he joined the *Record*, a Scripps paper in Los Angeles. Then he moved to the UP San Francisco office, where he was in charge of the "pony report." By 1918 the 28-year-old Baillie was chief of the Washington bureau. He then moved through executive posts to the presidency. Baillie loved nothing better than to whip his competitors with an exclusive story, preferably a vividly colorful one. He traveled extensively, impressing his own competitive drive for news upon his staff, and keeping his hand in by covering some big stories of the 1930's and World War II. When he moved up to board chairmanship in 1955, he was succeeded as president by Frank H. Bartholomew, also from the Pacific Coast and also a reporter.

The United Press jumped into several fields ahead of the AP, just as it did in developing its foreign news service. Newspaper Enterprise Association, an associate of the UP in the Scripps empire, was begun in 1902 as a feature service, 25 years in advance of the creation of AP Newsfeatures. Acme Newspictures began operating in 1925, two years earlier than the AP picture service was established. The United Press pioneered in supplying news to radio stations, and, with INS, was first into the television news field in 1951. Acme became United Press Newspictures in 1952 and handled UP Telephoto, rival to AP Wirephoto. In 1954 both services began supplying pictures by facsimile, over the UP Unifax and AP Photofax networks. The teletypesetter, producing a tape which automatically runs a typesetting machine, arrived in 1951 and both UP and AP set up teletypesetter circuits for smaller papers, sports, and financial services.

Earl J. Johnson, vice president and editor, was one of the UP veterans who became leaders, with Bartholomew, of the UPI after 1958. Others were Mims Thomason, first vice president and general business manager; Lyle C. Wilson, vice president and Washington manager; Joseph L. Jones, vice president and general foreign manager; Thomas R. Curran, vice president and general European manager; and Harry R. Flory, director of communications.

Other major figures included Roger Tatarian, executive editor; Harry Ferguson, European news manager; Earnest Hoberecht, who succeeded Miles W. Vaughn as vice president in Asia; and William H. McCall, vice president for Latin America. Webb Miller, Virgil Pinkley, and A. L. Bradford were earlier European news chiefs. Joe Alex Morris, Harrison Salisbury, Phil Newsom, and Joseph W. Morgan were foreign news editors.

Notable in the foreign service were W. R. Higginbotham, H. R. Ekins, Frederick Kuh, Norman Montellier, Henry Shapiro, Robert Musel, Jack V. Fox, Joseph W. Grigg, and K. C. Thaler. Russell Jones won a Pulitzer Prize in 1957 for covering the Budapest uprising. Merriman Smith, White House correspondent, was the best known of a Washington staff including editor Julius Fransden, political writer Raymond Lahr, and diplomatic reporter Stewart Hensley.

Byliners for the UP during World War II included Frederick C. Oeschner in Berlin, Ralph Heinzen in Paris, and war correspondents Webb Miller, M. S. Handler, Edward W. Beattie, Reynolds and Eleanor Packard, C. R. Cunningham, and Henry T. Gorrell in Europe. William F. Tyree, Frank Tremaine, and William B. Dickinson were leaders in the Pacific theater. Bert Brandt of Acme starred by getting the first pictures of the D-Day invasion.

The third American press association competitor has been the International News Service. Smaller than its rivals, and later in establishing itself as a comprehensive news service, INS nevertheless won prominence for its competitive spirit.

INS was founded in 1909 as an outgrowth of earlier leased wire facilities of the Hearst newspapers. Richard A. Farrelly was its first manager. By 1918 INS was serving 400 clients and had a leased wire system approximately half as extensive as those of the AP and UP. In that year INS and a Hearst morning paper news agency, Universal Service, were put under the direction of Moses Koenigsberg, also head of Hearst's King Features Syndicate. INS developed full 24-hour operations by 1928, but Universal Service was killed in 1937. Executive control of INS passed to Joseph V. Connolly, and on his death in 1945 to Seymour Berkson. Berkson, former INS managing editor, now became general manager.

The sparkplug of the INS after 1916 was Barry Faris, editor-in-chief. Faris worked for eight different midwestern and western newspapers in his first 10 years after graduating from college, then entered press association work with the United Press before joining INS. He found INS in trouble. The British and French governments in 1916 barred INS from use of their cables because the Hearst newspapers insisted on publishing German as well as Allied versions of the war news. The Associated Press then charged INS with stealing its foreign news before publication through the help of Hearst papers which were members of the AP. Similar charges had been made concerning INS collection of news in the United States, and even Hearst editors considered the service "reliably unreliable." [14] The U. S. Supreme Court upheld an injunction obtained by the AP against the INS, on the grounds of unfair competition. The INS was losing money, and its future seemed black.

But INS gradually won its place, through the efforts of Faris as editor, and Connolly and Berkson as business executives. It established fewer bureaus than the other services, concentrating its resources on the major news centers. Its most successful plan was to offer well-known bylines, and special coverage of major news events by talented writers. While only a few newspapers ever depended on INS as a single source of press association news, a substantial number subscribed to the service to obtain its well-written stories and occasional major news beats.

H. R. Knickerbocker, a Pulitzer Prize winner, and Floyd Gibbons were two longtime INS foreign correspondents. James L. Kilgallen began his roving coverage of major national stories in 1921. Later acquisitions as featured INS writers were Bob Considine and Inez Robb. Other glamor names on the INS wire were Quentin Reynolds, Frank Gervasi, Paul Gallico, Damon Runyon, Arthur "Bugs" Baer, Louella Parsons, and Edwin C. Hill.

The INS foreign service developed stature by the 1930's. Among

---

[14] M. Koenigsberg, *King News* (Philadelphia: F. A. Stokes Company, 1941), p. 454.

its leaders were J. C. Oestreicher, foreign editor, Pierre J. Huss, Berlin bureau chief, and J. Kingsbury Smith, who became European general manager. Top World War II correspondents were Howard Handleman, Kenneth Downs, Merrill Mueller, George Lait, Graham Hovey, Frank Conniff, and Kilgallen in Europe; and Richard Tregaskis, Lee Van Atta, and Clark Lee (a former AP man) in the Pacific. Leading Washington bureau chiefs were George R. Holmes and William K. Hutchinson, while George E. Durno and Robert G. Nixon handled the White House assignment. Jack Lotto and Malcolm Johnson of the New York bureau won awards for general news coverage. Among the INS women correspondents, Rose McKee achieved prominence for political reporting. In a final burst of glory, the 1956 Pulitzer Prize for international reporting was won for INS and the Hearst newspapers by William Randolph Hearst, Jr., Kingsbury Smith, and Frank Conniff, who conducted interviews with Communist political leaders behind the Iron Curtain.

There were lumps in many throats when the hard-hitting INS staff of 450 saw their agency merged with the UP in May, 1958. William Randolph Hearst, Jr., and two of his associates took minority seats on the board of directors of the new United Press International, and some INS staffers joined UPI. A few of the brightest INS stars went to work for the newly formed Hearst Headline Service. Otherwise INS was no more. UPI also acquired International News Photos. The INS was serving 334 American newspapers and some 2,000 worldwide clients at the time of the merger.

AP and UPI intensified their competition in the wake of the merger. The UPI opened a full double-trunk national wire circuit in 1959, giving it facilities comparable to those of the AP. As the 1960's opened, both associations leased more than 400,000 miles of telephone wires in the United States for transmission of news and pictures. Both used globe-girdling radio teletype circuits and underwater cables to carry their news reports to Europe and Asia. Both had teletype circuits covering more than 20,000 miles in Europe, where their news reports were translated and fed into national wires. Both had European picture circuits and radio facilities for worldwide picture transmission. News reports could go around the world almost instantaneously.

The UPI laid claim to the most direct client users of its news and picture services. The AP said it had the most outlets, including those receiving AP news through relay by a foreign news agency. Using these criteria, AP claimed 7,000 worldwide users, the UPI 6,400 by 1961. In the United States, the AP listed service to 1,760 publications and 2,122 radio and television stations; the UPI said it served 1,600 publications and 2,248 stations. Of 1,720 American dailies having press association teletypes, *Editor & Publisher International Year Book* listings showed approximately 1,200 receiving AP news and 950 UPI news. Approximately 45 per cent received AP news only, 30 per cent UPI news only, and 25 per cent both services. The UPI listed 248 news and picture bureaus and the AP listed 165 news bureaus. The UPI said its news went to 103 countries and territories; the AP figure was 80 countries. For both it was big business; the AP budget for 1960 was $38,500,000 and the UPI's was $35,500,000.

The tradition of individual newspaper coverage of foreign and Washington news continued despite the rise of the press associations. Some of the more extensive newspaper services were syndicated to other papers, just as they had been since the race for news developed in the 1830's and 1840's.

Among newspapers which emphasized their own foreign news coverage in the early years of the twentieth century were the *Herald, World, Tribune, Sun,* and *Times* in New York; the *Daily News, Tribune,* and *Record-Herald* in Chicago; the *Washington Post, Philadelphia Public Ledger,* and the *Baltimore Sun.* By the 1960's the *Times* and *Herald Tribune* in New York, the *Daily News* and *Tribune* in Chicago, the *Christian Science Monitor* and the *Baltimore Sun* led in foreign correspondence. Others with European bureaus included the *Minneapolis Star* and *Tribune, New York Daily News, Toledo Blade, Washington Post, Washington Star,* and *Wall Street Journal.* The *New York Times* led in staff abroad.

Washington bureaus of individual newspapers increased steadily. The number of American daily newspapers with some sort of special representation in Washington (as measured by Congressional press gallery membership) was 110 in 1890, 180 in 1910, 300 in 1930, and 405 in 1960. About one-third of the 1960 total had individual Washington correspondent representation; the others were served by correspondents writing for several different papers. The number of correspondents for newspapers in Washington jumped from 112 in 1890 to 150 in 1910, 214 in 1930, and 444 in 1960. Press associations and syndicates had altogether on their Washington staffs just 14 persons in 1890 and 24 in 1910. By 1930 the number was 112, and by 1960 it was 250. Foreign papers and agencies had just five representatives in Washington in 1910, 18 in 1930, and 73 in 1960. The over-all totals for Congressional press gallery membership were 126 in 1890, 179 in 1910, 344 in 1930, and 767 in 1960.

The elite of the Washington press corps have been the 50 members of the Gridiron Club, founded in 1885. The National Press Club was organized in 1908 and built the 14-story National Press Building in 1927. The White House Correspondents Association dates from 1914. Later on the scene were the Radio-Television Correspondents Association with 175 members in 1960, and the White House News Photographers Association, with 140.

Biggest of the Washington news bureaus in the early 1960's were, of course, those of the press associations. Associated Press bureau manpower was 100, that of the United Press International 80. Other staffs numbering in the twenties were those of CBS, the *New York Times*, NBC, the *Wall Street Journal*, and the Scripps-Howard newspapers. Next came *Time*, *Newsweek*, *U. S. News & World Report*, the McGraw-Hill Publications, and Fairchild Publications; Mutual and ABC; the *New York Herald Tribune*, *Baltimore Sun*, *Chicago Tribune*, *New York Daily News*, and the *New York Journal of Commerce*. Strong smaller bureaus represented the *St. Louis Post-Dispatch*, *Chicago Daily News*, *Christian Science Monitor*, *Buffalo Evening News*, the Cowles newspapers at Des Moines and Minneapolis, and *Look*. The Hearst, Knight, Newhouse, Ridder, and Gannett groups also had staffs of at least five. The three Washington dailies—the *Post*, *Star*, and *Daily News*—were strongly represented. Two foreign press associations, Reuters and Agence France-Presse, had Washington staffs of five (Reuters was serving some 40 American newspapers with its world news report). The United Nations Correspondents Association in New York had 200 members.

Biggest of the newspaper syndicates was the *New York Times* News Service. *Times* foreign correspondents won 10 Pulitzer Prizes in the 30 years beginning in 1932, and 11 more Pulitzer awards went to other leading *Times* writers in the same period. Best known of the *Times* foreign correspondents winning the Pulitzer citations were Walter Duranty, 1932; Anne O'Hare McCormick, 1937; Otto D. Tolischus, 1940; and Hanson W. Baldwin, 1943. From the Washington bureau, Arthur Krock won prizes in both 1935 and 1938, and James B. Reston in 1945 and 1957. Their stories, and those of other leading *Times* reporters, were available to newspapers subscribing to the syndicated news service.[15]

The *Chicago Daily News* Foreign Service grew out of the coverage begun in 1898 by Victor Lawson for the *Daily News* and *Record-Herald*. It won wide attention during World War I through the work of Edward Price Bell in London, Paul Scott Mowrer in Paris, and Raymond Gram Swing in Berlin. But it hit its most remarkable peak of performance in the 1930's and early 1940's under publisher Frank Knox and the foreign news director, Carroll Binder, himself a noted correspondent before he became head of the service in 1937.

Pulitzer Prizes were won by Paul Scott Mowrer in 1929 and by Edgar Ansel Mowrer in 1933. Ranking with the Mowrer brothers as among the best of American foreign correspondents of the day were John Gunther in London, William Stoneman in Moscow and London, Wallace Deuel in Rome and Berlin, Helen Kirkpatrick in Paris, and David Nichol in Berlin and Moscow. Other leading *Chicago Daily News* foreign correspondents of the World War II period were Leland Stowe, Robert J. Casey, William McGaffin, Paul Ghali, Ernie Hill, Nat A. Barrows, A. T. Steele, and George Weller, a Pulitzer Prize winner for distinguished reporting. Keyes Beech and Fred Sparks won Pulitzer awards for Korean War coverage. Paul Leach, Edwin A. Lahey, and Peter Lisagor were Washington bureau chiefs. Beech, Ghali, Lisagor, McGaffin, Nichol, Stoneman, and Weller were still on the staff in 1961.

The *New York Herald Tribune* foreign service was built on that of the old *Tribune,* which had Frank H. Simonds and Richard Harding Davis as World War I writers. Leland Stowe won a 1930 Pulitzer Prize as a *Herald Tribune* correspondent and Homer Bigart was similarly honored for his World War II work. Other leading

[15] Other *Times* foreign correspondents winning Pulitzer Prizes were Frederick T. Birchall, 1934; Arnaldo Cortesi, 1946; Brooks Atkinson, 1947 (better known as a drama critic); Harrison E. Salisbury, 1955; the entire staff, 1958; and A. M. Rosenthal, 1960. Winners for national reporting were Louis Stark, labor writer, 1942; C. P. Trussell, 1949, and Anthony Leviero, 1952. Distinguished reporting awards went to Lauren D. Lyman, 1936; William L. Laurence, science writer, 1937 and 1946; and Meyer Berger, 1950. Other leading *Times* foreign correspondents during the World War II era were Raymond Daniell, C. L. Sulzberger, Herbert L. Matthews, and Drew Middleton.

Herald Tribune correspondents of the war period were Joseph Barnes, Major George Fielding Eliot, Russell Hill, Joseph Driscoll, and John O'Reilly. A. T. Steele left the *Chicago Daily News* to join the *Herald Tribune*. Bert Andrews, while Washington bureau chief, won the 1948 Pulitzer Prize for national reporting. Jack Steele was a leading Washington staff member in the early 1950's before becoming Scripps-Howard's chief political writer. Bigart and Marguerite Higgins won Pulitzer Prizes as Korean War correspondents; Bigart later joined the *New York Times*. Other Pulitzer Prizes for reporting were won by William H. Taylor in 1935 and by science writer John J. O'Neill in 1937.

The *Chicago Tribune* foreign service had as World War I stars Floyd Gibbons, Frazier Hunt, John T. McCutcheon, and Sigrid Schultz. Serving the *Tribune* overseas for varying periods were such well-known journalists as Vincent Sheean, William L. Shirer, George Seldes, Jay Allen, and Edmond Taylor. Wilfred C. Barber won the *Tribune* news service's only Pulitzer Prize in 1936. In the following years, the leading correspondents of other foreign and Washington services outshone the *Tribune* men.[16]

Several special news and feature services were established for American newspapers after 1900. First was the Newspaper Enterprise Association, founded in 1902 by Robert F. Paine, E. W. Scripps' talented editor-in-chief. While NEA by the 1950's offered all types of features to newspaper clients, it also had foreign and Washington correspondence, highlighted by the work of prize-winning Peter Edson and of Fred Sparks, who transferred from the *Chicago Daily News*. A second Scripps contribution was Science Service, begun in 1921 and directed by Watson Davis as an authoritative science news agency. The Scripps-Howard Newspaper Alli-

---

[16] Other Pulitzer Prize winners for international correspondence were three *Baltimore Sun* men, Mark S. Watson, 1945, Paul W. Ward, 1948, and Price Day, 1949; Edmund Stevens, *Christian Science Monitor*, 1950; Austin Wehrwein, *Milwaukee Journal*, 1953; and Joseph Martin and Philip Santora, *New York Daily News*, 1959. Other Pulitzer awards for national correspondence went to three *St. Louis Post-Dispatch* men—Paul Y. Anderson, 1929, Charles G. Ross, 1932, and Edward A. Harris, 1946; to three members of the Cowles newspapers (*Minneapolis Star* and *Tribune, Des Moines Register* and *Tribune*) Washington bureau—Nat S. Finney, 1948, Richard L. Wilson, 1954, and Clark R. Mollenhoff, 1958; and to Dewey L. Fleming, *Baltimore Sun*, 1944; Edward T. Folliard, *Washington Post*, 1947; Edwin O. Guthman, *Seattle Times*, 1950; Anthony Lewis, *Washington Daily News*, 1955; Charles L. Bartlett, *Chattanooga Times*, 1956; Howard Van Smith, *Miami News*, 1959, and Edward R. Cony, *Wall Street Journal*, 1961.

ance, developed for the chain's own papers, had its share of Pulitzer Prize winners—science editor David Dietz, Washington correspondents Thomas L. Stokes and Vance Trimble, columnist Ernie Pyle, and foreign correspondent Jim G. Lucas.

Central Press Association, begun in 1910 by V. V. McNitt, achieved prominence, by having William Jennings Bryan cover the 1912 political conventions. George Matthew Adams, another leading syndicate organizer, helped several large newspapers found Associated Newspapers in 1912. David Lawrence began syndicating Washington news in 1919 under the name Consolidated Press. A major reorganization of the news syndicates took place in 1930 when the North American Newspaper Alliance was founded by a group of metropolitan newspapers under the managership of John N. Wheeler, head of the Bell Syndicate. NANA and Bell absorbed the Associated Newspaper, Consolidated Press, and McClure services and established NANA as the leading specialized news agency. Among its correspondents was military reporter and analyst Ira Wolfert, 1943 Pulitzer Prize winner. Central Press came under the control of Hearst's King Features Syndicate in 1930 and declined in importance.[17]

The impact of the syndicates upon newspaper content was heaviest in the non-news field. First to relieve newspaper editors of the necessity of clipping column material, fiction, poetry, and other entertainment features from newspaper and magazine exchanges was Ansel N. Kellogg, the Baraboo, Wisconsin, newsman who originated the ready-print service for small papers.[18] When Kellogg and another Wisconsin newspaperman, Andrew J. Aikens, founded feature services in Chicago after the Civil War the non-news syndicate idea began to flourish.

Kellogg's ready-print service—letters from New York, Washington, and foreign correspondents, serial stories, women's features, poetry, and other material printed on one side of newsprint sheets supplied to small publishers who printed their local news and ads on the other side—expanded rapidly. Another idea was the supply-

---

[17] Among other special news agencies were the Dow Jones News Service, with some 40 newspaper clients; the Jewish Telegraphic Agency, a world service headquartering in New York, and its Overseas News Agency; Associated Negro Press, largest for Negro papers; Religious News Service, serving 750 clients; and Copley News Service, specializing in Latin-American news.

[18] See pages 311-12.

ing of stereotyped plates to publishers, begun about 1875 and developed by the American Press Association. Editors could cut the plate material to fit, a process which its critics dubbed "editing with a saw." The ready-print and plate services spread throughout the East and South between 1870 and 1880, with Kellogg, Aikens, and others leading the way.

Destined to control the feature syndicate business for weeklies and small dailies was the Western Newspaper Union, a Des Moines enterprise dating from 1872. George A. Joslyn gained control of WNU in 1890 and set about to consolidate the businesses in his field, in keeping with the "big business" tendencies of the times. WNU bought the Kellogg company in 1906, added the Aikens enterprises in 1910, and snapped up other smaller services. Purchase of the American Press Association in 1917 gave WNU a virtual monopoly. WNU had by then become one of the "budget services," offering a wide variety of feature material to its customers rather than requiring purchase of a particular set of features. The ready-print service, which at its peak went to nearly 7,000 papers, gradually declined and was abandoned in 1952. But WNU's myriad of features, ranging from weekly columns by Drew Pearson and Walter Winchell to dress patterns, sold to nearly all the country's weeklies and many dailies. Under owner John H. Perry, who won full control of WNU in 1938, the sale of features and newspaper printing equipment became a 20 million dollar business. Perry also owned two trade publications, *Publishers' Auxiliary* and *American Press,* newsprint companies, and a string of Florida newspapers and radio stations.[19]

While Western Newspaper Union was developing in the weekly field, dailies were being offered syndicated literary material by the feature services of Irving Bacheller (1883), S. S. McClure (1884), and Edward W. Bok (1886). McClure and Bok sensed the public demand for entertaining reading, which led to their own more famous careers as magazine publishers. Hearst joined the syndicate movement in 1895, and in 1914 began his King Features Syndicate. George Matthew Adams entered the field in 1907 and John N. Wheeler in 1913. Wheeler's Bell Syndicate dates from 1916. The

<hr />

[19] The story of the Kellogg, Aikens, and other early syndicates is told in Elmo Scott Watson, *A History of Newspaper Syndicates in the United States 1865-1935* (Chicago: Publishers' Auxiliary, 1936).

Scripps-Howard United Feature Syndicate appeared in 1919 and the McNaught Syndicate was started by V. V. McNitt in 1922. Among leading newspaper-owned syndicates, Cyrus H. K. Curtis' *Public Ledger* service began in 1915, the *Chicago Tribune* Syndicate in 1918, and the *Des Moines Register and Tribune* Syndicate in 1922. By the 1960's there were some 225 general feature syndicates, and other special services, doing a total annual business estimated as high as 40 million dollars. The leaders were Hearst's King Features, Scripps-Howard's United Features and Newspaper Enterprise Association, the *Chicago Tribune-New York Daily News* Syndicate, Western Newspaper Union, AP Newsfeatures, Bell, and McNaught. The *Des Moines Register and Tribune* Syndicate, *New York Herald Tribune* Syndicate, *Chicago Sun-Times* Syndicate, General Features Corporation and the Post-Hall Syndicate (successor to the Curtis enterprise) were other important units. While the syndicates offered all manner of features, from crossword puzzles to "handy fillers," their part in the nationalization of columns, editorial page cartoons, and comic strips merits particular attention.

The early syndicates featured the writings of Robert Louis Stevenson, Rudyard Kipling, Mark Twain, Bret Harte, Henry James, Alfred Henry Lewis, Jack London, and other literary greats. They also could sample the work of a notable group of poetically-inclined columnists, and humorous writers, which appeared in newspapers throughout the country. Syndication spread the fame of humorists "M. Quad" of the *Detroit Free Press* and *New York Herald;* Bill Nye of Laramie, Wyoming, and the *New York World;* Opie Read of *Arkansaw Traveler* fame; Joel Chandler Harris of the *Atlanta Constitution;* and Finley Peter Dunne, the Chicago newspaperman whose "Mr. Dooley"—a saloon keeper who philosophized in a penetrating manner on current affairs—became a national institution. Also syndicated were the stories of George Ade of the *Chicago Record*, the verse of Edgar A. Guest of the *Detroit Free Press*, and the poems of Walt Mason and Ella Wheeler Wilcox.

To older newspapermen a column was "a little of everything"— wit, poetry, sentiment, and comment on personalities and events in the news. One such column conductor was Eugene Field, the St. Louis and Kansas City newsman whom Melville E. Stone brought to the *Chicago Daily News* to write his "Sharps and Flats" before

1900. Another was Bert Leston Taylor, who founded the *Chicago Tribune*'s famed "A Line o' Type or Two" column in 1901. A third was Franklin P. Adams, who wrote for the *Chicago Journal* and *New York Mail* before beginning his "Conning Tower" in the *New York Tribune* in 1914. On the *New York Sun* it was Don Marquis with his "Sun Dial" column, inhabited by "archie," the noncapitalizing cockroach. There were other gracefully literate columns in individual papers, among them the work of H. I. Phillips for the *New York Herald Tribune*, of Keith Preston for the *Chicago Daily News*, of Stoddard King for the *Spokane Spokesman-Review*, and of Christopher Morley for the *New York Evening Post*, in the 1920's. F.P.A.'s "Conning Tower" moved from the *Tribune* to the *World*, back to the *Herald Tribune*, and then to the *Evening Post*. Richard Henry Little and Charles Collins continued the *Chicago Tribune*'s "A Line o' Type or Two." Will Rogers was syndicated as the closest modern approach to the immortal "Mr. Dooley." But the older columns came to be overwhelmed by new kinds of syndicated columns, and polished writing with the light touch tended to retreat to such publications as the *New Yorker* and *Saturday Review*.

Walter Winchell set the pace for one kind of syndicated column. A New Yorker who entered journalism with the racy tabloids of the 1920's, Winchell promoted the "gossip" column as the Broadway reporter of the tabloid *Graphic*. He shifted to the *Mirror* in 1929 and became a star of Hearst's King Features Syndicate. No other columnist ever approached Winchell's sensationalism and intimate coverage of private lives, but such Hollywood columnists as Louella Parsons and Hedda Hopper did their best. Leonard Lyons and Dorothy Kilgallen were other New York scene columnists of the personal type, while O. O. McIntyre and Mark Hellinger wrote about the metropolis in an older literary style.

The political column began in the early 1920's with the writings of David Lawrence in his syndicated column and Washington publications, of Mark Sullivan in the *New York Herald Tribune*, and of Frank R. Kent in the *Baltimore Sun*. Walter Lippmann joined this trio as a *Herald Tribune* columnist when his editorship of the *World* ended in 1931. Their columns were concerned with current politics and issues of the day, as contrasted with Arthur Brisbane's philosophical commentary which began in 1917 and was front-paged by Hearst newspapers for nearly 20 years. But the coming of the New Deal in 1933 and a consequent revolution in Washington coverage brought a new version of the political column, to join the syndicated offerings of Lawrence, Sullivan, Kent, and Lippmann.

The four early leaders as political and current affairs columnists were identified as "pundits" who wrote in a sober style and with a serious-minded approach. Sullivan and Kent were masters of the practical political scene of the 1920's, but they were not responsive to the social and economic shifts which brought the widespread increase in governmental activity in the New Deal era. Sullivan, who had been an enthusiastic interpreter of Theodore Roosevelt's progressive program and an intimate of President Herbert Hoover, became far better known for his superb journalistic history of the 1900-1925 period, *Our Times*, than for his later columns. Lawrence continued to hold a place as a commentator on national affairs, as did Lippmann in the international field.

A new kind of political column after 1932 was the personalized or "gossip-type" column. The idea stemmed from the successful book, *Washington Merry-Go-Round*, published anonymously in 1931. The authors were soon identified as Drew Pearson of the *Baltimore Sun* and Robert S. Allen of the *Christian Science Monitor*. These two Washington correspondents quickly left their newspapers to co-author a behind-the-scenes column which Pearson eventually continued alone. Paul Mallon was in the personalized column competition from the start of the New Deal era; joining in as sympathetic commentators on the New Deal's activities were Ernest K. Lindley, Samuel Grafton, and Joseph Alsop. Pearson continued to lead in the race to obtain inside stories and "predictions."

United Features offered a particularly strong and varied group of columnists and commentators in the 1930's. Raymond Clapper, before his death in a 1944 wartime plane crash, was recognized as perhaps the best-balanced interpreter of the Washington scene. His opinions on national and international problems were widely respected, largely because they were based upon reporting ability and Clapper's long experience as a United Press newsman and political writer and as head of the UP Washington bureau and that of the *Washington Post*. Thomas L. Stokes, a hard-working reporter of the Washington scene for United Press and the Scripps-Howard newspapers, developed a large following for his vigorous and crusading columns. Stokes won a Pulitzer Prize for national reporting and a Clapper memorial award for his column before he died in 1958. Carrying on for United Features were Marquis Childs, distinguished Washington correspondent for the *St. Louis Post-Dispatch* who began his column after Clapper's death, and William S. White, from the *New York Times* Washington staff.

Also in the United Features group of columnists were some commentators of the personal variety. One was Westbrook Pegler, the caustic ex-sports writer and United Press and *Chicago Tribune* writer. Pegler had a distinctive, colorful style and won a 1941 Pulitzer Prize for his exposure-type crusading. Unhappily his work degenerated into monotonous and vicious attacks upon three small groups—labor unions, New Dealers, and members of the Franklin D. Roosevelt family—and Pegler switched from Scripps-Howard to Hearst sponsorship in the mid-1940's, becoming known as "the stuck whistle of journalism." Balancing Pegler was the witty, warm personality of Heywood Broun. Best described as "looking like an unmade bed," Broun was a deceptive writer who could switch from a gay and easy commentary to a hard-hitting defense of liberal traditions whenever his temper was aroused. His "It Seems to Me" ran first in the *New York Tribune,* then in the *World* during the 1920's, and finally in the Scripps-Howard papers. Broun's leading role in the American Newspaper Guild and his liberal line brought a break with Roy Howard and the column was headed for the *New York Post* when Broun died in 1939. Also writing columns for United Features were Mrs. Eleanor Roosevelt, first signed in 1935 in an unprecedented move for a president's wife, and the lovable Ernie Pyle, whose original cross-country tour columns about little people and things were followed by superb personal glimpses of American fighting men in World War II until Pyle was killed on a Pacific island in 1945.

Well to the right of the United Features columnists in political and social outlooks were the King Features group. Best known were Pegler and the conservative George Sokolsky; later in the field were George Dixon, radio commentator Fulton Lewis, Jr., and moral philosopher Bruce Barton. The Bell Syndicate offered the columns of two leading women journalists. One was Dorothy Thompson, a European correspondent for the *Philadelphia Public*

Ledger and *New York Post* before beginning a columnist career that closed in 1961. Her emotion-charged comments on international affairs were in contrast to the smooth political-type commentary of Doris Fleeson, who came to the columnist field from the *New York Daily News*. Miss Fleeson, a 1960's United Features star, became in 1954 the first woman to win the Raymond Clapper award for meritorious reporting. A third woman, Sylvia Porter, became the leading business columnist of the country for the Hall Syndicate. Edgar Ansel Mowrer left the *Chicago Daily News* to write a column for General Features. The *New York Herald Tribune* offered the writings of Lippmann, Lawrence, Joseph Alsop, and Roscoe Drummond as the 1960's opened. Drummond came from the *Christian Science Monitor* in 1953. Alsop's brother, Stewart, split their team in 1958 to become a *Saturday Evening Post* contributing editor.

Syndication also affected the profession of editorial cartooning. As in the field of columning, widespread readership offered fame and financial rewards to the talented. But easy access to their proved reader-drawing copy made it less likely that a newspaper would "bring up" its own cartoonist or columnist. Local columnists always had their field, of course, but serious commentary on national and international affairs by a local staff member became scarcer. So did locally-drawn cartoons, although the "package" services could not touch subjects affecting the local scene in each community.

The period after the Civil War saw the development of the political cartoon as an editorial device. Until then, the cartoon was more likely to be seen in magazines because of newspaper production difficulties, but the introduction of stereotyping enabled dailies to use illustrations more readily. Thomas Nast, the cartoonist who so savagely attacked the Tweed political ring, drew for the *New York Times* after 1870, as well as for *Harper's Weekly*. In the magazines of the times, Joseph Keppler's work for *Puck* was outstanding. The presidential campaign cartoons of Homer Davenport, drawn for Hearst's *New York Journal* in 1896, scored a new high point, both in prominence and in the bluntness of their attack (see page 459).

The first quarter of the twentieth century was a golden age for cartoonists. The issues were simple enough for easy pictorial interpretation, and they were elemental enough for clever satire. These are the ingredients of the political cartoon. One of the famous cartoonists was John T. McCutcheon, who began drawing for the *Chicago Tribune* in 1903 after serving on the *Chicago Record,* and who won a Pulitzer Prize before he retired in 1946. Clifford K. Berryman, who first appeared in the *Washington Post* as far back as 1889, was closely identified with the *Washington Star* after 1906. He and his son, James T. Berryman, were the only father and son combination to win Pulitzer Prizes for their work, after the younger Berryman succeeded his father in 1949. Reminiscent of the old school of flowery technique was Jay N. ("Ding") Darling, who began drawing for the *Des Moines Register* in 1906 and who was twice a Pulitzer Prize winner. His work was widely syndicated by the *New York Herald Tribune* feature service through the 1940's.

Lesser known to the public, but influential among his colleagues, was Arthur Henry Young, who always signed his cartoons "Art Young." He suffered because of his devotion to left-wing causes, especially during the World War I period, but in his day, Young was the cartoonist's cartoonist. He was the first to produce a daily panel, for the *Chicago Inter Ocean,* but the best of his work appeared in *The Masses,* the militantly socialist magazine. Young, unlike earlier cartoonists, strove for simplicity. His technique was to focus attention on a main issue; for example, one of his cartoons showed a ragged child of the slums looking up at the night sky and saying: "Ooh, look at all the stars; they're thick as bedbugs." Actually, of course, Young was as much a social as a political cartoonist.

Two other great masters of the cartooning art were Rollin Kirby of the *New York World* and Edmund Duffy of the *Baltimore Sun,* both three-time Pulitzer Prize winners. Kirby was a fiercely liberal spirit who began cartooning in 1911 and hit his peak on the old *World* in the 1920's. His "Mr. Dry," a gaunt, black-frocked, blue-nosed caricature of the bigoted prohibitionists, became famous. Duffy exhibited his mastery of satire and caricature for the *Baltimore Sun* for 25 years. In this era, too, was Nelson Harding of the *Brooklyn Eagle,* twice a Pulitzer award winner.

Beginning his work for the *St. Louis Post-Dispatch* in 1913 and continuing until 1958 was Daniel R. ("Fitz") Fitzpatrick, whose devastating cartoon attacks won for him two Pulitzer Prizes. He was succeeded by Bill Mauldin, of Willie and Joe fame in *Stars and Stripes,* who quickly won a second Pulitzer Prize in 1959.

From the Herblock Book (*Beacon Press*)

"Fire!"—Herbert Block defends freedom, in the *Washington Post*.

Courtesy, New York World-Telegram

Rollin Kirby's famous "Two chickens in every garage" barb at Hoover, 1932.

Several Pulitzer Prize cartoonists were syndicated in the 1960's. Outstanding among them was Herbert L. Block of the *Washington Post,* whose distinctive style and extremely effective liberal comment made the signature "Herblock" widely known. Vaughn Shoemaker of the *Chicago Daily News,* Jacob Burck of the *Chicago Sun-Times,* Reg Manning of the *Arizona Republic,* C. D. Batchelor of the *New York Daily News,* and Bill Mauldin of the *St. Louis Post-Dispatch* were other leading artists.

Highly lucrative for the syndicates was the distribution of the drawings of a different set of artists—the comic strip and humorous panel originators. The battle between Pulitzer and Hearst for possession of Richard F. Outcault's "Yellow Kid" in 1896 set off a fierce competition in Sunday color comic sections and gave the name to yellow journalism. Early favorites like "Foxy Grandpa," "Buster Brown," and "Little Nemo" tickled newspaper readers with portrayals of humorous episodes centering about the same set of characters, but not relating a continuing story. Charles E. Schultze's gay grandpa who played tricks on boys and Winsor McKay's childish wonderland of Little Nemo both appeared in the *New York Herald* at the turn of the century. But Schultze soon deserted to Hearst's *American*. There "Foxy Grandpa" joined Outcault's "Buster Brown" and other Hearst comics in the same vein.[20]

One was Rudolph Dirks' "Katzenjammer Kids," longest-lived of all American comics. Dirks began drawing Hans, Fritz, Mama, and the Captain in an 1897 color comic. When he transferred to the *World* in 1912, Hearst successfully sued to retain rights to the title and King Features continued the strip into the 1960's. So did Dirks and his son, for United Features, using the name "The Captain and the Kids."

Other Hearst comic successes before 1910 were James Swinnerton's "Little Jimmy," Frederick Burr Opper's "Alphonse and Gaston" and "Happy Hooligan," and George Herriman's "Krazy Kat." In the *World* were "The Newlyweds," drawn by George McManus of later Jiggs and Maggie fame. The doings of the "Toonerville Folks" were first portrayed by Fontaine Fox in the *Chicago*

[20] The lore of the comics is related in Coulton Waugh, *The Comics* (New York: The Macmillan Company, 1947).

Courtesy, D. R. Fitzpatrick and St. Louis Post-Dispatch

"You gambled but I paid"—Daniel Fitzpatrick in a 1947 crusade.

Courtesy, Baltimore Sun

"The outstretched hand"—Edmund Duffy, 1939 Pulitzer Prize cartoon.

573

Post of 1908. H. C. (Bud) Fisher's "Mutt and Jeff" was the first regular daily cartoon strip, appearing in the *San Francisco Chronicle* in 1907. When John N. Wheeler organized the Bell Syndicate he obtained Fox and Fisher as two of his major drawing cards.

Arising as major competitors in the comic strip business by the end of World War I were the Hearst-owned King Features Syndicate and the *Chicago Tribune-New York Daily News* combine, whose comics were master-minded by Captain Joseph M. Patterson and Colonel Robert R. McCormick. Some of the longtime Hearst favorites, distributed in *Puck* as a Sunday comic section to millions of Hearst readers and also sold separately, were George McManus' "Bringing Up Father," dating from 1912; Cliff Sterrett's "Polly and Her Pals," 1912; James E. Murphy's "Toots and Casper," 1918; Billy De Beck's "Barney Google," 1919; Elzie C. Segar's "Thimble Theatre" featuring Olive Oyl and Popeye, 1919; Russ Westover's "Tillie the Toiler," 1921; Rube Goldberg's "Boob McNutt," 1924; and the most popular of all American comics, Chic Young's "Blondie," 1930. Winning millions of readers, too, for the *Chicago Tribune-New York Daily News* group have been Sidney Smith's "Andy Gump," 1917 (drawn since Smith's death in 1935 by Gus Edson); Frank King's "Gasoline Alley," 1919; Carl Ed's "Harold Teen," 1919; Martin Branner's "Winnie Winkle," 1920; Frank Willard's "Moon Mullins," 1923; and Harold Gray's "Little Orphan Annie," 1924.

People still called them "the funny papers" in this period. But two developments were under way which would change the character of the comics. One was the continuing story strip originating with "Andy Gump" in 1917. Many adults of the 1960's remember how baby Skeezix was abandoned on Uncle Walt's doorstep in the "Gasoline Alley" of 1921 to begin a chronicle of family life now in a third generation. Far less satisfying was the continuity of "Little Orphan Annie," whose waif has been lost from Daddy Warbucks every little while and has never finished school.

The other development was the action story, entering the comic pages with United Features' "Tarzan" in 1929 and soon extending through countless strips involving detectives, cowboys, adventurers, gangsters, and finally, supermen. The greatest detective of the comic strip world has been operating in Chester Gould's "Dick Tracy" strip for the McCormick-Patterson syndicate since 1931. His principal competitors have been Alex Raymond's "Rip Kirby," begun in 1945 for King Features, and Alfred Andriola's "Kerry Drake," a 1943 discovery. Swashbuckling adventure has been most cleverly portrayed by Milton Caniff whose "Terry and the Pirates" was a 1934 McCormick-Patterson gold mine. When Caniff left the *Chicago Tribune* in 1947 to start "Steve Canyon" for the *Chicago Sun-Times,* George Wunder continued involving Terry and his friends in "real life" adventures. The McCormick-Patterson syndicate also featured Zack Mosley's "Smilin' Jack" strip and a comics heroine, "Brenda Starr," drawn by Dale Messick, only woman creating a successful comic. Ham Fisher's "Joe Palooka" began fighting in 1931. The first of the superhumans was Buck Rogers, whose twenty-fifth-century era began in 1929. Superman himself, drawn by Jerry Siegel and Joe Schuster, caught on in 1939.

There still was some humor left in the comic pages, despite the invasion of crime, tragedy, death, and lurid action in the 1930's. Harry J. Tuthill's "The Bungle Family," begun in the *New York Evening Mail* in 1918, and Sol Hess' "The Nebbs," dating from 1923, were family favorites. So were Cal Alley's "The Ryatts," Carl Grubert's "The Berrys," and "Hi and Lois," a 1954 entry by Mort Walker and Dik Browne. New heroines were "Ella Cinders" drawn by Charlie Plumb and Bill Conselman since 1925, and "Dixie Dugan," created by J. P. McEvoy and John H. Striebel in 1929. Children and their antics were not ignored; some of the favorites were Edwina Dumm's "Cap Stubbs and Tippie," Ernie Bushmiller's "Fritzi Ritz and Nancy," Robert Brinkerhoff's "Little Mary Mixup," Harry Haenigsen's "Penny," and four King Features offerings—Carl Anderson's "Henry," Percy Crosby's "Skippy," Charles H. Kuhn's "Grandma," and Jimmy Hatlo's "Little Iodine." Sweeping to fame in this field in the 1950's was Hank Ketcham's "Dennis the Menace." Right behind were Charlie Brown, Lucy, Linus, and Snoopy of the "Peanuts" strip by Charles M. Schulz, for United Features.

Of all the comic characters, none became better known than Al Capp's "Li'l Abner." Capp began his work for United Features in 1935, and by the time Li'l Abner finally married Daisy Mae in 1952 the event was featured as a news item in many papers. Capp's strip sometimes had a social message for its readers going beyond the doings in Dogpatch. Considerably more subtle in its satire was Walt Kelly's "Pogo" sequence dealing with animal characters, a

1950's offering appealing to the intellectuals among the comic page readers.

The best humor has been that of the panel artists. Stars of the 1920's were Clare Briggs of the *New York Tribune*, T. A. (Tad) Dorgan of the *American* and *Journal*, and H. T. Webster of the *World* and *Herald Tribune*. Briggs originated "Mr. and Mrs.," still a *Herald Tribune* feature. Dorgan's panels were "For Better or Worse" and "Indoor Sports." The master performer was Webster, who invented Caspar Milquetoast for "The Timid Soul" and who drew "The Thrill That Comes Once in a Lifetime," "Life's Darkest Moment," "How to Torture Your Wife," and a humorous series on bridge addicts. Webster's "The Unseen Audience" effectively criticised radio and television until his death in 1952. In a similar tradition were J. R. Williams' "Out Our Way" and "Born Thirty Years Too Soon," Otto Soglow's "Little King," and Clifford McBride's "Napoleon."

Some comic strips have had educational qualities. "Mark Trail," drawn by Ed Dodd, has encouraged an understanding of wild life and conservation policies. "Rex Morgan," by Marvin Bradley and Frank Edgington, has an authentic scientific approach. Frank King's "Gasoline Alley," in a virtuous but pleasant way, has introduced its readers to problems of the little business man. King once obligingly sold the values of newspaper advertising in his strip. The religious theme of "David Crane," by Winslow Mortimer, was a noteworthy addition to the comics. "Dondi," by Irwin Hasen and Gus Edson, portrays the Americanization of a foreign waif. Some of the best recent strips—"Pogo," "Mark Trail," "David Crane," and "Dennis the Menace"—came from the Hall Syndicate.

The impact of the comics is enormous. Chic Young's "Blondie," consistently first in reader preference surveys, runs in 1,200 papers. It and other strips claim from 40 to 80 million readers in up to 50 countries. Mort Walker's "Beetle Bailey" caricature of Army life swept into 800 papers in a few years. Today a capable editor must watch the pulling power of his comics, his cartoonists and columnists, and his features (use "Dear Abby" or Ann Landers, or stick to Dorothy Dix?). And he must choose between running them or news when space is limited. The choices are hard ones, for the common denominators of journalism have proved their effectiveness.

ANNOTATED BIBLIOGRAPHY

Books:

Alsop, Joseph and Stewart, *The Reporter's Trade*. New York: Reynal & Company, 1958. A discussion of Washington reporting and compilation of the Alsop brothers' columns, 1946-58.

Baillie, Hugh, *High Tension*. New York: Harper & Brothers, 1959. Readable autobiography of the former United Press president.

Becker, Stephen, *Comic Art in America*. New York: Simon and Schuster, 1959. Surveys comics, political cartoons, magazine humor.

Cater, Douglass, *The Fourth Branch of Government*. Boston: Houghton Mifflin Company, 1959. Surveys the Washington press corps.

Childs, Marquis, and James B. Reston, eds., *Walter Lippmann and His Times*. New York: Harcourt, Brace and Company, 1959. Twelve essays by admirers of the columnist.

Clapper, Raymond, *Watching the World*. New York: Whittlesey House, 1944. A collection of the writings of a great Washington correspondent and columnist, edited by his wife.

Cooper, Kent, *Kent Cooper and the Associated Press*. New York: Random House, 1959. Autobiography of the former general manager. For the story of the AP's restrictive news exchange agreements, see his *Barriers Down* (New York: Farrar and Rinehart, 1942).

Dennis, Charles H., *Victor Lawson: His Time and His Work*. Chicago: University of Chicago Press, 1935. Contains information about the building up of *Chicago Daily News* foreign service.

Desmond, Robert W., *The Press and World Affairs*. New York: D. Appleton-Century Company, 1937. Traces press association developments.

Drewry, John E., ed., *Post Biographies of Famous Journalists*. Athens: University of Georgia Press, 1942. *More Post Biographies*. Athens: University of Georgia Press, 1947. The first volume contains reprints of *Saturday Evening Post* articles about, among others, Edgar A. Guest, Roy Howard, O. O. McIntyre, Don Marquis, Westbrook Pegler, Dorothy Thompson, and Walter Winchell. The second volume has articles about Hugh Baillie, Raymond Clapper, Jay N. ("Ding") Darling, Arthur Krock, Bill Mauldin, Drew Pearson, and Ernie Pyle.

Ellis, Elmer, ed., *Mr. Dooley at His Best*. New York: Charles Scribner's Sons, 1938. Writings of Finley Peter Dunne.

Fisher, Charles, *The Columnists*. New York: Howell, Soskin, Publishers, Inc., 1944. A lively study, outdated but still valuable.

Gramling, Oliver, *AP: The Story of News*. New York: Farrar and Rinehart, Inc., 1940. Unreliable in its survey of early period of AP history, on which Rosewater is the authority, the book contains valuable details for the modern era. The author is an Associated Press executive.

Johnson, Gerald W., *The Lines Are Drawn*. Philadelphia: J. B. Lippincott Company, 1958. A study of Pulitzer Prize cartoons.

Kramer, Dale, *Heywood Broun*. New York: A. A. Wyn, Inc., 1949. Biography of a liberal columnist.

McCabe, Charles R., ed., *Damned Old Crank*. New York: Harper & Brothers, 1951. Contains a chapter in which E. W. Scripps explains why he started the United Press, and gives some financial details.

McKelway, St. Clair, *Gossip: The Life and Times of Walter Winchell*. New York: The Viking Press, 1940. An expansion of a *New Yorker* profile, unflattering to the gossiper.

"M.E.S." His Book. New York: Harper & Brothers, 1918. A book commemorating Melville E. Stone's first 25 years as Associated Press general manager. Much of Stone's own writing and his major speeches are included, along with other historical materials. See also Stone's autobiography, *Fifty Years a Journalist*.

Morris, Joe Alex, *Deadline Every Minute: The Story of the United Press*. New York: Doubleday & Company, Inc., 1957. By a UP staff member, observing the press association's fiftieth anniversary. Highly readable; much information about both UP executives and the men who covered the news.

Murrell, William, *A History of American Graphic Humor, 1865-1938*. New York: The Macmillan Company, 1938. The second volume of a work which reproduces many newspaper cartoons.

Nevins, Allan, and George Weitenkampf, *A Century of Political Cartoons*. New York: Charles Scribner's Sons, 1944. The cartoons are presented in historical setting.

Phillips, Cabell, et al., eds., *Dateline: Washington*. Garden City: Doubleday & Company, Inc., 1949. The Washington correspondents write about their work and about the National Press Club.

Rosewater, Victor, *History of Cooperative News-Gathering in the United States*. New York: D. Appleton and Company, 1930. The authoritative source for the rise of the press associations.

Salisbury, Harrison, *Moscow Journal*. Chicago: University of Chicago Press, 1961. Problems of reporting Soviet news, 1949-53.

Spencer, Dick, III, *Pulitzer Prize Cartoons*. Ames: Iowa State College Press, 1953. A history of the winning cartoons since 1922.

Stokes, Thomas L., *Chip Off My Shoulder*. Princeton: Princeton University Press, 1940. An autobiography which explains the background of a distinguished reporter-columnist.

Sullivan, Mark, *The Education of an American*. New York: Doubleday, Doran & Company, 1938. The autobiography of one of the first political columnists.

The Best of H. T. Webster. New York: Simon and Schuster, 1953. One of the best collections of newspaper humorous drawings.

UNESCO, *News Agencies: Their Structure and Operations.* New York: Columbia University Press, 1953. Includes discussions of AP, UP, and INS and examines their roles in worldwide news distribution.

Watson, Elmo Scott, *A History of Newspaper Syndicates in the United States, 1865-1935.* Chicago: Publishers' Auxiliary, 1936. Source for the story of Western Newspaper Union and for rise of other early syndicates.

Waugh, Coulton, *The Comics.* New York: The Macmillan Company, 1947. A first-rate history of the comic pages; detailed but well-written and well-illustrated.

Weingast, David E., *Walter Lippmann.* New Brunswick: Rutgers University Press, 1949. An impartial study of the political, social, and economic views of an essentially conservative columnist.

Periodicals and Monographs:

Abbot, Willis J., "Melville E. Stone's Own Story," *Collier's,* LXV (February 7, 1920), 51. A well-written portrait of the AP general manager.

Alsop, Joseph and Stewart, "Our Own Inside Story," *Saturday Evening Post,* CCXXXI (November 8-15, 1958). How the columnists operated, 1946-58.

Barcus, Francis E., "A Content Analysis of Trends in Sunday Comics, 1900-1959," *Journalism Quarterly,* XXXVIII (Spring 1961), 171. The first report from a major study of comics at Boston University.

Benét, Stephen Vincent, "The United Press," *Fortune,* VII (May 1933), 67. A compact treatment of UP history and its 1933 status.

Harrison, Richard Edes, "AP," *Fortune,* XV (February 1937), 89. The rise of the AP and a contemporary picture of its operations.

Irwin, Will, "United Press," *Harper's Weekly,* LVIII (April 25, 1914), 6. An estimate by a top-flight newsman of early UP progress.

Marbut, Frederick B., "Congress and the Standing Committee of Correspondents," *Journalism Quarterly,* XXXVIII (Winter 1961), 52. The history of the press gallery rules is traced from 1879.

Pearson, Drew, "Confessions of 'an S.O.B.'," *Saturday Evening Post,* CCXXIX (November 3-24, 1956). Story of an "inside" columnist.

Smith, Henry Ladd, "The Rise and Fall of the Political Cartoon," *Saturday Review,* XXXVII (May 29, 1954), 7. A well-illustrated essay.

Strout, Richard L., "Tom Stokes: What He Was Like," *Nieman Reports,* XIII (July 1959), 9. A portrait of a great Washington reporter.

"The Funny Papers," *Fortune,* VII (April 1933), 45. An excellent major study, well-illustrated.

Chapter **24**

THE PRESS IN MODERN WAR

> This is a people's war, and to win it the people
> should know as much about it as they can.
>
> —Elmer Davis

THE GREAT WAR WHICH BEGAN IN EUROPE in August,
1914, completely altered the pattern of civilization which a comparatively peaceful nineteenth century had produced. By 1917 it
had become a World War, with the embarking of the United States
upon a "great crusade" to make the world safe for democracy. But
men found at war's end that they neither could restore the old
order nor build a peaceful new one. Political and social disillusionment, economic depression, and the rise of modern dictatorships
brought a second great war in 1939, and the designations World
War I and II came into the language. After 1950, when the United
States found itself leading a United Nations army into Korea to
fight the forces of Communist aggression, the world peered fear-
fully at the fateful numeral III. What happened to the American
press in these periods of international war, interrupted by what
proved to be only brief interludes of fitful peace, thus becomes
a continuing story; equally important is the account of the role
played by communication agencies during the periods of conflict.

No one could foresee in 1914 the ultimate consequences of Germany's transformation of a "Balkan incident" into a general European war. Even though the United States had entered into the

world diplomatic arena after the war with Spain, most Americans probably felt secure behind two oceans and were interested only in preserving peace as far as this country was concerned. No doubt the jesting comment of the *Chicago Herald* summarized this attitude: "Peace-loving citizens of this country will now rise up and tender a hearty vote of thanks to Columbus for having discovered America." [1]

Yet underneath this denial of concern by Americans for what was happening in the Old World lay the first instinctive reactions to the shattering of peace, reactions which were to lead to the declaration of war in 1917. The war was real to Americans only insofar as newspaper stories and pictures were able to make it so. But the newspapers of Maine reflected a spontaneous anti-German reaction immediately upon the news of the German declaration of war and invasion of Belgium.[2] As Americans read the vivid account by Richard Harding Davis of the entry of the German army into Brussels—"one unbroken steel-gray column . . . twenty-four hours later is still coming . . . not men marching, but a force of nature like a tidal wave, an avalanche"—and as they looked almost unbelievingly at pictures of the sacked city of Louvain, they became increasingly uncomfortable. Neutral though they were by presidential proclamation, many Americans found themselves unable to be neutral in thought. Thus began a two-and-a-half-year struggle between a natural desire to stay out of the war, and a growing realization that this was more than "just another war" beyond the seas.

It is important to record these first American reactions, since in the depths of later disillusionment, when it was evident that our participation in the war had failed to bring a lasting peace, a literature appeared which told a different story. British propagandists, American munitions makers, and cynical politicians had led gulli-

---

[1] As quoted in Mark Sullivan, *Our Times*, Vol. V (New York: Charles Scribner's Sons, 1933), p. 32. Sullivan's six-volume journalistic coverage of the years 1900-1925 reflects both the life and history of America in an engrossing manner.

[2] Edwin Costrell, "Newspaper Attitudes Toward War in Maine, 1914-17," *Journalism Quarterly*, XVI (December, 1939), 334. This measurement of an immediate anti-German reaction, before the introduction of concerted propaganda by the belligerents and before the cutting of cable communications with Germany, is significant.

ble Americans to an unnecessary slaughter, the theme song ran, carrying with it the implication that American newspapers were duped by foreign propagandists and by war-mongering capitalists, and thereby misled their readers. A quite convincing case was built upon partial evidence for such a thesis—ignoring or overriding such important factors as these:

The impact upon American public opinion of crisis events, such as the sinking of the "Lusitania," which were predominantly unfavorable to the German side;

The effects of Allied censorships and control of overseas communications in shaping the available news (as distinct from overt propaganda efforts);

The effects of socially-important pressure groups in shaping American thought;

The natural ties between English-speaking peoples, and the distaste of Americans for German "Kultur";

The legitimate pro-Allied decisions of American officials and diplomats based upon German-caused events;

The feeling that a strong British navy was less hazardous to American interests than a strong German navy;

And, most importantly, the basic United States objection to one-nation domination of Europe—an objection which led to two wars with German militarism in defense of the American national interest.[3]

The American press quite definitely was handicapped in its presentation of the war news by the existence of wartime censorships and by Allied control of cable facilities. All of the belligerents exercised close control over correspondents in the fighting areas. News of military actions was delayed by both sides, and official communiques often attempted to conceal news of reversals. Some correspondents managed to obtain beats on news of important battles, but largely as a matter of luck. Front area reporters more often won recognition for their feature stories than for their straight factual accounts, while military analysts in the various European

---

[3] Among the more responsible, but still misleading, books of the era of disillusionment were C. Hartley Grattan's *Why We Fought* (1929), Walter Millis' *Road to War* (1935), and H. C. Peterson's *Propaganda for War* (1939). For criticism of Peterson's attitude toward newspapers, see Ralph D. Casey, "The Press, Propaganda, and Pressure Groups," *The Annals of the American Academy of Political and Social Science*, CCXIX (January 1942), 68.

capitals provided the continuing story of the fighting along the sprawling western and eastern fronts. This news, after clearing the military censorships, still had to funnel through the London communications center.

This was the result of the British action in cutting the German Atlantic cable on August 5, 1914. Stories written in Berlin, Vienna, and in neutral capitals thereafter had to travel through London to reach the United States. German attempts to use wireless for news transmission were relatively unsuccessful, although the powerful Nauen station on German soil was effective for a time and wireless reports were transmitted from German East Africa until Allied troops took over that colonial territory. Thus, while American correspondents remained with the German armies and were stationed in Berlin until 1917, their reporting of the German version of events was severely handicapped. In addition to this censorship of news in transit, the English had a domestic censorship under the Defense of the Realm Act (DORA), which affected all news published in Britain or originating there. Since it was easiest for American newsmen to take their news from English newspapers, censorship again had its effect upon what an American could read.[4]

Still, war maps in American newspaper offices reflected fairly accurately the positions of the contending forces. And both sides were able to put forth their military claims and political arguments to the rest of the world. Both circulated contrived propaganda, beginning with the Allied stories of German atrocities against Belgian and French civilians. The Germans countered with their own claims of Allied atrocities. But at this point the impact that events have upon public attitudes made itself felt. The heartless German sack of Louvain, to compel Belgian obedience, already was a demonstrated fact. The picture of a relentless German military machine was being built up in American minds by the sweep of the Kaiser's armies almost to Paris. The British "contemptibles" and the French poilus were the brave defenders, not only of Paris, but of western democracy against German authoritarianism. It was not hard to

[4] The best balanced picture of American press difficulties in covering the war is found in Ralph O. Nafziger's *The American Press and Public Opinion During the World War, 1914 to April, 1917* (Ph.D. thesis, University of Wisconsin, 1936). Nafziger ranks overt propaganda efforts as having less effect upon American news presentation than (1) rigid war censorships and (2) limited and controlled communications facilities.

believe stories of German atrocities and to discredit Berlin's counter-charges as propaganda when the weight of events pointed that way. Correspondents who attempted to pin down the atrocity stories could not do so, but as the war proceeded such factual proof seemed less and less necessary to increasingly partisan readers. Word-of-mouth rumors and embellishments of stories by public speakers added to the propaganda stream even faster than did newspaper stories. When, in the postwar years, the extremes of the Belgian atrocity stories became known, the disillusionment which resulted made it hard to convince Americans of the World War II era that there really were such places as Dachau, Buchenwald, and Belsen.

The course of events was rapidly bolstering pro-Allied sentiment in the United States. The *New York Times* printed the various "white papers" giving each belligerent power's version of the events leading up to the war, but Germany's obvious preparation for war and smashing early victories added reason to believe the Allied versions, imperfectly as they were presented. Natural ties of many Americans to the English traditions, which were particularly strong among social and intellectual leaders, made it fashionable to be pro-British. Yet large segments of the population opposed America's going to war up to the last, for various reasons. The Middle West was more isolationist than the seaboard sections and was suspicious of the pro-Allied easterners. The Irish, a strong minority, were naturally anti-British because of the Irish civil war, although this did not necessarily make them pro-German, it should be pointed out. The large groups of German-Americans who were, on the whole, loyal to the United States, were at the same time naturally sympathetic with the aims of the Fatherland. They regarded Germany's ambitions as being no more dangerous or imperialistic than the aims of Britain, France, and Russia.

All in all, there was never much pro-German sentiment expressed outside of German-American circles. But there was antiwar sentiment, and there was anti-British feeling. The latter was fanned by rigid British control of the high seas. The British greatly expanded the definition of war-contraband articles, and seized ships bound for neutral ports if they were suspected of carrying goods to be transshipped to Germany. Highhanded British control of sea trade brought numerous protests from Washington to London, which

American ambassador Walter Hines Page sympathetically handed to his friends in the British Foreign Office. The old issue of "freedom of the seas" was being raised in the American mind against the ancient enemy when suddenly a German action intervened to make the complaint against British maritime arrogance seem somewhat academic, involving as it did only the question of property rights.

This decisive event was the torpedoing of English Cunard line ship "Lusitania," then the queen of the Atlantic run. When the "Lusitania" went down off the Irish coast on May 7, 1915, with the loss of 1,198 of the 1,924 persons aboard—including 114 of 188 American passengers—Germany celebrated the accomplishment of her U-boat captain. But resentment ran high in the United States, particularly when it was remembered that an Imperial German Embassy advertisement warning travelers on Allied ships that they did so "at their own risk" had appeared in New York newspapers the morning the "Lusitania" left port. President Wilson held to his decision to remain neutral, uttering his famous phrase, "There is such a thing as a man being too proud to fight." Public opinion calmed somewhat, but many newspapers, civic leaders, and groups which theretofore had professed neutrality now swung to the Allied camp.

Confirming the rapidly growing American belief that the German cause was a dastardly one was another event of July, 1915. That month the *New York World, Providence Journal,* and other papers published the contents of some documents obtained by the Secret Service from pro-German circles. The story which was unfolded was one of an intricate system of espionage and sabotage organized in the United States by German agents and diplomatic officials. From that time on, all pro-German elements were suspect. Pacifists, who included many distinguished Americans, also fell from favor, particularly after the pathetic performance of those aboard Henry Ford's "peace ship."

Even though Germany relaxed its submarine warfare after months of diplomatic note-writing by President Wilson, the summer of 1916 was dominated by pro-Allied arguments and by talk of preparedness. Former President Theodore Roosevelt and General Leonard Wood opened a volunteer training camp at Plattsburg. President Wilson adopted the preparedness issue during his successful re-election campaign, even though his most effective slogan was "He kept us out of war."

In December, 1916, Wilson suggested that a "peace without victory" be arranged through the auspices of the United States. The peace would be kept in the future by a League to Enforce Peace, which for years had been advocated by former President William Howard Taft and other leading American internationalists. But Wilson's hopes of the United States serving as a neutral arbiter were dashed by two final German actions.

One was resumption of unrestricted submarine warfare by the Germans in February, 1917. This brought a break in diplomatic relations. Clinching the American decision was the Allied interception of German Foreign Minister Zimmermann's note to the Mexican government, offering Mexico the return of Texas, New Mexico, and Arizona after an American defeat, if Mexico would ally itself with Germany. The text of the note, given to the Associated Press unofficially, created a sensation. The sinking of three American ships by U-boats in March brought Wilson's war call on April 2—"The world must be made safe for democracy"— and the declaration of war on April 6. Wilson's masterful phrases played no small part in the determination of the issue. His denunciation of a group of 11 senators, led by Robert La Follette of Wisconsin, as "a little group of willful men" for filibustering against arming of American merchant ships in early March did much to discredit the bitter-end opponents of war.

Some periodicals had been pro-Ally almost from the start. Among the most outspoken were the old *Life* magazine, Henry Watterson's *Louisville Courier-Journal*, and the *New York Herald*. The *New York Times* was solidly pro-Ally, along with the *World* and most other New York newspapers. After the sinking of the "Lusitania" the number of anti-interventionist newspapers dwindled. William Randolph Hearst's chain of papers stood out as bitterly anti-British and was tarred as pro-German because Hearst made special efforts to obtain German-originated news to balance Allied-originated stories. Other hold-outs against war were the *New York Evening Mail* (which had been bought secretly by German agents), *Chicago Tribune, Cincinnati Enquirer, Cleveland Plain Dealer, Washington Post, Milwaukee Sentinel, Los Angeles Times, San Francisco*

Chronicle, and *San Francisco Call.*[5] All, of course, supported the war once it was declared. William Jennings Bryan's *Commoner, La Follette's Magazine,* and Oswald Garrison Villard's *Nation* and *New York Evening Post* were pacifist. And the German-language press was in the main pro-German.

Now that America was in the war, President Wilson turned to the problem of stimulating the country's morale and of educating the people to the task ahead. Himself a master of the art of creating public opinion, he knew the value of using the agencies of communication. And although he wanted those agencies to remain as free as possible, he knew that some control was necessary.

Only a week after the declaration of war, Wilson appointed a Committee on Public Information. Its job primarily was one of disseminating facts about the war. It also was to coordinate government propaganda efforts, and to serve as the government's liaison with newspapers. It drew up a voluntary censorship code under which editors would agree to refrain from printing material which might aid the enemy. Before it was through, the committee found itself "mobilizing the mind of the world," and Mark Sullivan characterized it as an American contribution to the science of war. George Creel, the newspaperman who was named by Wilson to direct the committee's work, explained that "it was a plain publicity proposition, a vast enterprise in salesmanship, the world's greatest adventure in advertising." [6]

Why the United States, entering the war so late, should be credited with taking a foremost part in informational and propaganda activities, might not seem clear. The work of Wellington House, a British propaganda agency, in mobilizing neutral opinion on the side of the Allies was a notable achievement. But the British did not unify the work being carried on in their various regular governmental agencies until January, 1917, when a Department of Information was created. It was February, 1918, before two British press lords were named to coordinate posts: Lord Beaverbrook becoming Minister of Information and Lord Northcliffe assuming

---

[5] Frank Luther Mott, *American Journalism* (New York: The Macmillan Company, 1950), p. 616.
[6] George Creel, *How We Advertised America* (New York: Harper & Brothers, 1920), p. 4.

the title of Director of Propaganda in Enemy Countries. This organization was popularly known as Crewe House. The Germans used a loosely organized Press Conference to coordinate the informational and propaganda activities of their various bureaus while the French operated only through the Maison de la Presse and their regular governmental agencies.[7]

The opportunity which Wilson gave to Creel was a greater one than any other person had enjoyed in the propaganda arena. Creel was a liberal-minded and vigorously competent product of New York, Kansas City, and Denver journalism. He was intensely anxious to achieve every possible task which his committee might embrace, and he eventually mobilized 150,000 Americans to carry out its varied and far-flung missions.

Creel's first job was to open up government news channels to the Washington correspondents. Officials were so fearful that any slip might give information to a German spy that they were treating much routine news as vital military secrets. Creel insisted that only news of troop movements, ship sailings, and other events of strictly military character should be withheld. He issued a brief explanatory code calling upon the newspapers to censor such news themselves, voluntarily. Throughout the war newspaper editors generally went beyond Creel's minimum requests in their desire to aid the war effort. In return they were rewarded by Creel's efforts to keep other news flowing.

What was needed, Creel said, was not censorship or suppression of news, but "unparalleled openness." The United States was "the arsenal of democracy," and factual reports upon its production achievements, its bumper food crops, its mobilization effort, and its growing war spirit would encourage both Americans and their allies. Neutral nations would be impressed by receiving evidence of America's war effort and the enemy peoples would be discouraged. In short, Creel used factual dissemination of news as a basic weapon in achieving the purposes of war propaganda: to mobilize his own people against the enemy, to preserve the friendship and morale of his country's allies, to win over neutral peoples, and to demoralize the enemy.

Creel soon found that the Washington correspondents needed

[7] Harold D. Lasswell, *Propaganda Technique in the World War* (New York: Peter Smith, 1927), p. 20.

help in covering the home front activities. His staff compiled information and served as an agency for the release of special war stories. In May, 1917, the CPI began publishing an *Official Bulletin* in which releases were reprinted in newspaper form. Before the war was over this publication reached a daily circulation of 118,-000. A weekly newspaperman prepared a digest of the news for rural papers. Still photographs, plates, and mats also were utilized.

There were only two serious incidents involving CPI news releases. One became known as the "Fourth of July fake" of 1917. The first military transports to sail for France reported that they had been attacked unsuccessfully by a German submarine pack during the night. Creel wrote a press statement for Navy Secretary Daniels which, as Creel admitted later, somewhat overplayed the incident and carried a patriotic Fourth of July flavor. The next day, however, the Associated Press released a message from its correspondent in Ireland, who said that there had been no submarine attack. A storm broke about Creel's head, in the press and in Congress. What never became known at the time was the fact that the transports were being convoyed in four separate units, and that the AP news source was not with the ships which were attacked. Creel was guilty only of overwriting, and not of fabricating a story, as charged. In the other principal case, a CPI picture caption writer said in March, 1918, that "thousands and thousands" of air frames were being rushed to France, when in reality the American aircraft manufacturing program was hopelessly bogged down. The offending material was quickly recalled from newspapers, but unfortunately for Creel, it appeared in his *Official Bulletin* and gave his enemies new ammunition.

A historian who studied the accuracy of CPI news releases years later came to this conclusion: "One of the most remarkable things about the charges against the CPI is that, of the more than 6,000 news stories it issued, so few were called into question at all. It may be doubted that the CPI's record for honesty will ever be equalled in the official war news of a major power." [8] The same high opinion of Creel's honesty and diligence in keeping news flowing was expressed by other students of CPI activities.

[8] Walton E. Bean, "The Accuracy of Creel Committee News, 1917-1919: An Examination of Cases," *Journalism Quarterly*, XVIII (September 1941), 272. The major study of the CPI is James R. Mock and Cedric Larson, *Words That Won the War* (Princeton: Princeton University Press, 1939).

Creel's imaginative conception of his job was fully expressed in the work of the CPI in other areas than the dissemination of news. It was in the use of several media and techniques that his publicity, advertising, and salesmanship talents came into full play. Creel rallied advertising men, painters, sculptors, illustrators, cartoonists, photographers, public speakers, writers, movie stars, singers—even college professors—to the colors. They used their skills to stimulate military enlistments, to obtain cooperation for Bernard Baruch's industrial mobilization and for Herbert Hoover's food conservation program, to sell Liberty bonds, and in every other possible way to propagandize in behalf of the war effort, both at home and abroad. Ultimately, the CPI's aim was to gain worldwide support for President Wilson's program for winning the war and the peace to follow.

Creel asked major advertisers and the publications themselves to donate space for various government campaigns, for the Red Cross, and other war-related activities. The advertising agencies were organized, and their copy men and artists were used to create newspaper and magazine advertising, streetcar placards, and outdoor posters. The artists in the CPI's division of pictorial publicity, headed by Charles Dana Gibson, contributed stirring posters. The infant motion picture industry produced films of both patriotic and instructive nature. Its stars, including Douglas Fairbanks and Mary Pickford, sparked Liberty bond sales, as did opera and stage personalities. Booth Tarkington, Mary Roberts Rinehart, Samuel Hopkins Adams, and other writers contributed their talents. Some 75,000 anonymous Americans, called the "four-minute men," stepped forward wherever a few citizens gathered, to deliver canned talks on such subjects as "Why We Are Fighting," "Maintaining Morals and Morale," "The Importance of Speed," and "Where Did You Get Your Facts?" The college professors served in a division of pamphleteering. It produced a *War Cyclopedia* and 75 million pieces of printed matter. Historian Guy Stanton Ford of the University of Minnesota headed the division, which numbered among its scholars such noted historians as Carl Becker of Cornell University, Evarts B. Greene of the University of Illinois, and Frederic L. Paxson of the University of Wisconsin.[9]

[9] Paxson eventually wrote a three-volume series titled *American Democracy and the World War*. The war itself is covered in detail in the second volume, *America at War, 1917-1918* (Boston: Houghton Mifflin Company, 1939).

"All the News That's Fit to Print."

The New York Times.

THE WEATHER

LXVIII . NO. 22,206. NEW YORK, MONDAY, NOVEMBER 11, 1918. TWENTY-FOUR PAGES. TWO CENTS

RMISTICE SIGNED, END OF THE WAR!
BERLIN SEIZED BY REVOLUTIONISTS;
NEW CHANCELLOR BEGS FOR ORDER;
OUSTED KAISER FLEES TO HOLLAND

WAR ENDS AT 6 O'CLOCK THIS MORNING

The State Department in Washington Made the Announcement at 2:45 o'Clock.

ARMISTICE WAS SIGNED IN FRANCE AT MIDNIGHT

Terms Include Withdrawal from Alsace-Lorraine, Disarming and Demobilization of Army and Navy, and Occupation of Strategic Naval and Military Points.

By The Associated Press.

WASHINGTON, Monday, Nov. 11, 2:48 A. M.—The armistice between Germany, on the one hand, and the allied Governments and the United States, on the other, has been signed.

The State Department announced at 2:45 o'clock this morning that Germany had signed.

The department's announcement simply said: "The armistice has been signed."

The world war will end this morning at 6 o'clock, Washington time, 11 o'clock Paris time.

The armistice was signed by the German representatives at midnight.

This announcement was made by the State Department at 2:50 o'clock this morning.

The announcement was made verbally by an officila of the State Department in this form:

"The armistice has been signed. It was signed at 5 o'clock A. M., Paris time, [midnight, New York time,] and hostilities will cease at 11 o'clock this morning, Paris time, [6 o'clock, New York time.]

The terms of the armistice, it was announced, will not be made public until later. Military men here, however, regard it as certain that they include:

Immediate retirement of the German military forces from France, Belgium, and Alsace-Lorraine.

Disarming and demobilization of the German armies.

Occupation by the allied and American forces of such strategic points in Germany as will make impossible a renewal of hostilities.

Delivery of part of the German High Seas Fleet and a certain number of submarines to the allied and American naval forces.

Disarmament of all other German warships

BERLIN TROOPS JOIN REVOLT

Reds Shell Building in Which Officers Vainly Resist.

THRONGS DEMAND REPUBLIC

Revolutionary Flag on Royal Palace — Crown Prince's Palace Also Seized.

GENERAL STRIKE IS BEGUN

Burgomaster and Police Submit—War Office Now Under Socialist Control.

LONDON, Nov. 10.—The greater part of Berlin is in control of revolutionists, the former Kaiser has fled to Holland, and Friedrich Ebert, the new Socialist Chancellor, has taken command of the situation. The revolt is spreading throughout Germany with great rapidity.

Dispatches received in London today announce these startling developments. The Workmen's and Soldiers' Council is now administering the municipal government of the German capital.

The War Ministry has submitted, and its acts are valid only when countersigned by a Socialist representative. The official Wolff telegraphic agency has been taken over by the Reds.

The red flag has been hoisted over the royal palace and the Brandenburg Gate. The former Crown Prince's palace is also in possession of the revolutionists.

There was severe fighting in Berlin between 8 and 10 o'clock last night and a violent cannonade was heard from the heart of the city.

Burgomaster and Police Join.

A Copenhagen dispatch states that Dr. Liebknecht, the famous Socialist, who spent many months in prison for antagonizing the German Imperial Government and who was recently released, has issued the following announcement in Berlin in behalf of the Workmen's and Soldiers' Council:

"The Presidency of the police, as well as the Chief Command, is in our hands. Our comrades will be released."

A dispatch from Berne states that the Burgomaster of Berlin has placed himself and his staff at the disposal of the new Government.

Some German newspapers describe the movement as Bolshevism. The people are shouting "Long live the Republic!" and singing the "Marseillaise."

Officers Shelled by Reds.

When revolutionary soldiers attempted to enter a building in Berlin in which they supposed that a number of offi-

Kaiser Fought Hindenburg's Call for Abdication; Failed to Get Army's Support in Keeping Throne

By GEORGE RENWICK.

Kaiser Shivered as He Signed Abdication

Socialist Chancellor Appeals to All Germans To Help Him Save Fatherland from Anarchy

GERMAN DYNASTIES BEING WIPED OUT

King of Wuerttemberg Abdicates — Sovereign of Saxony to Follow Suit.

PRINCES MAY BE EXILED

Socialists Are Demanding That Every Sovereign in the Empire Shall be Dethroned.

LONDON, Nov. 10.—A Havas dispatch from Basle says:

"Wilhelm II., the reigning King of the monarchy of Württemberg, abdicated on Friday night."

MORE WARSHIPS JOIN THE REDS

Four Dreadnoughts in Kiel Harbor Espouse the Revolutionary Cause.

GUARDSHIPS ALSO GO OVER

Those Protecting Mines in the Great Belt and the Baltic Abandon Their Posts.

The famous Armistice Day edition of the *New York Times.*

The publications of the college professors became a part of Creel's campaign abroad. Creel distributed materials directly in Allied countries, in neutral areas, and inside the enemy countries themselves. His principal weapons were the ringing phrases of Woodrow Wilson, who was offering freedom to submerged nationalities, a just settlement of political boundaries, open covenants of peace, protection for the vanquished enemy peoples once their rulers had been overthrown, and an association of nations which would preserve the peace. It was one of Creel's newsmen assistants, Edgar G. Sisson, who suggested that Wilson's speeches be condensed into a journalistic summary for distribution abroad, and thus prompted Wilson to produce his famed "Fourteen Points." The result was that when Wilson journeyed to Europe for the peace conference he was the object of mass worship. His political opponents in the United States, who feared Wilson's motives and his prestige, bitterly attacked Creel as Wilson's personal publicity man in this phase of CPI activity.

All in all, the Committee on Public Information performed extraordinarily well, thrown together hastily as it was for only a brief time. Among those who participated, and who admired Creel's techniques, were some leaders of the rudimentary public relations profession: Edward L. Bernays, Carl Byoir, and Ivy Lee. Creel had the money to experiment (although CPI cost but 5 million dollars when the books were balanced), and he opened the eyes of professional publicists to the uses of the various media. Most importantly, he demonstrated the importance of taking the public into the confidence of an institution, in this case the government, and the virtue of basing any opinion-forming campaign upon full dissemination of information.

It is evident that Creel and the Committee on Public Information had little to do with the problem of censorship, even though Creel sometimes was called the country's censor. The CPI had a few brushes with press associations and newspapers over cooperation in observing the voluntary code, the most persistent rebel being John R. McLean's *Washington Post*. There also were inadvertent disclosures of military information in the thousands of publications in the country. But the principal controversies involving freedom of speech and maintenance of individual civil liberties resulted from suppression and censorship of ideas rather than of news.

The Espionage Act of June 15, 1917, provided the opening wedge for suppression of those who were considered to be disloyal to the American and Allied war cause. A proposed amendment to the bill would have empowered the President to establish a mandatory censorship over publication of military or defense information deemed possibly useful to the enemy. Strong protests from newspaper publishers and many other citizens, and an insistence by a majority of the House of Representatives that a compulsory news censorship be avoided, resulted in the defeat of that amendment. But another section of the bill provided for a more remote censorship through use of the power of the federal government to control materials carried in the mails.

Among the crimes, punishable by heavy fines and imprisonment, which the Espionage Act defined were the willful making of false reports or false statements with the intent to interfere with the successful operation of the military or naval forces, and willful attempts to promote disloyalty in the armed forces or to obstruct recruitments. A section on use of the mails empowered the Postmaster General to declare unmailable all letters, circulars, newspapers, pamphlets, books and other materials violating provisions of the act. In the case of a newspaper or magazine, whenever the postal authorities declared a particular issue unmailable, the publisher affected had to make new application for second-class mail privileges, and usually had to carry his case against the Postmaster General into the courts. In practical application, the postal section of the Espionage Act gave Postmaster General Albert S. Burleson life-or-death authority over publications using the mails for distribution.

The axe fell most heavily upon Socialist organs and German-American newspapers, with a few other pacifist or anti-Ally publications losing their mail privileges. The *American Socialist* was banned from the mails immediately, and was soon followed by *Solidarity*, journal of the left-wing International Workers of the World—the much-feared anti-capitalistic IWW. A vociferous advocate of the Irish independence movement, Jeremiah A. O'Leary, lost mailing privileges for his publication, *Bull*, in July, 1917, for opposing wartime cooperation with the British. The magazine *The Masses*, brilliantly edited by socialist Max Eastman, felt the ban in August for publishing an issue containing four antiwar cartoons and a poem defending radical leaders Emma Goldman and Alexander Berkman. An indictment against the editors under the Espionage Act was dismissed in 1919.

Altogether some 75 papers either lost their mailing privileges during the first year of the Espionage Act, or retained them only by agreeing to print nothing more concerning the war. The best known were two Socialist dailies, the *New York Call* and Victor Berger's *Milwaukee Leader*. Berger, a Socialist member of Congress, was convicted on charges of sedition and disloyalty by a jury which considered his Socialist affiliation to be a wartime crime, and was expelled from the House of Representatives, to which he had been re-elected while under indictment. The U. S. Supreme Court upheld the Post Office ban on the *Leader* in a 1921 decision, and it was not until June, 1921, that the *Leader* and the *Call* had their second-class mail privileges reinstated. The German-language press likewise was hard hit by mail bans and prosecutions and declined one-half in numbers and in circulation during the war.

Other papers felt the weight of public opinion against those who did not wholeheartedly support the war. The Hearst newspapers, which had bitterly opposed American entry into the war and which continued to be clearly anti-Ally even though they supported the American war effort itself, were widely attacked. Hearst was hanged in effigy, his papers were boycotted in some places, and he himself was denounced as disloyal. The *New York Tribune*, itself a strong critic of the way in which the Wilson administration was conducting the war, ran a famous cartoon showing a snake coiled in the flag, with the snake's body spelling the legend "Hears-ss-ss-t." Oswald Garrison Villard's pacifist views and defenses of civil liberties brought such a decline in the fortunes of the *New York Evening Post* that he was forced to sell it in 1918, and one issue of the *Nation* was held up in the New York Post Office because it carried an editorial titled "Civil Liberty Dead."

The powers of the government to control expression of opinion were strengthened by the passage of two other laws. The Trading-with-the-Enemy Act of October, 1917, authorized censorship of all communications moving in or out of the United States and provided that translations of newspaper or magazine articles published in a foreign language could be demanded by the Post Office—a move to keep the German-language papers in line. The Sedition Act of May, 1918, amended and broadened the Espionage Act by making it a crime to write or publish "any disloyal, profane, scurrilous or abusive language about the form of government of the United States or the Constitution, military or naval forces, flag, or the uniform" or to use language intended to bring these ideas and institutions "into contempt, scorn, contumely, or disrepute." The application of these broad provisions by the Post Office in banning publications from the mails gave the Postmaster General immense powers which he hesitated to use. The memory of the blundering Sedition Act of 1798 kept him from using his authority to harass orthodox Republican opponents of the administration, and the brunt of persecution continued to fall upon the unpopular radical and pro-German minorities.

Former President Theodore Roosevelt was asking heatedly why the Hearst newspapers had not been denied mail privileges (some Republicans said Hearst escaped because he was a Democrat). Roosevelt also was writing editorials for the *Kansas City Star* criticising the administration, and was speaking strongly against what he called its incompetence and softness in dealing with the enemy. George Harvey, once one of Wilson's political supporters, was editorializing against members of the president's cabinet in the *North American Review*. Senator Robert La Follette of Wisconsin, who was politically crucified by an error which the Associated Press made in reporting one of his speeches,[10] likewise was a possible candidate for prosecution.

The Department of Justice, however, moved against lesser known persons like the IWW leaders, who were arrested and imprisoned, and like Mrs. Rose Pastor Stokes, who got a ten-year sentence for writing a letter to the *Kansas City Star* saying "No government which is for the profiteers can also be for the people, and I am for the people, while the government is for the profiteers." The verdict against Mrs. Stokes was reversed in 1920. But not so fortunate was the four-time Socialist party presidential candidate, Eugene V. Debs. When he told a Socialist convention in June, 1918, that the Allies were "out for plunder" and defended the Bolshevists in Rus-

---

[10] The AP committed a familiar journalistic blunder by adding a "no" to a La Follette statement concerning the American declaration of war, making it read "we had no grievance." An unsuccessful move to oust La Follette from the Senate resulted.

sia, he was jailed. Debs' conviction for violation of the Espionage and Sedition Acts was upheld unanimously by the Supreme Court. He received the record Socialist party presidential vote total of 920,000 while campaigning in 1920 from a federal prison, however, and was pardoned by President Harding in December, 1921.

The wartime atmosphere was favorable to restriction of civil liberties. State laws were adopted generally which contained anti-pacifist, anti-Red, and criminal syndicalism clauses designed to protect business and industry against radical-inspired strikes and violence. Mobs and citizens' committees took care of unpopular persons, including Americans of German ancestry. Many an American was persuaded by community pressure to buy more Liberty bonds than he desired to own. Prosecutors, juries, and judges went beyond the words of the Espionage and Sedition Acts, often because of public pressure. Zechariah Chafee, Jr., the distinguished Harvard law professor, documented the damage done to the spirit of the Constitutional guarantee of free speech in his 1920 work, *Freedom of Speech*.[11] In such circumstances the great bulk of the American press was fortunate to escape the harassments visited upon its Socialist and German-language fringe, or a direct and violent censorship.

Censorship of foreign communications sent by cable, telephone, or telegraph, as provided in the Trading-with-the-Enemy Act, was not a new device. Cable and telegraph communications had been under partial control in the Spanish-American War and use of telegraph lines was limited by the War Department during the Civil War. President Wilson ordered trans-ocean wireless stations in the United States put under government supervision at the opening of the war in 1914, as a part of the neutrality program. In April, 1917, an executive order put telephone and telegraph lines leading into and out of the United States under War Department authority, and submarine cables under Navy jurisdiction. The Trading-with-the-Enemy Act provided for a Censorship Board, which Wilson established in October, 1917, to coordinate control of communications facilities.

The board was mainly concerned with outgoing messages and news dispatches. Its principal operations involved communications

[11] Enlarged and brought up to date in his *Free Speech in the United States* (Cambridge: Harvard University Press, 1941).

with Spain, Latin-America, and the Orient. Censorship stations were established at control points along the southern borders. News filed to Europe also was checked. In some cases the censors intervened because news stories did not correctly represent the United States to the world. In a few other cases, news of labor disturbances in the United States was suppressed as detrimental to Allied morale. There were few causes for complaint against the Censorship Board, however, and it received a "job well done" commendation.[12]

Other censorship activities involved banning of some books from the mails, voluntary deletions from motion picture films at the suggestion of government authorities, and regulation of personal mail going to and from the armed forces.

American war correspondents in France found themselves freer to observe military actions of the American Expeditionary Force than those of the other Allied armies. In General Pershing's area correspondents could go into the front lines without military escorts, they could follow the fighting advances, and they could roam the rear areas, living where they chose. This had not been the case for correspondents with the British, French, and German forces in the early years of the war. But everything the correspondents wrote went through the censorship of the press section of the Military Intelligence Service, headed by Major Frederick Palmer, formerly of the Associated Press. News of general engagements, of casualties suffered, and of troop identifications was releasable only if it had been mentioned in official communiques. Press officers also were attached to the training camps and cantonments at home.

Notable among the early war reporting of Americans was Richard Harding Davis' story of the entry of the German army into Brussels, written for the *New York Tribune* and its syndicate, and Will Irwin's beat on the battle of Ypres, also printed in the *Tribune*. Irwin was one of several correspondents who represented American magazines in Europe, having been sent over in 1914 by *Collier's*. However, the brunt of the news coverage responsibility fell upon the men in the European capital bureaus and those who served as military analysts. Some of the leaders were Karl H. von Wiegand of the United Press, Sigrid Schultz of the *Chicago Trib-*

[12] James R. Mock, *Censorship 1917* (Princeton: Princeton University Press, 1941), pp. 81, 93.

une, and Cyril Brown of the *New York Times* in Berlin; Paul Scott Mowrer of the *Chicago Daily News* and Wythe Williams of the *New York Times* in Paris, and Edward Price Bell of the *Chicago Daily News* in London. Frank H. Simonds of the *New York Tribune* did distinguished work as a military critic.

There were some 500 American correspondents for newspapers, magazines, press associations, and syndicates in Europe by 1915 and the number was augmented when American troops joined the fighting. About 40 actually covered the actions of the AEF. Among the best known by-liners was Fred S. Ferguson of the United Press, who beat his competitors in reporting the battle of Saint-Mihiel by writing an advance story, based on the American battle plan, and having it filed section by section as the battle proceeded. Webb Miller of the United Press and Henry Wales of INS also won prominence, along with Edwin L. James of the *New York Times,* Martin Green of the *New York World,* and Junius Wood of the *Chicago Daily News.* Floyd Gibbons of the *Chicago Tribune* was hit by German machine-gun fire and lost an eye.

Also writing for the American reading public were such personalities as Irvin Cobb for the *Saturday Evening Post,* John T. McCutcheon and Ring Lardner for the *Chicago Tribune,* Walter Duranty for the *New York Times,* and Heywood Broun for the *New York Tribune.* Covering the Russian Revolution was a group of correspondents led by Frazier Hunt of the *Chicago Tribune.* Among them were two newspaper women, Rheta Dorr of the *New York Mail* and Bessie Beatty of the *San Francisco Bulletin.* Peggy Hull of the Newspaper Enterprise Association accompanied American troops to Siberia.

A soldiers' journalism also sprouted during wartime, the best known example being the *Stars and Stripes.* The eight-page paper was established in Paris in February, 1918, and quickly became the favorite reading matter of the AEF. Its editors were given freedom of action and comment unheard of in ordinary Army circles and they filled their pages with news, editorials, features, cartoons, and advertising. Harold Ross, later editor of the *New Yorker,* became the chief editor, assisted by such well-known newspapermen as Grantland Rice and Alexander Woollcott. Other overseas units had their publications, as did all of the camps in the United States.

With the coming of the Armistice, coverage in Europe turned

to the routine of the Army of Occupation in Germany, and to the postwar political and economic news, centering about the Versailles peace conference. In the United States a reaction set in against President Wilson's proposed League of Nations. Wilson's physical breakdown while on a nationwide speaking tour in defense of the League left the internationalists leaderless, and the assaults of the Republican Senate leader, Henry Cabot Lodge of Massachusetts, and of the tireless senatorial orators, Hiram W. Johnson of California and William E. Borah of Idaho, had their effect. The peace treaty was loaded with reservations affecting American participation in the League of Nations and the World Court to the point where the ailing Wilson refused to accept a compromise. The United States Senate failed to ratify the treaty, thereby backing out of the international association which Wilson had sponsored. As far as the newspapers and magazines were concerned, the League enjoyed a good press on the whole, right up to the end. Republican politics and Wilson's mistakes killed it.

The other major postwar reaction was a gigantic "Red scare," stimulated in part by the events of the Russian Revolution and also by the threat of the IWW movement. Attorney General A. Mitchell Palmer hustled groups of "Reds" to Ellis Island for deportation; the display of red flags was forbidden in New York and other states; the offices of the *New York Call* were raided and wrecked; Socialists were ousted from the New York state legislature and the U. S. Congress; bombings and a dynamite explosion in Wall Street added to the confusion. Many states passed "anti-Red" and criminal syndicalism laws. The conviction of Benjamin Gitlow, an obscure radical, in New York for his writings in the *Left Wing Manifesto* and *Revolutionary Age* was upheld by the Supreme Court despite the arguments of Justices Holmes and Brandeis that Gitlow offered no serious threat to the government. In general, the newspapers failed dismally to defend the civil liberties of those being questionably attacked. One of the worst records on this score was compiled by the usually stable *New York Times.* Civil liberties were best defended by the liberal magazines, led by the *New Republic* and the *Nation,* and by a few newspapers, including the *St. Louis Post-Dispatch, New York Globe,* and *New York World.*

Eventually the turbulence of the wartime period faded into the relatively complacent years of the 1920's. Each president after

Wilson attempted to obtain American adherence to the World Court, but the Senate failed to go even that far in international cooperation. The American government did sponsor the naval limitation treaty at the Washington Conference of 1922 and cooperated in a scaling down of the German war reparations and Allied war debts. In the happy year of 1928 Secretary of State Frank B. Kellogg and French Premier Aristide Briand won solemn promises from other nations that they would outlaw war as an instrument of national policy. But then the economic and political storm which had been brewing since the end of the war broke across the world.

Soberly the American people watched the steady march of new aggressive forces, beginning with the Japanese invasion of Manchuria in 1931. Working outside the League of Nations, the American government attempted to rally world opinion against the Japanese militarists, but there was no unity of diplomatic action. Mussolini's use of his war machine in Ethiopia, Hitler's defiance of the Versailles Treaty by occupying the Rhineland and later seizing Austria, the lining up of fascist and antifascist forces in the Spanish Civil War—each episode brought disturbing headlines and debate in the United States. The disillusionment which had produced the antiwar literature of the 1930's and set the stage for neutrality legislation was slowly passing. A nation which had found new social and economic strength during the years of the New Deal stood ready once again to play its part in the new world crisis.

Isolationism died hard, however. A Senate committee headed by Gerald P. Nye of North Dakota had advanced the thesis in 1935 that American munitions makers and bankers were almost solely responsible for the country's entrance into the first World War. The neutrality legislation which followed was designed to prevent American loans or sale of war materials to belligerents, on the theory that such a ban would prevent American involvement in "foreign" wars. Even after the Munich crisis of September, 1938, and Hitler's occupation of the remainder of unhappy Czechoslovakia in March, 1939, the isolationists held the upper hand.[13]

[13] One of the isolationists was historian Charles A. Beard, whose later writings attacking Roosevelt's foreign policy were ably answered in Basil Rauch, *Roosevelt from Munich to Pearl Harbor* (New York: Creative Age Press, Inc., 1950).

The diplomatic bombshell which signaled the opening of World War II was the signing of the German-Russian neutrality pact on August 23, 1939. A week later Hitler marched on Poland and the British and French answered with declarations of war. In November, President Roosevelt obtained a revision of the Neutrality Act as the first step in a reversal of the isolationist trend. Congress repealed the embargo on sale of arms and authorized a cash-and-carry trade with the Allies.

The full nature of Hitler's aggressive designs was revealed in the spring of 1940, when Nazi armies first invaded Denmark and Norway, and then on May 10 launched a gigantic offensive against Holland, Belgium, and France. The shock of Dunkerque, the fall of France, and the opening of the Nazi air blitz against Britain in August produced strong pro-Allied sentiment in the United States. In September the Selective Service Act was passed and President Roosevelt announced the trade of 50 destroyers to Britain in return for leases on air-sea bases in the Western Hemisphere. Many American newspapers supported both actions. So did the Republican presidential candidate, Wendell Willkie, who was unsuccessful in stopping Roosevelt's third-term bid.

By now the lines had formed between isolationists and interventionists. On one side was the America First Committee, headed by General Robert E. Wood and championed by Colonel Charles A. Lindbergh, the hero of the first New York-to-Paris flight in 1927. Senators Nye and Burton K. Wheeler were on the America First side. Unfortunately for their cause, so were such assorted rabble-rousers as Father Charles E. Coughlin, Gerald L. K. Smith, William Dudley Pelley of the Silver Shirts, Fritz Kuhn of the German-American Bund, and Communists William Z. Foster and Earl Browder. On the other side was the Committee to Defend America by Aiding the Allies, led by Kansas editor William Allen White. The White group attracted many influential newspaper editors, and carried out a newspaper advertisement campaign which brought the formation of hundreds of local committees. Among the journalistic leaders were columnist Joseph Alsop, radio commentator Elmer Davis, and playwright Robert E. Sherwood.

The Lend-Lease Act of March, 1941, which empowered the President to provide goods and services to those nations whose defense he deemed vital to the defense of the United States, represented a victory for the pro-Allied group. It also served to make America a non-belligerent ally of the British. In May, 1941, President Roosevelt proclaimed an unlimited state of national emergency to facilitate the American mobilization program. In August Roosevelt met Prime Minister Winston Churchill on the high seas and the two announced their peace aims in the Atlantic Charter. The isolationists were far from beaten, however; that same month the House of Representatives continued the military draft by the narrow margin of one vote. The subsiding of the Battle of Britain, as the Nazis launched their invasion of the Soviet Union, made American aid seem less urgent. Even with the torpedoing of two American destroyers in the North Atlantic in October, there was no growth of war sentiment. Not until December 7, 1941, when Japanese bombs fell on Pearl Harbor, was unity for war achieved. The isolationist minority of the American press, led by the McCormick-Patterson *Chicago Tribune* and *New York Daily News* and the Hearst chain, abruptly subsided in the face of this direct enemy attack.

With organization of the country for war, newspapermen recalled that the Espionage Act and Trading-with-the-Enemy Act of 1917 were still on the statute books. The more sweeping generalities of the Sedition Act had been repealed in 1921, however. Use of these acts to bar publications from the mails and to suppress free speech was more sharply limited than during World War I. Father Coughlin's *Social Justice* was discontinued after a warning from the Postmaster General. A Philadelphia German-language paper, the *Herold,* was barred from the mails. The editors of the magazine *Scribner's Commentator,* of the Rev. Gerald B. Winrod's *Defender,* and of the *New York Enquirer,* a Sunday paper, were indicted by a federal grand jury, along with publishers of a score of pro-Fascist and subversive propaganda sheets. The greatest invasion of civil liberties took place when Japanese living in the United States, including many American citizens of Japanese ancestry, were rounded up and kept in what amounted to protective custody in isolated camps during the early years of the war.

Military censorship by Navy and Army intelligence officers began on Pearl Harbor day. Within two weeks Congress passed the First War Powers Act giving the President power to establish censorship over all communications between the United States

EXTRA!

San Francisco Chronicle
THE CITY'S ONLY HOME-OWNED NEWSPAPER

FOUNDED 1865—VOL CLIII, NO 146 CCCC** — SAN FRANCISCO, MONDAY, DECEMBER 8, 1941 — DAILY 5 CENTS, SUNDAY 10 CENTS

COMPARATIVE TEMPERATURES

	High	Low		High	Low
San Francisco	60	50	Denver	60	46
San Jose	69	50	Fresno	64	44
Los Angeles	70	54	Chicago	35	24
Seattle	54	39	New Orleans	68	52
Honolulu	77	70	Salt Lake	44	34

Local Forecast: Fair

U.S. AT WAR!

Japan Bombs Hawaii, Manila, Invades Thailand, Malaya; 2 U.S. Battleships Claimed Sunk; FDR Talks to Congress Today!

America at War!
—EDITORIAL—

By the act of Japan, America is at war. The time for debate has passed and the time for action has come. That action must be united and unanimous. "Politics is adjourned," whether between parties, factions or economic groups. From now on America is one. Every man, woman and child a soldier in it, all joined to the one end of victory.

If war had to come, it is perhaps well that it came this way, wanton, unwarned, in fraud and bad faith, virtually under a flag of truce. For in war there can be only one side in action, and now there is only one side in thought or feeling. Its slogan is, "Americans unite, for victory and freedom."

We can not know how long this war will last, how wide it will range, nor what it will cost us, in toil, in sacrifice and in treasure. We do know that whatever the cost, we will pay it, and that our reward will be to hand down to our children the free America which our fathers bequeathed to us. Americans, unite!

Without Warning, Bombs Break the Peace

350 Slain—Then Tokyo Declares War on U. S., Britain
Pacific Coast, Electrified, Springs to Wartime Alert

Air Raid Precautions Taken; Military Leaves Cancelled; Coastal Guns Manned

The West Coast, from San Diego to the Canadian line, and the entire Western Continental United States was swinging to a wartime basis within a few hours of the air attack on Hawaii by Japan.

Air raid listening devices went into action. The fastest pursuit ships and bombers of the Army Air Corps were poised for any sign of raid by land, sea or air.

Leaves and furloughs of all officers and enlisted men of the 11th, 12th and 13th Naval districts were canceled and the men ordered back to their ships.

FACTORIES TIGHTEN WATCH FOR SABOTEURS

The outpost of the Nation's farflung Pacific Coast defenses at Alaska and the Panama Canal were blacked out last night.

Leaves of all soldiers in the 9th Corps Area — California, Nevada, Utah, Idaho, Montana, Washington and Oregon—were summarily canceled by the War Department and all men were ordered to their posts.

The United States Coast Guard ordered all Pacific Coast craft halted, and the Customs Department cancelled all departure permits and Movements of craft in harbors was restricted.

All enlisted men of Class M-2, Naval Reserve, were instructed by the navy to report today for mobilization orders.

FDR on Air
Network radio stations will carry President Roosevelt's address to the joint session of Congress this morning. Among them will be stations KGO, KPO and KSFO in San Francisco. Time here will be 9:30 a. m.

Raids Took a Heavy Toll, Hawaii Says
(This is the last uncensored Associated Press dispatch from Honolulu in the new war, from after this dispatch was telephoned a heavy censorship was imposed on dispatches from the Hawaiian islands by the Washington, some hours later, the War Department gave the White House a preliminary estimate that 104 were dead and more than 300 wounded in the bombing.)

HONOLULU, Dec. 7 (IP)—War struck suddenly and without warning from the sky and sea today at the Hawaiian islands, and Japanese bombs took a heavy toll in American lives.

In the Bay Area, where a spot of cargo ships are in the ways of shipbuilding plants, armed guards were called into immediate service to augment the patrols which have been on the alert against sabotage for months.

Officials of the Pacific Telephone and Telegraph Company and the Pacific Gas and Electric Company announced their properties were under strict guard and that only persons holding proper credentials were admitted.

Canada, Dutch Indies, Costa Rica Declare War on Japan; Wake Is Reported Taken

By the Associated Press

Japan assaulted every main United States and British possession in the central and western Pacific and invaded Thailand today (Monday) in a hasty but evidently shrewdly-planned prosecution of a war that began Sunday without warning.

Her formal declaration of war against both the United States and Britain came two hours and 55 minutes after Japanese planes spread death and terrific destruction in Honolulu and Pearl Harbor at 7:35 a. m., Hawaiian time (10:05 a. m., San Francisco) Sunday.

FDR Talks to Nation

Today at 9:30 a. m. San Francisco time, President Roosevelt will address a joint session of Congress and a declaration of war by the United States against Japan is expected. The speech will be carried on all major radio networks.

The claimed successes that this fell swoop included sinking of the U. S. battleship West Virginia and setting afire of the battleship Oklahoma.

From that moment, each tense tick of the clock brought new and flaming accounts of Japanese aggression in her secretly launched war of conquest or death for the land of the rising sun.

Japanese Surprise Attacks

As compiled from official and unofficial accounts from all affected countries, the record ran like this:

Honolulu bombed a second time.

Lumber-laden U. S. Army transport torpedoed 1300 miles west of San Francisco and another transport in distress.

Seizure or sinking of another U. S. transport, the former President Harrison.

Capture of the U. S. island of Wake.

Bombing of the U. S. island of Guam, which was reported by Tokyo to be surrounded by Japanese naval ships.

Bombing of many points throughout the Philippine islands.

Invasion of Northern Malaya and bombing of Singapore.

Invasion of Thailand (Siam) and bombing of Bangkok.

The first U. S. official casualty report listed 104 dead and more than 300 injured in the attack on Hickam Field, alone.

U. S. Faces War: Losses May Be Heavy, Nation Warned

WASHINGTON, Dec. 8 (Monday)—The Philippines were attacked today and as...

Continued on Page 2, Col. 1

Continued on Page 6, Col. 1

Chronicle News Conference Off
Air for Duration

INSIDE
You'll find full war coverage—news, background and pictures: See Pages A, B, C, D, E, F, G, H, 4, 5 and 6.

WE'RE READY! SAYS MARE ISLAND OFFICER

Continued on Page H, Col. 1

Hoover: Our Decision's Clear

Continued on Page C, Col. 7

Continued on Page 11, Col. 1

Big type announced the coming of World War II to America. This was the final edition of the *San Francisco Chronicle*, December 8, 1941.

and foreign countries—by mail, cable, telegraph, telephone, wireless, and radio-telegraph and telephone. President Roosevelt immediately created the Office of Censorship to handle this assignment. He also requested its director, in a letter based upon no legislative authority, to coordinate the efforts of the American press and radio in voluntarily withholding from publication military and other information of value to the enemy. Thus the patterns of censorship which were developed in World War I were reinstated for World War II.

Byron Price, executive news editor of the Associated Press and long a Washington newsman, was named director of the Office of Censorship. Probably no other man could have held the respect and confidence of newspapermen everywhere better than Price, who was temperamentally and intellectually equipped to handle the most difficult part of his job—the direction of the voluntary press censorship. He brought into his organization a score of seasoned newspapermen to handle press relationships, headed by John H. Sorrells, executive editor of the Scripps-Howard newspapers, and Nat R. Howard, editor of the *Cleveland News*.[14]

A *Code of Wartime Practices for the American Press* was issued on January 15, 1942. It carefully outlined to those who published newspapers, magazines, books, and other printed materials what would constitute improper handling of news having to do with troops, planes, ships, war production, armaments, military installations, and weather. Similar instructions were given radio stations. The code became a Bible for American newsmen, who usually erred in the direction of over-suppression of news possibly harmful to the war effort. The press and broadcasting divisions of the voluntary censorship program were small organizations, operating in Washington, handling inquiries about the code and requests for pre-censorship of stories and pictures. They also cooperated with officials in the mandatory censorship of the mails, cables, and radio whenever problems involving news stories and broadcasts were involved.

[14] The activities of the Office of Censorship and the work of other individuals are described by Theodore F. Koop, an Associated Press man and assistant to Price, in *Weapon of Silence* (Chicago: University of Chicago Press, 1946). Sorrells, Howard, managing editor Jack Lockhart of the *Memphis Commercial Appeal*, and Koop were successive heads of the voluntary press censorship division. J. Howard Ryan directed the radio division.

Usually a request from the Office of Censorship resulted in the voluntary cooperation of newspaper editors and radio news broadcasters. Price and his staff could not enforce any orders, and did not give any. However, there always remained the possibility of punishment for willful violations of military security, under the Espionage Act. And in wartime the authoritative voice of the Office of Censorship had all the qualities of command for most newsmen.

The Office of Censorship hewed to the policy of concerning itself with news only about the war itself. It took the position that information released by a responsible government official or legislator was publishable. Thus Price avoided becoming a censor of the government itself. Price also argued that information which already was known to the enemy, or which had been disclosed to a large number of persons, should not be kept from the American public. When the reasons for voluntary censorship of specific types of stories were not readily clear, Price took pains to issue explanatory off-the-record statements to newsmen. For all these reasons, the voluntary system worked well.

Several outstanding successes were chalked up to the credit of newspaper and radio men and the Office of Censorship. No hint of the successful development of the atomic bomb was published or broadcast despite the enormous activities preceding the trial explosion in New Mexico and its first use at Hiroshima. The secrets of radar and the proximity fuse likewise were protected. Details of the massing of troops in Britain for the D-Day invasion were kept from the Germans. Editors and broadcasters loyally refrained from mentioning cross-country trips by President Roosevelt even though thousands of their readers and listeners were aware that the President had been in their locality. Atlantic coast newsmen cooperated in censoring and delaying stories about ship sinkings offshore so the Germans could not accurately evaluate the near-success of their 1942 U-boat campaign.

There were some difficulties, of course. When the Japanese began sending thousands of explosive-laden balloons across the Pacific in late 1944 and 1945, the government sought to prevent enemy agents from learning anything about the success of the project. Censorship requests worked fairly well until six persons were killed in Oregon while investigating a fallen balloon. Army officers decided to launch a vast "secret" educational campaign in the West and the resulting confusion and spread of rumors forced release of the basic facts concerning the balloon invasion. Perhaps the most friction was generated over local coverage of the granting of war contracts, since military officers and government agencies often refused to authorize even generalized stories.

The Office of Censorship found two big areas of noncompliance with the code. One was the identification by military unit or ship of personnel overseas. Smaller papers and magazines, as well as club and church bulletins, were the principal violators. The other major violation was the running of interviews with returned soldiers without clearance from the Office of Censorship. Information which had been withheld by military censorship thus was sometimes published in the United States. The value of having such interviews cleared was demonstrated when the Office of Censorship killed several stories submitted to it which would have told the Japanese that their secret code had been cracked by American experts. One story involving the cracking of the Japanese secret code escaped the censors, however. It was an analysis of the Battle of Midway which appeared in the *Chicago Tribune,* and had the Japanese been more alert, the enormous advantage gained by American knowledge of the enemy code might have been lost. A federal grand jury investigated the incident, but found no willful intent to betray military secrets.

Throughout the war, Price rarely had to do more than softly remind violators of the voluntary press and radio censorships that they were being forgetful of their own best interests and those of the country to win renewed efforts to comply. He in turn was awarded a special Pulitzer Prize citation for his work and received genuine congratulations from the country's newsmen when he closed down the Office of Censorship at the end of the war, and became an official of the United Nations Secretariat.

Most of the 14,462 persons in the Office of Censorship were engaged in the mandatory censorship of mail, cables, and radio communications between the United States and other countries. Price inherited Army and Navy censorship organizations in these fields and also built a vast civilian force which was spread from Iceland to Honolulu. The censors checked as much of the mail addressed abroad as was feasible. They also passed upon as many as 350,000 cablegrams and radiograms in a single week and monitored 25,000 telephone calls in the same time. Not only did they prevent information of value to the enemy from going abroad, but they often intercepted incoming information of value to the military and other government agencies. As in World War I the censorship attempted to prevent news stories harmful to the morale of Allied or neutral nations from being sent overseas.

Price's Office of Censorship in World War II thus combined the World War I operations of the Censorship Board and the voluntary press censorship portion of George Creel's work. Price, however, had nothing to do with the originating of news or with the government's propaganda effort. Those aspects of the work of the World War I Committee on Public Information were handled during World War II by a separate agency.

This was the Office of War Information, established by an executive order of the President in June, 1942, to supersede four earlier government agencies. One of the original agencies had been the Office of Government Reports, headed by Lowell Mellett, which operated a clipping service, handled queries from the public concerning governmental activities, and coordinated the making of films by the government. Another was the Office of Facts and Figures, charged with correlating information about defense and foreign policies, and directed by poet Archibald MacLeish, Librarian of Congress. The third was the Division of Information in the Office of Emergency Management, headed by Robert Horton, which handled news of the war agencies. The fourth was the Office of the Coordinator of Information, established to collect and analyze all information bearing upon national security. Its foreign information section, which became a part of the OWI, was headed by Robert E. Sherwood. The remainder of the OCI, headed by William J. Donovan, became the Office of Strategic Services.

The Office of Government Reports was established in 1939, and the other three agencies in 1941, prior to American entry into the war. Work of the four agencies overlapped and there was dissatisfaction on the part of the press with some of the performances of the agencies. This led President Roosevelt to create the OWI. The President made a wise choice in the person of Elmer Davis as director.

Davis, like Price, was a veteran newsman. He had served on the

New York Times staff for 10 years and had been a news analyst and commentator for the Columbia Broadcasting System prior to his appointment. For his work with CBS, and after the war with the American Broadcasting Company, he three times won radio's Peabody award for radio news reporting and interpretation. A highly capable and conscientious newsman, Davis declared that the OWI would do its best to tell the truth and nothing but the truth, both at home and abroad.

"It is the job of OWI," Davis said, "not only to tell the American people how the war is going, but where it is going and where it came from—its nature and origins, how our government is conducting it, and what (besides national survival) our government hopes to get out of victory." [15] This concept of the total function of OWI also was applied to its work abroad.

One function of the OWI was to act as a city desk for the nation's war news. Government departments and war agencies continued to handle approximately 40 per cent of government publicity stories without reference to OWI. But those news releases relating significantly to the war effort or dealing with activities affecting more than one government agency had to pass through the OWI News Bureau. OWI thus was enabled to keep news flowing from the government agencies, to represent the interests of the press and of its readers in disputes with officials over what should or should not be said, to discourage official inclination to hide bad news and overplay good news, and to coordinate information given it by different agencies and put the news into proper perspective. OWI did not always win in its struggles with bureaucracy, but it succeeded in untangling poor news coverage situations far more often than it lost. The OWI also cooperated with the War and Navy Departments in handling military news, and the Army and Navy were required to consult with Davis about withholding of specific military information. The services, however, retained final authority over such withholding of news and Davis did not often win arguments with them. As a result, Davis took a steady drumming of criticism from those suspicious of any information agency.

Davis had as his associate director Milton Eisenhower, brother

[15] Elmer Davis, "OWI Has a Job," *Public Opinion Quarterly*, VII (Spring 1943), 8.

of the general and a trained public official. Gardner Cowles Jr., publisher of the *Des Moines Register* and *Tribune* and *Look* magazine, became director of domestic operations, being succeeded by Palmer Hoyt, publisher of the Portland *Oregonian*. George H. Lyon, former editor of the *Buffalo Times* and managing editor of *PM*, headed the News Bureau, most important sub-division of the domestic section.

The News Bureau operated on a million dollar annual budget, with 250 regular employes. Three hundred reporters and correspondents used its facilities, including some 50 reporters working full time in the OWI pressroom. Releases intended for daily newspapers were not mailed, but were made available in the pressroom to reporters for the press associations, larger newspapers, news magazines, radio networks, and larger trade papers. Special desks handled mailings designed for the business and trade press, rural press, labor press, Negro press, foreign language press, and other specialized publications.

Copy flowed from the general news desk, where policy decisions were made, to the domestic and foreign news desks, the radio news desk, the picture desk, and the feature desk. Cartoons, pictures, features, weekly digests, and fillers became a part of the OWI offering. Background information concerning desired propaganda and informational objectives of the government was given to editorial writers, cartoonists, and columnists.

The OWI domestic section had several other bureaus. One handled the preparation of copy for use by radio stations, and worked with radio commentators and analysts. Another supervised the making of motion pictures by the government. There was a bureau of publications and graphics, although domestic use of pamphlets was restricted. A bureau of intelligence engaged in audience research, analyzed basic public attitudes, and surveyed the contents of communications media. The division of campaigns directed appeals in behalf of war bond sales, salvage drives, fuel conservation, and victory gardens. In this work the OWI had the cooperation of the War Advertising Council and the nation's publishers. The government paid for recruiting advertising, but all other war-related newspaper, magazine, radio and billboard advertising space was donated by the media or by national and local advertisers.

Overseas operations of the OWI were directed by Robert E. Sherwood, with Joseph Barnes, foreign editor of the *New York Herald Tribune,* being deputy director for the important Atlantic area. The overseas news and propaganda programs of the OWI were far more extensive than Creel's work in World War I, particularly because of the availability of radio communication for what became known as the Voice of America. OWI cooperation with the military in the development of psychological warfare techniques also was an advance over World War I methods.

The overseas section received up to 30,000 words a day of tele-typed news from the OWI domestic News Bureau. The overseas offices in New York and San Francisco also used the news reports of the press associations, radio networks, and OWI's own regional offices. At its height of activity in 1943, the overseas news and features bureau, headed by Edward Barrett, cabled 65,000 words daily to all parts of the world, mailed hundreds of thousands of words of feature material, and airmailed or radioed 2,500 pictures.[16] This OWI overseas news service became an important factor in maintaining adequate news reports in many countries whose usual communications channels were disrupted by the war. OWI also produced motion pictures, posters, pamphlets, leaflets, books, magazines, and other materials for overseas use in Allied, neutral, and enemy countries.

OWI was given a 36 million dollar budget in 1943, of which 27 million dollars was allotted for overseas operations. Two-thirds of that sum went for radio operations, mainly the Voice of America, but it also covered programs for military and civilian personnel overseas. When the war began, the United States was making one radio broadcast a day, over the British Broadcasting Corporation's facilities. At the end of 1942 there were 21 American-run short wave transmitters, beaming 2,700 programs a week to Europe and Africa alone in 24 different languages. The number of transmitters was increased to 39 before the end of the war and the Voice of America was beamed increasingly into Asia.

Use of radio broadcasts in psychological warfare by the United States was first undertaken on a major scale in the invasion of

[16] OWI operated everywhere abroad except in Latin-America, where Nelson Rockefeller's Office of the Coordinator of Inter-American Affairs held jurisdiction.

North Africa. After that effort, radio broadcasts, pamphlets and leaflets, front-line mobile broadcasting units were utilized, but not always to the extent that psychological warfare advocates would have liked. One example was the dropping of 27 million leaflets along the invasion coast the morning of D-Day, while 100 radio transmitters carried messages from the Allies to the peoples of the German-occupied countries. By the time the war had ended the journalistic aspects of psychological warfare had fairly well proved themselves as weapons for use against enemy troops and civilian populations.

Military censorship for World War II picked up where it had left off at the end of World War I, with the added problem of controlling radio broadcasts. In the early months of the war British censorship was blundering and severe, and it remained tight even after the Ministry of Information became better organized. Nazi Germany was not so bady handicapped by Allied control of cables during World War II, since wireless and radio facilities were available. The Nazis did not censor foreign correspondents before publication, but if they sent stories which Dr. Joseph Goebbels' Ministry of Propaganda did not like, they were subject to expulsion from Germany. Two victims of this policy in the first few months of World War II were Beach Conger of the *New York Herald Tribune* and Otto D. Tolischus of the *New York Times*. Edgar Ansel Mowrer of the *Chicago Daily News* was compelled to leave by reason of threats against his person.

As the war developed newsmen found the British Admiralty and the U. S. Navy Department most prone to suppressing news of war actions. The American Navy withheld details of the Pearl Harbor disaster, and of the sinkings of ships in the Pacific, for long periods of time on the plea that the Japanese should not be given vital information on a confirmed basis. Newsmen grumbled, however, that evidence of inefficient naval operations also was being kept back. The British censorship in Egypt, conflicting British and American censorships in the India-Burma theater, the Chinese censorship in Chungking, and General Douglas Mac-Arthur's censorship in the Pacific also drew heavy fire from correspondents and editors. Many newsmen said MacArthur's information officers insisted unduly upon personal glorification of the commander. Techniques used by General Dwight D. Eisenhower in

Europe were, on the other hand, considered generally satisfactory. Coverage of World War II by the American press and radio was considered by most observers to be the best and fullest the world had ever seen. A great share of the credit for this achievement went to the overseas and war front correspondents for press associations, newspapers, magazines, and radio. As many as 500 full time American correspondents were abroad at one time. Altogether the U. S. armed forces accredited 1,646 different persons. The biggest staffs were those of the press associations and radio networks; the *Times* and *Herald Tribune* in New York; the *Daily News, Tribune,* and *Sun* in Chicago; the *Christian Science Monitor, Baltimore Sun,* and *Time, Life,* and *Newsweek.* Of the 37 American newsmen who lost their lives during the war, 11 were press association correspondents, 10 were representing individual newspapers, nine were magazine correspondents, four were photographers, two were syndicated writers, and one was a radio correspondent.

One of the early standouts among American correspondents was the veteran Leland Stowe of the *Chicago Daily News,* who reported the Russo-Finnish War and the Nazi invasion of Norway, and who was the first American to reach the Nazi-Soviet front lines after Hitler's invasion of Russia. Webb Miller of the United Press covered his eleventh war in Finland, then returned to London to be killed in a blackout accident. Frazier Hunt of International News Service and Marcel W. Fodor of the *Chicago Daily News* filed notable accounts of the French retreat in 1940. On the other side, with Hitler's triumphant army, were Louis P. Lochner of the AP, Pierre J. Huss of INS, and Frederick C. Oechsner of UP.

There were many distinguished examples of war correspondence, and many personal stories of performance in the face of danger by newsmen. Pulitzer Prizes went to Larry Allen of the AP for his exploits with the British Mediterranean fleet; to Hal Boyle and Daniel De Luce of the AP European staff; to military analysts Hanson W. Baldwin of the *New York Times* and Ira Wolfert of the North American Newspaper Alliance; to Mark S. Watson of the *Baltimore Sun* and Homer Bigart of the *New York Herald Tribune;* to AP war photographers Frank Noel, Frank Filan, and Joe Rosenthal; and to Ernie Pyle of the Scripps-Howard Newspaper Alliance. Clark Lee of the Associated Press and Melville Jacoby of *Time* were among the newsmen who shared the dangers of the Bataan evacuation; Jacoby died later in a plane crash but Lee survived to become an INS byline writer. Among other leading war reporters were Vern Haugland and Wes Gallagher of the AP, Quentin Reynolds of *Collier's,* Edward W. Beattie and Henry T. Gorrell of the UP, James Kilgallen and Richard Tregaskis of INS, Drew Middleton of the *New York Times,* and Russell Hill of the *Herald Tribune.*

World War II had its women correspondents. The INS sent its featured writer, Inez Robb, to North Africa and Europe. Three other INS women war correspondents were Lee Carson, with the U. S. First Army, Dixie Tighe with the British, and Rita Hume in Italy. Among the United Press women correspondents were Eleanor Packard and Dudley Anne Harmon, while the AP had Ruth Cowan and Bonnie Wiley in the field. Other correspondents were Helen Kirkpatrick, *Chicago Daily News;* Peggy Hull (Mrs. Harvey Deuel) of the *Cleveland Plain Dealer,* who served in World War I; Margaret Bourke-White, photographer for *Time* and *Life;* Iris Carpenter, *Boston Globe;* and Leah Burdette of *PM,* who lost her life in Iran.

Such radio voices as those of William L. Shirer from Berlin and Edward R. Murrow from London for the Columbia Broadcasting System, and that of the National Broadcasting Company's H. V. Kaltenborn, brought the war close to American homes. Bill Henry of CBS and Arthur Mann of Mutual became the first front line radio reporters in the fall of 1939. Development of mobile units and use of tape recordings soon brought greatly increased radio coverage. Direct reports came from battlefields, from bombers flying over Berlin and Tokyo, and other centers of action. Radiomen covered D-Day brilliantly, with George Hicks of the American Broadcasting Company doing an outstanding broadcast from a landing barge under German fire. Wright Bryan of the *Atlanta Journal* gave NBC and CBS the first eye-witness account from the cross-channel front by flying over with a planeload of paratroopers.

Usually acclaimed as the greatest reporter of the second World War was the columnist friend of the G.I., Ernest Taylor Pyle. Pyle had won attention before the war for his personal notes on life in the United States, as observed in his wanderings across the country. In 1940 he told his readers what the people of Britain felt as they resisted the Nazi air blitz. Then he attached himself to the American army, writing in a home-town style of the intimate daily life of the G.I. in Ireland, North Africa, Sicily, Italy, and France. His column for Scripps-Howard and his *Here Is Your War* and *Brave Men* won him a national reputation and a Pulitzer Prize. Pyle left Europe in 1944, but after a rest he flew out to cover the final stages of the Pacific war. When a Japanese sniper killed Ernie Pyle on Ie Shima during the Okinawa campaign of April, 1945, the saga of a great American war correspondent came to a close.

There was a soldiers' journalism again in World War II. The *Stars and Stripes* reappeared as the leading G.I. newspaper in 1942 and eventually had European and Pacific editions. *Yank,* a magazine with 22 editions, gained a circulation of 2½ millions. The resentments of the enlisted man were portrayed in the *Stars and Stripes* by cartoonist Bill Mauldin, while Sgt. George Baker's "Sad Sack" and Milton Caniff's sexy "Male Call" ran in both publications. Almost every major unit and camp had its own publication. And unlike World War I, the services developed extensive public relations units, of which the combat correspondents of the Marine Corps were most effective. Sergeant Jim G. Lucas of the Marines, formerly of the *Tulsa Tribune* staff, wrote one of the outstanding eye-witness stories of the war for American newspapers from the beach at Tarawa.

Coverage of World War II ended in Europe with the confusion of the Edward Kennedy case. Kennedy, Associated Press chief on the western front, was one of 16 Allied newsmen taken to the military headquarters in Reims to witness the German surrender. All were pledged not to release their stories until an officially prescribed time. Kennedy, angered by the news that the German radio was announcing the surrender in advance of the time set by American, British, and Russian political leaders, made an unauthorized telephone call to London and dictated part of his story for transmission. The AP thus had the official story of the German surrender a day in advance of V-E day. But Kennedy's 54 colleagues in Paris charged him with committing "the most disgraceful, deliberate, and unethical double cross in the history of journalism." Kennedy defended his action as necessary to counteract a needless political censorship, and eventually won reinstatement as a war correspondent a year after his suspension. But the AP disassociated itself from its stormy petrel, and he left its service in 1946.

The year 1945 brought hope to the world, with the defeat of the German and Japanese war machines, and the founding of the United Nations. But the failure of the Soviet Union to cooperate in the postwar era quickly renewed the feeling of tension and uncertainty which the world had endured since the early 1930's. Newsmen found barriers to the collection of news being erected higher than ever before, and the phrase "Iron Curtain" became a familiar one. The trial and imprisonment of Associated Press correspondent William Oatis in Communist Czechoslovakia clearly defined the issue of press freedom for American newsmen.

Realizing it had to work actively to tell the story of the free democracies to the world, the United States government continued to conduct international propaganda on a worldwide scale as initiated by the Office of War Information in 1942. The first such peacetime operation was the Office of International Information and Cultural Affairs, established within the State Department in 1945 with William Benton as head. In 1948, under the Smith-Mundt Act, the functions were split into an Office of International Information, headed by George V. Allen (later by Edward W. Barrett), and an Office of Cultural Exchange to handle exchange of scholars and students. But the annual budget was a third of OWI's, a mere 12 million dollars.

As the Soviet Union consolidated its grip on the satellite states of eastern Europe and attempted the 1948 Berlin blockade, and with the opening of the Korean War in 1950, Congressional appropriations rose swiftly. By 1952 the revamped International Information Administration, headed by Wilson Compton, had 87 million dollars, 25 per cent for the Voice of America.

Creation of an autonomous United States Information Agency in 1953 gave stability to the program. By 1961 its annual budget was 110 million dollars. The Voice of America was heard in 50 languages over 88 transmitters. The overseas United States Information Service was operating 164 information libraries and 91 reading rooms in 70 countries, and was distributing news services, motion pictures, magazines, and pamphlets. USIA heads have been Arthur Larson, George V. Allen, and, since 1961, Edward R. Murrow. But despite this increased activity, the United States was falling short of matching Communist propaganda efforts.

The news of the Communist North Korean attack upon the Republic of South Korea in June, 1950, was first flashed to the United States by Jack James of the United Press. His first message from Seoul reached the capital 20 minutes ahead of the American ambassador's cable. Soon American correspondents from Tokyo reached the fighting front. Among the first were Marguerite Higgins of the *New York Herald Tribune,* Keyes Beech of the *Chicago Daily News,* Walter Simmons of the *Chicago Tribune,* Burton Crane and William H. Lawrence of the *New York Times,* Russell Brines of the AP, Earnest Hoberecht of the UP, Howard Handleman of the INS, and David Douglas Duncan, *Life* photographer. Miss Higgins and Beech won Pulitzer citations for their front line coverage, along with Fred Sparks of the *Chicago Daily News,* Homer Bigart of the *Herald Tribune,* and Relman Morin and Don Whitehead of the AP.

General Douglas MacArthur, the United Nations commander in Korea, at first left correspondents to their own devices, refusing to institute the field censorship which had prevailed during both World War I and II. In the confused situation of the first months of the fighting, the press and radio men found themselves in the thick of battle, and several were killed or taken prisoner. They also found themselves subject to criticism for the stories they filed without benefit of adequate military supervision and censorship. Two press association men temporarily lost their accreditations on charges of giving aid and comfort to the enemy. Relations between Colonel Marion P. Echols, MacArthur's press officer, and the newsmen became even more strained than they had been during the years of the occupation of Japan, when dissenting reporters had found their accreditations endangered.

The September, 1950, victories following MacArthur's Inchon landing brought an easing of the correspondents' problems. Their interviews with critical and despondent soldiers, which had aroused MacArthur's ire earlier in the summer, were at an end. Nearly 300 correspondents from 19 countries were reporting the advance of United Nations troops to the Yalu. Then came the entry of the Chinese Communist army and a disastrous retreat of the UN's battered units. Keyes Beech of the *Chicago Daily News* reported that MacArthur had recommended an immediate withdrawal from Korea, and other correspondents criticised MacArthur's tactics in splitting the commands of his forces in northern Korea. The general's answer was the institution of a full and formal censorship, which he claimed had been recommended by the country's top newspaper executives.

Stringent regulations imposed in January, 1951, went further, however, than any newsman would have desired.[17] They covered not only censorship of military information but of all statements which would injure the morale of UN forces or which would embarrass the United States, its allies, or neutral countries. Correspondents complained that use of the word "retreat" was interpreted by the censors as being embarrassing, and they contended that MacArthur had brought about a political and psychological censorship, as well as a military one. The most dangerous provision of the new censorship was one making correspondents subject to trial by court-martial for serious violations of the rules.

The removal of MacArthur from the Korean command by President Truman brought another easing of the censorship situation, although his chief intelligence officer, Major General C. A. Willoughby, continued to attack such reporters as Hal Boyle, Hanson W. Baldwin, Homer Bigart, and Joseph Alsop as "inaccurate, biased and petulant." When truce negotiations began in Korea in July, 1951, the United Nations Command insisted that newsmen be permitted to cover the truce site. Reporting of the war during the prolonged negotiations became a routine affair, punctuated by excitement over the status of prisoners of war. The Defense Department issued new field censorship instructions in December, 1952, which transferred censorship duties from intelligence officers to public relations officers, and put the Army, Navy, and Air Force under a uniform plan. Censorship for reasons other than those involving security was forbidden, but as usual the differing between newsmen and censors about a definition of "security" continued. Signing of a truce in July, 1953, brought an end to the fighting phase of the Korean War. But the correspondents went on —to Vietnam, the Suez, Budapest, Algeria, Laos, the Congo, and Berlin—as warfare and crises punctuated the uneasy peace.

[17] Text of the censorship code was carried in *Editor & Publisher*, LXXXIV (January 13, 1951), 8.

ANNOTATED BIBLIOGRAPHY

Books:

The literature concerning the journalistic aspects of the two World Wars is voluminous. Listed here are the major works in the fields of wartime censorship, propaganda, and informational activity; the most important historical accounts; and a few of the dozens of excellent books by war correspondents.

Carroll, Wallace, *Persuade or Perish.* Boston: Houghton Mifflin Company, 1948. An excellent account of the World War II propaganda effort.

Chafee, Zechariah, Jr., *Free Speech in the United States.* Cambridge: Harvard University Press, 1941. The major study of the problem, by a Harvard law professor.

Creel, George, *How We Advertised America.* New York: Harper & Brothers, 1920. The chairman of the World War I Committee on Public Information makes his report to the public. See also Creel's autobiography, *Rebel at Large* (New York: G. P. Putnam's Sons, 1947).

Crozier, Emmet, *American Reporters on the Western Front, 1914-1918.* New York: Oxford University Press, 1959. Much detail about both star reporters and "specials."

Koop, Theodore F., *Weapon of Silence.* Chicago: University of Chicago Press, 1946. The story of the World War II Office of Censorship by one of its principal executives.

Langer, William L., and S. Everett Gleason, *The Challenge to Isolation, 1937-1940;* and *The Undeclared War, 1940-1941.* New York: Harper & Brothers, 1952-53. An exhaustive, well-documented analysis in two volumes, published for The Council on Foreign Relations under the joint title, "World Crisis and American Foreign Policy." It fairly and objectively traces the story of American entrance into World War II.

Lasswell, Harold D., *Propaganda Technique in the World War.* New York: Peter Smith, 1927. A standard source for World War I propaganda efforts in the major belligerent countries.

Lerner, Daniel, ed., *Propaganda in War and Crisis.* New York: George W. Stewart, Inc., 1951. A collection of writings in the field of psychological warfare, giving the background of twentieth-century war propaganda efforts.

Miller, Lee G., *The Story of Ernie Pyle.* New York: The Viking Press, 1950. Biography of the famed World War II columnist.

Miller, Webb, *I Found No Peace.* New York: Simon and Schuster, 1936. One of the best of the foreign correspondents' books, by a longtime United Pressman.

Mock, James R., *Censorship 1917.* Princeton: Princeton University Press, 1941. The major work on World War I censorship activities.

Mock, James R., and Cedric Larson, *Words That Won the War*. Princeton: Princeton University Press, 1939. Best account of the work of the Committee on Public Information during World War I.

Murray, Robert K., *Red Scare: A Study in National Hysteria, 1919-1920*. Minneapolis: University of Minnesota Press, 1955. A well-documented study of a period of violation of civil liberties. Lacks a summary evaluation of newspaper performance.

Palmer, Frederick, *With My Own Eyes*. Indianapolis: Bobbs-Merrill Company, 1933. Biographical account by a leading World War I correspondent who became military field censor.

Paxson, Frederic L., *American Democracy and the World War*. Boston: Houghton Mifflin Company, 1938 ff. A three-volume study of the 10 years, 1913 to 1923, that ranks at the top for its completeness, balance, and perceptiveness. The volume titles are: *Pre-War Years, 1913-1917, America at War, 1917-1918*, and *Post-War Years: Normalcy, 1918-1923*.

Pyle, Ernest Taylor, *Here Is Your War*. New York: Henry Holt and Company, 1943. A compilation of Pyle's columns.

Rauch, Basil, *Roosevelt from Munich to Pearl Harbor*. New York: Creative Age Press, Inc., 1950. An able and spirited answer to the isolationist argument.

Schreiner, George A., *Cables and Wireless*. Boston: Stratford, 1924. Analyzes effect of World War I on communications.

Sherwood, Robert E., *Roosevelt and Hopkins*. New York: Harper & Brothers, 1948. An intimate history of the wartime partnership by the writer-confidant of F.D.R.

Shirer, William L., *Berlin Diary*. New York: Alfred A. Knopf, Inc., 1941. The years 1934 to 1940 in diary form, by the CBS radio correspondent who covered Hitler's rise to power.

Slosson, Preston W., *The Great Crusade and After, 1914-1928*, A History of American Life, Vol. XII. New York: The Macmillan Company, 1930. An excellent social history.

Sullivan, Mark, *Our Times*. New York: Charles Scribner's Sons, 1926-35. Volume 5, *Over Here, 1914-1918*, and volume 6, *The Twenties*, are invaluable references for the period.

Thomson, Charles A. H., *Overseas Information Service of the United States Government*. Washington: Brookings Institution, 1948. Authoritative account.

Williams, Wythe, *Passed by the Censor*. New York: E. P. Dutton & Company, 1916. A World War I correspondent's story. Twenty years later his *Dusk of Empire* pictured the decline of Europe into another war.

Wittke, Carl F., *The German-Language Press in America*. Lexington: University of Kentucky Press, 1957. A history from 1732 to 1956; three chapters devoted to World War I period.

Periodicals and Monographs:

The files of the *Journalism Quarterly* and *Public Opinion Quarterly* contain many important articles published about World War II censorship and propaganda activities. See particularly the Spring, 1943, issue of *Public Opinion Quarterly* and *Journalism Quarterly* from 1942 to 1944. Other important articles include the following:

Bean, Walton E., "The Accuracy of Creel Committee News, 1917-1919: An Examination of Cases," *Journalism Quarterly*, XVIII (September 1941), 263.

Casey, Ralph D., "Propaganda and Public Opinion," a chapter in Willard Waller, *War in the Modern World* (New York: Random House, Inc., 1940).

————, "The Press, Propaganda, and Pressure Groups," *The Annals of the American Academy of Political and Social Science*, CCXIX (January 1942), 66. Reprinted in Wilbur Schramm, ed., *Mass Communications* (see Chapter 27 bibliography).

Fitzpatrick, Dick, "America's Campaign of Truth Throughout the World," *Journalism Quarterly*, XXVIII (Winter 1951), 3.

Larson, Cedric, "Censorship of Army News During the World War, 1917-1918," *Journalism Quarterly*, XVII (December 1940), 313.

————, "OWI's Domestic News Bureau: An Account and Appraisal," *Journalism Quarterly*, XXVI (March 1949), 3.

Miller, Robert C., "Censorship in Korea," *Nieman Reports*, VI (July 1952), 3.

Nafziger, Ralph O., "World War Correspondents and Censorship of the Belligerents," *Journalism Quarterly*, XIV (September 1937), 226. By the author of *The American Press and Public Opinion During the World War, 1914 to April, 1917* (Ph.D. dissertation, University of Wisconsin, 1936).

"The Truth Must Be Our Guide, But Dreams Must Be Our Goals," *Newsweek*, LVIII (September 18, 1961), 24. A substantial article about the USIA and its director, Edward R. Murrow.

United States Information Agency, *16th Review of Operations, January 1-June 30, 1961* (Washington: Government Printing Office, 1961). This semi-annual report, as well as earlier ones and those to follow, gives details of USIA activities.

Chapter **25**

FROM JAZZ JOURNALISM TO INTERPRETATIVE REPORTING

> It is much easier to report a battle or a bombing than it is to do an honest and intelligible job on the Marshall Plan, the Taft-Hartley Law or the Atlantic Pact.
>
> —Edward R. Murrow

A NEW CYCLE OF SENSATIONALISM IN JOURNALISM began with the close of World War I. Just as in 1833, when the penny press appeared, and in 1897, when the Pulitzer-Hearst duel climaxed the introduction of the new journalism, the times were right for a sensationalized appeal to the people. And there was an untapped audience awaiting such an appeal, just as there had been in 1833 and 1897. In the seven years between 1919 and 1926 three new papers in New York City found more than a million and a half readers without unduly disturbing the circulation balance of the existing dailies. Their sensationalism was accompanied by the use of two techniques which identify the period: the tabloid-style format and the extensive use of photography. As in earlier periods, the wave of sensationalism had its effect upon all of the press before it subsided; and, as before, a more substantial journalism followed the era of sensationalized appeal. The 1920's are known as the decade of "jazz journalism," [1] while the years which

[1] The title of a history of the tabloids: Simon M. Bessie, *Jazz Journalism* (New York: E. P. Dutton & Company, 1938).

followed were marked by a rapid rise in emphasis upon the techniques of interpretative reporting, not only in the newspaper field,
but in magazine publishing and radio broadcasting as well.

The tabloid format introduced so successfully in New York after
1919 was not a stranger to journalism. Before newsprint became
relatively plentiful in the middle of the nineteenth century, small-
sized pages were common. The *Daily Graphic* which was published
in New York between 1873 and 1889, and which carried Stephen
H. Horgan's early experimental halftone engravings, had a tabloid
format. So did Frank A. Munsey's ill-fated *Daily Continent* of 1891,
which like the *Daily Graphic* was heavily illustrated but no more
sensationalized than other newspapers. It was not these American
efforts which stimulated the tabloid era of the 1920's, however. For
better or for worse, America owes its tabloids to the cradle of English-language journalism, Great Britain.

Even though English journalistic preoccupation with crime news
and court stories played its part in suggesting the advantages of
sensationalism to the first American penny press newsmen in 1833,
newspapers for the masses lagged in Great Britain because of stamp
tax regulations which did not disappear until 1855. The *Daily
Telegraph* then became the first penny paper in England, but its
appeal was to the middle classes. Not until after the introduction
of compulsory education in England in 1870 was there a market
for a truly popularized newspaper. Into that market stepped a
discerning young man named Alfred C. Harmsworth, who as Lord
Northcliffe was to become one of Britain's great press lords. His
first project, in 1883, was a human interest weekly magazine named
Answers, which was modeled after George Newnes' *Titbits* of 1881.
Both publications used the contest idea as a means of enticing
working class readers, and Harmsworth had 250,000 of them within
10 years.

Meanwhile Harmsworth was watching the progress of Joseph
Pulitzer's *New York World* and of James Gordon Bennett's *Paris
Herald* with its short-lived London edition. He first adapted the
new American techniques to the *London Evening News*, which
he bought in 1894, and then to his far more famous *Daily Mail*,
founded in 1896. Soon Pulitzer was taking lessons from Harmsworth,
whom the *World's* publisher admired so greatly that he permitted
the Englishman, as guest publisher, to turn the January 1, 1901,

issue of the *World* into a tabloid representing "the newspaper of the twentieth century." New York was unimpressed however, and it remained for Harmsworth to do the job in England.

The first widely circulated tabloid was the *Daily Mirror*, which Harmsworth began in London in 1903 as a newspaper for women but soon converted into a "half-penny illustrated," small, sensational, and amusing. By 1909, its circulation had reached a million copies, and the *Daily Sketch* and *Daily Graphic* jumped into the tabloid field. Harmsworth had become Lord Northcliffe and a leading figure in English journalism by the time of World War I. He still felt that someone should be publishing a tabloid like his *Daily Mirror* in New York, and when he met an American army officer who was overseas from his newspaper desk, Northcliffe told him how lucrative the tabloid could be.

The army officer was Captain Joseph Medill Patterson, partner with Colonel Robert R. McCormick in the publishing of the *Chicago Tribune* since 1914. The two grandsons of Joseph Medill met later in France, and agreed to a plan to start a New York tabloid to be called the *Daily News*. The cousins had other reasons than the arguments which Northcliffe had advanced for undertaking the New York venture. Colonel McCormick, as will be shown in detail in a later chapter, was a king-sized chip off the conservative Medill block. Captain Patterson was unconventional enough to have written two novels (*A Little Brother of the Rich* and *Rebellion*) which constituted protests against social injustice and economic oppression, and was considered socialistic in his thinking by others of his wealthy class. The plan for Patterson to start a tabloid in New York would thus give him an opportunity to reach the many immigrants and least literate native-born, as he wished to do, and at the same time would rid Colonel McCormick of an embarrassing co-publisher arrangement in Chicago.

So the *Illustrated Daily News*, as the paper was called the first few months, made its bow in New York on June 26, 1919. Its half-size front page was covered with a picture of the Prince of Wales (later King Edward VIII and Duke of Windsor), whose forthcoming visit to America already had stirred anticipatory feminine heart-throbs. Its promotion gimmick was the sponsoring of its own beauty contest, which was announced to startled readers of the *New York Times* in a full page ad which read: SEE NEW

YORK'S MOST BEAUTIFUL GIRLS EVERY MORNING IN THE ILLUSTRATED DAILY NEWS. New York newsmen of 1919, like those of 1833 who had sniffed at Benjamin Day's newly founded *Sun*, dismissed the tabloid venture without much concern. But one of them, at least, foresaw the effect its sensationalism, its entertainment emphasis, and its reliance upon photography would have. He was Carr Van Anda, the astute managing editor of the *Times*, who while hardly in the sensationalized picture paper field himself, realized that the *Daily News* would satisfy a widespread postwar public craving and reach a new reading audience. "This paper," he said, "should reach a circulation of 2,000,000." [2] Patterson and his editors did not disappoint Van Anda. In 1924 the *Daily News* circulation of 750,000 was the largest in the country. By 1929 the figure was 1,320,000—gained while the combined circulation of the other New York morning papers stood still. And before World War II it had hit the two million mark.

The 1920's were made to order for the extreme sensationalism of the tabloid and for a spreading of its degrading journalistic features to the rest of the press. The great crusade of 1917 was over, and Woodrow Wilson's hopes for American leadership in world affairs were dissolving into a "Red scare" at home and a nationalistic-isolationist outlook toward events abroad. The country's cry was "back to normalcy" insofar as politics was concerned. This did not mean that America wanted to stand still; rather it wanted to forget the troubles of the war years and concentrate on "living." There were exciting new wonders to explore. The radio, airplane, and movie were just beginning to become familiar. A federal network of roads, started in 1920, opened the highways to every man and his "tin lizzie." Manufacturing and service industries built about the auto, radio, movie, and home appliances spurred industrialization and urbanization, and for a time buttressed the economy against the adverse effects of the disastrous postwar depression in agriculture. Mass production was the talisman which supposedly would make the nation rich, and solid economic accomplishment soon disappeared under a wave of overproduction and speculation.

Political conservatism and laissez-faire policies thus prevailed

[2] As quoted in Bessie, *Jazz Journalism*, p. 82.

over rebellious but out-voted progressivism. Occupying the White House were three Republicans, the sincere but scandal-plagued Marion, Ohio, newspaper publisher, Warren G. Harding; the close-mouthed Yankee believer in the status quo, Calvin Coolidge; and the efficient but depression-plagued Quaker, Herbert Hoover. Harding beat back the 1920 challenge of another Ohio newspaper publisher, James M. Cox, and his youthful running mate, Franklin D. Roosevelt, who vainly supported the League of Nations. Coolidge won over the colorless Democratic compromise candidate of 1924, John W. Davis, but he also shunted aside the colorful Progressive candidate, Senator Robert M. La Follette of Wisconsin. Hoover rode a high tide of prosperity, and benefited from vicious word-of-mouth attacks upon his 1928 opponent as he swamped the liberal Democratic candidate, Governor Alfred E. Smith of New York. America was a relatively complacent land, and business prosperity and the doings of Wall Street outweighed interest in political and social reform.

The press, preoccupied in many instances with sex, crime, and entertainment, reflected the spirit of the times. The majority of newspapers went with the tide, rather than attempting to give the country leadership either by determined display of significant news or through interpretation. There was good copy in the evidences of political laxity which emerge in all postwar periods, however, and even the tabloids played up the Teapot Dome oil lease scandal and others which issued from the unhappy Harding administration. Dapper Mayor Jimmy Walker's casual handling of New York City affairs was both entertaining and productive of graft exposés. The hue and cry against corruption were valuable, but sober examination of the country's own economic trend and of the world situation went begging in many papers.

And after all, the atmosphere of the 1920's made this inevitable. The national experiment called Prohibition brought rumrunners, speakeasy operators, and gangsters into the spotlight, and they were interesting people. Al Capone, Dutch Schultz, Waxey Gordon, Legs Diamond, and their rivals were sensational copy. Socialites caught in a speakeasy raid made good picture subjects. And the little man nabbed by the prohibition agents while making his own home brew or gin won the sympathy always extended to a rebel against a debatable law. Prohibition was a Godsend to the tabloid editors, but it was only a small part of the picture in the wacky 1920's.

Tabloid editors feasted, too, on stories about glamorous and sexy Hollywood and its stars—Rudolph Valentino, Fatty Arbuckle, Clara Bow. They gloried in the love affairs of the great and not-so-great —Daddy Browning and his Peaches, Kip Rhinelander, the Prince of Wales. They built sordid murder cases·into national sensations— Hall-Mills, Ruth Snyder. They glorified celebrities—Charles A. Lindbergh, Queen Marie of Rumania, Channel swimmer Gertrude Ederle. They promoted the country's sports stars—prize-fighter Jack Dempsey, golfer Bobby Jones, tennis champion Bill Tilden, football coach Knute Rockne, and homerun hitter Babe Ruth.

Joe College in his raccoon coat and Betty Coed in her tight short skirt were on the college campuses; the flapper was being emancipated, and according to the tabloids, every other flat was a Love Nest. The country was doing the Charleston and singing an inane song called, "Yes, We Have No Bananas." It tolerated H. L. Mencken but it listened to Elinor Glyn. John Held, Jr.'s flapper-days cartoons and the writings of F. Scott Fitzgerald best reflected the jazz age, which to the tabloid reader was a sensational mixture of sex, crime, conflict, and rags-to-riches stories. An imperfect picture of the real 1920's, yes; but nevertheless one which reflected the social mood.

The only complaint which a tabloid editor might have had was that the regular-sized dailies were panting nearly as avidly for the same stories. Big headlines, born of the wartime excitement, and pictures were not limited to the tabloids, nor were sensationalism and entertainment. By and large the tabloids were not much different from other dailies except in two important respects: the true tabloid of the early 1920's paid scant attention to the legitimate news of the day which other papers carried, and it went beyond the remainder of the press in raucous coverage of the most sensational material.

The *Daily News* did badly at first. Its initial circulation of 200,-000 dropped to 26,000 the second month, and two of its four reporters were fired. But Captain Patterson was discovering that his circulation potential was not among readers of the *Times*, but among the immigrant and poorly educated American-born population of

New York. The *News* was put on stands where only foreign language papers had sold before, and its pictures sold the paper. Patterson went on what he called snooping expeditions to find out what people read. He watched his readers scan the pictures, stop at the new comic strips which the *Daily News* and *Tribune* were developing, and favor crime news, sports stories, and other features. He was pleased to see that subway riders chose the *News* because it was easy to handle in the crowded cars. After a year he was more pleased to see that the *News* was selling to all types of readers. By 1921 it was second in circulation to Hearst's *Evening Journal*. Hearst's morning *American* tried to capture some of the readership going to the *News* by filling its columns with pictures and features but the tabloid won the verdict. The sharp battle between Hearst and McCormick circulation men in Chicago was transferred to New York, with lotteries, coupon prizes, and other inducements for readers. Patterson was the victor again with a limerick contest keyed to the popular taste.

Direct competition arrived for the *News* in 1924, the year it became America's most widely circulated newspaper. Hearst had experimented unsuccessfully with the tabloid format in Boston—always a poor town for journalistic innovations—but in despair of the *American's* ever whipping the *News*, he began his tabloid *Daily Mirror.* Close behind him was Bernarr Macfadden, publisher of *Physical Culture* and *True Story* magazines, and a bulging-muscle enthusiast. Macfadden selected Emile Gauvreau, up to that time the managing editor of the respectable *Hartford Courant*, as his chief editor, and the two brought out the *Daily Graphic*. The *Mirror* began to challenge the *News* on more or less straight journalistic terms, but the *Graphic* set out to see just how sensational and lurid it could be. The result was the battle of what Oswald Garrison Villard called "gutter journalism."

The *Graphic* quickly became the most notorious of the tabloids. Indeed, Gauvreau had no intention of running a newspaper. He did not bother with subscribing to a press association service, and played only the "gigantic" general news. He was trying to build a million reader audience on newsstand sales of a daily which was to be the *True Confessions* of the newspaper world. Reporters wrote first-person stories to be signed by persons in the news, and editors headlined them "I Know Who Killed My Brother,"

"He Beat Me—I Love Him," and "For 36 Hours I Lived Another Woman's Love Life." Love was a good headline word and it was paired in many ways: love pact, love thief, love slayer, love nest, love child, love cheat, love coward. A metropolitan area always has its grist of crime and sex news, murders, and court trials— but never before did one have tabloids making the most of each incident, big or grubby. Sensationalism in handling crime news aroused the ire of all responsible citizens, who were revolted by such banks of headlines as these: "Boys foil death chair. Mothers weep as governor halts execution. Would have kicked off with grin." Gauvreau's retort was that the public wanted "hot news," [3] and the evidence seemed to be on his side, as newsstand sales of the *Graphic* mounted.

Climax year of the war of the tabloids was 1926. First the Broadway producer, Earl Carroll, gave a party at which a nude dancing girl sat in a bathtub full of champagne. Before the furore had died down, the tabloids discovered a wealthy real estate man, Edward Browning, and his 15-year-old shopgirl bride. This was "hot" romance indeed and the pair became Daddy and Peaches to all of America. The *Graphic* portrayed them frolicking on a bed with Daddy saying "Woof! Woof! I'm a Goof!" Gauvreau decided to thrill his shopgirl audience with the details of Peaches' intimate diary, but at that point the law stepped in.

Next into the spotlight stepped wealthy socialite Kip Rhinelander, who charged in court that his bride of a few months had Negro blood, a fact he had not known at the time of the marriage. The sensation-hungry reporters were balked at the climax of the trial, when the judge ousted them before the attractive Mrs. Rhinelander was partially disrobed to prove a point for the defense. But Gauvreau hastily posed a bare-backed chorus girl among some of his reporters, pasted likenesses of court participants in place of the reporters' faces, and hit the street with a sell-out edition. The *Graphic* said in small type that its sensational picture was a "composograph" but most of its readers assumed that it was the real thing.

Meanwhile the desperate editors of the *Mirror* had dug up a four-year-old murder story in New Jersey. In 1922 a New Bruns-

---

[3] Gauvreau used this phrase as the title for a thinly fictionalized account of his editorship of the *Graphic:* Emile Gauvreau, *Hot News* (New York: Macaulay Company, 1931).

wick, New Jersey, minister named Edward Hall and his choir-singer sweetheart, Eleanor Mills, were found dead, apparently suicides. The *Mirror* succeeded in having the minister's widow brought to trial and for months the New Jersey town became one of the most important filing points for press associations and big newspapers in America. One witness became "the pig woman" to the 200 reporters at the trial. Unfortunately for the *Mirror*, Mrs. Hall was acquitted and sued the paper for libel.

While the Hall-Mills story was running Gertrude Ederle swam the English Channel to become America's heroine for a day. In late August of 1926 former President Charles Eliot of Harvard, and "the Sheik" of motion pictures, Rudolph Valentino, died. The *Daily News* gave Valentino six pages of space and Eliot one paragraph, thereby setting off more irate complaints from serious-minded folk. But "Valentino Dies With Smile as Lips Touch Priest's Crucifix" and "Rudy Leaped from Rags to World Hero" were tabloid copy, and the death of an educator was not. In most of the press, too, Valentino rated the most attention.

A second sensational murder trial was drummed up in the spring of 1927. A corset salesman named Judd Gray and his sweetheart, Mrs. Ruth Snyder, had collaborated in disposing of the unwanted Mr. Snyder. When it came time for Mrs. Snyder's execution in the electric chair at Sing Sing the *Graphic* blared to its readers:

Don't fail to read tomorrow's *Graphic*. An installment that thrills and stuns! A story that fairly pierces the heart and reveals Ruth Snyder's last thoughts on earth; that pulses the blood as it discloses her final letters. Think of it! A woman's final thoughts just before she is clutched in the deadly snare that sears and burns and FRIES AND KILLS! Her very last words! Exclusively in tomorrow's *Graphic*.[4]

It was the photography-minded *News* which had the last word, however. The *Graphic* might have its "confession" but the *News* proposed to take its readers inside the execution chamber. Pictures were forbidden, but a photographer, Tom Howard, strapped a tiny camera to his ankle and took his picture just after the current was turned on. The *News* put the gruesome shot on its front page, sold 250,000 extra copies, and then had to run off 750,000 additional pages later.

[4] As quoted in Helen M. Hughes, *News and the Human Interest Story* (Chicago: University of Chicago Press, 1940), p. 235.

Average net paid circulation of THE NEWS, Dec., 1927:
Sunday, 1,357,556
Daily, 1,193,297

DAILY NEWS FINAL EDITION

NEW YORK'S  PICTURE NEWSPAPER

Entered as 2nd, class matter Post Office, New York, N. Y.

Vol. 9. No. 174 28 Pages

New York, Saturday, January 14, 1928

2 Cents IN CITY | 3 CENTS

FUNERALS HELD For Gray, Mrs. Snyder

—Story on Page 3

WHEN RUTH PAID HER DEBT TO THE STATE!—The only unofficial photo ever taken within the death chamber, this most remarkable, exclusive picture shows closeup of Ruth Snyder in death chair at Sing Sing as lethal current surged through her body at 11:06 Thursday night. Its first publication in yesterday's EXTRA edition of THE NEWS was the most talked-of feat in history of journalism. Ruth's body is seen straightened within its confining gyves, her helmeted head, face masked, hand clutching, and electrode strapped to her right leg with stocking down. Autopsy table on which body was removed is beside chair.
—*Story and another electrocution picture on page 3.*

Fliers Up 40 Hours at 2 o'Clock Despite Accidents to Plane—Page 2

Courtesy, the News

The front page of the *New York Daily News* for January 14, 1928, represented the extreme in tabloid sensationalism. Tom Howard, photographer for the small Pacific & Atlantic agency took a picture of murderess Ruth Snyder in the electric chair at Sing Sing. The *News* heavily retouched his photo and had a sell-out edition.

Patterson's news and photo enterprise went beyond shocking people. When the steamer "Vestris" sank off the Atlantic coast with the loss of several hundred lives, Patterson sent all his staffers to interview the survivors on the chance that one of them had taken a picture. One had, and for $1,200 the *News* bought one of the greatest action news pictures ever taken, showing the tilted ship's deck and recording the expressions of the victims as they prepared to jump into the water, or go down with the ship. Patterson put $750,000 into Associated Press Wirephoto in the early 1930's, when other publishers were balking, and for a while had exclusive New York use of Wirephoto. The *News* developed its own staff of crack photographers and in addition welcomed shots taken by free-lancers in the vast New York area. The payoff was consistent.

With 1929 came the Wall Street crash, depression, and deepening years of unemployment; Herbert Hoover's promise of two chickens in every pot and a car in every garage gave way to soup lines and apple stands despite the president's conscientious efforts. Patterson, with his finger on the pulse of the people, told his editors and reporters that the depression and its effects upon the lives of all Americans was now the big story. What caused the bust, and what was going to be done for its victims, were more vital news subjects than the entertainment of the twenties. Not that the *News* and other papers stopped playing crime and sex news and features. But they also gave great space to the serious news of a people in trouble. America had stopped singing "My God, How the Money Rolls In," and it hoped desperately that the Franklin D. Roosevelt campaign song, "Happy Days Are Here Again," bore promise of a real New Deal in establishing genuine economic security for all classes of Americans. Patterson's *Daily News* became a firm supporter of Roosevelt's New Deal through the 1930's, to the disgust of the fiercely anti-New Deal Colonel McCormick in the *Chicago Tribune* tower.

The *Daily News* still wisecracked in its editorial columns, and still produced its headlines with a twist that caught any reader's eye. But after 1939 it had no gay greetings for the man in the White House. It broke with Roosevelt over involvement in World War II and became bitterly isolationist. Patterson's distrust of the President's foreign policy then led him to fight the administration all down the line. After his death in 1946, the *News* was under the control of Colonel McCormick, although its operations were directed by Patterson's former executives. Despite this political break with the Democratic party the *News* remained a "people's paper," climbing to peak circulations of 2,400,000 daily and 4,500,000 Sunday in 1947, before it felt the effects of a general slackening of metropolitan newspaper circulations which extended into the 1950's.[5]

Things did not go so well with the *Mirror* and *Graphic*. Hearst sold the *Mirror* in 1928, had to take it back in 1930, and then bolstered it by stealing columnist Walter Winchell from the *Graphic* and sending Arthur Brisbane in as editor. But the *Mirror* never became a profitable Hearst property. The *Graphic* never won any advertising support and died unmourned in 1932.

Two points should be made clear: very few of the other newspapers which adopted the tabloid format were of the racy character of the New York tabs; and the quest for sensational news did not die with the passing of the *Graphic* and the semi-transformation of the *Daily News*. One hopeful tabloid publisher was Cornelius Vanderbilt, Jr., who started crusading, non-salacious picture papers in Los Angeles, San Francisco, and Miami in the early 1920's. Vanderbilt won good-sized circulations for his papers, but failed to build up advertiser support, and the chain soon withered. The *Los Angeles Daily News* passed to liberal-minded Manchester Boddy, who built it into a pro-New Deal paper much like orthodox dailies except for a free-wheeling style of writing. The *Chicago Times,* founded in 1929, was likewise a liberal, tersely written paper, and less sensational than the Hearst Chicago papers, although still lively. When Marshall Field combined his *Chicago Sun* with the *Times* in 1947 he kept the tabloid format. The Scripps-Howard *Washington Daily News* and *Rocky Mountain News* were other tabloids of note, outside New York. No more than 50 dailies had adopted the tabloid format by the 1960's, however, and it was more popular with the small town and collegiate press. The curse of the old *Graphic* evidently was still feared.

Although the newspapers of the 1930's devoted far more space to stories about political and economic events and foreign affairs

[5] See Walter E. Schneider, "Fabulous Rise of N. Y. Daily News," *Editor & Publisher,* LXXII (June 24, 1939), 5, for an extensive account of 20 years of the paper's history. Patterson's obituaries appeared in *Editor & Publisher,* LXXIX (June 1, 1946), 9, and in *Time,* XLVII (June 3, 1946), 87.

than those of the 1920's, they did not lose the "big story" complex which characterized postwar journalism. The trial of Bruno Hauptmann in 1934 for the kidnaping and murder of the Lindbergh baby drew more than 300 reporters, who wired more than 11 million words in 28 days. The publicity-seeking judge turned the trial into a newsman's paradise and there was much criticism of "trial by newspaper." Lindbergh later accused the press of hounding him out of the country by relentless coverage of his private life. The Dionne quintuplets, major prize fights, the FBI's pursuit of John Dillinger, the "wrong way" flight of Douglas Corrigan to Ireland and other diverting stories were given concentrated news treatment. After World War II a fresh stream of murders and other sensational or entertaining stories hit the news wires, and in big cities competition in that field increased in intensity.

The rise of interpretative reporting was the most important development of the 1930's and 1940's, however. Proper backgrounding of news events, and covering of major areas of human activity by specialists, were not unknown before that time, just as uncritical and sensationalized treatment of news continued in the press after that time. But the impact of the political-social-economic revolution of the New Deal years, the rise of modern scientific technology, the increasing interdependence of economic groups at home, and the shrinking of the world into one vast arena for power politics forced a new approach to the handling of news. "Why" became important, along with the traditional "who did what," because the reader, more than ever, wanted and needed to know the meaning of the news. Coverage of politics, economics and business, foreign affairs, science, labor, agriculture, and social work was improved by reporter-specialists. Editorial pages also became more interpretative. The news magazines and some specialized newspapers and magazines joined in the movement, together with radio commentators. Old-style objectivity, which consisted in sticking to a factual account of what had been said or done, was challenged by a new concept of objectivity which was based upon the belief that the reader needed to have a given event placed in its proper context if truth really was to be served. Old beliefs that difficult subjects like science and economics could not be made interesting to readers likewise were discarded, out of sheer necessity.

Washington reporters found that a mere knowledge of political leaders and their ups-and-downs no longer sufficed with the coming of the New Deal. The banking crisis; the creation of the NRA, WPA, AAA, and many other new government agencies with vast socio-economic power; a rapid growth of labor unions under the NRA and Wagner Act collective bargaining guarantees; extensive government intervention in the affairs of business and agriculture; regulation of the security exchanges, and other events of the New Deal era presented one challenge after another to reporters and the desk men who handled their copy. And as international tensions built up before World War II, and as America assumed world leadership during that war and after, proper interpretation of international news became vital.

The Washington and foreign correspondents responded with increasing success to the demands thus made upon them by the pressure of the news. As the 1960's opened, there were talented Washington bureau chiefs like Raymond P. Brandt of the *St. Louis Post-Dispatch,* James B. Reston of the *New York Times,* Peter Lisagor of the *Chicago Daily News,* Robert J. Donovan of the *New York Herald Tribune,* Nat S. Finney of the *Buffalo Evening News,* and John L. Steele of *Time.* There were capable Washington reporters like Merriman Smith and Stewart Hensley of UPI, Marvin Arrowsmith and John Hightower of AP, Edward T. Folliard and Chalmers M. Roberts of the *Washington Post,* Felix Belair, Jr., of the *New York Times,* Mark S. Watson of the *Baltimore Sun,* Charles W. Roberts of *Newsweek,* and Douglass Cater of the *Reporter.* There were interpretative writers like James Marlow of AP and Lyle C. Wilson of UPI in Washington and foreign news analysts like Phil Newsom of UPI and William L. Ryan of AP. In Europe there were interpretative reporters like William H. Stoneman of the *Chicago Daily News,* Drew Middleton of the *New York Times,* K. C. Thaler of UPI, Graham Hovey of the *Minneapolis Star* and *Tribune,* and Don Cook of the *New York Herald Tribune,* in London; Preston Grover of AP and Henry Shapiro of UPI in Moscow; and A. M. Rosenthal in Geneva and C. L. Sulzberger in Paris for the *New York Times.* Many more could be named.

Specialists were required, however, both in Washington and in newspaper offices across the country. The rise of "big labor" to challenge "big business" under the collective bargaining guarantees of the New Deal brought the labor beat into full prominence.

Louis Stark of the *New York Times*, the paper's labor reporter and, with John Leary of the *New York World*, one of the first men in the field, transferred his base of operations to Washington in 1933. There Stark became the acknowledged dean of American labor reporters, as newsmen covered national labor-management bargaining in the steel and coal industries, the activities of the National Labor Relations Board, and legislative contests which culminated in the replacement of the Wagner Act by the Taft-Hartley Law. Coverage of strikes always had been a part of the nation's news report, but fuller interpretation of the problems of labor-management relations now became the good reporter's goal. He also sought to increase direct coverage of organized labor's activities and attitudes. Both Washington and local reporting were improved by numerous labor specialists.

The story of Louis Stark is an example of the manner in which some older newsmen met the challenge of specialized reporting. Stark grew up on New York's East Side and became a City News Association reporter. He joined the *Times* staff in 1917 and became a labor reporter in 1923. For the next ten years he made it his business to get acquainted with both leaders and followers in the labor movement, and studied the problems of labor and business. He covered the Sacco-Vanzetti case, the bloody coal riots in Harlan County, and other major news breaks.[6] When he went to Washington, Stark's intimate knowledge of persons and facts paid off with numerous beats and consistent leadership in labor news coverage. In 1951 he left Washington to become a *Times* editorial writer, taking with him a Pulitzer Prize and the plaudits of his newsmen associates. He told colleagues at a farewell dinner that newcomers to the labor reporting field had to be better prepared educationally than he had been, since they could not grow up with their subject as he had.[7] Stark thought there should be more full time labor reporters, but he noted with satisfaction that the list had grown considerably in 30 years. It included such men as Edwin A. Lahey of the *Chicago Daily News*, Fred Carr of the *Christian Science Monitor*, John Turcott of the *New York Daily News*, John F. Burns

---

[6] Stark's story of the execution of Sacco and Vanzetti is one of the most moving pieces of reporting of that period. Reprinted in Snyder and Morris, *A Treasury of Great Reporting*, pp. 454-60.

[7] "Louis Stark's Own Story," *Nieman Reports*, VI (January, 1952), 3.

of the *Providence Journal,* A. H. Raskin of the *New York Times,* and a score or more of equally competent associates.

The worlds of science and medicine were better covered, too, by men who repaired the damage done by the sensationalized science stories of the days of yellow journalism. Science Service, directed by Watson Davis, did much to improve the science coverage of its subscribers after 1921. The *New York Times* again was early in the field. Waldemar Kaempffert, an engineer, joined the paper as a science specialist in 1927, joined by William L. Laurence in 1930. Pulitzer Prizes were given in 1937 to a group of pioneer science writers, including Laurence, David Dietz of the Scripps-Howard newspapers, Howard W. Blakeslee of the Associated Press, John J. O'Neill of the *New York Herald Tribune,* and Gobind Behari Lal of Hearst's Universal Service. The National Association of Science Writers, formed in 1934, had 400 members by 1961. Top writers included Laurence, Dietz, Victor Cohn of the *Minneapolis Tribune,* Arthur J. Snider of the *Chicago Daily News,* Earl Ubell of the *New York Herald Tribune,* Nathan S. Haseltine of the *Washington Post,* Milton Silverman of the *San Francisco Chronicle,* Delos Smith of UPI, John Troan of Scripps-Howard, and Alton Blakeslee, Frank J. Carey, and John Barbour of AP. The elder Blakeslee and Kaempffert died during the 1950's.

Federal action to stabilize agricultural prices, to provide economic security for farmers, and to conserve soil resources became major news with the advent of the Agricultural Adjustment Administration. But the agricultural story had been an important one even before the concerted actions of the New Deal. Alfred D. Stedman of the *St. Paul Pioneer Press* and *Dispatch,* and Theodore C. Alford of the *Kansas City Star* arrived in Washington in 1929 as the first specialists in agricultural news correspondence. The press associations then did not sense the significance of many stories involving agriculture and even left some major stories uncovered or undeveloped. Early in the 1930's, however, the Associated Press selected an agricultural expert, Roy F. Hendrickson, and coverage from Washington by the AP and its competitors sharply improved. As in other specialized fields, however, lack of qualified manpower in bureaus around the country kept coverage from regional areas at a lower level than that developed in the capital. Farm editors like the veteran J. S. Russell of the *Des Moines Register* and *Tribune* and Stedman, returned to St. Paul from a long Washington career, kept their own regional coverage at a high pitch through their intimate knowledge of agricultural problems and trends.

Education writers became specialists, too, like Ruth Dunbar of the *Chicago Sun-Times,* Wilma Morrison of the *Portland Oregonian,* and Fred M. Hechinger of the *New York Times.* Civic and business news editors, reporters on social work and public health activities, food editors, religious editors who were more than church news rewrite men, automotive and aviation editors, and other new specialists joined the older established financial, book, music, fashion, travel, garden, theatrical, and sports editors. Coverage of crime news became a sociological problem for some newspapers, an advance over the usual sensationalized treatment.

Some larger dailies developed editorial-page staffs of a size and quality in keeping with the trend toward specialized news coverage and interpretation. Papers like the *New York Times,* the *Milwaukee Journal,* and the *St. Louis Post-Dispatch* had the resources and the inclination to keep their editorial pages staffed in this superior manner. Others, like the *Washington Post* and *Minneapolis Star* and *Tribune,* put emphasis upon editorial writers traveling or going directly to news sources as part of their work. No editor or editorial writer worth his salt could ignore the increasing number of specialized news fields and the pressure upon editorial page men became greater each decade. Fortunately an ever-growing amount of explanatory interpretation was being done by the reporters and specialized writers themselves, and the editorial-page role became more one of putting events into perspective and stating of opinion.

The newspaper thus became more interpretative in its style of writing and in its content. During the 1930's books appeared which urged backgrounding of the news, adequate preparation of reporters and editors for their specialized tasks, and a breaking away from old traditions.[8] Some newspapers attempted to departmentalize the news as a means of calling reader attention to various areas of significant news, but the idea did not catch on. Others used typographical devices to indicate insertions of background information

---

[8] Two of them were Herbert Brucker's *The Changing American Newspaper* (New York: Columbia University Press, 1937), and Sidney Kobre's *Backgrounding the News* (Baltimore: Twentieth Century Press, 1939).

and interpretation into news stories, but most papers preferred simply to give their writers greater latitude in adequately reporting their stories.

The extreme in interpretation was reached by the New York tabloid, *PM*, founded in 1940 and financed by Marshall Field. *PM*, under the editorship of Ralph Ingersoll, made it a policy to express its liberal point of view in its news columns, to the point where it became a daily journal of opinion. The paper had a notable staff and contributed a fighting spirit to New York journalism. But its hopes that it could exist on the basis of its intelligent writing, excellent pictures, and interpretative appeal—without solicitation of advertising—had faded by 1946. Even when it accepted advertising, *PM* languished financially. Field sold out in 1948, the paper became the *New York Star*, and fought for life under the editorship of Joseph Barnes. It backed President Harry S. Truman for re-election before suspending publication in 1949.

The *Christian Science Monitor* and the *Wall Street Journal* became nationally read as specialized newspapers of interpretation. The *Monitor* in 1961 was approaching 250,000 circulation, and was printing from mats airmailed to Los Angeles and London from its Boston offices. It had 12,000 British readers. The *Wall Street Journal*, however, was printing nearly 800,000 copies in eight nationwide plants. The *New York Times* led among regular dailies in national circulation with 150,000 daily and a half-million Sunday. It was also printing 45,000 copies daily in Paris, in competition with the *New York Herald Tribune*'s European edition of 70,000. And the *Times* was planning a weekday western edition, printed in Los Angeles, for late 1962.

The *Monitor* was begun in 1908 by Mrs. Mary Baker Eddy, founder of the Church of Christ, Scientist, in protest against the sensationalism of other dailies and their emphasis upon news of crimes and disasters. It was not intended to be, and did not become, a religious propaganda organ, but rather a serious-minded afternoon daily. Since by Christian Science tenets it avoided or minimized stories involving disasters, crime, or death, it had space in which to develop Washington and foreign correspondence, significant regional stories from around the country, and features dealing with literature, music, and art. Eventually it became noted for its ability to sit back periodically and take a long-view look at major news developments, thereby contributing interpretative analyses of problems and trends in government, world affairs, economics, and social development.

In its first ten years the *Monitor* gained 120,000 readers under the editorship of Frederick Dixon, then was temporarily disrupted by a dispute over its management. Editor Willis J. Abbot helped to restore its prestige in the 1920's. But the *Monitor's* outstanding editor has been Erwin D. Canham, who joined the staff in 1925 and served as a Washington and foreign correspondent before becoming managing editor in 1940 and editor in 1945. Canham's voice was often raised in discussions of journalistic problems and his professional associates soon came to regard him as an influential editor of a great newspaper. Paul S. Deland and Saville R. Davis followed Canham as managing editors. Donovan Richardson conducted the noncrusading but thoughtful editorial page. American news editor Robert R. Brunn supervised a network of bureaus and special correspondents, including a Washington staff of William H. Stringer, Richard L. Strout, Neal A. Stanford, and Josephine Ripley (Roscoe Drummond left to join the *New York Herald Tribune* in 1953). Overseas editor Joseph G. Harrison had staff members in seven bureaus. Among the most famous were Edmund Stevens, 1950 Pulitzer Prize winner for a series interpreting the Soviet Union, and Joseph C. Harsch, columnist from his NBC post in London. Charles Gratke, noted foreign news specialist, died in a 1949 airplane crash.

The *Wall Street Journal* was a solidly edited financial daily like its New York competitor, the *Journal of Commerce*, until Bernard Kilgore became its managing editor in 1940. It had been founded in 1889 by Charles H. Dow as the voice of the Dow Jones and Company financial news service. Clarence W. Barron became owner in 1902. Circulation was at a post-depression level of 30,000 daily when Kilgore took charge. He broadened the paper's coverage to include lucidly written summaries of important national and world news and comprehensive stories interpreting trends in industry. Circulation jumped to 65,000 in 1950, hit 360,000 in 1955, then leaped past 700,000 by 1960 as the *Journal* expanded to eight printing plants across the country, connected to the New York office by electric typesetting devices.

Kilgore, who became company president in 1945, had three former managing editors working with him on the *Journal* staff: William F.

Kerby and Buren H. McCormack, editorial directors, and Robert I. Bottorff, executive editor. Warren H. Phillips was managing editor. Editor William H. Grimes and his successor, Vermont C. Royster, both won Pulitzer Prizes for editorial writing, and Edward R. Cony won in 1961 for national reporting. The paper had 15 news offices in the United States, four in Canada, and five overseas. It also had the facilities of the Dow Jones News Service, headed by John O'Riley. A new venture of early 1962 was an affiliated national weekly newspaper of general appeal, the *National Observer*, edited in Washington with Don Carter and William Giles as news executives.

Some of the country's magazines became important factors in the trend toward interpretation and news specialization. There was a new element injected into the magazine world, however. The news magazines, as well as the magazines of opinion and general magazines, became important in magazine journalism's contribution to coverage of public affairs.

In the muckraking era, such general magazines as *Collier's*, *McClure's*, *Everybody's*, the *American*, and *Cosmopolitan* served both as entertainment media and as "people's champions," exposing industrial monopolies and political corruption and crusading for a broadening of political and economic democracy. But that phase ended by World War I and the old champions withered. *McClure's* went downhill before 1920 and flickered out in 1933; *Everybody's* died in 1930, and *Collier's* and the *American* in 1956. *Cosmopolitan* remained in the 1960's general magazine field, along with the much larger *Reader's Digest*, *Saturday Evening Post*, *Life*, and *Look*. These continued to carry significant articles on public affairs. The women's magazines—*Ladies' Home Journal*, *McCall's*, and *Good Housekeeping*—made some contribution to current affairs coverage. But the influence of the general magazines was far less than at the turn of the century.[9]

Most of the serious magazines which were important as sources of information and as vehicles of opinion before World War I fell by the wayside in the 1920's and 1930's. The *Century* was merged with the *Forum* and then both disappeared into *Current History*. *World's Work*, one of the best, had to combine with *Review of*

[9] For the modern era, see Theodore Peterson, *Magazines in the Twentieth Century* (Urbana: University of Illinois Press, 1956, rev. 1958). Economics of magazine publishing and current magazine empires will be covered in Chapter 27 of this book.

Reviews, which in turn was sold to the *Literary Digest.* The *Digest,* founded in 1890 and long a highly popular reporter on American newspaper opinion and current affairs, slumped away before the onslaught of newer-type news magazines and abruptly ended its career by publishing the results of a postcard poll which predicted that Alfred M. Landon would defeat Franklin D. Roosevelt for the presidency in 1936 (Landon carried two states). Of the distinguished literary magazines, *Scribner's* collapsed in 1939. *Harper's* became primarily a public affairs magazine after the mid-twenties and reached its hundredth anniversary in 1950 under the editorship of Frederick Lewis Allen. John Fischer succeeded Allen as editor in 1953 and furthered *Harper's* position among high-grade magazines. The *Atlantic Monthly* shifted toward public affairs articles, but to a lesser degree, after Edward A. Weeks replaced longtime editor Ellery Sedgwick in 1938. The *Atlantic* celebrated its centennial in 1957. *Harper's* and *Atlantic* pooled their advertising appeals and enjoyed considerable success, with circulations above 250,000.

H. L. Mencken's *American Mercury* was a bright new star of the magazine world in 1924, challenging American complacency, shocking solid citizens, and delighting the young rebels who already had enjoyed the work of Mencken and George Jean Nathan in *Smart Set* since 1914. But *American Mercury* declined after Mencken and his associates let it pass into other hands in 1933. Another newcomer of 1924 was the *Saturday Review of Literature,* founded by Henry Seidel Canby (who also was first editor-in-chief of the Book-of-the-Month Club). After Norman Cousins became editor in 1942, the *Saturday Review* (its title was shortened in 1952) expanded its interests beyond literature to include eventually music, science, education, communications, and travel. With circulation mounting to 265,000, the magazine put its business affairs in the hands of the *McCall's* publishing corporation in 1961.

Among the struggling magazines of opinion operating at the liberal left, the *Nation* (founded in 1865) and the *New Republic* (founded in 1914) survived into the 1960's. Godkin's *Nation* was owned by the Villard family from 1881 to 1934 and followed Oswald Garrison Villard's liberal, pacifist course. Freda Kirchwey became editor in 1937 and Carey McWilliams in 1955 as the magazine passed through financial crises and intra-staff dissensions over policy toward the Soviet Union. Its 1961 circulation was 25,000. The

New Republic, founded with money from the Willard D. Straight family in 1914, exerted influence during the Wilsonian era with the writings of editor Herbert Croly and Walter Lippmann. It again had force in the 1930's under editor Bruce Bliven. When Michael Straight took over its direction in 1946 he appointed Henry A. Wallace editor. Circulation touched 100,000, but Wallace's involvement in the ultra-liberal Progressive Party as its 1948 presidential candidate brought his resignation. Sales slumped, but were restored after 1956 by editor Gilbert A. Harrison. With 40,000 circulation the *New Republic* again was a liberal force. The *Reporter,* launched in 1949 by Max Ascoli as a fortnightly, won widespread praise for its high-grade research articles and sharply pointed opinion pieces, and had 170,000 readers by 1961. In Douglass Cater it had one of the best of the Washington correspondents.

Other opinion magazines with smaller circulations were publishing in the 1960's. The *Progressive,* founded in 1909 by the La Follette family in Wisconsin, continued its excellent work under the editorship of Morris H. Rubin. The *New Leader,* socialist but strongly anticommunist in its origins, appeared in 1924 as a tabloid and adopted magazine format in 1950. Samuel M. (Sol) Levitas made it a stronghold of intellectual thought and writing from 1930 until his death in 1961. The *Commonweal,* founded in 1924 by a group of Catholics but not connected with the church, won wide respect under the editorship of Edward Skillin. Another leading religious spokesman was the *Christian Century,* a nondenominational Protestant organ dating from 1884 which was given stature by editor Charles Clayton Morrison between 1908 and 1947. His successors were Dr. Paul Hutchison and Harold E. Fey. With 36,000 readers in 1961, the *Christian Century* was the most widely quoted of religious journals. The voice of the far right in American political opinion was best represented in the *National Review,* founded in 1955 by William F. Buckley, Jr. He had 32,000 readers and an $860,000 deficit by 1960.

Possibly the most distinctive of American magazines arrived in 1925, when Harold Ross began publication of his *New Yorker.* Ross was editor of the *Stars and Stripes* in World War I days and met Franklin P. Adams and Alexander Woollcott on that distinguished staff. In New York in 1925 they helped him to get his magazine venture under way, with the financial backing of Raoul Fleischmann. The magazine, Ross said, would be a humorous one, reflecting metropolitan life and keeping up with the affairs of the day, with a gay and satirical vein which would mark it as not "for the old lady in Dubuque." Ross was a demanding, irascible editor who hired and fired about 100 staff members in the first struggling year and a half before he began to find his stars: E. B. White, conductor of "Talk of the Town"; Rea Irvin, art editor who drew Eustace Tilley, the supercilious dandy who is the *New Yorker*'s trade mark; writers James Thurber, Ogden Nash, Wolcott Gibbs, S. J. Perelman; artists Peter Arno, Helen Hokinson, Otto Soglow, and a host of others who contributed the famous *New Yorker* cartoons. But the *New Yorker* was more than cartoons, whimsy, and curiously plotless fiction; it had its penetrating "Profiles," its "Reporter at Large," and other incisive commentaries on public affairs. When Ross died in 1951, his magazine was a solid success, both in circulation and in advertising, and under a new editor, William Shawn, it continued its career. There was some criticism as by-lines inevitably changed (*Time* reported in 1960 that Shawn's *New Yorker* had 97 subscribers in Dubuque, including several old ladies). But there were 430,000 subscribers and greater advertising profits, as well as such new talent as Washington correspondent Richard Rovere, writer John Updike, and jazz columnist Whitney Balliett.

Editing his magazine for the old lady in Dubuque, on the other hand, was George Horace Lorimer of the *Saturday Evening Post*. The solid success of that Cyrus H. K. Curtis enterprise enabled Lorimer to publish the fiction of the leading American writers of the first third of the twentieth century. With the fiction went inspirational biographies, articles stressing the material success of American business, and factual reporting pieces on a variety of current events. The *Post* became the reflection of a middle-of-the-road America, and its influence was spread to all corners of the country. After Lorimer's retirement in 1937 the *Post* had a shakedown, and under the editorship of Ben Hibbs its appearance and contents were modernized and strengthened. By 1961, when Hibbs passed the editorship to Robert Fuoss, the *Post* had 6½ million circulation. But it was caught in the same downswing of advertising that had caused the deaths of *Collier's* and other general magazines in the era of television, and Fuoss instituted makeup and content changes that would have left Lorimer speechless.

Very likely contributing to the demise of the quality magazines was the spectacular success of the *Reader's Digest,* which began in 1922 to print condensed versions of articles of current interest and entertainment value which had appeared in other magazines. The brainchild of DeWitt Wallace and his wife, Lila Acheson Wallace, the *Reader's Digest* slowly won readers during the 1920's, and then mushroomed to a one million circulation by 1935. The pocket-size style of the magazine, its staff's keen judgment of popular tastes, and skillful editing for condensation continued to make it a national best seller as circulation reached 3 million in 1938, 5 million in 1942 and 9 million in 1946. Wallace now began to develop his own articles, partly because some magazines began to refuse him reprint rights, and partly to support his personal outlook on life. Gradually during the 1940's, the magazine, which supposedly was an impartial digest of material in other publications, began to acquire a noticeable and conservative point of view of its own. Critics complained that its "inspirational" tone was unrealistic, if not Pollyanna-like, and offered little help in meeting major national and world problems. Nevertheless the *Reader's Digest* grew in size and potential influence. In 1961 it had 13 million circulation in the United States and 11 million more for foreign language editions in 60 countries. Wallace reversed an old ban and accepted advertising, beginning in 1955, further adding to the *Digest's* profits and to the woes of other publishers.

The other big new name in magazine journalism was that of Henry R. Luce. He, like Wallace, became extraordinarily successful and therefore a controversial figure. His weekly newsmagazine, *Time,* became dominant in its field, while his picture magazine, *Life,* became a runaway success in circulation and advertising.

The story of Time Inc. began in March, 1923. Luce and a fellow Yale man, Briton Hadden, brought out the first issue of *Time* that month. Both had been editors of the *Yale Daily News* and had worked briefly for New York newspapers—Hadden for the *World* and Luce for the *Daily News.* The young men in their twenties looked about them in the era of the 1920's and announced in their prospectus:

Although daily journalism has been more highly developed in the United States than in any other country in the world—
Although foreigners marvel at the excellence of our periodicals, *World's*

Work, Century, Literary Digest, Outlook, and the rest—
People in America are, for the most part, poorly informed.
This is not the fault of the daily newspapers; they print all the news.
It is not the fault of the weekly "reviews"; they adequately develop and comment on the news.
To say with the facile cynic that it is the fault of the people themselves is to beg the question.
People are uninformed because no publication has adapted itself to the time which busy men are able to spend on simply keeping informed.

Time, its editors promised, would organize and departmentalize the news of the week. Its slogan became: "*Time* is written as if by one man for one man." Its coverage of national affairs, foreign news, science, religion, business, education, and other areas was to be written not for people who had expert knowledge of each of the fields, but for *Time's* "busy man." The editors developed the use of the narrative story in telling the news and injected strong elements of human interest. To accumulate myriads of facts which could be woven into each story, *Time* developed an extensive research and library staff as well as a good-sized news-gathering organization of its own to supplement press association services.

Hadden died in 1929, after seeing *Time* reach a circulation of 200,000, and Luce went on alone. A "March of Time" radio program was begun in 1931 and its motion picture version in 1935. *Fortune,* Luce's lavish magazine for businessmen selling at a dollar a copy, was successful even in the first depression year of 1930. *Life,* hitting the newsstands in 1936, caught the interest of a photography-conscious people and had customers fighting for copies. *Sports Illustrated,* less of a success, was added in 1954. Time Inc. moved to Rockefeller Center in 1938, opened its own 48-story Time & Life building there in 1960, and counted a record-breaking 270 million dollars annual gross. *Time* had 14 domestic news bureaus and 19 abroad, while *Life* had other picture bureaus. *Time* claimed 3 million circulation for its domestic, Canadian, and three overseas editions (2½ million in the United States). *Life* reached 7 million at the start of 1962.

There were things about *Time* which aroused criticism, however. Luce and his editors made no pretense of sticking to the usual concepts of journalistic objectivity, which they considered mythical. Nor did *Time* want to be called impartial, it said; rather "fairness" was *Time's* goal. In a historical essay published on its twenty-fifth anniversary *Time* said: "What's the difference between impartiality and fairness? The responsible journalist is 'partial' to that interpretation of the facts which seems to him to fit things as they are. He is fair in not twisting the facts to support his view, in not suppressing the facts that support a different view." [10]

Some critics felt, however, that *Time* sometimes was not fair to its readers since it presented opinion and editorial hypothesis intermingled with the straight news. The editors thus were doing the thinking for the "busy man" reader. *Time's* editorial biases were accented by its use of the narrative and human interest techniques, and in its earlier years by its over-use of adjectives and its development of that journalistic "horror" called *Time*style (reverse word order, inverted sentences, and telescoped words). Still, *Time* had widespread influence and it served many readers by summarizing day-by-day news in its weekly digests. Particularly, its specialized departments brought news of science, medicine, religion, business, education, art, radio, the press, and other areas to many who never before had followed happenings in such diverse fields of interest.

After *Time* bought the remains of the *Literary Digest* in 1938 its only direct competitor was *Newsweek*, founded in 1933. *Newsweek's* format was almost identical to that of *Time*, but its editors injected less opinion into its columns. Financed by the wealth of the Astor and Harriman families and directed by Malcolm Muir after 1937, *Newsweek* grew steadily in influence. By 1961 it had 1½ million circulation, its own New York headquarters building, two overseas editions, and a network of six domestic and 10 foreign news bureaus. That year it was sold to the *Washington Post's* publisher, Philip L. Graham, for 9 million dollars. Graham took control as chairman of the board of *Newsweek*.

Devoting itself exclusively to news of national and international importance was *U. S. News & World Report*, a combination of David Lawrence's publishing ventures. Lawrence ran the *United States Daily* in Washington from 1926 to 1933, then changed it to a weekly. In 1946 he launched *World Report*, which he combined with his older journal in 1948. By 1961 the magazine had 1,250,000 readers, a large Washington bureau, and nine overseas bureaus. Specializing in news of business and industry was *Business Week*, founded in 1929 by the McGraw-Hill Publishing Company. It and

---

[10] *Time*, LI (March 8, 1948), 66.

34 other McGraw-Hill publications were served by the McGraw-Hill World News Service, headed by John Wilhelm, which had seven domestic bureaus and 10 more overseas. *Business Week's* circulation was 375,000.

The successful competitor to *Life* was *Look*, begun by Gardner Cowles in 1937. It at first adopted the rotogravure techniques of the Cowles family newspapers in Des Moines and Minneapolis, but gradually developed major articles on public affairs. A fortnightly, it reached 2 million circulation in 1945, passed 4 million in 1955, and, like *Life*, touched the 7 million mark at the start of 1962. Daniel D. Mich was its longtime editorial director.

The success of *Time* prompted some newspapers to start Sunday news-in-review sections. The *Cincinnati Enquirer* began such a feature in 1930, followed by the *New York Sun* in 1933. A "News of the Week in Review" section of the *New York Times* appeared in 1935 under the direction of the Sunday editor, Lester Markel. Its two pages summarizing the week's leading news developments, and its several pages of special articles by Washington and foreign correspondents, made the section a Pulitzer special citation winner. Another excellent summary was the *New York Herald Tribune's* "History in the Making." The *San Francisco Chronicle's* "This World" tabloid-style section followed the news magazine technique closely. Other extensive news-in-review sections were to be found in the *St. Louis Post-Dispatch* and *Washington Star*.

No one in newspaper or magazine work had the mass audiences which radio and television provided for their news analysts and commentators—a subject to be developed in the following chapter. For all, the job of trying to put the jumble of the news into true focus was an incredibly difficult one, considering the space and time limitations of print and electronic journalism, and some of their time-honored but hampering practices. The challenge remained the same: more qualified men and women with more time to do real jobs of interpretative reporting in increasingly complex news situations.

ANNOTATED BIBLIOGRAPHY

Books:

Allen, Frederick Lewis, *The Big Change*. New York: Harper & Brothers, 1952. Life in the first half of the twentieth century, as interpreted by the former editor of *Harper's*, who also covered the 1920's in *Only Yesterday* (1931) and the 1930's in *Since Yesterday* (1940).

Bainbridge, John, *Little Wonder*. New York: Reynal & Hitchcock, 1946. A critical study of the *Reader's Digest*, which originally appeared as a *New Yorker* profile.

Barck, Oscar T., and Nelson M. Blake, *Since 1900*. New York: The Macmillan Company, 1952. A general history of America starting at the turn of the century.

Beard, Charles A. and Mary R., *America in Midpassage*. New York: The Macmillan Company, 1939. Vol. III of the *Rise of American Civilization*, surveying life and thought in the 1920's and 1930's.

Bessie, Simon M., *Jazz Journalism*. New York: E. P. Dutton & Company, 1938. The best story of the tabloids, prefaced with a readable account of the rise of sensationalism.

Bird, George L., and Frederic E. Merwin, eds., *The Press and Society: A Book of Readings*. New York: Prentice-Hall, Inc., 1951. Chapter 14 deals with specialized news coverage.

Busch, Noel F., *Briton Hadden*. New York: Farrar, Straus and Young, Inc., 1949. The biography of the co-founder of *Time*, covering the magazine's early years.

Canham, Erwin D., *Commitment to Freedom: The Story of the Christian Science Monitor*. Boston: Houghton Mifflin Company, 1958. By the editor of the *Monitor*, tracing 50 years of service.

Goldman, Eric F., *The Crucial Decade: America, 1945-1955*. New York: Alfred A. Knopf, Inc., 1956. A sequel to *Rendezvous with Destiny*.

Hofstadter, Richard, *The Age of Reform*. New York: Alfred A. Knopf, Inc., 1955. A study of reform leaders from Bryan to F.D.R.

Hughes, Helen M., *News and the Human Interest Story*. Chicago: University of Chicago Press, 1940. A sociological study of the feature story and sensationalism, with some discussion of the tabloid era.

Kramer, Dale, *Ross and the New Yorker*. Garden City: Doubleday & Company, Inc., 1951. A biography of Harold Ross, editor of the *New Yorker*, which appeared just before Ross died. Ross didn't like the book. See also *The New Yorker Twenty-fifth Anniversary Album: 1925-1950* (1951), for the magazine's delightful cartoons.

Link, Arthur S., *American Epoch*. New York: Alfred A. Knopf, Inc., 1955. A history of the United States since the 1890's.

Manchester, William, *Disturber of the Peace*. New York: Harper & Brothers, 1950. Best of the biographies of H. L. Mencken, whose autobiography is titled *The Days of H. L. Mencken* (New York: Alfred A. Knopf, Inc., 1947).

Morris, Lloyd, *Postscript to Yesterday*. New York: Random House, Inc., 1947. An unconventional but valuable social history which surveys the

American scene of the past 50 years. Included is a section on the newspapers and magazines.

Mott, Frank Luther, *The News in America*. Cambridge: Harvard University Press, 1952. Chapters 6, 7, and 8 of this study of news cover problems discussed in this chapter.

Peterson, Theodore, *Magazines in the Twentieth Century*. Urbana: University of Illinois Press, 1956, rev. 1958. A gold mine of interpretation and factual detail about the magazine industry and hundreds of publications.

Preston, Charles, ed., *Main Street and Beyond: The World of the Wall Street Journal*. New York: Simon and Schuster, 1959. A compilation of reprints, with a brief history of the paper.

Schlesinger, Arthur M., Jr., *The Age of Roosevelt*. Boston: Houghton Mifflin Company, 1957 ff. A multi-volume history of the New Deal years, ranking at the top.

Stewart, Kenneth, and John Tebbel, *Makers of Modern Journalism*. New York: Prentice-Hall, Inc., 1952. Includes discussions of Joseph M. Patterson, Henry Luce, DeWitt Wallace, Erwin D. Canham, and the *PM* experiment.

Sullivan, Mark, *The Twenties* (*Our Times*, Vol. VI). New York: Charles Scribner's Sons, 1935. This volume provides the political and social background for the era of jazz journalism in a delightful manner.

Tebbel, John, *An American Dynasty*. Garden City: Doubleday & Company, Inc., 1947. The story of the McCormick and Patterson newspapers, including the *New York Daily News*.

———, *George Horace Lorimer and The Saturday Evening Post*. Garden City: Doubleday & Company, Inc., 1948. Both a biography of Lorimer and a history of the *Post*, which he edited from 1899 to 1937.

Thurber, James, *The Years with Ross*. Boston, Little, Brown, 1957. A first-rate biography by a *New Yorker* writer; Ross might have liked it.

Wecter, Dixon, *The Age of the Great Depression, 1929-1941*, A History of American Life, Vol. XIII. New York: The Macmillan Company, 1948. Excellent social history.

Willey, Malcolm M., and Ralph D. Casey, eds., *The Press in the Contemporary Scene*, Annals of the American Academy of Political and Social Science, CCXIX (January 1942). Contains several articles on interpretative reporting trends.

Wish, Harvey, *Contemporary America: The National Scene Since 1900*. New York: Harper & Brothers, 1955. Excellent social history.

Wood, James Playsted, *Magazines in the United States*. New York: The Ronald Press Company, 1956. Social background is provided.

———, *Of Lasting Interest: The Story of the Reader's Digest*. Garden City: Doubleday & Company, Inc., 1958. Friendly tone.

Periodicals and Monographs:

An extensive selected bibliography covering books and articles about magazine journalism, edited by John E. Drewry, appeared in the *Journalism Quarterly*, XXV (September 1948), 260.

Alexander, Jack, "Vox Populi," *New Yorker*, XIV (August 6-20, 1938). A profile of Captain Patterson.

Allen, Frederick Lewis, "The American Magazine Grows Up," *Atlantic Monthly*, CLXXX (November 1947), 77. An admirable survey of magazine publishing trends.

Childs, Marquis, "The Christian Science Monitor," *Saturday Evening Post*, CCXVIII (September 15, 1945), 14. Reprinted in Drewry, *More Post Biographies*.

"The Common Touch," *Time*, LVIII (December 10, 1951), 64. *Time* takes an extensive look at the *Reader's Digest*.

Erwin, Ray, "Wall Street Journal Grows into a National Newspaper," *Editor & Publisher*, XCIV (August 19, 1961), 12. An extensive article with historical background. See also press section of *Time*, LXXIV (October 12, 1959), 44, and LXXVIII (November 10, 1961), 46; *Newsweek*, LVIII (November 6, 1961), 94.

Gibbs, Wolcott, "Time—Fortune—Life—Luce," *New Yorker*, XII (November 28, 1936), 20. A dissection of the Luce empire.

Krieghbaum, Hillier, *American Newspaper Reporting of Science News*. Manhattan: Kansas State College Bulletin, XXV, No. 5, 1941. A brief historical summary. See also his *Science, the News, and the Public* (New York: New York University Press, 1958), and the press section of *Newsweek*, LVII (January 9, 1961), 72.

Lasch, Robert, "PM Post-Mortem," *Atlantic Monthly*, CLXXXII (July 1948), 44. An excellent analysis of the *PM* experiment and of the reasons for the newspaper's failure.

Tebbel, John, "The *New York Times* Goes West," *Saturday Review*, XLIV (November 11, 1961), 69. Report on national newspapers.

"The Reader's Digest," *Fortune*, XIV (November 1936), 121.

"The Story of an Experiment," *Time*, LI (March 8, 1948), 55. *Time* evaluates itself after 25 years.

"The Troubled Press," *Fortune*, XLV (February 1952), 124. An analysis of the problems of Washington news coverage and of the capital press corps.

White, William S., "News in Washington," *Harper's*, CCXVII (August 1958), 76. Criticism of the press corps by a member.

Chapter 26

RADIO AND TELEVISION: NEW COMPETITORS

> Radio broadcasting is an essential part of the modern press. It shares the same functions and encounters the same problems as the older agencies of mass communication. On the other hand, radio exhibits significant differences. Its ability to draw millions of citizens into close and simultaneous contact with leaders and with events of the moment gives it a reach and an influence of peculiar importance in the management of public affairs.
> —Commission on Freedom of the Press

THE FIRST AMERICAN RADIO STATIONS to seek regular public listenership made their bows in 1920. Forty years later, there were nearly three times as many radio and television stations in the United States as there were daily newspapers. In the interval the scratchy-sounding crystal sets of radio's headphone days had been transformed into big-screen television whose picture tubes could give home viewers on-the-spot journalistic coverage of history in the making. The reader of the printed page thus also had become a listener and a viewer for new communications media competing with newspapers, magazines, and books.

Competition among the media for the attention of the mass audience involved competition to inform as well as to entertain, for radio almost from the first sought to capitalize on the intrinsic drama of news events. And inevitably the growth of broadcasting

651

led to a sharp battle with the print media for advertising revenue. This chapter, and the one which follows, will trace the varying fortunes of the mass media in the years of vast economic and social change which followed the advent of radio.

The name De Forest has the same relationship to the history of radio broadcasting as that of Marconi to wireless telegraphy.[1] While the Italian scientist was perfecting wireless transmission of messages, other inventors were seeking a way to transmit the sounds of the human voice. Radio was the product of many individual efforts, but the improvement made by Dr. Lee De Forest in 1906 in the vacuum tube was essential to the development of voice broadcasting. Within the year both De Forest and Reginald A. Fessenden achieved successful voice transmissions. Public attention was attracted in 1910, when De Forest broadcast Enrico Caruso's tenor voice from the stage of the Metropolitan Opera in New York. It was De Forest, too, who did the first newscasting in the United States when he broadcast the 1916 Wilson-Hughes presidential election returns from his Highbridge, New York, experimental station, using bulletins furnished by the *New York American*.

Despite these successes in voice broadcasting, there was no immediate attention paid to the possibilities of mass radio listening. Marconi and other wireless telegraphy pioneers had been interested primarily in point-to-point message communication. The government, too, had an interest in using the new process. The U. S. Navy had 20 wireless stations in operation by 1904, sending code messages, and it was interested in De Forest's success in voice transmission. The Navy quickly had become a rival of the American Marconi Company in developing what the Navy dubbed "radiotelegraph."

Primarily to prevent interference with government broadcasting, Congress enacted a 1912 law which provided that the Department of Commerce should issue licenses to private broadcasters and assign a wave length for commercial operators which would not conflict with government wave lengths. During World War I all use of wireless was placed under government control and experimentation was concentrated upon military uses. But by March 1, 1920, private operation of broadcasting facilities was fully restored.

[1] See page 495 for the story of Marconi's development of wireless.

The radio experimenters now found that they had an audience of some size. It was composed of amateur enthusiasts who had built their own receivers and transmitters to become wireless "hams," and of crystal set owners who could pick up broadcasts on their headphones. When Dr. Frank Conrad, a Westinghouse engineer who operated experimental station 8XK, used music rather than spoken signals to test reception of his 1919 broadcasts in Pittsburgh, he got fan mail from hundreds of radio amateurs. A local department store began advertising Westinghouse crystal sets for sale to hear "Dr. Conrad's popular broadcasts." Westinghouse decided that there was a new sales market awaiting it and applied for the first full commercial license for standard broadcasting. Its station, KDKA, began operating November 2, 1920, with a broadcast of returns from the Harding-Cox presidential election.

But KDKA was not the first station on the air with news. The University of Wisconsin station, WHA, was broadcasting weather and market reports in 1919. Regular daily programs first began in Detroit, where a De Forest sales organization had obtained a license for experimental station 8MK. On August 20, 1920, that station began daily operations from the *Detroit News* building, under the newspaper's sponsorship. August 31 it broadcast the results of a Michigan primary election and from that time on it carried music, talks, and news for a part of each day. The *News* obtained its full commercial license for what became station WWJ in October, 1921.[2]

Radio broadcasting thus began as a means of promoting another enterprise. The *Detroit News* looked upon WWJ as a service to the public which would gain goodwill and sell papers. Other newspapers soon followed in establishing stations, among them the *Kansas City Star, Milwaukee Journal, Chicago Tribune, Los Angeles Times, Louisville Courier-Journal, Atlanta Journal, Dallas News,* and *Chicago Daily News.* Department stores also built stations which would promote their names and wares. But the most important elements in the growth of national radio broadcasting were the big companies of the communications and electric manu-

---

[2] The best account of the development of radio newscasting is in Mitchell V. Charnley, *News by Radio* (New York: The Macmillan Company, 1948). An interesting, but not always accurate, history of radio is Francis Chase, Jr. *Sound and Fury* (New York: Harper & Brothers, 1942).

facturing industries: American Telephone & Telegraph, Westinghouse, and General Electric. Radio's growth would mean expansion of outlets for their products and services.

The pioneer Westinghouse station, KDKA, scored many radio firsts as it pointed the way toward achieving public interest in buying radio sets. During 1921 it broadcast a series of public speeches by national figures, an on-the-spot report of a prize fight, and major league baseball games. Westinghouse also opened stations in New York, Chicago, Philadelphia, and Boston. General Electric built WGY, its powerful Schenectady, New York, station, and American Telephone & Telegraph built WEAF (now WNBC) in New York City.

More importantly, the three companies had gone together in 1919 to form the Radio Corporation of America. At government urging, stimulated by U. S. Navy officers interested in the new medium, the companies had bought up British-owned Marconi patents on radio equipment, which they pooled with their own patent rights in the new RCA. They thus brought into being the future giant of the radio industry, although at first RCA devoted itself to wireless message service.[3]

In 1922 the big companies began a competitive struggle for control of radio. American Telephone & Telegraph held two trump cards. Under the patent-pooling agreements with its competitors AT&T held considerable power over many stations' rights to charge fees for broadcasting. And the telephone company observed that KDKA had been successful in using telephone lines to bring church and theater programs into the studio for broadcasting.

So when WEAF went on the air in August, 1922, American Telephone & Telegraph announced that it would be an advertising-supported station. Within seven months it had some two dozen sponsors using air time, and the era of commercialization of radio had dawned.[4] At the same time WEAF was experimenting with use of telephone lines to air inter-city broadcasts—telephone lines which AT&T now withheld from its competitors.

[3] The full story of RCA's rise and of other concentration of radio control is told in Llewellyn White, *The American Radio* (Chicago: University of Chicago Press, 1947).

[4] The *Kansas City Star* offered a combination newspaper-radio rate for advertising users of the *Star* and its station WDAF in 1921 but there were few immediate takers.

But despite AT&T's advantage, and its withdrawal from the RCA consortium, its rivals were not discouraged. Coming to power in RCA was David Sarnoff, son of a Russian immigrant family who had got his start as a Marconi wireless operator. Sarnoff had been an advocate of mass radio broadcasting since 1916 and he saw promise long before 1923 that radio could become a major industry.

And indeed it was clear that radio could become a paying proposition for many. The number of stations in the country had increased from 30 in January, 1922, to 556 in March, 1923. The number of receiving sets jumped from some 50,000 in 1921 to more than 600,000 in 1922. Newspapers found the story of radio's growth one of continuing interest—in June, 1922, the *New York Times* was averaging 40 column inches of radio information daily.[5] The public was demonstrating avid interest in radio's newly developing stars —announcers Graham MacNamee and Milton Cross, the vocal duet of Billy Jones and Ernie Hare, and the performers on the Eveready Hour, sponsored by a radio battery company. There were objections to radio's introduction of direct advertising to pay the costs of programming, but they were to prove unavailing in the onward rush of the new medium.

Sarnoff's problem was to break the hold AT&T had won on big-time radio. The outlook appeared grim so long as RCA was hampered in accepting advertising fees or in using telephone lines for inter-city programming. WEAF, after broadcasting the 1922 Chicago-Princeton football game from Stagg Field, expanded its experimental circuit to Boston, Washington, Providence, and other cities. In early 1924 the Eveready Hour bought time over a dozen stations —the first use of national radio advertising. A year later the chain headed by WEAF had 26 outlets, reaching as far west as Kansas City. RCA and General Electric set up a competitive network, headed by WJZ, RCA's New York station, and WGY, Schenectady, but it had to use telegraph wires which proved to be inferior in transmitting voices and music. And only by straining the agreement concerning advertising could RCA accept payment of program costs by sponsors.

---

[5] From testimony by Ralph D. Casey, director of the University of Minnesota School of Journalism, before the Federal Communications Commission, reprinted in part by the Newspaper-Radio Committee in *Freedom of the Press* (booklet, 1942), pp. 5-21.

Then, at the moment Sarnoff was planning to create an RCA broadcasting subsidiary which could accept unrestricted advertising, the telephone company offered to withdraw from the broadcasting business. WEAF was sold to RCA in 1926. Immediately RCA, General Electric, and Westinghouse incorporated the National Broadcasting Company as an RCA subsidiary, with Merlin H. Aylesworth as president. Networks were extended coast-to-coast in 1927 as the WEAF-led chain became the Red network of NBC and the WJZ-led chain the Blue network. In 1930 a federal antitrust action forced General Electric and Westinghouse to dispose of their holdings in RCA and the management headed by Sarnoff became supreme. RCA had acquired the Victor phonograph interests and had established the RCA-Victor manufacturing unit to produce phonographs, radio sets, and tubes. RCA Communications, Inc., operated a world-wide radiotelegraph system. And two big coast-to-coast NBC networks were under RCA control.[6]

NBC's first competition came in 1927 when rival radiomen and the Columbia Phonograph Company formed the Columbia Broadcasting System. William S. Paley, a CBS advertiser, was so delighted with radio's ability to increase sales of his company's cigars that he bought control of CBS in 1928 and began giving it the vigor and enterprise that were to bring it to equal stature with NBC. By 1934, CBS had 97 affiliated stations, to 127 for the two NBC networks. That year four independent stations, headed by WOR, New York, and WGN, the *Chicago Tribune* station, organized the Mutual Broadcasting System, which primarily served to affiliate smaller stations. Chains of a regional nature developed, such as the Yankee network in New England, the Texas and Michigan networks, and the Don Lee network on the West Coast. Networks, radio found, could produce more costly and successful programs because they could draw upon the support of national advertising, and their growth made radio a more formidable competitor each year for the advertising dollar.

None of this development of radio would have been possible, however, had not the federal government's power been used to

[6] Pressure by the Federal Communications Commission brought the sale of the Blue network in 1943 to Edward J. Noble, who renamed it the American Broadcasting Company in 1945.

David Sarnoff (*left*) was instrumental in creating Radio Corporation of America and NBC, while William S. Paley (*right*) developed CBS.

Two famous radio newsmen's voices were those of Elmer Davis (*left*) for the ABC network and of the veteran H. V. Kaltenborn (*right*) for NBC.

Two radio news commentators who early developed television programs were Edward R. Murrow (*left*) and Eric Sevareid (*right*), both of CBS.

Publishers of groups of magazines included Cyrus H. K. Curtis (*left*), a pioneer, and Henry R. Luce (*right*), founder of *Time, Life,* and *Fortune.*

Famous as owners of groups of newspapers were Robert R. McCormick (*left*), *Chicago Tribune-New York Daily News,* and Roy W. Howard (*right*).

John S. Knight (*left*) and John Cowles (*right*) rose to prominence as publishers of important groups of newspapers developed in the 1940's.

avert chaos on the airwaves. Secretary of Commerce Herbert Hoover had endeavored to regulate the growing number of stations, but he lacked sufficient authority under the 1912 law to prevent one station from interfering with the broadcasts of another. By early 1927, when the number of stations had increased to 733, listeners found stations jumping about on the broadcast band to avoid interference, which in metropolitan areas particularly had reached the point of curtailing sales of radio sets.

National radio conferences held in Washington each year after 1922 urged additional federal regulation of use of the limited number of available broadcast channels, which by common consent were recognized as being in the public domain. Radio manufacturers wanted the government to unscramble the situation. So did the National Association of Broadcasters, which had been formed in 1923. So did the listening public. The American Newspaper Publishers Association, a substantial number of whose members owned stations, also wanted the government to resolve the problem. Walter A. Strong of the *Chicago Daily News* served as chairman of a coordinating committee which sought passage of a new federal radio act. The bill was approved by Congress in February, 1927.

The Radio Act of 1927 established a five-man Federal Radio Commission which was empowered to regulate all forms of radio communication. The federal government maintained control over all channels, with the Commission granting licenses for the use of specific channels for three-year periods. Licenses were to be granted "in the public interest, convenience, or necessity" to provide "fair, efficient, and equitable service" throughout the country.

Under this authority the Federal Radio Commission set about eliminating confusion on the broadcast band. The number of stations fell by approximately 150, and the total remained just above the 600 mark for the next ten years. The commission established a group of "clear channels" on which only one station could operate at night. Of the 57 clear channel stations in 1947, designed to give rural areas unimpeded reception of a powerful metropolitan station's programs, 55 were owned by, or affiliated with, the networks. They were the lucrative prizes of radio.[7]

Federal authority was broadened by passage of the Communica-

[7] White, *The American Radio*, pp. 144-147.

tions Act of 1934, which established the seven-man Federal Communications Commission. It took over not only authority to regulate radio broadcasting, but also jurisdiction over all telecommunications. The responsibility of the license holder to operate his radio station in the public interest was more clearly spelled out, with the commission having the power to refuse renewal of a license in cases of flagrant disregard of broadcasting responsibility. The law forbade, however, any attempt at censorship by the commission; no station can be directed to put a particular program on or off the air. The FCC rarely used its power to cancel the licenses of broadcasters; for the most part it resorted only to indirect pressure in carrying out its supervision of station operations. However that pressure was to become substantial in later years.

With the development of widespread network broadcasting, and the unscrambling of the airwaves by exercise of federal authority, radio had come of age. But radio's development ran head-on into the interests of other media, particularly incurring the wrath of the newspaper publishers. The major conflict involved radio's growing income taken from the nation's advertising budget. A second involved radio's broadcasting of the news.

Newspaper reaction to radio in the early days of broadcasting was mixed. Newspapers carried the radio log as a reader service and publicized radio's progress and stars. A report by the American Newspaper Publishers Association's radio committee in 1927 showed that 48 newspapers were owners of stations, that 69 sponsored programs on unowned stations, and that 97 gave news programs over the air. More than half the high-grade stations had some newspaper affiliation. The ANPA's radio committee took the position that radio reporting of news events stimulated newspaper sales—a belief borne out fully by later experience.[8]

But others took a different view. The Associated Press tried to retain its 1924 presidential election returns for newspaper publication only, and fined the Portland *Oregonian* $100 for broadcasting them, but some 10 million Americans listened in on 3 million radio sets to hear of Calvin Coolidge's victory. By 1928, the NBC and CBS networks could reach many of the nation's 8 million receiving sets. Both Republican Herbert Hoover and Democrat Alfred E.

[8] The story of the newspaper-radio struggle and ANPA's part in it is told in Edwin Emery, *History of the American Newspaper Publishers Association* (Minneapolis: University of Minnesota Press, 1950), chap. 13.

Smith took to the air, spending a million dollars on campaign talks. That year the press associations—AP, UP, and INS—supplied complete election returns to radio stations.

Stimulated by public interest in radio's coverage of the election, a few stations began to expand their news operations. In December, 1928, KFAB in Lincoln, Nebraska, employed the city editor of the *Lincoln Star* to run its newscasts. Stations followed suit in other cities. The most elaborate early news effort was made by KMPC in Beverly Hills, California, which put 10 reporters onto Los Angeles news runs in 1930.[9] Some newspaper publishers complained, justifiably, that radio was using public interest in newscasts as one selling point in attracting advertising.

In 1929 newspaper fear of radio seemed unjustified. It was true that radio had advanced spectacularly in advertising revenue, from 4 million dollars in 1927 to 40 million in 1929. But that year newspapers carried a record 800 million dollars' worth of advertising, according to the U. S. Census of Manufactures.

Then came the depression, whose opening phase was recorded with the simplicity that has made *Variety* famous for its headlines: WALL ST. LAYS AN EGG. The financial collapse of October, 1929, brought industrial slowdown, decreasing retail sales, growing unemployment, and, by 1933, a virtual paralysis of business and banking and 10 million unemployed. Newspaper advertising revenue fell 45 per cent from the 1929 peak by 1933, while that for magazines was cut in half. But radio advertising revenue doubled in those depression years. It seemed logical for newspaper publishers to eye radio as a source of trouble.

Actually, however, radio was not taking much advertising away from newspapers in those early depression years. Newspapers' loudest complaints were that national advertising was being lost to radio. But out of the total amount spent by national advertisers each year in just the three major media—newspapers, magazines, radio—how much did each of the media receive? According to ANPA Bureau of Advertising estimates, newspapers got 54 per cent in 1929, still received 50 per cent in 1935. Magazines lost some ground, from 42 per cent in 1929 to 35.5 per cent in 1935. Radio increased from 4 per cent to 14.5 per cent. By 1939, however, the figures for this three-way split of national advertising showed a

[9] Charnley, *News by Radio*, p. 9.

different picture: newspapers, 38 per cent; magazines, 35 per cent; radio, 27 per cent. The publishers' fears had been justified.

Another set of figures—estimates of total expenditures for all forms of advertising by both national and local advertisers—is available for the years after 1935. These estimates, made by McCann-Erickson, Inc., advertising agency, include all types of advertising-connected expense in addition to the direct revenues of the media. Besides the major media, they include direct mail, business papers, farm papers, outdoor, and a large miscellaneous category. Table 1 shows the varying fortunes of newspapers, magazines, radio, and, beginning in 1950, television.

TABLE 1

ADVERTISING IN THE MASS MEDIA AS A PERCENTAGE OF TOTAL
ADVERTISING EXPENDITURES

Year	Newspapers	Magazines	Radio	Television	All Other
1935	45.2	8.3	6.5		40.0
1940	39.2	9.6	10.5		40.7
1945	32.0	12.5	14.6		40.9
1950	36.5	9.0	10.7	3.0	40.8
1955	34.0	8.0	6.1	11.2	40.7
1960	31.0	7.9	5.8	13.3	42.0
1961	30.2	7.7	5.9	13.9	42.3

Source: McCann-Erickson, Inc., estimates. Current estimates appear in *Printers' Ink* in February, with revisions in August. Original estimates for years prior to 1945 were later substantially revised.

Again, what hurt most in the 1930's was that among the mass media only radio was taking in more dollars; newspapers and magazines suffered heavy cuts in actual cash revenue because of declining dollar advertising volume. Some could stand the cuts; some could not. As the depression deepened, newspaper publishers took out after the well-heeled culprit, radio, with new vengeance.

The furnishing of 1932 presidential election returns to the radio networks by the Associated Press, to forestall sale of election coverage by the United Press, precipitated action by the ANPA board of directors in December, 1932. The board recommended that press associations should neither sell nor give away news in advance of its publication in the newspapers. Broadcasting of news should be confined to brief bulletins which would encourage newspaper readership. And radio logs should be treated as paid advertising. There were many qualified observers who felt radio was too well established as a news medium to be hobbled in this way.[10] But the ANPA recommendations led to a futile two-year effort to eliminate radio news competition. After a spirited fight, the 1933 AP membership meeting voted not to furnish news to the radio networks and to limit broadcasting of news by AP members to occasional 35-word bulletins. The UP and INS bowed to their newspaper clients' desires and stopped their sale of news to radio stations. The answer of the radio industry was to undertake the job of gathering news itself.

Columbia Broadcasting System set up the leading network news service under the direction of Paul White, former UP newsman. White staffed bureaus in New York, Washington, Chicago, Los Angeles, and London with other newspapermen, built up an extensive system of correspondents, and imported the British Exchange Telegraph agency's news report. By the fall of 1933 commentators H. V. Kaltenborn and Boake Carter were doing daily CBS newscasts. NBC organized a less extensive news service. Local stations continued to broadcast news regularly, all the while, by the simple expedient of using early editions of newspapers.[11]

The networks found the collection of news expensive, while the publishers disliked the new competition. So in December, 1933, a new solution was proposed. This was the Press-Radio Bureau, which would present two five-minute unsponsored news broadcasts daily on the networks from news supplied by the press associations. Bulletin coverage of extraordinary events also would be provided. In return, the networks would stop gathering news.

The Press-Radio Bureau began operating in March, 1934, and after a year had 245 subscribers. But it was doomed from the start. Not only was it unrealistic, but it left the door open for the founding of new news-gathering agencies not bound by the agreement. Five new services jumped into the field, led by Herbert Moore's Transradio Press Service, which at its peak in 1937 served 230 radio clients and even signed up several newspapers.

[10] Including *Editor & Publisher*, which expressed skepticism in its issue of December 10, 1932, p. 5.

[11] The AP won suits against KSOO, Sioux Falls, South Dakota, and KVOS, Bellingham, Washington, to stop this practice. Eventually the period of time during which there is a protectible property right in news came to be recognized as a minimum of four to six hours after publication.

Collapse of the effort to curtail news broadcasting came in 1935. The United Press and International News Service obtained releases from the Press-Radio Bureau agreement, so that they could meet Transradio's competition by selling full news reports to stations. UP began a wire report especially written for broadcasting, which AP matched after it joined the race for radio clients in 1940. The Press-Radio Bureau suspended in 1940; Transradio slumped away, and died in 1951. The United Press International and the Associated Press, which were serving 2,248 and 2,122 American radio and television stations, respectively, in 1961, became dominant in both the newspaper and broadcast news fields.

The networks continued to develop their own news staffs and news analysts and commentators. Hans Von Kaltenborn was the first of a long line of radio commentators. A foreign correspondent, managing editor, and associate editor of the *Brooklyn Eagle* in his first journalistic assignments, Kaltenborn started broadcasting in 1922, two years after the first stations went on the air. He became a CBS commentator in 1930, leaving to join NBC in 1940. Radio was building audiences in many ways, but coverage of major news events of the 1930's helped: President Roosevelt's "fireside chats," the presidential nominating conventions and campaigns, King Edward VIII's abdication talk delivered for world-wide shortwave broadcast. The voices of Kaltenborn, Boake Carter, Gabriel Heatter, Lowell Thomas, and other pioneers became familiar to millions of Americans. So did those of many regional and local radio newsmen.

The Munich crisis of 1938 and the outbreak of war in 1939 gave radio newsmen their big chance, which they took in stride. Kaltenborn went to Europe for NBC. Such voices as his and that of William L. Shirer, CBS Berlin correspondent, brought the war close to American homes. The outstanding performer was Edward R. Murrow, whose "This is London" broadcasts for CBS made the 1940 Battle of Britain come alive for his American audience. His graphic reporting in a quiet but compelling voice did as much to awaken the still neutral United States to its responsibility in the second World War as any other type of journalistic effort. Bill Henry of CBS and Arthur Mann of Mutual became the first front line radio reporters in the fall of 1939. George Hicks of ABC took honors on D-Day.

Taking Kaltenborn's place at home on CBS was former *New York Times* staff member Elmer Davis. Davis, in his three years with CBS before becoming OWI director, and in his work with ABC after the war, won high praise for his clear-eyed reporting, his dry humor and telling barbs, and his ability to cut through conflicting news reports and statements to find the truth. He and Murrow came to represent the best in interpretative broadcasting in the 1940's. Coming to the top, too, was Eric Sevareid, whose analyses from Washington won top professional awards.

Radio was now reaching its maturity. As Table 2 shows, the number of stations on the air more than doubled between 1940 and 1950. Program quality improved, despite increasing emphasis upon advertising messages and despite radio's tendency to permit advertising agencies to control the content of their sponsors' entertainment shows.[12] Then came television as the 1950's opened.

Television had written radio's obituary, many observers said. But time proved there was room for both. Network radio withered, as

TABLE 2

NUMBERS OF RADIO AND TELEVISION STATIONS AND SETS IN USE

Year	AM Stations	FM Stations	TV Stations	Radio Sets	TV Sets
	(on the air)			(millions)	
1930	612			13	
1935	605			30	
1940	814			51	
1945	943	53	9	60	(8,000)
1950	2,086	743	97	80	6
1955	2,669	552	439	115	33
1960	3,506	753	533	156	55
1961	3,624	931	548	168	60

Source: Broadcasting Yearbooks. Radios were in 96 per cent of all U. S. households in 1950, 97 per cent in 1961. Television household figures were 13 per cent in 1950, 68 per cent in 1955, 89 per cent in 1961. Of the 1961 radio sets, 115 million were in homes, 43 million in cars, 10 million in public places. There were 14 million FM sets in 1960.

its established stars moved (with the advertising budgets) to network television. The value of time sales for national radio networks was 40 million dollars in 1935, rose to a high of 133 million in 1948,

---

[12] A policy thoroughly criticised in White, *The American Radio*, and in Charles A. Siepmann, *Radio's Second Chance* (New York: Holt, Rinehart and Winston, Inc., 1946).

then dropped back to 35 million by 1960. But the time sales for all of radio increased each year. The "music, news, and sports" pattern proved successful for the spreading number of smaller stations. Incessant newscasts, rather than longer and more meaningful ones, proved annoying, but radio still produced many excellent network and local news and public affairs broadcasts.

The networks, with the exception of the loosely-organized Mutual, moved into television, but they also stayed in radio. American Broadcasting Company (the NBC Blue network until 1943) merged with Paramount Theatres in 1953 in a mutual defense pact against television. ABC had 375 radio station affiliates in 1961, CBS had 210, and NBC had 205. Mutual, serving 428 stations, went into bankruptcy in 1959 but was reorganized by a maker of magnetic tapes for sight and sound recording, Minnesota Mining and Manufacturing Company. The number of regional radio networks increased to 81 by 1961.

FM (frequency modulation) radio made a bid against the normal AM (amplitude modulation) radio in the 1940's, as Table 2 shows. FM radio was looked upon as the means of providing smaller towns with thousands of radio stations, since FM covers a smaller area with better reception. But only a few hundred FM stations developed and survived, primarily as "better listening" stations, because transistor radio sets produced by mass methods did not tune in FM channels. Appearing on the scene with FM was facsimile broadcasting, also limited in scope of reception. Facsimile broadcasting, begun on a daily basis by KSD, St. Louis, in 1938, was viewed as a possible way of delivering printed newspapers into the home. But the innovation failed to reach mass-production use.

Television became the successful competitor, combining the appeals and techniques of film and radio. As early as the 1860's there were efforts to achieve the illusions of depth and movement by projecting pictures on screens. Thomas A. Edison used some of George Eastman's early Kodak film in inventing the Kinetoscope in 1889, and one of his assistants projected *The Great Train Robbery* in 1903, the first motion picture to tell a story. Sound motion pictures were developed by Warner Brothers in 1926; color arrived in 1935. Newsreels had been popular since 1897; in the 1930's documentaries, focusing on a social problem or economic issue, were filmed. By the time of the arrival of commercial television the technological processes and artistic techniques of film making were well established.

Experimental television broadcasting began in the 1920's in the United States. A picture was televised between New York and Philadelphia in 1923, and WGY, the General Electric station in Schenectady, was televising regularly in 1928. By 1937 there were 17 experimental stations on the air. Commercial broadcasting began in 1941, but World War II put a halt to production of sets and equipment. Stimulated by the development of the coaxial cable and the microwave relay, which made possible network television, 108 stations were broadcasting by 1949. Some soon failed.

That year the Federal Communications Commission ordered a "freeze" in channel allocations. For three years the FCC replanned and reallocated channels, to permit more than 2,000 channel assignments to nearly 1,300 communities, including 242 channels for noncommercial educational stations. To do this, the FCC extended television broadcasting from the established VHF (very-high-frequency) channels (numbered 2 through 13) to 70 more channels called UHF (ultra-high-frequency). There were more than twice as many UHF as VHF assignments. But different equipment was needed to tune a set to the UHF and VHF stations, and the established patterns of set-making and broadcasting were VHF. By 1961 there were 466 commercial VHF stations, only 82 commercial UHF stations. And there were only 55 educational stations.

Even if the mechanical problems had been overcome, the FCC's hopes for thousands of television stations probably could not have been realized. For the profits were made by big-time network stations. During the freeze period, the transcontinental relay was completed, and the nation's television viewers saw the Japanese peace treaty conference in San Francisco during September, 1951, as their first cross-country program. The networks grew, with stations served numbering 205 for CBS, 187 for NBC, and 127 for ABC in 1961. DuMont also had a network, and there were 10 regional chains. The national television networks had just 2½ million dollars in time sales in 1948; by 1960 the figure was 471 million dollars, more than 3½ times radio networks' high.

The FCC reported that in 1960 the three major networks made profits of 8 per cent before taxes. Their 15 owned-and-operated television stations earned 42 per cent before taxes, and some other big-city network affiliates did nearly as well. The typical television station earned 15 per cent before taxes, the typical radio operation 7.5 per cent. But some smaller television stations, a third of AM stations, and three-fourths or more of UHF and FM stations were losers. In television, production costs were so heavy that high-grade programming could be achieved only by the networks and largest stations—a factor not true in radio.

Color television was authorized by the FCC in 1953 after a false start in 1950 when the CBS noncompatible color system was given preference over the eventually adopted RCA compatible system—i.e., a system which enables either color or black-and-white sets to receive the same broadcast. The networks expanded telecasting in color, but high prices of color-receiving sets kept their use at only 600,000 in 1961.

As Table 2 shows, there were 548 commercial television stations in 1961, and 60 million sets in use. TV was in 89 per cent of all American homes, and radio in 97 per cent. Both had come as close as the newspaper to reaching the saturation point of usage. Sixty million Americans had heard President Roosevelt address Congress the day after Pearl Harbor; now, with television, at least 85 million saw one of the "Great Debates" of 1960 between John F. Kennedy and Richard M. Nixon, with the presidency at stake. Thus half the country could sit in television's town meeting.

Radio's pioneers were still active—David Sarnoff as board chairman for RCA and William S. Paley for CBS. Sarnoff's son, Robert, became NBC board chairman and Robert E. Kintner became president. Dr. Frank Stanton was an intelligent spokesman for broadcasting as CBS president. The two top officials of CBS News, Sig Mickelson and John F. Day, resigned in 1961 and were replaced by Richard S. Salant and Blair Clark. John Daly was replaced as head of ABC News by James C. Hagerty, President Eisenhower's press secretary. William R. McAndrew headed NBC News and Stephen J. McCormick the Mutual news operation.

Covering the news was a 50 million dollar annual operation for the networks in 1961, with CBS and NBC each budgeting more than 20 million (much of it reclaimed from sponsors). CBS and NBC each had some 40 correspondents and as many staff cameramen in the United States, a dozen key overseas bureaus, and hundreds of stringers. The development of cable film enabled the networks to show live film two or three hours after an event had occurred abroad. And radio could call in correspondents at will, around the world.

Edward R. Murrow became a CBS vice-president in 1946. His "Hear It Now" became "See It Now" in 1951 and ran until 1958. Other CBS News specials were "CBS Reports," "Eyewitness to History," and "The 20th Century," with Walter Cronkite a familiar figure in many. Other leading CBS newsmen included commentator Eric Sevareid, from Washington; Howard K. Smith, senior European correspondent for a decade; Charles Collingwood, Harry Reasoner, Winston Burdett, Robert Trout, David Schoenbrun, Bill Henry, Daniel Schorr, and White House correspondent Robert S. Pierpoint. Douglas Edwards conducted the leading CBS television news program, and veteran Lowell Thomas held forth on radio.

NBC's top stars were two seasoned newspapermen, Chet Huntley and David Brinkley, whose mixture of news and comments on the "Huntley-Brinkley Report" made it the best known television news program. They also bested the CBS commentators during the 1960 presidential campaign. Morgan Beatty and Merrill Mueller had leading newscasts. Other NBC newsmen included Joseph C. Harsch, senior European correspondent; Martin Agronsky and Richard Harkness in Washington; Ray Scherer, White House correspondent; Pauline Frederick at the UN; John Chancellor, Alex Dreier, and Irving R. Levine.

Hagerty's arrival at ABC brought additions to its budget and staff. Added were Washington newsmen William H. Lawrence, from the *New York Times*; John Scali, from AP; Robert Clark, former INS White House correspondent, and Peter Clapper, son of the famed columnist. Lisa Howard joined ABC from Mutual. Edward P. Morgan was ABC White House correspondent. Quincy Howe and John W. Vandercook achieved prominence with ABC as commentators. John Daly conducted the network's top television news show. For Mutual, Stephen J. McCormick headed Washington operations, with Bill Costello at the White House.

Radio and television were still under public regulation, through the Federal Communications Commission. The FCC held license control over stations and limited holding of multiple licenses. No person or group could own more than five television, six FM, or seven AM stations. No one could own more than one radio and one television station in the same city. And the FCC frowned on ownership of stations by newspaper publishers (a subject to be discussed in the following chapter).

The problem of editorializing on the air was another involving the stations and the FCC. In a 1941 ruling, called the "Mayflower decision" because it involved renewal of a Boston station license held by the Mayflower Broadcasting Corporation, the FCC said, "The broadcaster cannot be an advocate." Radiomen presented arguments against this policy, and in 1949 the FCC decided broadcasters could—and should—"editorialize with fairness." Station owners were cautious in taking up the invitation, but by 1961 a *Broadcasting Yearbook* survey showed 37 per cent of radio and television stations were presenting editorial opinion, one-third of them either daily or weekly, the rest occasionally. Some problems of covering politics were removed in 1959 when bona fide newscasts and news programs were exempted from the FCC's "equal-time" rule.

Radio stations were stimulated to increase their use of local live programs—including news and public affairs—by publication of the 1946 FCC "Blue Book," called "Public Service Responsibility of Broadcasting Licensees." The Radio-Television News Directors Association and the National Association of Broadcasters also upheld the importance of high-level news and comment. Broadcast newsmen won their way into public events previously covered by newspapermen, beginning with the successful fight by Fulton Lewis, Jr., of Mutual to get radiomen into the Congressional press galleries in 1939. By 1961, President Kennedy's press conferences were sometimes televised live—full recognition of the importance of radio and television as news and opinion-making media.

ANNOTATED BIBLIOGRAPHY

Books:

Bulman, David, ed., *Molders of Opinion*. Milwaukee: Bruce Publishing Company, 1945. Includes chapters on H. V. Kaltenborn, Gabriel Heatter, Fulton Lewis, Jr., and Raymond Gram Swing.

Burlingame, Roger, *Don't Let Them Scare You: The Life and Times of Elmer Davis*. Philadelphia: J. B. Lippincott & Company, 1961. A good biography of a top-flight news analyst.

Charnley, Mitchell V., *News by Radio*. New York: The Macmillan Company, 1948. The best source for the growth of radio news.

Chase, Francis, Jr., *Sound and Fury.* New York: Harper & Brothers, 1942. An informal history of radio with much information, but sometimes inaccurate in precise details.

De Forest, Lee, *Father of Radio: The Autobiography of Lee De Forest.* Chicago: Wilcox & Follett, 1950. The early years.

Emery, Walter B., *Broadcasting and Government.* East Lansing: Michigan State University Press, 1961. An encyclopaedic survey of all aspects of government interest in, and regulation of, U. S. broadcasting.

Head, Sydney W., *Broadcasting in America: A Survey of Television and Radio.* Boston: Houghton Mifflin Company, 1956. Covers the physical bases of broadcasting, its history, economics, and problems of social control. The best source for television.

Kaltenborn, H. V., *Fifty Fabulous Years, 1900-1950: A Personal Review.* New York: G. P. Putnam's Sons, 1950. Autobiography of a commentator who began on the air in 1922.

Levin, Harvey J., *Broadcast Regulation and Joint Ownership of Media.* New York: New York University Press, 1960. A study of radio and television economics and public regulation.

Seipmann, Charles A., *Radio, Television, and Society.* New York: Oxford University Press, 1950. Social criticism of the media, by the author of *Radio's Second Chance* (1946).

White, Llewellyn, *The American Radio.* Chicago: University of Chicago Press, 1947. A publication of the Commission on Freedom of the Press. Best single discussion of radio's growth.

Periodicals and Monographs:

Principal sources are the trade journal *Broadcasting* and *Broadcasting Yearbook.* The Summer, 1957, issue of the *Journalism Quarterly* was devoted to articles about radio and television, and an extensive bibliography.

Cranston, Pat, "Political Convention Broadcasts: Their History and Influence," *Journalism Quarterly,* XXXVII (Spring 1960), 186. A survey from 1924 to 1956.

"First Team," *Newsweek,* LVII (March 13, 1961), 53. A report on NBC's Chet Huntley and David Brinkley. See also the press section of *Time,* LXXIV (October 19, 1959), 92.

Morgan, Thomas B., "Crisis, Conflict and Change in TV News," *Look,* XXV (November 7, 1961), 48. Network news policies and programs.

Price, Wesley, "Murrow Sticks to the News," *Saturday Evening Post,* CCXXII (December 10, 1949), 25. About a leading commentator.

Shaplen, Robert, "A Farewell to Personal History," *Saturday Review,* XLIII (December 10, 1960), 46. Summarizes radio and television network coverage abroad in the 1950's.

Wertenbaker, Charles, "Profiles," *New Yorker,* XXIX (December 26, 1953), 28. An excellent profile of Edward R. Murrow.

Chapter *27*

ECONOMIC PRESSURES
ON THE MASS MEDIA

> It is often made a matter of boasting, that the
> United States contain so many public journals. It
> were wiser to make it a cause of mourning, since
> the quality, in this instance, diminishes in an in-
> verse ratio to the quantity.
> —James Fenimore Cooper (1838)

COMPETITION AMONG THE MEDIA, in the years after
the rise of radio and television, was intense, both for advertising
revenues and for attention from the reader, listener, or viewer. But
the effects of inter-media competition upon the fortunes of any one
were less important than were the effects of general changes in the
country's economy, fashioned in turn by a great depression, a world
war, and a postwar boom. Deflation, inflation, and war accentuated
the already well-developed trend toward newspaper suspensions
and mergers which was discussed in Chapter 22, and likewise adversely affected magazine publishing. On the other hand, a tremendous expansion of the gross national product and a population
explosion beginning in the 1940's served to bulwark the publishing
industry's position by providing a wider base for the support of
both the old and new media.

At the same time the socio-economic pressures inherent in modern American society, which had brought about concentration of
newspaper ownership throughout the twentieth century, continued
to have their effects, both on newspapers and other media. Com-

petition for the mass market encouraged further standardization at the expense of individuality—common denominators for mass readership, listenership, or viewership to win mass advertising. Failure of individual enterprises to keep pace with the requirements of a modern socio-economic situation also continued to play a part. And increasingly heavy investment costs in both publishing and broadcasting lessened ability to compete. Small radio stations, like small daily and weekly newspapers, could and did spread across the country as community enterprises. But big-time radio and television, like big-time newspaper and magazine publishing, was conducive to concentration of ownership—and radio and television proved to be easily adapted to chain operation. Finally, the natural tendency of publishers to become interested in new communications agencies, and their desire to spread their investments into radio and television, led to extensive interlocking ownership among the media.

As explained in Chapter 26, only radio made gains in advertising revenue during the 1930's.[1] During that decade of depression, recovery, and recession, expenditures on radio advertising rose from 40 million dollars in 1929 to 225 million dollars in 1941, last peacetime year. Newspaper advertising revenue, peaking at 800 million dollars in 1929, fell 45 per cent by 1933 and was still down 20 per cent in 1941, at 650 million. Magazine advertising revenue followed a similar pattern, being cut in half by 1933 from its 240 million 1929 high and recovering to 210 million by 1941. Then came the general advances in the economy of the war years, and corresponding gains in advertising revenues.

The story of competition for advertising among the media after 1945—and of the rise of television—can be told in two statistical tables. Table 1 shows the total dollar costs of all advertising expenditures by both national and local advertisers, including advertising-related costs. The percentage figures make it clear that television's inroads were made most heavily against radio, with magazines taking the next heaviest percentage drop. Radio's rather steady dollar volume in the 1950's, in contrast to the gains of other media, was due to its substantial cutting of advertising time rates (and parallel cutting of operating costs), and declines in national advertising.

[1] See pages 659-60.

TABLE 1

DOLLAR VOLUMES (IN MILLIONS) AND PERCENTAGES OF TOTAL
ADVERTISING EXPENDITURES ALLOTTED TO MASS MEDIA

Year	Newspapers Dollars	%	Magazines Dollars	%	Radio Dollars	%	Television Dollars	%
1945	920	32.0	360	12.5	420	14.6		
1950	2,080	36.5	510	9.0	610	10.7	170	3.0
1955	3,070	34.0	720	8.0	550	6.1	1,010	11.2
1960	3,700	31.0	940	7.9	690	5.8	1,590	13.3
1961	3,630	30.2	925	7.7	705	5.9	1,665	13.9

Source: McCann-Erickson, Inc., estimates. The percentage for all other advertising expenditures was approximately 40 per cent for each period.

Total advertising expenditures increased from 2 billion, 870 million dollars in 1945 to 11 billion, 930 million dollars in 1960, according to McCann-Erickson, Inc., estimates. But total disposable income in the country was also increasing greatly, and the amount
of advertising expenditures stayed at a range between 2 and 3 per
cent of disposable income. Thus the sizable dollar gains only kept
the mass media roughly even in their financial race. Another measure of the support of the mass media is found in a study of average
expenditures per household by advertisers, made by Scripps-Howard's research organization. It shows that, keeping dollar purchasing power constant, advertisers spent 10 per cent more per household in 1957 than they did in 1929,[2] with two new media present.

Table 2 shows the division among the major mass media of the
national and local advertising revenues spent on them alone. In
other words, the four major media together were allotted varying
amounts of advertising expenditures each year by national and local advertisers. How were these total sums split among the con-
testants? Table 2 shows that television made its gains in this division of national advertising mostly at the expense of radio, but also
trimmed the percentages of newspapers and magazines (particular
victims among the magazines were large general magazines appealing to mass audiences, rather than specialized ones).

The changes in divisions of local advertising were small, with
television taking relatively small amounts from radio and newspapers, percentagewise. The percentage of total newspaper advertis-

[2] "Economic Support of Mass Communications Media, 1929-1957," Scripps-
Howard Research, New York, 1959.

ing revenue coming from local advertisers increased from 70 to 77 per cent between 1950 and 1960; the percentage of total radio advertising revenue coming from local sources jumped from 41 to 62 per cent. Television decreased in percentage of local advertising during the same 10 years, from 27 to 17 per cent, as its volume of national advertising revenue increased so dramatically. Radio thus joined newspapers as primarily a local advertising medium. Magazines have no advertising categorized as local, although in the late 1950's they began to offer regional and state split-runs so that advertisers could buy space in copies being distributed in restricted areas.

TABLE 2

DIVISION OF ADVERTISING EXPENDITURES ALLOTTED AMONG
THE MASS MEDIA (PERCENTAGES)

| | National Advertising in | | | | Local Advertising in | | |
Year	News-papers	Maga-zines	Radio	Tele-vision	News-papers	Radio	Tele-vision
1948	33.5	37.0	29.5		84.1	15.9	
1950	33.6	32.4	24.8	9.2	82.4	14.6	3.0
1952	28.8	31.5	18.9	20.8	80.6	13.6	5.8
1956	28.6	28.8	8.0	34.6	80.3	11.3	8.4
1960	25.0	28.0	7.9	39.1	80.2	12.0	7.8
1961	24.0	27.4	7.7	40.9	79.5	12.5	8.0

Source: McCann-Erickson, Inc., estimates.

What were the effects upon newspapers of this inter-media competition, and of the ups and downs in the economy from 1930 to 1960? In broad strokes, the number of dailies decreased, then stabilized near the 1,750 figure; ownership concentration increased as the number of competitive dailies declined; circulation steadily increased; and while financial problems were many, newspaper publishing economy tended to stabilize comfortably.

The sharp drop in advertising revenue in the early 1930's wiped out many newspaper profit margins despite cutbacks in salaries, production costs, and newsprint prices, which fell as low as $40 a ton. There were 145 suspensions of dailies during 1931-33, and 77 more in the recovery years of 1934-36. Then came the business recession of 1937, dropping advertising revenues at a time when labor and production costs had mounted to substantially higher post-depression levels. Some newspaper managements, hit by these new disasters after surviving the great depression, were too tired to struggle any longer. Daily newspaper suspensions and mergers accelerated, totaling 165 in the years 1937 to 1939. These were in many respects the blackest years in the history of American newspapers, with one-third of salaried employes in the newspaper industry losing their jobs, according to census statistics. The war years of 1940 to 1944 brought another 197 newspaper deaths, most of them small dailies pinched by production problems. With 584 suspensions and 386 new starts of dailies since 1931, the number of English language general-circulation daily newspapers dropped from 1,942 in 1930 to a twentieth-century low of 1,744 in 1944.

Postwar expansion brought an excess of new starts over suspensions in the daily field. The mid-1940's and mid-1950's were profitable years for newspapers in general. Despite the loss of 350 dailies between 1945 and 1960, their number rose to 1,786 in 1952, then settled back to 1,763 in 1960.

Circulation of dailies was approximately 40 million copies in 1930 for a population of 122 million; by 1960 it was close to 59 million for a population of 180 million. Thus newspaper circulation stayed even with population expansion, thanks to a heavy increase in circulation in the 1940's which counterbalanced the population explosion of the 1950's. The number of papers for each household decreased slightly, however, from 1.32 to 1.16 in the period.[3] In early 1961, the Audit Bureau of Circulations reported that the dailies had at last passed the 60-million figure. Their Sunday editions had 49 million circulation.

Table 3 shows the extent of the decline in competition in cities having daily newspapers, since 1930.[4] The number of one-daily cities steadily increased, and there were more one-combination cities (one owner of two papers). Joint-printing cities are those in which two owners have merged their printing and business operations, and thus are not fully competitive.

Of the 1,461 cities with dailies at the close of 1960, there were competitive dailies in only 29 of 1,334 cities of 100,000 population or less, and competitors in only 15 of the 105 cities with populations between 100,000 and 500,000. The 17 cities of a half-million

---

[3] Wilbur Peterson, "Is Daily Circulation Keeping Pace with the Nation's Growth?," *Journalism Quarterly*, XXXVI (Winter 1959), 12.

[4] See page 516 for similar data from 1880-1930.

TABLE 3

COMPETITION IN DAILY NEWSPAPER CITIES

	1930	1940	1944-45	1953-54	1960
Number of English language general circulation dailies	1,942	1,878	1,744	1,785	1,763
Number of cities with dailies	1,402	1,426	1,396	1,448	1,461
Number of one-daily cities	1,002	1,092	1,107	1,188	1,222
Number of one-combination cities	112	149	161	154	160
Number of joint-printing cities		4	11	19	18
Number of cities with competing dailies	288	181	117	87	61
Percentage of daily cities with competing dailies	20.6	12.7	8.4	6.0	4.2
Total daily circulation (millions)	39.6	41.1	45.9	54.5	58.9

Sources: For number of dailies and circulation, *Editor & Publisher International Year Books.* For other data, Raymond B. Nixon and Jean Ward, "Trends in Newspaper Ownership and Inter-Media Competition," *Journalism Quarterly,* XXXVIII (Winter 1961), 3. In cases of double years, numbers of dailies and circulation figures are for first year; other data extends into the following year.

to a million had competition in only 12 cases. There were, however, competing papers in all five cities of more than a million. The prevailing pattern was one daily for cities under 100,000 in population, and single ownership or joint-printing of a morning-evening combination in cities from 100,000 to 500,000.[5] But if there were only 155 competing voices of daily newspapers in 61 competitive cities in 1960, radio and television added other voices. With 1,946 stations in the same 1,461 cities, the total of competing voices rose to 3,324 in 1,106 cities. Only 355 single-voice cities with no competition between newspapers or between a newspaper and a broadcasting station remained.[6]

Only four cities had three or more daily newspaper owners at the opening of 1962: New York, with six owners of seven dailies; Boston, three owners of five dailies; and Houston and Washington, three owners of three dailies. Only seven other cities supported more than two dailies (all had just two ownerships): Chicago, with four dailies, and Philadelphia, Baltimore, San Francisco, San Antonio, Indianapolis, and Fort Worth, with three dailies each. Ten of the largest 25 cities had two separately-owned dailies: Los Angeles, Detroit, Cleveland, St. Louis, Milwaukee, Dallas, Pittsburgh, Seattle,

[5] The *Jackson State Times* of Mississippi, founded in 1955 to compete with a morning-evening combination, was the only new daily begun in a city of more than 100,000 in the 1950's. It suspended in 1962.

[6] Nixon and Ward, *op. cit.*

Buffalo, and Denver. Six of the largest 25 cities had just one owner of their two dailies: New Orleans, San Diego, Cincinnati, Memphis, Atlanta, and Minneapolis. Oakland, California, thirty-third in size, was the largest one-daily city.

Newspaper managements could cite several reasons for these contractions and for continued concern over newspaper financial stability: a steady increase in the price of newsprint, which did not level off until it reached $135 a ton in 1957; increasing supply costs; rising wages and salaries; losses of national advertising to television. Their critics, however, generally agreed that a major difficulty was one of rigidity of advertising rates, which had not been advanced sufficiently in light of circulation increases and rising production costs. Many dailies, however, advanced sale prices to 7- or 10-cent levels. Annual *Editor & Publisher* surveys of newspaper profits showed expenses increasing slightly more than revenues in all but two years after 1947. Nevertheless, informed estimates of newspaper profits, as the 1960's opened, put them at 10 per cent of gross income as a general picture. Smaller dailies, and non-competitive larger ones, were likely to be making greater profits than highly competitive big-city dailies. Fourteen major metropolitan dailies were suspended between 1950 and early 1962, and five others were sold to competitors. Some were losing a million dollars a year at the end.

Circulation gains were going to moderate and smaller-sized dailies, especially in the suburbs. Metropolitan papers were hardpressed to stay even; of the 10 largest dailies in 1960, only two (the *New York Times* and *Los Angeles Times*) had larger circulations than in 1950. The largest, the tabloid *New York Daily News*, lost 240,000 circulation during the decade. Hearst's *Mirror* and *Journal-American* in New York lost 200,000 and 107,000. The *Chicago Tribune* and *Philadelphia Inquirer* each lost 60,000. The *New York Times*, by contrast, gained 139,000. Sunday circulation losses were even heavier for the decade: 900,000 for the *New York Daily News*, 790,000 for the *New York Mirror*, 300,000 for the *Chicago Tribune*. Papers depending heavily on entertainment appeal were the heaviest losers. The *New York Times* gained 184,000 Sunday sales.[7]

---

[7] The other leaders in daily circulation were the *Philadelphia Bulletin, Detroit News, Chicago Sun-Times,* and *Chicago Daily News.* Other top Sunday circulations were those of the *Los Angeles Examiner* and *Minneapolis Tribune.* The five leading papers in advertising linage during the 1950's were the *Los Angeles Times, New York Times, Miami Herald, Chicago Tribune,* and *Milwaukee Journal.* Circulation figures for the *New York Daily News* in 1961 were 2,006,-983 daily and 3,147,219 Sunday. No other daily had a million.

The suburbs offered opportunity for new papers, both daily and weekly. By 1961 there were some 2,000 suburban papers and as many more big-city neighborhood sheets. Major centers for this growing journalism included Los Angeles, Chicago, New York, Philadelphia, and Detroit. Suburban dailies were growing particularly rapidly in the Los Angeles and New York areas. One conspicuous success was *Newsday*, founded in 1940 on Long Island by Alicia Patterson. Its excellence in publishing both local and world news gave it a circulation above 330,000 by 1961 and a standing as one of the leading evening newspapers in the country. Such growth of the suburban press was a factor in big-city journalism's decline.

New York City lost Hearst's *American* (his pride and joy as the old morning *Journal* of the 1890's) in 1937. The evening *Sun* was sold to Scripps-Howard in 1950 for merger with the *World-Telegram*. The *World-Telegram and Sun* thus boasted a melting pot heritage: Pulitzer, Bennett, Dana, Scripps, Howard, and a dash of Munsey. Its competitors were the *Times, Herald Tribune, Post, Daily News,* and Hearst's *Journal-American* and *Mirror*. Brooklyn lost its *Citizen* in 1947 and its 114-year-old *Eagle* in 1955.

Boston saw two suspensions: the 111-year-old staid *Transcript* in 1941 and the 125-year-old *Post* in 1956. Two Hearst tabloids were combined as the *Record American* in 1961. Other survivors were the two *Globes* and the jointly-owned *Herald* and *Traveler*. In Washington, Mrs. Eleanor Patterson bought the *Times* and *Herald* from Hearst and merged them in 1939. Ownership passed to her cousin, Robert R. McCormick, in 1949; he in turn sold the *Times-Herald* in 1954 for merger with its morning rival, the *Post*. Evening competitors were the *Star* and the Scripps-Howard *News*. Houston's three dailies were Oveta Culp Hobby's *Post*, the Jesse Jones family's *Chronicle*, and the Scripps-Howard *Press*.

Chicago was cut to two morning-evening combinations owned by the McCormick and Marshall Field interests. After Hearst killed his *Herald & Examiner* in 1939 in the wake of a Newspaper Guild strike, Field launched the *Sun* in 1941 to do battle with McCormick's *Tribune* in the morning field. Finding the going rough, he bought the *Times* in 1947 and made the merged *Sun-Times* a tabloid. The *Tribune* purchased Hearst's *American* as an evening affiliate in 1956. The *Sun-Times* countered by buying the *Daily News* from John S. Knight in a record 24 million dollar 1959 transaction.

Six other cities dropped to two ownerships but retained three dailies. In Philadelphia, Walter H. Annenberg's *Inquirer* bought the tabloid *Daily News* in 1957, to step up competition with the Mc-Leans' *Bulletin*. The liberal *Record* died in 1947 after a Guild strike. San Francisco's Hearst and Scripps-Howard evening papers were combined as the jointly-owned *News-Call Bulletin* in 1959; the morning dailies were Hearst's *Examiner* and the *Chronicle*. In Indianapolis, Eugene C. Pulliam bought the *Star* in 1944 and the *News* in 1948 as a morning-evening rival to the Scripps-Howard *Times*. Baltimore's survivors were the two *Suns* and the Hearst *News-Post*. San Antonio's trio were the jointly-owned *Express* and *News* and Hearst's *Light*. Fort Worth had Amon Carter Jr.'s two *Star-Telegrams* and the Scripps-Howard *Press*.

Los Angeles, the third largest city, dropped to two dailies, joining nine others of the largest 25 cities in that class. The Chandler family's *Times* began the tabloid *Mirror* in 1948 to give it a breezier afternoon entry against two Hearst papers, the morning *Examiner* and evening *Herald-Express*. The competition was fatal for a fifth paper, the liberal tabloid *Daily News*, which suspended in 1954. The *Mirror*, edited drably after a 1957 management shakeup, faltered and was suspended in January 1962. The Hearst group at the same time elected to kill the *Examiner*, naming their evening paper the *Herald-Examiner*.

Detroit lost Hearst's *Times* in 1960, victim of a battle with the *News* and *Free Press*. In Cleveland, the *Plain Dealer* disposed of its evening paper, the *News*, to the Scripps-Howard *Press* in 1960. The *St. Louis Star-Times*, published by Elzey Roberts and ably edited by Norman Isaacs, fell before the *Post-Dispatch* and *Globe-Democrat* in 1951. Pittsburgh saw Hearst's *Sun-Telegraph* merged with the Block family's *Post-Gazette* in 1960, with the Scripps-Howard *Press* the remaining rival. Seattle's *Star* blinked out in 1947, leaving the *Times* and Hearst's *Post-Intelligencer*. Milwaukee's survivors were the *Journal* and Hearst's *Sentinel*; Buffalo's the *Courier-Express* and *Evening News*. Dallas had its *News* and *Times Herald*; Denver its *Post* and Scripps-Howard *Rocky Mountain News*.

Six of the 25 largest cities of 1960 had two papers but only one ownership. Memphis fell to this status in 1936 when Scripps-Howard added the *Commercial Appeal* to its *Press-Scimitar*. Minneapolis saw John Cowles complete his *Star* and *Tribune* ownership in 1941. In San Diego, James S. Copley's *Union* and *Tribune* eliminated the *Journal* in 1948. James M. Cox added Clark Howell's *Atlanta Con-*

stitution to his *Journal* ownership in 1950. The *New Orleans Item* was merged with the *States* in 1958, under the ownership of the *Times-Picayune*. In Cincinnati, Scripps-Howard won control of the *Enquirer* in 1956, then merged the Taft family's *Times-Star* with its *Post* in 1958.[8]

Among the chain ownerships, Scripps-Howard dropped from 25 dailies in 1935 to 20 in 1962, with 10 Sunday editions. In the late 1930's papers were disposed of in Akron, Toledo, Youngstown, Oklahoma City, San Diego, and Buffalo. In addition to later changes already described, Scripps-Howard in 1950 merged its *Birmingham Post* with the *Age-Herald* to form the *Post-Herald*, and in 1959 merged its *Columbus Citizen* with the *Ohio State Journal* to form the *Citizen-Journal*. In these and five other cities the chain had common printing and business operations with rivals.

The Hearst chain's 26 dailies of 1935 were cut to 12 by 1962, with 10 Sunday editions. Sold or killed between 1937-40 were nine dailies: the *Rochester Journal*, *Syracuse Journal*, *Omaha News-Bee*, *Wisconsin News*, *Washington Times* and *Herald*, *Chicago Herald & Examiner*, *Atlanta Georgian*, and *Pittsburgh Post-Gazette*. The *Oakland Post-Enquirer* died in 1950. Then came the 1956-62 withdrawals from Chicago, Pittsburgh, and Detroit and contractions in Boston and Los Angeles. On the plus side, the *Albany Knickerbocker News* was added in 1960 as a companion to the *Times-Union*.

Rising rapidly among the group owners was Samuel I. Newhouse. He bought the *Portland Oregonian* in 1950 for 5 million dollars; the *St. Louis Globe-Democrat* in 1955 for 6 million; the *Birmingham News* in 1955 for 18 million; and the *Oregon Journal* in Portland in 1961 for 6 million. This gave him 14 dailies with 10 Sunday editions. His other major holdings included the *Jersey Journal*, *Long Island Press*, *Newark Star-Ledger*, and the dailies in Syracuse and Harrisburg. Newhouse's reputation was primarily that of a successful busi-

---

[8] Among other cities which dropped to one-owner status were Akron and Toledo, through Scripps-Howard withdrawals of the late 1930's, and Omaha (one paper status) and Rochester by 1937 Hearst sales. Other dates for elimination of competition included Louisville, 1936; Providence, 1938; Richmond, 1940; Kansas City, 1942; Syracuse, 1943; Harrisburg, 1948; Dayton and Tacoma (one paper), 1949; Oakland (one paper), 1950; Raleigh and Augusta, 1955; Tampa and Grand Rapids (one paper), 1958; Charlotte and Jacksonville, 1959; Wichita and Albany, 1960. Among well-known dailies disappearing not mentioned in the text above were the *Louisville Herald-Post*, *Providence Tribune*, and *Kansas City Journal-Post*.

nessman-publisher with seemingly inexhaustible funds. He tightened up the operations of his acquired papers, but proclaimed a policy of leaving their editorial pages alone.

John S. Knight, starting with the *Akron Beacon-Journal*, bought the *Miami Herald* in 1937, the *Detroit Free Press* in 1940, and the *Chicago Daily News* in 1944. He sold the latter in 1959, but had added the *Charlotte Observer* in 1954 and *Charlotte News* in 1959 to make a group of five. The importance of Knight's papers and his signed personal opinion column made him a major figure.

John Cowles, whose family owned the *Des Moines Register* and *Tribune*, invaded Minneapolis in 1935 by purchasing the evening *Star*, into which he merged the rival *Journal* in 1939. Two years later the heirs to William J. Murphy's morning *Tribune* sold out to Cowles. The *Tribune's* evening edition, the *Times*, was killed in 1948. Cowles bought the *Valley Times Today* in San Fernando, California, in 1960. His brother Gardner purchased the *San Juan Star* in Puerto Rico in 1961 to give the family six dailies.

Another growing multi-newspaper ownership was that of the Ridder family. The founder was Herman Ridder, publisher of the *Staats-Zeitung* in New York City. His three sons—Bernard H., Joseph E., and Victor F. Ridder[9]—bought control of the *Journal of Commerce* in New York in 1926. The next year they acquired the *St. Paul Pioneer Press* and *Dispatch*, eliminating the rival *Daily News* by 1938. Added to the chain were the *Duluth News-Tribune* and *Herald*, two papers in the Dakotas, and a 49 per cent interest in the *Seattle Times*. Then, in 1952, the Ridders invaded California by buying the *San Jose Mercury* and *News*, and the previously competing *Long Beach Press-Telegram* and *Independent*. The *Pasadena Star-News* and *Independent* were added in 1956 to make a total of 14.

James M. Cox built a sizable empire by acquiring the *Miami News* and *Atlanta Journal* in the 1930's and the *Atlanta Constitution* in 1950. Other Cox holdings were four Ohio papers in Dayton and

---

[9] Bernard H. Ridder headed the family's newspaper expansions from St. Paul. His son, Bernard H., Jr., became publisher in St. Paul and Duluth. His other three sons became publishers in California—Joseph B. in San Jose and Herman H. and Daniel as co-publishers in Long Beach. Joseph E. Ridder centered his attention on the *Journal of Commerce*, of which one of his sons, Eric, became publisher. The other, Bernard J., published the Pasadena newspapers. Victor F. Ridder's son Walter headed the Ridders' Washington bureau, son Robert the family's radio-TV interests.

Springfield. The 15 Gannett newspapers, largely concentrated in New York state, ranked well up in total circulation.

Large national newspaper chains were no particular menace, however. The 63 chains of 1935 controlled 328 newspapers with 41 per cent of daily circulation and 52 per cent of Sunday sales.[10] In 1960 a more exhaustive study by Raymond B. Nixon, editor of *Journalism Quarterly*, uncovered the existence of more smaller chains, so that the totals became 109 groups controlling 560 dailies with 46.1 per cent of daily circulation and 54.2 per cent of Sunday's.

The Hearst group, which had 13.6 per cent of the country's daily circulation and 24.2 per cent of Sunday sales in 1935, had dropped to 6.8 per cent daily and 9.9 per cent Sunday by 1960. The McCormick-Patterson holdings (*Chicago Tribune* and *American, New York Daily News*) ranked next with 5.7 per cent daily and 12.1 per cent Sunday. Scripps-Howard had 5.5 per cent daily and 4 per cent Sunday; Newhouse 3.5 per cent daily and 5 per cent Sunday. In total daily circulation, Hearst was at the 4 million level, McCormick-Patterson and Scripps-Howard above 3 million, Newhouse at 2 million. The Knight newspapers were above 1 million in circulation, Ridder and Cowles papers above 900,000, and Cox and Gannett papers above 800,000. Among leading smaller-circulation groups were the Lee Newspapers of Iowa and Montana, with 18; the Scripps League in western states, with 16, and the James S. Copley group in California and Illinois, with 15.[11]

Weekly newspapers followed the same general trends. In 1930 only 13.5 per cent of country weekly towns had competing papers; by 1960 the figure was 5.2 per cent. The number of weeklies of all types stood at 10,000 in 1940, at 9,800 in 1950, and at 9,000 in 1960. Most of the decrease was in the smallest towns. True country weeklies numbered some 5,800 in 1960; a typical one had a circulation of 1,500 copies in a small town and agricultural countryside, and a net income of $9,500. Larger county seat weeklies and the fast-growing suburban weeklies were more profitable—some of the

---

[10] See pages 532-38 for development of chains prior to 1935.

[11] See Nixon and Ward, *op. cit.*, for a complete listing of numbers of papers and circulations for the 109 groups. Other chains with more than 10 dailies and their headquarters were Southwestern, Arkansas; John H. Perry, Florida; Stauffer, Kansas; H. C. Ogden, West Virginia; Harte-Hanks, Texas; R. C. Hoiles' Freedom Newspapers, California and Texas; C. E. Palmer, Arkansas; and Westchester-Rockland, New York.

suburban press chains were major businesses.[12]

Those who found the country's newspapers too closely conforming in socio-economic opinion—whether published in one-owner or competitive cities—attempted to publish their own papers, with mediocre success. The Socialist labor press was led by the *New York Evening Call* (1908-23) and the *Milwaukee Leader* (1911-42), both of which achieved substantial circulations before succumbing. However, the Jewish language Socialist paper *Vorwärts* (*Jewish Daily Forward*), published in New York with editions in other cities, attained more than 100,000 circulation under editor Abraham Cahan. The Communist *Daily Worker*, founded in 1924, had 100,000 circulation in the late 1930's, but only 5,600 when it dropped to weekly status in 1958. In the Middle West, farmer-labor groups founded the *Minnesota Daily Star* and the *Oklahoma Leader* in 1920, but the *Leader* ceased daily publication in 1922 and the *Star* went into receivership in 1924.

In other specialized newspaper publishing fields, the foreign language press steadily declined during the twentieth century. In 1914, peak year for foreign language newspapers, there were approximately 1,000 papers, of which 140 were dailies. By 1961 there were fewer than 70 dailies and perhaps 600 other papers. German-language dailies, dominant in 1914, declined 90 per cent. *Editor & Publisher* listings show dailies in 21 languages, with Chinese, Spanish, Polish, Japanese, Russian, Italian, Yiddish, German, and Lithuanian the most numerous. New York, Chicago, San Francisco, and Cleveland were major publishing centers.

Negro newspapers, which by 1961 numbered 175 weeklies and two dailies, have a history dating back to pre-Civil War days. The *North Star*, founded in 1847 by Frederick Douglass in Rochester, New York, was the most famous of the early papers. The *New York Age*, dating from 1879, became the oldest Negro newspaper currently publishing. Other 1961 leaders were the *Atlanta Daily World*, the *Chicago Defender* (daily and weekly), *Pittsburgh Courier*, the *Afro-American* newspapers, the *Journal and Guide* of Norfolk, Virginia, and the *Amsterdam News* of New York. Leaders among Negro magazines were *Ebony*, *Jet*, and *Sepia*.

---

[12] See Wilbur Peterson, "Loss in Country Weekly Newspapers Heavy in 1950s," *Journalism Quarterly*, XXXVIII (Winter 1961), 15, and John Cameron Sim, "Weekly Newspapers Again Facing Challenge to Move," *Journalism Quarterly*, XXXV (Spring 1958), 195.

Variety of reader appeal and diversity of opinion were more possible in the magazine field, where periodicals of every shade of interest could find countrywide audiences. By 1961 there were 8,400 periodicals of all types. Of these, however, no more than 600 were magazines of general interest (a figure which nevertheless was more than double that for 1900). Approximately 50 had circulations of more than a million. The larger of these mass circulation magazines exhibited the same characteristics of bigness and ownership concentration as other media. Time Inc. and the Curtis Publishing Company received more than 40 per cent of all magazine advertising revenue and had annual grosses between 250 and 300 million dollars.

The major groups and their leading magazines were: Time Inc. (six, including *Time, Life, Fortune, Sports Illustrated*); Curtis Publishing Company (five, including *Saturday Evening Post, Ladies' Home Journal, American Home, Holiday*); McGraw-Hill (*Business Week* and 34 trade publications); McCall Corporation (*McCall's, Redbook*); Hearst Magazines (14, including *Good Housekeeping, Cosmopolitan, Popular Mechanics, Sports Afield, Harper's Bazaar*); Samuel Newhouse (11 Condé Nast and Street & Smith magazines purchased in 1959, including *Vogue* and *Mademoiselle*); Meredith Publishing Company (*Better Homes and Gardens, Successful Farming*); Cowles Magazines (*Look*); and Walter H. Annenberg's Triangle Publications (three, including *TV Guide* and *Seventeen*).[13]

Of nine major general interest magazines remaining in 1961, all but *Reader's Digest* were group-owned. The others were *Saturday Evening Post* and *Life* (weeklies), *Look* (fortnightly), *Redbook* and *Cosmopolitan* (general monthlies), and *McCall's, Ladies' Home Journal,* and *Good Housekeeping* (women's monthlies).

Gone were the famous Crowell-Collier magazines—*Collier's,* the *American,* and *Woman's Home Companion*—which dated from the 1870's and 1880's. They suspended in 1956 due to mismanagement, top-heavy costs, and loss of advertising to television. *Collier's* had almost 2 million circulation, the other two more than 4 million each.

---

[13] Leading circulations in 1961, in round numbers, were *Reader's Digest,* 13 million; *TV Guide,* 7½ million; *Life, Look, McCall's,* and *Ladies' Home Journal,* 7 million; *Saturday Evening Post,* 6½ million; *Everywoman's Family Circle,* 6 million; *Better Homes and Gardens, Good Housekeeping,* and *Woman's Day,* 5 million; *American Home* and *Redbook,* 3½ million; *Farm Journal,* 3 million; *Time* and *National Geographic,* 2½ million.

Coronet, running mate of *Esquire,* was a 1961 casualty, despite a 3 million circulation. Shaky, for all its income, was the Curtis group, which was showing a deficit in 1961 after sharp advertising losses. Curtis disposed of its 102-year-old *Country Gentleman* in 1955 (absorbed by the *Farm Journal*) and picked up the *American Home* in 1958. Best money makers were the *Reader's Digest, Life, Look,* and such specialized circulation magazines as the *New Yorker, Business Week,* and the news magazines.

Badly hurt, too, was Hearst's 65-year-old Sunday newspaper magazine supplement, the *American Weekly,* which was withdrawn from all but the Hearst papers and the *Chicago American* early in 1962. The leading Sunday supplements then were *This Week,* with 14 million copies; *Parade,* with 10 million; and *Family Weekly,* with more than 5 million. Working for economic stability in the industry was the Magazine Publishers Association.

Those who complained about a sameness in their newspapers and their mass-circulated magazines fared little better when they turned to television and radio. The major radio networks grew steadily, having 228 station affiliates in 1934, 702 in 1944, and 1,324 (55 per cent of all stations) in 1953. The decline in network broadcasting and expansion in number of stations changed the figures to 1,218 affiliates (34 per cent of all stations) in 1961. The 548 television stations of 1961 had 519 network affiliations (two or three for some stations). Of 272 television market areas, 132 were served by only one station and 69 more by just two, leaving many areas with limited choice.

Group, or chain, ownership became strong in radio, and stronger in television than in daily newspaper publishing. A 1949 study arrived at this picture: group ownerships controlled 281 AM radio stations, or 13.2 per cent of the total; 24 television stations, or 40 per cent of the total; and 386 dailies, or 21.6 per cent of the total.[14] Ten years later the figures for group ownership were 776 AM radio stations, or 23.5 per cent of the total; 278 television stations, or 53.3 per cent of the total; and 560 dailies, or 32.3 per cent of the total.[15] More than half the groups were involved in more than one medium.

---

[14] Warren K. Agee, "Cross-Channel Ownership of Communication Media," *Journalism Quarterly,* XXVI (Fall 1949), 410.

[15] Harvey J. Levin, *Broadcast Regulation and Joint Ownership of Media* (New York: New York University Press, 1960), p. 41; and Nixon and Ward, *op. cit.*

A final threat to diversity of communications ownership thus became such cross-channel ownership of the mass media. The Hearst organization led in 1962, with 12 dailies, 14 magazines, three AM stations, three FM stations, three TV stations, a news service, a photo service, a feature syndicate, and the Avon paperback book firm. Samuel Newhouse was not far behind, with 14 dailies, 11 magazines, four AM stations, three FM stations, and five TV stations. Scripps-Howard controlled 20 dailies, three AM stations, one FM station, four TV stations, a press association, a photo service, and a feature syndicate. The other six largest newspaper groups— McCormick-Patterson, Knight, Ridder, Cowles, Cox, and Gannett— together owned 16 AM, five FM, and 15 TV stations.

There were many other cross-channel combinations. Two magazine groups were in broadcasting, Meredith Publishing Company with 10 stations (four TV) and Time Inc. with eight stations (four TV). Walter H. Annenberg owned the *Inquirer* and *Daily News* in Philadelphia, 14 stations (five TV), and three magazines. The Chandler family had the *Los Angeles Times,* a suburban daily, a TV station, and the Signet and Mentor paperback book companies. Philip L. Graham owned the *Washington Post, Newsweek,* and four stations (two TV). The Cowles family owned *Look,* six dailies, six stations (three TV), and the *Insider's Newsletter.*

The Federal Communications Commission looked askance at this inter-media ownership. In 1940 newspapers owned 30 per cent of AM radio stations. They were heavily interested in FM broadcasting, and led by the *Milwaukee Journal* in 1939, they applied for 28 of the first 60 television licenses. Extensive hearings on the problem were held in 1941, with the publishers forming a Newspaper-Radio Committee. The FCC closed the issue in 1944, commenting that licenses would be granted on the merits of individual applications, under the guiding rule of as much diversification as possible. In general, newspapers won licenses without undue difficulty.

As the numbers of stations increased, the percentages of those affiliated with newspapers and magazines declined. In 1961 the percentages were 11.4 for AM stations, 15.8 for FM stations, and 29.3 for TV stations. In 76 cities there was single ownership of all daily newspaper and broadcasting facilities, while in 29 towns the weekly owned the only radio station. This meant that only 4.2 per cent of the 2,475 cities or towns with radio or television stations had a newspaper-broadcasting monopoly.[16] Few Americans did not have access to a variety of news or opinion, if they wished, despite the economic pressures affecting the mass media.

ANNOTATED BIBLIOGRAPHY

Books:

Ellis, L. Ethan, *Newsprint: Producers, Publishers and Political Pressures.* New Brunswick: Rutgers University Press, 1960. Study of costs, 1940-60; includes his earlier *Print Paper Pendulum.*

Ernst, Morris, *The First Freedom.* New York: The Macmillan Company, 1946. Discusses press and radio ownership concentration problems.

Levin, Harvey J., *Broadcast Regulation and Joint Ownership of Media.* New York: New York University Press, 1960. Contains a wealth of statistical information on the problem.

Peterson, Theodore, *Magazines in the Twentieth Century.* Urbana: University of Illinois Press, 1956, rev. 1958. The most comprehensive discussion of magazine industry economics.

Schramm, Wilbur, ed., *Mass Communications.* Urbana: University of Illinois Press, 1949, rev. 1960. Selected readings, including sizable portions of Llewellyn White's *The American Radio* and Neil Borden's *The Economic Effects of Advertising,* and articles on communications ownership and income problems.

Stewart, Kenneth, and John Tebbel, *Makers of Modern Journalism.* New York: Prentice-Hall, Inc., 1952. Contains chapters on the Knight, Cox, Cowles, Gannett, Luce, Field, and other major ownerships.

Periodicals and Monographs:

Agee, Warren K., "Cross-Channel Ownership of Communication Media," *Journalism Quarterly,* XXVI (Fall 1949), 410. Summary of Master's thesis, 1949, University of Minnesota.

Akers, Milburn P., "Chicago's Newspaper Concentration," *Nieman Reports,* XIII (July 1959), 20. Factual reasons for Chicago's two-ownership situation, by *Sun-Times* editor.

Bogart, Leo, "Magazines Since the Rise of Television," *Journalism Quarterly,* XXXIII (Spring 1956), 153. A study of magazine readership and economics from 1946-55.

"The Cowles World," *Time,* LXXII (December 8, 1958), 55. An extensive press section report on the Cowles family enterprises.

"Knight of the Press," *Newsweek,* XLV (April 25, 1955), 97. A special report on John S. Knight and his newspaper group.

Nelson, Harold L., "The Political Reform Press: A Case Study," *Journal-*

---

[16] Nixon and Ward, *op. cit.*

ism Quarterly, XXIX (Summer 1952), 294. An analysis of an almost successful farmer-labor newspaper, the *Minnesota Daily Star* (1920-24). Summary of Master's thesis, 1950. University of Minnesota.

Nixon, Raymond B., and Jean Ward, "Trends in Newspaper Ownership and Inter-Media Competition," *Journalism Quarterly*, XXXVIII (Winter 1961), 3. The most comprehensive study of the subject. See bibliography for Chapter 22 for Nixon's 1945 and 1954 studies.

Peterson, Wilbur, "Is Daily Circulation Keeping Pace with the Nation's Growth?," *Journalism Quarterly*, XXXVI (Winter 1959), 12. Covers the period 1929-57 with extensive statistical analysis.

————, "Loss in Country Weekly Newspapers Heavy in 1950s," *Journalism Quarterly*, XXXVIII (Winter 1961), 15. An evaluation of the community weekly's situation, with full data.

Scripps-Howard Research, "Economic Support of Mass Communications Media, 1929-1957," New York, 1959. A statistical analysis in brochure form of consumer and advertiser expenditures on media.

Shaplen, Robert, "The Newhouse Phenomenon," *Saturday Review*, XLIII (October 8, 1960), 55. Analysis of the rise of Samuel Newhouse, group owner of newspapers, magazines, and broadcasting stations.

Sim, John Cameron, "Weekly Newspapers Again Facing Challenge to Move," *Journalism Quarterly*, XXXV (Spring 1958), 195. Suburbia's effect on the weekly. See also Charles E. Hayes, "Journalism Grows New Roots in Suburbs," *Quill*, XLIX (September 1961), 6.

Small, Collie, "Little Publisher, Big Empire," *Collier's*, CXXVIII (August 4, 1951), 31. An earlier article on Samuel Newhouse.

"Some Publishers May Read Their Own Magazines, Books," *Editor & Publisher*, XCIII (April 23, 1960), 25. Cross-ownership report.

Survival of a Free Competitive Press, Senate Print No. 17. Washington: U. S. Government Printing Office, 1947. Senate committee hearings on newspaper economic problems.

Wertheimer, Jerrold L., "The Community Press of Suburbia." Ph.D. dissertation, Northwestern University, 1960. Chicago case study.

Chapter **28**

GOVERNMENT AND THE PRESS:
THE NEW DEAL ERA AND AFTER

> There can be no such thing as a free press and
> no such thing as the integrity of the news if the
> men and women who write the news live in fear
> of the security of their jobs.
>
> —Heywood Broun

A NEW ERA IN THE HISTORY of the United States opened in 1933 when Franklin D. Roosevelt inaugurated the New Deal. Driven by the impact of the great depression, the nation sought for new patterns of social and economic justice and security. In doing so, it adopted philosophies concerning government participation in socio-economic affairs extending well beyond those which arose from the Theodore Roosevelt and Woodrow Wilson eras early in the century.

The press, as a result, entered into a period of sharply intensified concern about its relationships with government and with groups that utilized the powers of government in ways which affected the press. Its business operations, like those of all private enterprises, were affected by New Deal social and economic legislation inaugurating federal social security and unemployment insurance, providing guarantees for collective bargaining, extending wage and hour controls, stiffening federal trade regulations, and otherwise utilizing governmental authority to intervene in economic affairs for the welfare of the individual or of society as a whole. A new chapter in newspaper labor relations was opened with the rise of the American Newspaper Guild under the collective bargaining laws. And, in the turbulent New Deal era and afterwards, the question of freedom of the press was raised steadily by those who either feared or resented the strengthened hand of government. There was also a constant battle for reporters' access to news sources.

The first job of the Roosevelt administration in 1933 was to restore confidence in the country's banking system, on the verge of collapse after a wave of fear swept the nation in the winter months. This was done by emergency action, reinforced by establishment of the Federal Deposit Insurance Corporation. The second job, with some 17,000,000 persons unemployed, was to coordinate relief activities under the Federal Emergency Relief Administration, which later became the famous Works Progress Administration. By the end of 1934, one-sixth of the population was on relief. Young men were enrolled in the Civilian Conservation Corps and college students in the National Youth Administration.

But the main task of the New Deal was to stimulate recovery in industry, business, and agriculture. The agencies involved were the Reconstruction Finance Corporation, established by the Hoover administration to make credit available to businesses; the Public Works Administration, which financed job-giving construction projects; the Agricultural Adjustment Administration and the Farm Credit Administration; and, most important of all, the National Recovery Administration. The National Industrial Recovery Act, passed by Congress in June, 1933, was an ambitious effort to plan the return to prosperity. American employers were to cooperate, under government leadership, in shortening working hours, raising wages, and pledging themselves to increase employment. The act called for establishment of NRA codes of fair competition for all industries.

Two sections of the recovery act in particular affected newspaper publishers. One was the famous Section 7-a, which guaranteed the right of collective bargaining and freedom of labor union organization. Under the shelter of its provisions the American Newspaper Guild came into being. The other was the licensing section, which gave the President power to license individual companies in an industry not cooperating under the NRA program and to revoke such licenses for continued noncompliance if he deemed it necessary and proper. Operation of a business without a license under such conditions would be unlawful. Only those who cooperated could fly the "Blue Eagle," the NRA's publicity and public opinion symbol.

Trade associations in the communications industries were called upon to write voluntary codes to which individual businesses could subscribe. Deciding that there was work to be done to protect newspapers from the NRA legislation, the American Newspaper Publishers Association took the lead in the writing of a code for daily newspapers which would contain the safeguards and requests the ANPA leadership believed publishers wanted. The association's general legal counsel, Elisha Hanson, played a leading role in influencing the code negotiations. His intense fear of possible government regulation and his stern disapproval of any unionization of newspaper editorial workers made him, and the ANPA, the objects of intense criticism by those who thought that the official spokesmen for organized daily newspaper publishers were both too conservative and unrealistic. The critics included not only outside observers and newspaper workers, but also a substantial number of newspaper publishers and editors.

The ANPA's code committee feared the licensing provisions of the NRA legislation. At the urging of Colonel Robert R. McCormick, chairman of the association's committee on freedom of the press, the publishers correctly insisted that their code deny the application of the licensing power to newspapers. But General Hugh S. Johnson, the outspoken former cavalry officer who headed NRA, raised his eyebrows at some of the other reservations. So did some newspaper publishers, newspaper editorial workers, and others who felt that the ANPA was asking for a privileged position for daily newspapers that was not in keeping with the recovery effort.[1]

After eyeing the NRA guarantee of the right to collective bargaining, Hanson and the committee had written into their code an open-shop provision assuring any employer or employe the right to bargain individually. The code also proposed that carrier boys be exempted from NRA provisions limiting child labor. Reporters and other editorial workers who were doing "professional work" were not to be subject to the maximum hour provisions of the law.

[1] *Editor & Publisher*, LXVI (August 12, 1933), 3, carries some of the dissents, as do subsequent issues.

To cap their requests, the publishers insisted upon a clause stating: "Nothing in the adoption and acceptance of this code shall be construed as waiving, abrogating, or modifying any rights secured under the Constitution of the United States or of any state, or limiting the freedom of the press."

Those surrounding President Roosevelt regarded the inclusion of such a statement in the proposed code as an insulting gesture, and a vigorous debate ensued over the intentions of the New Deal toward the newspapers. After obtaining modification of the child labor and open-shop clauses, General Johnson accepted the code with the remark, "I don't want to fight the press of America but I can't afford to lay down for them." When he approved the final draft of the daily newspaper code in February, 1934, President Roosevelt called the publishers' proposed press-freedom clause "pure surplusage," and added: "The freedom guaranteed by the Constitution is freedom of expression and that will be scrupulously respected—but it is not freedom to work children, or to do business in a fire trap or violate the laws against obscenity, libel and lewdness." This was strong medicine, and it was the publishers' turn to feel unjustly and falsely accused.

The final version of the daily newspaper code provided for a 40-hour week only for employes of newspapers published in cities of more than 50,000 population. Its minimum wage scale ranged from $15 a week for employes of papers published in cities of more than 500,000 population down to $11 a week in cities of less than 25,000 population. "Learners" would receive at least 70 per cent of the scale. Mechanical employes were guaranteed wages of 40 cents an hour. The minimum age for carrier boys remained at 12 (subject to regulations in the various states), with the added provision that those under 16 would work only in the daytime. The "professional worker" clause was clarified so that ordinary news-editorial employes came under the maximum hour clause. The President asked metropolitan papers to put newsmen on five-day weeks to increase employment, and most of them did so.[2]

Newspapermen received the wage and hour provisions of the daily newspaper code with little enthusiasm. The $11 to $15 weekly salary minimums did nothing to further the professional status of

[2] *Editor & Publisher*, LXVII (February 24, 1934), pp. 3, 36, gives Roosevelt's executive order and the text of the code.

journalism, or the economic security of its workers—an obvious conclusion to which thoughtful leaders of the profession agreed. The code provisions were far from the $40 a week minimum for newsmen with two years or more experience, which New York newspapermen considered equitable at the time. Surveys made for the NRA in 1934 showed median weekly salaries of reporters, photographers, and deskmen running between $30 and $45, but the going figure in many places for experienced men was $25. Beginning reporters sometimes worked free, or for less than $5 a week; and $12 a week for a six-day week with no limit on the number of hours worked each day was not uncommon. Living costs were low, but so were the spirits of those who hoped the New Deal was meant for them, too.

Reporters and deskmen around the country began talking about formation of collective bargaining units in the summer of 1933 when the trend of the code negotiations became apparent. Heywood Broun, the liberal and combative columnist for the *New York World-Telegram,* sounded a call for action in his syndicated column for August 7, 1933, which sparked the translation of talk into deeds. Broun deftly chastised his fellow newspapermen for not having formed a union like those of the better-paid printers, and gently chided those who feared "the romance of the game" would be lost if they organized. Then in typical Broun style he concluded:

> But the fact that newspaper editors and owners are genial folk should hardly stand in the way of the organization of a newspaper writers' union. There should be one. Beginning at nine o'clock on the morning of October 1, I am going to do the best I can in helping get one up. I think I could die happy on the opening day of the general strike if I had the privilege of watching Walter Lippmann heave a brick through a *Tribune* window at a non-union operative who had been called in to write the current "Today and Tomorrow" column on the gold standard.[3]

The cautious Lippmann ignored Broun's call to arms, but the newspapermen across the country who read his column didn't, nor did they wait until October 1. Cleveland's newsmen were the first to respond, forming what became the first local of the American Newspaper Guild on August 20. The Twin Cities, Minneapolis and St. Paul, were second in line. New York, Rockford, Newark, Akron,

---

[3] Broun's column is reprinted in the *Guild Reporter,* XVI (December 9, 1949), which contains several pages reviewing early Guild history and Broun's career.

Duluth—Superior, Cincinnati, Philadelphia, and Youngstown locals followed in rapid order. There had been newswriters' locals chartered by the American Federation of Labor and its affiliated International Typographical Union as early as the 1890's, but few had lived for any length of time. Broun himself had headed a New York effort in 1923.[4] But if newsmen had lagged up until 1933 in creating a union, they hesitated no longer, despite the reluctance of some of their colleagues to go beyond the stage of the press club or professional organization.

The movement toward unionization was not an automatic one, however. Long discussions were held in newspaper offices and press clubs about the advisability of newsmen becoming a part of the trade union movement. Broun was one of the few established newspaper writers who plumped wholeheartedly for the Guild. There were those who conscientiously felt that a union would endanger the professional status of newspapermen. Others warned that newspaper managements, which in general were friendly to the local organizations and to the idea of a professional guild, would not welcome a national union. Disappointment over the wage and hour provisions of the NRA code, and failure of most newspapers to answer the stirrings among their newsmen with concrete salary proposals, led however to a full-blown union movement.

New York newsmen, headed by Broun, issued the first number of the *Guild Reporter* on November 23, 1933, and called for a national convention to be held in Washington December 15. Delegates from 30 cities responded, and formed the American Newspaper Guild. Broun was elected president, a post he held until his death in 1939, and Jonathan Eddy became the first executive secretary. The newspapermen and women were seeking, they said, "to preserve the vocational interests of the members and to improve the conditions under which they work by collective bargaining, and to raise the standards of journalism."

By the time the first annual convention met in St. Paul in June,

---

[4] The early AFL efforts are summarized in National Labor Relations Board, *Collective Bargaining in the Newspaper Industry* (Washington: Government Printing Office, 1939), and in Alfred McClung Lee, *The Daily Newspaper in America* (New York: The Macmillan Company, 1937). The most successful locals were in Scranton, Milwaukee, Boston, New York, Philadelphia, and Columbus, Ohio.

1934, the Guild had 8,000 members. But only one of its local units had a contract with a publisher. The 1934 Guild convention called for more contracts covering minimum wages and maximum hours, paid holidays and vacations, overtime pay, sick leave, severance pay, and other usual trade union contract provisions—goals which remained to be gained by the average newspaper staff. Publishers who disliked seeing the Guild take on the form of a trade union organization were further antagonized when the convention approved a code of ethics which listed what the Guild regarded to be harmful practices of newspapers. The publishers viewed the listing as a harmful public indictment of all newspapers, regardless of degrees of individual newspaper integrity, and wondered how far the Guild was going in demanding a voice in newspaper operations. The Guild, rebuffed in its effort "to raise the standards of journalism" on a philosophical plane, and realizing that it faced a hard fight to win union contracts, thereafter stuck closely to problems of salaries and working conditions when dealing with employers. Local units sponsored Guild discussions and competitions designed to improve journalistic practices.

The first contract to be signed by a publisher and a Guild unit included a Guild objective that was to meet determined opposition from the publishers. J. David Stern, liberal-minded publisher of the *Philadelphia Record,* signed a contract in April, 1934, which provided for a Guild-shop agreement, stipulating that all newsmen must join the Guild within 30 days of initial employment. Insistence by the national Guild in 1937 that all local contracts should include the Guild shop provision led to a mass meeting of representatives of publishers' groups in Chicago, where more than 500 newspaper executives agreed to oppose mandatory Guild membership. A compromise form of the Guild shop agreement became one which required that 80 per cent of the employes covered by a contract must be Guild members. In either case the publisher was free to employ whomever he chose, without regard to prior Guild membership, thus differentiating the Guild shop from typical closed shops. And in many cities the Guild-shop agreement was not included in local contracts.

Stern guaranteed his *Philadelphia Record* employes a $20 a week basic minimum, a 40-hour week, vacation and overtime pay, and severance provisions. The second Guild contract, signed by the

Madison Capital Times and *Wisconsin State Journal* in September, 1934, offered a $35 top minimum after two years' experience, one month of dismissal notice, a Guild shop, and a 48-hour week (down from 55 to 65 hours).[5] The third contract, signed with the *Cleveland News* in December, called for $40 a week top minimum after four years' experience, a 40-hour week, severance pay, and overtime compensation. Vacations, holidays, and sick leave went unmentioned. These contracts were regarded as Guild achievements in 1934.

Strike action was taken by the Guild for the first time in November, 1934, after publisher L. T. Russell of the *Newark Ledger*, in New Jersey, discharged eight Guildsmen. Heywood Broun walked the picket line and the Guild campaigned for a public boycott of the newspaper and a secondary boycott of advertisers. Both publisher Russell and the ANPA called the strike a showdown, but after 18 weeks Russell sold the paper, leaving the newsmen with little more than a moral victory. Three strikes of minor importance followed in 1935. Then, between February, 1936, and June, 1938, Guild locals were constantly involved in one or more strikes, for a total of 16 in this period. The biggest were against four Hearst papers, the *Wisconsin News* in Milwaukee, the *Seattle Post-Intelligencer,* and the *Chicago American* and *Herald & Examiner.* The Chicago Hearst papers were merged during a year and a half struggle with the Guild.

These years of peak strike activity were years of decision in many ways for the Guild. By 1936 it still had only 30 contracts and 33 "bulletin-board" agreements with newspaper managements. That year the Guild joined the American Federation of Labor, only to switch in 1937 to the newly formed Committee on Industrial Organization. In 1937 the national Guild office was given a veto power over contracts negotiated by the locals, and a comprehensive national collective bargaining plan was established. Special negotiating councils were set up for employes of the press associations and of the principal newspaper chains. The 1937 convention broadened the Guild membership base to include commercial office employes, in addition to the news-editorial and advertising personnel—a move which was opposed by quite a few Guild members and which

---

[5] *State Journal* employes later withdrew from the Guild, as did some of the other early organized units.

resulted in some locals withdrawing to form independent units. Passage of resolutions on controversial topics also angered some Guild members. But as a result of over-all strengthening of the national organization, the Guild had 75 newspaper contracts by 1938 and had signed its first with a press association, the United Press.[6]

But the biggest Guild victory was gained in a court case involving one Associated Press staffman, Morris Watson. Watson, who had been discharged by the Associated Press in 1935, asserted he had been dismissed for Guild activities. He appealed to the National Labor Relations Board for an order compelling his reinstatement under the provisions of the Wagner Labor Relations Act of 1935, whose collective bargaining guarantees had replaced those of the NRA codes outlawed by the Supreme Court that year. When the NLRB ruled in favor of Watson in 1936, the AP carried the case to the Supreme Court, contending that the Wagner Act was unconstitutional and that in any event it did not apply to newspapers or press associations.

Elisha Hanson brought the American Newspaper Publishers Association into the case as *amicus curiae,* and asserted that unionization of editorial employes under government compulsion destroyed freedom of the press. Not waiting for the court's decision, he told ANPA members to "flatly refuse to have anything to do with the National Labor Relations Board other than to notify it that it is without power under the Constitution to interfere with their business." [7] The ANPA board of directors followed up in December, 1936, with a flat statement that a publisher who agreed to a Guild shop thereby destroyed or restricted freedom of the press, arguing that unionization could only lead to biased news writing. J. David Stern, publisher of the *Philadelphia Record* and first signer with the Guild, resigned in anger from the ANPA, telling the board: "Ever since the NRA code, the American Newspaper Publishers Association has been using the pretext of protecting the freedom of the press to gain special privilege in purely business obligations. That

---

[6] The details can be followed in the *Guild Reporter* and *Editor & Publisher,* and are summarized in the NLRB's *Collective Bargaining in the Newspaper Industry* and in the special issue of the *Guild Reporter,* XVI (December 9, 1949).

[7] *Editor & Publisher,* LXIX (October 10, 1936), 7.

is why I say *you* are endangering the freedom of the press, one of the most important essentials of our democracy." [8]

The smashing re-election victory won by President Roosevelt in November, 1936, made it evident that the country had accepted the basic New Deal reform measures, including approval of the principle of collective bargaining. Newspaper publishers, recognizing the situation and desiring to abide by the majority decision, shied away from the ANPA's Guild policy in growing numbers, without awaiting the Watson case ruling. The *New York Daily News,* the country's largest newspaper, signed a contract for a Guild shop, and William Randolph Hearst ended the long *Seattle Post-Intelligencer* strike, putting President Roosevelt's son-in-law and daughter, John and Anna Boettiger, in charge of the paper. Many metropolitan papers granted higher salaries and shorter hours.

Then the Supreme Court, which had ruled adversely on key New Deal legislation in 1935 and 1936, announced a series of decisions in April, 1937, upholding the constitutionality of the Wagner Act. Among the cases decided was that of Morris Watson. Justices Hughes and Roberts swung to the liberal side to join Justices Brandeis, Stone, and Cardozo in ordering the Associated Press to reinstate Watson in his job. The five justices ruled that Watson had been illegally discharged for union activity, and it was upon that point that the case turned. [9] But the majority also observed that "The publisher of a newspaper has no special immunity from the application of general laws." Four justices agreed with the AP and the ANPA that freedom of the press was being endangered if the Wagner Act henceforth was to apply to news organizations. These were the four justices who were to become the objects of President Roosevelt's ill-fated "court-packing" plan, advanced with the intention of bringing the court back into step with the country's dominant economic and social philosophies. They were Justices McReynolds, Butler, Van Devanter, and Sutherland.

Upholding of the Wagner Act was a great Guild victory. It assured the American Newspaper Guild a permanent place in newspaper life. Gradually contracts were won in larger cities, including one with the *New York Times,* whose staff had long been skeptical

[8] *Editor & Publisher,* LXIX (December 19, 1936), 57.
[9] *Associated Press v. NLRB,* 301 U. S. 103 (1937).

of the Guild. Strikes declined after the 1936-38 flurry, in part because the Guild eased up on aggressive efforts to organize staffs of smaller papers.

But the road was still a rocky one. The recession years of 1937-39 brought widespread newspaper closings and staff prunings which left thousands of newspapermen unemployed, and made contract negotiation difficult. The Guild, after the tragic death of Heywood Broun at age 51 from pneumonia, became engaged in a bitter fight between conservative or "pro-Guild" members and left-wing elements who were strongest in the New York City locals. Forcing of election of officers by nationwide referendums, however, brought victory to the "pro-Guild" group. Under the leadership of presidents Milton M. Murray and Harry Martin, and executive vice-presidents Sam Eubanks and Ralph B. Novak, the Guild remained vigorously liberal, but shunned Communists and fellow travelers, after 1941. Like other AFL-CIO unions, the Guild continued this anti-Communist policy during the next two decades.

World War II brought a general "freezing" of labor relations activities. Industries and unions agreed to no-strike and no-lockout pledges and wages and prices were regulated by the government. Salaries for reporters on metropolitan dailies had reached the $50 to $55 level for experienced men and women by 1941, under Guild contracts, but were at the $40 to $45 level for medium-sized dailies, and lower still in many newspaper offices. The Guild was aided by the maintenance of membership provisions of wartime labor legislation, which required union members to remain in good standing during the life of a union contract. Such provisions were written into many postwar contracts, if Guild shop or modified Guild shop agreements were not obtainable.

As the war ended, the Guild's goal was a $65 a week top minimum for all contracts. Then in 1946 the goal was set at a seemingly impossible $100 level. Postwar inflation made the $100 a week salary not only feasible, but reasonable, both in the eyes of Guild members and newspaper managements before 1950. Strikes broke out in 1946, however, the principal ones being against Hearst's *Los Angeles Herald & Express* and, ironically, J. David Stern's *Philadelphia Record*. Stern accused the Guild of making unfair salary demands upon him, and sold his paper to the *Bulletin* after a three months' strike, but the Guild insisted he had planned to sell before the strike started. A new strike technique was demonstrated in 1950 when 500 striking Guild employes of the *New York World-Telegram and Sun*, principal Scripps-Howard paper, were supported by 1,000 AFL mechanical unions members who refused to cross the Guild's picket lines. Such inter-union cooperation ensured that a struck paper could not publish and the Guild used the threat in other cities, closing the *Seattle Times* in similar fashion in 1953, the *Brooklyn Eagle* in 1955, the Cleveland dailies in 1956, and the *St. Louis Globe-Democrat* in 1959. The Guild also was involved in major strikes begun by other unions in Detroit in 1955, in St. Paul in 1957-58, in San Jose in 1959, and in Portland, Oregon in 1960.

Too much emphasis can be placed upon strikes, however; in the main, Guild locals and newspaper managements were able to negotiate contracts at the conference table in friendly, if determined, fashion. Most Guild locals had not been on strike during the first three decades of Guild history.

There were more than 31,000 Guild members by 1961. They worked on approximately 180 newspapers in some 115 cities and towns, for the press associations and feature services, and for a dozen magazines. In the main the Guild was concentrated in metropolitan areas, although a good number of middle-sized dailies and a sprinkling of smaller ones were represented. About 2,000 Guildsmen were members of a Wire Service Unit begun in 1957. A Canadian unit founded in 1951 had 3,000 members.

Salary scales continued to move upward. By 1954 the $100 top minimum goal had been reached in 90 per cent of the contracts. In 1957 the Guild set as new goals a $200 a week top minimum and $100 a week for beginners. *Newsweek* granted the $200 scale in 1961 and the *New York Times* and *Wall Street Journal* the $100 beginning wage. The best 1961 newspaper contract guaranteed at least $165 a week for both newsmen and women after six years of experience. The median of 178 contracts called for at least $130 a week. Most Guild contracts included at least 37 weeks of severance pay, three-week vacations, paid sick leave, paid holidays, a pension plan, and a work week of 40 hours or less.

Joseph F. Collis served as Guild president during 1953-59, and was succeeded by Arthur Rosenstock, a *New York Times* librarian. William J. Farson became the executive vice president in 1955.

Remembering the role Broun had played in making such gains possible, the Guild in 1941 established an annual award for newspaper work "in the spirit of Heywood Broun."

While the NRA and the Wagner Act thus had been stimulating the growth of the American Newspaper Guild as an organization of major social and economic importance, other New Deal reform proposals had become law. Some of the reform legislation affected the newspaper business directly; more of the laws affected newspapers only indirectly; and some affected newspapers not at all. But the total impact of the New Deal reform legislation of the 1930's was great upon those who preferred traditionalism to change. Conservative-minded spokesmen for the American Newspaper Publishers Association found occasion to criticise or oppose, for varying reasons, the Federal Securities Act of 1933, establishing the Securities Exchange Commission; the Social Security Act of 1935; the Wagner Labor Relations Act of 1935; the Fair Labor Standards Act of 1938, prescribing minimum wages and maximum hours; revisions of the Agricultural Adjustment Act; the Wheeler-Lea bill giving the Federal Trade Commission power to regulate unfair or misleading advertising; the Copeland pure food, drugs, and cosmetics bill; and child labor legislation.

In their many challenges to federal legislation, the spokesmen for organized daily newspaper publishers had a valid, material argument to present. They asserted that should the prevailing tendency toward government regulation of business continue unabated, a press that was regarded solely as a business enterprise might find its freedom of economic action so restricted that it would wither. If society wished to have a free press, the publishers felt, it must safeguard newspapers against restrictive actions which would endanger their economic security and would curtail their enterprise as forceful organs presenting news and opinion.

The ANPA spokesmen did advance this argument against specific legislative proposals which they thought would impair the financial integrity—and therefore the freedom—of the press. Too often, however, the argument was lost because the association's leadership talked more loudly about a "press freedom crusade" than about the problem of maintaining a healthy newspaper economy. Furthermore, the ANPA spokesmen did not concentrate their opposition upon those legislative proposals which, if adopted, would seemingly jeopardize press freedom. Rather, they attempted to oppose a great variety of New Deal measures of varying potential effects upon newspapers' well-being, without balancing the extent of public interest in the measures against their own narrower interests. So the impression was left that newspaper publishers were crying "freedom of the press" because they did not want to make reasonable adjustments to new socio-economic conditions.

Some voices within the press itself expressed the fear that such indiscriminate opposition to legislation and constant appeals for protection of press freedom would dissipate public support—upon which that freedom eventually depends—and would render the press unable to fight effectively against those governmental actions that could be shown clearly to endanger the welfare of newspapers, and therefore the public welfare. One such voice was that of Arthur Hays Sulzberger, publisher of the *New York Times,* who suggested at the 1936 ANPA annual convention that perhaps the association was going too far in its campaign. He said that while safeguarding of press freedom was necessary he was not convinced that the Roosevelt administration "has or had designs upon the freedom of the press." And he reminded his listeners that the freedom of the press guarantee in the Constitution "is the statement of an essential liberty of a free people and not a grant of immunity extended to a particular trade or profession . . . the responsibilities that the franchise entails are greater than the privileges it bestows." [10]

More bluntly critical was Virginius Dabney, noted editor of the *Richmond Times-Dispatch,* who wrote in the aftermath of Roosevelt's smashing 1936 re-election victory:

> The publishers association has indulged in an unabashed campaign of self-laudation; it has over-emphasized the "freedom of the press" to a ludicrous extent, thereby incurring the suspicion that it is using this shibboleth as a red herring; and its members have banded together to defeat legislation, such as the Child Labor Amendment, and have thereby created the impression in many minds, whether justly or not, that they put their own private profit above the general good.[11]

Thus in a period of economic stress and social insecurity, when the press, business, and all other institutional activities were under

[10] *Editor & Publisher,* LXIX (April 25, 1936), 4.
[11] *Public Opinion Quarterly,* I (April 1937), 124.

close scrutiny, the ANPA legislative and anti-Guild activities constituted the association's public front. Little was known about the substantial work done by the ANPA as a trade association, representing 850 dailies with 90 per cent of total daily newspaper circulation. In contrast to its position on the Guild, the ANPA had sponsored an imaginative policy of voluntary arbitration in cooperation with the printing trades unions in 1900. Its Bureau of Advertising was publishing the *Continuing Study of Newspaper Reading*, in cooperation with the Advertising Research Foundation, to determine readership of advertisements and news. It had encouraged research in printing processes. And it had done a good job of defending newspapers' interests in obtaining cheap and plentiful supplies of newsprint, and in using the second-class mail privileges, although these activities brought complaints about self-interest.[12] Its New York central office operations, directed from 1905 to 1939 by Lincoln B. Palmer and subsequently by Cranston Williams, constituted capable trade association work. But all this was submerged in a "press freedom" crusade which seemed little concerned with improvement of press standards of performance.

What were the specific complaints of the ANPA's legal counsel, Elisha Hanson, and of its committees on federal legislation? In 1933 they protested the regulation of financial advertising copy in newspapers as proposed by sponsors of the Federal Securities Act in order to protect investors from a repetition of the financial fiasco of the 1920's. And they asserted that various food and drug regulation bills under consideration in Congress "involved censorship." This contention that advertising has constitutional protection was to be persistently advanced by the ANPA, although the Supreme Court twice flatly denied the claim.[13] It was part of the general argument that business activities of newspapers either were exempted under the First Amendment from government regulation, or should be protected against any adverse effects of Federal general business laws—an argument never recognized by the Supreme Court but sometimes accepted by Congress.

In 1934 the ANPA convention was warned about a 30-hour work

---

[12] See pages 396, 402, and 409-12 for earlier ANPA history.

[13] J. Edward Gerald, *The Press and the Constitution* (Minneapolis: University of Minnesota Press, 1948), p. 75.

week bill which did not exempt newspapers; about new proposals for child labor legislation which did not exempt newspaperboys; and about the Wagner bill and the Social Security bill. In 1935 the ANPA spokesmen reported on their losing battle against the Wagner Act, which was termed "one of the most obnoxious of bills," and which was to be fought as inapplicable to newspapers under the First Amendment. They also said they had again sought revisions in the advertising safeguards of the Securities Exchange Act, because of a drying up of financial advertising. A brief had been filed against the Copeland pure food, drugs, and cosmetics bill because amendments advocated by the ANPA and designed to modify the proposed advertising safeguards of the bill had not been included. Publishers were warned that amendments to the Agricultural Adjustment Act would "control advertising of farm products." And a suggestion was made that newspapers receive special consideration in the assessment of payroll taxes under the Social Security Act. In 1937 and 1938 the ANPA opposed, without success, the granting of increased authority to the Federal Trade Commission to regulate unfair or misleading advertising of products in interstate commerce. Newspapers, however, were released from responsibility for any false advertising the FTC might find.

In the debate over the Fair Labor Standards Act, popularly known as the Wage and Hour Law, the ANPA again contended that the First Amendment applies to the business operations of newspapers. The act looked forward to the establishment of the 40-hour week and 40 cents an hour minimum pay. Congress exempted weekly newspapers with circulations of less than 3,000 copies from the provisions of the act, but refused the exemption pleas of larger papers, despite their showing that they too were being burdened with difficult financial problems by the Wage and Hour Law provisions. Having lost the battle in Congress, the ANPA then contended that the Wage and Hour Law "was not intended to apply to the newspaper publishing business" and supported publishers who went to court rather than let federal investigators inspect their records. But the Supreme Court in 1946 ruled that newspapers were bound to observe the requirements of the law, like other businesses.[14] Hanson, by the mid-1940's, found this crusade

[14] *Mabee v. White Plains Publishing Co., Inc.,* 327 U. S. 178 (1946).

unpopular; he complained that editors were giving him "plain un-shirted hell for even challenging the power of Congress to destroy the press."

The end of the New Deal reform period by 1938, the coming of World War II, and a shift in ANPA leadership brought a soften-ing of the association's voice in matters of public issue. Newspaper publishers were aroused by the press freedom implications of the suit brought by Marshall Field's *Chicago Sun* in 1943 to have the Associated Press' restrictive membership provisions declared illegal restraints of trade. But when the Supreme Court in 1945 decided against the AP, and forced it to open its membership to legitimate applicants,[15] no one found that any damage had been done, or that any Constitutional safeguards of the press had been endangered. The ANPA scored a legislative victory when, after the Supreme Court had ruled in 1944 that adult newspaper vendors came under Social Security Act provisions, it joined in persuading Congress to pass a 1948 bill removing the vendors from the protection of the law, despite two vetoes of such legislation by President Truman.

Passage in 1947 of the Taft-Hartley Act, replacing the Wagner Act, also pleased the ANPA leadership. But the Taft-Hartley law's outlawing of the closed shop brought newspaper publishers into a major conflict with the powerful International Typographical Union. The typographers, as a powerful traditional craft union with an organizational history running back for more than a century, were logical candidates among the closed shop unions to challenge the provisions of the Taft-Hartley law. The ANPA, with 60 years of experience in the daily newspaper labor relations field, was quick to take up the challenge.

After two decades during which all the printing trade unions and the ANPA observed the provisions of national voluntary arbi-tration agreements as a means of preventing labor disputes, the typographers' arbitration agreement foundered in 1922. The union refused ANPA demands that provisions of union law, including those which the publishers labeled as "featherbedding" practices, be subject to arbitration. The same year the ANPA established an Open Shop Department for the benefit of non-union publishers; during the 1930's this department furnished crews of non-union printers to strike-bound publishers until Congress made such inter-

[15] *Associated Press v. United States,* 326 U. S. 1 (1945).

state activities illegal. While relations between the ANPA and the unions of pressmen, photo-engravers, and stereotypers remained on a cordial note—the pressmen retaining their national arbitration agreement throughout the entire period—those with the typographers steadily deteriorated.

Late in 1947 the ANPA filed a complaint with the National Labor Relations Board, charging the International Typographical Union with violations of the Taft-Hartley Act. Almost immediately the ITU answered by selecting the Chicago newspaper publishers as the object of a show-down strike. The strike lasted 22 months, but the Chicago newspapers got along without typographers by substituting typewritten copy and photo-engraved pages for regular makeup processes. In the end, the Chicago publishers in effect recognized the closed shop. When the NLRB finally ruled on the ANPA-ITU case in 1949, it found the ITU guilty of violating the closed shop ban, and agreed with the ANPA that union law provisions should be subject to arbitration, but upheld the union's "featherbedding" practices, including the controversial "bogus matter" rule which permits union members to reset advertising furnished the paper in ready-to-print form. The Supreme Court in 1953 upheld the union on the "bogus" setting dispute, and in 1961 approved a revised ITU version of a closed shop contract.

More than half of newspaper strikes between 1946 and 1960 involved the ITU. But other unions also made initial strike calls. The photo-engravers closed New York City newspapers for 11 days in 1953; a drivers' union strike closed them again for 18 days in 1958. Other major closedowns—in Detroit in 1955, Boston in 1957, and San Jose in 1959—involved the mailers as well as the ITU. Papers in Portland, Oregon, were crippled by a strike begun by stereotypers in 1959 and still continuing in 1961. During the period 1946-60, however, newspapers and their unions reached 829 arbitration agreements, compared to 322 strike calls.

The ANPA expanded the activities of its Research Institute in the 1950's, seeking to pare production costs and to find new printing processes. Under a new general manager, Stanford Smith, who took office in 1960, the association began a Newspaper Information Service and aided journalism teachers and students in high schools and colleges. It seemed definitely to have dropped the ultra-conservative role of the troubled 1930's.

Significant episodes involving freedom of the press, and the right of the people to know, became a part of the record beginning in the 1930's, along with the furor over comparatively transient matters. There were landmark cases in which newspapers appealed to the courts to uphold the historic right to freedom of expression without prior restraint and without punitive action by government. And there were revitalized efforts by newsmen to keep channels of information open by insisting upon their right of access to news.

An obscure Minnesota publisher provided a case in which the Supreme Court, in 1931 for the first time, applied the freedom of the press guarantees of the First Amendment against the States through the due process clause of the Fourteenth Amendment. The case of *Near v. Minnesota* thus served as a turning point in the battle to hold states as strictly accountable for invasions of liberty as the federal government. What was known as the Minnesota "gag law" of 1925, permitting the suppression of malicious and scandalous publications, had been applied by a court to the *Saturday Press* of Minneapolis in order to stop its smear attacks upon public officials. Calling the law a threat to all newspapers, no matter how unworthy the *Saturday Press* might be, chairman Robert R. McCormick of the ANPA committee on freedom of the press retained counsel to carry the case to the Supreme Court. There Chief Justice Hughes, speaking for the majority in a 5-4 decision, held the Minnesota law unconstitutional because it permitted prior restraint upon publication.[16] Suppression, the court said, was a greater danger than an irresponsible attack upon public officials, who in any event had proper recourse through libel action.

Huey Long, the Louisiana political boss, provided the next major case in 1934. The Long machine obtained passage by the state legislature of a special 2 per cent tax on the gross advertising income of Louisiana papers with a circulation of 20,000 or more. Twelve of the 13 papers affected were opposed to the Long regime. They appealed to the courts, again with the assistance of Colonel McCormick's ANPA committee, and in 1936 the Supreme Court found the punitive tax unconstitutional. Justice Sutherland wrote a unanimous decision, holding that Long's bill was "a deliberate and calculated device . . . to limit the circulation of information

[16] *Near v. Minnesota ex rel. Olson,* 283 U. S. 697 (1931).

to which the public is entitled by virtue of the constitutional guarantees."[17] A Baltimore city tax on advertising was voided in 1958.
Newspapers, however, often have had to appeal to higher courts
for relief after they have been held in contempt by lower courts.
A landmark case in giving newspapers more latitude in commenting
upon judges' activities was decided by the Supreme Court in 1941.
This was the case of *Bridges v. California*, with which a companion case involving the *Los Angeles Times* was affiliated. Harry
Bridges, the longshoreman labor leader, had been cited for contempt because newspapers had published the text of a telegram he
had sent the Labor Department threatening to call a strike if a
court decision went against him. The *Times* was cited for publishing editorials deemed threatening by a court. The California Bar
Association asked the Supreme Court to declare the two contempt
citations unconstitutional. This the court did by applying the sanc-
tions of the First Amendment against the state court under the due
process clause of the Fourteenth Amendment, and by utilizing the
clear and present danger test first applied in the Schenck case.[18]
Newspapers henceforth in theory could comment upon a court
action not yet closed, without fear of punishment, unless a judge
could hold that press comment created so great and immediate a
danger that his court could not continue to function. But state
courts continued to resist this trend in thinking, and hard battles
were fought by the *Miami Herald* and the *Corpus Christi Caller-
Times* in 1946 and 1947 to avoid the penalties of contempt
charges.[19]

The Post Office Department, with its power to exclude publications from the mails under certain conditions, also has at times been
a threat to freedom of the press. Over the years, court decisions,
administrative actions, and the sweeping use of the postmaster's
power during World War I to throw Socialist publications out of
the mails, built up a spirit of censorship in the Post Office. Matters
came to a head in 1943 when the Postmaster General proposed to
withdraw use of the second-class mailing rate from *Esquire* maga-

---

[17] *Grosjean v. American Press Co.*, 297 U. S. 233 (1936).
[18] *Bridges v. California*, 314 U. S. 252 (1941).
[19] *Pennekamp v. Florida*, 328 U. S. 331 (1946); *Craig v. Harney*, 331 U. S.
367 (1947).

zine. The second-class rate, it was contended, was a privilege, which the government could withdraw if the publication using it was not making a "special contribution to the public welfare." The Post Office thought *Esquire* was not worthy of the use of the second-class rate. The magazine's publishers, who were faced with paying a half million dollars a year additional in postal charges, carried the case to the Supreme Court. There *Esquire* was upheld, with Justice Douglas commenting: "But to withdraw the second-class rate from this publication today because its contents seemed to one official not good for the public would sanction withdrawal of the second-class rate tomorrow from another periodical whose social or economic views seemed harmful to another official." [20] The decision put the Post Office Department back into its normal role of excluding publications for reasons of obscenity.

Those who are the faithful champions of freedom recognize that arbitrary action against the weak and the obscure, against the non-conformist and the radical, against the foolish and the crafty, usually leads to later arbitrary action against others. Freedom of the press, save when publication constitutes a legally determined clear and present danger to society, cannot be denied in one case without jeopardizing the constitutional guarantees of all.[21]

Freedom of the press can of course be jeopardized by a newspaper publisher. This was found true by the Supreme Court in the case of the *Lorain Journal*, an Ohio daily. When a radio station was established in the nearby town of Elyria in 1948, the *Journal's* management refused to carry the advertising of any merchant who also bought time on the radio station. The radio station obtained an injunction against the newspaper, under the antitrust laws, which the *Journal* insisted was unconstitutional. But the Supreme Court held that the First Amendment was not intended to protect monopolistic practices which would destroy a competing medium and in a unanimous decision forced the *Journal* to recant.[22]

This was a clear-cut case, involving the use of boycott to destroy a competitor. Less clear-cut was the government's subsequent contention that the selling of advertising in jointly owned morning and

[20] *Hannegan v. Esquire*, 327 U. S. 146 (1946).

[21] This thesis is examined exhaustively in J. Edward Gerald, *The Press and the Constitution*. The cases discussed here and many others are treated in detail, for the period 1931-47.

[22] *Lorain Journal v. United States*, 342 U. S. 143 (1951).

evening papers under a unit rate plan also constituted an illegal action. A complaint brought by the *New Orleans Item* against the jointly owned *Times-Picayune* and *States* reached the Supreme Court in 1953. The court held, in a 5-4 decision, that the *Times-Picayune* and *States* were not violating the antitrust laws, but the decision was limited to the New Orleans situation alone.[23] The *Item* sold out to its rivals in 1958.

The government's next case was stronger. In 1955 it obtained a jury conviction of the *Kansas City Star* and its advertising manager on charges of monopolizing dissemination of news and advertising in the Kansas City area. The *Star*, together with its morning edition, the *Times*, and its broadcasting stations, WDAF and WDAF-TV, accounted for 85 per cent of mass media advertising income in the metropolitan area. The government charged that forced and tied-in sales of advertising and of newspaper subscriptions had brought about the death of the competing *Journal-Post* in 1942. The Supreme Court declined to review the case in 1957, and the *Star* agreed to end its combination sales and to sell the two stations, which in both instances had been pioneering efforts.[24] The *Wichita Eagle's* advertising and circulation price policies for morning, evening, and Sunday editions were brought under regulation in a 1959 antitrust suit, but the action did not save the rival *Beacon* from being forced to sell out in 1960.

The battles for freedom to print and freedom to criticise, carried on in the courtrooms, were important ones. But just as important were the fights put up for the right to have access to the news— for the right to publish news is worthless if the sources of information have been dried up.

Freedom of information campaigns have been carried on since the late 1940's by the American Society of Newspaper Editors, the Associated Press Managing Editors Association, the Radio-Television News Directors Association, and Sigma Delta Chi, professional journalism society. Through their efforts, and those of others, 33 states had laws requiring open public records, and 25 states laws requiring open meetings for conduct of public business, by 1960. Leaders of the fight included James S. Pope, *Louisville Courier-*

[23] *Times-Picayune Publishing Co. v. United States,* 345 U. S. 594 (1953).
[24] *Kansas City Star Co. v. United States; Emil A. Sees v. United States,* (8th Circuit) 240 Fed. 2d 643 (1957).

Journal; J. R. Wiggins, *Washington Post*; V. M. Newton, Jr., *Tampa Tribune*; and Harold L. Cross, ASNE legal counsel.

Creation of the House Subcommittee on Government Information in 1955, headed by Congressman John E. Moss of California, brought a campaign against secrecy at the federal level. Aided by the newsmen's groups, the Moss committee won revision of the 1789 "housekeeping statute" in 1958 to stop its use in denying access to records. It also won some ground in opposing the claim of executive privilege by the President and his subordinates, and reported success in 95 of 173 cases exposing undue federal censorship of information during 1955-60.

A campaign by the ASNE, the National Press Photographers Association, and the National Association of Broadcasters to win access to courtrooms by photographers was less successful, although the American Bar Association in 1959 agreed to review its Canon 35 regulating such activity.

Much depended on the public, whose right to know was at stake in the unending battle by newsmen to tell the news.

ANNOTATED BIBLIOGRAPHY

The most important sources are the files of *Editor & Publisher* and the *Guild Reporter*, and the proceedings of the annual meetings of the American Society of Newspaper Editors, the American Newspaper Guild, and the American Newspaper Publishers Association. Of books previously cited, Edwin Emery's *History of the American Newspaper Publishers Association* and A. M. Lee's *The Daily Newspaper in America* tell the story of newspaper relationships with the Guild and mechanical unions.

Books:

Bird, George L., and Frederic E. Merwin, *The Press and Society*. New York: Prentice-Hall, Inc., 1952. Chapter 26 concerns the Guild.

Chafee, Zechariah, Jr., *Government and Mass Communications*. Chicago: University of Chicago Press, 1947. A two-volume specific study of areas involving government and press, for the Commission on Freedom of the Press.

Cross, Harold L., *The People's Right to Know*. New York: Columbia University Press, 1953. Scholarly, detailed study of problems of access to news, sponsored by the ASNE. A supplement was issued by the Freedom of Information Center, University of Missouri, 1959.

Gerald, J. Edward, *The Press and the Constitution*. Minneapolis: University of Minnesota Press, 1948. The best source for freedom of the press cases, 1931-47. See its extensive bibliography.

Hocking, William E., *Freedom of the Press: A Framework of Principle.* Chicago: University of Chicago Press, 1947. Discusses philosophical problems; written for the Commission on Freedom of the Press.

Kramer, Dale, *Heywood Broun.* New York: A. A. Wyn, Inc., 1949. Biography of the Guild's founder, a famous columnist.

National Labor Relations Board, *Collective Bargaining in the Newspaper Industry.* Washington: Government Printing Office, 1938. Studies both the Guild and printing union movements.

Nelson, Harold L., *Libel in News of Congressional Investigating Committees.* Minneapolis: University of Minnesota Press, 1961. Scholarly study of problems faced in reporting attacks on individuals.

Siebert, Fred S., Theodore Peterson, and Wilbur Schramm, *Four Theories of the Press.* Urbana: University of Illinois Press, 1956. Philosophical discussions of concepts of press freedom.

Wiggins, James Russell, *Freedom or Secrecy.* New York: Oxford University Press, 1956. A summation of access-to-news problems by an ASNE leader, the executive editor of the *Washington Post.*

Periodicals and Monographs:

Barth, Alan, "Freedom from Contempt," *Nieman Reports,* III (April 1949), 11. A study of the contempt cases of the 1940's.

Broun, Heywood, "An Army with Banners," *Nation,* CXL (February 13, 1935), 154. The Guild president's own account.

Cross, Harold L., "The Myth of 'Executive Privilege,'" *ASNE Bulletin,* No. 411 (August 1, 1958), 7. A documented attack.

Keating, Isabelle, "Reporters Become of Age," *Harper's,* CLXX (April 1935), 601. One of the best early articles about the Guild.

Mollenhoff, Clark R., "Secrecy in Washington," *Atlantic,* CCIV (July 1959), 54. A critical view of executive privilege.

Pringle, Henry F., "The Newspaper Guild," *Scribner's,* CV (January 1939), 21. A review at a turning-point time in Guild affairs.

Scher, Jacob, "Access to Information: Recent Legal Problems," *Journalism Quarterly,* XXXVII (Winter 1960), 41. An authoritative summary for the 1950's by a Northwestern University journalism professor who was special counsel for the Moss subcommittee.

Swindler, William F., "The AP Anti-Trust Case in Historical Perspective," *Journalism Quarterly,* XXIII (March 1946), 40. Scholarly analysis.

U. S. Congress, House Committee on Government Operations, *Availability of Information from Federal Departments and Agencies,* H.R. No. 2084, 86th Congress, 2nd session. Washington: Government Printing Office, July 2, 1960. A five-year summary of the trend toward secrecy. Reports with a similar title were issued every six months by the Moss subcommittee.

Chapter 29

THE CHALLENGE OF CRITICISM

> Partisanship, in editorial comment which know-
> ingly departs from the truth, does violence to the
> best spirit of American journalism; in the news col-
> umns it is subversive of a fundamental principle
> of the profession.
>
> —ASNE Canons of Journalism

CRITICISM OF THE PERFORMANCE of American news-
papers became particularly pointed during the liberal resurgence
of the 1930's. That there was criticism of newspapers, or even extensive criticism, was nothing new; press critics had been having
their say since the dawn of newspaper publishing, and public concern was widespread during such periods of major change in the
American press as those which ushered in the penny press of the
1830's and the modern newspaper of the 1890's. But while much
of the earlier criticism had dealt with the cultural and social values
of the press, the emphasis in the 1930's was upon its political power.
The press as an institution thus came under challenge more directly
than at any time since the Federalist attacks upon press freedom in
the 1790's.

The favorite targets for the critics were those publishers dubbed
"the press lords"—notably William Randolph Hearst, Robert R.
McCormick, and Roy W. Howard. Their prominence kept them
at the center of an upsurge of criticism which affected newspapers
generally, in a time when America was engaging in a searching re-

712

examination of all its social, political, and economic institutions. Analysis of their journalistic roles thus becomes a factor of major importance in any study of public reaction to press performance in recent decades.

But more significant is the story of how the press reacted to criticism. When criticism from outside the press continued at a heightened tempo in the 1940's and 1950's, newspapermen engaged in an increasing amount of self-analysis. A strengthening of the professional spirit in journalism resulted. Growth of professionalism, in part at least in response to the challenge of criticism, offered the best hope for improvement of the newspaper's character and public service. Constructive criticism of press performance, coming both from within the ranks of the press and from outside groups, could reinforce public confidence in the newspaper—upon whose strength and freedom all other democratic institutions depended. Recognition of these facts grew as newspapermen and their critics came to see that neither angry rejection of criticism nor sweeping and extreme attacks upon the press could solve any problems.

Much of the criticism which developed during the 1930's and later was based on issues already discussed in earlier chapters of this book. The growth of one-publisher cities and of chain newspaper ownership aroused opposition among many of the critics. Decreasing opportunity for variety of expression of opinion by differing socio-political groups occupied the attention of others. Complaints were made that newspaper content was standardized, that there was overemphasis of entertainment and sensational material, and that there was insufficient interpretation of important news.

Certainly there was merit in general discussions of these problems. Such discussions served to warn publishers who had been slow to recognize their responsibilities to their readers. No thoughtful newspaperman would deny the validity of much of the criticism; but on the other hand, newspapermen would have been less than human had they not resented some of the charges leveled at them in sweeping terms and without regard for changing conditions of society which forced acceptance of conditions not to everybody's liking. For example, the arbitrary assumption by some critics that a "monopoly" newspaper situation is automatically bad for a community was an unfair generalization. Some so-called "monopoly" newspapers rose to superior levels of performance; others, like some newspapers in competitive cities, failed to meet their responsibilities to their readers.[1]

Criticism of newspapers since the 1930's centered about, more than anything else, their editorial positions in political campaigns. Historically a small but definite majority of daily newspapers giving editorial page support to a presidential candidate was to be found on the side of the Republican party. As Franklin Roosevelt entered the first of his four presidential campaigns, in 1932, he had the support of 38 per cent of the nation's dailies, compared to 55 per cent for President Hoover. In 1936, Roosevelt was backed by 34 per cent of the dailies, Republican Alfred M. Landon by 60 per cent. These figures are approximations gathered by *Editor & Publisher* when it launched, beginning in 1940, a comprehensive pre-election poll of dailies concerning editorial page support. Approximately three-fourths of all dailies, with 90 per cent of total daily newspaper circulation, responded to the polls. Table 1 shows the percentages of the responding newspapers giving editorial page support to the Republican or Democratic candidate each four years, and the percentages of circulation they represented.

TABLE 1

EDITORIAL PAGE SUPPORT OF PRESIDENTIAL CANDIDATES

	Republican		Democratic		Uncommitted	
	Per Cent of	Per Cent of	Per Cent of	Per Cent of	Per Cent of	Per Cent of
Year	Dailies	Circulation	Dailies	Circulation	Dailies	Circulation
1940	63.9	69.2	22.7	25.2	13.4	5.6
1944	60.1	68.5	22.0	17.7	17.9	13.8
1948	65.1	78.5	15.3	10.0	15.6	10.0
1952	67.3	80.2	14.5	10.8	18.2	9.0
1956	62.3	72.3	15.1	12.8	22.6	14.9
1960	57.7	70.9	16.4	15.8	25.9	13.3

Source: Editor & Publisher polls. In 1948, Progressive party candidate Henry A. Wallace had the support of 4 per cent of the dailies with 1.5 per cent of circulation. See *Editor & Publisher*, XCIII (November 5, 1960), 9.

[1] See Raymond F. Stewart, "Surveys of Reader Attitudes Toward Newspaper Combinations," *Journalism Quarterly*, XXX (Summer 1953), 315. The article reports surveys showing that approximately three-fourths of readers in Louisville, Des Moines, Minneapolis, and Atlanta—all one-ownership cities—believe their newspapers try to be fair in presenting all sides of news to the public.

The figures show that the number of dailies supporting Roosevelt declined for his 1940 and 1944 races with Wendell Willkie and Thomas E. Dewey, as did the circulation they represented. Harry S. Truman reached the low point of support in his successful 1948 contest with Dewey. Dwight D. Eisenhower enjoyed the most support in 1952, for his first race against Adlai E. Stevenson. John F. Kennedy's position was improved as he defeated Richard M. Nixon in 1960. Kennedy was endorsed by 22 of 125 dailies above 100,000 circulation, while 12 endorsed no candidate. This represented more large pro-Democratic papers, with a better geographic spread, than at any time since 1944.[2]

Stevenson called it "a one-party press in a two-party country." But partisan critics did not acknowledge the impact which day by day coverage of the news has on voter decisions, and available studies of campaign news coverage indicate at least larger dailies were essentially fair in their news columns. Research shows, too, that voters are often strongly affected by social pressures, group associations, and "opinion leaders." Radio and television can become highly important factors.[3]

A study of how news comes to Paducah, Kentucky, made in 1947 by *Fortune* magazine (August 1947), also illustrates the point that it is impossible for a single newspaper to exercise a monopoly in the realm of opinion-making. Paducah's one daily newspaper had a circulation of 12,000 copies within the city. There was also a small weekly, and the city had two radio stations, one owned by the daily paper. Outside publications came into Paducah in the following numbers: *Louisville Courier-Journal*, 1,400 copies daily and 2,400 on Sunday; New York, Chicago, St. Louis, and Memphis newspapers, 428 daily and 2,770 Sunday; weekly news magazines, 429 copies; picture weeklies, 1,968 copies; other general weeklies, 1,769 copies; monthly magazines, 13,037 copies. The public library had 110 magazines on file and circulated about 10,000 books a month. Motion pictures, public meetings, and club and luncheon

[2] Among major dailies supporting Kennedy in 1960 outside the South were the *New York Times, St. Louis Post-Dispatch, Milwaukee Journal, Louisville Courier-Journal, New York Post, Newsday, Long Island Press, Pittsburgh Post-Gazette, Toledo Blade, Hartford Times, Denver Post,* and *Sacramento Bee.* The *Washington Post* did not endorse, but favored Kennedy.

[3] See Bernard Berelson, Paul F. Lazarsfeld, and William N. McPhee, *Voting* (Chicago: University of Chicago Press, 1954). For studies of campaign news coverage in large dailies, see the bibliography for this chapter.

gatherings also brought information to Paducah's 33,000 citizens.

Political tension, and accompanying criticism of the newspaper's role in elections, made for extensive public acceptance of a literature of criticism of the press. Upton Sinclair's bitter book, *The Brass Check* (1919), unrealistically painted a picture of a false, cowardly press dominated by its business offices and its advertisers. While there were newspaper situations which fitted these patterns, in isolated instances of time and place, the Sinclair thesis did not ring true generally. Suspicious individuals, however, continued to quote the book as evidence of advertiser domination of the press long after that bugaboo had been exploded as a serious charge.

Caustic surveys of the "press lords" began in earnest with Oswald Garrison Villard's *Some Newspapers and Newspaper-Men* (1923). They flourished in the 1930's, which saw the publication of such books as George Seldes' *Lords of the Press* (1938), Harold L. Ickes' *America's House of Lords* (1939), and individual studies such as Ferdinand Lundberg's *Imperial Hearst* (1936). These books were valuable as exposés, but their influence was undue in that they enjoyed wider public circulation than such counterbalancing and more constructive discussions as Casper S. Yost's *Principles of Journalism* (1924), Villard's brief *The Press Today* (1930), Herbert Brucker's *The Changing American Newspaper* (1937), Silas Bent's *Newspaper Crusaders* (1939), and such products of the growing journalism schools as Leon N. Flint's *The Conscience of the Newspaper* (1925), Willard G. Bleyer's *Main Currents in the History of American Journalism* (1927), and *Interpretations of Journalism* (1937), edited by Frank L. Mott and Ralph D. Casey.

In any event, the dynamic and intriguing personalities of some of the "press lords" provided more interesting fare for the American reading public than any other material about newspapermen and newspaper problems. To understand, therefore, the bitterness and extent of criticisms of the press since the 1930's, it is necesary to examine the roles played by the most often discussed newspaper publishers of the times.

William Randolph Hearst, as has been suggested in previous chapters,[4] is one of the most difficult men of journalism to study

[4] Chapters 19 and 20 deal with Hearst's earlier career. See also page 532 in Chapter 22 and page 679 in Chapter 27 for the extent of his newspaper operations.

and to estimate, considering the complex nature of his personality, the variegated social and political impact of his many ventures, and the length and extent of his career. Those who wrote about Hearst were never permitted access to the publisher's private papers and to the records of the Hearst empire. So the literature about Hearst ranged from reasonably fair evaluations to vehement attacks combining facts and rumors.[5] As a result, the official Hearst biography released by International News Service when the publisher's 64-year newspaper career closed in 1951 noted in its second paragraph: "And as he fashioned his vast enterprises, there grew progressively in the public mind a picture of the builder himself. It was a strange portrait, obscured by myth and legend, confused by controversy and distortion."

When Hearst had lived out his 88 years, the question became: Did he deserve the criticism which had been heaped upon him, more vehemently than upon any other publisher? There was some tendency to accord him a place in the ranks of journalistic leaders, despite the extent of criticism of him and his newspapers. The points most often made in support of the thesis that Hearst made notable contributions to American journalism are these:

1. Hearst built the world's biggest publishing empire, in terms of newspapers and their combined circulations. At the peak, in 1935, Hearst printed 26 dailies and 17 Sunday editions in 19 cities. The papers had 13.6 per cent of the total daily circulation in the country and 24.2 per cent of Sunday circulation. In addition, he controlled the King Features Syndicate, largest of its kind; the money-coining *American Weekly;* International News Service, Universal Service, and International News Photos; 13 magazines, 8 radio stations, and 2 motion picture companies. This, it is argued, spells a success which must be recognized.

2. Hearst's methods and innovations in newswriting and news-handling—particularly in makeup and headline and picture display—and his utilization of new mechanical processes were highly important. Hearst journalism changed the character of American journalism, it is argued, and therefore it must be recognized.

3. Hearst newspapers were edited to appeal to the mass of read-

---

[5] The best balanced and most analytic book is John Tebbel's *The Life and Good Times of William Randolph Hearst* (New York: E. P. Dutton & Company, 1952). See the bibliography in this chapter and in Chapter 19 for other citations.

ers, and encouraged millions to increase their reading habits. Because of this, and because of Hearst's editorial policies and his own political activities, Hearst newspapers exercised a powerful influence in American life which must be recognized.

4. Hearst was in many ways a constructive force: stalwart in his Americanism; a believer in popular education and in the extension of the power of the people; and during different phases of his long career an advocate of many progressive solutions to national problems. These included early advocacy of popular election of senators, of the initiative and referendum, of a graduated income tax, of widespread public ownership of utilities, of breaking up of monopolies and trusts, and of the rights of labor unions.

These points, the argument runs, are in the record for all to see. Hearst's critics, and the public record, provided counter-arguments. They should be prefaced, however, with this general observation:

The building of a great publishing empire does not in itself assure Hearst or anyone else a high standing in the journalistic profession. The newspapers which the craft recognizes as great are those which demonstrate their integrity and zealousness in the telling of the news, and which at the same time possess the social conscience which is acquired by their recognition of the needs of society, and by a proper and reasonable adjustment to society's desires. Honest and comprehensive coverage of the news is of course the first essential. The second is a demonstration of responsibility in community leadership. The great newspapers—whether conservative or liberal, Republican or Democrat, in their political beliefs—are those which are aroused whenever basic principles of human liberty and progress are at stake in a given situation, and which are constantly on guard against intolerance and unfairness. Operating within a consistent social framework, they do their best to be the kind of progressive community leaders America expects.

Keeping these two tests of the greatness of a newspaper in mind, then, the rebuttals to the points listed in Hearst's favor may be considered:

1. The Hearst empire, for all its one-time size, was not the roaring success which the accumulated figures would indicate. Hearst began to borrow from banks as early as 1924. In the early 1930's he had his newspapers publicize and sell a 50-million-dollar stock issue to keep themselves afloat. The intricate nature of the Hearst

corporate structures makes a clear determination of the publisher's financial standing impossible. Hearst poured money into his publishing ventures from the profits of mining, ranch land, and other business operations. He also spent fabulous sums—an estimated 40 million dollars on art treasures and oddities, untold millions for his personal life—and sank more than 50 million dollars into real estate holdings which by the depression times of the 1930's became enormous liabilities. How much of this spending represents a drain on the journalistic properties, no one knows. But it is known that great sums were both made and lost in journalism; on the loss side, for example, Hearst's effort to win a foothold in Atlanta cost him 21 million dollars before he gave up.

The crash came for Hearst in 1937, when he was forced to abdicate temporarily, and watch a group of trustees liquidate a portion of his empire. Nine dailies and five Sunday editions were dropped by 1940; Universal Service was consolidated with INS; movie companies, radio stations, and some magazines were sold. Arthur Brisbane, Hearst's longtime associate who had become a front page columnist-philosopher and wealthy newspaper and real estate operator, died in 1937, and the trustees began liquidating 40 million dollars worth of New York City real estate which Brisbane had helped Hearst to accumulate. Many of the art treasures which were Hearst's pride were auctioned off by Gimbels and Macy's. Eventually even many of San Simeon's 275,000 acres were sold to help reclaim some of the 36 million dollars invested there.

Through it all, however, Hearst continued to live in regal style. The man who had bought a castle in Wales, Egyptian mummies, Tibetan yaks, and a Spanish abbey (which was dismantled stone by stone and shipped to a New York warehouse, after which Hearst never saw it again), had a truly pre-capitalistic attitude toward money as such. His guests at San Simeon, who were legion, continued to dive into an indoor pool from a sixteenth-century Italian marble balcony, to pick flowers in a mile-long pergola stretching along Hearst's private mountain range, and to eat from kingly silver plate. Before World War II had ended, the trimming down of his empire and wartime publishing profits had accomplished the desired miracle, and the Hearst once thought to be broke was back in full command again.

When death had claimed its founder, the Hearst organization

had 16 dailies and 13 Sunday editions appearing in a dozen cities. They had 9.1 per cent of the country's total daily circulation and 16.1 per cent of the Sunday total, a substantial decline in Hearst influence from the 1935 figures of 13.6 per cent daily and 24.2 per cent Sunday. The Hearst estate was valued at some 56 million dollars, based on estimated stock values, but the profit margins of the Hearst enterprises were below those of other newspapers of their size for which financial reports are available. All in all the record scarcely bears out the picture of tremendous success which is claimed for Hearst.

2. Undoubtedly Hearst editing and printing methods made their impress on American journalism. Particularly Hearst's sponsoring of mechanical innovations, and the Hearst format techniques, spurred others on. But these were contributions which were largely technical in their nature, and in the judgment of most newspapermen they were more than matched on the negative side by Hearst proclivities for sensational treatment of the news.

3. Undoubtedly, too, Hearst drew many new readers of newspapers to his fold, and held more than 5 million daily and 8 million Sunday to the day of his death. But what was the end result? Pulitzer defended the use of sensationalism in his *World* by arguing that it attracted readers who then would be exposed to the columns of his carefully planned, high quality editorial page. The same could never be said of a Hearst newspaper.

Nor did Hearst ever exercise the powerful influence in American life which his great circulations might indicate. Among the men whom he wanted to see become president of the United States were William Jennings Bryan, Champ Clark, Hiram W. Johnson, William Gibbs McAdoo, John Nance Garner, Alfred M. Landon, General Douglas MacArthur, and William Randolph Hearst. Among the men whom he fought while they were in the White House were William McKinley, Theodore Roosevelt, William Howard Taft, Woodrow Wilson, Herbert Hoover, Franklin D. Roosevelt, and Harry S. Truman. Hearst got on the bandwagons of Warren Harding, Calvin Coolidge, and Hoover in the 1920's largely because he disagreed with their Democratic opponents. He rode the Wilson bandwagon in 1912 and the Roosevelt bandwagon in 1932, but promptly got off in high dudgeon both times, even though he considered himself a Democrat. His own personal political ambitions, which bloomed strongest from 1900 to 1910, were permanently smashed in 1922. When he wanted to run for senator in New York state that year, Al Smith refused to let him on the Democratic ticket and made a bitter speech attacking Hearst's isolationist record in World War I.

4. What then of Hearst as a constructive social force? Certainly he was an advocate of Americanism. But to many his continued espousal of nationalistic policies bordering on jingoism, in a time which demanded American cooperation in international security efforts, was the most distressing feature of his newspapers. And the "Red hunts" which his newspapers fostered in the 1930's among the ranks of political leaders, educators, YMCA secretaries, labor leaders, and other citizens were based on the familiar tactics of the demagogue: those who disagreed with Hearst were "Communists." Indeed, part of the strong criticism of Hearst which developed during the 1930's centered about these tendencies, and about his apparent admiration of the Nazi government in Germany when it first emerged. Hearst newspapers ran syndicated articles by Hermann Goering and praised the Nazi economic program, until wiser heads prevailed upon the publisher to recognize the uglier features of Hitlerism.[6] To the end, however, Hearst opposed the basic foreign policy adopted by the American people during and after World War II and distrusted the United Nations as thoroughly as he had distrusted the League of Nations.

In domestic affairs, Hearst newspapers continued to give stalwart support to public education and to the idea of public ownership of utilities. But they backslid during the 1920's and 1930's on many of the other progressive features of the Hearst editorial platform as written before World War I. The change became particularly apparent during the first years of the New Deal. Hearst had helped to obtain Franklin Roosevelt's nomination for the presidency, largely to settle an old score with Al Smith, and in the spring of 1933 his newspapers applauded vigorously as Roosevelt undertook unemployment relief, suspended exports of gold, and proposed the NRA—which, a Hearst editorial said, "embodies several basic policies long advocated by the Hearst newspapers."[7]

By 1935 the tune had changed. It was the "Raw Deal" and the

[6] Tebbel, *The Life and Good Times of William Randolph Hearst*, p. 256.
[7] *San Francisco Examiner*, May 6, 1933.

"National Run Around" in both news and editorial columns. The Supreme Court decision outlawing the NRA, which Hearst papers once had proudly claimed for their own, was greeted with an American flag and the headline: "Thank God for the Supreme Court!" President Roosevelt was on his way toward establishing a "personal dictatorship" according to Hearst editorials. And a special squad of Hearst newsmen was installed in Washington, called the "smear bureau" by the cynical, whose sole duty was to unearth anti-New Deal stories for the chain's papers to run.

There are other examples in the columns of the Hearst papers of 1935 which illustrate the extent to which the earlier beliefs of Hearst had changed. The publisher who before World War I had been perhaps the most aggressive in supporting the power of labor unions said now: "The Wagner Labor Bill . . . is one of the most vicious pieces of class legislation that could be conceived—un-American to the core, violative of every constitutional principle and contrary to the whole spirit of American life. Congress in passing it is betraying the country." [8]

The publisher who had fought so long against monopolies and trusts said now: "The Wheeler-Rayburn Bill, decreeing death to the holding companies, is PURE VENOM distilled by a PERSONAL and MALIGNANT OBSESSION, without a pretense of economic or legal justification." [9]

The publisher who always believed that he understood the common people, and was understood by them, sparked an extensive front-page coverage of WPA activities in 1936 with headlines like this one: "Taxpayers Feed 20,000 Reds on N. Y. Relief Rolls." And his newspapers warned that the Social Security Act was "A Pay Cut for You! . . . Governor Landon, when elected, will repeal this so-called security act." [10]

Hearst newspapers threw every resource of the editorial and news pages into the campaign to elect Governor Alfred M. Landon of Kansas president in 1936. When President Roosevelt was re-elected by the greatest majority in history, carrying all the states but two, Hearst's enemies cried for his scalp. Liberals pointed to

[8] *Ibid.*, May 29, 1935.
[9] *Ibid.*, June 21, 1935.
[10] *Ibid.*, October 30, 1936.

the obvious and heavy slanting of news column material in Landon's favor as evidence of Hearst's professional irresponsibility. Boycotts reminiscent of those carried out in World War I against Hearst papers were attempted. The Hearst name on a widely shown newsreel was hissed. Hearst's troubles with the American Newspaper Guild added to the furor. And when it seemed in late 1937 that the Hearst empire was collapsing, his critics gleefully wrote him off as a broken-down old man.

But the triumphant liberals overreached themselves in launching the Supreme Court reorganization bill of 1937, called the "court packing bill" by those who defeated it. The New Deal reform period came to an abrupt halt. Just as the Hearst papers weathered their economic difficulties in the next few years, they weathered public attacks against them and moved into a different political climate in which they once more could go on the offensive. Vicious personal attacks on President Roosevelt continued during the war years, and when Scripps-Howard dropped columnist Westbrook Pegler because of his monotonously vituperative assaults upon the Roosevelt family, labor leaders, and Communists, Hearst welcomed Pegler into the fold of rancorous Hearst columnists. Politically the Hearst papers descended to a ridiculously synthetic, but fully publicized, boom for General Douglas MacArthur for president in 1948, giving every appearance that they believed he was a major contender for the Republican nomination that year (MacArthur received 11 votes in the party convention).

With Hearst's death came some changes in the empire. His longtime friend, at whose home he died, Marion Davies, no longer found her wishes carried out by Hearst editors (it had been she who sponsored the Hearst papers' antivivisection campaign which harassed American medical schools). William Randolph Hearst, Jr., one of the publisher's five sons, undertook to exert leadership in toning down some of his father's policies. Local editors were given greater autonomy; they were told to "use the greatest care to avoid bias or lack of objectivity in the handling of the news"; and in other ways the new Hearst executive team sought to wipe out some of the memories of the past. The once crudely sensational *American Weekly* was completely revamped and modernized. Hearst magazine and television holdings were expanded. The younger

Hearst made it clear, however, that he would not ignore "the pool of wisdom and experience accumulated by my father and his associates through the passing years." [11] Such key Hearst executives as Richard E. Berlin, president of the Hearst corporation, and J. D. Gortatowsky, board chairman for its publishing divisions, continued as advisers of the sons into the 1960's. William Randolph Hearst, Jr., took the title of editor-in-chief of the Hearst newspapers in 1955. Randolph A. Hearst became second most powerful of the brothers, as president of Hearst Consolidated Publications. Randolph's twin, David, headed West coast operations. The eldest of the brothers, George, did not choose active leadership. A fifth son, John Randolph, died in 1958.

The Hearst organization undertook a 35 million dollar plant modernization program, and streamlined the papers' typography. Hearst editors sought to rejuvenate circulation in competitive city situations. Still, in 1962, the Hearst newspaper empire was down to 12 dailies and 10 Sunday editions with 6.6 per cent of daily circulation and 9.5 per cent of Sunday. Hearst Consolidated Publications ran more than 11 million dollars in deficits during 1958 to 1960. The *American Weekly* was cut back to be a Hearst-only supplement. Fabulous San Simeon became a California Historical Monument in 1958, open to tourists for a $2 fee. Hearst, Jr., had one major triumph: the Pulitzer Prize for international reporting went to him, J. Kingsbury Smith, and Frank Conniff in 1956 for stories from the Soviet Union. "I have a feeling that Pop and Joe Pulitzer are getting almost as big a kick out of it as we are," he told his readers.

Second only to Hearst in stirring up the wrath of critics was Colonel Robert R. McCormick, publisher of the *Chicago Tribune.* McCormick was for two decades chairman of the committee on freedom of the press of the American Newspaper Publishers Association. In that role he helped newspaper publishers and editors win court battles waged in defense of constitutional guarantees. But, ironically, McCormick's insistence on perpetuating his kind of personal journalism—which made his newspaper distort the news picture according to the dictates of a powerful but extremely opinionated mind—was at the same time imperiling freedom of the press. Those who defended McCormick said personal journalists

[11] *Editor & Publisher,* LXXXV (March 22, 1952), 7.

play important roles, as indeed some had in the history of the newspaper, and reiterated the essentials of press freedom: (1) the right to print without prior restraint; (2) the right to criticise; (3) the right to report. Those who claim these rights, however, owe society in turn a conscientious effort to criticise fairly and in the public interest, and to report the news fully and honestly. This is implicit in the contract by which the press accepts protection under our fundamental law in exchange for its valued service to the public. McCormick, by ignoring public complaints that he was not living up to his obligations, and by brushing aside similar judgments by many leaders of his profession, continued to be the kind of personal journalist he wanted to be. He also exposed the journalistic profession to the danger of loss of public confidence by providing a vast amount of ammunition to those who used the *Tribune* and similar newspapers as proof that the press was irresponsible.[12]

The quarrel with McCormick was not so much that his *Tribune* clung to an outmoded and dangerous nationalist-isolationist point of view in the face of overwhelming public support of efforts to find peace and security through international cooperation. Nor was it so much that his *Tribune* became the principal spokesman for the ultra-conservative right wing in American politics, and rejected a President Eisenhower as violently as it had rejected a President Truman. The real quarrel McCormick's critics had with him was that as he tried so hard to prove that the *Tribune* was right, and most everybody else was wrong, editorial columns became bitter personal proclamations whose prejudiced approaches to matters of public interest spilled over into the news columns. McCormick's answer, until death stilled his voice in 1955, was that his *Tribune* was the "World's Greatest Newspaper."

This claim would have had merit if newspaper greatness were measured only in terms of financial success, circulation, and mechanical excellence. In the mid-1950's the *Tribune* carried as much advertising as its three Chicago rivals combined. Its circulation, while down to 900,000 daily from a 1946 high of 1,075,000, was still the largest of any standard-sized American newspaper, and was spread through five states in an area McCormick called "Chicago-

[12] For a book-length documentation, see John Tebbel, *An American Dynasty* (New York: Doubleday & Company, Inc., 1947).

land." Its 450-man news staff, operating from the 36-story Tribune Tower, provided blanket coverage of local and area news events which was the despair of rival city editors. Its comics, sports pages, woman's pages, financial and business reporting, and advertising columns attracted readers at all levels. Technically the *Tribune* excelled in writing, editing, and typography. And what its critics called outrageously prejudiced and insufferably insulting editorials (the *Tribune* called them "the hair on our chest") had a "gutty prose" quality which commanded reader attention, if not always respect. For a venture that rated as the single most often criticised American newspaper, the *Tribune* was doing all right, and Colonel McCormick frequently reminded his critics of that fact.

Not all of this success was due to McCormick. The *Tribune* has a long history, beginning in 1847. The builder was Joseph Medill, who from 1855 to 1899 devoted his energies to the creation of a prosperous, powerful newspaper. In an era of personal journalism, Medill was not outdone; he belligerently stood for nationalism, for conservatism, for civic progress, and for giving a free hand to business in the days of unrestricted individualism. When he died, Medill left a financial trust which provided for the families of his two daughters—the McCormicks and the Pattersons. One son-in-law, Robert W. Patterson, and a grandson, Medill McCormick, assumed leading roles at the *Tribune* but Patterson died in 1910 and Medill McCormick retired from the paper to become U. S. Senator from Illinois. During the period 1895 to 1914, while the family control was thus undergoing change, James Keeley rose to brilliance, first as city editor and then as managing editor. Under his direction the *Tribune* developed a crusading spirit and a community service record typical of newspapers published in those years of muckraking and reform.

The Robert R. McCormick era began in 1914. His brother Medill retired from the paper that year, and Keeley, sensing that his talents would not be appreciated by the new family representatives, joined in an ill-fated effort to resuscitate an opposition paper, the *Chicago Herald.* Sharing responsibility for the *Tribune* with the future colonel was his cousin, Joseph Medill Patterson, later the founder of the *New York Daily News.* The fourth Medill grandchild, Eleanor Medill Patterson, was to become owner of the *Washington Times-Herald.*

Building on the foundations Medill and Keeley had laid, the young cousins doubled *Tribune* circulation and advertising during the World War I period. Patterson had a particular brilliance for spotting the best comic strips and other features; McCormick proved to be an excellent business man. Circulation was boomed, too, by the hoodlum tactics in which Max Annenberg, *Tribune* circulation boss whom McCormick thoughtfully lifted from Hearst, excelled. McCormick bought Canadian forests and built paper mills which gave him an advantage when newsprint prices soared in the 1920's.

The success of the *New York Daily News*, and the disappearance of Captain Patterson into that venture, further entrenched McCormick's position. The two papers made as much as 13 million dollars a year. The *Tribune-Daily News* feature syndicate, radio station WGN, and more Canadian paper and power investments followed. When Captain Patterson died in 1946, McCormick became the head of the *New York Daily News*, although he preferred to exercise influence by remote control. When Eleanor Patterson died in 1948, she willed the *Washington Times-Herald* to seven of her executives, but they sold it to McCormick in 1949 for 4½ million dollars. The Colonel first installed a favorite niece, Mrs. Ruth McCormick (Bazy) Miller, daughter of Medill and Ruth Hanna McCormick, as *Times-Herald* editor. But Mrs. Miller fell from grace in 1951 and McCormick took over personal control of what became the Washington "outpost" of the *Chicago Tribune*. The *Tribune* formula did not work in Washington, and in 1954, ill and weary of a paper which was losing $500,000 a year, McCormick sold the *Times-Herald* for 8½ million dollars to Eugene Meyer's *Washington Post*, which incorporated the *Times-Herald* nameplate in its own. But despite this retreat, no one except the Hearst heirs had more readers than McCormick had, with his two big dailies.

The memos signed "R.R.Mc." were law in the *Tribune* empire. The six-foot four-inch colonel turned eyes of ice-water blue on all aspects of the business. His private domains were the Tribune Tower and his 1,000-acre farm and estate outside Chicago, named Cantigny for the World War I battle in which McCormick participated. Those who worked for him enjoyed a paternalism which provided high salaries, health and welfare protection, and job security. They learned to follow the Colonel's lead in business affairs, in news and editorial policies, and in such McCormick specialties as military strategy and foreign relations. McCormick made a deep study of military history; but his opinions about international affairs were based upon a belief that foreigners, especially Englishmen, were dangerous. Almost as dangerous, the *Tribune* said, were New York financiers, Eastern internationalists, and educators and intellectuals.

Among the men who helped to build the *Tribune* as McCormick's aides were Edward Scott Beck, managing editor from 1910 to 1937; J. Loy Maloney, managing editor from 1939 to 1951, when he became executive editor; W. D. Maxwell, city editor who became managing editor in 1951; and sports editor Arch Ward, business manager Elbert M. Antrim, and circulation manager Louis Rose. Heading the Washington bureau were Arthur Sears Henning and his successor, Walter Trohan, who learned to shape their coverage to back up the Colonel's opinions. Such *Tribune* foreign service stars as William L. Shirer, Edmond Taylor, and Vincent Sheehan disappeared when the Colonel's personal direction of their work interfered with their coverage.

McCormick opposed President Franklin Roosevelt and the domestic policies of the New Deal with every resource. As a result the *Tribune* was voted in a 1936 poll of Washington correspondents as runner-up to the Hearst papers for the title "least fair and reliable." When the World War II crisis began to develop, the *Tribune* bitterly denounced cooperation with Great Britain, the ancient enemy; a typical eight-column banner when the lend-lease bill was under debate read: "HOUSE PASSES DICTATOR BILL." It was this combination of extreme conservatism and nationalism which incited Marshall Field to start the *Chicago Sun* as a rival morning paper (the *Tribune* having inherited the field alone when Hearst retired from it in 1939).

But McCormick's luck held. Three days after the *Sun* appeared its principal issue of isolationism *v.* interventionism was exploded by the bombs which fell at Pearl Harbor. McCormick supported the American war effort although the *Tribune* called American entrance an "FDR war plot." Marshall Field's hard-pressed *Sun,* Colonel Frank Knox's *Chicago Daily News,* and the pro-New Deal tabloid, the *Chicago Times,* opposed McCormick valiantly but without noticeably denting its readership until the merged *Sun-Times* made headway in the 1950's. The Washington correspondents again estimated the *Tribune's* standing in 1944, voting it "the newspaper . . . most flagrant in angling or weighting the news." [13]

How much the *Tribune's* activities could embarrass all American newspapers was driven home the morning after the presidential election of 1948, when re-elected Harry Truman was photographed gleefully holding a home edition of the *Tribune* whose banner line read: "DEWEY DEFEATS TRUMAN." An over-confident *Tribune* Washington bureau had let its hopes override the facts, to the delight of press critics, and to the dismay of newspapermen who had conscientiously tried to maintain news page objectivity. The *Tribune* was not embarrassed; next morning its banner was back to a more usual theme: "CONFESSES DOUBLE KILLING."

Key McCormick executives took over his *Tribune* in 1955 and continued its policies. Chesser M. Campbell, the new president and publisher, died in 1960 and was succeeded by J. Howard Wood. W. D. Maxwell became editor. The *Chicago American* was purchased in 1956. The *Tribune's* circulation of 854,000 in 1961, down 220,000 from its top, was still 300,000 ahead of the *Sun-Times*.

Hearst and McCormick were not the only newspaper publishers who aroused the ire of those who spoke out against journalistic irresponsibility in the momentous years after 1930, when domestic and international crises demanded the best efforts of the press in obtaining and interpreting the news. Readers of other dailies than the Hearst and McCormick-Patterson papers had justifiable complaints about fairness and devotion to the public interest, although in over-all perspective, American newspapermen succeeded in raising their sights during that quarter century. It was Hearst and McCormick, however, who got the spotlight.

Receiving special attention, too, was Roy W. Howard, the man who by the 1930's had come to dominate the newspapers founded

[13] *Time*, XLIX (June 9, 1947), 68. The 1936 survey of Washington correspondents, cited above, was taken by Leo C. Rosten for his book, *The Washington Correspondents* (New York: Harcourt, Brace and Company, 1937). Cited most often as "least fair and reliable" by 93 correspondents were, in order, the Hearst newspapers, the *Chicago Tribune*, the *Los Angeles Times*, and the Scripps-Howard newspapers. Cited most often as "most fair and reliable" by 99 correspondents were, in order, the *New York Times, Baltimore Sun, Christian Science Monitor*, the Scripps-Howard papers, and the *St. Louis Post-Dispatch* (pp. 356-57).

by E. W. Scripps. Howard was held responsible by his critics for a rightward shift in the outlook of the 20 surviving Scripps-Howard dailies, which ranked third behind Hearst and McCormick-Patterson papers in circulation. The complaints were not of the same character as those made against Hearst and McCormick; they reflected rather the disappointment and dismay of the liberals that the "people's papers" of Edward Wyllis Scripps had become in many respects conventionally conservative in tone.[14]

Robert Paine Scripps, the founder's youngest son, inherited the controlling interest in the newspapers, the United Press, Acme Newsphotos, Newspaper Enterprise Association, and United Feature Syndicate when his father died in 1926. Robert Scripps had been at the editorial helm as family representative since 1918, while Roy Howard, the architect of the United Press, had taken over business management of the newspaper chain in 1922, the year the Scripps-McRae newspapers were renamed Scripps-Howard.

The son was imbued with the philosophy of the father, although his quiet and sensitive nature kept him from exercising a firm control over policy. When editor Carl Magee of Albuquerque, New Mexico, was persecuted and driven from business in 1922 because of his efforts to expose the political machine headed by Secretary of the Interior Albert B. Fall (later convicted of bribe-taking in the Teapot Dome scandal), Robert Scripps bought the paper, the *Tribune*, and restored Magee to its editorship. In 1924 the Scripps-Howard papers supported Robert M. La Follette, Progressive party candidate for the presidency. The Scripps-Howard editors, called into session periodically to decide matters of national policy, backed Herbert Hoover for the presidency in 1928, but swung back to Franklin D. Roosevelt in 1932 and 1936.

Howard's ascendancy in Scripps-Howard affairs became apparent in 1937, when the chain's papers broke with Roosevelt over the Supreme Court reorganization bill. Lowell Mellett, editor of the *Washington News,* and other old Scripps men left the organization. Robert Paine Scripps, who had been in virtual retirement, died aboard his yacht in 1938. The Scripps wills provided for eventual distribution of the family holdings among Robert Scripps' six

[14] See Chapter 20, pages 535-36 in Chapter 22, and page 679 in Chapter 27 for the earlier Scripps story.

children and their heirs. Howard, William W. Hawkins of the United Press, and George B. Parker, editor-in-chief of the newspapers, were named trustees, to serve until the sons of Robert Scripps reached the age of 25.

Under this regime the Scripps-Howard newspapers opposed a third term for President Roosevelt in 1940 and supported Republican presidential candidates every four years through 1960. The newspaper chain was cut from 25 to 19 dailies during the depression years, with such old fighting Scripps papers as those in Akron and Toledo disappearing. Organized labor no longer found the chain's papers to be stalwart champions. The papers still reflected considerable variety in outlook and reader appeal, however, and exercise of local autonomy made outstanding such dailies as those in Memphis and the *Cleveland Press*, edited by the strong-minded and community-conscious Louis B. Seltzer. The United Press developed stature as a press association under presidents Karl Bickel and Hugh Baillie and the United Feature Syndicate became noted for its array of offerings from such capable columnists as Raymond Clapper, Marquis Childs, and Thomas L. Stokes. Liberal columnist Heywood Broun broke with Howard in 1939, but Howard also broke with extremist Westbrook Pegler in 1944. Howard's major desire was to build a powerful paper in New York City, but the result of his efforts, the *World-Telegram and Sun*, was disappointing.

After World War II, Hawkins and Parker were replaced as trustees by Robert Paine Scripps, Jr., and Charles E. Scripps. In 1949 Charles Scripps became chairman of the trust. Neither was interested particularly in editorial matters, however, and eventual leadership in that direction seemed likely to fall to Edward W. Scripps II, who assumed the third trusteeship from Roy Howard when his brother Samuel declined his option. One of Robert Scripps' daughters, Margaret Scripps McCabe, also showed interest in the newspapers' editorial policies, as was demonstrated when her husband, Charles R. McCabe, criticised the turn Scripps-Howard policy had taken in an introduction to a collection of E. W. Scripps' writings.[15]

[15] Charles R. McCabe, ed., *Damned Old Crank* (New York: Harper & Brothers, 1951), p. xii.

Roy Howard remained powerful, however, as president of the *World-Telegram and Sun,* and his son Jack was high in the councils as president of the parent E. W. Scripps Company. In the Far West, the family of James Scripps, eldest son of the founder who quarreled with his father in 1920, was successfully rebuilding the once nearly defunct Scripps League by developing small daily newspapers in Utah, Idaho, Montana, and Oregon. Another Scripps grandson, John P. Scripps, had built a chain of small California dailies. The name Scripps seemed certain to remain an important one in the business.

Too much attention can be centered upon the "press lords," important and interesting as they always prove to be. More vital to the future of American daily newspapers is the trend taken by the bulk of lesser-known publishers, editors, and newspapermen in response to pressures for improvement of the press coming both from without and within the profession. In this regard, the years since 1930 proved to be heartening ones for those who sought to improve journalistic practices and to stimulate greater concern in the exercise of public responsibilities. National, regional, and state organizations of publishers, editors, and other newspapermen; professional societies and such groups as the Nieman Fellows; journalism educators and other students of the press; and organized study groups such as the Commission on Freedom of the Press made varying contributions to newspaper progress.

The American Society of Newspaper Editors was organized in 1922, under the leadership of Casper S. Yost of the *St. Louis Globe-Democrat,* to fill a long-felt need. As the group's constitution pointed out, "Although the art of journalism has flourished in America for more than two hundred years, the editors of the greater American newspapers have not hitherto banded themselves together in association for the consideration of their common problems and the promotion of their professional ideals." State and regional newspaper associations had considered news and editorial problems, but the American Newspaper Publishers Association had virtually excluded all but business topics from its agendas.

Membership in the ASNE was limited to editors in chief, editorial page editors, and managing editors of dailies published in cities of more than 100,000 population, a figure soon reduced to 50,000.

Limited numbers of editors of smaller dailies were admitted to membership in later years.

Early meetings of the society were enlivened by a bitter dispute over the power of the group to expel a member, Fred G. Bonfils of the *Denver Post,* who stood accused of blackmailing oil millionaire Harry Sinclair in connection with the Teapot Dome scandal. At one point a vote of expulsion was taken, but the action was rescinded and the Denver editor was permitted to resign. Later the ASNE clarified its power to expel a member for due cause, but the Bonfils incident made it clear that the group did not propose to serve as a policing organization. Willis J. Abbot of the *Christian Science Monitor* and Tom Wallace of the *Louisville Times* were leaders in the fight for a stern policy, but Yost and others held to a middle course.

A code of ethics, called the "Canons of Journalism," was presented to the first annual meeting in 1923. Chief author was H. J. Wright, founder of the *New York Globe.* Some of the key paragraphs read as follows:

The right of a newspaper to attract and hold readers is restricted by nothing but considerations of public welfare. The use a newspaper makes of the share of public attention it gains serves to determine its sense of responsibility, which it shares with every member of its staff. A journalist who uses his power for any selfish or otherwise unworthy purpose is faithless to a high trust.

Freedom of the press is to be guarded as a vital right of mankind. It is the unquestionable right to discuss whatever is not explicitly forbidden by law, including the wisdom of any restrictive statute.

Freedom from all obligations except that of fidelity to the public interest is vital.

Partisanship, in editorial comment which knowingly departs from the truth, does violence to the best spirit of American journalism; in the news columns it is subversive of a fundamental principle of the profession.

Annual meetings of the ASNE are held each April in Washington. Proceedings are reported in a series of books, dating from 1923, titled *Problems of Journalism,* which offer in their pages some significant discussions of professional matters.[16]

[16] The proceedings of the twenty-fifth annual ASNE meeting, in 1947, contain on pages 39-53 historical reminiscences of three early members, Grove Patterson of the *Toledo Blade,* Marvin H. Creager of the *Milwaukee Journal,* and Donald J. Sterling of the *Oregon Journal.*

Editorial page editors and editorial writers who wanted a smaller and more vigorous "working" organization than the 450-member ASNE formed the National Conference of Editorial Writers in 1947. The idea came from a group attending an American Press Institute session at Columbia University[17] and was promoted by Leslie Moore of the *Worcester Telegram* and *Gazette,* Ralph Coghlan of the *St. Louis Post-Dispatch,* John H. Cline of the *Washington Star,* Robert H. Estabrook of the *Washington Post,* and Forrest W. Seymour of the *Des Moines Register* and *Tribune,* among others. Annual sessions were held beginning in 1947, which featured small-group critique panels in which members appraised the editorial page efforts of their colleagues. A quarterly magazine, the *Masthead,* and convention proceedings were published. A code of principles was adopted in 1949 "to stimulate the conscience and the quality of the American editorial page."[18] Membership stood at 350 by 1961.

Another important national group, the Associated Press Managing Editors Association, was formed in 1931 by news executives who found the annual meetings of the ANPA and the Associated Press too little concerned with improvement of the news columns' content. The organizers in this case included Oliver O. Kuhn of the *Washington Star,* Roy Roberts of the *Kansas City Star,* Sevellon Brown of the *Providence Journal* and *Bulletin,* W. C. Stouffer of the *Roanoke World-News,* and Roy Dunlap of the *St. Paul Pioneer Press* and *Dispatch.* The AP news report was analyzed and criticised orally in annual meetings until 1947 when a printed report was prepared by a Continuing Study Committee. Although the studies of the different portions of the Associated Press news report were penetrating enough to arouse replies from the AP management, they were made public as the *APME Red Book* beginning in 1948.[19] Setting the pattern for the Continuing Study reports were the first chairmen, William P. Steven of the *Minneapolis Tribune* and Lee Hills of the *Miami Herald.* Attendance at APME conventions rose to 300 by 1960.

[17] The American Press Institute was founded in 1946 through the efforts of Sevellon Brown of the *Providence Journal* and *Bulletin.*

[18] The NCEW code of principles appears in *Editor & Publisher,* LXXXII (October 29, 1949), 7.

[19] The *APME Red Book* for 1948 opens with a history of the organization and its Continuing Study activities to that time.

The equivalent newsmen's organization in broadcasting is the Radio-Television News Directors Association. It was founded in 1946 as the National Association of Radio News Directors. First leaders were John Hogan, WCSH, Portland, Maine; John Murphy, WCKY, Cincinnati; Sig Mickelson, WCCO, Minneapolis; Jack Shelley, WHO, Des Moines; and Edward Wallace, WTAM, Cleveland. Its publication is the *RTNDA Bulletin*. The group set broadcast news standards and worked closely with journalism schools.

Other professional groups were concerned with varying aspects of journalistic problems: the American Newspaper Guild, with its *Guild Reporter*; the American Newspaper Publishers Association, representing dailies; the National Editorial Association, representing weeklies and some smaller dailies; the Magazine Publishers Association; the National Association of Broadcasters; the United Press International editors; and many regional organizations. Some schools of journalism joined with newsmen in sponsoring various professional conferences dealing with journalistic problems. Awards for outstanding achievement were inaugurated by Sigma Delta Chi, men's professional journalism society begun in 1909 at DePauw University and expanded to include both undergraduate and professional chapters. Research about journalism was encouraged by annual awards of both Sigma Delta Chi and Kappa Tau Alpha, journalism scholastic society founded in 1910 at the University of Missouri. Theta Sigma Phi, women's journalism society founded in 1909 at the University of Washington, stimulated interest through its annual Matrix table gatherings and its scholarship awards.

The ties between campus and city room were strengthened greatly in the second quarter of the twentieth century. The famous cartoon showing a city editor asking a young hopeful, "And what, may I ask, is a school of journalism?" no longer held true by the 1950's. It was likely that the city editor by that time was a journalism school graduate himself—or at least a college graduate with an appreciation of the necessity for sound educational training for newspapermen.

Talk about education for journalism began seriously after the Civil War, but little action resulted until the turn of the century. General Robert E. Lee, president of Washington College (later Washington and Lee University), attempted to establish training in printing in 1869, but the program languished, as did another effort at Cornell University in 1875. Kansas State College instruction in printing dates from 1873, and courses in history and materials of journalism were given at the University of Missouri from 1878 to 1884. The first definitely organized curriculum in journalism was offered at the University of Pennsylvania from 1893 to 1901 by Joseph French Johnson, a former financial editor of the *Chicago Tribune*. The University of Illinois organized the first four-year curriculum in journalism in 1904 under the direction of Frank W. Scott. The first separate school of journalism, with newspaperman Walter Williams as dean, opened in 1908 at the University of Missouri.[20]

In this first period of journalism education, emphasis was placed upon establishment of technical courses. But journalism teachers, often getting their starts in English departments, had to win academic recognition as well as the confidence of the newspaper profession. Their most successful early leader in this regard was Willard G. Bleyer, who began his journalism teaching at the University of Wisconsin in 1904. Bleyer advocated integration of journalism education with the social sciences, and through his development of this concept and his own journalism history research, established Wisconsin as a center for graduate study by future journalism teachers. Other early leaders were Eric W. Allen of the University of Oregon, H. F. Harrington of Northwestern University, Leon N. Flint of the University of Kansas, Arthur L. Stone of Montana State University, J. W. Piercy of Indiana University, Merle H. Thorpe of the University of Washington, Everett W. Smith of Stanford University, and Talcott Williams and John W. Cunliffe of Columbia University, the first two men to head the Pulitzer School of Journalism, opened in 1912 with a two million dollar endowment from the *New York World* publisher.

The second phase of journalism education saw emphasis placed upon the study of journalism history and of the press as a social institution, as well as a widening of instruction to areas other than

[20] See Albert A. Sutton, *Education for Journalism in the United States* (Evanston: Northwestern University Press, 1945), for an historical treatment. For a current picture, see Edwin Emery, Phillip H. Ault, and Warren K. Agee, *Introduction to Mass Communications* (New York: Dodd, Mead & Company, 1960), chap. 18. An historical analysis of trends was made by Ralph D. Casey in *Journalism Quarterly*, XXI (March 1944), 55.

that of the daily and weekly newspapers. Pioneer textbooks had been written by Bleyer, Harrington, James Melvin Lee of New York University, Grant M. Hyde of Wisconsin, and M. Lyle Spencer of Syracuse. In the early 1920's the books of Bleyer in journalism history and of Flint and Nelson Antrim Crawford of Kansas State College in newspaper ethics pointed the way toward integration of technical training with analysis of the social responsibilities of the journalist. Coming into importance were the American Association of Teachers of Journalism, founded in 1912, and the American Association of Schools and Departments of Journalism, established in 1917. The latter group sought to give recognition to well-established journalism curricula and thereby stimulate improved instruction in the growing number of colleges and universities offering courses.

Other newspapermen than Pulitzer aided in the establishment of journalism schools. Second in size to the Pulitzer gift to Columbia University was the endowment fund provided in 1918 by William J. Murphy, publisher of the *Minneapolis Tribune*, for journalism education at the University of Minnesota. The fund's value by the 1950's was $800,000. The owners of the *Chicago Tribune* established the Medill School of Journalism at Northwestern University in 1921 and continued to assist the school financially in subsequent years. State press associations and individual newspapermen played parts in the establishment of other schools and departments of journalism.

The 1920's saw the founding of the *Journalism Quarterly*, devoted to research studies in the field of mass communications. It began as the *Journalism Bulletin*, issued in 1924 by the teachers' group, and edited by Lawrence W. Murphy of the University of Illinois. Frank Luther Mott of the University of Iowa (later dean at the University of Missouri) became *Journalism Quarterly*'s editor in 1930, followed by Ralph D. Casey of the University of Minnesota in 1935, and Raymond B. Nixon of Emory University and Minnesota in 1945.

A third phase of journalism education was developing by the 1930's. Fuller integration of journalism education with the social sciences was the goal, and the leading schools and departments undertook research and teaching in the field of communications as a whole. Journalism students, it was recognized, should receive a broad liberal arts education, sound journalistic technical training, and an understanding of the social implications of their chosen profession. Northwestern University established a five-year plan for professional training in 1938; the Pulitzer School at Columbia had restricted its year's course to holders of a bachelor's degree in 1935. Graduate level instruction was expanded at other institutions, along with research in mass communications. In 1944 the Minnesota School of Journalism set up a journalism research division, the first of its kind. Among early leaders in mass communications research were Chilton R. Bush of Stanford University, Ralph O. Nafziger of Minnesota (later at Wisconsin), Wilbur Schramm of Iowa (later at Illinois and Stanford), Paul F. Lazarsfeld of Columbia University's Bureau of Applied Social Research, and Douglas Waples of the University of Chicago.

Closer ties between newspapermen and the schools were established during the 1930's. The idea of a joint committee which would include representatives of the principal newspaper associations and the schools and departments of journalism was suggested by Fred Fuller Shedd, editor of the *Philadelphia Bulletin* who had been instrumental in the founding of the department at Pennsylvania State College (later University). Journalism educators, led by Bleyer of Wisconsin, Allen of Oregon, and Frank L. Martin of Missouri, joined in the plan in 1931. The project lapsed during the depression years but was brought into full operation in 1939 through the efforts of Kenneth E. Olson of Northwestern University. The American Council on Education for Journalism was formed by journalism educators and five major newspaper organizations—the American Society of Newspaper Editors, the American Newspaper Publishers Association, the National Editorial Association, the Inland Daily Press Association, and the Southern Newspaper Publishers Association. The National Association of Broadcasters and the Magazine Publishers Association later joined in the council's work. The ACEJ established an accrediting program and approved work in one or more phases of journalism at 40 schools and departments in the late 1940's. The number of accredited institutions increased to 48 by 1961.

In 1949 the American Association of Teachers of Journalism reorganized as the Association for Education in Journalism. Accepting coordinate roles within the AEJ structure were the American

Association of Schools and Departments of Journalism (now composed of the accredited schools) and the American Society of Journalism School Administrators, founded in 1944 by heads of other schools. The ASJSA published the *Journalism Educator*. Serving in the American Council on Education for Journalism for long periods of time were Olson of Northwestern, Casey of Minnesota, Mott of Missouri, Fred S. Siebert of Illinois (later Michigan State), John E. Stempel of Indiana, and Alfred A. Crowell of Maryland. Active in supervising the accrediting program were Earl F. English of Missouri, Norval Neil Luxon of North Carolina, Leslie G. Moeller of Iowa, Burton W. Marvin of Kansas, Quintus C. Wilson of Utah (later West Virginia), I. W. Cole and Baskett Mosse of Northwestern, and DeWitt C. Reddick of Texas. Newspaper representatives who gave leadership to the work of the council included Jerome D. Barnum of the *Syracuse Post-Standard*, David W. Howe of the *Burlington Free Press* in Vermont, A. H. Kirchhofer of the *Buffalo News*, Dwight Marvin of the *Troy Record*, Edward E. Lindsay of the Lindsay-Schaub Newspapers in Illinois, Joyce A. Swan of the *Minneapolis Star* and *Tribune*, and Herbert Brucker of the *Hartford Courant*.

Journalism schools, by the 1960's, were thus well established in the fields of teaching, research, and service. They had close ties with the profession through short courses, consultative services, and, in some states, through joint operation of a field manager service for the state press association. Their scope of interests included daily and weekly newspapers, magazines, radio and television, photography, advertising, the graphic arts, industrial editing, public relations and information writing, journalism teaching, and research in mass communications. The concept of integrating journalism education with the social sciences was fully recognized by leaders in both the schools and the profession.

A million dollar endowment left to Harvard University in 1936 by the widow of Lucius W. Nieman, founder of the *Milwaukee Journal*, was used for a different type of educational opportunity. The Nieman Foundation, beginning in 1937, annually selected a dozen highly-qualified working newspapermen for a year of study at Harvard as Nieman Fellows, on leave from their newspapers or press associations. Louis M. Lyons, curator of the foundation, established a thoughtful quarterly magazine, *Nieman Reports*, in 1947.

Nieman Fellows also produced two cooperative books, *Newsmen's Holiday* (1942) and *Your Newspaper* (1947), about newspaper problems. The year at Harvard was regarded generally by Nieman Fellows as a high-point experience, giving them an opportunity to broaden their education in selected fields.

Other attempts to study the responsibilities and the character of the American press were made in the years after World War II. Magazine publisher Henry R. Luce financed an important private study by the Commission on Freedom of the Press. The commission was headed by Chancellor Robert M. Hutchins of the University of Chicago and was composed chiefly of social science professors outside the field of journalism. Its summary report, *A Free and Responsible Press* (1947), covered newspapers, radio, motion pictures, magazines, and books, and consisted of a general statement of principles. The commission itself conducted only a limited research program in the making of its report, but it sponsored the publication of a number of books, including Zechariah Chafee, Jr.'s *Government and Mass Communications,* William E. Hocking's *Freedom of the Press,* and Llewellyn White's *The American Radio.*

The presidential elections of 1948 and 1952 brought flurries of activity in the analysis of press behavior in relation to public questions. *Editor & Publisher,* trade journal for the daily newspapers, sponsored a meeting in March, 1949, of a panel on the press, composed of 10 newspapermen and educators. The panel suggested studies for press self-improvement but an ASNE committee appointed to consider the problem came to no specific conclusions. Before the 1956 election journalism educators and Sigma Delta Chi urged a major study of press election coverage, but a group of hesitant publishers and editors vetoed action. However, effective voices have been raised within the profession, in analysis of press behavior. A partial list would include J. Russell Wiggins and Alan Barth, *Washington Post;* Herbert Brucker, *Hartford Courant;* Barry Bingham and Norman Isaacs, *Louisville Courier-Journal;* James B. Reston, *New York Times;* Erwin D. Canham, *Christian Science Monitor;* columnists Marquis Childs and Thomas L. Stokes; and commentators Elmer Davis and Edward R. Murrow.

Important recent books include Frank Luther Mott's *American Journalism* (1941) and *The News in America* (1952), J. Edward

Gerald's *The Press and the Constitution* (1948), Brucker's *Freedom of Information* (1949), Wiggins' *Freedom or Secrecy* (1956), and Wilbur Schramm's *Responsibility in Mass Communication* (1957). Criticism of newspapers' technical performance has taken two forms: lack of sufficient research about their product and audience and failure to keep pace in technological progress. Both criticisms are valid, but recent efforts to meet them should be recognized. Since the 1930's newspapermen—as well as magazine, broadcasting, and advertising men—have paid ever-increasing attention to audience and motivational research, readership and listenership studies, readability formulas, and design and layout. Some dailies have employed their own research directors.

In technological progress, the major effort has been to produce a "cold type" revolution, involving the introduction of photography into the printing process. Such machines of the 1950's as the Fotosetter, Linofilm, and Photon produce words on film and transfer them directly to a printing plate. Already widely used in advertisement composition, they promised to make further inroads on "hot metal" typesetting. Offset printing, based upon the age-old lithography process, avoids both typesetting and photo-engraving by use of paste-ups photographed onto flexible printing plates. But time-lag and other problems have restricted its use so far to weeklies and magazines, in the main. The *Opelousas Daily World* in Louisiana, begun in 1939, was the first successful daily to print by offset. It was joined by 40 other small dailies by 1961. By comparison, there were 431 weeklies printed by offset. The Phoenix *Arizona Journal*, founded in February, 1962, as a rival to the jointly-owned *Arizona Republic* and *Gazette*, was the first attempt at producing an offset daily in a metropolitan competitive situation.

Use of perforated tape for automatic operation of improved typesetting machines—such as the Mergenthaler Blue Streak Comet and the Intertype Monarch—brought a doubling of production during the 1950's in the traditional "hot metal" process. Engraving processes also were improved. The Fairchild engraving machine, producing plastic printing plates simply and cheaply, was a boon to smaller publications beginning in the 1940's. The newspaper industry, united in such efforts as the ANPA Research Institute, expected technological advances in the 1960's rivaling those of the revolutionary period of the 1880's and 1890's.

ANNOTATED BIBLIOGRAPHY

Most of the important references are referred to in the text of this chapter. Discussions involving press criticism are to be found in the American Society of Newspaper Editors' *Problems of Journalism* series, in the Associated Press Managing Editors' *APME Red Book* series, and in the periodicals *Journalism Quarterly, Masthead, Nieman Reports, Editor & Publisher,* and *Guild Reporter.* Bibliographies for Chapters 19 and 20 should be consulted for earlier references to Hearst and Scripps.

Books:

Blumberg, Nathan B., *One Party Press?* Lincoln: University of Nebraska Press, 1954. How 35 large dailies covered the 1952 campaign; news columns found to be essentially fair.

Brucker, Herbert, *Freedom of Information.* New York: The Macmillan Company, 1949. Able defense of press by *Hartford Courant* editor.

Clark, Wesley C., ed., *Journalism Tomorrow.* Syracuse: Syracuse University Press, 1958. A symposium on future of mass media.

Commission on Freedom of the Press, *A Free and Responsible Press.* Chicago: University of Chicago Press, 1947. A penetrating summary.

Drewry, John E., ed., *Post Biographies of Famous Journalists.* Athens: University of Georgia Press, 1942. Contains excellent articles about Hearst, Roy Howard, McCormick, and Eleanor Patterson.

Emery, Edwin, Phillip H. Ault, and Warren K. Agee, *Introduction to Mass Communications.* New York: Dodd, Mead & Company, 1960. Current status of all mass media, research, journalism schools.

Ford, Edwin H., and Edwin Emery, eds., *Highlights in the History of the American Press.* Minneapolis: University of Minnesota Press, 1954. Contains articles about Hearst, Scripps-Howard, and McCormick.

Lindstrom, Carl E., *The Fading American Newspaper.* New York: Doubleday & Company, 1960. A strong critique of trends and methods by a 40-year newspaperman (*Hartford Times*).

Mott, Frank Luther, *The News in America.* Cambridge: Harvard University Press, 1952. An excellent discussion of news-gathering and news-distribution and of socio-political responsibilities.

Mott, Frank Luther, and Ralph D. Casey, eds., *Interpretations of Journalism.* New York: F. S. Crofts & Company, 1937. The most important historical collection of statements on press problems.

Pollard, James E., *The Presidents and the Press.* New York: The Macmillan Company, 1947. Carries through the Roosevelt administration.

Rowse, Arthur E., *Slanted News.* Boston: Beacon Press, 1957. Analysis of how 31 large dailies reported the "Nixon fund" episode in 1952.

Schramm, Wilbur, ed., *Communications in Modern Society*. Urbana: University of Illinois Press, 1948. Contains essays on press responsibility by Paul F. Lazarsfeld, Ralph D. Casey, and Robert J. Blakely.

——, *Responsibility in Mass Communication*. New York: Harper & Brothers, 1957. The best recent study of the problem.

Swanberg, W. A., *Citizen Hearst*. New York: Charles Scribner's Sons, 1961. A highly readable, detailed biography.

Tebbel, John, *An American Dynasty*. New York: Doubleday & Company, 1947. An analysis of the McCormick-Patterson publishing empire.

——, *The Life and Good Times of William Randolph Hearst*. New York: E. P. Dutton & Company, 1952. Best single book about both Hearst and his publishing empire.

Periodicals and Monographs:

Bigman, Stanley K., "Public Reactions to the Death of a Daily," *Journalism Quarterly*, XXXII (Summer 1955), 267. Little public concern found after merger of *Washington Post* and *Times-Herald*.

"The Chicago Tribune," *Fortune*, IX (May 1934), 101. Detailed study.

Columbia Journalism Review staff, "Campaign Coverage: An Appraisal of 1960—and Implications for 1964," *Columbia Journalism Review* (Fall 1961), 6. A 14-page report on newspaper "fairness" in 1960 presidential election coverage, appearing in the "pilot issue" of a journal produced by the Columbia University Graduate School of Journalism. Includes comments on 25 metropolitan areas.

Danielson, Wayne A., and John B. Adams, "Completeness of Press Coverage of the 1960 Campaign," *Journalism Quarterly*, XXXVIII (Autumn 1961), 441. A report on a sample of 90 dailies, based on completeness of coverage of 23 campaign events.

Ethridge, Mark, "Fateful Crisis of the Newspaper," *Nieman Reports*, XIV (October 1960), 14. By *Louisville Courier-Journal* publisher.

Hutchison, Earl R., "Kennedy and the Press: the First Six Months," *Journalism Quarterly*, XXXVIII (Autumn 1961), 453.

Liebling, A. J., "Publisher," *New Yorker*, XVII (August 2-23, 1941). Critical profile of Roy W. Howard.

Lyons, Louis M., "A Glance Backward at the Press," *Nieman Reports*, XIII (January 1959), 7. Analysis of past 20 years.

Meyers, W. Cameron, "The Chicago Newspaper Hoax in the '36 Election Campaign," *Journalism Quarterly*, XXXVII (Summer 1960), 356. Criticism of *Chicago Tribune* by the biographer of *Chicago Times* editor Richard J. Finnegan (Ph.D. dissertation, Northwestern University, 1959, "Chicago's Mister Finnegan: A Gentleman of the Press").

Nixon, Raymond B., "Changes in Reader Attitudes Toward Daily Newspapers," *Journalism Quarterly*, XXXI (Fall 1954), 21. Reinforces findings that readers approve of quality "monopoly" dailies.

Nixon, Raymond B., and Robert L. Jones, "The Content of Non-Competitive vs. Competitive Newspapers," *Journalism Quarterly*, XXXIII (Summer 1956), 299. No major differences were found.

Pollard, James E., articles on "Truman and the Press," *Journalism Quarterly*, XXVIII (Fall 1951), 457, and XXX (Summer 1953), 273; on "Eisenhower and the Press," XXXII (Summer 1955), 285; XXXIII (Winter 1956), 3; and XXXVIII (Spring 1961), 181.

Stempel, Guido H., III, "The Prestige Press Covers the 1960 Presidential Campaign," *Journalism Quarterly*, XXXVIII (Spring 1961), 157. Fifteen leading papers divide news space almost evenly between Kennedy and Nixon when figures for the 15 are added together.

Taylor, Frank J., "The Incredible House That Hearst Built," *Saturday Evening Post*, CCXXXII (May 9, 1959), 38. Hearst's San Simeon estate becomes a California Historical Monument.

Tebbel, John, "The Quiet Offset Revolution," *Saturday Review*, XLIV (December 9, 1961), 60. A report on newspaper use of the offset printing process.

Chapter *30*

SOME REPRESENTATIVE NEWSPAPERS

> . . . it is as difficult to apply objective stand-
> ards to newspapers as it is to people, and the
> greatest newspaper is as difficult to identify as the
> greatest man. It all depends upon what you
> require.
>
> —Gerald W. Johnson

THE OBLIGATIONS OF ANY NEWSPAPER to its commu-
nity are to strive for honest and comprehensive coverage of the
news, and for courageous expression of editorial opinion in support
of basic principles of human liberty and social progress. Those
newspapers which have been most consistent in fulfilling these
obligations have been rewarded with public and professional acclaim. Other factors which have operated to give some newspapers
greater professional recognition are brilliance of individual leadership on the staff, and the maintenance of a steady and sound publishing tradition. No one, however, can with any certainty rank
America's leading papers in numerical order. But the results of
three opinion polls on the subject, taken in 1960 and 1961, offer
some at least interesting results. One was of 335 editors, one of
311 publishers, and the third of 125 journalism professors.

The *New York Times, Christian Science Monitor, St. Louis Post-
Dispatch, Washington Post,* and *Milwaukee Journal* were rated
among the top six dailies in all three polls. The *Louisville Courier-*

Journal was in the first eight of all three polls. The *Chicago Daily News, Wall Street Journal, New York Herald Tribune,* and *Chicago Tribune* were in the first ten of two of the polls. Included in the top 15 dailies by one or more polls were the *Baltimore Sun, Atlanta Constitution, Minneapolis Tribune, Kansas City Star, Los Angeles Times, Miami Herald, Detroit Free Press,* and *Des Moines Register.*[1] Threads of journalistic achievement can be woven together by examining the current status of these and some other representative daily newspapers whose accounts were not completed in earlier chapters of this volume.[2]

The *New York Times* ranked first in all three polls, continuing to hold its place in the forefront of American journalism by maintaining the tradition of telling the news with completeness and integrity. Arthur Hays Sulzberger, who became publisher when his father-in-law, Adolph S. Ochs, died in 1935, lived up to his responsibilities as the head of the country's "newspaper of record." Throughout the 1930's and 1940's, the news staff was led by the team of Edwin L. James, managing editor, and David H. Joseph, city editor. Responsibility for the editorial page, which rested briefly with John H. Finley after the death of Rollo Ogden in 1937, passed in 1938 to Charles Merz. Merz had been managing editor of *Harper's Weekly* and an associate editor of the *New York World.*

Turner Catledge, well-tested as a Washington correspondent, became managing editor in 1951, the *Times'* centennial year. Catledge named two *Times* veterans, Theodore Bernstein and Robert E. Garst, as assistant managing editors with responsibility for enlivening the paper's writing and news presentation. Frank S. Adams became city editor, presiding over a block-long city room in the 18-million-dollar Times building down 43rd Street from the old Times Square location (the Times Tower was sold in 1961). Major changes came in 1961 when Sulzberger turned over the publisher's chair to his son-in-law, Orvil E. Dryfoos, and Merz retired as

---

[1] For the poll of editors, see *Editor & Publisher,* XCIII (April 2, 1960), 12. For the poll of publishers, see *Editor & Publisher,* XCIII (April 9, 1960), 66. For the poll of journalism professors, see John Tebbel, "Rating the American Newspaper," *Saturday Review,* XLIV (May 13 and June 10, 1961).

[2] The stories of the *Christian Science Monitor* and *Wall Street Journal* are told on pages 638-40 of Chapter 25, and that of the *Chicago Tribune* on pages 724-29 of Chapter 29. See page 638 for *New York Times* as a national newspaper.

editorial page chief in favor of John B. Oakes (a nephew of Adolph Ochs), who had won distinction as an editorial writer. Lester Markel remained as editor of the Sunday edition.

Editorially the *Times* was staunchly internationalist in world outlook, progressive-conservative in domestic affairs. It supported Democrats Franklin D. Roosevelt in 1936 and 1944 and John F. Kennedy in 1960, and backed Republicans Wendell Willkie in 1940, Thomas E. Dewey in 1948, and Dwight D. Eisenhower in 1952 and 1956. Like other responsible newspapers it vigorously defended individual freedoms against reactionary attacks which characterized the years of stress following World War II. By 1961 the *Times* and its staff had won a record number of 32 Pulitzer Prizes, including two for meritorious public service in 1918 and 1944.

The *New York Herald Tribune* proved to be a distinguished morning rival of the *Times*. Ogden M. Reid and his wife, Helen Rogers Reid, succeeded to control of the *Tribune* when editor Whitelaw Reid died in 1912. With the purchase of the *Herald* from Frank Munsey in 1924, and the creation of the *Herald Tribune*, a distinctive newspaper emerged. Ogden Reid was content to have his wife assume the major responsibilities of the publisher's office.

Like the *Times*, the *Herald Tribune* became known for its foreign and Washington correspondence, and for its coverage of cultural news. Its syndicated columnists included Mark Sullivan, Walter Lippmann, Joseph Alsop, and Roscoe Drummond. Geoffrey Parsons, a Pulitzer Prize winner, served as chief editorial writer from 1924 to 1952. Stanley Walker became one of New York's best known city editors, and assistant editor Wilbur Forrest was an important journalistic figure. When Ogden Reid died in 1947 his sons, another Whitelaw Reid and Ogden R. Reid, joined their mother in directing the paper's affairs. But difficulties piled up, and in 1958 the Reids reluctantly sold the *Herald Tribune*.

John Hay Whitney, millionaire new owner of the paper, first selected Robert M. White II, co-owner of the *Mexico Ledger* in Missouri, as *Herald Tribune* president and editor. But Whitney assumed direct control of the paper in 1960 as publisher and editor-in-chief, and chose John Denson, former editor of *Newsweek*, to replace White as editor. Denson revamped the *Herald Tribune's* makeup, adopting a magazine-style format. Dwight E. Sargent became editor of the editorial pages.

Consistently conservative in its outlook, the *Herald Tribune* won wide respect for fairness and for high quality interpretative writing. It supported the internationalist wing of the Republican party and early promoted the presidential bids of Willkie and Eisenhower, as against that of Senator Robert A. Taft.

No American newspaper rose more rapidly in esteem in recent decades than did the *Washington Post* after Eugene Meyer, a civic-minded financier, rescued it from a receivership in 1933. Meyer's object in buying the *Post* from the McLean family heirs was to give Washington a newspaper with a sound and intelligent editorial page. This he achieved with two editors who won Pulitzer Prizes for editorial writing: Felix Morley, editor until 1940, and Herbert Elliston, who served until 1953. Robert H. Estabrook then became editor of the editorial page. Giving the page added distinction were the cartoons of Herbert L. Block. Through its editorial page and its interpretative coverage of national news, the *Post* won recognition as the most independent paper in the capital. It also carried a large volume of foreign news.

When Meyer became president of the International Bank in 1946, he named Philip L. Graham, his son-in-law, as publisher, but he and his wife, Mrs. Agnes E. Meyer, remained influential in the newspaper's continued progress. Purchase of the *Post's* morning competition, the *Times-Herald*, in 1954, ensured the *Post's* economic stability. With James Russell Wiggins as editor and Alfred Friendly as managing editor, the paper had effective news-side leaders. They joined Graham in raising voices in behalf of improved journalistic practices and in defense of fundamental press freedoms. Editorially the *Post* avoided direct endorsements, but it favored the Dewey, Eisenhower, and Kennedy candidacies. It was strongly internationalist in outlook, and became known for its outspoken and early criticism of Wisconsin Senator Joseph R. McCarthy's political movement of the early 1950's which became known as "McCarthyism."

Vying with the *Washington Post*, the *New York Times*, and the *Herald Tribune* for position on important Washington breakfast tables was the *Baltimore Sun*. The *Sun*, giving special attention to Washington coverage since its founding in 1837, had developed one of the strongest capital bureaus as well as a notable foreign service. Rejuvenated in the decade preceding World War I by Charles H. Grasty and Van-Lear Black, the *Sun* prospered under

Arthur Hays Sulzberger (*left*), publisher of the *New York Times,* and Mrs. Helen Rogers Reid (*right*), who guided the growth of the *Herald Tribune.*

The second Joseph Pulitzer (*left*), publisher, *St. Louis Post-Dispatch,* and Barry Bingham (*right*), owner-editor, *Louisville Courier-Journal.*

Harry J. Grant (*left*), board chairman, *Milwaukee Journal,* and Philip L. Graham (*right*), publisher of the *Washington Post and Times Herald.*

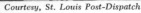

Courtesy, St. Louis Post-Dispatch *Courtesy, Post-Dispatch*

Reporter Paul Y. Anderson (*left*) and managing editor O. K. Bovard (*right*) formed a great team for the *St. Louis Post-Dispatch* in the 1920's.

Courtesy, Washington Post and Times Herald *Courtesy, Louisville Courier-Journal*

Two news executives: J. Russell Wiggins (*left*), *Washington Post and Times Herald*, and James S. Pope (*right*), *Louisville Courier-Journal* and *Times*.

Courtesy, New York Times *Courtesy, Harris & Ewing*

James B. Reston (*left*), *New York Times* Washington bureau chief, and Erwin D. Canham (*right*), editor of the *Christian Science Monitor*.

the effective leadership of Paul C. Patterson, publisher from 1918 to 1950. Hamilton Owens directed an aggressive editorial page. Washington columnist Frank R. Kent, H. L. Mencken, and Gerald W. Johnson were well-known staff members, followed by four Pulitzer Prize winners of the 1940's—Dewey L. Fleming, Paul W. Ward, Mark S. Watson, and Price Day. Day became editor-in-chief in 1960, succeeding J. Hamilton Owens. The *Sun* won the Pulitzer Prize for meritorious public service in 1947.

Among other leading newspapers of the East was the *New York Post*, which completed 160 years of continuous daily publication in 1961, a record for currently-published American dailies. The *Post* entered a new phase when Dorothy Schiff bought it in 1939. With editor Ted O. Thackrey, she made the paper a streamlined tabloid, departmentalized the news, and added feature content. Its columnists, led by Max Lerner, were prominently displayed. James A. Wechsler, from the staff of *PM*, became editor in 1949. The *Post* was the only New York City daily supporting Democratic candidate Adlai Stevenson in 1952 and 1956, and backed John F. Kennedy in 1960. Joining the *Post's* political leanings in 1956 and 1960 was Alicia Patterson's *Newsday*, the Long Island tabloid which in two decades rose to major circulation status. *Newsday* won a Pulitzer Prize for public service in 1954.

The *Washington Star*, solid if unspectacular, celebrated its centennial in 1952, still in the possession of the Noyes and Kauffmann families which took control of it in 1867. Its editors have been Crosby Noyes, 1867 to 1908; Theodore Noyes, to 1946, and then Benjamin M. McKelway. Frank B. Noyes, president of the *Star* from 1909 to 1948, was succeeded by Samuel H. Kauffmann. Equally as civic-minded as the *Star* was the *Philadelphia Bulletin*, purchased in 1895 by William L. McLean and later published by his son, Robert McLean, with Walter Lister as executive editor. The Butler family's *Buffalo Evening News*, edited by Alfred H. Kirchhofer, also excelled in news coverage.

Achieving distinction for editorial page leadership and substantial news presentation were the *Providence Journal* and *Bulletin* and the *Hartford Courant*. Sevellon Brown, an executive of the Providence papers from 1921 to 1957, made them "the conscience of Rhode Island." His son, Sevellon Brown III, became editor in 1953. The *Hartford Courant*, begun as the weekly *Connecticut Courant* in 1764 and claimant to the longest publishing record in America, was kept at a high level by publisher John R. Reitemeyer and editor Herbert Brucker.

In Ohio, publisher Paul Block, Jr.'s *Toledo Blade* advanced rapidly in the 1950's in comprehensive news coverage, community leadership, and independence of opinion. With its morning edition, the *Times*, it was allied in ownership with the *Pittsburgh Post-Gazette*, published by William Block. The two brothers were among owners of major dailies supporting Kennedy in 1960. The *Blade* also was one of the few American dailies to have a European correspondent. The *Cleveland Press*, edited by Louis B. Seltzer, remained the best of the Scripps-Howard group, and a strong civic leader. John S. Knight's *Detroit Free Press*, survivor with the *News* in that city's circulation battle, won the Pulitzer Prize for public service in 1945, and editor Royce Howes won for editorial writing in 1955.

The revolution of the 1870's and 1880's known as the "new journalism" gave the Middle West nationally known newspapers which continued to demonstrate their leadership in the 1960's. None was more consistently in the foremost rank of American newspapers than the *St. Louis Post-Dispatch*, founded in 1878 by the first Joseph Pulitzer, edited from 1911 to 1955 by the second Joseph Pulitzer, and since then by the third of the line, Joseph Pulitzer, Jr., who began assuming authority in the late 1940's.

Continuity, both of Pulitzer family ownership and of the *Post-Dispatch* editorial policies, proved to be the key to greatness. Hammering away consistently to make the editorial page an independent, liberal voice have been six editorial page editors: George S. Johns, who served from 1897 to 1928, Clark McAdams, Charles G. Ross, Ralph Coghlan, Irving Dilliard, and Robert Lasch. Daniel R. Fitzpatrick's incisive cartoons dramatized *Post-Dispatch* crusades from 1913 until 1958, when Bill Mauldin took over his duties.

O. K. Bovard, one of America's great newsmen, provided the necessary complement of leadership during his 30 years as *Post-Dispatch* managing editor, from 1908 to 1938. Under his tutelage, such brilliant reporters as Paul Y. Anderson, Charles G. Ross, Marquis Childs, and Raymond P. Brandt advanced from St. Louis to the Washington scene to help win a national reputation for the paper. Anderson proved to be the mainspring of Bovard's effort after World War I to expand *Post-Dispatch* coverage of the national scene. Through his efforts the paper successfully led a campaign in 1923 to obtain the release of 52 Americans still imprisoned five years after the war's end for expression of radical antiwar opinion. Anderson and his paper were the first to realize the significance of the Teapot Dome scandal. And as a Washington correspondent, Anderson aided in the impeachment, for improper conduct, of federal judge George W. English of East St. Louis in 1926. English resigned before his impeachment trial.

What *Post-Dispatch* men called the "dignity page"—the opening page of the editorial section—was developed by Bovard to carry special articles on political, economic, scientific, and cultural subjects. When Bovard resigned in 1938 after differences with his publisher, Benjamin H. Reese became managing editor. Raymond L. Crowley succeeded Reese in 1951.

During the 15 years beginning in 1937 the *Post-Dispatch* won five Pulitzer Prize gold medals for meritorious public service, two more than the number won by the *New York World*, second-ranking in this awards category.[3] In its campaigns, the paper obtained abatement of the city's smoke nuisance and exposed two political scandals in St. Louis and two in nearby Illinois. Politically, *Post-Dispatch* support has usually been given to Democratic presidential candi-

[3] A series of articles on the Pulitzer Prize public service awards, by Ray Erwin, began in *Editor & Publisher*, XC (December 7, 1957), 13. Large daily winners not mentioned in the text of this chapter were the *Boston Post*, 1921; *Memphis Commercial Appeal*, 1923; *Indianapolis Times*, 1928; *Indianapolis News*, 1932; *New York World-Telegram*, 1933; *Miami Daily News*, 1939; *Omaha World-Herald*, 1943, and *Brooklyn Eagle*, 1951. Smaller dailies won, too: the *Columbus* (Ga.) *Enquirer-Sun*, 1926; the murdered Don R. Mellett's *Canton* (Ohio) *Daily News*, 1927; *Medford* (Ore.) *Mail Tribune*, 1934; *Cedar Rapids* (Iowa) *Gazette*, 1936; *Bismarck* (N. D.) *Tribune*, 1938; *Waterbury* (Conn.) *Republican* and *American*, 1940; *Scranton* (Pa.) *Times*, 1946; Lincoln *Nebraska State Journal*, 1949; *Whiteville* (N. C.) *News Reporter* and *Tabor City* (N. C.) *Tribune* (weeklies), 1953; *Columbus* (Ga.) *Ledger* and *Sunday Ledger-Enquirer*, 1955; *Watsonville* (Calif.) *Register-Pajaronian*, 1956; *Utica* (N. Y.) *Observer-Dispatch* and *Daily Press*, 1959; *Amarillo* (Tex.) *Globe-Times*, 1961. Winners of revised Pulitzer Prizes for local reporting were from the *Vicksburg* (Miss.) *Sunday Post-Herald* and *Kansas City Star*, 1954; *Alice* (Tex.) *Daily Echo* and *Guere* (Tex.) *Record* (weekly), 1955; *Detroit Free Press* and *New York Times*, 1956; *Salt Lake Tribune* and *Portland Oregonian*, 1957; *Fargo* (N. D.) *Forum*, 1958; *Washington Star*, 1958, 1959, 1960; *Scranton* (Pa.) *Tribune*, 1959; *Atlanta Constitution*, 1960; *New York Herald Tribune* and *Buffalo Evening News*, 1961. Winners for national and international reporting are listed in Chapter 23.

dates—but not to some Missouri party leaders. Franklin D. Roose-- velt incurred the paper's wrath in 1936, although it endorsed him three other times, and it opposed Harry S. Truman in 1948. Its devotion to liberal principles led also to unrelenting attacks upon McCarthyism and other right-wing movements.

The morning *St. Louis Globe-Democrat* was the *Post-Dispatch's* only rival after closing of the *Star-Times* in 1951. The *Globe-Democrat*, built to prominence by Joseph B. McCullagh before 1900, also worked vigorously for civic progress, although less dramatically and in a conservative political atmosphere. E. Lansing Ray was publisher from 1925 to 1955, when the paper was sold to Samuel I. Newhouse. Editorial editor Louis LaCoss won the Pulitzer Prize for editorial writing in 1952, the paper's centennial year.

While the *Post-Dispatch* was expanding its staff reporting of national news, the *Kansas City Star* was sticking principally to the local and regional area coverage which William Rockhill Nelson had emphasized from the time he founded the *Star* in 1880 until his death in 1915. Fine writing of news and features, and vigorous crusading in the community interest, were special ingredients which kept the *Star* high in newspaper ratings. Continuity was ensured for the paper when the staff bought stock control in 1926, with some 90 employes raising 2½ million dollars in cash and assuming an 8½ million dollar mortgage which was paid off by 1939.

Two men became particularly prominent in *Star* affairs. One was Henry J. Haskell, named editorial page director in 1910 and editor from 1928 to 1952. The *Star* won two Pulitzer Prizes for editorial writing during his tenure. Overshadowing him, however, was the bulky, jovial Roy A. Roberts, who came to be Kansas City's leading citizen. Roberts joined the staff in 1908, served as the paper's Washington correspondent 15 years, and then became managing editor in 1928. He was elected president and general manager of the *Star* and its morning edition, the *Times*, in 1947. Roberts loved politics as well as newspapering and he became an important, if unofficial figure, in Republican party affairs, maintaining the paper on that political course into the 1960's.

The *Milwaukee Journal* stood in the uppermost level of the country's newspapers by the 1960's as a conscientiously edited, well-written, community-conscious daily blessed with one of the nation's largest volumes of advertising and space for comprehensive news coverage. Its editorial page ranked in stature with those of the *St. Louis Post-Dispatch* and *Washington Post*.

The *Journal*, founded in 1882, faced strong competition through all its early years. Publisher Lucius W. Nieman set the trend for its community leadership and first attracted national attention when he courageously exposed disloyal elements among Milwaukee's large German-American population during World War I. For this the *Journal* won the Pulitzer Prize for public service.

Under Nieman's guidance the *Journal* developed an international outlook, supporting the League of Nations and the United Nations. The paper clashed with the isolationist-minded La Follette family and Milwaukee's Socialist leader, Victor Berger, on foreign policy. But as a middle-of-the-road, independent paper it tended to support progressive-minded politicians of whatever party. Nationally, it supported Roosevelt in 1932, 1936, and mildly in 1944; Willkie in 1940, Dewey in 1948, and then the Stevenson and Kennedy candidacies. Its fiercest battle was with Senator Joseph R. McCarthy on his home ground; when McCarthy won reelection in 1952 he failed to carry Milwaukee.

A dominant personality appeared on the *Journal* staff in 1916 when Harry J. Grant became business manager. Grant acquired 20 per cent of the stock and the title of publisher in 1919. He imported Marvin H. Creager from the *Kansas City Star* and Creager, as managing editor and later as editor and company president, reinforced the *Journal's* local coverage and writing qualities with an insistence born of his *Star* experience. The Kansas City paper, indeed, long had an important influence on *Journal* policies. In the years which followed, the *Journal* became a paper which made its influence felt in every Milwaukee activity, big or little.

Nieman died in 1935 and his wife in 1936. Part of the Nieman fortune was left to Harvard University, which used it to establish the Nieman Fellowships for newspapermen. The Nieman stock holdings in the paper were up for sale, but Grant saved the situation by organizing an employe-ownership plan similar to that of the *Star* in Kansas City. Eventually the employes obtained more than two-thirds of the stock. Grant, as board chairman and a substantial stockholder, remained in firm control. J. Donald Ferguson succeeded

Creager as president and editor in 1943. In 1961, publisher Irwin Maier became president and Lindsay Hoben editor. Wallace Lomoe was named executive editor and Arville Schaleben managing editor in 1959. All have had long careers with the paper.

The *Chicago Daily News* retained its traditional place among newspaper leaders despite a series of ownership changes after the deaths of owners Victor F. Lawson in 1925 and Walter A. Strong in 1931. Colonel Frank Knox, former general manager of the Hearst newspapers and a leading Republican political figure, then became publisher. Knox kept the *Daily News* operating in its old traditions until his death in 1944. Its famous foreign and Washington news service reached brilliant heights. Henry Justin Smith, a news executive from 1901 to 1936, ran a "school for reporters."

Sale of the *Daily News* to John S. Knight in 1944 brought in Basil L. Walters as executive editor. Walters introduced new typographical and readership techniques he had learned while with the Cowles newspapers in Des Moines and Minneapolis. The paper emphasized local news and developed crusades on local issues. As a result, the *Daily News* printed the stories of its own foreign staff in less depth, although the service remained a strong one. The paper won two Pulitzer Prizes for public service, in 1950 and 1957, and gained in circulation and financial position.

Chicago newspaper ownership was streamlined in 1959, when Marshall Field, Jr., owner of the *Sun-Times*, bought the *Daily News* as an evening affiliate. Field became publisher of both papers and editor of the *Daily News* after Walters retired in 1961. Milburn P. Akers became editor of the *Sun-Times*, with Larry S. Fanning as executive editor. Thomas H. Collins was named executive editor of the *Daily News*. A. T. Burch headed the *Daily News* editorial page and Robert E. Kennedy that of the *Sun-Times*. Both papers favored Republican presidential candidates, but backed those from either major party in seamy Chicago and Illinois politics. Both were internationalist in outlook.

When journalism educators were asked in a 1961 poll to select the best combinations of morning and evening newspapers published by the same organization, they placed the Cowles-owned *Minneapolis Star* and *Tribune* and *Des Moines Register* and *Tribune* second and third, close behind the *Louisville Courier-Journal* and *Times*. Of the four papers owned by John and Gardner Cowles, the *Minneapolis Tribune* ranked highest as an individual daily.

Under publisher John Cowles the morning *Tribune* and evening *Star* developed wide upper Midwest circulations from their Minneapolis base. Gideon Seymour, after a successful career with the Associated Press, joined the papers in 1939 and was named executive editor in 1944. Carroll Binder, *Chicago Daily News* foreign editor, became editorial page editor of the *Tribune* in 1945.

Cowles, Seymour, and Binder teamed together to give the papers broadened news coverage, strong interpretative qualities, and independent-minded editorial pages strongly internationalist in outlook. Seymour died in 1954 and Binder in 1956. William P. Steven became executive editor and Wilbur E. Elston editorial pages editor. Steven resigned in 1960 when John Cowles, Jr., took direct control of the news pages as editor. Joyce A. Swan was named publisher, with the elder Cowles as company president. The Minneapolis papers placed staff correspondents in the European and Mediterranean areas. Republican in national politics, they developed under Elston a reputation for independent editorial endorsements from both parties for local and state offices, and a crusading opposition to right-wing political movements.

In Des Moines, editorial editors W. W. Waymack, Forrest W. Seymour, and Lauren K. Soth all won Pulitzer Prizes for editorial writing. The Cowles Washington bureau won three Pulitzer awards for national reporting, and the four papers won the 1957 Sigma Delta Chi award for public service. Kenneth MacDonald became chief operating officer for Gardner Cowles in Des Moines.

The South and West, with more slowly developing industrial economies, smaller populations, and fewer major cities, did not match the East and Middle West in producing newspapers which could win the highest possible rankings in the estimate of the craft. But they did produce several dailies which stood well up in the listings and undoubtedly would produce more. At least one—the *Louisville Courier-Journal* from the border state of Kentucky—became a newspaper which ranked among the nation's best.[4]

The retirement in 1919 of Henry Watterson, editor of the *Courier-*

---

[4] It is interesting to note that Baltimore, Washington, Louisville, St. Louis, and Kansas City, all border state cities, developed outstanding newspapers.

Journal since 1868, brought the Bingham family to the fore. Judge Robert Worth Bingham bought the *Courier-Journal* and the after-noon *Times* in 1917. Before he died in 1937 he saw his son, Barry Bingham, well established as directing owner of the newspapers. At his right hand was Mark Ethridge, former associate editor of the *Washington Post* and publisher of the *Richmond Times-Dispatch*, who came to Louisville as general manager in 1936 and became publisher in 1942. Bingham took the title, and writing responsibili-ties, of editor of the *Courier-Journal*.

Events moved rapidly at Louisville under the Bingham-Ethridge regime. James S. Pope became executive editor of the two papers. Norman E. Isaacs, managing editor of the *St. Louis Star-Times* when it closed down in 1951, came to Louisville as managing editor of the *Times*. Bingham, Ethridge, Pope, and Isaacs all were recog-nized as vocal, intelligent leaders in the journalistic profession. Russell Briney became editor of the *Courier-Journal* editorial pages and George Burt editor of those for the *Times*.

Steadily Democratic in its political preferences, the *Courier-Jour-nal* exerted a strong influence as a progressive, fair-minded news-paper dedicated to defending basic democratic principles. In news play, it excelled in international and national coverage, but it also paid close attention to Louisville, where it did effective work in behalf of the Negro, union labor, education, music, and art.

Atlanta gave the South two strong newspapers, the *Constitution* and the *Journal*. Clark Howell, Sr., who succeeded Henry Grady at the *Constitution* in 1889, became the paper's owner and served as editor until 1936. His son, Clark Howell, Jr., named Ralph Mc-Gill as editor in 1938. McGill opposed the Ku Klux Klan and the Talmadge political machine in Georgia, and won a Pulitzer Prize for editorial writing in 1959. James M. Cox, owner of the *Journal*, obtained control of the *Constitution* in 1950, but the papers con-tinued to have separate editorial policies. The *Constitution* won a Pulitzer Prize for public service in 1931, and both papers won Sigma Delta Chi awards for public service in the 1950's.

There were other famous names in southern journalism. Josephus Daniels continued his interest in the *Raleigh News and Observer* until his death in 1948, and passed on his editorship to his son, Jonathan, who also exerted influence in community and political affairs. Editor Virginius Dabney of the *Richmond Times-Dispatch* eyed traditional attitudes skeptically and jarred complacent conservatives with his editorials from 1928 into the 1960's. He won a Pulitzer Prize in 1948. Dr. Douglas Southall Freeman, editor of the *Richmond News Leader* from 1915 to 1949, won Pulitzer Prizes for his biographies of Robert E. Lee and George Washington. In Little Rock, J. N. Heiskell was completing 60 years as editor of the respected *Arkansas Gazette* in 1961. His paper won the Pulitzer Prize for public service, and executive editor Harry S. Ashmore the award for editorial writing, for leadership during the 1957 school desegregation crisis in Little Rock. Lee Hills, executive editor of the Knight newspapers, was instrumental in the growth of the group's *Miami Herald* into a paper of major size and influence. It too won a Pulitzer Prize for public service, in 1951.

In the Far West, the *Los Angeles Times* led all the nation's dailies in total advertising linage by a wide margin, and also led in space allotted to editorial material. Long known for its conservatism, and ranked by the Washington correspondents in 1937 as close behind the Hearst and McCormick newspapers as "least fair and reliable," the *Times* began to show a change of direction after Otis Chandler succeeded his father, Norman, as publisher in 1960. It won the Pulitzer Prize for public service in 1942, for fighting a contempt of court charge, and again in 1960 for an exposure of narcotics traffic.

The *San Francisco Chronicle* was famed under publisher George T. Cameron, editor Chester Rowell, and general manager Paul C. Smith in the 1930's and 1940's for its comprehensive national and foreign news coverage. But in the 1950's, under new direction, the *Chronicle* turned heavily toward features, columnists, and circulation-getting news. It passed the Hearst-owned *Examiner* in readers, but saw the *Examiner* surpass it in solid news.

The McClatchy-owned *Bee* newspapers in California, published in Sacramento, Fresno, and Modesto, won a reputation as fiercely independent dailies. The *Sacramento Bee*, founded in 1857, became well known under its publisher-editor, C. K. McClatchy, who served from 1883 to 1936. The *Bee* crusaded for public power, spoke out for individual liberties, and won a Pulitzer Prize for public service in 1935 for exposing political corruption. Eleanor McClatchy succeeded her father as publisher and kept to his usually pro-Democratic political beliefs.

In Portland, the long respected *Oregonian* ran into difficulties. Its famous editor, Harvey W. Scott, died in 1910, and manager Henry L. Pittock in 1919. Their heirs found a strong editor in Palmer Hoyt, from 1933 until he left to become publisher of the *Denver Post* in 1946. Control of the *Oregonian* passed to Samuel Newhouse in 1950, as did ownership of the rival *Oregon Journal* in 1961. The papers were badly hurt by a prolonged strike beginning in 1959 which sharply reduced their staff morale.

Palmer Hoyt's entry into Denver journalism as publisher of the *Post* signaled a definite end of the Tammen-Bonfils type of newspapering. Hoyt gradually modified the *Post*'s gaudy makeup, increased its interpretative news coverage, and gave the paper a better editorial balance. The *Post* developed a strong internationalist point of view and an independent editorial page which swung the usually Republican paper to the Kennedy camp in 1960.

Rapidly growing Texas fostered a journalism which was in keeping with the state's free enterprise economic atmosphere. Vigorous competition existed in many cities, but among dailies essentially conservative in their editorial outlooks. The *Dallas News*, inherited by E. M. (Ted) Dealey in 1946 from his father George, became an arch-conservative voice in Republican-voting Dallas. Houston's two largest papers, the morning *Post* and evening *Chronicle*, were carefully conservative, leaving the crusading role to the Scripps-Howard *Press*. The *Post* was built into prominence by William P. Hobby and his editor-wife, Oveta Culp Hobby. The *Chronicle*, owned by financier Jesse Jones until his death in 1956, obtained William P. Steven as editor in 1960. Another financier, Amon G. Carter, firmly established the *Fort Worth Star-Telegram* as a leading Texas daily. Noteworthy for taking a strong liberal stand on the integration issue were the *San Antonio Express* and *News*. Among Texas editors who achieved national prominence professionally were Felix R. McKnight of the *Dallas Times Herald* and Walter R. Humphrey of the Scripps-Howard *Fort Worth Press*.

Few of the present-day newspapers whose stories have been told date back more than 100 years. Indeed, only a little more than two and a half centuries separate the crudely printed news sheets produced in Boston by Benjamin Harris and John Campbell from the modern dailies of the mid-twentieth century. But vast changes have been recorded. The story of the growth of newspapers—and the addition of magazines, books, radio, and television to create the mass media—is the story of both the development of communications and the maturing of a nation. It is the story of journalism in American life—of the press and America.

ANNOTATED BIBLIOGRAPHY

Books:

Berger, Meyer, *The Story of the New York Times, 1851-1951.* New York: Simon and Schuster, 1951. The best history of the *Times.*

Encyclopaedia Britannica Book of the Year. Issued annually, it contains summaries of changes in newspapers, magazines, other media.

Garst, Robert E., ed., *The Newspaper—Its Making and Its Meaning.* New York: Charles Scribner's Sons, 1945. Addresses by 12 *New York Times* staff members, describing their work.

Hart, Jim Allee, *A History of the St. Louis Globe-Democrat.* Columbia: University of Missouri Press, 1961. Tells the story of St. Louis' "other paper" in a social and political framework.

Johnson, Gerald W., et al., *The Sunpapers of Baltimore.* New York: Alfred A. Knopf, Inc., 1937. An outstanding newspaper history.

Kobre, Sidney, *Modern American Journalism.* Tallahassee: Florida State University Bookstore, 1959. Traces the twentieth-century histories of many leading newspapers, in detail.

Markham, James W., *Bovard of the Post-Dispatch.* Baton Rouge: Louisiana State University Press, 1954. A discerning biography.

Stewart, Kenneth, and John Tebbel, *Makers of Modern Journalism.* New York: Prentice-Hall, Inc., 1952. Contains extensive comment on many of the newspapers and men covered in this chapter; see index.

Periodicals and Monographs:

Several *Saturday Evening Post* articles—about the *Philadelphia Bulletin, Christian Science Monitor, Denver Post,* Eugene Meyer, Mrs. Helen Rogers Reid, and John S. Knight—are reprinted in John E. Drewry, ed., *More Post Biographies.* Bibliographies in the *Journalism Quarterly* annotate articles in *Editor & Publisher, Nieman Reports, Saturday Review, Time, Newsweek,* and other periodicals. See the bibliography for Chapter 27 for references to Knight, Cowles, and Newhouse.

"The Challenger," *Time,* LXXVII (January 20, 1961), 60. Marshall Field, Jr., and the *Chicago Sun-Times* and *Daily News.*

DeVoto, Bernard, "Always Be Drastically Independent," *Harper's,* CCVII (December 1953), 42. The *St. Louis Post-Dispatch* is nominated as the "finest practitioner of liberal journalism."

"The Fair Lady of Milwaukee," *Time*, LXIII (February 1, 1954), 44. An extensive report on the *Journal*.

"Guest at Breakfast," *Time*, LXVII (April 16, 1956), 64. A major feature on the *Washington Post*.

Patterson, Alicia, "This Is the Life I Love," *Saturday Evening Post*, CCXXXII (February 21, 1959), 19. *Newsday's* story.

Shaplen, Robert, "Denson's Revolution at the Herald Tribune," *Saturday Review*, XLIV (July 8, 1961), 36. Latest in a long story.

Tait, Samuel W., Jr., "The St. Louis Post-Dispatch," *American Mercury*, XXII (April 1931), 403. An analysis of editorial policy.

Tebbel, John, "Rating the American Newspaper," *Saturday Review*, XLIV (May 13 and June 10, 1961). Ratings by 125 journalism educators.

Waldrop, A. Gayle, "A Chinook Blows on Champa Street," *Journalism Quarterly*, XXIV (June 1947), 109, and "Reborn Denver 'Post' Has Prestige and Power," XXVIII (Summer 1951), 327.

Walker, Jerome H., "Dryfoos Now Publisher, Oakes Editor of Times," *Editor & Publisher*, XCIV (April 29, 1961), 23. *New York Times*.

White, Llewellyn, "Papers of Paradox," *Reporter*, II (January 31, 1950), 22. *Louisville Courier-Journal* and *Times* analyzed.

————, "A Good Paper Pays Off," *Reporter*, III (August 29 and September 12, 1950). Excellent reports on the *Milwaukee Journal*.

INDEX

INDEX